The *Sankofa* is an Adinkra symbol from the ancient language of the Akan people of Ghana. The symbol can be literally translated "Go back and fetch it." It instructs one to go back to one's past and reclaim the essence of the culture's knowledge and wisdom to use as a foundation for the future.

Contemporary Etiquette

HowtoBe
for African Americans

Harriette Cole

Simon & Schuster

SIMON & SCHUSTER
Rockefeller Center
1230 Avenue of the Americas
New York, NY 10020

Designed by Karolina Harris

Manufactured in the United States of America

1   3   5   7   9   10   8   6   4   2

Library of Congress Cataloging-in-Publication Data
Cole, Harriette.
How to be: contemporary etiquette for African Americans /
Harriette Cole.
p.   cm.
Includes bibliographical references and index.
1. Etiquette—United States.   2. African Americans—Conduct of life.
3. United States—Race relations.   I. Title.
BJ1857.A37C65   1999
395'.089'96073—dc21`   98-48335   CIP
ISBN 0-684-82645-3

Dedication

With sincere devotion and respect, I dedicate this book to my ancestors and elders, those from my own family and community, as well as from the cultural continuum that defines, supports and enlivens Black folks the world over.

To My Ancestors

I offer libation to my heart, Carrie Elizabeth Alsup Freeland, my mother's mother, the angel lady who stayed with us for 101 years to guide us on our way; to Rosina Thompson Cole, my father's mother, whose powerful presence kept all of us in line; to Esther Rosina Thompson Cole Arrington, my father's eldest sister, who made her transition as I was writing this book, a woman whose style, grace and quiet resolve reminded us to love each other always; to my father's youngest sister, Audrey Robinette Cole Johnson, who also took her transition in 1998, Organizing Audrey who never gave up, not once, who carried the torch of love and stick-to-it-iveness every day of her life; to Audrey's husband, Henry Addison Johnson, whose soothing presence promised that it was all okay; to George Edward Hill, my sister Susan's husband, whose subtle humor and gentle strength assured that we were all welcomed and protected (and fed!); to Cousin Lucille, Aunt Ida, Granddaddy Freeland, Uncle Walter and, and, and . . .

To My Elders

I bow to my parents, Doris Irene Freeland Cole, the most exquisite mother, whose smile I share, for devoting her entire life to the care, sustenance and protection of my sisters, Susan Elizabeth Cole Hill and Stephanie Irene Cole Hill, and me, Harriette Ann Cole Chinsee; and Harry Augustus Cole, for whom I am named, who at the beginning of his career was the first Black assistant attorney general in Maryland, then elected as first Black state senator in Maryland and, at the end, the first Black judge on the Maryland Court of Appeals, for his commitment to excellence, duty, family and ethics and his insistence that I do my very best. I offer my love to Uncle Wendell and Aunt Jane, Mommie's brother and his wife, my godparents, for proving that love and intelligence bloom eternal; to Aunt Pearl, Daddy's sister, who demonstrated that a woman can be independent and strong; to the "girls" in Jersey City, Hortense, Betty, Marguerite and Helen, for illustrating the elegance and sweetness that define our family; to Aunt Alice, who is ever a ray of sunshine; Aunt P., a.k.a. G.G. a.k.a. Luna Thomas, my husband's sweet grandmother who has cared for all of the hearts who have come her way, including mine; Olga Buchanan, George's mother, whose quiet presence and thoughtful ways continue to make me feel welcome: my cousins Patricia and Gina; Mama Davis; Bennie and Dottie Hill. . . .

I extend my hands to so many elders in our Baltimore neighborhood and beyond—my extended family—for helping to mold me into the woman I have become: Aunt Etta and Uncle Ted, who proved that marriage could last, with a marriage sixty-two years strong; Aunt Sarah, who showed me that four eyes could be fabulous; Uncle Oney, who engineered me into Howard University; Judge Robert Bell, who carries the torch that Daddy lit as Chief Judge of the Maryland Court of Appeals and who became the son my father never had; to Aunt Margaret, a light of love and Mommie's best friend since age four; Aunt Ellen, another Doris girlfriend, who became my champion; Uncle Howard Mitnick, John Earl Stokes, . . . and the list goes on.

I *pranam* to my spiritual teacher, Gurumayi Chidvilasananda, who has opened my heart and eyes to the magnificence of my own true Self.

I extend prayers of thanks for all of those who have contributed to my life. Though I cannot possibly name you all, I pledge my love and gratitude to you. Your spirits live in my heart. Without this great family I would not know *how to be.*

Our deepest fear is not that we are inadequate. Our deepest fear is that we are powerful beyond measure. It is our light, not our darkness that most frightens us.

We ask ourselves, who am I to be brilliant, gorgeous, talented and fabulous? Actually, who are you not to be?

Your playing small doesn't serve the world. There's nothing enlightened about shrinking so that other people won't feel insecure around you.

We were born to make manifest the glory that is within us. It's not just in some of us; it's in everyone. And as we let our own light shine, we unconsciously give other people permission to do the same. As we are liberated from our own fear, our presence automatically liberates others.

NELSON MANDELA,
INAUGURAL SPEECH, 1994

Contents

Invocation

Listening minds began to grow connections. The remembrances were separate, but underneath them all
ran connected meaning.

ARMAH

BELOVED readers, I want you to know that this is a work in
progress. A few years back as I was traveling the country talking to
African-American people about incorporating our cultural traditions
into wedding rituals, I realized that there was a book that needed to be
written—a book that could help Black people in this country manage
social, business and other situations. I had seen books like these before—they're often called etiquette books—but none for Black people.

I asked myself over and over, *Do I really want to write an etiquette
book?* The answer was no. At least not an etiquette manual in the accepted, traditional sense, I didn't. I wasn't so much interested in promoting superficiality or cursory nonsense as some things considered
etiquette seemed to be. I didn't see the value of describing to Black
people how to put on airs, as the old folks used to call it, either. At the
same time, it had been my experience growing up in an upper-middle-
class Black family and neighborhood that learning all that stuff made it
easier for me to navigate Western society. So I realized what I was
searching for was balance. What I wanted to do was provide information pertinent to everyday living—the niceties and challenges—and
make it relevant for African Americans. The message needed a foundation, a guiding spiritual force that would allow for Black people to tap
into the strength our ancestors and parents used to survive our *Maafa,*
a Kiswahili word coined by scholar Marimba Ani, meaning "great disaster" (the Middle Passage, enslavement, the postdeconstruction period,
Jim Crow, busing, ghettos).

The three years it has taken to birth this book have opened my eyes, but my vision is still not crystal clear. My research team and I have crisscrossed the country, asking questions everywhere, finding out from our people the questions about how to live their lives that are most important to them. We have conducted focus groups, talking to every kind of Black person you can imagine—from the art crowd to angry and happy young people, from what my husband calls *bourgie* old-school elite to some of the kids in my Harlem neighborhood, from elders at every point across the country to African scholars and spiritual advisers. And every day that I have worked on this project, every time I have looked over the results of these discussions, I have discovered in each of our chosen topics a huge new dimension of a glorious whole: the magnificent and simple lives of our people.

One of the wonders and frustrations of *How to Be* is that it has felt as if every chapter is its own world, worthy of ten books for full exploration. Because of this, one of the ways that *How to Be* resembles a traditional etiquette manual is that it skims the surface of innumerable topics that need to be explored, researched and developed further. I trust that they will be.

One of the joyous discoveries that I have made in the years since I completed *Jumping the Broom* is that that book became a springboard for thought. And that is what I hope will happen with *How to Be*. About two years into the development of *How to Be,* I had an inspiring discussion with the late Thurlow Tibbs, an African-American art dealer in Washington, D.C. I told him that I was writing this book about conscious living for African-American people, that it was to help them, us, to become conscious. An intuitive spark prompted Tibbs to say, "What you're writing is a book to promote thinking. Maybe this is a book for thinking people *and* for people who haven't begun to think yet." The merit of his comment was undeniable.

What we all need to do is use our brains to think, research and study, because when we don't, we suffer. Even more, as I've learned with this work, from the perspective of the African worldview—our ancestral context—we hurt the community when we don't think, when we don't study, when we don't research. When we don't know anything about ourselves that we have not learned from the popular media that often degrade us, we're doomed. In turn, we don't choose to offer our hands in support and love to our people. So this book is an offering of support and love, and it is also a push. What I offer here are ways that African people in America, in the West, can develop tools to live our lives, meet our goals, take care of our families and plant seeds for a real future for our children and theirs. The only way we can do this is if we gain a sincere and deep appreciation for who we are—and who we have been, both the best and the worst, so that we have faith in our ancestral ability to do anything, so we don't keep making the same mistakes or feeling as if we have to start all over again with each generation. Only then, when we have a clear sense, a deepening understanding, of who we are can we really know *how to be*.

While engaged in the process, we need tools, instruments and sometimes armor. Some of these tools in today's society are Western, as is some of the armor. But the foundation is partly what you learn from the elders of your own family and the elders in your community. And I invite you to look just a little further back to our African ancestors and to their power and presence in your life today for the rest of that foundation. Part of the purpose of this book, in fact, is to let you know that it's okay to look all the way back, past Slavery, and to know that Slavery did not destroy all of the best we have ever been. Chances are you experience remnants of our historical strength in your own family—in living elders and ancestors. I surely have, in the presence and spirit of my maternal grandmother, Carrie Elizabeth Alsup Freeland. Grandma Carrie, as I call her in this book, was dear to my heart. She truly was a beautiful lady. Born in 1889 in Baltimore, Maryland, she spent her whole life working for white folks *and* supporting her family—with the intention of providing a better life for her family. Grandma Carrie had a way of bridging our two cultures—of being in Western culture and understanding that she had to support the community, an essential component of African life. In the process, she always found a way of offering love. I believe that this process that we are going through of learning who we are and *how to be* has got to be fueled with love.

What really made me understand that it was vital to look at the cultural continuum of African people for guidance was a trip that I took in 1984 to the Ivory Coast. It was there that I saw African people, on their turf, displaying a quiet dignity and presence of *being* that were undeniable. All that I saw was contrary to anything that I had ever been told was African. It didn't have a dollar figure attached to it, this state that I witnessed; it didn't have descriptions that I can even put into words in English. But it was that quality of seeing what was true and what was real about people I was connected to that made me feel connected to them. Not in some romanticized way, but in a concrete, clear way, I could see that I was a part of these people. I realized that there was something that I could learn from them too, because they had something that I thought I didn't have: an African home, a connection to the land of our original people. There was a power in them, a beauty in them that was astonishing, and it wasn't attached to anything other than who they were and their connection to the Divine. As I experienced these exquisite people, I thought about the folks back home. I wanted every Black person to see the magnificent image that I was seeing, to realize how tall and strong and focused indigenous African people seemed to be, because I knew that it would inspire us all to see with new vision.

Upon my return, I looked at Black folks in America differently, watching for a glimpse of that power in us. And it was there, most evident in the elders. I believe the greatest challenge for us, in this society, is to reconnect to that space of *being* where we can find the support we need in each other—as we used to and as Africans still do. We can look to the elders for guidance. We must also seek strength from faith in the Creator and trust in the ancestors. The balance lies in discovering an artful way of counterbalancing the requirements of our Western experience with the grounding power and guidance of our African legacy. Depending on where you are in your life and what you need, this book will affect you in different ways. For me, I know that I am a work in progress. I am in the midst of a process that I invite you to join. Using this book as a launching pad, you can read and learn and grow so that you can know *how to be.*

> May the vision of the ancestors and the connection to brothers and sisters across the planet guide and direct you as you begin your journey. I love you.
>
> ASHÉ
> (YORUBA INVOCATION OF PERSONAL AND COMMUNAL POWER THAT COMES FROM THE CREATOR)

Introduction

Our way, the way, is not a random path. Our way be-gins from coherent understanding. It is a way that aims at preserving knowledge of who we are, knowl-edge of the best way we have found to relate each to each, each to all, ourselves to other peoples, all to our surroundings. If your individual lives have a worthwhile aim, that aim should be a purpose insepa-rable from the way.

A R M A H

R E M E M B E R when your Mama used to talk to you in that firm tone of voice about how to behave? Listen, and you can probably hear her sweet yet stern voice calling out to you just as you were on the brink of getting into mischief. *You better act right, chile.* If you already were full throttle into naughtiness, her words might be, *You don't know how to act!* alive with the promise that she would show you how to behave once she got next to you. Elders have long called the practical instruc-tion that parents give their children "home training." Those fundamen-tal dos and don'ts about daily living, which form the basis for relationships between people, are guidelines that people generally learn during their formative years in the intimacy of their homes. In the African-American community, where both Mama and Daddy (that is, all adults in the home) *had* to work, the knowledge was gained under the loving supervision of the extended family—grandparents, older sib-lings, aunts, uncles, cousins, neighbors and friends. It was there that young people learned how to live their lives respectful of others. Then they would go out into the world and practice their home training, first on friends, then at school and at work, in romances, in times of cele-bration and crisis, all the while developing relationships with the like-minded as well as those who thought differently.

Today as we become more mainstream, primarily through integra-tion (not to be confused with desegregation), the structure of the

African-American family reflects the changes of the past few generations. Even beyond the dual-income necessity, the idea that a "real family" should be limited to mother-father-sister-brother, and then the frequent lack of this type of unit, has left many children to fend for themselves. In turn, we have all but lost the traditional or extended family support system—and with it traditional African home training. That loving neighbor who had the responsibility of our youth's care and discipline in Mama's absence is now an uninterested stranger who doesn't want to get involved because *"That ain't my chile!"* while the in-laws and siblings who were once there to provide added support now frequently live many miles away. That is my experience. I live 500 miles from my parents and one sister, and 3,000 miles from the other sister, and that distance is affecting the choices I am making now about how to live my life and grow my family.

America is on the move. That mobility, which has sent our folks to every possible corner of the globe, has made it very difficult for our children to receive all of the needed guidance and support that historically was available to them from the Black community. Is it any wonder that when it comes to a grasp of good manners, people are often stumped? What has happened is that many people are growing up without a clear understanding of *how to be* with others. Even some of the most intelligent among us are often starved for basic information on how to manage in today's complex world. As a result, adults who otherwise should be looking mainly to fine-tune their social skills find themselves in serious need of the basics. You might be amazed at how many people don't even understand the mechanics of common courtesy. Another component that adds confusion to the etiquette question is this: What is the definition of "cultural diversity"? We use the term, but do we know what it means as it relates to thought and behavior differences? People from all walks of life commonly sit down to eat, conduct business and otherwise interact, yet the guidelines that they follow for dealing with these very basic activities often conflict, simply by the way that they have been taught to view the world. As simple as life sometimes seems to be, on the level of human interaction, it is also filled with subtle complexities.

Even so, the question remains, In a world as busy as ours, who has time to explore those nuances? What we should really ask is who can afford *not* to take a hard look at such things. It has been said that bad manners can get a Black man killed—"manners" in this case meaning the expected behavior for pressured situations, such as wrongful arrest. Read any newspaper and you'll see what I mean. Being too busy to learn the ins and outs of what's ahead may be too great an expense to pay. To figure out how you feel about exploring the intricacies of etiquette, consider this: Have you ever found yourself in a situation when you weren't quite sure what you were supposed to do? It could be as simple as knowing which fork is yours at an important business luncheon or as complex as discovering the protocol of a given situation, such as what to do when you forget someone's name just as you are about to make an introduction, or how to invite a guest to leave who has overstayed his or her welcome. No matter how well educated you are (or are not), chances are that you have walked into a set of circumstances where you weren't certain how to respond. Visualize such a scenario now. Replay the whole scene slowly. As you recall the details, what's physically happening to your body? Is your chest tightening? What about your facial muscles? How did your actions affect those around you? I know, for me, I ended up damaging a friendship *and* losing a contract simply because my insensitivity turned people off. I didn't consider others' level of comfort before my own. Now switch to another scenario when you *did* know what to do. It might have been handling a bill at a restaurant when you were with a large group, helping an elderly person at a crosswalk when you were in a hurry, or diffusing a racially charged situation gracefully that was about to blow up on your job. When you responded in a thoughtful manner that took into consideration others' circumstances and possible perspectives, it worked out well, didn't it? That's because a healthy dose of common sense, selflessness and respect for differences—even if you don't know their specific details—are key components of good manners. The essence of all of the structures that have been erected to help people get along with each other peacefully and effectively finds its root in living honorably. We learn this today through the Golden Rule: *Do unto others as you would have them do unto you.* An African priest and teacher of ethics, Ptahhotep, said, *"Each man teaches as he acts."* If you can grasp the full meaning of these simple truths, all the rest will follow. Cultures have and continue to come up with their own formulas for managing in daily and special event situations, because that's not easy to do.

Hence, *How to Be.* This book exists to help you navigate through your life in the most effective and fulfilling manner. Its foundation is the magnificent wellspring of inspiration and knowledge that comes directly, to borrow from the words of the great thinker W. E. B. Du Bois, from the "souls of Black folk." *How to Be* is meant to be a resource for the empowerment of people of African descent. It is a manual that offers guidance on how to live your life in a responsible, confident and inspired way, all the while being respectful and thus affirming the liberties of those who cross your path. Because this book reaches into the tried-and-true experience and wisdom of Black folks, it also gives power to an often unspoken reality: that the ancient and contemporary cultures of people of Africa and their descendants are rich with integrity and insight. All it takes is a moment of conscious awareness for you to discover and treasure this knowledge.

Being aware is a critical component of living a fulfilling life. The list of things that require your attention and awareness can seem staggering. Rather than being overwhelmed by what lies in front of you, slow down. Take pages out of the elders' book. Cultivate the spiritual practices of prayer, meditation and contemplation. By contemplating the import of your thoughts, words and deeds and then acting based on those considerations, you can reach your goals *and* sleep soundly at night.

How to Be gives voice to the village invoked in the Yoruba proverb that tells us that it takes a whole village to raise a child. This book is an exploration of the codes of conduct that govern the various environments in which people find themselves on a daily basis—from family life to the office, dating to travel, eating to getting dressed. The premise is that it is best to walk into a situation with an understanding of the fundamental guidelines that define that environment. From that perspective, you can make conscious choices about *how to be* when you are there. What I hope to do here is teach, not preach, to show you how to be respectful of others as you live your life. In fact, throughout the book I offer my own experiences of trial and error to show you how I am discovering *how to be*. I welcome you to use this book as a resource that has evolved out of the wisdom of leaders and regular folk of Africa and African descent today and from generations past. *How to Be* puts forth a collective best effort to address some of today's most pressing and basic questions, providing suggestions on what is considered appropriate in a wide variety of circumstances. Finally, this book can serve as a jumping-off point for you and your family to begin considering more deeply how to live your lives in such a way that you can reach your goals as you consciously support those in your midst. With great respect and love, I offer it to you.

Codes of Conduct

Seek the most perfect way of performing your responsibility so that your conduct will be blameless.

PTAHHOTEP

A GROUP of sister elders gathered one Sunday afternoon to talk
about what life was like when they were growing up. Oh, the stories
they told! Stories of Miss Mary's correcting one of them when she spoke
unkindly to her brother, or of Reverend Wilson who preached about
the need for folks to treat each other right. They spoke of how it just
wasn't acceptable in their neighborhoods to let loose and say whatever
you wanted to say or do whatever you wanted to do. You had to have
manners—good manners. And that meant you'd better be nice to folks,
speak to people with a smile on your face, shake hands politely while
looking kindly into the other's eyes and remember to say, "Thank you,"
and "Please," when you're talking to folks. The basics.

The conversation started with everyone chiming in about how different things are nowadays. "Children will say anything to adults," Miss
Cora declared, horrified. "They don't have any home training. My Mama
wouldn't stand for that nonsense!" What's more, these days, those old
enough to know better don't always speak up to tell a child what's right.
People regularly turn a blind eye to children's and adults' misguided actions and words, perhaps out of fear, perhaps out of lack of interest.

Everyone agreed that there's a lot of nonsense being allowed in
communities now—basic stuff that's not being considered as people interact with each other. That old saying, *"You can catch more flies with
honey,"* seems to be a thought from a prehistoric age, what with children and adults alike displaying weapons rather than kind words to get
their way.

Political activist Haki Madhubuti, founder of the Third World Press, takes this one step further, back to the core of our community structure. "The community plays a pivotal role in stabilizing itself," he explains. "We have to work together to be strong." This means conscious disavowal of individualist ideology or thinking, which essentially is what was given to our community and others as a means to divide and conquer. Working together includes each of you. You must remind yourself that being kind is the honorable way to live, and it builds character. Although it doesn't always seem possible to be kind and strong at the same time—that is, if you assume that everything breaks down according to the Western logic that considers information in polar opposites as either/or—both can happen, it can be done. Just remember the adage, *Don't mistake kindness for weakness.* You do have to be ready to defend yourself when the time comes. And, yes, others may challenge you when they see you coming before them wearing a genuine smile or a face of gentle calm. Yet even for people in the toughest environments, kindness can win. Half the time a pleasant state will appear as an unexpected approach that disarms people. In other instances, it can be infectious, rubbing off on a sourpuss to the point that the person discovers a willingness to work as a team player. Give it a try. The challenges will come no matter what. It's how you choose to face them that defines the art of life. A shield of kindness can be very powerful.

Today, what we often hear people say is "We live in what's supposed to be a free country. Why do we have to follow other people's rules?" Perhaps no more profound question has been asked during the time that I have spent preparing this book. What's the difference between people seeking to explore their own dreams without care for others' interests or needs, and those who work to balance their goals with the needs and desires of others in their midst? African scholars will tell you it's the difference between a Western worldview and an African worldview. If you consider the ultimate need for balance in the world, what is known as *Maat* in Khamitic (ancient Egyptian) philosophy, the answer is that the difference is "Everything."

The United States is supposed to be the freest country in the world, but what does that mean? What is freedom, in its truest sense? In *Webster's New World Dictionary, freedom* is defined as "the condition of being free of restraints," as well as "the capacity to exercise choice." Essentially, from a Western philosophical perspective, the quality that this intangible thing called freedom offers is the ability for each of us to think, speak and act as we please—potentially without concern for others. Common courtesy and common sense, however, both say that this should not be so.

Theoretically, we can accept that the premise of this country's being a free land of opportunity for all was a noble cause. The reality is that Black folks were left out of the mix from the start—as people, that is. The Constitution did not afford people of African descent the same liberties as white folks; they were relegated to being property, or chattel— the very property that early Americans had given themselves the inalienable right to *own*! Thanks to many bloody battles, our people have been given some of the same rights as other Americans—on paper, that is, since being able to exercise them has often proved challenging, to say the least. Still, the promise of freedom on so many fronts is ours to embrace. Learning how best to wear the cloak of freedom effectively is, in my view, the mission of human life.

For African-American people, the journey must begin with a change of perspective. For starters, we must embrace a fundamental truth about our African ancestors: that freedom was very different for them than it is for us here in the United States. From an African perspective, freedom is not conceived in terms of the individual. Instead, African philosophy considers freedom in the context of the community—the state in which all members enjoy physical, spiritual and social liberties while simultaneously honoring the needs and boundaries of each other and the community as a whole. From this vantage, freedom becomes an empowering state for all, because it is grounded in an unshakable belief: that true freedom requires responsibility and respect for your individual Self, your family, your elders, your community, your environment, your ancestors and your Creator.

This way of understanding freedom as communal response and responsibility was all but erased from our collective consciousness by the route that we traveled to get to this country. Individual liberties were stripped away from our ancestors, followed by a series of denials of their even being human. It only follows suit that in the Western world, we have faced varying degrees of discrimination that have left many of us feeling socially disabled even today. Many Black folks are walking around right now not believing that they are empowered even to have a dream, let alone pursue one. Thus, the first freedom to embrace is that which releases you from the bondage of negative thinking. The *"I can't, I'm afraid to try . . . , I don't know how . . . , No one would let me if . . ."* and other doubtful comments have got to go! Starting with your very words, you must replace negative self-images with verbal affirmations, such as *"I can . . . , I will make a plan . . . , I am Black and I'm beautiful . . . , I am worthy of this life."* The Reverend Jesse L. Jackson's powerful affirmation, *"I Am Somebody!"* belongs to you.

Being Black in America means that you are descended from survivors, from people who dared to discover unique and creative ways to enjoy whatever liberties were afforded to them. Today, your responsibility is to walk farther along the powerful path that has already been paved. To do so with style and grace requires a heavy dose of self-confidence (*not* arrogance), along with humility (not to be confused with self-deprecation, which holds you back; but humility that shows "I don't know everything and can learn from anyone"), perspective and patience. Otherwise, you risk seeming cocky, demanding. This is not a healthy option for anyone, certainly not us. Selfishness, shortsighted-ness and violence are the very strategies that have been used to op-press us. In most situations, a more subtle approach is better. Enter social graces, protocol, etiquette.

This chapter examines how best to manage your personal freedom in Western life, which requires being conscious, or aware, of *how to be,* wherever you are. If you think about it, graceful life management is the definition of etiquette for all people. Etiquette represents the guidelines that provide boundaries of behavior for a particular group of people or situation. Every society has explicit rules, be they written into law or unspoken tenets, so that people can function together in a relative de-gree of harmony. This, in fact, is the foundation for common sense, which *is* culturally determined and relevant in daily life. Depending on where you find yourself in the world or in your city, these codes of conduct may change, which is why it is of great value to know what is expected in a certain place before you arrive. Good manners are the foundation of etiquette. They represent a person's ability to honor or show respect for himself or herself and other people—their humanity and idiosyncrasies, their commonalities and differences, their selfless ways and their egos, their strengths and frailties.

This chapter will help you begin the process of making informed de-cisions about your behavior based on the knowledge of what behavior is expected from you in any situation. Here you will be able to explore the basics of being with people—from how to cultivate such virtues as kindness and compassion to the art of making introductions and exits.

Developing Good Judgment

One thing is for sure: you must learn how to make decisions for your-self that are both informed and honest. Following anyone or anything blindly is a sure way to ruin, be it spiritual, financial or political. There's a wonderful African story that illustrates this point, as told by Jamal Koram the Storyman:

> *"You can't always do what you see everyone else do."*
> A monkey was on the roof. He was dancing and jumping around and
> making funny sounds. The owner of the house laughed and laughed

at the monkey's antics. That afternoon, the donkey, who had watched the monkey, climbed up on the roof, and he commenced dancing and shouting, "Hee Haw," "Hee Haw!" While he was jumping, he made a big hole in the roof. The owner climbed up on the roof and whipped the donkey. "Get off of here!" he shouted.

"Why are you hitting me when you didn't hit the monkey?" whined the donkey. "You laughed at him." "You, my friend," said the owner, "are not a monkey."

"What is good for one is not necessarily good for another."

This story brings to life a fact that many of us don't want to accept: people are treated differently for countless reasons, including race, education, economic status, physical presence, political views, fashion, you name it. You must develop the ability to look at a situation and assess it in relation to your identity, needs and values—so that you can respond appropriately in any given moment.

First, you must figure out what your own value system is. Ask yourself, *"What do I believe? How do I want to live my life? How do I live my life?"* Most people find that the values they were taught as children are their strongest guides. Does this mean that what you learned as a child makes your decisions today?

For Sharon, a sister born and reared in a Christian home in Washington, D.C., that set of easily identifiable values, traits and issues was put to the test. Being in a committed relationship for several years, she and her man, who live now in Brooklyn, New York, decided that they wanted to live together. They found an apartment and were really excited. When Sharon called her mother to share the news, she got a big surprise. Her mother and sister were very upset. "I could hear the disappointment in my Mama's voice over the phone," Sharon says. "She told me that she didn't think it was a good idea for me to live with a man without being married to him, regardless of how old I was or how committed we are to one another." Sharon had to question her decision. Did she, underneath it all, as a thirty-year-old woman, agree with her mother? Did she think she was doing something "wrong"? More to the core of the issue, had she changed her value system from the one that her mother and sister had chosen to judge her decision? As it turned out, Sharon and her man did move in together. Because her values had evolved away from her family's values, Sharon decided to stick to her decision but also to assure her mother that she felt solid in her decision, that she was serious about her relationship, and that even though she did not choose to follow her mother's advice, she was okay. Sharon knew that there would be consequences: her mother might not change her views and never welcome the two of them with open arms while they were living together. Even so, Sharon committed to maintaining a loving and open relationship with her mother rather than shutting down or pulling away.

Sharon not only exercised her personal judgment; she acted as a responsible adult in the way that she communicated with her family. (She subsequently married her man, so everybody is happy.) I could name a dozen other sisters now living in cities away from their families—and with their boyfriends—who simply lie. "What they don't know won't hurt 'em," is their motto. For some, not revealing information may be the best decision. Why worry Mama unduly if you've made up your mind and you believe she will never understand, and more, that you will hurt her in the process? If you withhold information out of love, it may be fine. Know, however, that retreating out of cowardice holds no honor. What you are ultimately looking to reach is a level of honesty and integrity that allows you to be who you are—without apology, with grace. Unless you have this basic integrity, nothing you do can be real.

Countless brothers and sisters who were polled for this book said they felt their value systems were not as much set as a work in progress. Yes, they have certain fundamental beliefs about *how to be,* but they are open to possibilities. Isn't this kind of change the stuff of life? Change is the one guarantee in this world. Allow flexibility to be an integral part of your life as you develop your discrimination skills, and you can become friends with change and truly go with the flow without drowning!

Learning to Listen

Sometimes the most obvious things are the most difficult to grasp. One of the biggest stumbling blocks that people must overcome is the failure to communicate effectively. Don't assume that others will automatically understand you, or vice versa. Slow down long enough to give yourselves time to be with one another. We need to think more, remember better, listen carefully and not be afraid to talk until we are sure we are understood—if it is important and the person is willing to listen. Those mottos that the elders told you over and over again ring loudly now: *Think before you speak* and *If you don't have anything good to say, don't say anything at all.*

To be able to understand others and what they really mean requires patience, humility and good listening skills, a recipe repeated frequently throughout this book. If you want to actually and fully communicate, follow the time-honored Vedic (ancient East Indian) test, known as the Four Gateways of Speech. The test invites you to ask yourself four questions before you open your mouth: *Is it true? Is it timely? Is it necessary? Is it kind?* By using these key questions as a filter for what you communicate to others, you will be able to use your words productively as you go about your day.

Learning to listen is the essential ingredient in successful communication and cannot be overemphasized. When you are in someone's company, start off by making friendly eye contact and then greeting the person with a warm, firm handshake and a smile. As your conversation develops, listen for key words or phrases that can serve as guideposts to the person's message and attitude. When you are unsure what he or she is trying to say, gently interject a question that rephrases what you believe to be the core of the person's intent: "Do you mean that . . . ?" If you are incorrect, you may follow up with, "I'm not sure I understand yet. Would you tell me again what you mean?" By participating in your conversation using an even, friendly tone and showing sincerity through your words and body language, the other person will probably be happy to help you come to a clear understanding of what he or she means.

Two prominent psychologists, a married couple, Derek S. Hopson, Ph.D., and Darlene Powell Hopson, Ph.D., wrote a wonderful book, *Friends, Lovers and Soulmates: A Guide to Better Relationships Between Black Men and Women* (1994), in which they spent time exploring how to have a successful relationship. Following is some guidance from them on the art of assertive communication:

> It is important that a non-threatening climate be established to encourage meaningful dialogue. Nonverbal cues are also an important part of assertive communication. Making direct eye contact, listening attentively, sitting in a relaxed manner and nodding at appropriate moments all convey a message that you are a respectful, attentive and open-minded listener.
>
> Too many discussions begin with a negative statement: "We really have a problem," or "You messed up big time." This approach immediately puts the other person on the defensive and heightens a confrontation. Using "I" messages is much more effective: "I need to have more time to myself." "I felt hurt that you did not call me to tell me you were going to be working late." "It is important to me that you visit my family more often." With an "I" message, you accept ownership of your own feelings while also affirming and validating those of your partner [or the person with whom you are speaking]. This sets the stage for candid dialogue.

Although this may seem laborious at times, it's worth it. Adding to the Hopsons' strategy, I suggest that you also ask questions about the other party's feelings. Find out what the person was thinking when he or she made a particular comment. Take the time to really hear what the other person intends to communicate.

If, after making a concerted effort, you still fall short of getting the person's meaning, invite someone nearby to help you out. Sometimes language or cultural differences make it hard to deliver or grasp a clear message. That includes cultural usage of the same language, like between Caribbean and American use of English. Keep trying until you get there, though. It's worth it.

What Is My Standard?

So often I've heard folks complain—after the fact—that they are mad about how somebody treated them. *"I can't believe he did that to me!"* or *"How dare she talk like that in front of me?"* And the list goes on. I too have been a singer in that chorus. Chances are, so have you. There are times when you have probably accepted wrongful action from others too.

Dating back to our deceptive roots in this country, our ancestors bore the brunt of tremendous hardship that was downright inhuman. Even back in those horrific days of our *Maafa,* there were those who said "No," who refused to compromise the standard of how they saw fit to live their lives. The Ibo of Nigeria stepped off the slave ship and walked into the water to drown rather than endure the unendurable. Nat Turner and Henry Hyland Garnet, Denmark Vesey and Haiti's Jean Jacques Dessalines led uprisings, challenging slave owners to free their people from the wretched bondage forced on them. Harriet Tubman led people through the dead of night into the light of freedom, fortified by the knowledge that as African people, they deserved to be free of the oppression that was destroying their families.

Through the decades, it has been the same. Leaders have sprung up among our people, propelled by the spiritual and temporal knowledge that life had been and should be different, that what they believed in their hearts to be the righteous way to live was reattainable. Think of Marcus Garvey and Martin Luther King, Jr., Taharqa of Nubia and Kwame Nkrumah of Ghana, Malcolm X and Angela Davis, the Kentake queens of Ethiopia (Candace) and Yaa Asatewaa of Ghana, Thurgood Marshall and Dr. Dorothy Height, Huey P. Newton and Nelson Mandela.

What does that say for the common folk? For you and me? When we hear stories or witness tragedies of physical and emotional abuse in the home, at work, on the street, what can we do? We must use our brains and our bodies to change our lives. When I worked at *Essence* magazine, I used to hear editor in chief Susan Taylor say all the time, "We have to become active in our communities. We can't afford to sit back and let things happen. We have to do something." Susan implored all of us on staff to get involved in community organizations that help people to become strong. She also reminded the readership of the magazine and the staff on a regular basis to find their source of strength within first.

Starting at home is key. Discovering who you are and what you believe is the only way that you can stand firm among others. You must take the time to find out what your standard is for living in this world. What are the nuances of that standard? Where does it come from? Is it working? Are you—and the people you learned it from—happy *with* other people, and not at their expense? And more, once you know what you believe, promise yourself that you will not sink below that basic level. It is when you are unsure or weak as well as when you don't love your Self that you allow abuse of many kinds into your life. Learning how to be a productive and viable member of the community requires that you become strong. As you discover *how to be,* you will find that support is all around: through your faith, your family, your community, brothers and sisters throughout the Diaspora and many other bright lights who illuminate the path. You simply have to open your eyes to see them. Sister Iyanla Vanzant, bestselling author of *In the Meantime* (1998), and *One Day My Soul Just Opened Up* (1998), often reminds us that miracles happen every day. We just have to be prepared to see them.

Let There Be Virtues

There has been a lot of talk, especially in political circles, about the re-institution of "family values." A Black family revolution is in order! Many of our families are in crisis. They suffer tremendous stress due to economic insecurity, unsafe neighborhoods, latchkey children lacking supervision, single-parent households without the community support that we used to have and a general lack of constructive value development in the home. We must invigorate the village, allowing it to reinvent itself through us, in our daily lives. Starting in our own families, we must make the commitment to embrace those qualities of goodness that build integrity for ourselves—such as hard work, honesty and kindness—as they also inspire others to be the best that they can be. Some call them virtues. So did St. Peter in the New Testament. In a verse that talks about the importance of choosing to live by our divine nature rather than the aspect that has been corrupted, he says:

> And . . . giving all diligence, add to your faith virtue,
>   and to virtue, knowledge;
> And to knowledge temperance; and to temperance patience;
> And to patience godliness;
> And to godliness brotherly kindness; and to brotherly kindness
>   charity. (II Peter 1:4–7)

The way to energize the village is by example. One by one, you can study the virtues of life and make them your own. From our own historical tradition, you can learn the forty-two admonitions of *Maat,* which espouse how to live an honorable life. (See the chapter "Your Spiritual Life" for a listing of them.)

Honesty

Honesty *is* the best policy, and it starts at home. Daily meditation, prayer and contemplation in the morning and in the evening support honest, conscious living. In every spiritual tradition, it is recommended that you begin your day by asking the Creator through prayer for blessings to carry you through each moment. Ericka Huggins, a former Black Panther who now lives in San Francisco, says, "Throughout the day, I look to see how my actions might affect others. By stopping to pay attention to that, I can tell what I should do next. Coming from a place of honesty is the basic criterion, and it requires tremendous willpower and contemplation." That doesn't mean that you have license to say anything you think, whenever you think it. Brutal honesty—just telling it like it is—can hurt feelings. In comes your good judgment or discrimination. Without being dishonest, you can selectively determine when it is appropriate to reveal to others your assessment of any given situation. You have to be kind to yourself first to be able to reach a space of true honesty in your life. Meditation on God—an effective tool for unlocking that honest place inside—doesn't always reveal sweet thoughts and feelings either. Sometimes tumultuous things come up. Old concepts may get shot down. Memories of past actions may shake your steadiness at its core.

You may discover that a foundational area of your thinking must change, because it was based on faulty understanding. All of this is good. It means that you are allowing yourself to go through spiritual growth. As you discard the layers of baggage that you have been carrying around for years, you will find that lightness and gentleness can be your daily companions. It just takes time.

This is exactly what Gwynn Gladden's father taught her when she was growing up in Winston-Salem, North Carolina. "He taught us not to throw rocks. He taught us being honest was not when somebody was looking. It was when they weren't looking. That's how to stay honest, how to stay true to yourself," Gladden, a librarian, explains. "My father taught us to learn to stand for what you believe in and to stand by yourself when no one else will stand with you." By being honest with yourself first, you can then find the proper and honest way to be with others.

Compassion

Compassion has been the cornerstone of the development of African-American culture. We have been genuinely sensitive to the suffering of others and interested in relieving it. Our generations-old cry has been for fairness. We have stood up for our rights in hundreds of ways, demanding to be treated fairly while also appealing to others' human nature, to their compassion—their ability to empathize with and support our struggle. "How could it be," so many of our ancestors have asked, "that one cannot see the plight of African-American people as a fundamental effort toward goodness and integrity for all?" If you look historically, you will see that appealing to a sense of morality hasn't worked very well. Dr. Martin Luther King, Jr., wrote these words in a letter from his Birmingham, Alabama, jail cell, on April 16, 1963: "Injustice anywhere is a threat to justice everywhere. We are caught in an inescapable network of mutuality, tied in a single garment of destiny. Whatever affects one directly affects all indirectly." His words, though true, have gone largely unheeded. That double standard again. Fairness has frequently slipped from our grasp since our earliest days in the Western world. Still, we have the choice to reconnect to the African belief that we can offer love and respect to each other—to offer comfort and compassion—to all. Taking the time to consider others and offer compassion is a sign of respect, an example we must set for our children and for others who need the reminder.

This applies to family members and romantic relationships, too. As quick as you may be to support coworkers, sorority sisters and fraternity brothers or the neighbor down the street is as tough as it can be to look on your loved ones with compassionate eyes. And when you are too hard on your family, chances are you're beating up on yourself as well.

Patience

Think of your grandmother rocking slowly in her chair watching the scene at hand. Her feet aren't shaking. She's not trying to race you to your goal. She's just observing and rocking. In this fast-paced world, people are so quick to expect everything NOW. The job, the money, the man, the woman, the car, the house—everything NOW. Folks also want understanding, compassion and love pronto. In truth, this is the mentality of a child. In an adult it reflects a mentally immature attitude. Life doesn't always come to you as you want it. You often have to wait. Having patience requires faith and builds character. It means letting go of wishing for something that someone else has and resting in the certainty that what is yours will come. This doesn't allow you to sit around and do nothing, however. Patience must be coupled with honest and steadfast work in order for you to reach your goals. It's just that you can't expect to meet your objectives *and* be satisfied when you get there if you don't relax and enjoy the journey. Every moment does count. By living fully in the moment, you can lead a productive, serene and exciting life. Resist the temptation to worry over past action or plot too hard about what's next. Live *in* the moment; live *for* the future; learn *from* the past; avoid old mistakes. You can exercise the patience that allows you to enjoy the here and now. Only then can you lead a conscious and inspired life.

Acknowledging Others

What do you do when you are walking down the street and you see someone you know? Do you make eye contact and nod your head? Look off quickly in the other direction? Quicken your pace so that you can greet the person and strike up a conversation? Duck into a nearby alley? Going out of your way to avoid someone is generally not the best strategy to employ. If you see someone you recognize as you are intent on doing something else, a nod of the head with a friendly gaze will suffice. If you keep your pace even and your focus on your goal, the person will see that you have something else to do. If the other party, on the other hand, clearly wants to strike up a conversation, you can easily greet the person in stride and let her know that you are very happy to see her but that now is not the best time to talk. End your communication with a warm yet firm "Have a great day," and be off.

That's only one point of acknowledgment. So many occasions present themselves when you see people. How you choose to recognize them does matter, so think about how you normally respond to see if your behavior matches your true intention. Here are some guidelines to consider:

- When you see someone you know, greet the person with enthusiasm. Speak clearly when you say "Hello." Say the person's name: "Good afternoon, Mrs. Williams. It's so nice to see you."
- Extend your hand and gaze at the person as you greet him or her.

- As you are going about your day and you see familiar faces, offer a smile. Stay centered—comfortable and content within your own being—so that you don't overdo it. You cannot spend all of your time looking at others. Keep your goal at the forefront of your mind.
- If you are in a restaurant, don't get out of your seat, walk to another person's table and interrupt the meal to say hello to a relative stranger or, worse, a celebrity. Let the person have his peace. That goes for any other situation where the party you want to acknowledge is unavailable to you. Pick your moments wisely.
- If you are from the South, it is customary to give a nod or a "Hello" to people as you pass them on the street. In the North, people are not as likely to be as friendly to strangers on the street. When I first moved to New York, in fact, I spoke to most people who passed me on the street, only to have strangers start following me. I quickly learned that the Baltimore way did not translate well in the Big Apple. Pay attention!
- Audrey Smaltz, an entrepreneur and a member of the U.S. Commission for Protocol, says that when you are in a professional setting, you should speak to all of the Black folks even when you aren't able to greet everyone.
- Don't gawk at people from a distance or up close. People deserve to have their personal space.
- Give celebrities their privacy. You can acknowledge them if you naturally find yourself in their company. Otherwise, stick to your own agenda. It is terribly unsettling for people to have no sense of personal space when they are out in the world. Those who have risen to celebrity status in contemporary society have reached a point where they sometimes cannot even walk out of their homes without being accosted. Don't fall into the unnatural place of invading others' space. Be respectful, and remain at a distance.
- Be mindful of touching people. Keep your hands to yourself unless there's a natural moment for a physical connection. Even then, reserve physical contact to a handshake or a touch on the shoulder for casual acquaintances.

Making Introductions

There is an art to introducing people to each other so that they will feel comfortable. The key is to share just enough information about each person in a clear and warm manner that will allow for the two (or more) of them to find a common interest or point of reference. Traditionally, in many African countries greetings were not only a time of introduction, but also a time of wishing the other person prosperity or success. In villages in the small West African country of Burundi, the Twa (misnamed by Europeans as the "Pygmies"), who migrated from Central Africa, spoke the language of Kirundi. Upon seeing each other for the first time, they would say, *"Amashyo,"* or "May you have herds [of cattle]," as the other person responded with *"Amashongore,"* which meant "I wish you herds of females." Cattle were a metaphor for health and happiness. In the West African country of Senegal, long greetings are customary with lengthy handshakes until you have sincerely learned about each member of the person's family. A Senegalese responds by asking about the health of your family, your work and if the weather agrees with you, to which it is customary to respond that everything is fine. In the Senegalese language of Wolof, *Yamangahfahnin* means "Good morning," and *Yamangahyenlou* means "Good evening."

In the United States, there are many details about introductions that include all of the niceties, such as remembering to greet people with a smile and an affirmation, such as "Good afternoon." As well, there are specific guidelines when it's your turn to make the introductions. The degree of formality depends on the circumstances surrounding the introduction:

- Always introduce a junior person to a more senior person. For instance, when you and your assistant meet the president of the local YMCA, you would say, "Mr. Lake, I would like to introduce my assistant, Katherine Wallace. Katherine, Mr. Lake is the new president of our local Y."
- Include a few details about each party as you introduce them, such as job titles, your relationship to them or any points that would be common for them to note.
- Out of respect, address elders using Mr., Mrs. or Ms. Do not address an elder by a first name. When you can, greet elders first.
- Use proper titles for people who have them. A judge, a medical doctor, a professor and anyone else with a title should receive the proper title upon introduction.
- When introducing someone to a group of people, go from left to right, unless there is clearly a senior person present. Then, start with that person and resume from left to right, unless you know the rank of each member of the group. Give people a chance to shake hands before you move on to a new introduction. Treat everyone, including the most junior person, with respect.
- When introducing a group of people to each other, seek out the most senior person, and introduce the others to him or her, or go from left to right and announce each person's name and affiliation so that everyone can hear you.

- When introducing a spouse with a different last name, state the first and last name clearly without drawing attention to the fact that you don't share a surname. Instead, just say, "I'd like for you to meet my wife, Shondra Brown."
- If you get the chance to meet the President of the United States (or of any other country, for that matter), *you* should be introduced to him or her. For instance, if you were meeting President Robert Mugabe of Zimbabwe, one would say, "Mr. President, may I present Mr. Blake, a businessman from Tallahassee, Florida, in the United States." You should then extend your right hand to shake the President's, look the President squarely in the eye and acknowledge that you are pleased to meet him or her.
- Similarly, if you find yourself in the company of a king, queen or other member of a reigning family, only your name should be spoken along with your title or a description of who you are. The person doing the introducing should say, "Your Majesty, may I present Ms. Jones. She is the director of staffing for the local community college." A king or a queen is initially called "Your Majesty," and thereafter "Sir" or "Madam." This is the one time other than in the company of elders that you should address a person in that way.
- Traditionally women curtsy and men bow when meeting the Queen of England. If you meet on American turf, a slight bow of the head will suffice.
- In the Catholic Church, it's pretty straightforward. When you're meeting the Pope, one introduces you by saying, "Your Holiness, may I present Mr. Lewis." A cardinal is referred to as "Your Eminence." Further, if you are Catholic and meeting the Pope or another high-ranking official, you should drop to your knees, take the dignitary's extended hand and kiss his sacred ring. If you aren't Catholic, a bow will be fine.

When Someone Is Disabled

Chances are that someone in your life, if not in your family, is disabled. For many years in this country, disabled people were ostracized. In African societies, such as the Bantu people who reside throughout the Continent, disabled people are considered special and require extra love and attention. To them, no one is thrown away. Thanks to public education here, we now know that being disabled does not make a person unfit for society or otherwise unwelcome. Actually, the *Disability Etiquette Handbook* defines a disability as "a condition caused by an accident, trauma, genetics or disease which may limit a person's mobility, hearing, vision, speech or mental function." It is up to each of us to treat everyone with respect. Disabled people are just like you and me: have no fear. When it comes to introductions, use these guidelines from the *Handbook*:

- Offer to shake hands with a disabled person at the point of introduction.
- Shake the left hand when that is necessary.
- When shaking hands is not an option, make physical contact by touching the person on the shoulder or arm.
- Speak directly to the disabled person even if he or she uses an interpreter or is traveling with a companion.
- Treat a disabled adult as you would any other adult. Don't patronize or talk down to the person.

The Handshake

There's nothing worse than a limp handshake. Yet I continue to be surprised by how many people offer their hands without paying much attention to this key greeting. For some women, this could be a throwback to the days when a gentleman greeted a woman with a kiss on the back of the hand. Trust me, I've heard that said. But let's be real. How many sisters get their hands kissed these days? And when we do, it seems creepy and phony, unless it's offered by a loved one. Anyhow, you hold your hand differently for that interaction. Plus, for many African-American women, those days of yesteryear did not represent frequent moments of curtsies and kisses. For the record: it's not cool, cute, attractive or otherwise smart to shake hands without some strength and intention coming through your grip.

It took a trip to Switzerland for me to get a sense of the full import of this simple Western ritual. I was on a business trip and had been briefed by coworkers about what to expect. The most immediate lesson was that when you shake someone's hand, extend your right hand matter-of-factly, grip the other's right hand with strength but without being overbearing (you don't want to break any bones!) and look straight into the person's eyes. They cautioned me by noting that even the firmest grip is lost when your eyes wander. Eye contact conveys interest and honesty. Over the years, I have seen time and again that I remember people better when we complete that initial contact. A warm, welcoming glance from another person ensures that the exchange matters to him or her as much as it does to me.

However, only a few generations back, our ancestors could have been whipped until bloody from the hide of leather straps for daring to look a white person in the eye. You've probably heard stories about "shuffling Negroes" and conjured up images of a Black person in servitude who walked slowly along with eyes cast downward. Well, that posture was not assumed by choice. When an enslaved African looked directly into the eyes of a white man, woman *or* child, what he was most likely assaulted with was, "Don't eyeball me, boy!" After years of being forced to lower our eyes, a practice that lasted until recent times in some areas of the South, it's no wonder that some of us don't feel comfortable making eye contact. What we must do now is wake up out of the spell that we were placed under upon arrival in this country. We can meet anyone eye to eye. And we must.

As it relates to the mechanics of the handshake, even for left-handed people, it is traditional to shake hands using your right hand, throughout most of the Western world and in many African and Caribbean countries that have been Westernized. The exception generally comes for people with disabilities. Here are some other pointers:

- Remove your gloves before shaking hands, so that the contact is skin to skin.
- When you want to convey warmth along with conviction, you can shake hands while placing your left hand over the shaking hands, thereby cupping the other party's hand.
- If you suffer from sweaty palms, carry a handkerchief in your pocket. Before shaking someone's hand, surreptitiously dry yours off. You will not make a good impression by leaving behind a moist palm print.
- When shaking hands with an elder, be gentle but still firm.

When Not to Shake

Depending on where you grew up, it may be a knee-jerk reaction for you to extend your right hand when you first meet someone, but a firm handshake is still largely a universal Western way of greeting someone.

When meeting a dignitary (or anyone else of a traditional background) from the Far East, bring your hands together in the form of praying hands and bow your head slightly—instead of shaking hands. This gesture, called *namaste* in Hindi, an Indian language, is a sign of welcoming another in the highest way.

In some Islamic communities, men do not touch women unless they are family. It is considered disrespectful. Women doing business with Islamic men will need to check to see what the codes of conduct for business are—whether they have been relaxed in your particular setting. If you cannot shake, acknowledge your associate by name and brief eye contact, because prolonged eye contact is considered offensive.

Do your research. In this way you will be prepared no matter whom you meet. For instance, when Bob Dole ran for President of the United States, he met many people on the road. Because Dole has a lame right hand, his advance team had the responsibility of reminding people to shake his left hand. Really, though, an aware person in his company should not have needed to be told. When you aren't sure, watch what others do. Being observant is the best preparation.

What's in a Name?

One of the hardest basics of being with people is being able to identify them properly. It starts with remembering a person's first and last name. People really appreciate it when they are acknowledged personally. The finest way of honoring another person may be by greeting him or her with a firm handshake and a verbal acknowledgment: "It's so great to see you, Patricia. It has been six months since we last saw one another at the Johnson family reunion, hasn't it?" This greeting will definitely make Patricia feel good. You remembered her, her name *and* where you last saw her. If someone were to approach you at that moment, you would be prepared to introduce Patricia (I trust along with her last name!) and tell a bit about her. Such awareness goes a long way.

Everyone is special. When you treat them that way, you reap many unknown rewards. That goes for when you write people's names too. When you correspond with another person, take the time to check the spelling of the person's name and title carefully. One of my pet peeves is seeing my name spelled every way other than how it is actually spelled. It baffles me, too. If someone can spell an unusually difficult-to-spell or foreign name, why can't he spell *Harriette*? In the end, I think it's because the person isn't paying attention. As Terrie Williams describes in her book of wisdom, *The Personal Touch* (1994), correspondence with the correct spelling and other pertinent details is the one to receive the first response.

That said, I have to admit that I have a lot of nerve being ruffled about my name spelling when I often literally forget people's names— people I know! One of my greatest nightmares is that I will forget someone's name when it comes time to introduce people. It's as if a part of my brain was born dead in the memory department. There are exercises that you can practice to jump-start the memory, and sometimes they work for me. They include making an immediate association with a person and his or her name. For instance, a young woman named Faith recently began interning with my company. Her first day at work was at the beginning of the year, right after Kwanzaa. I had just celebrated Kwanzaa and was therefore keenly aware of the Swahili term for "faith," *imani*. To remember Faith's name, I immediately thought *imani* in my head. Not only did I memorize her actual name, but I also told her of the Swahili and Arabic translation of her name—both of which are *faith*—and everyone in my office began to call her Imani!

Since I'm not always so swift, I have come up with an alternative plan that allows me to greet people kindly and respectfully—causing minimal, if any, discomfort. Because I usually travel with a business associate or my husband, I let the other party know *before* we arrive at our destination that I may not remember everyone's name, so I may need help. I let the person know that as we approach someone or someone approaches us, I will introduce my companion in the following manner, "I would like you to meet my husband, George Chinsee." I may add, "He's a fashion photographer and has worked with me on many projects." This often will trigger the person's saying his or her own name. If that doesn't happen, George knows to ask, "What is your name?" Another point to note here: Since George and I have different last names, it is important that I say his whole name. Brothers may have become more relaxed about their wives' keeping their maiden names, but rest assured they don't want to be called by her name. Your husband will appreciate your speaking up in the beginning.

If I am alone and I greet someone whose name I can't remember, I speak to something that I know about the person. Recently, for example, I saw an accessories designer who is mentioned in *Jumping the Broom*. Although her name escaped me, how I knew her did not. When she asked me if I knew who she was (people will do that, although I strongly discourage putting people on the spot in that way), I said, "Of course. You design those great scarves. I know who you are. I have just forgotten your name."

What people want most is to be acknowledged and remembered. When in doubt, rather than avoiding someone by ducking to a distant corner of the room, go right up to the person, say hello and if necessary ask to be reminded of the person's name. Then, as Terrie Williams suggests, repeat the name out loud and silently to yourself several times in an attempt to lock it into your memory. Attach the name to a familiar idea, place or item so that you will have a way to cross-reference it later.

To Hug or Not to Hug?

Greetings are not as simple as they seem, so make your intention your focus. Take a moment before you greet someone to ask yourself, *"What do I want to convey to this person?"* Your answer will help to guide you to the appropriate greeting. A handshake is the safe and appropriate greeting for most business encounters. A hug is a different matter altogether. Like many of my colleagues, I am an affectionate person. I like to greet people I have known for some time, even professional acquaintances, with a hug. The gesture is usually cheek to cheek, and maybe shoulder to shoulder, but not full body contact. My guess is that a good 40 percent of the people I greet regularly receive a "professional" hug.

Several years ago, I learned a valuable lesson on the hug front, though. I was at a spiritual retreat among many people I had grown to know and like. While on a break, I ran into several friends, and we shared hugs and kisses. After a few of these greetings, I came upon a woman I hadn't seen in some time. As we approached one another, I got the clear message that it was not appropriate to hug her. A handshake would have been awkward too, so we ended up not touching at all. We greeted one another warmly with our eyes and our words. Amazingly, I didn't feel that anything was missing from that exchange. Later, I remembered that moment and examined it carefully for lessons. I learned that there is a time and a place for physical contact, but that it is not always necessary. Further, I saw that whether a person touched me or not did not determine how much respect or love he or she had for me. Since that time, I have been more reserved with my hugs. Instead, if I do shake hands with someone who is more special than a general business associate, I often extend my left and cup it over the other person's, so that I am gently embracing the hand between my own. If I do not want someone to embrace me, I communicate that subtly through my own body language, by standing firmly planted and extending my hand to that person or holding my hands together in front of me and smiling broadly at them.

So, when is it okay to hug? You must be the judge of this in your own life. Knowing yourself and how you may be perceived by others can also help you gauge how physical contact will be accepted. Here are a few suggestions for when you may hug:

- When you are greeting a loved one or a family member. Unless the person is a spouse or significant other, your bodies should not touch below the waist. In public, all such greetings should be discreet.

- When you are greeting a coworker who has just gotten engaged or married, had a baby or had a death in the family—that is, when you are sharing love.
- When you are greeting others of equal status with whom you are friends at social events.
- When not to do so would create discomfort for yourself or others.

Don't feel that you have to hug someone when you really don't want to do so. There are spiritual reasons to avoid being touched by people whom you know don't like you or vice versa. Ask an elder whom you think will be open to discussing this with you for greater insights. In the here and now, accept the responsibility that you are the guardian of yourself, and that includes your body. Be aware of people who are inebriated or otherwise off balance, even if they are your friends. You may want to keep your distance for both of your sakes.

Greetings with a Kiss

In these days of heightened awareness of sexual misconduct, people have become more sensitive to how they greet one another, particularly as it relates to kissing. There are a few general guidelines that you can follow, ones that have evolved out of a global context.

- If you are meeting someone for the first time, don't greet the person with a kiss. A handshake will suffice. If the other person is European or from a French-speaking African country, however, it may be that he or she quite naturally will shake your hand and then offer first the right cheek and then the left. This cheek kissing is traditional and widespread in Europe and more frequent in the United States. No lips are involved, and often faces don't even touch. So as not to be rude, extend your right cheek to meet your acquaintance and then your left. Follow the lead of the foreigner on this one.

Making Exits

Leaving graciously is an art unto itself. Whether you're leaving a party, your office, your home or an argument, you can do so with grace. Although the basics are the same for everyone, it does seem to be true that the rules shift a bit for men and women. For instance, one sister from South Carolina explained that her mother taught her never to be the last person to leave the party. "It's un-ladylike." One's manhood is not questioned, however, by the hour that he leaves an event. For a man—a gentleman—what would be more important is whether he has taken care of any woman he escorted to the event and/or any woman who might have needed help. Tips for graceful exits:

Events
- Thank the host before you leave a party or other event, even if the affair is casual.
- Make sure that everyone who came with you is accounted for and safe.
- Don't consume too much alcohol or food before leaving. Be able to leave on solid feet.
- If you think you will have to leave early, quietly let your host know in advance as well as anyone who came to the event with you.
- If you are uncomfortable with the subject of conversation, the company at an affair or other situation, gently stand and make your way to the host and let him or her know that you will need to leave. Save the reasons for your departure until another time, unless the offense is grave.
- Don't overstay your welcome. If it turns out that it's just you and the host left at an affair, stand up, thank the host for a lovely event and head toward the door.
- Offer to help clean up at a more casual or home party when it feels appropriate. Black folks have done this since the beginning of time!

At Work
- Out of courtesy and practicality, let somebody know when you are leaving your office, whether for the day, an errand or a break.
- Even if you punch a time clock, it's a good practice to greet your boss and your coworkers when you arrive, and say "Good evening" when you prepare to leave. In this way, you will establish a pattern of consistency and reliability. Should the occasion arise when you need someone to support you if you have to leave early, your coworkers and boss will remember your openness and team spirit and work to assist you.

In Tense Situations
- If you find yourself in an uncomfortable situation in which you are unable to dispel anger or other strong emotions, attempt to remove yourself as soon as possible.
- Speak up and recommend that everyone take time to cool off and then reconvene with a clear head.

- Excuse yourself to go to the rest room—a great strategy if you fear yourself getting out of control. A splash of cold water on your face is far better than inflammatory words that you may regret later.
- Stand and gesture to shake everyone's hand and let others know you must go. It's not rude. It's called self-preservation.
- If you can explain your perspective calmly, do so!

Watch Your Words!

The elders have whispered about it for years. There's a time and place for conversation, and sometimes it's best to keep your mouth shut. The art of using your voice and its messages to your advantage is something that you cultivate over time. Yet many people waste their energy by spouting off about absolutely everything, paying no heed to what they are actually saying or how their words are affecting others. Such irresponsible speech represents unconscious action.

It all starts with our youth. One summer afternoon I was at the beach with my husband when I overheard a young girl barking out orders at her mother. I opened my eyes and sat up, so that I could see who it was who dared to speak so disrespectfully to her own mother. The child was a white girl about five years old. As I listened to her in amazement, I thought, "If that had been my Mama, she'd have shot me a look that said: 'Take those words back in your mouth and swallow them so they can come back out as something that makes sense.' " You know that look! There would be no way that any Black child in my neighborhood could get away with yelling or smart-mouthing her Mama or any other grown person for that matter. Yet I couldn't just chalk this scene up to white family life. I've seen similar things happen in my Harlem neighborhood in the company of children who spend too much time on the street unsupervised. The bravado that they are developing has extended as far as speaking in unconscionable ways to their parents.

Our words really do matter. Here are a few ways that you can be the guardian of your speech:

- Choose to make affirming statements; it is a healthy practice.
- Decide to remain silent when nothing of value can be contributed.
- Use discrimination when offering criticism. Otherwise, you simply end up backing folks into a corner.
- Paint a picture through anecdote to make it easier for others to receive your message, especially when you are offering recommendations for change. Allegory and metaphor are the most African of teaching methods.

- Eliminate gossip from your verbal communication and thought. In the teachings of Ptahhotep, an ancient Khamitic (Egyptian) priest who lived some 2,500 years before the birth of Christ, we are advised: "Do not repeat slander, nor should you even listen to it. It is the spouting of the hot bellied. Just report a thing that has been observed, not something that has been heard secondhand. If it is something negligible, don't even say anything. He who is standing before you will recognize your worth. Slander is like a terrible dream against which one covers the face."

On Profanity

I will never forget my first foray into the use of profanity. I was no more than ten years old, and I had just learned a "bad" word at school. I didn't have any idea of what it meant, but knew enough to want to try it out nonetheless. There I was in my room, throwing my dolls, one by one, into my closet—with a vengeance. As each doll sailed through the air, I yelled, "F— you!" What a release I felt. I was doing something bad, and it felt oh-so-good! Until my mother heard me. All of a sudden she appeared from around the corner. "What did you say?" she asked. "Nothing," I responded. "What did you say?" she asked. "Nothing," I responded. "What did you say?" she repeated, this time with steam coming out of her eyes. I remained silent. "Come with me," she said as she took my hand, turned and stalked into her bathroom. There she did the undoable. She did what she had threatened to do before. *She washed my mouth out with soap!* She literally put a bar of Ivory soap in my mouth and held my lips shut for what seemed like forever. (I'm sure it was only a few seconds.) While she was holding it, she promised to do it again if I ever repeated such a thing. Shaking my head remorsefully, with silent tears streaming down my face, I swore off cursing. So, when I first broke my promise a half-dozen years or so later, the taste of Ivory soap brought me back to reality: *Don't do it!*

A single father from Oklahoma, Dekar Lawson, explained that it took his aunt to set him straight on profanity. As a young boy, he too had come home with a *bad* word, the worst: *mother f—r.* After putting down his book bag, he found himself repeating it under his breath over and over again, while his aunt, who watched him until his Mama came home, was busy fixing dinner in the kitchen. When she deciphered his mutterings, she stopped her food preparations, collected some paper and crayons and then called him into the room with her. "What did you say?" she calmly inquired. "Nothing," he responded. "What did you say?" she insisted. When finally he uttered what he now knew to be a bad word, she surprised him. No regular punishment was in store. She asked him to write that word down, along with every other curse word. Slowly putting crayon to paper, he wrote the few words he knew in big, fat, child-made letters. She filled in the words he didn't know and then proceeded to define each one indi-

vidually, saving *m-f* for last. When she got to that word and graphically described what that word meant—what someone wanted to do to somebody else's Mama—Dekar lost all interest in cursing. That lesson has paid off with his preadolescent daughter. Dekar teaches her to respect everyone, especially somebody's Mama.

And a final note about codes of conduct. Saying a curse word used to be grounds for punishment in my house. As I polled adults around the country about the ground rules when they were growing up, the punishments varied, but in most homes, cursing was not allowed. Parents went to all manner of extremes to prevent their sweet babies from hearing profanity. Spelling words rather than saying them was one method. Substituting naughty words that ran just short of profane was a favorite in my house. My mother consistently used "durn" for "damn."

When it comes to profanity, times surely have changed. The lyrics of rap and hip-hop music are laced with profanity and echoed in the halls of the public schools. Mrs. James, a retired teacher from the Baltimore City public school system who now volunteers several days a week at her old stomping grounds, is infuriated and afraid. "For many of these young girls and boys, if they don't use profanity, they'd have to close their mouths. They can't talk to you. I've gotten to the point that I hear so much profanity from the kids until I *have* to listen to it. They aren't swearing at me, they aren't swearing about me. They have no other vocabulary. They don't *want* to learn anything else, and nobody makes them whether they want to or not. Because if they do learn something else, their friends won't understand what they're talking about."

Is there a way to turn the tide? Some educators argue that it is possible to expand a student's vocabulary. Following in Mrs. James's footsteps, more of us need to get out there among our youth and offer them the opportunity to learn more about what is available to them. As far as profanity goes in general, here are some guidelines to follow regarding its use:

- Get creative and use descriptive language instead of profanity whenever you can. Make up words. My new literary assistant, Raven Rowe, says "Razen Frakken," instead of *m-f,* and it cracks us up every time.

- Avoid using profanity in a work environment under nearly all circumstances. Even if others are bandying it about, you don't have to.
- If you're in the company of people who normally use light profanity and you also engage in the practice, do so with discretion.
- Don't curse in front of your elders, unless it is common practice. Even then, I don't recommend using profanity. The same goes for your boss, leaders in your spiritual community, your children—anyone who might take offense.
- Lead by example. Maybe others will stop cursing to keep from offending you!

YOUR QUESTIONS ANSWERED

1. Who should walk through a revolving door first? A man with a woman, a woman with an older woman or a parent with a child?

Back when we were consistently taught respect for our elders, the elder female would always be the first to enter a space, whether it was a revolving door or not. Today, such rules have relaxed quite a bit, in part because in business settings especially, it can seem quite awkward for a group of men to wait to let the lone woman enter first. Some women consider any special treatment a form of discrimination, when, in fact, it may mean that they are confused about how they should be treated. Choosing to exert so much energy on being treated exactly like men has been mistaken for the pursuit of equality. (What Black women more accurately need to do is to work to restore womanhood to its rightful place. That place is understood through Khamitic culture through forces of nature that have complementary counterparts that are different but of equal value.) The bottom line in this topic is you should do what is practical as it relates to the door.

As far as elders go, it still is in good form to honor them. In the case of a revolving door, the kindest gesture might be to go ahead of the elder so that you shoulder the weight of the door and the elder moves through effortlessly. In a social setting, some women still appreciate being invited to enter a space first. If a group of people is standing at a revolving door, those in the front should proceed rather than waiting to let others pass. A parent and small child will likely prefer to wait until the crowd has died down.

2. Is it rude not to take off your sunglasses when being introduced to someone?

Yes. Part of the introduction is eye contact. Connecting with a person visually seals communication, so if you keep your sunglasses on at any time other than when you are outdoors in the blazing sun, you may come off as being pretentious and untrustworthy.

3. My parents always told me to take off my hat inside someone's home and definitely when sitting down to eat a meal at home or in public. Is that still a rule?

Men should take their hats off when they enter a building and certainly when they sit down to eat a meal. Traditionally men's hats are worn to protect them against the elements, whereas women often wear hats as fashion accessories that can stay on all day. Even though men today wear caps and other toppers for fashion purposes, it's not fitting to walk around in one when you are under a roof.

4. When you want to sit down on a bus or a train, shouldn't you say "Excuse me" or "May I sit down?" instead of just standing there staring somebody down?

Unless you have a good reason to need to sit down—such as a disability, pregnancy, frailty from age or feeling faint—you should just stand until a seat becomes available. Why should you be afforded a seat that already is occupied by someone else? If you do have a valid reason, by all means look for a welcoming face and quietly ask the person if he or she might let you sit. Explain in a few words the nature of your malady. If you are declined, don't get an attitude. Breathe deeply, and continue to stand. To those who are seated, pay attention to the people around you. If you see a person in need of sitting, immediately offer your seat.

5. In a grocery store, after I pay for my groceries or as I'm packing them up, often the next person is standing right beside me, trying to hurry me up. I think that is rude.

It is. Instead of getting into a debate with the person, pay attention to the task at hand. As quickly as you can, gather your belongings and move on. If you feel that the person is invading your space, you may say—firmly and with a smile—that you would appreciate the person giving you a few extra moments and some extra room.

6. Isn't after 9:30 P.M. too late to call someone on the phone?

It depends on the nature of your call and your relationship with the person you are calling. Business calls typically should end by 6:00 P.M. unless you have established other ground rules. Close friends with whom you regularly speak at a late hour or who would not find it an imposition if you need to place a late emergency call are fine. On the other hand, anyone who goes to bed early will be annoyed. When it comes to using the telephone, think about the person you are calling with compassion rather than just yourself. When your call first connects, find out if it is a good time to talk or if you should call back later.

7. When you're waiting to use a pay phone and the person ahead of you is taking a long time, what should you do or say?

Look around to see if there are any other phones in sight. If so, go there. If your call is urgent and you don't know of another available phone, you may stand in view of the person and gesture that you really need to use the phone. You may also say in a few words that you need to make a quick and urgent call. If the person becomes hostile, move on. If you are the one on the phone, keep in mind that a pay phone is for public consumption, not to be used like the phone in your home. Be fast. If others are lining up, that's your cue to say goodbye and hang up.

8. If you're in line for an event and someone in front of you lets her friends cut in, what should you do?

Assess the situation. How long have you been waiting in line? How many people are behind you? Was the person in front of you always holding a space for the friends? If you feel that the new group of people are infringing on your space, by all means speak up and graciously let the person in front of you know that many people have been waiting before these friends arrived. Otherwise, ignore them.

9. If you buy tickets for a group of people and one of them cancels at the last minute, should the person pay for his ticket anyway?

Yes. If the person had committed to buy the ticket, he or she should be responsible for paying for it or finding someone else to buy it. One way to head off this problem is to let everyone know in advance what the ticket price is and that each person is responsible. If you can, collect the money in advance.

10. When you are talking to someone who is long-winded, and you really need to go or get back to work, what should you say?

Find a space in the conversation and gently interrupt. Let the person know that as interesting as the conversation is, you must leave. Make your exit as brief as possible. You may offer to shake the person's hand and then begin to walk away.

11. I'm embarrassed to say that I really don't know how to accept a compliment. I always feel uncomfortable when people say nice things about me. Any advice?

Many people have difficulty accepting praise. Rather than clamming up, consider who is offering the compliment. By graciously thanking the person for thinking so kindly of you, you will complete an important circle. The person who made the gesture will then feel good, and you will be able to experience this momentary celebration of you with humility. If someone else is deserving of the compliment extended, thank the person who offered it and immediately say, "Wanda is the one who made this project happen," or "It was a team effort. I will be sure to let everyone know how you feel."

YourSpiritualLife

God and nature first made us what we are, and then
out of our own created genius we make ourselves
what we want to be. Follow always that great law.
Let the sky and God be our limit and Eternity our
measurement.

MARCUS GARVEY

A L L of the rules, all of the social graces, all of the codes of conduct
that we possibly can engage to govern our lives mean absolutely nothing if we don't have a good grasp on why we are here. Instead of being
supported by practical social conventions that help to make personal
interactions more comfortable, people end up almost sleepwalking if
they don't get the true meaning of life: that we are on this planet to
care for ourselves, for our families, for our communities, for our environment and, as the Yoruba believe, to develop character. Life is not
about keeping up with the Joneses, movin' on up like the Jeffersons or
any other upward movement unless our efforts include reaching back
and supporting our fellow brothers and sisters along the way. As our
ancestors well knew, the role of a human being is to offer love and respect to everyone and everything on the path. That essentially is the
reason that etiquette exists in the first place—to provide a framework
for honorable living.

Yet without a strong sense of Self, an understanding of who you are,
all of the exercises you could possibly master are essentially for naught.
And tapping into that sacred space of Self requires a spiritual connection. When it comes right down to it, the essence of learning *how to be*
finds its source in spirituality. Whether you are aware of it or not, the
nature and health of your soul are defined by your connection to the
Divine. How in sync you are with your spiritual Self really does determine if you will prosper or perish—but not in the traditional meaning,
as it relates to things external. Common African philosophy says that

we are spirit beings who are on a spiritual journey. Thus, prosperity in the sense that I now mention it has to do with your entire being. From the inside out, a person is prosperous when he or she lives in alignment with the Creator. Because this is true, it is essential in the course of daily living for you to live your life as if you are awake—as if you are conscious. I am reminded of the last line in Spike Lee's film *School Daze* (1988), which proclaimed to Black America: "WAKE UP!" At the time that I saw the film, I thought this loud statement was overkill. Now I see differently. Both individually and as a community, Black folks need a wake-up call in a big way. It is our responsibility to live conscious and responsible lives.

A conscious being has a keen awareness of the world in which he or she lives as well as the condition of his or her inner state. This is the minimum requirement of a conscious life and cannot be attained without a spiritual connection. You might liken a conscious person to being an electronic appliance with a backup battery that is plugged into a live socket. The force of energy that flows from the socket through the wire into the appliance affords the appliance the ability to perform its function. Further, the energy stored in the battery makes the appliance capable of working even after it is unplugged, although at limited capacity. In time, however, the appliance will lose its strength unless it is reconnected to its power source. By remaining connected to your Higher Power, whatever it is, you can live a fulfilling and inspired life. Tapping into the wellspring of grace and knowledge that is the Divine, you can rise above all challenges. Without the essential connection to the power source, you will eventually lose your way, which leads ultimately to death, at least of the spirit. In the Black community, as well as the rest of the world, there are too many lost souls—people who essentially are dead inside largely because of their lack of faith. Our ancestors' disconnection from their own spiritual traditions certainly helped to foster our people's current state of spiritual confusion. Misguided souls wander and frequently fall prey to reckless behavior that is both self-destructive and potentially dangerous to the community at large. Disconnection will do that.

Our African ancestors understood that and walked through their lives with a tremendous faith and respect for each other and Nature. They maintained a spiritual connection. And so must you.

For our ancestors, their faith promised that their God would carry them when they could not go on any longer. For this reason, they did not have to fall victim to negative thinking, hopelessness, defensiveness and the range of other ills that create waves of destructive energy in our world. I encourage you to consider your spiritual life as a basic component in cultivating good manners, which really is conscious living. Evaluate your spiritual life. How did you learn about God, worship and integrity when you were a child? Did you grow up in the Baptist Church? A mosque? The AME congregation in your town? Where? How did your mother interpret religion? Spirituality? What were the guidelines for your father? For others in your family? Have you evolved spiritually over the years? What are your beliefs today? Do you follow a spiritual path? Once you have considered these basic and vital questions, make a conscious decision about how you will cultivate your spirituality so that it can serve you throughout life.

This process has yielded exquisite treasures for me. I remember the powerful example that my mother and her mother, Grandma Carrie, presented for my sisters and me when we were growing up. Their brand of religion was more than just a few hours in church on Sunday. These two powerful ladies showed us that it was possible to be strong *and* kind. Although my Daddy was not a regular churchgoer, his brand of spirituality showed its face in his own powerful virtues. A judge for more than thirty years, my Daddy has been a man of principle and ethics. For him, honesty and clarity have been basics for a good life. And so, the foundation of my spiritual life was strong. When I look a little deeper, I also see that I experienced a long period of searching, during which I looked outside my family, my Self and my religious upbringing to fill the void that developed during my adolescence and early adulthood. Instead of an inward journey, mine became a search for some sort of friend/school/work/boyfriend connection that would make me whole. That search fell far short of satisfaction and led me right back to the place that my family had presented so many years before, although not before some ugly stumbling. It says in the Bible, "The kingdom of Heaven dwells within." I rediscovered this wisdom just before crossing the threshold of my thirties when I heard from my own spiritual teacher, Gurumayi Chidvilasananda, that *God dwells within you as you.* When I received that message, it was as if a light went on inside my soul.

There is a proverb that says, *"As above, so below."* Inside me, I discovered, was not just my personal body but the body of my people *and* the pure presence of the Divine. And so, the core message of *How to Be*: get to know yourself, learn your history, have faith in God and find that connection within. Only then can you live a fulfilling, honorable and worthy life. Our grandparents knew this truth, as did their parents and those who came before them. Through ritual and song, ceremony and dance, they nurtured and celebrated it.

To help you develop a strong spiritual center, this chapter will explore the historical, spiritual and religious roots of our people, painting a brief picture of how we have come to practice faith. We will also consider what conscious living means in a spiritual context as a basis for your entire life. Some of the questions that have been most prevalent will be answered. And finally, we will look at the deepest issues that face all people: worthiness and identity.

Our Spiritual Legacy

A good starting point is to take a look at our spiritual legacy. Many routes led African people to the United States, one of them the slave trade. As our enslaved ancestors were finding their way in this hostile "New World," they consistently invoked God's guidance. First, they followed their own spiritual practices. Quickly, however, recognizing our spiritual systems as a source of unity among our people and access to power that they did not understand and could not control, slave owners and others forced Christianity on them. To be fair, many white Christians truly believed that everyone should embrace their religion so that all could experience redemption. It may be noteworthy that as a result of voluntary acceptance of Christianity, many of our ancestors were afforded liberties. Evidence reports that some of them were actually allowed to worship alongside their enslavers; others were allowed to attend services where the master's own minister presided—making sure the enslaved were receiving the religious instruction that would best maintain them in a state of acquiescent servitude. Those who learned to read, however, discovered the promise of freedom in Christ's message.

There were two conversion movements in the early days of American life that affected everyone, including our ancestors. The Great Awakening began in 1734 in New England under the leadership of Jonathan Edwards. This minister preached that only absolute dependence on God in concert with divine grace could save a person, regardless of his race. The teachings of the Great Awakening, as translated by the enslaved, sparked tremendous enthusiasm as well as a search for ways to connect the message to their unique experience. What was born of this great desire as early as the 1750s was a call to song that led to some of the great Negro spirituals that we know today. Musically, Black folks truly put their mark on Christianity, claiming it in their own way and cultivating it so that it included the essence of their ancestral spiritual traditions and it served their spiritual needs. In many cases, the spirituals called for freedom and redemption, such as this Underground Railroad song whose code meant, "Tonight we go to where freedom is":

Steal away, steal away,
Steal away to Jesus;
Steal away, steal away home.
I ain't got long to stay here.

With the next great movement, the Azusa Street Revival, founded in California, Pentecostalism was born and Black people finally had a more familiar version of Christianity that soothed their souls, even though they had long been practicing Methodists and Baptists. Unlike the Great Awakening, this movement was created by African Americans in 1906 (a year after W. E. B. Du Bois founded the Niagara Movement, which would become the National Association for the Advancement of Colored People) and featured several remnants of the African religions brought over during Slavery, among them "speaking in tongues." These people believed, as they do today, that a person's soul can become filled with The Holy Spirit and that Spirit will speak through him or her, albeit through a language different from that commonly spoken. Being filled with the spirit was tangibly illustrated on the day of Pentecost as described in Acts 2, when several days after Christ's resurrection The Holy Spirit descended on them in the form of tongues "like as of fire" along with a rushing wind. In that story, those present were blessed with the capacity to understand that language, even though they themselves were not multilingual. This and other gifts of the Spirit are still in operation today: word of wisdom, word of knowledge, faith, gifts of healing, working of miracles, prophecy, discerning of spirit, diversity and interpretation of tongues. These are manifestations of The Holy Spirit and are given to "every man to profit all" (1 Corinthians 12:7).

In 1787 Richard Allen founded the African Methodist Episcopal Church in Philadelphia, much like the Pentecostal Church, in an effort to claim dignity and worthiness for a Black Christian congregation. When Black folks weren't welcome in white churches, our ancestors made their own. And so it has been over time. Unfortunately, much like other communities, Blacks have often been conservatively judgmental about people of different denominations within the Christian faith. When it comes to African Americans of other spiritual traditions, we can be downright biased. Sometimes by learning about the origins of people's views and what those views really are, opinions change.

The Spirituality of Our Ancestors

What influences have our ancestors' spiritual practices had on our lives today? How have their philosophies influenced or informed our thinking today? According to Dona Marimba Richards (Marimba Ani) in *Let the Circle Be Unbroken: The Implications of African Spirituality in the Diaspora* (1991), our ancestral legacy is profound and long lasting:

> Various theorists maintain that the trauma of slavery severed all ties between us and our ancestors; culturally as well as physically. If that were the case it would have meant "death" for us as a people, given the African understanding of the meaning of life. . . . Ironically . . . while we persist in denying our [Africanness], it is that very Africanity that allows us to survive in . . . America. . . . What is it that makes us the "best Christians," for instance? [It is the] deep spirituality that we have inherited from the motherland.

Not everyone would agree with Ani's contention. The African-American philosopher Howard Thurman dedicated his life to discovering the meaning and validity of the Judeo-Christian tradition for our people. Surely many of our ancestors embraced Christ's teachings, as we continue to do so today, recognizing the purity of His message—apart from the politics of the culture. One of the points Thurman makes is that our ancestors' plight was similar to that of the people of biblical times. They were persecuted, disillusioned and in great need. The message that Christ brought to them was one of hope and love. What essentially happened is that many of our ancestors embraced and transformed Christianity into an expression that satisfied their needs, as evidenced through the call-and-response-style relationship between preacher and congregation that was reminiscent of their ways of communing back home.

Many ways of our ancestors, in fact, found a new residence in the religious philosophies they practiced in the "New World." Because the slave trade harvested most of its prey from West African shores, each of the many religious influences that have resulted originates from the Yoruba people. The enslaved established creative ways of embracing the principles of the Catholic Church, particularly throughout the Caribbean, while also aligning their pantheon of gods with the saints of Catholicism. What's remarkable is that the similarities were quite natural; in the traditional African faiths and Catholicism, the belief is that there is one omniscient God who is expressed in countless ways, through actual beings. Regardless of your personal religious views, it is valuable to see how inventive and full spirited our ancestors' religious views and practices were. Many African Americans have rediscovered these ancient practices as they have looked to gain peace and spiritual wholeness.

The Yoruba Faith (The Ifa Oracle—
or Way of Knowing the Spiritual Path)

One of the most powerful and popular African spiritual systems to take hold in America is that of the Yoruba people of West Africa. When I visited Cote D'Ivoire in the mid-eighties I got my first taste of Yoruba culture and spiritual philosophy, and it was remarkably different from the vague impression I had had. While in the home of a wealthy, Westernized African couple, I noticed exquisite weavings hanging on their wall. When I asked what the symbols represented, I was told that these were weavings of the *Orisha,* or forces of nature. As my hosts attempted to explain their spiritual philosophy, I was captivated. Here were two level-headed individuals who had thriving careers and two healthy and "normal" children, but who practiced some ancient spiritual system that considered God, whom they called *Olodumare,* to be many. My Christian and American education unconsciously told me to reject them and their spiritual views as dangerous and "pagan." Yet these people didn't seem dangerous or antireligious at all. The journalist in me allowed me to sit tight and listen to what they had to share. What I learned opened my eyes to a world that I had been made too afraid to consider. These people, along with thousands of others in their town and from their ancestral heritage, followed a belief system that incorporated a tiered understanding of the Divine that turned out to be not so different from my own evolving views.

Although I am hardly a scholar of Yoruba, I have gleaned the following as the basic tenets of the Yoruba belief system: The Yoruba teach that we are here to develop character *(Iwa)* and that it is good character *(Iwa pele)* that is our ultimate goal. The purpose is to take the lessons that can be learned only in the physical realm (which results in a special type of energy), back out into the metaphysical (or beyond the physical) realm to feed the universe:

- There is one God who created and controls the universe—*Olodumare.*
- There are forces of nature or aspects of God—*Orisha*—who deal with the affairs of people on earth as well as the governing of the entire universe. For *Olodumare,* they are his intermediaries.
- The human spirit lives on after death and can recycle back into the physical realm.
- Ancestral spirits must be remembered, honored and consulted by the living, so that we may be whole and sane and celebrate our collective and historical successes and learn from our mistakes.
- Divination exists as an integral part of life.

- Offerings and blood sacrifices are used to elevate prayers to the *Orisha* and their ancestors—food offerings every day and animal sacrifices to restore severe imbalances in mind/body/spirit.
- *Ashé* (personal power bestowed by *Olodumare,* the source of all *Ashé*) transforms prayers and offerings to action. That's why people say *"Ashé"* after prayers and during the practice of libation.
- Yoruba believe in the power and medicinal use of herbs.
- A person can commune with *Olodumare* through trance states, now popularly known as channeling.
- Ritual song and dance are essential in the communion with *Olodumare.*

More than 300,000 people in the United States today practice this spiritual system and its synchronistic derivatives such as Vodun, Candomble and Santeria. All traditional African spiritual systems developed and practiced by our ancestors prior to Islamic and then Christian conversion invasions were similar to *Ifa* (Yoruba) with *Ewe* (God) and a system of *Orisha,* which takes us to the Diaspora.

Santeria
The roots of Santeria reflect those of the other religions that were brought from African shores to the western points of the slave trade. Rather than representing pagan practices that demand annihilation in order to enforce communal safety (negatively called "black magic" or "voodoo"), Santeria actually represents the ingenuity and community strength of an oppressed people. Many Westerners frown on Santeria and other spiritual practices, considering them far from sacred and instead dark and demonic. The spiritual systems that grew out of the Ifa tradition, however, are hardly "pagan" or unsophisticated. The Yoruba people were and are a highly cultured people with great history and a tradition that lives on today, despite the many efforts to suppress it and them, including hundreds of years of Spanish efforts to "purify" their minds. The Spanish-speaking Caribbean, especially Cuba, is the real home of the religion known as Santeria, which means "way of the saints." It is also known as *La Regla Lucumi* in Cuba and *Macumba* in Brazil.

This syncretistic religion combines the *Orisha* and beliefs of the Yoruba with the Bantu peoples in southern Nigeria, Senegal and the Guinea Coast with the God, saints and beliefs of Roman Catholicism. As you will see in the box, the deities, called *Orisha,* had very specific functions and were approached depending on a person's or community's needs. What's of particular interest is how easily these *Orisha* translated into Christian saints. For example, *Eleggua* became St.

Anthony, who controls the roads and gates. *Obatala* became Our Lady of Las Mercedes, who is the source of spirituality.

The central beliefs of Santeria that have been revealed to nonpractitioners include the following:

- Deities govern the universe. All answer to God or *Olorun,* the owner of heaven and creator of the universe, who interacts with the world and humanity through emissaries—a variety of *Orisha.*
- Ritual sacrifices occur. Mainly chickens and doves are used, from which blood is offered to the *Orisha* being invoked in a symbolic gesture. Sacrifices are called *ebo.* Blood symbolizes life and power, or *Ashé,* and it is of a type that spirits do not have in their realm; therefore, its physical presence is contributed by spiritual practitioners.
- Trance states induced by *Orisha* occur regularly. During intensive drumming and dancing, people are believed to be entered by the *Orisha* invoked, such that the person takes on that *Orisha's* qualities.
- Ancestor communion, or *Ara Orun* (people of Heaven), is an integral part of Santeria ritual. Ancestors are regularly called on for guidance.
- *Patakis* are the legends that tell the stories of the *Orisha,* much like the stories told of the Roman and Greek gods and the Khamitic *Ntrw* (ancient Egyptian pantheon).

As with all other well-developed spiritual philosophies and all Yoruba traditional practices, to become a practitioner of the system one must go through many years of study. To become a priest or *Babalawo* (father of the Mystery), or *Santero,* one must be willing to make tremendous personal sacrifice and undergo rigorous study and purification of the mind, body and spirit.

Considerable controversy has arisen with regard to animal sacrifice, which led to a U.S. Supreme Court ruling in 1993. The question of whether ritual sacrifice constituted inhumane slaughter of animals was the primary issue. Because there are so many other forms of slaughter that are legalized in this country, including killing for food, killing as pesticides and killing as euthanasia to control the population, religious practitioners who practice animal sacrifice continue to have the legal right to do so. It should be noted that such sacrifice is performed in a nearly painless manner, and all such sacrifices result in meals. For generations throughout the continent of Africa and even in ancient Israel, ritual sacrifice was a given.

Luis Manuel Núñez elaborates on this topic in his book, *Santeria: A Practical Guide to Afro-Caribbean Magic* (1992):

It can't be a strictly moral objection. With all our Burger Kings, Colonel Sanders, steaks, barbecues, American daily life requires an enormous amount of slaughter. Our supermarket shelves are full of it. Whether these creatures are killed for food or for ritual surely is all the same to the creatures. A culture that considers it just fine to throw a live lobster into boiling water and then eat it can't claim a moral superiority to Santeria's treatment of animals.

Vodun

The African religion that grew out of Haiti during European colonization is known as Vodun or Voodoo. This spiritual system incorporated aspects of many African peoples, including mostly the Fon, along with the Nago, the Ibos, the Senegalese and others. They withstood all manner of persecution by the French for three centuries without losing their spiritual base. This religion was developed much like Yoruba and Santeria and reflects a pantheon of *Orisha*. Vodun, like Santeria, evolved and was shaped in defense against forced and violently enforced conversions to Catholicism.

Whether you follow one of these paths or not, it is important that you see the value in them as part of our cultural continuum. Coming to faith is both a personal choice and part of a powerful legacy.

Our First Spiritual System?

Scholars of African civilizations have become aware of a spiritual system that predates all other such systems that have been found so far—one believed to be the genesis of all the rest. It is *Maat*. If we can understand the Oracle Ifa as the Yoruba "religion," then the same can be said about *Maat* for the ancient African people of Khamit (the ancient name for Egypt, a Greek word). *Maat* is the order of the universe. In this spiritual tradition, everything that *is* comes from *Maat*. *Maat* is the first thing the Creator created: order, balance, harmony, reciprocity, truth, justice and righteousness. The most important thing that can be said about *Maat* is that it should be understood as a total way of life; everything was understood to come from *Maat* and had to return to *Maat*. *Maat* was not something you went to do or talk about on Sunday. Every day (of the ten-day Khamitic week) one was expected to do *Maat*, speak *Maat,* think *Maat* and live *Maat* so that when the person made transition out of the physical life, he or she would stand before

HOW TO BE

Deities or *Orisha* at Home and in the Diaspora

God is differentiated by His many aspects in traditional African religions by various smaller deities or *Orisha*. Westerners have often grouped such philosophy into a pagan category when, in fact, it is just another way of understanding the breadth of God's presence in the universe. In Haiti, the traditional religion is called Vodun, and its spirits are called *Iwa*. In Santeria, which is found in many Spanish-speaking regions, and Candomble, whose origin is Brazil, spirits are called *Orisha*. Both Santeria and Candomble draw their traditions from the Yoruba spiritual pantheon, while Vodun finds its spirits from what were Dahomey and the Kongo.

The Deities

Elegba (Yoruba) Elegua (Santeria) Legba (Vodun) Exe, Eshu (Candomble)	This *Orisha* guards the doorways and crossroads. He is a warrior and a trickster who often creates confusion in people's lives.
Ogun (Yoruba and Santeria) Ogoun or Ogou (Vodun) Ogum (Candomble)	This deity governs iron and war (technology). He is a hunter, a warrior and a blacksmith.
Babalu-Aye (Yoruba and Santeria) Obaluaiye (Candomble)	This is the deity that governs sickness and healing.
Obatala (Yoruba and Santeria) Batala (Vodun) Oxala (Candomble)	This deity reigns supreme as the god of creation, morality and purity.
Shango (Yoruba and Vodun) Chango (Santeria) Xango (Candomble)	He is the god of thunder and lightning and is a great warrior dancer, drummer and lover.
Oya (Yoruba and Santeria) Aida (Vodun) Yansa (Candomble)	She is the goddess of the wind. She represents both softness and violence. She is associated with the cemetery.
Oshun (Yoruba) Ochun (Santeria) Erzulie (Vodun) Oxum (Candomble)	She is the goddess of the river, of love, beauty, femininity and prosperity.
Yemoja (Yoruba) Yemaya (Santeria) Agwe (Vodun) Yemanja (Candomble)	She is a river goddess in the Motherland and the *Orisha* of the ocean in Cuba. Her association is with motherhood and fertility.

Ausar, the Ntr or *Orisha,* who sat in judgment at the point of transcending the physical plane, and declare:

1. I have done no wrong.
2. I have not robbed.
3. I have not acted with violence.
4. I have not killed.
5. I have not been unjust.
6. I have not caused pain.
7. I have not desecrated holy places.
8. I have not lied.
9. I have not wasted food.
10. I have not spoken evil.
11. I have not committed sodomy.
12. I have not caused the shedding of tears.
13. I have not sown seeds of regret.
14. I have not been an aggressor.
15. I have not acted guilefully.
16. I have not laid waste the ploughed land.
17. I have not entered into a conspiracy.
18. I did not bear false witness.
19. I have not been wrathful or angry except for just cause.
20. I have not committed adultery.
21. I have not committed adultery [abused my sexual power].
22. I have not polluted myself.
23. I have not caused terror.
24. I have not polluted the earth.
25. I have not spoken in anger.
26. I have not turned from words of right and truth.
27. I have not uttered curses except against evil.
28. I have not initiated a quarrel.
29. I have not been excitable or contentious.
30. I have not been prejudiced.
31. I have not been an eavesdropper.
32. I have not spoken overmuch.
33. I have not committed treason against my ancestors.
34. I have not wasted water.
35. I have not done evil.
36. I have not been arrogant.
37. I have not blasphemed the one most high.
38. I have not committed fraud.
39. I have not defrauded temple offerings.
40. I have not plundered the dead.
41. I have not mistreated children.
42. I have not mistreated animals.

Food for thought, eh?

Without Religion

As people wrestle with personal questions of faith, they frequently reach beyond the parameters of organized religion to quench their thirst. If information about ancient and contemporary spiritual practices makes you uncomfortable, by all means don't let it keep you from exploring your connection to God in a more familiar way. The fundamental reason that people the world over have developed religions is to reveal their proper relationship to God. That too can be your personal mission. Establishing a conscious connection with your Higher Power may be the greatest gift that you can give yourself. Regardless of the road you travel to get there, the fruits of the journey make the traversing worthwhile.

Remembering

If there's one singular piece of advice that I can offer to myself and others, it is, "Remember God." However you understand that Great Power that created each of us and every aspect of the universe in which we live, remember Him. In so doing, you will be keeping the door of your heart open and allowing yourself the opportunity to live a conscious, noble life. My mother offered a beautiful prayer a couple of days after Christmas in 1997 that seems applicable here. My parents, my husband and I were sitting in a restaurant in Baltimore, having breakfast before the two of us headed back north. A beautiful light snow was dusting the roads, and we were having a warm and quiet time together. We four joined hands and my mother said, "Dear Father, we want to thank you for all that you have given us today and every day. Please help us to remember that even when we are experiencing good things, great things, that it is because of You that they happen. Please help us to remember You in all that we do, in all that we say. Please help us to follow in your Steps and do your Will."

My Mama spoke something that I have learned consistently, from childhood to today. We are *not* the doers in this world. Although it can be hard to recognize that the world doesn't revolve around you or me, believe it. Most important is the clear fact that God created everything and everyone. Baba Muktananda, a great being from the Siddha Yoga tradition, once said the world we live in is not more than "a play of Consciousness." We are actors in this great play. We did not create the roles. A power far greater than any one of us or all of us combined set the stage. For me, this is one of the hardest parts of life to accept: that I am *not* the doer. To believe in my heart that I am a vessel of the Creator's Will is *my* job in this world. From here, it is my responsibility to act in a manner that supports my being as pure a vessel as possible. To help you remember God in your daily life, do the following:

- Begin your day with a prayer. Get up a little earlier each day and take time to talk to God in the quiet of the new day. In many spiritual traditions, the hours between 3:00 and 6:00 A.M. are considered auspicious for prayer and meditation. Regardless of your hour of prayer, make it consistent. Find a place in your home where you can go to pray. Set up the space so that it is comfortable and clean. You may want to place sacred items at the center of this space, creating a holy place for prayer. In many Christian homes, this takes the form of a "prayer closet" (not a literal closet, but wherever you pray). A picture of a deceased relative you were personally close enough to can also serve that purpose. A small candle is perfect as well. As you kneel, make a concrete prayer thanking God for providing another day and asking Him to guide your steps through the day.

- Sit for meditation. In your same sacred space, you can sit for a few minutes of silent meditation after you offer your prayer. Find a comfortable upright posture. Close your eyes. Now breathe deeply, inviting your body to fill itself with oxygen. Exhale slowly. Repeat this deep breathing three times. Now breathe normally. Pay attention to your breath as it goes in and as it comes out. Know that the breath is the life-sustaining energy that we all share. Allow your focus on the breath to remain strong. As thoughts about your day, your work, your family or anything else come in, invite them to wait for a few minutes. Instead, refocus on your breath, on the clean, purifying action of simple breathing. You may want to say a silent prayer, or mantra, which vibrates the chakras or spiritual centers, as you watch your breath. Perhaps your spiritual tradition has provided you with a sacred mantra. If not, consider these: "I am one with the love of the Divine," or "I am all goodness and light," or "The Divine dwells within me as me." By taking time each day to become centered in the presence of God, you can then go about your day with greater conviction and grace. Meditation is a powerful practice. It represents the moment that you listen to God. This is what I do.

- Read spiritual literature. If you are actively involved in your spiritual tradition, read the supporting scriptural texts that delineate how to live. The most sacred ancient texts include the Bible, the Tao Te Ching, the Torah (or the book of coming forth from darkness into light), the Qur'an, the Upanishads, and the Vedas. Many African spiritual traditions were not recorded but rather passed down on the words of *domas, djelis* or sages (sometimes called by the French word, *griots*). In recent years, these spiritual stories have been recorded as well, including those in the Metu Neter of the ancient Khamitic tradition. In addition to the original texts, many other pieces of inspirational literature now exist to help people to enter upon and stay their spiritual course. Whether it's a book of aphorisms or sacred poetry, read positive spiritual literature daily. Queen Afua, Khamitic priestess of Heal Thyself Smai Tawi in Brooklyn, New York, recommends a minimum of half an hour a day of reading. It will help to inspire your thoughts, words and actions throughout the day and remind you of who is in charge and what you are doing here.

- Listen to your inner voice. For generations, people have talked about some internal force that speaks to them from within their own beings. Some call it intuition. Others have labeled it ESP (extrasensory perception). Still others have called it an internal alarm clock, which we also have. I've heard stories where that "little" voice actually saved people from horrific accidents, loss of employment and other catastrophes. You must become quiet to hear it.

- **Pause before you speak.** Especially when you are facing a confrontation or a delicate situation, take a few moments to consider your words and actions *before* you do anything. So often people think they are being either rude or incapable if they don't react immediately to whatever lies before them. Timing is critical in life; however, timing is different from speed. By giving yourself an opportunity to assess a situation carefully and decide on a course of action, you will be doing yourself and anyone else involved a real favor. Too often the wrong thing gets blurted out of people's mouths when they are overcome with emotion and starts an out-of-control cycle of tumult. Find your center before you take action. During your moment of silence, invite God to step in and lead the way.

- **Pray for forgiveness.** Throughout the day, positive and negative things happen. It may be a rare day when somebody doesn't get on your nerves, push your buttons or hurt your feelings at least a little bit. Half the time people don't realize that they are doing harmful things. That includes all of us. The Lord's Prayer says, "Forgive us our trespasses as we forgive those who trespass against us." Forgiveness is a virtue that is an absolute requirement for a happy and wholesome life. Holding on to grudges, no matter how large or small, hurts the one holding on to them, and often others as well. Refusing to forgive can turn into a dangerous virus that feeds on the person holding negative thoughts, to the point of self-destruction. To counteract the negative affects of resentments and grudges, pray each day for the ability to forgive yourself for anything that you may have done that was wrong, as you also ask the Lord to grant you the ability to forgive others for what they may have done to you. By practicing inner forgiveness daily, you will prevent resentments, jealousies and other pain from festering and growing out of proportion. When necessary, apologize face-to-face to the party you hurt. Offer your forgiveness, and don't attach yourself to the person's reaction. Move on.

- **Assess your day before you go to sleep.** Even when you are tired, take a few minutes to review your day. What worked well? What didn't? How did you spend your time? With whom did you interact? Did you follow your plan for the day? Did you cause yourself or anyone else pain? Did you make amends for any pain that you may have created? Did you offer love and support to others? Can you sleep with a guilt-free conscience? If not, what can you plan to do tomorrow that will relieve your heavy feelings? You may want to keep a journal that answers these and other questions that you may have. If you develop a discipline in assessing your day, you will find that no problem is insurmountable, because with each day something new comes along to replace it with either positive or negative effects.

- Make a plan for the next day.   A vital tool of my day came from a simple spiritual teaching. I was told it is smart to make a plan the night before, outlining what you intend to do the next day. In this way, when you wake up, you are simply executing your plan rather than stumbling about trying to figure out what to do. I write down my day's plan and prioritize it. The next day I check off the projects that I have completed and the status of those that must carry over to the next day. I can't fool myself into thinking that I've accomplished anything that is left undone, because proof is right in front of me. This also enables me to relax. I don't have to keep every detail of my responsibilities in my head. I can use my brain space for creating solutions rather than remembering my to-do list.
- Pray before you retire.   Once again, get down on your knees—an act of humility that will help you to focus—and thank God for providing you with yet another day of life. Offer your gratitude for all that you have learned and received during this one day. Pray for the grace to live through the night and see the light of another day. According to Luis Manuel Núñez, "Before going to bed a Santero will ask *Olodumare* to give him the strength to get up the following day by chanting *'Ologinewa Wo'* (May *Olodumare* help us get up!)."

How Do You Think?

We have long been taught that how we think is how we are. Do you believe that? It's easy enough to test for yourself. Consider for a few minutes what thoughts occupy most of your waking moments. Are they about work, your family, a lover, bills, new purchases, a vacation? Now travel with your thoughts to their final destination. What is your goal when you have these thoughts? What do you hope to accomplish? Even in your daydreaming, what is your goal?

It seems that the American landscape has been inundated with advertising that takes strategic steps to harness and then direct your thinking even further than your own efforts. Even more, history, certainly since Slavery days, proves that Black folks' thinking has been considered an entity to control. To ensure that as little as possible would be learned about the opportunities of life, slave owners forbade our ancestors to learn to read. In the Bible was the promise of freedom and free thought. Access to such knowledge was too great a risk for slave owners to allow. The mandate was to practice Christianity as it was presented to them in lieu of their own religious practices, which were labeled "dark" and pagan. When Jesus Christ's teachings have been permeated to facilitate political objectives, they sometimes have become

weapons used against others, including our people. Yet that's only part of the story. And, as always, our ancestors were able to synthesize the essence of Christianity so they could grow and prosper spiritually. Regardless of the perverse intentions of some, they survived.

Today African-American people have the "benefit" of distance from our historic roots and generations of proof before, during and after that we can be freethinkers with full lives. Still, many of us fall short when it comes to developing our intellectual and spiritual muscles. As Carter G. Woodson assured in *The Mis-education of the Negro* (1933), such behavior is dangerous: "When you control a man's thinking, you do not have to worry about his actions. You do not have to tell him not to stand here or go yonder. He will find his 'proper place' and will stay in it. You do not need to send him to the back door. He will go without being told. In fact, if there is no back door, he will cut one for his special benefit."

We cannot allow anything or anyone to control our thinking. To become free of mental indoctrination, ridicule and self-deprecation is far from easy, but this must be the goal of each one of us in order for any of us to achieve true liberation. Reconnecting to God and consciously cultivating a spiritual base can and will enable us to stretch beyond other people's thinking, including the current limitations of our own. We don't all have to throw away Christianity (or any other religion), as many have chosen to do. The tenets of Christianity remain steadfast and powerful. We must each look at our lives carefully, stop taking any aspect of our experience on face value, which may be out of context, and run our intentions through the filter of our religious beliefs. This may require you to reassess your spiritual needs. Look in your own heart to see what is important to you. To what values do you subscribe? What is important to you now and in the long run? What are you willing to sacrifice to reach your goals? Are your goals in line with the order of the universe? Do you know what this is? If not, are you willing to find out and then adapt your goals to be in alignment?

When in doubt, do your research. Explore different faiths and interpretations of God, or ways of worship, until you find a philosophy that suits your inner development. Suspend judgment and accept the fact that none is "wrong"; but all were designed by peoples of a specific culture to express their feelings about God and their connection to Him, regardless of what each of the three Western religions (Judaism, Christianity and Islam) proclaim about the universal and exclusive nature of their version. The fact that wars are fought and people die over such absolutism should clue us in to a possible flaw in such logic. I bet not one Dogon ever perished over whether to call the Divine *Amma,* as He is known in their language, or *Onyame,* His name in Akan. Be wise and tolerant as you learn.

Spiritual Practice

The reason that elaborate and simple rituals have been created throughout the generations of human life, spanning all spiritual traditions, is to quiet the mind and allow an individual to experience a conscious connection with God. What some view as pomp and circumstance, particularly of some of the more elaborate ceremonies of the Catholic Church, for example, stems from an effort to focus the mind in the highest way. Turning the most basic activity into a spiritual experience, then, is largely practiced as an effort to calm a person down and to free him or her to experience the inner realm.

As a tool of etiquette, such practices as prayer and meditation make it possible for a person to learn *how to be* in the world, from a grounded place. Some of the other more common practices that have worked for people over time include these:

- Singing. The power inherent in using one's voice to "praise the Lord" cannot be overstated. The simple act of using the vocal chords in song creates a powerful reverberation in the body similar to the *om* chanted by people of Eastern faiths. Our ancestors and many others have known for generations that the vibrations produced in spiritual reverie provide tremendous healing to the body and spirit. You may choose to sing hymns or chant mantras or other spiritual material, alone or in a group. My spiritual teacher says that chanting is one of the easiest and most powerful ways to tap into God's love. Go for it!

- Contemplation, prayer and meditation. The three are intimately connected—inseparable in fact. When you act in a knee-jerk kind of way, you're bound to make mistakes and create conflict in your life. The practice of daily contemplation, deep and quiet introspection when you consider an issue, offer it to God for guidance (prayer) and then listen for answers (meditation), can serve as a useful aid in making wise and informed choices in life. Like any other discipline, it takes time and patience for the practice of contemplation to yield results, but it's well worth the wait.

- Communal worship. Being in the company of fellow seekers of the Truth and participating in worship with them can be a transforming experience. As powerful as private daily worship is, there's nothing like going to a sacred place of worship and being with others who share your commitment and resolution. You will find that in times of need, your spiritual family can provide you with support that you may not be able to muster from within or from your biological family. This is particularly true if you are on different spiritual paths and your family is not as accepting of your way of worshipping.

- Service. Giving freely from your heart is one of the most beautiful and rewarding experiences in this life. When offered on a regular basis, the act of selfless service to humankind, to your place of worship, a charity or any other good cause will yield you more than you could ever imagine. Your heart will become full if you give freely, truly expecting nothing in return. In that spirit, what you then receive is an inner experience of love. Don't confuse such giving, however, with allowing yourself to be taken advantage of. In the Khamitic faith, weakness is considered a sign of imbalance or *Isfet,* which never fails to result in some form of evil.

How You View the World

Many people believe that reality has one face. In actuality, what is real for people is largely shaped by their perceptions and what they are taught to believe about the nature of reality. For instance, if a person has been taught, trained, conditioned or convinced to believe that there is no such thing as spirit communication with humans and a spirit does speak to this person, he might consider himself utterly mad or evil rather than accept that his belief might not be "true" after all. Writer Dennis Kimbro spoke on this topic, echoing many before him by saying, "We see things not as they are, *but as we are.* Our perception is shaped by our previous experiences." And so it is. You can test this truth yourself by examining a situation, relationship or challenge that you may have faced some years ago that has cropped up again. How did you respond to it five years ago? What did you believe was the right thing for you to do given the circumstances? How did you weigh right and wrong? Is your perception today any different from your original point of view? Have your actions changed based on your perspective or new information you have acquired since then? Chances are that the

The Lord's Prayer

Our Father, who art in heaven, hallowed be Thy name. Thy kingdom come, Thy will be done, on earth as it is in heaven. Give us this day our daily bread. And forgive us our trespasses as we forgive those who trespass against us. And lead us not into temptation, but deliver us from evil. For thine is the kingdom, the power and the glory forever and ever. Amen.

way you look at a situation directly influences the way you respond to it—even when the issue is exactly the same. You have changed; therefore, your reality and how you see it have changed as well.

Because your perspective is ever changing, or certainly should be, it is not entirely possible for you to see everything as it is in absolute terms—nor should you.

Recognizing this may come as an eye-opener for you. It surely did for me. What I have assessed from this reality is that I must be more tolerant of myself (I don't know everything, even when I would like to think that I do), others of my culture (their reality today may be different tomorrow) and others from different cultures (their reality now may be different from my own). Looking down on others "less fortunate," especially when it could have been you, is what all our Grandmamas would have called ugly, and it will limit your spiritual growth. Cultivating a tolerant acceptance of first myself and then others allows me to view the world with friendlier eyes. You may find that you will have more compassion and acceptance for others when you take a look at your own changing views of the world in which you live and your experiences in relation to it. Lighten up!

Further, and perhaps more important, is a call for action. Because you don't know everything, you must continue to learn and grow. A requirement of a good life is education, and that includes gaining knowledge about yourself, your community, your legacy. The only problem is that many people don't want to do the work that is necessary. A combination of ego and apathy often gets in the way. When you fall into such lethargy, you are demonstrating the worst of bad manners—because you know better. As sister-poet Sonia Sanchez so beautifully explained at the 1998 National Black Arts Festival to a group of young and old, "You ain't got time to be alienated from yourself, your culture, your people, your life. What you must have time for is to learn *how to be.*"

Spirituality and Work

A great battle ensues for some people when it comes to creating a balance in their lives between work and spiritual principles. Somehow we have been led to believe that this is a dog-eat-dog world, so it is okay to prey on others during working hours, even if we are conscientious and kind the rest of the day. Particularly for people who work in areas of finance or law, questions of appropriateness seem to rise to the surface with regard to how one can earn money and remain honorable. "Is it possible?" many ask.

The answer has to be "Yes!" One can rise above the misconception that it is all right to hurt or deceive someone at work in order to make ends meet. In traditional African life, there is no separation between the secular and the sacred. In the African worldview, all work is divine work; all work is perceived, conceived and performed for the benefit and continuation of the community. This does not mean that everyone is happy all the time or that no problems occur in human situations. It does mean, however, that there are both societal recognition and institutionalized provisions for resolutions and restoration of balance between parties, or within the Self, that cannot be arrived at in a despiritualized version of secular life, like that lived in the West. The point here—and whenever else traditional African references are made—is that we have a whole legacy from which to draw.

Because we are African descendants, descendants of the oldest people in the world, people who had centuries to figure out *how to be* in the world, we had people who laid out plans for living that have far more depth, diversity and flexibility than we have been allowed to imagine in contemporary Western life. It is ours—like a house your Grandmama left you, down South—and we don't have to feel lost and hopeless when these Western ways don't work for us. Even so, throughout our history here, there are examples of people who have lived wholesome and profitable lives, and so can you. It may mean that you won't make absolutely every dollar possible, but being able to sleep at night with a clear conscience has got to be worth something.

Expressing an African orientation toward material possessions (if only unconsciously) Sister Nannie Burroughs said, in 1927, "It will profit the Negro nothing to enter into ungodly competition for material possessions when he has gifts of greater value. The most valuable contribution which he can make to American civilization must be made out of his spiritual endowment." Amen, Sister Burroughs. In the midst of so much excess and opportunity, even the most aware of us can lose sight of what is truly important. What we can remember during times of conflict at work is that as African-descended people, we come from great stock that has yielded both divine and questionable qualities, as do all other peoples. Two of the lessons that we needed to learn relate to the unbalanced degree to which we tolerated and welcomed others who did not share our belief system. As a result of such an extreme form of tolerance (religious) and political naïveté (inability to perceive threat), we allowed a seeming handful of foreigners to overrun a 12 million–square–mile continent and then helped them to take over.

We have a lot to learn! Because of our breadth of historical roots, we can choose—out of our *own* ancestral and current experience—to embrace the good qualities and learn from the "bad" or useless. From our African, Caribbean and early African-American heritage, we were taught to put God first, as our African ancestors did. We were encouraged to run our experiences and choices through the filter of spiritual awareness in order to decide what is the right move to make. From our Native American and African experience, we were taught to cherish the earth on which we live. We were shown how it would serve us if we honored it. From our European experience, we were taught that industry and commerce could create wealth and political power while unconsciously destroying the very earth we learned to cherish from the other two. Only by balancing these three can we today have the skills needed to survive and thrive. What's important, however, is that we not stray too far into convincing ourselves that our well-being can be achieved at the expense of another. History shows that sacrificing others for success was part of the effort that European settlers used to develop this country. Rather than accepting and claiming that concept, we must reject it and opt for our rightful African orientation toward others that requires collective growth and development for all. Only then can our greatest strengths rise to the surface and support not only us but also many generations to come.

Practically speaking, when people consider their work life and their spiritual beliefs, they sometimes are moved to change how they earn money. One brother, for example, developed a career in computer technology, and became a leader in the development of missile systems. Although he was really good at his job, his conscience didn't allow him to sleep well at night, particularly when he knew that his work was being used to launch dangerous missiles in developing lands (inhabited by people of color). Because of his strong faith and its tug that told him his work didn't work for him, he began to pursue his life-long dream of opening a school. By enrolling in an education program at his local college while on the job, he was able to make the transition to something more meaningful to him.

A great Vedic text, the Bhagavad Gita, presents another take on this issue. In this text, a warrior is faced with going to battle—something that has been his responsibility for his entire life. This particular battle made him weak in the knees, though, because on either side of him were members of his family and loved ones. How could he, in good conscience, fight any of these people? As he wonders, he calls out to the

Lord, asking for guidance. What he learns is that he must follow his *dharma,* a Sanskrit term that means "duty." He must do his job with love and humility, praying for the ability to follow his path and God's will at once, without being attached to the results. This didn't mean that he should not care about those who would get hurt in the battle. Instead, it meant that in some instances we may not like the task that lies before us.

Sometimes we have to perform our duty and move on. If it is not honorable for us to walk away from it, we must ask God for guidance and then do our best without holding on to what may or may not be the results. There are many rich lessons in this great spiritual text. What I have been able to discover from it in my own work is that if I remember God in all that I do, I will be guided to the right action. That action may lead me to change my path or live through a difficult situation with confidence. Learning to do my work without being attached to what gain may appear on the other side of it has been one of the greatest challenges. But it works just as Nannie Burroughs said, holding on to my spiritual endowment and not allowing myself to fall into ungodly competition because I turn it all over to God, praying only to be able to be a vessel of His work. Miraculously, this keeps me sane and clear-headed. Perhaps it will do the same for you.

Surah 2, Verse 286 (from the Qur'an)

Our Lord! Punish us not if we forget or fall into error, our Lord! Lay not on us a burden like that which You did lay on those before us, our Lord! Put not on us a burden greater than we have strength to bear. Pardon us and grant us forgiveness. Have mercy on us. You are our protector; help us against those who stand against faith.

You and Worthiness

Nelson Mandela said it best at his inaugural address in 1994 when he became president of South Africa: "Our deepest fear is not that we are inadequate. Our deepest fear is that we are powerful beyond measure. It is our light, not our darkness, that most frightens us." Mandela's words resonate with power and meaning, especially for people of color. It is our light, in fact, that has often caused great turmoil and discomfort in our lives and others'. Over the years, Black folks in America have surely had to learn how to cloak that light so as not to draw too much attention to ourselves. In covering up our inner beauty and strength, many of us inadvertently stepped into dangerous and impotent positions, thus steeping us in feelings of unworthiness. Rather than allowing our spirits to soar, many of us have begun to believe the harmful and untrue things that were said about us and to us: that we are not good enough, that we are inferior to others, that we do not deserve equal rights, that we are second-class citizens, that we are unattractive, even downright ugly, that who we are is less than human. First and foremost untrue, such thinking has proven very damaging to the individual and collective psyche of our people. I would be remiss, however, if I didn't note that people of all backgrounds suffer from feelings of unworthiness that fuel their spiritual lethargy. This is why we should draw on the decades of historical and theoretical work done by Black scholars here and abroad about African thought and behavior. (See the Selected Bibliography at the end of the book.)

Mandela said, "There's nothing enlightened about shrinking so that other people won't feel insecure around you. We were born to make manifest the glory that is within us." By tapping into our own inner glory, we have the capacity to move beyond our fears and limitations into our greatest Selves. But how can we release ourselves from the clutches of unworthiness? One of the best solutions is to make a gratitude list. Don't you remember your Mama telling you to count your blessings when you started feeling down in the mouth? That's what a gratitude list is all about. Everyone has something for which he or she can be grateful, no matter how bad life seems at the moment. Maybe it's your children or your spouse, your new job or even your recent firing. Out of every single experience something of value can be learned. It's how you choose to look at the situation that will color your perspective. If you find yourself stumped, use this exercise: Say to yourself, "I am grateful for _____ in my life." Leave a blank where your point of gratitude should be and then say a little prayer asking God to reveal it to you—and He will! Then wait quietly and listen for the answer.

A Thousand Points of Faith

Most people will agree that there is a power in this world that is greater than our individual selves, even though the eighties tried hard to get us to think otherwise! In truth, there is no question but that there is a Higher Power. The questions come regarding the ways in which people choose to honor that Power. What is It called: God, Yahweh, Jah, Jehovah, Olodumare, Rastafari, Shiva, the Inner Self? How do we choose to worship? These two questions reveal many answers. For our ancestors, depending on where they lived, this Power manifested in the earth and the animals and the foods they ate. For African-American people during and after Slavery, the Baptist Church, the African Methodist Episcopal (AME) Church and then other Christian denominations provided a blanket of comfort. In the Caribbean, because of active missionary work,

About the Ancestors

One of the more precious jewels that I have discovered about our African roots is the relationship that people across the Continent have to their ancestors. Those who have passed on and who lived honorable lives are commonly revered and remembered as sources of spiritual strength. The belief is that the souls of the ancestors live in the hearts and minds of those who continue on. During times of sorrow, joy, fellowship and need, the elders and others invoke the ancestors for guidance. The ritual of pouring a libation to the ancestors—the first drink of water or another clear liquid—to begin a sacred celebration is commonplace in many West African communities today and, interesting enough, is retained and manifested (albeit unconsciously) every time you see a young brother tip his "40" (beer) for his "dead homies" and call names out! I suggest that we, as contemporary African-American people, consciously embrace this way of thinking and learn to practice ancestor communion.

One sister from North Carolina, Shelly, told me that as a child, she too intuitively knew this concept. When she was just fourteen years old, her paternal grandmother passed away. The two of them had had a distant relationship, but they definitely shared a sense of love and respect. After her grandmother died, Shelly spent a lot of time thinking about her grandmother's ways. As she would go about her day, just before she was going to do something wrong, she says she would hear her grandmother's voice, *"Chile, you know better!"* At first, Shelly said that she was surprised. Clearly her grandmother was gone, yet her voice rang clearly in Shelly's ears. After some time, Shelly grew to like her grandmother's presence. Now, as an adult, Shelly says that she carves out time to remember her grandmother and other loved ones who have passed on. She tells stories to her children about them and stokes the flames of their memory. In this way, she says that when she is in need, their spirit is right there at her side offering support.

the Roman Catholic Church took on a predominant role in ministering to the people, even as the ancient Vodun and Santeria stood their course. Today the choices vary widely: Christianity, Judaism, Islam, Taoism, Jehovah's Witnesses, Seventh-Day Adventists, Yoruba, Khamit, Eastern yogic paths (Siddha Yoga Meditation, Buddhism) and many more. What happens when so many points of faith are practiced? America was designed to be open and free, a welcoming homeland for one and all, no matter how people choose to worship. We know now that this viewpoint does not represent reality. Under many circumstances people find themselves in awkward, even potentially life-threatening positions as they seek to practice their faith.

How can this change? What can we do within our own communities to promote a supportive and tolerant way in which to coexist with people of different religious and spiritual backgrounds? The answers are far from simple, at least at first glance. Sure, we can remind ourselves to "live and let live," yet that is much easier said than done. Depending on your affiliation, the dogma of your particular religious home may at the same time fortify your spirit as it degrades another. Perhaps this (coupled with higher education, when caution often gets tossed to the wind) is why so many young people have cast aside the religious viewpoints and practices of their families. Dogma has clouded some folks' vision. In discounting what a person has had as a spiritual foundation, however, what happens next can be dangerous. The period of floundering about "in search of" the Truth, God or one's Higher Power is usually fraught with great tension and missteps. Again and again, people discover that without faith, they are lost. Whether it's the belief system that your Mama taught you or one that you have embraced after years of trial and error, your connection with that which is greater than you that also connects you internally to God is absolutely vital to your survival. Each one of us must discover that connection and nurture it.

In the end, what spiritual seekers come to is the Truth. Back in 1907 George Washington Carver said, "Our creator is the same and never changes despite the names given Him by people here and in all parts of the world." From his lips, people were able to accept the message. When it has come from more controversial leaders, it is often more difficult. For example, the Honorable Louis Farrakhan essentially said the same thing in 1993: "If we can put the names of our faiths aside for the moment and look at principles, we will find a common thread running through all the great religious expressions." Pearls of wisdom do come from people who believe in God with their full hearts. Developing religious tolerance comes when we can look beyond the messenger to the purity of message and take from it that which will empower us and ultimately set us free. In day-to-day life, maintaining that tolerance and learning to see the Truth require constant awareness. Tolerance isn't a compromising of spiritual beliefs, it's a way of agreeing to disagree.

Who Am I?

What is the purpose of human life? Why are we here? Such questions occupy precious space in our heads for much of our lives. In a Western context, the age-old question *Who am I?* leads the list of curious questions with no clear answer. To answer that question takes both introspection and research. As the Western philosopher George Santayana said, "Those who cannot remember the past are condemned to repeat it." The Akan of Ghana have another way of expressing this important message, using a symbol in their *Adinkra* vocabulary that is known as

Sankofa. This symbol, one version of which is seen at the beginning of this book, is also represented by a bird standing with its feet facing forward and its head turned back. In its mouth is an egg, meant to symbolize essence or worldview. The message is that we must go back and fetch our essence in order to move forward in our lives, with vision, so that we can take forward the best of what we are without having to carry the baggage of our mistakes. For African-American people, the past has been fraught with many political and emotional ramifications.

The question of identity has been perhaps the most significant source of discomfort. By the very nature of our physical selves, we have been defined as second-class citizens by our neighbors. For those of us who are brown skinned, we have been immediately pointed out and ostracized by countless faceless beings as inherently flawed. The fight to break free from the figurative and too often real noose of being "not good enough" has proved to be a bloody battle. Many of our kinfolk have lost their lives in their efforts to prove our validity in a culture that survives in part by demeaning some part of its own. What has happened to others of us is either a self-destructive pattern of imbibing the negative images that have been thrust upon us or a knee-jerk hatred spewed back at the initiator. And thus the cycle has continued over the years.

When rooted in a spiritual context, we can rise above such indignities and lead in the national and global revolution of spirit by our thoughts, words and actions. Yes, we must continue to stand up for our right to live and prosper in the world as equal citizens. In order to do this, we must first believe that we deserve that right. The great writer Ralph Ellison wrote, "When I discover who I am, I'll be free." How prophetic. Too many of us live under burdensome cloaks of insecurity, self-righteousness, delusion, self-hatred, poor self-esteem, fear and anger. This weight forces us to act without thinking, without contemplating our true value. Answering the *Who am I?* question becomes a real problem when you consider the following, as expressed by Malcolm X in his *Autobiography* (1965):

> Europeans created and popularized the image of Africa as a jungle, a wild place where people were cannibals, naked and savage in a country side overrun with dangerous animals. Such an image of the Africans was so hateful to Afro-Americans that they refused to identify with Africa. We did not realize that in hating Africa and the Africans we were hating ourselves. You cannot hate the roots of a tree and not hate the tree itself.

In this attempt to impart insight into the traditional African worldview, I do not wish to make it sound idyllic or romantic. All human societies had and have problems. We realize that our brothers and sisters on the Continent had to have helped in the colonization effort for it to work. Furthermore, because of the overwhelming success of enslavement and colonialism, we understand that the traditional lifestyles of African peoples were largely destroyed. (Or is that just what we are supposed to think so that we will feel homeless and hopeless, resigning ourselves to just dealing with things as they are?) In any case, even if the traditional African world were completely extinct, the African world*view* is alive, well and waiting for us to come on home! As an extension of our ancestors, I would like to invite African-descended people around the world to tap into the ancient spirit of *how to be* in the world, by explaining and thus demystifying as much as we can of the negative stigma that was attached to being African in order to justify enslavement. This effort is not to try to *make* you African; instead, think of it as our flag of love waving a message that promises, "It's all right to be African—again." Scholar Marimba Ani, elaborates in *Let the Circle Be Unbroken*:

> We, as Black people, have been told that we are not African for so long and with such social scientific "expertise," that we have great difficulty believing otherwise. . . . Our oppressors have emphasized the loss of language, dress, living patterns [spiritual practices] and other tangible and surface aspects of culture, just as they do in discussions of African culture on the continent. They emphasize differences in language and customs—even physique—from one society to another. Until we learn that it serves our [regeneration and unification] objectives to emphasize the similarities . . . ties . . . unifying principles . . . common threads . . . themes [and essence] that bind us all as "African," we will continue to be politically and ideologically confused.

Just as Ellison said, "When I discover who I am, I'll be free." From a spiritual point of view, we are all manifestations of God. All equal. All one. Regardless of our ethnicity. To embrace the spiritual philosophy that permeates every major spiritual tradition—that we are one in the presence of God—is to have a full life. To see God's light in everyone, no matter who that person may be, is to live a conscious and complete life. To do so does not mean that you must allow indignities to be perpetrated on you. Instead, it empowers you to inform others with kindness and conviction, as needed. Even more, it challenges us all to look within our own hearts and lives to discover what we can do ourselves to make our own Selves better. It inspires us to stoke the flames of our own internal evolution that will allow us to help others. The balance that we must strike lies between our inherent political and social needs to build solidarity in the Black community and our spiritual need to evolve beyond our cultural identifications to become humble and powerful servants of the Lord. It is my belief that the brown-skinned people of the world will be the leaders in this essential journey. To be prepared for that which lies ahead of us and future generations, we must decipher and embrace the legacy of our ancestors, positive and negative, taking the best forward and transcending the rest. Through faith and tremendous self-effort, introspection and prayer, we can do it. And we must. For this is truly *how to be.*

YOUR QUESTIONS ANSWERED

1. What can I do when my child comes home proclaiming that he has changed his religion?

Relax, remain open and listen. One of the biggest challenges facing a parent is the complete realization that your child is different from you. Your child is unique, with personal thoughts, ambitions, philosophies and ways of being of his or her own. Because your child has decided to pursue another path to God does not mean that he or she has "fallen from Grace" or that you have somehow failed as a parent. Do your best to remain open to hearing about your child's experiences and reasons for changing. Ask questions with the intention of learning, not with suspicion. Ask your child what benefits he is receiving from joining this faith. Was there something your child felt she could not get from the religion she was reared in? What are the tenets of the religion? Who else belongs to the faith? Anyone you know? Who is the leader? How old is the faith? Continue on in this manner, gathering information. Most of all, pay attention to your child's behavior. Look for signs of centeredness or discomfort. Listen for your child's own experience as opposed to the dogma of his faith.

If you are worried about the organization that your child has joined, tread lightly. Telling your child not to participate will only isolate you further from him. Remain open. As soon as you can, do some research. Contact the organization and request literature. Look it up on the Internet. Be mindful, though, that there is a lot of uncensored, negative information written by followers of competing faiths floating about on the Internet about every religious organization. Don't consider the Internet your sole source of research. Ask your child to invite you to a prayer meeting or service. Participate in the activity fully, so that you can have your own experience that you can assess later. Try not to judge.

Be aware that you really cannot change your child's mind or actions. You can offer your own advice from your personal experience about the value of your religious beliefs or spiritual pursuits. You can also let your child know that you don't approve of his choice, if that is so. If possible, let your child know that you will continue to love him no matter what his religious affiliation.

2. What can I do if I learn that my child has joined a cult?

During the sixties and seventies, there was a lot of talk about cults in America. (For the record, any religion can look like a cult to another religion.) Various religious organizations from other parts of the world found their way West to the United States, the presumed home of religious freedom, and began to attract disillusioned young people. In many cases, these groups were loving and wholesome, yet faced tremendous scrutiny and ridicule. In others, the leaders took on great power and twisted the message into something vile and unhealthy. Such groups, of both types, continue to exist in America today. A young woman who grew up in Denver found her way into the clutches of a "cult" when she was in college. Christine had always been a quiet, thoughtful girl who had a troublesome upbringing. In college, she remained introspective. She was also a bit naive. She discovered a religious organization when she graduated and moved in, along with a number of other singles and couples, under the leadership of one strong man, who professed that they were a Christian sect. What made this organization a cult were the following: (1) family members were not allowed to visit or call, (2) people were told what to think and monitored accordingly, (3) members were not allowed to leave without permission. Christine stayed for several years because she felt secure and happy in her new life—until the leader of the group approached her about having sex with him. It turned out that this man had been rotating which women he would bed over the years. Christine's turn had come up. When Christine let a male friend who would later become her husband know what was going on, he encouraged her to leave. Christine gathered up the courage and left the group, moving with her beloved to a nearby area. Clearly, she had been in an unsafe, unhappy place.

During the entire period of her religious sequestering, her family had little or no recourse. Since Christine had cut off ties from her family several years prior, no one knew that she *could not* reach out regularly during her period in the commune. What her mother and family members did was to pray. They offered continuous prayers asking for God to protect Christine from harm. Other things they could have done include:

- Finding the name of the organization and researching its origins as fully as possible

- Contacting local authorities if they suspected questionable activity
- Demanding that they be able to visit on a regular basis
- Sending regular registered correspondence to their daughter updating her on their lives (the registration allows for tracking of its receipt)
- Enrolling the help of the local authorities or news organizations to pursue their suspicions

3. I want to get married, but my fiancé does not practice my religion. I don't know how to get my parents to accept him. What can I do?

Part of the reason that both your parents and your spiritual adviser may initially frown on your union is that they understand that the commitment of marriage requires a spiritual foundation in order to cultivate a productive and healthy relationship. This doesn't mean that husband and wife they must be of the same spiritual persuasion, although that would be ideal in many folks' eyes. More than sharing the same membership card, so to speak, you need to develop a common perspective that you both can respect and trust. To secure the blessing of your families, you also need to share with them a clear sense of your own spiritual foundation. Patience is important here, especially if either of you is from a very religious family. It may take time for your parents to warm up to your partner. Give them time.

4. How do we determine the religion of our children if my husband and I are of different faiths?

That's one of the first questions that a spiritual adviser will ask of you during premarital counseling. If the two of you have separate beliefs, you will need to decide. Leaving it up to your child, as many couples have done, is not necessarily the best solution. Children's minds are impressionable. They do need a spiritual foundation that is unwavering or at least asserted with confidence. When they grow up, of course, they should be free to make their own decisions. During their youth, however, it is important for them to receive some clear guidance. Many parents choose the religion of the parent who has the more disciplined practice, so as to provide a structured spiritual environment for the child.

If you are finding it difficult to reconcile your religious perspective with that of your potential life partner, take some conscious time out to address your concerns. You may want to seek spiritual counseling, in which case it is wise to look for someone who is broad-minded and has some sense of the value systems of your different beliefs. It is possible to maintain two different religions in a household. What's smart, however, is for the two of you to come to an agreement on a shared way of acknowledging your faith. This may come as a morning prayer and meditation that you do together, a generic prayer you repeat at mealtime or something else. In order to make your relationship work, you need to respect your partner's views, even if they are different from your own. Otherwise, you will experience constant conflict throughout your life together.

5. I am a practicing Muslim, and find it difficult to honor the holy season of Ramadan while I am working. Islamic holidays are overlooked here. What is the appropriate way to address this with my boss?

Be calm, kind and clear. Explain to your boss, well in advance of the month of Ramadan, that your holy season is approaching. Explain what that means to you and how it will affect your work. One Senegalese sister worked in a hair salon as a braider, a job that often kept her until after 7:00 P.M. During Ramadan, she asked her boss if she could leave at 5:00 P.M. so that she could go home to cook a meal for her family, since no one is allowed to eat during daylight hours. Because she asked in advance, her boss accommodated her. You will find that being up front about your needs is always best, so that your boss can prepare.

6. Is psychotherapy necessary for spiritual maintenance?

Many psychotherapists, psychiatrists and other mental health professionals have shown that people who suffer from mental illness often also suffer a crisis of spiritual identity. Trying to fill that pit inside with all of the outer accoutrements of life hasn't worked for anyone. Therapy can serve as a bridge to sanity, by helping people to discover how to manage their lives better. It also often leads people toward a spiritual awakening. Yet for years, Black folks have been afraid to go to therapy, many fearing that it showed a sign of weakness in their spiritual practice and faith. Today research shows that therapy can be of tremendous value to people as they sort through the pressing issues in their lives so that they can discover peace. When you think about it, it makes sense to seek as much assistance as possible to be able to peel away the layers of misunderstanding and delusion that lead people to unhappiness. Knowing that we live in a time when help abounds means that we need only the courage to reach out for it in order to heal. If you have questions about therapy, ask your local health center, your medical doctor or your spiritual adviser for recommendations.

Further, know that in the African worldview, one's mental and spiritual identity are one. There is no separation between secular and sacred. The mind is considered an aspect of the soul, so when your mind is troubled, it is seen and treated, primarily as a manifestation of a spiritual imbalance. This means seeking help is imperative when you need it, and it is understood historically as an act of strength.

7. I practice the Khamitic faith. I find that other Black people often speak in disparaging ways about my religion. What can I do?

Unfortunately, many people have been taught to see God in just one way. For this reason many of our people remain close-minded to unconventional beliefs, especially when they look "African." We have been taught that our own spiritual systems are pagan. The shroud of negativity that once covered all of African history and culture is lifting, though, largely thanks to African-centered scholarship (see the Selected Bibliography at the end of the book). We need to have respect for that and find a gentle way to express that many of the vague impressions we have of things we have no firsthand information about can lead to inaccurate conclusions. I have found that if you are clear in your convictions about your choices, whatever they may be, you can speak from a place of calm as you inform others. Share insights about your spiritual history that will explain your faith to naysayers. Many people do not know that the Khamitic (Egyptian) path is that of the ancient African people, considered the first people of the world who developed a level of civilization that was so advanced and enduring that it has not been completely destroyed or fully understood—and our ancestors made it. Describe how your commitment to this path has strengthened your life and broadened your knowledge of our history. In this way, you can open the door for others to consider alternative paths to spiritual wellness.

8. *Because of my religious convictions, I am supposed to keep my head covered at all times. How can I honor my spiritual beliefs and work in the Western world?*

As the saying goes, *Where there's a will, there's a way.* A young Islamic sister told me that her religious beliefs require that she keep her head covered and that she wear garments that cover her body completely. When she first entered the job market, she thought that she would have great difficulty getting past her first job interview wearing a head wrap. To her surprise, the first temporary agency that she visited in Atlanta hired her on the spot because her skills were excellent for the job. To her credit, she had also modified her head wrap to make it as acceptable as possible—and she wore a business suit, a jacket with a long skirt. What's key here is to look for the solutions to your concerns rather than feeling that anything so powerful as your religious beliefs would stand in the way of your success.

9. *I was invited to a bar mitzvah by a friend. When I arrived, I was told that I had to put on a yarmulke. I refused, because I am not Jewish. Was that wrong?*

It all depends on why you refused. Traditionally, when men visit Jewish sanctuaries and sacred events, they are given yarmulkes to wear—out of respect. My father has adorned his bald spot with hundreds of them over the years, without ever feeling that his religious views were being compromised. I recommend that you wear the yarmulke out of respect unless you feel that something about your action disrespects others' religious beliefs or your own. Usually, though, people with such strong religious views don't enter sanctuaries outside of their religion. Otherwise, when in Rome . . .

10. When visiting an unfamiliar house of worship, do I participate in all of the rituals?

Absolutely not. Ask the person who invited you to the service—in advance—about the order of service. Find out what is expected and what is required. Talk to your friend about your levels of comfort, if you can. If you do find yourself at a house of worship in the midst of service, pay attention. You do not have to take communion, feign the sign of the cross over your heart or anything else that you don't understand or practice. Instead, you can sit or stand quietly until that particular ritual has passed. In general, don't do anything you don't understand.

WeAreFamily

God created us so that we should form the human family, existing together because we were made for one another. We are not made for an exclusive self-sufficiency but for interdependence, and we break the law of being at our peril.

DESMOND TUTU

FOR thousands of years, our ancestors lived in communities that reflected the strong, solid family bonds that created them. In contemporary times, even when things were at their worst, when we were suffering under *Maafa* (catastrophic) conditions in this country, we maintained an unshakable family strength that allowed our children to grow strong and lead productive, meaningful lives. Our families endured. We took care of each other. It was a given. In some cases, we were all we had.

Our ancestors fully understood that they had to rely on each other in order to live complete lives. And that's what they did. We have always known that the primary building block of any community is family. As all spiritual traditions maintain and history proves, both the condition and the health of the family unit individually and collectively directly determine the health of the community and society at large. This is something that Black folks used to know like the back of their hands. This knowledge is informed by our ancestral memory.

Today it's as if we're suffering from amnesia—some of us, anyway. Many of us have forgotten the basics, and we are paying the price as a result. The health of the African-American family stands in serious jeopardy. Of course, there are explanations for the many issues that plague our households. During the period of our enslavement, our ancestors were not allowed to establish traditional family unions, even as they were forced to proliferate. Slave narratives and newspaper clippings point to the fact that Black men and women were sold from plantation to plantation in order to make more babies, who would be able to participate in the landowner's agricultural pursuits. Yet the men typically were not allowed to take up housekeeping with their women and children, largely out of fear of family strength, but also due to the mind-set of slaveowners that encouraged a male's fertility to go a long way. Sick, yes. But this is part of our ancestral reality.

On the surface, it may seem as if these brothers and sisters were defeated, as many of them weren't ever able to live under one roof with their families. If you dig a little deeper though, you will see that it was their African-ness, their spirit and connection to the ways of their ancestors that kept the community going. Many men spent their entire lives trying to stay close to their families, even when it meant traveling great distances to stay in contact with their wives and children after they'd been "sold." The integrity of the men and women who endured enslavement and managed to rear strong families and respectful children with good hearts and spirits cannot be emphasized enough. The faith and perseverance that they demonstrated are undeniable. They are qualities that we would do well to emulate today, yet just as we need to align ourselves with that which is powerful about our collective experience, we too often pull away.

Of course I know that there are many thousands of African-American families across the country who are taking care of business. I grew up in one of those homes, as did many of the people I interviewed for this book. It is inspiring and hopeful to see a brother teaching his son, a family headed to church together, a meeting of elders and youth. Conscious efforts are being made to fortify our families. Yet it is glaringly clear that many African-American families are in crisis—which means that we all are.

With a 200,000-year cultural legacy, why are so many of us lost? What has happened? Many of us have forgotten *how to be* with our families. Otherwise we wouldn't be in this predicament. There's a Hausa saying, *"Relatives are like a part of your body; if anything touches it, however small, you feel it."* Could it be that some of us have become numb to the feelings and needs of our children, our relatives, our Selves? It sure seems that way. In this moment, many of us, across all class lines, are not taking care of business. Our children are often growing up unsupervised. With frightening frequency, brothers are dropping seeds left and right and not looking back. Our jobs sometimes leave us without enough money to put food on the table and books in our children's hands. We are stretched. Or we use our resources to pay for care but remain distant from our kids. In this hour of need, many of us have forgotten how to reach within for strength and to our communities for support.

To discover the fundamentals of how to live your life, you must take a close look at family, the primary building block of all communities. In this chapter, we explore the full life cycle of the family from an African point of view, highlighting the ways in which you can honor your family life today and in the future to keep it and the community at large strong. Information will include how healthy families are formed, the dynamics of having and caring for children, supporting the elders and remembering our past, dealing with death, participating in celebratory rituals and facing tough issues and troubles.

Marriage

The most common thread that links us all together is the bond of family. We all emerge from some kind of family structure. The particulars certainly change depending on the location of your birth, your family's economic and social status, your neighborhood and other such elements. But every living being came from some kind of simple family unit. Marriage was—and is—the primary means of creating family. A few generations ago, the guidelines for marriage were a lot more specific than now. Before a couple could even "date" seriously, in fact, wedding plans often had to be in place—especially in the African-American community.

Apart from the period when our ancestors could not legally become a family, our people have been honoring the tradition of initiating two people into familyhood through spiritual and legal means for generations. Even during our enslavement, we figured out ways to honor our unions, because we *knew* that they represented the sacred foundation for our lives. Living together, eloping or otherwise not becoming one with the sanction of family and community spirit has *never* been looked on favorably and in traditional African communities was *just not done.* And, in truth, even now, after the efforts of the bra-burning seventies and the introduction of the Pill, Black folks commonly still expect their children to become family the old-fashioned way—pre-pregnancy, standing up before family and loved ones in a house of worship or other spiritual environment. So when a couple announces that they want to take the giant step and commit to each other, what steps should they take? What is the etiquette of such a personal and public commitment?

One of the first things that I tell people when they start talking about marriage is to slow down. Marriage represents one of the most sacred bonds that two people can share. To that end, as ministers so routinely point out, "it is an institution not to be entered into lightly." So why do people seemingly jump into marriage before they are truly ready?

Among the reasons is that people decide that they want to get married when they are experiencing the euphoria of "being in love," a somewhat short-term condition that tends to distort one's perception a bit. Now, I'm not trying to be a wet blanket. Instead, I want couples to think before they act. It all goes back to the same premise: to live a conscious life, you must take the time to consider your actions, especially those of significant lifetime importance, with a clear and level head. That's why there are traditional checks and balances in every culture around the world—to ensure that couples about to tie the knot are actually prepared to make the commitment inherent in their union. Some of the best advice comes from the traditions of our African ancestors.

Although Africa represents many countries and many peoples, each with its own set of customs and social mores, several key requirements about marriage ring true throughout the Continent:

- Before a couple can get engaged, they must receive permission from *all* of their family members. This doesn't just mean that the young man has to go to Daddy all the while trembling, although that is a practice too! Historically, it meant that your parents, grandparents and other elders, aunts and uncles, brothers and sisters and even cousins had to give their approval in order for a marriage to happen. That may seem like a tall order in modern times. But think about it for a minute. Basically, this is a kind of insurance policy that our ancestors created. They understood that marriage is challenging for *all* couples. By engaging the participation of the entire family on both sides, you secure support for yourselves and your growing relationship. Knowing how much people today dislike the idea of asking for anybody's opinion, let alone permission, especially since people are getting married much later and therefore after they are free of their parents' household rules, I see a viable, contemporary interpretation of this practice. Rather than thinking of it as permission, understand that the couple must secure the blessing or support of their blood relatives as well as those whom they have invited into their lives as family. This makes sense. If you and your husband or wife are experiencing tough times, for example, when you go to your Aunt Sarah for refuge, she won't tell you, "I told you so," *because she didn't.* Likewise, your best friend Dwight won't be able to tell you, "I've got somebody I want you to meet," because he has made a commitment to support you in your relationship. You'll be surprised at just how powerful their blessings of encouragement can be during the hard times.
- In concert with the blessing is the core understanding of an African marriage: that it is a union of two families, as well as two individuals. His-

torically, this was simply practical. For nomadic peoples especially, in moments of conflict you could have a civil war on your hands— literally. So, a group "We do" was significant. Isn't that true today as well? We certainly experience violence in our communities and families, too regularly for anyone to find real comfort. By taking the time first to cultivate relationships with family members and receive their blessings, and then during the ceremony pay tribute to the powerful union of hearts being made, you are already creating a support system that you will need on occasion through your married life. How is this union sanctioned? In traditional African weddings, this occurs in a family home where all of the family members are gathered, after many months of preparation and preliminary gifting. Prayers are offered along with a libation to the ancestors, asking for their protection and guidance, followed by a transfer of gifts from the groom's family to the bride's. At this point, the families are considered one unit. In contemporary Western weddings, many couples include a prayer of unification in their ceremonies, during which the wedding officiate invites all family members (and sometimes all who are gathered) to join hands and hearts in their commitment to become one in supporting the budding union.

- A dowry must be secured to seal the union. Before your judgments set in, wipe your mind clean of the images you may have seen in old African movies or in certain skewed documentaries. The concept of bride-price or bride-wealth, also known as *lobola* (and many other African names), is not a "price" paid to *purchase* a woman. In the African worldview, humans are divine and cannot be owned. In many African countries, a young man must give to a young woman's family a set of gifts. Those gifts range from community to community, but typically they used to include goats, cattle and chickens, as well as clear, homemade liquor, and a small portion of cash. In contemporary urban African settings, the bride-wealth has included Western clothing, furniture, electronics and larger amounts of money. Beyond the actual gifts is the purpose of the bride-wealth itself: an offering of gratitude for the opportunity to marry a treasure of the family household, who in her own right generates income for the family who will be deprived of her efforts when, in patrifocal communities, she will go to live among her husband's family and generate an income for them. In one sense, her loss means a loss of services, which should be compensated for in some way. The additional understanding on the part of both families is that the intention of the young man to marry this woman and provide for his family must be demonstrated. If he has to stretch his resources and include his family in his effort to show his love and devotion tangibly, he will become more fully immersed in the knowledge and understanding of the sacred life he is now entering. Bride-wealth can be seen as a beautiful practice used to teach family values. At the same time, it can be, and has been, abused by parents who get greedy and want to use the opportunity to get that great stereo they never had or some other expensive item. This ritual will bear proper fruit only if it is handled appropriately and exercised with the original intent. I suggest an evolution in the bride-wealth philosophy by recommending that couples embrace the spirit of the gift and together offer gifts of love to both of their families for preparing them to be the adults they now are and for providing them with the love and support that have gotten them to this sacred point in their lives. Try it. Your families will love it!

• No wedding is complete without the ceremonial feast. Unlike many wedding receptions today, where standard catered fare looks more like bland baked chicken, white rice and green beans, the feast of a traditional African wedding is replete with all of the delicacies of the community. The thinking behind the feast has been that now is the time for the newly married and their families to invite the community to support and love them in their new life. Through the bond of breaking bread, drumming and dance, the two—this time the families and neighbors—confirm their union. Because marriage represents the primary building block of community, this moment is an auspicious one that must be acknowledged with precious gifts of food and drink. Generally the families prepare the food, with the men often securing and preparing the meats and the women making the vegetables, desserts and beer.

In Western weddings today, the scenario is quite different. The "community" represents, in part, people you love and others you feel obliged to invite. And the reception itself often takes place at a location where it seems you have no control over the food—hence, the bland hotel food that so many people pay exorbitant prices to feed their guests. I challenge you not to fall into this trap. Instead, be empowered by the strength and conviction of our ancestors who understood the sacred nature of sharing special foods at such an important event. If your caterer says he or she cannot prepare a certain dish, don't feel that you have to give in or necessarily walk out. Instead, give the caterer a recipe and some ideas on how you can work together to honor your choices. Collective effort is vital to the success of your big day.

Once you have made the decision to get married, put on your seat belts and prepare for the most extraordinary ride of your life! And, just think, it all begins with your wedding. The list of things to do to plan a wedding could go on indefinitely. Because this is true, you must make a plan, enroll the support that you need and pay attention to every detail along the way.

First Things First

You are a contemporary couple. Keeping in mind that you will be forming a union of two families—whether you thought about that before or not—you still owe it to each other and to the overall happiness of everyone involved to establish clarity about your wedding plans early on. That means that both the bride and the groom need to sit down and talk about the wedding. Ask yourselves what you envision your wedding to be like. Consider divination to discern the opinion of the ancestors and other spirits (*Orishas,* angels, *Ntru*). Did you make the best choice? Is this supposed to be the parent of your child? Do you have compatible ancestral lineages? Do you have complementary destinies? These are the questions that would be asked in a traditional African community.

Find out what dreams the two of you share, as well as the financial restrictions that you believe will exist for you. Be frank about money. Now is the time to put your cards on the table. Trying to seem as if you have more (or less) money than you actually have is deceptive and can prove to be disastrous if you mislead your partner. Determine what resources you can realistically allocate to a wedding, and then consider who else might be able to help. In Western tradition, the bride's family has been responsible for paying for all of the wedding bills, save the rehearsal dinner and the alcohol at the reception, which are the responsibility of the groom's family—two hefty checks. It is more common today for couples to make significant contributions and for those family members who are financially able and interested in supporting the big event to pool their resources accordingly. Beyond the money, the couple needs to organize their plans so that they will know how to ask for the help that they need. Basically, you should make an ongoing list that you check off as each item is handled and how much each costs.

Sharing Responsibilities

Both families have a role in the planning of a wedding in African-American and West African tradition. As a matter of respect, you should meet right away with both sets of parents to find out how they want and are able to participate. To avoid potential conflicts, I recommend that the two of you sit down first and map out how you think they can be of help in planning the wedding that you really want. So often, couples flounder about in the early stages of their planning, which makes communication poor. What then happens is that loved ones get hurt feelings, because they want to do one thing and you want them to do another, and no one is perfectly clear on the final decision. In cases of confusion, what ultimately happens is that the wedding suffers, because someone drops the ball.

There is a workable solution. Take each family member and loved one into consideration. Ask yourself what you think each one is willing and potentially able to contribute to your wedding. Make a master plan that incorporates the responsibilities that will need to be fulfilled, with a blank next to each point. Then, in pencil, record the initials of the person you would like to ask to take on a particular role. When you receive confirmation of acceptance or decline for the role, mark your schedule accordingly. In the end, you will have a clear picture of how your plans will come to fruition and with whose assistance.

As far as your parents and elders go, be sure to keep them up to date on your plans. Let them know how things are going, so that they can provide their own insights and feel that they are being included in this very sacred event.

Cultural Kisses
Only a few years ago, the majority of African-American couples rarely considered including aspects of their cultural history in our weddings. As the trend to personalize weddings has swept the country and couples have continued to get married later in life, and, most important, the stigma of identifying with things that are culturally specific has begun to lift, more and more Black folks are looking for ways to incorporate what I call "cultural kisses" into their weddings. A cultural kiss essentially is a detail in the wedding that relates immediately to the couple's cultural heritage. For people of African descent, the choices are vast. Here are a few ideas:

- Take a cleansing bath. In the Khamitic tradition, you must go through a complete cleansing ritual, from purifying the body internally by fasting and eating sacred foods to cleansing the body first in pure water and then in rare oils. All of this happens well before you get dressed—the idea being that you work from the inside out. Begin this process several months before you are married for optimal benefits. On the day of the wedding, each of you can take your final bath as you prepare to offer yourselves to each other. See Queen Afua's *Heal Thyself for Health and Longevity* (1993) for more ideas.
- Wear body incense. Rather than choosing commercial fragrances, anoint your body with oils, such as Egyptian musk, frankincense, heena, amber or lavender. Women in Mali used to make body incense specifically to arouse their husbands and remind them of their

scent. Although they were in polygamous marriages and had extra incentive to mark their mates, you (meaning both bride and groom) can enjoy the excitement of enlivening every one of your spouse's senses on your wedding day—a day to remember forever!

- Purify the space. During traditional African ceremonies (much like those in the Catholic Church and other religions), the location of the wedding is purified through the burning of sage, frankincense and myrrh and/or other sacred incenses. A responsible person is assigned the task of waving the container with the incense to the four corners of the universe, inviting the good spirits to enter while urging all negative forces to leave the premises at once.
- Pour a libation to the ancestors. To pay tribute to the power and presence of the ancestors is a must at a traditional African ceremony. You can include this in your wedding by having your officiate make a prayer to the ancestors, including names of departed honorable members of your families and other personally respected ancestors such as Malcolm X, Fannie Lou Hamer, Yaa Asantewaa, John Henrik Clarke, your grandmother's minister, your first-grade teacher—those you love. This prayer should occur early on in your ceremony and can be accompanied by a sprinkling of holy water directly on the ground, if possible, or on a plant. If not, you can use two wooden bowls that you either purchase or have made for this purpose, to pour water from one to the other in order to keep water off the floor.
- Create an ancestral altar. A subtle way of honoring your ancestors is to set a private space on or near the site of your wedding and place pictures of your ancestors on it. Use beautiful fabric with a candle and incense to enliven the table. Either before your ceremony begins or during the wedding itself, you can go to the altar and make a silent prayer. That's what Lisa Miller and music executive Deric Angelettie did at their wedding. In the midst of a traditional Christian wedding, they wanted to make sure that they invoked the grace of their ancestors to support their marriage. Standing together, they invited their mothers to call out the names of their ancestors, after which the mothers lit the unity candle together. Their guests loved it!
- Wear cultural clothing. You don't have to wear white to your wedding in order to be an appropriate bride. In African communities, couples wore the most sumptuous of their village's cloth. Much like the plaids of Scotland, African cloth ranges from village to village and bears the most extraordinary patterns. The most popular African patterns in this country are *kente* from Ghana, *asooke* from Nigeria and mudcloth of Mali, although many other choices are currently available. African and Caribbean cloth are frequently replacing white

satin for African-American brides and grooms. Sometimes the cloth appears in trim on white dresses or as vests, bow ties and cummerbunds. Other weddings showcase traditional African designs and fabrics. In your home town there are bound to be designers who make these culturally inspired garments. I have a listing of many of them in *Jumping the Broom: The African-American Wedding Planner* (1995). Just so you know, white as the color of a wedding dress became popular during Queen Victoria's reign. Before that, throughout Europe, brides wore richly colored velvets and brocades, the finest threads they could afford—just as Africans do. Because white is so prevalent today, many culturally inspired brides are incorporating African brocade and other patterns on a white dress with a Western silhouette.

- **Serve cultural cuisine.** Whatever the food is that speaks to both of your family traditions—the food that gets spread out on Thanksgiving Day or when special guests come calling—serve it at your wedding. Your wedding should be a celebration of your unique style and heritage. Find a caterer who will work with you to make your dream meal come true.
- **Present a culturally designed wedding cake.** Cake designers across the country now produce cakes featuring African and Caribbean motifs. Look at African reflective fabrics and textile designs for ideas, and then talk to your cake designer about a cake that suits your interests.
- **Jump the broom.** This ceremony, during which a couple literally jumps over a broom, was born during our enslavement when our ancestors were denied legal marriage. Instead of giving in to the pressure to procreate without a proper ceremony, our ancestors recreated their own. They used a broom, which is a symbol of householding the world over. They often decorated the broom and gave it to a male loved one to hold before them. The two shared vows and then, at the crescendo of the big-bellied West African drum (before it was outlawed)—which indicated the call for grace to the ancestors—they jumped together over the broom. Their jump symbolized their transition into "married" life. This ritual remained popular in the South well after Slavery, and many white couples also included it in their ceremonies. Thanks to Alex Haley's *Roots,* the world got to see the ritual come alive, and it has been embraced once again by countless couples.

Keeping It All Together

For most people, the biggest event they will ever plan is their wedding, and the details can seem overwhelming. It is possible to stay on

How to Jump the Broom

Slave narratives paint beautiful pictures of the ways in which our ancestors honored their unions. When it came to jumping the broom, there
wasn't just one way of participating in this ritual. The enslaved jumped together over the broom as well as with bride first, groom second and for-
wards and backwards. One belief was that the one who didn't trip would
be the ruler of the household. In recent years, couples here have discovered a number of ways that work in contemporary ceremonies. Here are
the two top suggestions:

- **End your wedding by jumping the broom.** After you have recited your
  vows and sealed your union with a kiss, if you have incorporated drums in
  the ceremony, turn and face your loved ones, wait until the drummers reach
  a crescendo and then jump. It is believed that at the crescendo, the ancestors are in the house! You can have your wedding officiate explain the history of jumping the broom—how our ancestors found a way to celebrate
  each other even in their darkest hour—as the drumbeat quickens. You also
  may invite a trusted friend, family member or a "broom mistress" to recite
  the history of this ritual. At the crescendo, take each other's hands, look
  into each other's eyes, then turn and jump over the broom. The broom can
  be on the ground in front of you or held slightly above the ground by your
  best man or an usher.
- **Reserve the ceremony for your reception.** For many reasons, couples opt
  to jump the broom after the wedding. Sometimes the house of worship objects to the ritual; other times the couple want a different environment.
  Some couples have worn Western dress at the wedding and change into
  African garb at the reception, where they jump. This concept is similar to
  that of contemporary African weddings. Even now when couples marry in
  church in Africa, they also *must* partake of a traditional marriage ritual at
  home, or the marriage is not considered valid by the community. If you decide to jump the broom at your reception, select a time when your guests
  have settled down, as this is a sacred ceremony. It can be after you make
  your entrance with your bridal party. Your host can invite everyone to be
  seated after which your drums—live or on tape—can play. Someone should
  explain the ritual so that everyone understands what you are doing. Make
  sure that you have a beautifully decorated broom to honor the occasion.

top of all of your plans, have a beautiful and memorable wedding and
reception *and* stay within budget. The key is organization. Following
are some tips to help you stay on track:

- Select a date as soon as possible, preferably a year in advance.
- Determine how much money you intend to spend and how much
  time you need to collect the funds. Then add a little to your wedding
  fund for unanticipated expenses. (Experts suggest a 25 percent al-

lowance for unanticipated expenses. I know that seems like a lot, but it's the going overage average.)

- Select your wedding party, including maid and/or matron of honor, best man and other attendants. Invite them to be a part of your wedding. Stay in touch with them, giving each specific duties that will help you to handle the many details of your plans.

- Make a preliminary guest list, so that you can get a count. You need this information in order to shop for wedding and reception sites, as well as to get estimates on caterers. Consult your family on their lists. Do your best to secure the invitation lists in writing, with correctly spelled names, addresses *and* telephone numbers at least three months before the wedding. This is not easy to do, so don't leave it until the last minute. If you can put it on a diskette in alphabetical order, you will save yourself and whoever is helping you a lot of time.

- Secure the location for your wedding and reception, and lock in the dates as soon as possible. Provide security deposits *before* the deadline has passed, so that you can hold the space even if you aren't certain that it is your final choice. Many couples have forfeited a few hundred dollars when they've decided to change the location, while others have found themselves with nowhere to assemble their guests because they waited too long.

- Secure a wedding officiate, especially if you are getting married outside a spiritual sanctuary. Sign a contract with this person, as well as all other professionals working with you.

- Set a meeting for premarital counseling sessions with your mate and a spiritual adviser. Be honest in these meetings, so that you can identify any issues that you should address before you marry. (This is another reason for setting the date early: so you can resolve these issues.) You can discuss specifics of the wedding ceremony that you would like to incorporate. Keep in touch with your officiate throughout your plans.

- Earmark a contribution for the house of worship where you will be marrying, to include use of the church or other facility, the organist and other musicians and the officiate. Find out if there is a set fee for these services. If not, offer at least $100 for each. Prices can run much higher, so check with the officiate or church secretary.

- Determine what type of food you want to serve. Shop for menus that you like. If you use a catering facility for your reception, work with the staff to create a menu of your own choosing.

- Define the style, colors and overall look of your wedding. Then focus on finding the right attire for your wedding party, as well as the decorations for the wedding and reception sites.

- Select a florist who can implement your theme.

- As soon as you secure your date and location, select your invitations. There's a wide assortment of culturally inspired invitations available on the market these days. You may also want to have your invitations hand-made. Give yourself at least two months, preferably longer, to secure your invitations. They should be mailed six to eight weeks before the wedding. Be sure to have your RSVP cards stamped, so that your guests can easily return them.
- Research photographers and videographers. Be sure to select a professional whose work you like. Some traditional wedding photographers present mostly formal photographs. I strongly recommend that you work with a photographer who offers a balance of formal portraits and candid shots. You may want to put disposable cameras on each table at your reception so that guests can take photos as well.
- Hire a coordinator if you can. This person can help you to keep track of the details, source goods and services that you want and oversee the little things along the way. Even if you work with a coordinator, make sure that you stay actively involved.
- Review all details with coordinator in advance. Assign trusted friends and family to backup roles, such as signing of the guest book.
- Select gifts for each other, your parents and grandparents, the wedding party and guests. (See "Gifting and Giving Thanks" for ideas.)
- For a large wedding (100 or more guests), have a formal greeting time, as people exit the ceremony, enter the reception or when the two of you go to each table to say hello. In a formal receiving line, the bride's mother comes first, then the groom's mother, then the bride at the right of the groom. Next is the maid of honor, then the bridesmaids (optional). Although fathers do not need to stand in the line, I recommend it so that guests can see a strong family. The other men should mingle.
- Be sure to get thank-you notes and send them out right away for all of your gifts. Ideally you should send all thank-yous within two weeks. Each guest should receive a personalized, handwritten note.

Same-Sex Unions

Can gay people marry? Is it condoned in the African-American community? What happens if gays and lesbians want to acknowledge their committed relationships? These continue to be tough questions that homosexual couples face. There are still a lot of questions across the country as to the legality of same-sex marriages, with most states not giving their approval. The Black community, which is generally pretty conservative, does not wholeheartedly cheer same-sex couples on in these pursuits. In African communities, there are no established rituals that I could identify that recognize homosexual relationships or unions.

At the same time, my research did show that in some African societies, homosexuals are not necessarily tossed to the side. Instead, they are given roles within the community structure just like everybody else, such that they can make meaningful contributions. Traditionally, African communities honor the spirit of a person and the gifts that he or she brings to the village.

In contemporary Western culture, the question of how to honor same-sex unions is coming up with increasing frequency. And the answers that couples have come up with are creative. I get questions all the time from homosexual couples about how they should handle the logistics of solidifying their unions. A friend in San Francisco called to tell me that she and her girlfriend are getting married soon. She wanted to know what would be appropriate for the two of them to wear, what type of service they should have and all the other intricacies involved in planning a wedding. Although the legalities are very different for same-sex couples, the basics of putting together a beautiful event that acknowledges your union are largely the same:

- Secure the blessing of your family members, including the people you have enrolled as family over the years. As with other couples who have experienced familial conflict, if you are experiencing rejection from your folks, you will have to decide how you want to proceed. I always recommend that couples take the time to win over family members, so that the family bond can be secure. Whether you are heterosexual or homosexual, that dream doesn't always come true. You will have to evaluate for yourselves how to respond to your hearts' calling.
- Choose a wedding location that will allow you to have the ceremony that you desire. Before you get your heart set on having a wedding at a sacred site, make sure that the sanctuary allows for same-sex marriage rituals. Many do not. If you cannot find a spiritual facility to house your wedding, consider myriad other choices, including anything from a beautifully landscaped garden to a private home, a yacht or a gazebo at a public park.
- Find a wedding officiate who will honor your union. In order to have a spiritual acknowledgment of your union, you must find an ordained officiate to conduct your ceremony. Your religion will determine where to look. Often, homosexual couples are able to have only spiritual unions; most states do not acknowledge same-sex marriages legally.
- Create a program for your wedding that illustrates your commitment to each other. The purpose of marriage is to create family and to be a pillar in the community in which you live. The genesis of the

strength needed to serve in those ways comes from the commitment that two people share with each other. In your ceremony, pledge your commitment to each other and before those gathered to support you.

- Invite only people who will offer you love. This is true for every wedding, and especially for yours. To avoid making a spectacle of your sacred moment, limit your guest list to people who respect and affirm you for who you are and what you are pledging on that day. Others can receive an announcement or nothing.
- Find out which publications will run your wedding announcement. Again, the more traditional newspapers will not likely run your photo and story, unless they do so as a point of news, which you may not appreciate. In most metropolitan communities, gay-friendly media exist that may welcome your announcement.

Our Children, Our Future

Ask any parent, and you will hear a deep echo: *Having children changes your life forever. There is no greater experience than that of being a parent.* No greater responsibility exists either. Children are the extension into the future of the family unit. It is through them that a family lineage grows. Because that is so, parents shoulder a tremendous responsibility when it comes to rearing their offspring. That's why Haki R. Madhubuti, author and founder of Third World Press, consistently urges our families to build a strong foundation for our children, one that includes the active participation of the grandparents and other extended family. We must be conscious about how we bring children into this world and how we provide for them. From an African perspective, we know that the spirit of a child is valued as the most precious source of love and inspiration. It is believed that children enter this world with a purpose, a destiny the entire community must help them to fulfill. The only way that parents and community can accept this charge is by paying attention all the time.

Being Responsible

Congratulations on making the decision to become a parent. As a parent, you will discover the core meaning of responsibility as you nurture your offspring and help to mold them into healthy, strong people. Whether you have spent years planning, have found yourself with child, are adding to a family with children, or adopting, you should keep your personal responsibility for the family lineage at the forefront of your mind. In the tradition of our ancestors, you can draw on the community for advice and counsel as you also enlist contemporary outlets to assist you in establishing your home. Following are some important areas that require your attention:

- Health care. Both yours and your child's health care are critical to the development of your family. If you are not already enrolled in a health care plan, research options on your job, through your partner's job or through the government. You will need adequate insurance to take care of the many visits that young children need to make to the pediatrician, as well as your own care before and after pregnancy.
- Savings. Start now to save money for your family's future. Set up a savings account in the name of each of your children. Even if you put only a few dollars away every paycheck, you will be surprised at how fast that money grows. When you need resources for your child's education, the funds will be there.
- A safe home. The environment where you and your children live should be clean, neat and welcoming. Then you will be free to care for your family without worries about your physical space. For a newborn, make sure that the space the child will occupy is clean and out of reach of pets or toddlers.
- Elder wisdom. Consult sister and brother elders about their experiences in rearing children. Their knowledge expands generations and can never be discounted even if you decide to use more modern strategies on occasion.
- Loved ones. Consult family members, friends and coworkers about strategies and services they may have used to have a smooth birth and introduction to child care. They can help you set up your network of support. Find out who is willing to pitch in even before your child arrives. In that way, when your hands are full, you won't be scrambling around for assistance.

Baby Showers

Family members and close friends generally organize baby showers for expectant moms and dads. These joyful events are best scheduled at least one month before the due date, so that Mommy can feel relatively comfortable and there is less chance of early labor getting in the way! Loved ones should be invited. The list may include coworkers, family and friends but should not extend to people who aren't really close to the mother or the couple. In other words, leave the politics out.

Some of the most successful baby showers have themes that relate to the new parents' needs, although most first-time parents need just about everything, from infant wear to furniture, diapers to reading material. If the host knows that the couple have a certain sensibility about products or services that they hope to maintain, that information should be communicated on the invitation or by word of mouth. For example, if they plan to use cloth diapers, a group of friends might want to give three-months' free diaper service, whereas others will know not to give a commercial brand of disposables. Likewise, if parents intend to use natural fibers exclusively for the baby, that information will help direct purchases of clothing and bedding. The point here is to make the shower count, and avoid wasting anyone's time or money.

You may also want to get more culturally creative. When entertainer Erykah Badu was about to have her baby, several friends brainstormed to come up with the perfect baby shower for her. Being a spiritually minded sister, Erykah didn't seem like the type of woman who would really want an average party. So the group invited Queen Afua, a priestess in the Khamitic faith, to re-create an ancient birthing ritual that dates back to Khamitic times. Five of Erykah's friends (myself included) were assigned to be honorary midwives. Dressed in white, we stood surrounding a chair that would be Erykah's seat on her arrival. When Erykah walked through the door, expecting to hang out with friends, she was greeted with uproarious drums, horns and bells as well as a joyful *"Ankh"* cry, the symbol of enduring life. For the next hour, Erykah was treated to a ceremonial foot bath in sacred oils and a burning of sage to purify the passageway for the child's birth. Then, seated in front of her mother and grandmother, "the great wombs of her heritage," she was heralded with prayers recited by each of the midwives on behalf of the gathered assembly. The afternoon was magical and inspired. After the ceremony of blessings, everyone ate a delicious vegetarian feast, followed by the traditional opening of gifts. The only male present was her partner, who was invited to stay.

You too can create a special baby shower for your loved ones. Take a few minutes to consider what would be most appropriate for them and then work with others to make it happen.

Note: It is considered in poor taste to have a baby shower for anyone outside of immediate family when the event is hosted for a second or third child. The going wisdom is that the parents already have the necessary items to take care of the child, so another shower for which people have to spend money may be considered greedy. To that, I suggest that you follow your intuition. If the children are spaced closely together, the shower may be unnecessary. When the births are more than four years apart or the sexes are different, the needs may be just as great as with the first child.

Note: Be sure to record the pregnancy, birth and early days of all of your children. Being the middle child, I experienced a bit of an identity crisis during my puberty when I saw that both of my sisters had lots of photographs of them when they were small. There were not as many of me. What happened, of course, was that my parents, like so many others, were just plain tired. They had overdone taking pictures with the first child, and decided to enjoy *being* with their second child (me) rather than recording everything. For the record, it's best to have a record. Pull out that camera.

Naming Ceremonies

In many African traditions, "baby showers" happen after the birth of a child. It is considered bad luck to have a party before birth, since you don't know if a child will "decide to stay" (live or die, in Western terms). Actually, they happen after divination (the consultation with the *Orisha* and the ancestors), which determines what spirit has decided to take its form in the child and what reason it has returned. For this reason, the child is not normally named until at least seven days after birth.

Then, as was illustrated in *Roots,* the child is held by the father and pointed to the heavens in an outdoor ceremony. Through prayer, the father, the rest of the family and the spiritual elder ask for the ancestors' blessings for the child's happy and strong life. At that moment, the child is given a name, which the father whispers into the child's ear and later proclaims to all assembled.

The naming ceremony is being reintroduced, displacing the christening in many African-centered enclaves around the country as brothers and sisters work to discover their identity through every means available. Invoking the African in us through naming (and renaming ourselves) has been popular for more than thirty years. Claiming one's heritage through name has been considered essential in rebuilding the community. As men and women joined the ranks of the Nation of Islam, for example, they immediately received Islamic names that were symbolic of their personalities and temperaments. (This continues today.) Additionally, people have traveled to African shores to receive names, as they have also sought out spiritual leaders, academicians, and anybody else with knowledge and authority who can help them to take a name that ties them to their African lineage with dignity.

When children and older people receive African names, they do so through a similar process. Following are some of the basics included in naming ceremonies:

- Those receiving a name often eat a bitter herb, sip honey and drink water to cleanse themselves of their old identities.
- Loved ones walk together in procession to the site of the naming

ceremony. An outdoor location is optimal, as it places everyone in the presence of the power of Nature.

- African *Ashanti* stools—of the Akan peoples of Ghana—are popular choices for the seat of the one to be named. The child or adult can be seated on the stool during the ceremony and blessed with his or her name while seated there.
- Before the ceremony begins, a parent or the officiate traditionally pours a libation of clear water or clear liquor on the ground as an offering to the ancestors, inviting their presence and their assistance.
- Drums invoke the ancestors' grace and unite all assembled in one love.
- The naming occurs after the libation and prayers and words of inspiration are spoken. First, the recipient of the name hears his or her name whispered. Then the name is announced to the entire congregation, along with its meaning.
- African names often have two or three components, one representing the day of the week on which the person was born and the other two defining attributes that are part of his or her personality. Many traditions also use the father's name as what we might think of as a middle name.
- Much like a christening ceremony, the officiate encourages the community gathered to serve the child or adult being named. In a ceremony in Baltimore, Maryland, the Reverend Vashti McKenzie asked all the women to serve as spiritual mothers to a girl who was being named and all the men to take on the role of spiritual fathers for a boy being named. She explained that this meant paying attention to them and gently urging them in the direction of goodness throughout their life.

How to Use Your New Name

When Pamela and Lushon Neferkara got married, they found a surname that represented their love for each other and respect for their African heritage: *Nerferkera,* which means "beautiful are the blessings of God." To make it official, the two changed all of their legal documents and fully became Nerferkara. Other adults have chosen a variety of ways of using their new names, much like women who change their names when they marry. Here are some choices:

- Use your African name at all times. Be prepared to explain the meaning of your name. When you offer the definition, do so with great love. Tolerance for the inquirers' ignorance—even when they aren't asking with the intention to learn but rather to be "smart"— should still be handled carefully. They don't know that their reaction

Adoptive African Names

Girls' Names	Language	Meaning
Adedoja	Yoruba	Crown becomes a thing of worth
Adeola	Yoruba	Crown brings honor
Aziza	Swahili	Gorgeous, precious
Duniya	Hausa	Earth
Fabayo	Yoruba	A lucky birth is joy
Folami	Yoruba	Honor and respect me
Ife	Yoruba	Love
Ifetayo	Yoruba	Love brings happiness
Iliroza	Zulu	Rose
Imbali	Zulu	Blossom
Isandla	Zulu	Careful
Jamila	Kiswahili	Beautiful
Jehlani	Kiswahili	Strong, mighty
Kada	Hausa	Blow of slight breeze
Keisha	Kiswahili	Jealous
Kibibi	Kiswahili	Princess
Lulu	Kiswahili	Pearl
Malaika	Hausa	Angel
Nayo	Yoruba	We have joy
Nkosi	Shona	"God"
Ododo	Yoruba	Flower
Olaniyi	Yoruba	There is joy in wealth
Qhakaza	Zulu	Flower
Rashida	Kiswahili	Righteous
Rawa	Hausa	Dance

HOW TO BE

GIRLS' NAMES	LANGUAGE	MEANING
Rhadiya	Kiswahili	Agreeable
Rukiya	Kiswahili	She rises on high
Sade (short for Folashade)	Yoruba	Honor bestows a crow
Sahra	Kiswahili	Flower
Siti	Kiswahili	Lady of the house
Thandisisa	Zulu	Adore
Undoli	Zulu	Doll
Zakiya	Kiswahili	Intelligent
Zuma	Hausa	Bee

BOYS' NAMES	LANGUAGE	MEANING
Abdullah	Islamic	Servant of God
Aje	Yoruba	Wizard
Attajiri	Hausa	Businessman of prominence
Iligeza	Zulu	Handsome
Imbudle	Zulu	Hero
Injitimane	Zulu	Gentleman
Inzalamizi	Zulu	Patriarch
Issa	Swahili	God is our salvation
Jabari	Swahili	Fearless person
Jaha	Swahili	Dignity, glory
Jakuta	Yoruba	Stone thrower
Jaruntaka	Hausa	Courage
Jumoke	Yoruba	Everyone loves the child

(continued on next page)

Adoptive African Names *(cont.)*

Boys' Names	Language	Meaning
Karimi	Hausa	Charitable
Khalfani	Kiswahili	Born to lead
Khamisi	Kiswahili	Born on Thursday
Kito	Kiswahili	Precious
Kitwana	Kiswahili	Pledged to live
Konata	Yoruba	A man of high station
Kufere	Yoruba	Do not forget
Kunle	Yoruba	His home is filled with honor
Mbwana	Kiswahili	Master
Nassor	Kiswahili	Victorious
Nuru	Kiswahili	Born during daylight
Obasi	Ibo	In honor of the Supreme God
Obi	Ibo	Heart
Odudua	Yoruba	First ruler of the city
Ogbon	Yoruba	Wisdom
Okorie	Ibo	Born on market day
Ola	Yoruba	Wealth
Ologun	Yoruba	Warrior
Olujimi	Yoruba	God gave me this
Simba	Kiswahili	Lion
Umofo	Zulu	Fellow

stems from the Willie Lynch program—the agenda put forward in 1713 that negated the very humanity of our people—but *you* do. So take a breath; be thankful that you are no longer where they are and that you are now empowered to teach others.

- Use your given name at work and your African name outside work. On face value, this seems accommodating, which can be dangerous for your psyche. Why be ashamed of your African identification? But it can also be practical. If you have come to be known by one name and it works for you in a business environment, you may choose to remain under that appellation. If your hesitation has to do with being judged, understand that this is but a symptom of a deeper issue. We all suffer with questions of our worthiness from time to time. Focused contemplation and historical study about our people should help you to develop the self-confidence needed to assert your re-Africanized self-image. Then, whatever you decide about your name will be of secondary consequence.
- Put forth that your African name is the name you should be called, but keep your given name on your legal documents. People tend to follow this path when they want to save money. It can be a bit costly to change your social security number, driver's license, and other documents. The only problem is that in cases of emergency, you could experience difficulty if no one knows you by your given name. The wise choice is to make all documents the same by going to the expense of legally changing your name. Until you choose or can afford to do so, be sure to share with key coworkers and loved ones your legal name.

One last point concerns how to respond to questions about your name. If coworkers, neighbors or others approach you in a ridiculing manner regarding your African name, resist the urge to get angry. Ignorance and fear tend to be the reasons that people poke fun at each other. Instead of getting mad and lashing out at the person, remember why you chose to be renamed. Continue to study the tradition of your name's origin. Read as much as you can about people from the area of your name. As you delve more deeply in African culture, you will become more properly oriented and empowered. Then, when others challenge you, you can welcome the discussion because you have a bounty of information that you can pass along. Being of African descent in the world means that you stand as a potential target of ridicule. Becoming a more conscious African-descended being means you can stand tall and strong and know that part of your purpose on this planet is to help reeducate others so that we can all see both the uniqueness and the commonality that we all have and share.

A word to parents: Make sure that if you select an African name for your child you research it fully and know what it means. Too many of our children are walking around right now with beautiful African names that have nothing to do with who they are. *Then* we do seem

Basket Names

Chances are you or somebody close to you grew up with a nickname—a term of endearment that somehow described your personality more intimately than your formal given name. Nicknames tend to come from family members and friends who grow to know you over the years; and they often remain private, used only among loved ones. Our practice of giving love names to people is African. A beautiful story that portrays the gifting of these special names is told in the film *Family Across the Sea Is Roots* (1991), a story of the Gullah people of the South Carolina Sea Islands. In the film, directed by Tim Carrier, this story is told:

Many Gullahs kept private names, basket names, they called them. Names that no outsider ever heard. Names like "Limba," and "Roko," are strange to our ears, but are very African. Over a hundred years ago, a friend of Eugenia Dee's, Agnes Brown was born into a world where Slavery was a recent memory. Her husband's name "Mundee" [Monday] is a hint of the strong spice of Africa that seasons her life.

Agnes: I don't know why they call him so. All I know is his name was Mundee. That was the name he gave me, Mundee. He was a good old Mundee Brown.

Eugenia: . . . that came from Africa. They used to name their children after the day of the week in which they're born. If they didn't give them the whole name, they gave them part of that name.

ridiculous. Why go so far as to gift a child with a spiritually charged name if the child and you don't know what it means?

The Christening

To invite the Lord's blessings into the life of a newborn child is a moment that many parents await with great expectation. Even though the infant may be as young as a few months on the earth, the energy of the moment is palpable for everybody present. It is powerful to invoke the grace of God, especially for a new life. That is the purpose of a christening in the Christian church. The child is dressed in white clothes and presented to the presiding officiate, who administers prayers and anoints the child with holy water. Traditionally, the godmother holds the child, as she and the godfather have been identified as the spiritual guardians of this new life. It is their duty throughout the years to honor the child and his or her parents by staying close and providing loving support and guidance.

Protocol says to the parents that family members and very close friends should be invited to the christening, followed by a meal at home or at an outside establishment. Attendees often bring gifts for the child.

Godparenting

One of the joys that many parents experience is inviting other family members and loved ones to serve as godparents to their children. Coming out of Christian tradition, this practice was created to ensure protection and loving spiritual care for young ones in case any disaster or hardship would befall the parents. The name *godparent* is no accident. The spiritual well-being of a child was entrusted beyond the nuclear family to specific individuals with the clear intention that these few people would remain consciously aware of the child's spiritual development and would be willing to take full responsibility for the child if the need were to arise. To sanctify the relationship, at a ceremony in a church, a minister bestows God's grace on the child, his or her parents and the godparents, asking the godparents to proclaim their love and commitment to the child while at the same time inviting God to watch over and guide their steps. Though a simple ritual that often includes other families in a group ceremony, the intention and focus of it are powerful.

My Aunt Audrey, who is my father's youngest sister, was godmother to my two sisters and me. From the time that we were little girls, she used to take care of us regularly. In fact, spending the night over her house was a treat for us. As the years progressed, she made it her business to stay in our lives and offer her love and support in whatever way she could, clearly the African way of being with family. When I look back over the years, I see just how important her role was for us and for my parents. Without her support and that of our other godparents and family, I can't imagine what our lives would have been like. Quite often, godparents are not family members. In their godparent capacity, they take on the role of family for life.

In theory, people think they understand the role of godparent. In practice, it's often another story. Participating in the ritual of godparenting is a sacred event. In the moment, it makes everyone feel great and willing to contribute to a child's welfare. What doesn't always sink in is that the commitment is supposed to be for life—and through life. Some folks are good at it. My sister Susan, who lives in Los Angeles, is an ideal godmother. She has several godchildren in our home town of Baltimore; she calls them regularly and sends them gifts on special occasions, as well as throughout the year. She pays attention to them. As a result, they listen to her and are open to her guidance.

When children are very young, such care is nice but not always vital to a child's mental well-being. As they get older, it can mean the difference between a healthy life and a troubled one. A godparent, after all, isn't Mommy or Daddy, so he or she isn't the supreme disciplinarian. That means that when a child is going through puberty, for instance,

Ten Ways to Be a Good Godparent

1. Remember your godchild. As basic as those words sound, that's where it starts. Include him or her on your list of things to do, such as "Call Kofi on Friday to say hello."

2. Acknowledge birthdays and other special events. Send a card or gift (and on time). Pick up the phone and call to let your godchild connect with you on this special occasion and encourage phone calls from the child.

3. Send photos. Especially if you live some distance from your godchild, be sure to send pictures of yourself, of you and your family, of your pet, your new home—whatever is of meaning to you at that time. This will help you to stay close across the miles.

4. Check in with your godchild's parents regularly. Inquire as to how the child's education is going, how his or her social skills are developing, at what stage the child is. Find out what strategies the parents have been using to teach the child. Offer your assistance, but be sure not to contradict the methods being used by the parents.

5. Do what you say. The worst thing that a loved one can do to a child is to commit to something and renege on that commitment. Don't overextend yourself or be too ambitious about what you can offer to your godchild. Make a clear and careful assessment of your abilities and resources, and then agree only to that which you can and will make happen. If you find that you cannot honor a commitment, let the child know immediately, and apologize. Your open and loving apology will help the child learn how to apologize and how to forgive.

6. Remember to listen. So often children (and adults) simply need to get out what's on their minds without fear of judgment. Offer a compassionate ear to your godchild. Exercise restraint when you find yourself wanting to tell the youngster what to do.

7. Provide advice through anecdotes. People hear better when information is not targeted directly at them. Keep a reservoir of information available—in the form of stories, allegories and analogies—so that when you do feel the need to offer guidance, you can do so in a gentle way. Telling a story about someone else's life and struggles can be a powerful means of delivering a message.

8. Have fun. One of the benefits of being a godparent is that you spend focused yet limited time with a child. Use that time to your advantage, and make it a joyful experience. Discover ways that you can have fun together.

9. Be responsible. As tempting as it may seem just to run off and throw caution to the wind sometimes, keep a level head. You can do that by discovering balance with your godchild—a mixture of fun and inspired direction.

10. Cultivate a spiritual connection. Your title of godmother or godfather was created for a reason. Your accepted and blessed responsibility is to help guide this person on a spiritual path.

---

and separating from parents is a vital part of his or her growth, the teenager is more likely to turn to an attentive godparent for advice. If there is no such person and no relative or close family friend who can offer wholesome guidance that will be heard, the teenager stands a greater chance of falling into harm's way.

The Nanny or Au Pair

Mary Poppins was a nanny, as was Ole Golly in *Harriet the Spy*. Do we have fairy tales that sing of nannies for our children? I haven't been able to dig up any, although I have read countless stories about our mothers, sisters and aunts serving in that role for white youth. The more likely characters—and, by the way, the better trusted with the task—for taking care of little Black boys and girls have been grandparents, aunts and uncles, neighbors, sisters and brothers and cousins. In other words, when there traditionally has been full-time help for our children, it has usually been somebody living in our home or nearby at the time. And Lord knows, we've had plenty of folks spending time with us over the years. An open-door policy for family from down South or relatives from wherever they came has been a part of the tradition for generations that has not abated in the Diaspora. And truly these people who lived with our families for certain periods also often took on nanny proportions as they helped to maintain our homes.

Today things are a lot different. As African Americans are becoming more affluent (some of us, anyway), families often live far away from their relatives, making the need for outside help more prevalent. Luckily, the resources are also more widely available to make live-in help a viable option. A few extra dollars usually means that both parents are working (nothing new), so consistent help—if it is responsible—is a wonderful possibility. For some, it seems a luxury; for others, a requirement. If you're thinking about hiring a nanny or au pair, as Europeans have titled the role of live-in child care attendant, be mindful of who the person is you invite into your home. Here are some guidelines you can follow:

- Do your research. Ask your friends and coworkers who have nannies how they found them and what the relationships have been like. Get candid responses to your questions about what has worked and what has not. Do your best to find someone who is part of your network of support, who understands your values and culture.
- Get referrals, and check them out. If you find a nanny through an agency, check the organization's credentials through the Better Business Bureau and your local chamber of commerce. Get names of previous employers, and interview each one. Check all educational institutions, and make sure that the person is telling the truth. Contact the police department to determine if the person has a criminal record. (Whenever you start feeling uncomfortable about your research, think of your child. Too many cases of child abuse at the hands of nannies and baby-sitters have cropped up for you to have any feeling of guilt. What you are being is responsible.)

- Interview prospective candidates in your home. Paint pictures of potential problems that could occur in the home to learn how the person handles crisis and how quickly the person thinks on his or her feet. Look carefully at the person to see how neat, clean and attentive he or she is. How well does the person speak English? If the nanny's primary language is other than English, do you know how to speak that language? Do you want your child to learn how to speak that language in this way? (This *could* be the best way to learn colloquial Spanish, for example, without having to send him or her for formal lessons!) If you think you like the person, invite your child to come into the room. Introduce your child to the person and watch their interaction from a distance.

- Make sure the person is either an American citizen or a legal alien. Thousands of citizens have been caught by the Internal Revenue Service for not reporting income to household workers, not to mention the Immigration and Naturalization Service. Sneaking around when it comes to your child is not worth it. Check the prospect's records carefully, and then pay the extra money for taxes. And report the income to the IRS.

- Set the ground rules from the beginning. Obvious rules include no smoking, no alcohol, no mind-altering drugs, no guests, no long-distance phone calls, no profanity. Others include spending quality interactive time with the children, preparing meals and feeding the children, reviewing homework, getting them dressed as needed, listening to their concerns and giving parents a daily update. It should go without saying that having a live-in nanny or even a regular babysitter does not take away any real responsibility from parents. You still must monitor your children as well as your helper to ensure that your family is getting quality care and that you are the foundation for that care.

The Art of Discipline

> It is etiquette for a son or daughter to talk to the father in a gentle and polite tone, and the parent, except when reprimanding or correcting his children, is required by custom to reciprocate the compliment in the same way as his children extend it to him.
>
> JOMO KENYATTA, ON GIKUYU CUSTOM

Hands down, when you talk to elders, you frequently hear stories of the harsh discipline they endured. Whether it was being whipped with a switch (a thin green tree branch), a belt, a bare hand or a slipper, they got it up close and personal when they stepped out of line. And for the most part, that form of discipline worked. Even in school, teachers used to be allowed to crack students lightly over the knuckles with a ruler if the students were unruly or inattentive. Discipline in the old school was physical.

Today, physical discipline has cost many a teacher, parent and day care worker their jobs or even their freedom. It seems that people don't quite understand where to draw the line—both the disciplinarian and the child, that is. Abuse in any form is unacceptable. When it's directed toward a child, it should be considered criminal. Yet what we are now facing is a generation of many out-of-control children.

A teacher recently explained that she would rather turn her head than reprimand her own students when she catches them cursing, spitting or otherwise exhibiting bad conduct. Why? Because she is afraid for her life. And she has every reason to be. In her Michigan school, a teacher recently got stabbed for less. When the teachers are afraid of the students, you know you're walking in deep and murky waters.

And the question is: *What's going on at home?* Some psychologists suggest that many parents are experiencing such high levels of stress that they are taking their frustrations out wherever they can. The innocent, the children, are bearing the brunt of their frustration. This must change. It all goes back to consciousness. Rather than reacting to circumstances and staying on that dreaded treadmill that leads to nowhere, we have to step off and take a good, hard look at our lives. When we have children, that means that we must be able to look straight at them and assess who they really are and how we can guide them responsibly into adulthood. Here are some workable forms of discipline that folks are using today:

- Time out. This works if you start it at a very early age. When a child does something that is unacceptable, speak to him or her in a firm voice, lead the child to a corner (that will become the child's time-out spot) and tell the child that he now has to stop whatever he is doing for *x* amount of time. That's what time out is. The clock gets stopped on any other activity other than sitting in silence. The duration can be a matter of minutes. What's important is initiating the time out as soon as the unacceptable behavior starts.
- Explain what was done wrong. Let your child know immediately when her action is unacceptable. Then briefly explain what was wrong with it, so that the child can develop skills of discernment. One man in a video store used this strategy on his son. The boy, who was about six years old, was looking at videos and strayed from his father. In a stern voice, the father called to his son and told him

to stay at his side while they were in the store. At first the harshness of the father's voice was startling. Then the father explained that children are often kidnapped in stores when they wander off. He told his son that because he loves him, he wants to take care of him and that they can do that together by staying next to each other.

- Take away privileges. Anything from watching television to talking on the phone or participating in a sport will usually work—if you stick to it. Children (and adults) treasure their free time and don't want anything to stand in the way of it. If their bad conduct means that they will lose cherished privileges, they may think twice before taking that action again.

- Do what you say. If you tell your child he will not have television privileges for a week, act on your words. Unplug the television, and put it away if you must. And make sure it stays put away for the whole week. Otherwise, he will consider you a pushover, and then no disciplining will work.

- Use your eyes. My mother used to give us "the eye," and all we wanted to do was take back what we had done. Because her eyes are hazel, they would change color, and you'd never know what color they'd be that day. If you've ever spent time with someone who had light eyes, you might notice that it seems that light passes through them. Well, when she was angry, it seemed as if *extra* light would come through them, and she'd be shooting those beams at us. We knew we were about to get in trouble. Those eyes set us straight, because behind them was the promise of a serious punishment if we made another infraction. Other such subtle expressions are commonly used by African parents, such as clearing the throat or moving the fingers a certain way. Loud, violent gestures are actually less common among us.

- Spank if you must. Some parents vow never to use physical force with their children. I agree that you shouldn't beat your children, not even close. But a slap on the hands could prevent a burn. Similarly, good old-fashioned discipline may keep your child out of harm's way. Just recognize that violence begets violence, so don't spank your child when you are angry. Wait until your anger or fear has subsided. The discipline should be for principle, not to satisfy your rage or loss of control. God does not like ugly!

The Family That Prays Together Stays Together

This familiar saying has a lot of merit. Starting from an early age— usually just at the point when the child begins to talk—parents teach that child to recite a very simple prayer. Establishing a connection with the Divine is essential to a good life. By creating the discipline of prayer in children at a young age, parents build an environment that can make it easier later on for children to reach out to God in their times of need and of gratitude.

Family prayer is powerful. Beyond the evening prayers that you may do by yourself or with your children, other times are recommended for prayer with your family members:

- At meals. First thing in the morning—even on busy or late days—take a few moments and offer a prayer of thanks for the meal that you are able to eat. This time will allow each of you to connect with each other and God. Even more, it will give you a chance to slow down and focus within before starting your day. Whenever you eat meals together, pray beforehand. Take turns offering the prayer, so that everyone has a vested interest in paying attention to the message of the meal.
- Before pivotal moments. At any significant turning point in the life of your family, remembering God is a good practice. Rites of passage represent moments for spiritual reflection. A prayer of gratitude that also asks for strength and guidance is a great marker for your family. In some Native American homes, after such prayer, a physical marking is etched into the family broom (which could also be your wedding broom). At each pivotal moment in the family's growth, a mark is added to note the evolution of the family.
- When tragedy occurs. During the course of daily living, painful things happen, including the death of loved ones, loss of employment, serious accidents and illnesses. How we deal with these tragedies is important to the well-being of our families, our communities and ourselves. Asking for God's grace and guidance through difficulty is a clear way of inviting positive energy into your experience. You may still feel pain and discomfort. Tragedies are heart-wrenching, and it seems impossible to function in the midst of the storm. Join with your family and other loved ones during crises, and pray together for strength and guidance. Further, you can call on the ancestors for help. In many African communities, ancestral guidance was one of the first prayers made. The understanding was—and is—that the wisdom of the ancestors is even more powerful now that they live in the spirit world. One way that I like to consider this concept and make it real is to think about my Grandma Carrie. She was a strong and sweet woman who lived through countless tragedies given her 101 years on this earth. When I remember that she grieved with dignity and continued to remember to care for those around her, I feel better.
- In times of fear. Fear is a fact of life. Some fear is quite healthy, such

as the fear of getting burned that keeps people from sticking their hands into a flame. Other fears are not as easy to understand or identify as being healthy, unhealthy or unfounded. Whether the fear is about illness, financial woes, communication issues—whatever it is—you can ask for the strength to work through the fear and find the courage that will replace it and help to propel you and your family to the next level. Fear can be paralyzing. Before it gets to that point, if you can remember to ask for help, you may be able to discover a simple solution that will bring your family together.

Honoring the Elders

Every solid Black family knows that the elders are the rock of the community. It is they who provide wisdom, insight and inspiration during times of need. The elders are the ones with perspective, simply because they have lived long lives and witnessed its ups and downs. As our older population has become a larger portion of American society in the last decade or so, the question of what to do with the elders has become a big issue. Whose responsibility is it to take care of the older members of the community? How will we all manage?

In some discussions, the fact that our elders are still with us actually seems like a "problem." Not if you are a conscious member of the community. Learning *how to be* has its roots in discovering creative and appropriate ways to honor our wisest members. There is no concept in African cultures of "throwing away" anybody in the community, especially the older people. Instead they are revered and cherished, as they are also considered vital participants in family life. Kongo wisdom suggests that African people do not want their elders to live in loneliness. According to K. Kia Buneski Fu-Kiau, coauthor of *Kindezi* (1988), "Loneliness is an illness; it can kill." Malidoma Some, an African medicine man and professor from Burkina Faso, describes the spiritual understanding of the elders:

> For the Dagara of Burkina Faso, every person is . . . a spirit who has taken on a body. So our true nature is spiritual. This world is where one comes to carry out specific projects. A birth is therefore the arrival of someone, usually an ancestor that somebody already knows, who has important tasks to do here. The ancestors are the real school of the living. They are the keepers of the very wisdom the people need to live by. The life energy of ancestors who have not been reborn is expressed in the life of nature, in trees, mountains, rivers and still water. Grandfathers and grandmothers, therefore, are as close to

an expression of ancestral energy and wisdom as the [community] can get.

To care for our elders, we must constantly look for ways to include them in our lives. This may mean frequent telephone calls and visits, and family conferences to listen to great wisdom. Children need to understand that their elders are precious—just as they are—and that they are to be celebrated and respected. As our parents, grandparents, aunts and uncles grow old, we also need to identify ways to take care of them. We must ask ourselves who will be responsible for either living with an elder or visiting as needed. Who in the family will invite elders to live with them during their twilight years? Haki Madhubuti said that he and his wife decided when their children were young to invite her mother to live with them. In this way, they had a built-in loving caretaker for their children—what the people of the Kongo call the *ndezi*. They created a traditional African family environment, even when they had the financial resources to handle their child care needs in another way.

Elders and Institutions

When illness and death come knocking at your family's door, you often realize that theoretical solutions for caring for your elders don't always translate into workable plans. What do I mean? Many people have told me that they had every intention of providing for their elders until their transition. They have understood the importance of not "throwing their relatives away" and instead keeping them in the family home structure. They have organized ways for everyone in the family to pitch in and value the time that they have with the elders. Yet when illness strikes, things often change. This is due, in large part, to the uncomfortable nature of health care in this country. If anyone becomes ill and requires around-the-clock care, the person will be hard-pressed to stay at home to receive that care—unless the dollars are extremely plentiful. So what can we do, knowing that putting our loved ones in nursing home facilities, at least in part, goes against the grain of our collective conscience?

First, stop beating yourself up. Guilt about care for our elders is a huge problem these days. For years, there was a buzz simmering that said that only white folks would dare send their family away to an institution. "They don't care," people claimed. Over time, though, our own families have discovered that nursing homes, retirement facilities and other such locales are real options that we must consider. What you should do instead of feeling bad is to learn as much as you can about the retirement market and take careful steps toward taking care of your elders as best as you can. Well before an elder possibly needs to move, he or she undoubtedly needs help handling medical issues and daily living. If you are younger and vital, you can help.

- Secure details of your elder's medical history. Get permission from your elder to review the records; it's the law. By remaining clear and calm about your elder's needs, you will be able to get to this vital information without ruffling too many feathers. Have a consultation with the primary physician as well so that you can be advised about the details of the care that will be needed.
- Ask the primary care physician, friends and relatives, your spiritual adviser and coworkers for recommendations for elder care housing. Chances are someone you know has had experience with finding reliable facilities. When you hear about a place that sounds interesting, continue to ask as many pertinent questions as you can to get an accurate picture of the establishment. Many facilities provide elder day care, a perfect option for working supporters.
- Research health insurance while your elders are still healthy. Some families have purchased extra insurance for their parents, including nursing home insurance while they are still healthy, so that if the need arises, their loved ones will be provided for.
- Be patient with your elders. Don't mistake them for members of your age set. Remember to slow down and speak clearly when you communicate. Build in enough time in your schedule, so that when you do spend time together, you are not rushing them. Allow the telephone to ring a minimum of ten times to allow an elder to reach the phone.
- Stay in touch. Especially if you live far away or your elder has moved into a home, write letters and send notes, photographs and cards. Keeping in touch with little tidbits about your life can light up your elder's day. Plus, the item is something that he or she can cherish for days and months to come. Practicing remembrance is the point here. When your child loses a tooth and you have a photo, send it with a few lines on the back of the card. If you passed a test with flying colors, send a copy of the essay that you wrote.
- Make dates with your elders. The activities can range from getting your nails done to going to the theater, a jazz concert or a church function. Or you could simply invite your elder over to spend time at your home.

Holiday Gatherings

Being together and sharing love is one of the wonderful definitions of family. Although family gatherings do occur throughout the year, particularly when family members live in the same city and when folks visit from out of town, holiday gatherings are special. To ensure that you and yours make the best of your moments together, take the time to prepare in advance.

Juneteenth

It took more than two years from the time that President Abraham Lincoln signed the Emancipation Proclamation for Texas to get word. So it wasn't until 1865 that Black folks in the state of Texas celebrated their Emancipation. The official day was June 19, and what a joyous day that was. Every year since that historic date, people in Texas have been remembering their prized freedom, and the spirit has spilled over to other parts of the country. Now, across the United States many African-American people consider Juneteenth to be a national family day. (FYI: It took the Thirteenth Amendment to end Slavery.)

Martin Luther King, Jr., Day

When I was in college, there was a huge March on Washington, led by the Reverend Jesse L. Jackson, in an effort to commemorate the late great leader, Dr. Martin Luther King, Jr.'s birthday as a national holiday. My mother came to Washington, D.C., as did one of my best friends, who is now deceased, Todd McDaniels. Together we walked slowly toward the nation's Capitol, planting our steps so that our fearless leader's life would mean something for generations to come. The walk was significant for many reasons, not the least of which was the criticism that it received from mainstream America. More than a few leaders, not to mention run-of-the-mill right-wingers, laughed at the prospect of turning King's birthday into any kind of holiday. That experience reminds me of those that others have shared about the sit-ins of the sixties when our people demanded the right to eat in the same restaurants as whites, or the long marches to polling booths and educational institutions in an effort to gain equal treatment under the law. Even so, King Day is only registered as optional among the holidays recognized by government offices and many other businesses across the country.

At my company, I have made the decision to claim King Day as a holiday and instead relegate Columbus Day to secondary status. After all, Dr. King led so many of our people on the path to freedom. Christopher Columbus ran roughshod through our idyllic islands and called them Spain's. It's so easy to accept a holiday at work just because you get the day off. If you consider what the word *holiday* means, "holy day," you may spend a little more time thinking about your choices and your actions. In recognition of the life that was sacrificed for us, request Martin Luther King, Jr., Day as a recognized holiday for yourself. On your day off, learn something more about King and/or the struggle. Take your children to a museum or to view a film about King's life. Make this *holy day* count.

Thanksgiving

When the day of feasting draws near, the season for family cheer has definitely begun. Historically, Thanksgiving Day represents the day that the Pilgrims in America sat down to break bread with each other and their Native American brothers and sisters. The day of thanksgiving was supposed to be a day of peace. Never mind, it signaled the theft of Native American land by European settlers. For the most part, people today just celebrate a feast without really knowing the genesis of the holiday.

That said, I am incorporating information about how our people spend Thanksgiving because it is so popular among us, a time when family members from near and far come together to share in a fantastic meal. (On one level, then, it is an opportunity for familial communion. We have always found ways to make something good out of something bad.) For those who have to choose which holiday to travel, being with friends at a potluck dinner has become a welcome solution. As you plan your family gathering, be conscious of your intentions and aware that it is your duty to share the full history of what your gathering means. In this way, you can make it mean something else. Beyond your dinner, you can take time to explore aspects of African-American culture and wisdom so that you practice remembering all that is good and powerful about our people. Whether you are going to your family's home or to someone else's, here are a few considerations to keep in mind:

- Bring something to the table. You really should never go to another person's home empty-handed, especially not at Thanksgiving. If you don't cook, you still have lots of choices. Find a great bakery and bring a sweet potato pie, a sugar-free apple pie or some other treat. Offer to bring the centerpiece—anything from freshly cut flowers to a beautiful and fragrant candle.
- Be on your best behavior. In the spirit of the holiday, come in peace. That means that if you have issues with your family, don't spoil the

day by picking fights or holding on to past resentments. Be fully present, in the moment, and enjoy the company around you.

- **Keep a clear head.** Stay away from too much alcohol. Holiday gatherings are prime occasions for rum-spiked punches and other such drinks. Watch your intake. Many a party has turned sour when someone has had too much to drink and starts getting loud and ugly. Pay attention, particularly if you are feeling uncomfortable or tense about your surroundings.
- **Be of service.** There's always some help needed at these big functions. Make yourself useful. Ask the host, even if it's your mother, what you can do to lighten her load. Be genuine in your offer, and then do the work that you've accepted.
- **Leave when it's time.** Thanksgiving Day celebrations can run on into the wee hours of the next morning. In some homes, that's perfect. In others, it's a source of discomfort. Pay attention to your hosts. If you get a sense that you should leave, do so. When in doubt, feel free to ask if they want to spend time alone, if they are ready for bed or just ready for you and your family to go home. If you are spending the night with your hosts, go to your room or other private space when you sense that they want some downtime.

Christmas

People of many religious backgrounds have come to celebrate Christmas as a time to be with family and friends. Just as with Thanksgiving, you should be mindful of how you interact with others. In the spirit of the season, which honors the birth of the son of God, Jesus Christ, you should live at your best. Remembering your loved ones with positive thoughts and prayers, cards, gifts and personal interaction is a highlight of the season.

Don't spend your last dime trying to impress people by buying them expensive gifts. The practice of giving gifts at Christmas came from the original giving of gifts from the Three Wise Men to acknowledge Christ's birth. Give in this spirit. If you embrace the memory of Christ and his great gift to humanity of spreading love, peace and goodwill to every living being, you can approach the Christmas season with great joy.

It's also interesting to discover that December 25 was chosen to represent the birthday of Christ because it points to a high spiritual time. Christ's actual birthdate is unknown; however, as Anthony Browder points out in *From the Browder File* (1989): "Christian bishops in the fourth century adopted December 25 because it was the most universally celebrated day for the birth of numerous [deities] throughout the world.

There were over a dozen religious figures who were said to have been born on December 25, and they all lived before the birth of Jesus."

As you celebrate Christmas and other holidays, do some research so that you know both the historical and the spiritual motivations behind your celebrations.

Kwanzaa

In 1966 Professor Maulana Karenga, Ph.D., an African-centered scholar in California, developed a national African-centered holiday based on Swahili principles. With the intention of reclaiming principles that are African, Kwanzaa, or *first fruits,* occurs from December 26 through January 1. Its meaning is to instill in African-descended people a sense of purpose and clarity about the life-sustaining laws of nature and its values that our ancestors have cherished for thousands of years. Kwanzaa's main focus is the family. Each day of Kwanzaa is honored with a different principle of life that we are encouraged to incorporate into our daily experience:

Umoja—unity
Kujichagulia—self-determination
Ujima—collective work and responsibility
Ujamaa—cooperative economics
Nia—purpose
Kuumba—creativity
Imani—faith

During the weeklong celebration of Kwanzaa, families and communities get together to share creative expression and inspiration and food. For more on Kwanzaa, see the chapter "Breaking Bread."

Single Parenting

It's no secret that many of our families are run by single parents. What a lot of people don't realize, however, is that sisters *and* brothers have been accepting this responsibility for generations—and doing a good job of it. For a variety of reasons, parents sometimes end up going it alone with their children. And the path is often not easy. At the same time, African-American parents have had years of experience in managing children and personal time successfully. There's no question but that issues of etiquette do come up for single parents, as well as those who are coparenting due to joint custody agreements or other arrangements. Here are some suggestions gleaned from successful single parents about taking care of their families:

Symbols of Kwanzaa

Mazao. Fruits and vegetables literally represent the harvest or first fruits, as the name *Kwanzaa* literally means. In the tradition of the collective effort of the harvest throughout African agricultural communities, the *Mazao* symbolizes the historic coming together of the community to honor one another.

Mkela. The placemat, usually made of handwoven straw, has come to signify the importance of honoring tradition and ancestry among African-American people.

Kinara. The candelabra, much like the menorah used by Jews, finds its origins among the Zulu. It was originally used to symbolize *Nkulunkuku,* the firstborn, and has expanded to represent all of our ancestors.

Vibunzi. The ears of corn reflect the children in a family, as Dr. Karenga explained in his book *The African American Holiday of Kwanzaa: A Celebration of Family, Community, Culture,* "the potential of the offspring to become stalks or producers and reproducers themselves, thus insuring the immortality of the people or the nation." Each family should include an ear of corn to represent each child.

Zawadi. Gifts given at Kwanzaa should be offered, with the intention of celebrating great merit and providing inspiration for personal growth and development. They should never be given out of obligation. Educational material, such as books by and about African Americans, and handmade treasures are encouraged.

Kikombe Cha Umoja. The communal unity cup celebrates the fundamental principle of Kwanzaa, the unity of the community. In the tradition of many ancestral African families, it is used to pour *Tambiko,* libation to the ancestors. Customarily, a family elder pours the libation to each of the four winds—north, south, east and west—after which it is passed among family and friends who take a sip (or make a sipping gesture out of respect). The *Tambiko* and subsequent passing of the cup unite our link to the ancestors and with each other.

Mishumaa Saba. The seven candles used in the *Kinara* represent the *Nguzo Saba* or seven principles of Kwanzaa (*Umoja,* unity; *Kujichagulia,* self-determination; *Ujima,* collective work and responsibility; *Ujamaa,* cooperative economics; *Nia,* purpose; *Kuumba,* creativity; and *Imani,* faith.)

- Don't think that you are alone.   There's no reason to feel that you are isolated. Participate in the Bakongo (Kongo) tradition of *kindezi,* which invites all nonworking members of the family and community to participate in child rearing, through the art of baby-sitting. Everyone in the community participates in watching and caring for the children so that their parents can work. Remember the village, and establish your network of support.

- Do what's best for the child.   Keep your child's welfare at the top of your mind. Ramon Hervey, a brother who shares custody of his children with his former wife, actor Vanessa Williams, says that if you keep your children's well-being at the top of your mind, you can handle any situation. He says that you have to decide what kind of parent you want to be: "I don't think that just because your marriage fails, you have to fail as a parent. There's no excuse for being a poor parent. You just have to realize it's a lifetime commitment."

- Agree on values you want to instill in your child.   If the other parent is in the picture, it's essential that you come to terms with basic principles that you intend to teach your child; otherwise, the child can become confused. Establish bedtime hours, time for homework, types of chores and so forth that are to be honored in each household.

- Keep your dates away from your children unless you are serious.   A single father in Detroit told me that the sacrifice for him as he has been rearing his two daughters is that he rarely dates. Because he feels good about the way that his children are developing, he is fine with that. When he does have female companionship, it is off premises. A single mom in New York explained that when she really likes a guy, she includes him in a family meal or activity. She makes sure not to show outward affection toward him, instead opting to treat him like a friend.

- Affirm the positive in your children and in the other parent.   No matter what happens between the two adults, keep that information to yourself. Remember that your children were born of both of you. Honor that bond.

- Be true to your word.   If you say that you are going to do something with the children, especially on your weekend, be there. Children's feelings are fragile. Don't let them down.

- Get creative.   When you don't quite know how to handle a situation, consider it an opportunity for creative expression. If it's appropriate, present the concern to your children, and work together to discover a way to handle something that may be baffling you. We are an enormously creative people. What's imperative is that you remember that you can tap into that creative expression at any time.

Having your children as the motivator behind that effort should yield you incredible results.

The End of a Marriage

'Til death do we part has not been the reality for thousands of married couples, including brothers and sisters. Any honest person who is married will tell you that being married isn't easy, at least not all the time. That's why the traditional Western wedding vows remind couples that the commitment is supposed to be "through thick and thin." Being married essentially means that you gain a partner in life who in many ways is really a reflection of you—your positive qualities *and* those that you would rather not address.

Staying married takes commitment on both sides. If you feel that things are headed toward disaster, try a few of these healing exercises before you give up:

- Pray. Especially if you don't want to, literally get down on your knees and ask for Divine guidance. Pray for the ability to see what you should do next. Pray together if possible.
- Go to a therapist. Chances are you have been talking to close confidants, sharing the details of your misery. But they don't always have the best advice, even when they are well meaning. A trained professional, whether a psychologist, psychiatrist, couple's therapist or spiritual adviser, will be able to listen to each of you and help to identify your core issues. In this way, you will be able to discuss what's really going on for you and attempt to work through your problems. You have to be willing if therapy is to work.
- Take a vacation. Really! You'd be surprised what time off from the pressures of work, the children and other stresses can do for your relationship. Sometimes we get so caught up in dealing with everyday life that we forget to pay attention to each other. Time alone, whether it's at a hotel right there in your home town or on an exotic tropical island, may do wonders for your marriage. If you see that it helps, plan mini-vacations throughout the year.
- Consider a sabbatical—not a legal separation. And call it a break, not a separation. Go on separate vacations, possibly to visit family members or other loved ones who have supported your relationship. Talk to them and listen to their advice.

After you have exhausted all avenues of renewal, if you think you need to end your marriage, work to do so with dignity. For your own well-being, make a list of the things you like and those you don't about your relationship. Remember the things that you like about your spouse when you find yourself about to lash out. Make a written list of your intentions for the future, including what happens to the children, possessions you would like to keep, where you will live and other important matters. Talk to your spouse about your plans. Hire a lawyer, and review everything. Although it will be challenging, be sure to give your lawyer details of your marriage and the reasons for your breakup; this information may be needed in court.

If you and your spouse are able to part ways amicably, the divorce can be cheaper both financially and emotionally. When children are involved, be absolutely clear about how you intend to provide for them, and then follow through on your commitment. It is unconscionable to allow the demise of your relationship to affect your children's health and well-being. The era of the deadbeat dad or mom needs to end now!

Extended Family and Friends

The family in traditional African cultures extends far beyond the so-called nuclear unit that is so treasured in the West. Family consists of blood relatives along with neighbors and friends—in other words, the people who love you. In the Black community, we have naturally been drawn to this concept, inviting our neighbors, church members and other associates to be called "Aunt Jackie" and "Uncle Rob" by our children, so that they would be treated with proper respect. Everybody really gets a love-name that welcomes each one into the family covenant. On a spiritual level, this serves to fortify the entire community. It gives rights and responsibilities to each "family" member to watch over each other—elders, children and working folks alike. In today's busy society, it is ever more important for us to revisit this African concept for holistic living. We must not move into neighborhoods and shut ourselves off from those around us. Yet many of us, particularly in urban areas, seem to have put on blinders, not even seeing the people who live next door. Then, in times of need, we wonder why no one came to help. Let us reconnect to this humanistic principle that says that we must love and honor all in our midst—and welcome those with good hearts into our lives.

When it comes to establishing and maintaining friendships, people have many considerations. *How do I cultivate a friendship when I am busy? How much do I tell a friend? What is a friend?* We all can search our souls for answers to these questions about our relationships. In terms of *how to be* with other people as friends, you can also consider these suggestions:

- Devote time to your friendships. Do not assume that you can be a true friend to anyone with whom you do not communicate. Nurture your bond through visits, phone calls, letters, e-mail.
- Give your friends gifts that acknowledge your love for them. The "just 'cause" gifts are the best. When you are inspired and a friend comes to mind, pick up or make an item that celebrates that person and share it in a beautiful way.
- Enjoy the life of your friendship without neediness. Many people believe that they must stay friends with someone forever—in the same way they started out. Life often doesn't work out this way, though. If you believe that God puts people into each other's lives for a reason, have faith that your friendship's intensity and closeness will be regulated by Divine order. Many people experience short, intense periods of involvement with others followed by years of fondness and infrequent yet meaningful connections.
- Be clear about what your friendship means. Don't allow unspoken questions to create discomfort between you and your friend. If you think that your friend is becoming intimately attracted to you, and you do not feel the same, address the issue carefully and with an even tone before it escalates. You can express how much you value your friendship, adding that you want to remain friends and not move the relationship any further. Work to come to an agreement about your relationship, and then give your friend time to adjust to this emotional turn.
- Find a kind way to end a friendship that is making you uncomfortable. Whenever possible, establish a meeting in person where you can talk to one another. Let your friend know the positives about your relationship first, what you have enjoyed and respected. Then express what is causing you discomfort now. Let your friend know that you think it's important to step back from each other but that you wish him or her the very best. If you cannot handle this conversation in person, write a loving handwritten letter that shares your sentiments. Remember that anything in writing takes on greater power, so be kind, clear and direct.

Dealing with Death

Miss Mary's matter-of-fact wisdom (what I now know to be African retentive wisdom) was that "death is a part of life." Whether it's put bluntly or sugar coated, the reality of being a living, breathing human being is a promise that one day the body will perish. How people have viewed the occurrence of the body's losing its vitality is what makes differences in societal values and considerations so interesting. Now I understand that many people see death as transition to spirit, nothing to dread or lament.

In African-descended communities all over the world, the transition of a human being from life to afterlife has been the focus of great ritual and ceremony. Ultimately, the society's cosmological assumptions and resulting spiritual beliefs define the way they consider everything, including death.

In many Christian faiths, children are taught that there is life after death, that just as Christ lay dead and buried and was resurrected, so can we all experience a spiritual resurrection for our souls. The philosophy of Christ and the Apostles asserts that by living a wholesome, honorable life in the now, our souls will be worthy of entrance into heaven in the hereafter. It's all about the soul, isn't it? Young and old people alike contemplate the existence and meaning of the soul.

Many of us question what gives us life and what purpose we have on the planet. Looking a little deeper, people also wonder how it is that we are alive. Spiritually, there are different answers based on one's particular spiritual foundation. But at the core, most traditions assert that there is a soul that exists within our being. It may be called by other names, but the essence of this soul is what makes us think, feel, taste and experience life. This soul is often considered to be eternal, so when the body perishes, it does not. So where does the soul go? Heaven or hell, depending upon how good you were in life? Purgatory? The afterlife? The other side of the river?

A resounding global pulse indicates the universal belief that life does not end at death. For this reason, the rituals that surround the passing of the spirit into the next realm are significant. Even more, once the soul has passed into the other space of being, many believe that we are able to communicate with that soul in an intimate and meaningful way. That's why great reverence is paid to the ancestors—those who came before us and lived as examples from whom we can draw strength.

Note: In African tradition, one does not automatically become an ancestor by dying. That role is one of honor and is ascribed to those who achieved great merit in their lives by helping others and building their community; the torch of their life's flame gives light and strength to their family. Among the Zulu, a ceremony occurs two years after one's death. During the *ukubuyisa idlozi* ceremony, or "bringing home of the spirit," the community invites the soul of the ancestor to stay with them. According to one study, when the deceased is an elder of high position, an ox is sacrificed to the ancestors, followed by his name's being added to the praise list. Finally, the elder son drags a tree branch from the grave site to the homestead. For the Shona of Zimbabwe, a similar ceremony, the *kugadzira,* occurs a year after death. Only after this important rite of passage is the spirit able to settle and be elevated to the role of ancestor.

Celebrations of Transition

In many parts of the Diaspora, a person's departure from the physical realm represents a point of great celebration. Death marks the last rite of passage for an individual and a turning point for an entire community. Through dance, song, a feast and prayer, the fellowship gathered can assist in ushering their beloved from this life to the next. These ceremonies also serve another important purpose: they allow loved ones to grieve even as they remember the joyful moments that made their lives with the one who passed so special.

During Khamitic antiquity, food, elaborate gifts, libations and other offerings were placed in and around the burial site on behalf of the deceased, to be used during the journey from this world to the next. In Sierra Leone, the Men people hold a crossing-the-river ceremony that occurs a few days after the loved one's death. Their belief is represented by the metaphor that the other side of the water is the resting place of the soul. They also maintain that right before the person's death, his last gasps for air reflect his effort to climb the hill of leaving his physical body. A number of other African family groups, including the Bsuto, Lozi, Lgbara, Shilluk, Mbuti and San of the Khalahari, believe that the souls of the dead go directly to the sky in order to be closer to God.

Jazz funerals in New Orleans are among the most elaborate celebrations. A marching band plays uplifting jazz pieces during a walk through the city with family, pallbearers and attendants, celebrating the joy of the life that has passed on.

Children and Death

When loved ones die, the issue arises about what to tell the children. There is no simple answer; it depends on the child's ability to process the information and your ability to share it. The only rule is to tell the truth. My sister Stephanie, then mother of a three-year-old, had to share the news about the death of our sister's husband. Kori-Morgan and her uncle had developed a telephone relationship, as they lived far away from each other, and the child knew to ask for Uncle George whenever she spoke to her Mommy's sister. George was ill for some time, and rather than hiding the illness, Stephanie decided to include her daughter in a prayer vigil for Uncle George. Each night the two of them prayed for him, as well as the rest of the family. After George made his transition, Stephanie waited until her daughter asked her again about Uncle George. Stephanie's response was, "He's gone to heaven." Her daughter nodded and said, "Oh." Later she asked for Uncle George again. Stephanie reminded her gently, "Uncle George has gone home. He has gone to heaven." To that, her daughter asked, "Is he coming back?" When Stephanie said, "No," her daughter left it alone.

You will have to find a way in your heart to talk to your child about death. If you have a loved one who is ill, it is best to let the child know about the illness. You can do as Stephanie did and invite the child to pray with you on behalf of your loved one. You may need to talk a little bit about the disease that is crippling the person but without going into any greater detail than necessary. For example, instead of explaining the detailed nature of brain cancer, you can say simply that Aunt Betty has cancer, a disease that can be very serious. That could be enough. Telling the truth appropriately means not withholding information but sharing what's necessary. When you do that, you will experience relief, as will your child. Children can read a cover-up in a flash. You can find comfort in being real with your children and bringing them along in the process, so that if or when the loved one dies, the child is already part of the cycle of grieving. On the other hand, if your loved one survives, the child will be able to see the miracle of physical restoration and build a greater reservoir of faith and hope.

The Funeral

The logistics of organizing a funeral can be incredibly detailed, particularly at a time of great stress on a family. Depending upon your spiritual tradition, you may follow different rituals to acknowledge your loved one's passing, but a few basic pointers remain the same:

• Tell your loved ones right away of the death. You may inform one family member and ask him to make a list of everyone who needs to be called, including coworkers. Be mindful of where people are when you deliver this information. If you reach an answering machine, you may just want to ask the person to call you back.
• Secure the official, typed death certificate immediately. With this in hand, signed by the attending physician, you can then plan the funeral. Let the doctor know of any organ donation.
• Contact your loved one's spiritual adviser. If he or she belonged to a

congregation, it will be easier to organize the funeral at the church. If the clergy member knew the person, the service will also be more personal. If not, get referrals from loved ones or the funeral director.

• Contact the funeral director of your choice. Assign someone to handle the details who is clear-thinking and knows your budget. Too many people have been ripped off during their time of grieving. The funeral director should handle all of your wishes—from the choice of casket to the details and location of the service. Funerals can be very expensive, with many details. Pay attention, and don't assume that things will be handled as you want unless you have approved them.

• Assign someone to write a newspaper announcement that briefly states your loved one's birthplace, accomplishments and survivors, and date of death. You do not have to include the cause of death. If you know where the wake and/or funeral or memorial service will be, include that information.

• Invite a family member to accompany you (as a balance) as you handle the details.

• At a Christian funeral, there is commonly a wake where the family gathers separately to view the body and sit together for a few hours, followed by a two- to three-hour period when loved ones gather and a clergy member leads a simple service. The funeral can be as elaborate or as simple as you like. Check with the location of your funeral to determine what is allowed. Make sure that the eulogy that details the person's life is full and reflective of his or her merit. Select singers and sacred readings that will uplift those gathered. If you will have pallbearers, select them in advance, making sure that they are strong men (although women sometimes fill these shoes). These people will carry the coffin out of the sanctuary after the ceremony. Honorary pallbearers walk two by two in front of the casket.

• Your family members sit in the first few pews, with immediate family in the front row to receive guests. As guests approach family, they should extend their hand to each member and offer their love. They may express their sympathy for your loss, or a specific quality about the person that they admire. They should hug those grieving only if it seems appropriate.

• Mourners often send flowers to the wake and funeral sites, although many people today request that donations be made to specific charities. Should you prefer this option, be sure to let your guests know— through the newspaper announcement and via your phone tree.

• Organize your procession to a funeral via the funeral director. You will need limousines to transport immediate family. Make sure in advance that there are enough cars to transport everyone else. When you drive in a funeral procession, put on your lights and drive slowly, but in sync with the other cars. Do the same if you are going to the burial site, an option for everyone except for immediate family.

• Make sure that the family home is prepared to receive guests after the funeral. We generally gather afterwards and share a meal—food that is organized by the family, although loved ones usually bring many covered dishes too.

• If you are a guest at a funeral, be sure to sign the guest book and include your address. The family will send you a thank-you note as soon as they settle down, preferably within a couple of weeks.

• Attire at funerals today is more relaxed than years ago. You do not have to wear black, although many do. Consider the person who has passed, and wear something modest that he or she would consider appropriate.

• After the funeral, stay in touch with the bereaved to provide support and love.

• When a body is cremated, you can still have a full funeral, where you display a photograph of the deceased. This is also done at closed-coffin funerals. The funeral director handles the cremation and the family determines where and how to place the ashes.

• Memorial services are often like testimonials. They can take on dramatic or simple proportions. Most important is to have people speak who will celebrate the life of the one who passed. A memorial service can be held in a sanctuary or another beautiful location.

Dying with Grace: Beyond Wills

Proper etiquette when it comes to death and dying is generally a subject reserved for the living. But there are considerations for the dying as well—in particular, those who have no real plans to die. Sound confusing? Well, perhaps *etiquette* is not the proper word here. *Thoughtfulness* would be more appropriate, which, in reality, is the essence of etiquette.

Many times people with terminal illnesses or chronic diseases or those who are simply getting up in age have faced the eventuality of death and have planned accordingly, if they are able. Historically, many couples have bought space for their grave site right after they get married to ensure that they will have a final resting place. Yet so many deaths are tragic, especially nowadays, or completely unexpected, and they hit survivors unaware, leaving families and loved ones devastated. And too often the devastation of the loss is exacerbated by the confusion and turmoil created when the dying person has left his or her business unattended.

Here are some ways to ease the pain:

Cataloguing
- Get organized now. Decide how you want to distribute your belongings, and write your plans down.
- Leaving a child your favorite watch is a fine gesture. But wouldn't it be wonderful if that watch came with a story? How did you acquire it? Why did you buy it? What is its value—financial and intrinsic? Why did you want the child to have that item in particular? Write a note describing your thoughts, and put it in a safe place with your other important papers, addressed to the child.
- Chances are your home is filled with hundreds of items that represent special moments, important events, original thoughts. From books and records to memorabilia, jewelry, poems, essays, school papers, furniture and collectibles, the stories behind these items are often more interesting and more cherished than the pieces themselves.
- Get a looseleaf notebook and start one room or one shelf at a time. Begin taking about ten minutes a day and increase as you need or wish. Ask friends and family to help jog your memory about gifts and other items picked up on trips abroad or conventions out of state.
- If you don't already do so, go through your photo albums and write down the names, places and events associated with each photograph.
- Developing a thorough catalogue of the things that are important to you is a good practice, if only to enhance your own appreciation of the life you've lived. You've been more places than you thought, known more people than you realized. And the things in your home are proof. Share that with generations to come, not just in the oral tradition of our *djeli* ancestors (those who carried the legacy of our families through storytellings), but also through documentation that will last beyond any individual's memory.

Destroying Evidence
Those pictures you hide in that secret place next to the love letters from an old flame provide fine memories when you're home alone and want to reminisce. But do your family or parents or spouse know they are there? And what about that diary that you demanded no one ever touch? What will happen when your private thoughts become not so private? In an already painful situation, why add fuel to the fire?

Ask yourself these three questions before surveying your possessions. Purge accordingly:

1. Is there anything in my home that would prove potentially embarrassing or hurtful to my loved ones if I were to die tomorrow?
2. Is there anything in my home that would prove damaging to the reputation and image that I have spent my life building?
3. Why am I keeping these things around the house anyway?

Before you finish this exercise, ask the same questions about your workplace. Often people leave confidential, personal and/or damaging material at work. This is a dangerous practice, and it can prove humiliating for your family after your death.

Note: A safe deposit box is a viable alternative for storing confidential documents and items of a sensitive or valuable nature. The cost is nominal, as peace of mind is invaluable. Be sure to include the name of a responsible party in your will who will manage the contents of your safe deposit box upon your death. Give that person an idea of what's in it.

Your Will

It is a myth that you should wait until you get old or ill to create a will. It is never too early to write out a will, but for many slow movers, it has been too late. Further, you don't have to be wealthy to need a will. Your pots and pans may be of great interest and value to your niece or nephew who is in college on a fixed income. Similarly, your record collection might be the greatest treasure for your next-door neighbor who has been a family friend for years. Leave the excuses and fears behind, and make a will.

A will is a legal document that describes in detail your personal intention for sharing your physical belongings, financial and otherwise, in the event of your death. There are many ways to make a will, the simplest being that you write out a list of your belongings in chart form and write next to each item who will receive the item. If you know the party's contact information, that is good. Also the value of each item will be important for the recipient and the IRS. Your loved ones will have to pay estate tax for each gift received. Once you have created your list, take it to an attorney who will review it with you and notarize it, thereby making it a legal document.

If you do not leave a will after your death, confusion sets in. Your family may end up fighting over your belongings, especially if you have financial assets. People have been known to duke it out over a piece of furniture too. Also you run the risk of the government's taking over your belongings. Take the steps today to direct the future of your assets, and review your will yearly to ensure that you are of the same mind about your divisions. A will can be updated as often as need be.

Currently there are hundreds of thousands of legal (and illegal) aliens of African descent living in the United States. For a variety of reasons, many legal aliens decide to maintain their status as citizens of their birth countries while enjoying the privileges of living and working in America. One right that these legal aliens are denied during their lives is the right to vote here, which is reserved for full citizens of this country. We already know that apathy plays a big role in our communities when it comes to the political structure and our efforts to change it. Beyond that, there are real concerns about one's citizenship when the end comes. As of 1997, a non–U.S. citizen's estate retains only $600,000 of personal assets for distribution. For many people, this figure may seem out of reach, but for others it is not. Assets include cash, stocks, bonds and other financial instruments—a home, a car, a boat, jewelry, clothing, artwork and more. You'd be surprised how quickly your assets add up, even after you subtract your debt. For those who have reached a level of financial success that measures beyond the $600,000 figure, tough luck. The government gets the rest.

No offense to the government, but do we want to give them any more of our belongings? Our families, loved ones, favorite charities, any of the above and more would greatly appreciate the fruits of our labor. If you are one of the many brothers and sisters living in this country under alien status, revisit your decision to do so. Consider carefully the pros and cons so that you can make a conscious decision about this vital issue, and then act.

Dealing with Addiction

It's one of those things that you think happens to other people's families, except that more and more frequently addiction to alcohol or drugs is finding its way into many American families. Conspiracy theories abound too. Stacks of supporting evidence suggest that during the Civil Rights Movement, when Blacks gained momentum in their efforts to unite and stake a real claim in American society, the government allowed our communities to be flooded with drugs. These lethal substances rendered thousands of able-bodied, intelligent and progressive African-American people powerless. Instead of being down with the struggle as they had been, they were suddenly nodding on the corner, largely incoherent and oblivious of their surroundings. This horrific tragedy has repeated itself over and over again since the sixties. The Great Escape has come in many forms—a bottle, a needle, a joint, a line of lethal white powder, a series of pills, the crack pipe. Checking out became in vogue several decades ago and still lurks in the corners of our hallways and bedrooms in the faces and lives of our very own loved ones. Just listen to the news for five minutes, and you will hear horror stories of heinous crimes that were committed by people who were high on something. A recent study showed a clear correlation between cocaine and crack use and violent crime. When I was growing up, there was a commercial that warned parents about marijuana, saying that a joint would definitely lead people to harder drugs. People laughed at that ad. I remember hearing lots of folks say that that message was pure propaganda. "Herb," as it was called then, was holistic, good for you, helped you to get in touch with your soul. So how could it lead you to disaster?

History has painted a different picture. In some instances, marijuana has helped people. In fact, some medical doctors today recommend its use for alleviation of nausea for patients undergoing chemotherapy. Still others, namely the Rastafarians, have long heralded the medicinal and spiritual value of marijuana, claiming that it provides a window into a deeper realm of humanity—and every Castaneda reader knows that various "power plants" have been used for centuries to "shift levels of awareness." So why all the fuss? Because we so often hear stories of people who moved from a casual brew and puff to a heavy-duty cocaine habit. All it takes is learning that your brother, sister or child is strung out in some crackhouse, scratching around on the floor for loose rocks, to take this seriously.

Drugs and alcohol are addictive for many people. The Great Escape is alluring for lots of folks, most notably those who see little hope for a vibrant future.

So what can you do if you discover that someone in your family is hooked on drugs or alcohol? The greatest caution that health professionals offer is to take it easy. No one who is actively using drugs or overusing alcohol wants to hear you preach about why he should stop. Preaching won't cut it. Here are some recommendations that have worked over the years:

- Pick a time when your loved one is sober. If it is possible to have a talk during a sober moment, you are more likely to insert a wedge of clear thinking into his head. Someone who is high rarely wants to talk about or even hear about why he shouldn't do it.
- Approach suffering people with love, for they know not that they suffer. If you can treat your loved one as if she has a disease, no different from any other life-threatening ailment, you will show greater compassion. This, in turn, may provide a window of opportunity for you to talk. Rather than accusing the person of anything, use anecdotes

that illustrate what has happened to other people who are having addiction problems.

- Recognize that your concern may be viewed as meddling, or worse. If your interest is taken the wrong way, back off for now, but don't give up.
- Research facilities or programs that may help. Many twelve-step programs provide support for people suffering from all manner of addictions, from alcohol and drugs to sex and gambling. Find out what's available in your area, how much it costs for treatment and what the requirements are for bringing your loved one there. Also, request literature that discusses the problems your loved one is experiencing. This literature will help you to understand addiction better, and it's also a great tool to leave in strategic locations for your loved one to find and read.
- Find out if your insurance company will cover treatment, if the person is your dependent. Try to find out discreetly about your loved one's own insurance carrier if the plan is different from yours. Note that many twelve-step programs operate free of charge, with contributions offered on a volunteer basis.
- Call a help line to get support as you work through your family crisis. You may request a referral for someone who may be able to help by talking to your loved one about his problem. Listening to a third party talk about addiction is often easier to swallow than listening to your own family member or friend.
- Put your foot down. Recognize your own boundaries, and draw the line when you can manage no longer. For example, if your loved one begins to steal from your home, you may have to change the locks or even report her to the authorities—for her and your own good.
- Don't be judgmental. As hard as it may be to bite your tongue, lashing out with criticism or accusations won't help. Instead, your behavior may drive a deeper wedge between you and make it harder for you to communicate.
- Go to Al-Anon or another support group that will help you to manage your reaction to your loved one's condition. Because you are a feeling being (as we all are), you are being affected by this addiction and need to keep your head on straight in order to be able to help anyone else.
- Pray. During times of crisis, it can feel as if there is no hope. Ask for guidance and strength for yourself and for your loved one to find his way back to sobriety. Many people have kicked their habits; the possibility does exist.

Mental Illness

Who knows why some people are able to manage better in life than others. What is clear, though, is that in many families, at least one person suffers from some form of mental illness. Being able to cope in daily life with a measure of clarity and optimism just doesn't work for these people. In some families, the illness is hereditary. Depression is one of the most common of these; it often affects generations of families in differing degrees of severity. What's most important to know about mental illness is that you don't need to be ashamed or afraid. So many options are available for help these days that you don't have to worry about your loved one's being given shock treatments until her hair stands on end, God forbid, or being locked away for the rest of his life without hope of recovery. Respecting one's personal liberties even as mental illness is treated is highly regarded in the medical profession now.

The African take on mental illness is worthy of noting. According to Yaya Diallo in *The Healing Drum* (1989):

The Ibo and Yoruba people of Nigeria, like the Minianka [of Mali] . . . see physical and mental illness as the result of contact with . . . spirits who may have been provoked by some violation or invisible order. A healer acts, in part, as an intermediary between worlds to determine which spirits are at work and how to bring the ill person back into harmony with them. For the traditional [healer], one cannot speak of mental health without taking the invisible world into account. The goal of life is to be able to fulfill a good life and then to occupy a peaceful place in the parallel community of ancestors.

When a Loved One Is Behind Bars

Nearly 40 percent of young African-American males are incarcerated. That's a frightening number that basically tells us that it is likely that in nearly every one of our families, somebody is in jail. We can argue the politics of incarcerating our men and women forever. And some of us need to stay on top of this issue to fight the injustices that put some of our people in jail.

When we have loved ones in jail, what we deal with is often a lot grittier than a moral issue. Feelings of shame, remorse and failure plague many parents whose children are behind bars. Yet we don't have to give up on our family members or lose sight of hope. For Malcolm X, spending time in prison altered his life—for the better. He became a spiritual man with a mission to uplift our people. Nelson Mandela endured the life of a political prisoner in a jail cell in South Africa for twenty-seven years, only to become the president of the newly freed nation upon his release. As part of the support network for your incarcerated loved one, you must search for the strength to "keep hope alive," as Jesse Jackson professes, and provide constant support and encouragement. Some ideas:

- Visit regularly. A connection with the outside world is vital to the incarcerated person's sense of reality. Bring your love, good news and wishes when you visit.
- Pray together. If he or she is open to it, make a brief prayer asking for insight and patience, justice, discernment, clarity and reflection to carry you through this troubled time.
- Provide inspirational literature. Apart from the Bible, the Qur'an and other spiritual texts, there are hundreds of books available that celebrate different expressions of spirituality and leading a good life. Look for biographies from people who hit rough spots and survived them, so that your loved one can see transformation at work.
- Follow the case in close detail. Depending upon the circumstances for the person's incarceration, appeal may be an option. Get as much information as you can on parole, and keep your loved one posted on his case. This will show your dedication and interest, which can be a great relief to your loved one. A lot of the violence that goes on behind bars is a result of despondency, of thinking, "No one cares whether I live or die."
- Don't baby your loved one. Showing pity has never helped anyone.

Instead be strong and show the power of positive example. If the crime that was committed was worthy of punishment, talk about the nature of the crime with the person and discuss the reasons why it happened. Work with her to come to peace about the matter so that she can heal.

- Upon release, set ground rules for how your loved one must behave if he or she will be living with you. Don't be a pushover. Now is the time to accept only estimable behavior. Otherwise, help the person to find other housing. Tough love is a must.

YOUR QUESTIONS ANSWERED

1. I am planning my wedding and am really baffled about where to put my parents. You see, they are divorced and don't get along at all. Where should they sit?

Before you even get to seating, sit down with your parents, one-on-one and talk to them about your plans for the future. Ask them for their blessing and also for their pledge to be peaceful and respectful to each other at your wedding. Sometimes this invitation is enough to get divorced parents to work together on your behalf. If you don't think they will be happy in close proximity to each other, seat them apart. The parent who is closest to you should sit in the front pew during the wedding. Your other parent—and certainly any other married partners—can sit farther back. You may want to give all of them honorary flowers. At the reception, place them at different tables in the company of people they will enjoy.

2. What is the etiquette of addressing problems in a marriage constructively, without causing undue conflict, so that your relationship can deepen? It seems almost too hard to try sometimes.

To that, our African ancestors would likely say that you are looking at marriage the wrong way. When you consider your relationship with your mate as a lifelong partnership, you look upon it as an opportunity for growth and expansion, not in a way that considers the chance for an "out" or dooms the marriage as a "lost cause." Ruby Dee, who celebrated her fiftieth anniversary of being married to Ossie Davis in 1998, had this to say about marriage: "It takes a long time to be really married. One marries many times at many levels within a marriage. If you have more marriages than you have divorces within the marriage, you're lucky and you stick it out." When you feel as if you don't know how to move on, seek help. Traditionally, your support can come from the married elders in your community who can share wisdom with you about how they and others stayed married. You may also seek spiritual or psychological counseling. Look for real assistance before giving up. Throughout your difficulties, treat your partner with love *and* respect.

3. How do I maintain a loving relationship with my mother and still remain in charge with my children?

Stories go on and on about conflicts between the matriarchal elder in a family and her daughter. *Who has the final word regarding discipline?* What is required is a meeting of the minds between the adults on how the children will be reared. Regular discussion with your mother or other elders—in private—is the only way that you can effectively reach an agreement on how issues, conflicts and other situations should be handled in your home. Otherwise, you will experience what so many husbands and wives do: Mommy says one thing, and Daddy (Grandma, Auntie) says another. And before you know it the children are becoming undisciplined because they have successfully pitted their parents against each other. Not the way to go. One father suggested that you tell your children not to attempt to play adults against each other. Let the child know that the adult's word goes. In that way, whatever Grandma says carries weight, the same as your words. Whoever is minding the child, then, will have control.

4. I don't live near my family, and my father has become quite ill. Although I am able to visit frequently, what is an appropriate way of giving support in line with African teaching?

Communicate with your father every day. Pick up the telephone and call. Send notes and small gifts. Send photographs with brief handwritten messages describing what you are doing. By staying in touch you will provide a support of love that your father will experience. Also, be in touch with your mother and the rest of your family to ensure that everyone is okay. When our elders become ill, it is often hard for the entire family to face. By staying in touch with each other, you all get to rely on the support of the group.

5. My godmother recently died, and she didn't leave me in her will. I know that she had some little memorabilia, and I would like to have them as a reminder of her. What is the appropriate way to request a memento of hers?

Find out who the executor of your godmother's estate is. Contact that person and express your grief as well as your interest in having a tangible memory of her. If you approach the person from your heart, rather than out of greed, indignity or anger, you are likely to receive a favorable response. Be sure to follow the directions of the executor, and don't be a nag.

6. I have been "best" friends with a woman for many years. Now she seems jealous because I have developed new friendships. How can I handle this?

Be careful. Consider your friend's situation. Basically, she is telling you that she feels threatened by your other friends; she's afraid that she may lose you. Decide how you intend to nurture your friendship with her—or if you still want to maintain it. Then speak to her from the heart, letting her know how you feel and what your intentions are. If you do want to remain friends, carve out the time to be with her alone *and* invite her to spend time with you and your friends so that she won't feel isolated.

7. I am in an uncomfortable situation. Sometimes when I go out with a close male friend who is not my lover, he hits on other women while we are together. I think this is rude. What should I do?

First of all, know that your friend's actions are rude. If you commit to going out with a friend, unless it is understood that he or she will be shopping for dates, the two of you should be focused on each other. Quite often, though, people think that in social environments finding a date is fair game when they are with others. On this point, you need to establish the ground rules that will make both of you feel comfortable and valued. Allowing yourself to get upset without speaking up is not honoring your friendship. Discuss the issue when you are in a private setting. If you believe that your friend disagrees with you or will not follow your wishes, limit your social contact to environments where you will feel comfortable.

8. My mother-in-law has agreed to take care of my newborn while I go back to work. Since she is family, do I have to pay her?

According to the philosophy of the *ndezi,* a retired family or community member is supposed to fulfill this role. This doesn't mean, however, that some form of reciprocity is not in order. Decide together *before* your arrangement begins what fair compensation is. Quite often money is of little significance, whereas help around the house, grocery shopping and other such needs are. If financial compensation is preferred, agree on a price and honor that payment as you do all others.

ToBeYoung

Though it be a thrilling marvelous thing to be merely
young and gifted in such times, it is doubly so, doubly dynamic—to be young, gifted and black. Look at
the work that awaits you!

L O R R A I N E   H A N S B E R R Y

W H O   are the jewels of our community? The trailblazers? The inspiration? The future? Our youth. It is the young people, those golden and
chocolate, honey and caramel, crystal black and café au lait, who will
carry the torch of who we are and who we can become into the new
millennium. Knowing this, we all must cherish our youth and prepare
them to lead in the noble tradition of those who have come before
them. Throughout our history, it has been our youth who have led uprisings, made scientific discoveries, championed freedom marches and
taken care of elders. Our youth have consistently been great contribu-
tors to the overall welfare and development of our people—and of this
country. Through their strength and untiring will, their charm and ingenuity, we have risen, again and again. This we must never forget. At the
same time, we must look at the state of our youth today, because many
of them are in turmoil. And if they are, so are we all.

I went to a panel discussion that explored the relationship between
poetry and music at the 1998 National Black Arts Festival in Atlanta,
Georgia. On the panel sat many distinguished artistic figures. From the
"old school" were poet-writers Ntozake Shange, Sonia Sanchez and
Amiri and Amina Baraka. Representing the young folk were Joan Morgan, a hip-hop journalist, and Charlie Braxton, a poet. At a certain
point, a young brother stood up and challenged the audience, saying
that he didn't think it was necessary to know jazz or bebop to know
hip-hop music. "Jazz is my Daddy's music," he defiantly explained. Ms.
Sanchez, who loves hip-hop and jazz alike, tried to show him that jazz

is everybody's music by discussing the connectedness of all of our music, old and new, from all over the Diaspora, to each other. Others on the panel tried to reinforce her message, but the brother wasn't listening. He seemingly had made up his mind when he approached the microphone that the panelists would refuse to hear him, so he unconsciously blocked his mind to hearing them.

When I left that panel, I was troubled and inspired. Although the discussion had been about music and art, so much more had come to the light. Everybody on that dais was really talking about how to live rather than how to hear a note or craft a poetic line. So much goodness came forth, and so much was lost because it wasn't heard—on both sides of the mike. At a certain point, Sanchez made the point that all of us are allowed to think whatever we may choose, but, she said, "What is not allowed is ignorance or unwillingness to study. You can only come out of confusion by listening and studying." What I know in my heart is that we all must acknowledge our historical continuum in order to continue to grow as a powerful people *(Sankofa)*.

That discussion reinforced for me one of the greatest lessons of all for young and old—that we must learn how to listen to each other and to the sounds and messages of the world in which we live. What with all of the inner movements that occur on a physical, spiritual and emotional level within young souls, it is often supremely challenging for them to sit still long enough to hear anything, let alone the words of the elders. According to the teachings of Ptahhotep some 2,500 years ago, "The fool who does not hear, he can do nothing at all. He looks at ignorance and sees knowledge. He looks at harmfulness and sees usefulness." In the context of learning *how to be,* it is essential that we teach our young people to understand that the first thing they must embrace to create a firm foundation for life is respect for the elders, the world and their own magnificent Selves.

Honor the Elders

Watch your Grandmama as she moves. How graceful is her step? With what precision and clarity does your Great-Uncle impart his words?

Take a moment and watch your elders through loving eyes. I find this exercise rewarding every single time I practice it. Whether the elder is a family member, a neighbor, a sister or a brother in the congregation or even a passerby, I revel at the mystery of that person's life— how he or she got to this point in time and what this wise soul has to offer me.

When I adopt the mind-set of respect for the elders, I automatically slow down. Try it out. Your day may be action packed, moving at what feels like light speed. Particularly when you are young, your physical energy usually far exceeds those only a generation older than you. For those with many decades, silver hairs and tender facial lines more than you, the pace is far slower, more deliberate. So when your Mama or Daddy says, *Go be with your elders,* be grateful for the opportunity.

Learning to treasure the elders is key in building character and strength, for both individuals and the community. From the perspective of the African worldview, it is one of the primary components in honest, wholesome living. One of the initial points of connection and sources of balance for our people is our elders. It used to be that if an older person walked into a room, the young people immediately stood up. It was the responsibility of the youth to lead an elder to a seat, to give up a seat when necessary, to prepare food and otherwise tend to an elder's needs, to speak clearly and with reverence. (Now we need signs on buses to remind people to give their seats to those in need.) The neighbor down the street was Mr. Phillips to you, even if he was Butch to your Mama and even if he wasn't that much older than your oldest brother. Elders were considered with the highest regard. When they spoke, everybody listened.

On African shores, the role of the elder was, and is, even more pronounced. Often the elders of a community are consulted during family conflict, business crises, rites of passage—everything. In fact, there was a council of elders in every traditional African government; there was no such thing as a king ruling alone. Ultimately, elders are treated with the greatest of respect and reverence, being considered repositories of wisdom and grace. This way of considering the elders needs to be relearned. Instead of saying, *"This is how it used to be,"* we need to be able to say, *"This is how it is. This is the way we must treat our elders, with the utmost of respect."* There is no more room for the young person who ignores his older relatives or community leaders simply because he is intent on another goal. To be fair, we must acknowledge that the systems that our ancestors used to cultivate respect and intimacy were largely destroyed upon arrival on these shores. The time that was traditionally spent in preparing youths for each turning point in their lives—through rites-of-passage initiations led by elders—are nearly extinct.

In today's society, young people are pushed to grow up. The unfortunate reality is that this country operates on a gotta-do-everything-yesterday mentality that doesn't welcome quiet, intimate moments with others, certainly not with elders. Rather than giving in to this unhealthy way of being, we must encourage our youth and each other to slow down and carefully consider how we manage our lives. From the legacy of our ancestors, it is absolutely clear that we must start by turning the tide that currently allows for little communion between elders and youth. Consider these suggestions:

- Create regular time for being with the elders. You may spend Sunday afternoons every week or once a month with your family's wise ones. During that time, turn the television off. Create a forum where you ask questions of your elders and then truly listen to the answers. You may want to videotape the discussion for future generations.
- Seek out the elders in your neighborhood. You may pass Miss Mary every morning, but how often do you stop to see how she's doing? On your way to school, to visit with friends, to play, carve out a few minutes to sit with your neighbor and talk. Approach the moment with faith that you will leave with a great pearl of wisdom. It's amazing how much you can learn if you are open.
- Speak so that you can be heard. Remember that as folks grow older, their hearing can diminish. Speak clearly, slowly and at a high enough volume that you can be easily understood. Your goal should be to make your elder comfortable in the communication.
- Don't interrupt. Develop patience. Older people often are long-winded, so you need to reserve enough time for being with them. When you want to move on to another subject or you must excuse yourself, interject by saying, "Excuse me, Nana. Would you tell me about how you and Granddad moved from South Carolina again?" or "I'm sorry, Uncle Walter, but I have to go back to my chores now. I love speaking with you and look forward to seeing you again soon."
- Express your opinion with love. There once was a saying that young people should not speak unless they are spoken to. That is not a philosophy that I endorse, although many Black families still follow it. At the same time, tactfulness is imperative when communicating with anyone, especially elders. Start off by knowing that your opinion may not always be heard or accepted. (Sound familiar?) And that's okay. You still are entitled to share your opinion constructively. It is best to search for a context in which to talk about your beliefs that relates them to something that your elders will understand. If your intention is to explain your beliefs clearly—not to convert anyone—you may succeed. If you face opposition, you don't have to begin fighting. Listen for the wisdom that your elders have to offer. And later assess your own views.
- Introduce your life to your elder. Bring your friends to meet your grandfather. Show him the work that you have been doing, and explain what it means to you and the world. Provide a context for the hairstyle that you currently wear. Explain the music that you love the most. You'd be surprised at how much your elders actually want to

learn from you when you are willing to share a part of yourself with them. Even more, your respect for and interest in them may grow when you hear stories that directly relate to your own experience. The continuum of experience within our community is astounding. What you may learn is how beautifully your current insights connect to those elders who may have gone through adolescence or young adult life more than fifty years ago. I can just hear Grandma Carrie saying, "There's nothing new under the sun."

- Don't lie. If asked about something that may be of controversy, do not skirt the issue by lying about it. Instead, you may say that you would rather not talk about the subject. You can attempt to change the subject gracefully as well. But stating an out-and-out lie will only provide further separation between you. In the Khamitic tradition, to lie is to dishonor your very existence. It is the opponent of *Maat,* or universal truth.

- Be tender when you embrace. A bear hug is usually not appropriate for older bones. Be genuine as you embrace, careful not to cause physical damage. When shaking hands, be firm but light. If you take the time to pay attention to your elder and really absorb the person's presence and state into your awareness, you will intuitively know the proper approach.

- Offer to be of help. My seventy-something Aunt Hattie invited me to address holiday cards for her every year when I was a child. My hands could easily write out her thirty or so cards. As we sat together, I learned all about my father's family tree, something that my working Dad was too busy to share, if he even knew all of the details that Aunt Hattie so generously offered. When you give freely from your heart, great gifts always come back to you.

- Encourage exercise. Put your energy to use. Invite your elders to take a walk or go swimming with you. Rather than criticizing them, get them moving. It will make you both feel better.

- Use the telephone respectfully. When you call an elder, it's not the same as calling your buddy from school or work for a quick conversation. You have to build in time for everything—including at least ten rings on the phone before you hang up and at least ten minutes of conversation. If you hang up at ring five, your aunt may have just made it to the phone, only to be reminded of her slow pace without benefit of the promise of a voice on the other end. If you rush on the phone while talking, once again you will put your elder in an uncomfortable position. Be thoughtful.

- Write. Send cards whenever you think of it, making sure that your handwriting is legible and big. If you live a distance from your elders, drop a line or send a photo of you during some exciting activity. Include your family and elders in your life, no matter where you are.

- Be attentive. By paying attention to your elders' needs, you will learn how to pay attention to yourself. Look for the little things that will make your elders comfortable, and be honored that you have the opportunity to provide some comfort in their lives. There are things you can learn from old people that you can't learn anywhere else.
- Value the message over the money. Seek out elders who will share their insights, their stories, their inspiration with you. Historically, the *djelis,* also known as *griots,* of West African cultures—those wisdom bearers who recounted the history of a culture—offered their information freely. Today, the lure of fancy gifts and expensive opportunities often diminishes the value of the elders' messages. Don't let that happen to you.

Growing Pains

It is essential to have guidelines on *how to be* with others, especially for young folks who are evolving so fast that the world sometimes seems as if it's visibly spinning. Part of the reason that it is so hard to follow codes of conduct when you are young in contemporary Western society is that so much other stuff gets in the way. The world today is brimming with distractions. The pressures of growing up make life challenging, no matter what the circumstances. For me, it seemed as if the rules were all switched around from what my parents had taught me and what my social life dictated. My growing-up years were happy *and* conflicted. During the years of my puberty and adolescence, I discovered my ability to write and draw and sew and be creative. At the same time, being in this body that was doing things that I didn't understand, having feelings that were unreconciled, competing with friends and foes—all of that made for rough times. What I thought about seemed off the mark; what I attempted seemed awkward; how I looked was unsettling; everything seemed askew. Even now as I recall moments during my preteens through my early twenties, I shudder a bit. It was a rocky road. And contrary to what some kids thought, it didn't matter that I came from a family of some privilege. That too was a point of contention. So was the fact that I did well in school. It was as if everything that was supposed to make it easier got turned around, convoluted into being wrong. It was as the saying goes, *You're damned if you do, and you're damned if you don't.* Kareem Abdul-Jabbar had a similar experience. In his autobiography, *Giant Steps* (1983), he says:

I got there [Holy Providence School in Cornwells Heights, outside Philadelphia] and immediately found I could read better than anyone in the school. My father's example and my mother's training had made that come easy; I could pick up a book, read it out loud, pronounce the words with proper inflections and actually know what they meant. When the nuns found this out they paid a lot of attention, once even asking me, a fourth grader to read to the seventh grade. When the kids found this out I became a target. . . . It was my first time away from home, my first experience in an all-Black situation, and I found myself being punished for doing everything I'd ever been taught was right. I got all A's and was hated for it; I spoke correctly and was called a punk. I had to learn a new language simply to be able to deal with the threats. I had good manners and was a good boy and paid for it with my hide.

Although as a girl I didn't find myself in fights over being a good student, I did feel like a pariah even as I was doing all in my power to be my best. Now that I have some years between me and my adolescence, I realize that no matter what a person's situation, that period of accelerated growing up when we move from being a child to being a young adult is defined by rapid and uncertain change. In the path of such motion, people generally wrestle with mixed emotions and a seeming roller coaster of thoughts, feelings and responses to what lies before them. Parents do their best to guide their children during this tumultuous period, but it's hard for them too. All of a sudden, their sweet daughter or strong-minded son turns into Mr. or Ms. Hyde.

Adolescence marks the beginning of one's search for consciousness. It is at this point in life that independence becomes a possibility. We yearn to know ourselves. Yet the elusive nature of the Self—our connection to the Divine—that dwells within us is seemingly even more distant because we have to face a metamorphosis on a physical level at the very same time as we attempt to look inside. Adolescence was hell for me, but I survived. With the dedication of my mother; the unconditional friendship of my younger sister, Stephanie; the protection of my big sister, Susan; and the guiding force of the Divine (which I didn't recognize or acknowledge at the time), I made it out alive and well. I wish we could say that for all of today's youth. Too many African-American adolescents are succumbing to peer pressure, gang involvement, violence of all forms, drug and alcohol abuse, teenage pregnancy, sexually transmitted diseases, suicide and other roads that lead to self-destruction.

Adolescence isn't easy. It truly is at this point that we see the wisdom of the Yoruba that it *takes a whole village to raise a child*. We all have to work together to ensure that our youth make it to the other side as strong, viable members of the community. We can start by reembracing the ways of traditional African society. The search for individuality is not an African concept. Young people in traditional African societies did not grow up void of the tools needed to move into the next stage in their development or with the hope that they could release themselves from their parents' clutches. Yearning to evolve certainly is a universal trait of youth, but not in the sense of wanting to break free of family tradition and life. From the perspective of African worldview, the years of youth represent the time for fertile, organized opportunities for instruction and development. This is why rites of passage rituals were integral parts of the community experience. The youth were taught what was expected of them, from birth through the end of their lives—by those older and wiser. Supervision was a given, and is something that needs to be reinforced today.

The Basics of How to Be

It's one thing to do research and present to parents strategies for preparing their children for life. It's another to gain access to the psyche of our youth such that they will be willing to consider a different way of living in the world. I conducted several focus groups with young people to find out how they live, what's important to them and how to reach them. Following is a combination of their ideas and those of the elders that can serve as basics for young folks to follow:

- Learn the unwritten rules. At home the guidelines may be clearly articulated, but once you leave the front door, things change. Find out the expectations of school, your neighborhood, those who cross your path. And then create a strategy for managing in your environment. This may mean downplaying your wardrobe in a particular environment or soft-pedaling your academic accomplishments (even as you continue to strive hard to succeed). It also means that you observe your environment closely to see who is considered to be in control. Make sure that you establish a respectful relationship with that person, as with everyone else.
- Keep good company. There's a lot more on this topic below, but it bears mentioning now. Stick with the winners, even when the tough kids seem to be more interesting. The tough kids who always picked fights or talked bad to the teacher when I was in high school never graduated. Most of them ended up in jail or in abusive relationships. Steer clear of those people. Earvin "Magic" Johnson has said, "If peo-

ple around you aren't going anywhere, if their dreams are no bigger than hanging out on the corner, or if they're dragging you down, get rid of them. Negative people can sap your energy so fast, and they can take your dreams from you, too."

- Don't travel alone. The word from young folks is that traveling solo can get you in big trouble. Make plans with your friends during the day and in the evening so that you have each other's back. You may also follow a rule that my family has in place: When you reach your destination, call somebody and say that you have arrived safely. In this way, nobody worries unnecessarily, and in times of trouble, no time will be wasted. Even if you are battling for space with your parents, you can offer to give a call to state your safety. They will appreciate your call and will probably lighten up on their discipline. All they really want is for you to be safe.

- Mind your own business. One of the greatest ways to command respect *and* stay out of trouble is to keep the focus on yourself. What you see and hear that relates to other people is *their* business. As compelling as it may be to discuss other people's business, don't do it. One young sister told me that she ended up suffering what is known as a telephone cut—a slice along the side of her face with a switchblade—because she started running off at the mouth about something that didn't concern her. The information she shared ended up hurting someone else, who retaliated with violence.

- Be humble. As compelling as it may seem to jump in someone's face when the person says something off-color, improper or otherwise hurtful to you, don't do it. Stay quiet. Likewise for when you do something that you think deserves applause. Look within. Humility is one of the greatest virtues. To acquire it, you must look inward for affirmation rather than to others for their opinions. In this way, whether good or bad comes your way, you can remain in an even state. Don't confuse humility with weakness and self-deprecation.

- Be kind. You know how it can be. With all the hype that surrounds your life, it may seem much cooler to diss somebody than to give the person support. When in doubt, think about yourself. How would you want to be treated in the situation? Chances are you would love for someone to stroll by with a kind remark, a thoughtful gesture, a momentary smile. Be that someone. In the most discreet way, you can offer kindness to others. It is true what your Mama taught you— that what goes around comes around. Your kind words or actions will rescue you one day through someone else's good deeds.

- Speak to people. Don't be shy or rude. When you enter a room, come with a greeting that may be as simple as, "Good morning, everyone." Acknowledge your elders first and then your peers. Your greeting may be with a smile or a small gesture, depending on the circumstances. Remember that everyone appreciates acknowledgment.

- Look people directly in the eye. When you shake hands, with each greeting and during conversation, be confident and clear. Eye contact immediately shows your inner strength and conviction. Many young people, however, look away as they speak, which can be rude and disconcerting. Be strong and connect with others. It may be your shyness that keeps you from looking up, but other people don't know what it is and may think that you are rude. Also, know that you may need to reprogram your way of communicating. When our ancestors were enslaved, they were not allowed to look any white person in the eye. After generations of practicing a downward glance, we sometimes naturally look away when participating in communication. Now is the time to let go of that negative behavior. Own only that which will empower you. Look up!

- Honor your word. If you say you are going to do something, do it. If you find that you cannot honor a commitment—for any reason—let the other party know. Pick up the phone, write a note, get the message to its proper place. All that you have is your reputation. Keep that in the forefront of your mind as you live your life. Being young is no safeguard against your own actions.

- Get busy. A song of the 1980s popularized an age-old saying, *"The idle mind is the playground of the devil."* To keep the mind growing rather than lying dormant or straying down the wrong path, to discipline the mind when it is young, you have to stay busy. That's why parents encourage after-school activities, sports, arts and crafts. Explore your interests. Go against the flow of your friends and find out where the programs are that highlight your dreams. You deserve it.

- Find a mentor. One of the most effective ways to encourage positive growth is to align yourself with someone who knows more than you—someone you respect, who can serve as a role model. Yes, many programs exist. But you need to open your eyes. Chances are that in your own community, there are people who would love to serve as mentors to you. You pick a mentor by studying the person, getting a sense of who he or she is, what the person represents on many levels. Ask yourself if you think you would get along. Then approach the person to see if you can establish a mentor-mentee relationship. Many people are honored to be asked and delighted to participate.

- Become culturally aware. The Reverend Martin Luther King, Jr., spoke a vital message that is reflective of the Adinkra *Sankofa* symbol which reminds us to look back to reclaim our history before moving forward: "We must teach each Negro child that rejection of heritage means loss of cultural roots, and [that] people who have no past have no future." As unique as you actually are, you remain part of a powerful historical continuum that you must own. So much has happened to pave the way for all of us to exist in this world at this level of involvement. By paying homage to that legacy, we all gain the opportunity to expand more fully.

- Read! There's a terrible thing that has been said about our people: "If you wanna hide something from a nigger, put it in a book." Don't let this be true about you. Know that even when we weren't allowed to read, we found a way. Nat Turner taught himself how to read using the Old Testament. Turn that TV off, and pick up a book.

- Respect your family. As basic as this may seem, times show that family members often take each other for granted. Part of growing into consciousness is treating your family, your elders, your community, your environment, your ancestors and yourself with the utmost respect. That translates into paying attention to your loved ones, listening to them in times of happiness and pain, choosing to be with them on occasions when you think you'd rather be with your friends, making it your business to eat meals together, sharing information about how you are living your life. The balance that you must strike between your life as a growing-up individual and as a member of a sacred unit requires that you offer love and nourishment to your family first. Remember that the African model of conscious living affirms that we are part of an extended spiritual family, not individuals on separate courses.

- Be a good friend. Speak well of your friends. Be kind and thoughtful. Support them in times of joy and need. Resist the urge to ridicule them publicly or prey on their weaknesses. Be generous. As Ptahhotep recommended, "Help your friends with things that you have, for you have these things by the grace of God." One more point: When your heart tells you it is time to move beyond a friendship, do so gracefully. Rather than abandoning another human being, explain to your friend how you intend to move on and live your life. Separate respectfully by affirming the goodness in your friend.

- Give yourself a break. Everything seems so intense for young folks. Slow down—from the inside out. Lighten up on yourself. You don't have to get everything perfect. Know that you are probably your biggest critic. Have fun and be aware. Look at yourself with love. That is what you truly deserve.

- Remember the Divine. The elders always have the last word, and this is it. When things are going well—beyond your wildest dreams —and when everything seems rotten, remember God. We are here on this planet as beams of God's light. Keep that in mind as you live your life. Through that filter alone, you will be able to walk a steady, honorable path.

Pursue Education

Part of leading a conscious life is learning. From the day we are born, we have the opportunity to learn, and that chance doesn't end until we leave. For young people, education is key in personal and community evolution. Just think of a three-year-old and how the toddler soaks up information like a sponge. As human beings, we want to learn, even when society tells us otherwise. For African-descended people, access to education has been fraught with difficulty—everything from segregated schools to outdated textbooks, a lack of information about the depths of our cultural legacy to denial of access to resources.

To gain knowledge that will help you to negotiate in a Western world using the holistic principles of African life requires that you seek out education that will empower you. This includes formal and informal training. In terms of formal education, we already see that the American public school system is in crisis. Scholar Asa Hilliard has asked whether a thinking person should question whether it was actually set up to educate us in the first place. Our children are not faring well, on the whole, in their formative years. Psychiatrist Edwin J. Nichols suggests that the reason for much of the difficulty that our children are facing is the way in which they are taught. Nichols says that European Americans look at the world and therefore teach from the perspective of Man-to-the-Object, while African Americans use the model of Man-to-Man. In our school systems, the objectified way of presenting information and rewarding students on merit ensures that some do better than others, and it sometimes leaves a Black child cold, whereas the more intimate person-to-person interaction of the African model benefits all by ensuring that everyone succeeds. Nichols says that we have different ways of looking at the world—one being dichotomous, looking at situations from an either/or perspective, and the other being diunital, essentially meaning that two things can be true at the same time (e.g., I can be Black *and* pretty, not black *or* pretty), considering the whole as the point of continuum.

What does this mean? Basically, we have to reexamine the way that our children are educated, at school and at home, so that they will be prepared to navigate daily life. The whole movement toward African-centered education has its roots in solving this problem. Some scholars suggest that a mainstream education is one of assimilation rather than identification with one's own culture. In order to address many of the problems that we have had with formal Western education, we need to understand culture as more than just its physical manifestations—food, dress, music, and so forth. We need to understand culture as a system of thought that creates all those things. Those sharing this point of view believe strongly that in order to produce capable torchbearers for our communities, we have to train our young people to embrace the morals, values and mind-set that come from an African-based philosophical perspective that points to the development of Self while embracing community for survival. According to Molefi Asante, a scholar and leader in the Afrocentric movement, the path to wholeness requires this cultural embrace. In his book *The Afrocentric Idea* (1987), he writes: "Afrocentricity can be defined as a quality of thought and practice rooted in the cultural image and human interest of African people [and their descendants]. To be rooted in the cultural image of African people is to be anchored in the views and values of African people as well as in the practice which emanates from and gives rise to these views and values." Asante asserts that we must respect and embrace our heritage in order to grow. This means often moving beyond mainstream educational institutions to meet the needs of our own communities, as well as seeking our own scholars at mainstream institutions. This does not negate an Ivy League or other such education, either. We just can't stop there. We must also develop extracurricular activities that support our children's growth. These come in many forms, including rites of passage, during which principles of spirituality, interdependence, cooperation, respect, reciprocity, intergenerational balance, understanding and development of purpose and cultural competence are emphasized. The goal of rites of passage, as recorded by Lathardus Goggins II, author of *African Centered Rites of Passage and Education* (1996), is "to make conscious the development of self, which fosters (1) internal locus of control, (2) the ability to transform and interpret information, (3) historical continuity, (4) development of purpose, and (5) [fictive] kinship among community members."

Developing a sense of self-worth and self-love is essential to leading a conscious life. These programs have proved that it does work for young people to participate in rites of passage that affirm who they are within the context of their heritage, as do other groups (e.g., Jews and Japanese). When we don't enroll our youth in such programs or other constructive activities, however, we find that they still frequently involve themselves in their own versions of rites of passage, such as gang involvement, violent acts, early and unprotected sexual activity and various other forms of inappropriate behavior. The choice is ours. I recommend that we engage an African point of view and seek out education and rites of passage that support the redevelopment of an African worldview, along with programs and initiatives that reveal and explain the Western educational model. Our youth must understand both in order to be fully prepared and empowered.

Coming of Age

When a society's youth reach the threshold of maturity, the community acknowledges the turning point in some significant way. Quite often in traditional African cultures, the rituals that transform youth into adults include instruction and are directly related to their sexuality. For the Gikuyu of Kenya, for example, the practice of male *and* female circumcision is one element that marks the evolution of youth into adult. You may be familiar with the battles that have been waged recently about the legitimacy of female circumcision in particular. Writer Alice Walker brought national attention to this custom on the heels of many public outcries. Personally, I cannot imagine being a part of such a painful and seemingly unnecessary practice. But as I have continued to research the origins of African rituals, working to understand them from an African perspective, I have gained a much clearer understanding and appreciation for them. Male and female circumcision in African cultures represents a coming of age and is required as a component of community development. Author Jomo Kenyatta describes in vivid detail the steps leading to initiation of youth into adulthood in his book *Facing Mt. Kenya* (1938). Kenyatta illustrates the social order and organization inherent in bringing youth to the next stage in their lives, explaining the roles that elders and sponsors play in teaching the youth about their new expectations and roles. For the Gikuyu people, the time of initiation of youth, called *irua,* is considered sacred. Leading up to the circumcision and weeks after, the initiates participate in spiritual rituals where they invoke the ancestors and learn how to live as adults. When the initiation is complete, Kenyatta says, "This signifies that the children have now been born again, not as the children of an individual, but of the whole tribe."

This point is perhaps the most significant about African coming-of-age ceremonies. As the youths move into adulthood, they do not consider it time to move away and live individual lives. Instead, they learn that they must become responsible members of their community.

In Western society, rites of passage are also used to mark the development of youth, although the depth of their teachings is often not as profound as that of African communities. To initiate our youth, Black families have participated in a number of these rituals, including the cotillion, a coming-of-age dance where young girls are introduced to the community—and to boys, presumably for the first time. When my cousin Patricia Johnson Branch turned eighteen, back in the fifties, she participated in one of these dances. She remembers that the preparations seemed endless. "My father, my date and I had to take dance lessons, so that we would be able to do the father-daughter dance, and the 'first' dance with a man that we were officially allowed. We practiced hard, so that we would do a good job." She and her girlfriends got sponsors, mainly local women's groups who supported the costs and efforts of the girls. And then they focused on the many preparations: getting dresses made, finalizing hairstyles, preparing brief speeches, practicing walking gracefully in heels, and more. Patricia's party, much like so many others across the country, represented her evolution into adulthood. Although she and her friends had already been dating, their lives had been governed largely by their parents. At age eighteen, they were taking the first steps into the world as adults, preparing for college or for work, and they were having a formal party to acknowledge it all.

The relevance or necessity of learning to waltz, as my cousin did and many young women today agonize over, has been questioned by African scholars. Why not teach codes of conduct and disciplines as well as artistic forms that are part of our own cultural landscape—including our own music forms such as jazz, the blues, gospel and *djembe* (style of drumming with corresponding dance)? Because so many have questioned what essentially is the validity of patterning coming-of-age ceremonies after European traditions, complete with white dresses and gloves, new rites of passage events have begun to develop throughout this country. I certainly believe that our youth need all the training possible to manage in contemporary society. Learning Western *and* African codes of conduct makes sense to me.

Making a Pledge

Young adults create a bond together in Western society through sororities and fraternities. Our own Greek letter organizations are patterned after those white organizations on college campuses throughout the country that originally did not allow Black folks entry. In fact, they started out as exclusive social clubs, like their white counterparts. Quickly, though, these organizations laid deeper roots of commitment to the community. Now all Black sororities and fraternities have service as an integral part of their makeup. What's worthy of note here is that our ancestral memory is so powerful that as a people we did not allow ourselves to create organizations only to have fun. There had to be a reaching-back component to give support and love to others. That's the way of African people. Even more significant is the fact that Europeans patterned their Greek organizations after Egyptian, or Khamitic, "mystery" schools—our ancestors. As George G. M. James describes in *Stolen Legacy* (1954, reprinted 1992):

> The Egyptian mystery system was also a Secret Order, and membership was gained by initiation and a pledge to secrecy. The teaching was graded and delivered orally to the neophyte; and under these circumstances of secrecy, the Egyptians developed secret systems of writing and teaching, and forbade their Initiates from writing what they had learnt.

> After nearly 5000 years of prohibition against the Greeks, they were permitted to enter Egypt for the purpose of their education. . . . From the 6th century B.C., therefore, to the death of Aristotle (322 B.C.), the Greeks made the best of their chance to learn all they could about Egyptian culture; most students received instruction directly from the Egyptian priests, but after the invasion by Alexander the Great, the royal temples and libraries were plundered and pillaged, and Aristotle's school converted the library at Alexandria into a research centre.

The current pledge process is reflective of African rites of passage. Conceptually, initiates are supposed to spend an intensive period of time together during which they learn how to support and protect one another even as they work to transcend to the next level of development. When the pledge process in our contemporary organizations is conducted with awareness and respect for the intention of creating a brotherhood or sisterhood of inclusion, initiates cross to the other side having become stronger people with greater respect for the group. When the intention is lost, the power of our collective strength is dissipated. Since both happen today in our organizations, I can only recommend that parents and youth take careful steps before agreeing to participate in the initiation process. Talk to the leaders in the organization that attracts you, and listen for signs that point to conscious, respectful attitudes. You may also research African-centered spiritual systems that provide initiation rites directly steeped in African tradition.

Embracing Faith

It's time to look at the question of faith in young people's lives. For most Black folks, part of being a child means going to church or mosque or temple or some other holy place for regular worship. I went every Sunday to our United Methodist Church with my sisters and my

Mama. Like many children, I squirmed in my seat as the minister talked on and on about the way God lived in our lives. I have to admit that a lot of times counting hats and giggling at the ones we thought were comical was more captivating than listening to the drone of our Methodist minister's words. Even so, I was there—every week. As I grew up, there was a whole crop of us at church. We got involved in youth activities, from singing in the choir to doing service in our neighborhood. It was there I first started noticing boys. In those environs, I see now, that was probably good. Nothing *could* happen. There were way too many eyes watching us, so the most we could do was sneak a kiss or two!

One of my mother's Sunday practices used to puzzle me to no end. As soon as we would walk into the church and reach "our pew," she would kneel, bow her head and say a silent prayer. I always wondered what she was saying. But this activity somehow seemed reserved for her and God, and I never felt comfortable asking her what transpired in those quiet moments. Many years later, after I rediscovered my own connection to the Divine, I asked her. I learned that her prayer was really a request of sorts. Before sitting, my mother always asks God to allow her to hear His message and accept it in her own heart.

To our youth, I put forth the challenge that right now you can look to the Creator for inspiration. Try it today. Ask God for guidance on one simple issue that you may be facing now. Sit for meditation and listen for God to tell you what to do. This connection of spirit will protect and guide you. It can become your secret weapon against the unknowns in the world.

For parents, guardians, lovers of our youth, we must never give up looking for ways to introduce our young people to the presence of the Divine in their lives. Surely it is by our example that they can learn to have faith. As well, without the development of a strong spiritual connection, however they understand that Presence, life will be fraught with difficulty. We must show them the way.

YOUR QUESTIONS ANSWERED

1. How can I teach my sons to stay safe in the face of police brutality?

In some instances, what's required is no less than an art form. You must be able to teach your children, including your sons, to be strong and brave. Yet we have seen that that very bravery can trigger fear and contempt in the dominant culture, including the law. Teach your male children to walk with dignity and honor, to pay attention to their environment at all times, to be aware of the rules wherever they find themselves, to be able to articulate who they are and what they are doing with an evenness of tone and to be patient. Encourage your sons not to travel alone or in large groups.

It's tragic that Black people are viewed with such trepidation, but it is also real. Many will argue that the society structure was designed that Black masculine traits would be automatically perceived as threatening and therefore ample reason to "defend" oneself. To shake off those old "chains" and stand strong in the face of the law—and anyone else—requires grace and intuition. Make your sons aware of their environment, educate them fully and pray.

2. How can I escape drugs when they're all around me?

There is a spiritual understanding of life: that one can be in the world but not of it. Part of the reason that it is so important for young people to imbibe positive teachings from their families, communities and traditions is so that they will be able to stand strong against negative influences and know that there's something *to be* besides what they see in the streets. The lure of drugs and alcohol is great in Western society—as both a means of "checking out" and not dealing with one's problems and as a source of major income. Learn about the origins of drugs in this country—their entry and distribution—and how they have been used to annihilate the power of thinking Black people. It has been proven, for example, that during the Civil Rights Movement when so many powerful Black men and women were exercising their intellectual and physical rights *to be* viable members of the community, a covert government scheme was set in motion to thwart their momentum. Instead of seeing a brother reading a book, we began to see brothers "nodding" on the street, courtesy of the introduction of heroin into our communities. Drugs are available in huge numbers where Black people reside. When you understand how destructive the use and sale of drugs are to the foundation of our community structure, you then have the opportunity to stand strong against them in your life.

3. I often go to the mall with my friends. Sometimes I get followed by salespeople or security guards. What should I do?

Unfortunately, people have been trained in this culture to believe that Black people are untrustworthy. That translates into a "need" for us to be watched whenever we are around other people's property. You have several choices: (1) don't spend your money where you are not treated with respect (which can be very limiting), (2) present yourself such that no one can suspect you of concealing a weapon (a sign of potential danger for you), (3) go into stores with a clear intention of what you want and be prepared to inform the salesperson of your goal, (4) keep your cool (it could save your life).

4. I know that Jack & Jill of America is a Black youth organization. Will my children be empowered to learn about their culture if they join this middle-class organization?

Part of the reason that Jack & Jill was created was to provide an opportunity for Black middle-class youth to grow up together. Yes, the membership was and is primarily representative of the middle- and upper-middle-class segments of the Black community. But that has not necessarily meant something bad. Thinking that Blacks with means automatically desire to negate their historical legacy is dangerous and unproductive. I learned a lot in Jack & Jill. If you are interested in enrolling your children in this organization, do your research. Find out what programs are being offered in your area through Jack & Jill and other such organizations. If you want to see more culturally specific activities, roll up your sleeves and offer to bring them in, or seek out other organizations that more immediately serve those needs.

5. I go to school with white children and have become friends with some of them. My Black friends ridicule me for this. What can I do?

You are entitled to be friends with anyone who treats you fairly and with respect. This does not always mean that all of your friends will agree with your choices or support you. Historically, Black people have grown suspicious—for good reason—of personal relationships with white folks. Your Black friends may be responding out of an innate sense of self-preservation when they attempt to draw you away from your white friends. Rather than assume that anyone means you harm, listen to your heart. What has your relationship been like with your white friends? Have you been treated warmly? Have you had any interaction with the family members of your friends? Have you been treated with respect? This is how you should judge all of your relationships. Actually, that's why parents normally have the role of "interviewing" children's families before they allow their own children to visit—to ensure that their children will be both welcomed and protected. I have white women and men whom I love and trust. We have built our bond of friendship over years of communication, and I believe that we consider ourselves brothers and sisters in our hearts. You will have to decide the value of your own relationships and then learn how to negotiate them such that you live in comfort.

6. I currently attend a majority-white school and often feel isolated.

Contact the Black Student Union, and participate in their functions. This is why they were created. Or you can create your own. Get involved in extracurricular activities that will support your culture. Find a member who can support you.

7. Young people are so impressionable. As my husband and I teach our children about their history, how can we talk about our beginnings and even our situation today without teaching them to hate white people?

Hatred is a vicious character defect—a real sickness that should be avoided at all costs. No one has ever benefited from hating another. Furthermore, there is no reason to hate anyone. Instead, you need to do your research so that you can present a clear and accurate picture to your children of who they are and what this country has meant to them. There is a powerful 1998 PBS documentary, *Africans in America,* that illustrates in great detail the history of our origins in this country. It presents the cold realities of Slavery along with stories of those who encouraged its development and those who fought for its demise. Children of all ages can learn from this carefully presented document. Find other books and films as well to share with your children about our origins. What you will discover is that there were many greedy settlers who discovered quickly that indentured servitude (which was how most people of all races first came to these shores) didn't work well enough. The enslavement of Africans became the necessity for economic growth. Many of the Founding Fathers had slaves, including Thomas Jefferson, who also had many children with one of his enslaved, Sally Hemings. At the same time, many whites rejected the premise of Slavery that eventually stated *in the Constitution* that our ancestors represented only three-fifths of a man. The Abolitionist movement found Frederick Douglass and Frank Lloyd Garrison, a white man who ran a paper called *The Liberator,* working side by side to free our people. Throughout history, there have been white sympathizers to our struggle, including the Quakers, the Jews, the Freedom Riders, participants in marches, petitions and hand-to-hand combat, as well as corporations and individuals today who have not given up. The point is that we cannot fall prey to the very logic that has hurt us so deeply. We cannot judge a group of people entirely as one. Yes, African-American people deserve to receive reparations and respect. Yes, we need to stand up and require that our efforts to build this country count for something. (Whatever happened to those forty acres and a mule?) Yes, we need to understand the horrific and heroic roles that many whites have played over the years in our struggle and learn to use our discrimination to distinguish friends from foes with care. *This* is what we can teach our children.

TheDanceofDating

The kind of passion, the kind of emotion, feeling and connection that people look for in the West, from a romantic relationship, [people in the village] look for from spirit. The power of romantic love in the West is really a symptom of a separation from the spiritual.

SOBONFU SOMÉ

I WAS a late bloomer. Hardly had a boyfriend when I was a teenager. As the middle of three girls, I always got to see my superfine big sister get her guy, while being the egghead myself, I basically stayed solo. Time I did meet my "man," in high school, I fell in love and felt fabulous. Everything was beautiful, and it was all because of *him*. As insecure as I was about my slowly developing body, I met a guy who seemed to like me just the way I was. Even more, he didn't pressure me at all. We turned intimate corners without crossing adult boundaries. Our time together was exciting and new. For sure, I was gliding along on a golden carpet of love—until it was time to go to college, that is. When high school was over, so was our relationship. My "man" was going away, and I was not. For him that meant it was over. The end. Just like that. I couldn't believe it. I thought that we were going to get married. Isn't that what was supposed to happen? As my magic carpet came crashing down, so did all of my fantasies about being in love.

Chances are you have experienced some version of this story. Whether it was at age seventeen or thirty-five, somebody broke your heart, and you may have felt as if it was just too much to bear. That crash is often a part of life, but does not need to be blown out of proportion. The problem lies in the way that people in Western societies have come to view intimacy. Look around at the images that reflect the nature of relationships today. You see "romantic" dramas on television all day long and into the night, "romance" novels that detail the exploits of people who seem *too* everything to be true, "romantic" love stories in feature films that illustrate too-good-to-be-true lives, erotic hideaways and videos that elicit expectations of immediate sexual gratification and a barrage of advertisements everywhere you look that tease consumers with promises of intimate fulfillment—*right now*. With all of this, teenagers and grown folk alike dream about the prince (or princess) who will come along and make their lives sublime.

In *The American Heritage College Dictionary, romance* is defined as "a strong, sometimes short-lived attachment, fascination, or enthusiasm for something." Another definition is, "a fictitiously embellished account or explanation." This makes sense, doesn't it? When people recall incidents and make them sound larger than life, they are often accused of *romanticizing* the situation. It is no wonder, on the whole, that people have difficulty making romance work. The expectations that Western culture has placed on people who are seeking love are virtually unattainable, and certainly unsustainable. Just witness how many people go from one relationship to the next looking for the "perfect fit," only to end up alone, disillusioned or miserable. The 50 percent divorce rate is a clear indication that something is going wrong.

That said, it *is* possible to have healthy relationships, both short- and long-term commitments. Dating is the process of going out with someone to see if you want to spend more in-depth or quality time with a person. But, by definition, dating is a short-term thing. Courtship, on the other hand, is personal interaction between people of the opposite sex designed for marriage and "mating." Both of these are under siege today. Part of my purpose in explaining *how to be* is to express that even though we are in a Western situation, we are African people, and we have an ancestral paradigm from which to draw. When Western ways don't work for us, we have a home to go to, not just physically but conceptually.

When it comes to dating and courtship, the African worldview says that nothing is done without the support of the community, including the short- or long-term joining of two people. Contrary to the stereotypes that suggest that African people are savage sexual beings, the codes of conduct that govern how people develop intimate relationships have been carefully established in order to allow for exploration and mutual respect without repression. What's most important is that all members of the community be prepared by the time of their first sexual contact, thanks to ritual and initiation. In this way, the potential for exploration and learning far outweighs the potential for devastation and fear of rejection. Contemporary culture really doesn't provide for the extensive preparation that was part of our ancestors' daily life; we must use all of the resources that are available to us to reembrace the practices that they followed so that we can keep our families and communities strong. And—guess what?—you can have fun in the process!

What can we do to incorporate the African way of *being* with each other intimately in our lives today? In this chapter, we look closely at all aspects of dating—from first loves (and first dates) and how parents can prepare their children for dating all the way to dating between mature people. Our goal will be to find ways to synthesize the reality of our lives in Western society with the foundation of African principles, which provide clarity and direction. By the way, we already know this stuff; it's just trapped in our ancestral memory waiting to be revealed.

Initiation

"How you gon' win when you ain't right within?" This question, posed in hip-hop songstress Lauryn Hill's 1998 hit, "Doo Wop (That Thing)," is the core issue facing relationships today *for everyone*. All of the rules in the world won't make your dating life right if you don't have your act together.

The way our ancestors took care of this concern was through rites of passage and initiation. In traditional African communities, parents do not sit around and wonder how to talk to their children about the birds and the bees. From birth, children participate in family building and witness many aspects of intimate life. One of the principal lessons that they learn is that intimacy is sacred (as opposed to being "forbidden," "sinful," "nasty," "heathenish" or "dirty"). At the point of puberty, young men and women participate in initiation rites during which they receive formal training from their elders about *how to be* responsible adults and *how to be* with each other. Jomo Kenyatta describes young "love" among the Gikuyu of Kenya in his book *Facing Mt. Kenya* as follows:

> Among the things taught during this period are the matters relating to rules and regulations governing sexual indulgence. In order not to suppress entirely the normal sex instinct, the boys and girls are told that in order to keep good health they must acquire the technique of practicing a certain restricted form of intercourse, called *ombani na ngweko* (platonic love and fondling). This form of intimate contact between young people is considered right and proper and the very foundation stone upon which to build a race morally, physically and mentally sound. For it safeguards the youth from nervous and psychic maladjustments.

In the face of rising numbers of teenage pregnancy and sexual exploitation, we need to reassess how our youth look at their first intimate encounters with each other to help them explore their sexuality responsibly. The challenge, of course, is to balance lessons about "petting" and other light intimacies with the overwhelming number of overt sexual messages that American society nearly pushes down our throats. There is beauty in being young and curious. Learning *how to be* safe, both emotionally and physically, during the vulnerable days of youth requires guidance.

What parents and elders can do is to tell the truth to young people about their own life experiences. Sharing stories about how you managed puberty and adolescence will certainly help assure a young person of how he or she may respond if faced with a similar situation and will offer relief, because the youth will learn that she is not alone. People learn through anecdote and action far better than through direct inquiry or evaluation of their own behavior. Writer James Baldwin put it this way: "Children have never been very good at listening to their elders, but they have never failed to imitate them."

To that end, by adopting a traditional African perspective on dating, you can show your children that elders do participate in all aspects of one's development, without needing to be intrusive. Once a girl starts menstruating and a boy grows pubic hair, it doesn't mean that they are suddenly adults with license to do whatever they want. The African worldview does not support the notion that puberty represents a countdown to independence or the assertion of individualism—a Western concept that negates the cohesion of the community. Instead, it indicates that the community is evolving. The support of family members and elders throughout one's intimate explorations allows for essential guidance along the way.

Further, spiritual cultivation must be a requirement for everyone in a traditional African community, so that no one mistakenly looks to the possibility of a relationship as a cure-all for spiritual emptiness. The process of initiation invokes the grace of the ancestors and the Creator to provide a blanket of support and inner peace as a young person's body and thoughts develop. Young people are traditionally taught to value family, elders and friends first, to look upon each other as true brothers and sisters, and only secondarily to consider those of the opposite sex as sexual partners. Having a spiritual anchor balanced with a strong community presence eliminates the distractions that many families face today: when people are so hungry to find a partner who looks the part or who has the dollars rather than one who will respect and support them for *who they are*.

Dos and Don'ts for Parents

Dos

Talk to your children about intimacy, sex and friendship when they are still children. Explain to them what the changes in their bodies mean.

Ask questions. Find out what's going on at school and in extracurricular activities. Talk to your children with their friends to get a sense of how they are developing. Establish a respectful and welcoming environment for open communication so that your children will feel comfortable coming to you for support and guidance.

Encourage personal responsibility. Talk to your children about the need for understanding the potential rewards or repercussions for their actions.

Be mindful of how much information you believe will be helpful to share with your children about your own life. Give examples to illustrate your points.

Listen to your children when they talk to you. Pay close attention so that you understand what's really on their minds.

Give practical advice about dealing with sexual pressure and using contraception.

Establish rules, including the age at which children can begin to date, curfews, approved activities and dress.

Don'ts

Wait until your children reach puberty to explore topics related to sexuality.

Snoop around or eavesdrop in the hope of learning what's going on with your children.

Lie about your own experience.

Make assumptions about your children's thoughts or behavior. And don't interrupt.

Judge your children when they are questioning and exploring their sexuality; but always pay attention.

Allow your children to establish their own rules, no matter how "grown" they may seem. Youth need structure in which to function respectfully.

Chaperoned Dating

When I was finally old enough to date, I was not allowed to do so without my mother or father—or another child's parent—serving as chaperone. Somebody was always nearby, watching out to make sure that we behaved properly. Although my friends and I didn't love the idea of having our parents around, it did virtually eliminate the possibility of sexual intercourse, or anything more than light fondling really, when we were growing up. Today, many young people live during the day and weekend largely independent of their parents and elders by the time they reach their mid-teens. This means that they travel without chaperones into environments with people of the opposite sex. What many young folks have told me is that they travel in same-sex groups from the ages of fifteen into their early twenties, a practice that establishes peers as chaperones. As a point of relief, I learned that there is a whole lot less sexual activity going on than reports might lead us to believe. This group restraint is reflective of the influence of a traditional African youth support system. Peer pressure can be good!

What could be even better is for parents to encourage controlled intimacy—for example, having their youth "keep company" at home, but in a private area where they have the opportunity to kiss and share other intimate actions, while obviously not sanctioning intercourse. This is where the community network comes into play. All of the parents have to be of one accord in order for this sanctioned youthful intimacy to be enforced. The Gikuyu actually had a location as part of their youth's activities that was designed for young people to share intimate interaction without intercourse. The place for *ngweko,* or fondling, was a special hut, the *thingira.* This rendezvous location was designed as a private youth location for everything from games and food to *ngweko.* Young people were taught the parameters of the practice of *ngweko,* which allowed them to be nearly naked, lying next to one another caressing. (In this culture, people walk around nearly naked anyway, so nakedness is not a shock or a revelation.) Intercourse and even touching of the genitals were strictly forbidden and enforced by peer pressure. Hence, young people were provided a structured opportunity for intimate and innocent relations that prohibited intercourse even as it validated the need for relief from the young people's raging hormones.

The modern lesson from the Gikuyu practice, I believe, is that parents need to recognize that their adolescents will be participating in some form of intimate activity as they enter puberty. This is not a sin. In fact, if you look back at your own life, you're bound to remember your own first steps in this direction. By respecting the activities of the age group and talking with your children about what's going on in their lives—and allowing them space to be together alone at least for short intervals—you will be doing everyone a great service. Rather than using threats to attempt to avoid pregnancy or disease, you can use trust and dialogue to guide your youth to responsible action.

First Things First

As we consider *how to be* in the context of dating, we already see the need to look through a different filter than the one currently in favor that promotes romantic love. That distorted way of thinking essentially drops a veil of ignorance over people's eyes when they step into the world of attraction. Yet dating can and often does represent a glorious time. It can be an exquisite dance. It reflects what the Tao calls *yin* and *yang*. An aspect of our lives that can be ripe with exploration, discovery and possibility, dating can also be fertile ground for fear, disappointment and unfulfilled desires. The way that we can reconcile what appear as opposing thoughts about a very sensitive subject is to assess who we are and what we want in life and in a relationship. For example, if you don't know what's important to you, how will you be able to communicate that to a potential partner, whether it's a first or tenth date? Do a personal evaluation of who you think you are; what your likes and dislikes are; what makes you happy, sad or uncomfortable; what you are looking for in a relationship; your willingness to compromise; your vision of a date and/or potential partner. Once you have taken the time to figure these things out, you will be much better able to behave in a comfortable and meaningful way when you participate in the dance of dating.

A question to keep in mind is: *How can I fully experience someone else—whether it's for one date or for a lifetime—and still be myself?* Mutual respect is the answer. Basically, this means there's nothing wrong with casual dating or going out every now and then with a new person. In African situations, such activity is considered natural to daily life— that we get to know each other as people and as friends. The Western need arises in the requirement that you be clear that this is what you're doing; otherwise, people following the romance paradigm often get confused thinking that each one needs to be "the one."

Don't forget worthiness. When my husband, George, proposed to me, I was skeptical about getting married, particularly since I had been down that road before, and it hadn't worked out. With great love and conviction, he looked into my eyes and asked, "Don't you think you are worthy of happiness?" This was a profound question for me. In one sense I thought I *was* happy. I had a very successful career. Dreams were coming true left and right. But truth be told, I had not figured out *how to be* in a relationship comfortably. I think I had been living with the fantasy idea that a man was supposed to be a chocolate-covered Prince Charming for me and make everything perfect. George's question extended beyond my childhood fantasy. He spoke of worthiness. As I contemplated that concept, it occurred to me that to consider myself worthy took action in my thinking and in my being. I had to affirm that I would choose to make decisions with and without my man that would support my own value. It was a simple and basic concept, yet something that had eluded me for so long.

I mention this because many sisters echo the sentiment. We spend so much time taking care of everybody else or building our careers so that we can *be* somebody that we can forget who we really are, what's on the inside. *Yet if we don't have the inside together, nothing can work out there.* It's not possible. The road for brothers can be pretty tough too. Working within the belief system that you must provide for your woman, your children, your family—be the so-called breadwinner —can seem overwhelming even as it seems basic. Many sisters are outpacing brothers in their earning capacity. (Brothers currently suffer a 36 percent unemployment rate.) Historically, brothers were emasculated, not allowed to be with their families, even after participating in creating them. Over the years, we have seen ramifications of this tortuous start in today's single-parent households and thwarted dreams. There is a lot going on in our lives and homes. And nobody said it was going to be easy to handle. What needs to happen for each one of us is to take a look at who we are and discover how to nurture ourselves. In turn, we will discover how to bring our best selves to the table to share with someone else. Every conscious African elder will tell you that you have to have a strong spiritual foundation in order to succeed.

When it comes to relationships, that generally means it's best to take it slow. Admittedly, that's not always easy. When the adrenaline is flowing and the attraction is intense, it can be hard to put on the brakes and get to know somebody. But if you can do it, it's worth it. Psychologists Darlene Powell Hospon, and Derek Hopson, authors of *Friends, Lovers and Soulmates* (1994), strongly suggest that you get to be friends first with anybody you find interesting. For the Hopsons, the dance of dating starts at friendship. Although temptation may entice you to jump into bed with somebody right away, chances are it will be more difficult to find your way back emotionally or even intimately if you don't have a sense of the person you're with. This is primarily because clear communication and a common goal were not established first. The same goes for all other kinds of relationships, even those that you don't intend to last forever. People often fall into their old patterns of thinking and behaving when they don't take the time to get to know themselves or someone who is a potential date first. By traveling the friend route, you get to explore one another as people, before becoming intimate. You have an opportunity to establish a relationship that fosters openness that can enable you to move beyond any stereotypes about relationships or personal inhibitions that may otherwise bind you. This is the African way.

Dating the Ancestral Way

It would be inaccurate to say that all traditional African people date in the same way. First of all, the concept of dating as trying a partner out really doesn't exist. For the most part, young people across the Continent historically spent time together in groups as they learned *how to be* responsible adults in their lives. Depending on the community structure, couples were predetermined as marriage partners, and many groups marry exogamously anyway, outside their family group. That said, there are some beautiful stories of courtship that reflect the respect and understanding that our ancestors had for young love.

Among the Samburu of Kenya, men and women are not allowed to date until they reach a certain level of development. For the men, it is when they become *moran,* or the warrior class. In this period, young men are taught how to be brave warriors who can protect their homes and families. At this point they are allowed to have relations with young women. Both sexes are actually allowed to engage in intercourse during their youth. To prevent pregnancy, they are encouraged to practice withdrawal. The Masai, also primarily of Kenya, are similar. They allow their young people to spend time together, including time for intimacy. Among the Masai, there is an art to courtship that includes young men giving their female lovers beaded necklaces that speak of their affection. The young girls revel in receiving these necklaces and wear as many as they are given. Even so, the relations that these young people have during puberty do not mean that they will marry, as marriage is exogamous. The Wodabe have a style of courtship similar to the Masai. During an elaborate dance, which resembles Sadie Hawkins dances, young men labor for hours painting their faces and bodies, working to make themselves look attractive. Then, right before sunset, the men line up and begin a dance during which each of them attempts to make the most unusual and provocative gestures he can imagine in an effort to attract a young woman. Here, the women choose the man. Each does so by dancing up next to him and then continuing to dance with him until the two wander off together.

The incorporation of sexual activity on whatever level in African societies has not been looked upon in the same way as in the West. Life is seen as the most important thing. Women and sex are seen as the conduit for bringing life to the planet, so they are considered sacred. The saddest part about the disintegration of at least some of our communities in Africa postcolonization is that they're facing the very challenges that sisters and brothers face here today: a rise in sexist behavior that degrades women, misinterpretation and misuse of traditional forms (such as female circumcision, which wasn't originally about the control of women's sexuality), the embrace of the dollar above the family and the abandonment of the ancestors for individual pursuits. In the midst of all of this, being on the dating scene isn't easy, even as it can be fun and rewarding. Somewhere in the swell of feelings that bubble up during the dance of dating, we also must find respectful grounding ways of being with each other intimately so that we can stay on the path to community strength.

That First Date

Even if you are the most culturally grounded person, chances are that when it comes time to go on that first date, you're going to get the jitters just like everybody else. Whether you're fifteen, and it's your first date ever, or you're forty-five, and it's the first time going out with someone new, it's natural for you to get a little nervous about it. A flurry of questions goes through your head: *What will he think about me? What should I wear? Will she think I'm attractive? Will he like what I have to say?* What can you do when your stomach doesn't want to calm down? Lighten up on yourself. Experts have documented proof that when a person feels comfortable in his or her body, chances are that others will be attracted. Here are a few pointers to help you keep it together:

- Remember to breathe. Whenever you feel tense, take a few deep breaths and invite your spirit to settle down. As excited as you become, it is possible to be euphorically happy and grounded at the same time. Staying in touch with your breathing will help you. You may also want to make a list of what you need to do before your date. Write down your thoughts, and then check them off one by one as you accomplish them.
- When in doubt, affirm yourself. *I am smart. I am beautiful. I am worthy of being happy. I will have a great time.* You really are special. Wear your confident smile; it's contagious.
- Agree to an activity that makes you feel comfortable. You may prefer a restaurant over a bar, for example, because eyes often wander in bars. You want the focus to be on the two of you, right? Feel free to recommend an activity that allows the two of you to spend time together and have something to talk about.
- Don't tell your whole life story. On a first date, it's best to keep things light. You can definitely talk about yourself and your interests, but you might not want to give all the details of your family history, complete with Uncle Alex's mental illness. Be positive and honest.
- Listen. Especially if you are a talker, remember to listen to your date so that you can learn more about him. Participate in the conversation, too, so that you both get a flavor of each other.
- Bring your own money. Although I still think it's right for a man to pay for the first date—whatever it entails—that doesn't mean that it will happen. Follow your Mama's advice and have your own money, so that if you need it, it's right there. When the check comes for your meal, don't sit around too long waiting to see what your date will do. If he seems apprehensive about paying, pipe right up and offer to pay your portion. If his behavior bothers you, you don't have to

Dos and Don'ts of Dating

The etiquette of dating has changed to a certain extent over the years. What your parents taught you, what the cultural background of your date is and what both of your personal views are will all affect how you go about the dance of dating, whether you are male or female. Nevertheless, a few central rules have withstood the test of time. Although many people challenge them all these days, the following are worth serious consideration, especially if you are going out with someone for the first time:

- **Plan to have fun.** Sounds basic, but too often people get serious, especially on the first date. The whole idea of going out with somebody is not to be on display but to enjoy one another's company. If you go with the objective of having a nice time, the odds grow in your favor.
- **Dress modestly.** Your activity will determine what is appropriate, but modest dress is the best choice—even after you've changed outfits in the mirror more than a few times. You want the person you're going out with to see you for who you are, not for what you are wearing. Obviously first impressions make a huge difference. People do see you before they get to know you. But isn't that the point? If you dress modestly and comfortably, which doesn't mean boring or corny, in something that flatters you and that can be sexy, what your date will focus on is your face. Then your intellect and personality can take over. What a relief!
- **Choose an activity that you both like.** What's the point of pretending that you want to do something that doesn't interest you at all? Pretension is what you want to avoid at all costs. Presenting the true you should be your objective. If you participate in an activity that interests you and can occupy part of your time, you will have built-in tools for managing your time together. Once you select an activity, find out the price range, the dress code and business hours.
- **Avoid a lonely restaurant or other remote place.** Unless you already know that you like your date a lot *and* that the two of you have a lot to talk about, going out to eat for several hours in a quiet place could be the kiss of death. What happens if you get tired of talking—or listening for that matter?
- **Bring your own money.** You may participate in heated debates about who pays for a date, whether it's your first or your thirty-first. No matter what, be prepared. The general rule still remains that the man is responsible for footing the bill for food, at least on the first date. Afterward, you can decide together. Some people "go dutch" periodically or trade off, depending on who does the inviting, who's got cash that day or some other arrangement. For both of you, it's best to discuss it beforehand and be prepared. That means to be able to pay your own way without an attitude.
- **Avoid compromising situations.** For women especially, this includes being alone with a man in a private area, such as his home, bedroom or hotel room, unless you are clear in your own mind about what you want. You don't want to send mixed messages.
- **Pay attention to your date.** Listen to *what* he or she has to say so that you can get a sense of whether you really like the person. Check body language—his and your own. Is it open? Tight? Uncomfortable looking?

(continued on next page)

- **Know when it's time for your date to end.** If you pay attention, you will sense a natural ending point for your date, whether it's thanks to the activity or a predetermined agreement. Build in flexibility by creating an activity that could naturally end earlier or later, depending on how the two of you hit it off. Coffee could turn into dinner, for example. If things are going well and you discover that time has slipped away, work to end your date before the magic is over. You can do this by saying, "I have had such a great time. We should do this again," as you stand up to get your coat or move toward the door. If the date turned sour, you can bow out gracefully when you feel it's time to go.

write him off automatically either. Instead, go out with him again, and find a way to let him know what you like.

- Have an exit plan. What if your date is lousy? Or offensive? Or boring? Stay as long as you can without being miserable. If you feel that your integrity or self-worth has been attacked or compromised, by all means get up and leave. You can thank the person for the date, if there is anything to thank the person for. Then stand up and head out. This is the time when it's really good to have your own money or transportation. A hostile car ride home with a date is not cute.

- Don't give it up on the first date. Come on! Especially if you are really attracted to the person, don't ruin the opportunity for a meaningful relationship by giving over the goods too fast. It sends a message that you're "easy" and "too available," particularly if you are a woman. If you are a man, it can say that "all you want me for is sex," or "You're not really interested in me for who I am."

Updates from the Old School

There used to be clear-cut rules about behavior when it came to dating in Western life. Now most dating codes of conduct are blurred. That doesn't mean that certain expectations don't still exist. Some things considered ladylike or gentlemanly still carry a lot of weight with young and old:

- It's good to hold the door open for a woman who's getting out of a car. This practice seems almost obsolete, and it's not a requirement. But I assure you, brothers, that you will score big points with most sisters if you walk around to the passenger side of the car and offer your arm to your date as she gets out. It's a nice gesture, *and* it creates an opportunity for physical contact.

- Go for other doors, too. If you are going to a restaurant, for example, it's wonderful for a man to hold the door open as a woman

The Background Check

Years ago in Mali, it was the responsibility of the women of the family to check out a prospective date, that is, a marriage partner, before two people were allowed to meet. The female elders did what amounts to a background check: they visited the town of the young man or woman and snooped around. They researched the family's reputation, the family's status in the community, the way in which the family lived, the degree of harmony or discord and the level of respect that the young person and his or her family held in the community. Further, they looked to find out details about the young person's level of responsibility and overall quality of life and health. Only after the young person and his family checked out were the two allowed to see each other.

A modern version of this analysis has gained in popularity. Shy of hiring a private eye, people are recognizing the importance of discreetly finding out about the foundation of their loved ones. Often people miss basic signs about a person's behavior, largely due to the blindness caused by romance. Although you should never base your decision to date someone solely on your research, you can learn a lot about a person by asking a few simple questions. Using an elder or a respected friend who is *not* a busybody or jealous to help you can be great. Confide in someone who loves you, knows you well and wants the best for you about your feelings for the person, and give your confidante a list of what you want to know. The list should include things about his or her family background, upbringing, friends, work life, habits and so forth.

passes through. It is unnecessary, however, for a woman to stand at a door waiting for a man to come forth to open it for her.

- A kiss will do. When you greet your date, a kiss on the cheek is appropriate. When the date is over, how good it was will determine your next move. Make sure you seal your date with some type of closure. If you like the person, you can allow a kiss on the cheek or lightly on the mouth. The move should be on the brother's part, though. Otherwise, a sister should say, "Thank you," and be off.

- The man should see the woman safely home. This means by whatever mode of transportation necessary. If you are driving, brothers, get out of the car, open the door and walk your date to her door. Under no circumstances should you drive off before your date gets safely inside. If you are riding public transportation, you have to ride to her destination with her and then get back on to go to your place.

- Men call; women don't. Oh, if only we followed this one. My Mama used to forbid us to call boys when we were children. It was "unladylike," she explained. Ask any parent these days, and you will hear that the girls are ringing boys' phones off the hook. Remember the notion of playing hard to get? Well, it still works. The dance of dating requires strategy. Being too available doesn't work. If a brother is interested in you, he knows how to pick up the phone. It's okay to return a call, though.

- Meet his Mama. *The apple doesn't fall far from the tree* is an old saying. Well, there's a reason that African people do background checks on potential partners for their children: to make sure that the two are compatible and that they come from respectable families. Chances are you will get a good insight into your date's way of *being* by spending just a little time around his Mama (or the person who raised him). Don't wait until you get serious. Get to meet her right away.

Adult Dating

Because so many people these days put their careers first, many don't stop even to think about making a family until they are well beyond their twenties. That's why the average age that people marry has continued to rise over the years. For brothers and sisters, that means that there are an awful lot of single people who are twenty-five years old and above. Chances are, if you are a woman and fit into this group, you live by yourself, have a job and your own money and have begun to wish for serious companionship. If you are a man, the scenario may be similar, although lots of brothers still live at home. What else is true is that you have likely developed a solid sense of what you like and dislike and what you are willing to tolerate. You may have adopted a Western value system that says that your date or potential life partner has to have a certain résumé in order to be worthy of your time. In some senses, this is true. African families traditionally took great pains to check out a potential partner for their children, looking into the personality and character of the person and his or her family. That didn't require, however, that the intended have a certain amount of money in the bank, drive a specific car or wear designer clothes. The research was not done for superficial reasons, but rather to discover something about the person's family lineage and integrity.

As an adult with a set way of living your life, you do need to be flexible as you participate in dating. Here are a few ideas from veteran adult daters to make your experience easier:

- Look forward to each new experience. No matter what your age, going out with someone new can be lots of fun if you look at it that way. Remind yourself of your great qualities, and take time to prepare carefully so that you feel good about yourself. Then affirm that you *will* have fun. In this way, you empower your date to have fun with you.

- Be honest about your intentions. Whatever you are looking for in a relationship needs to be stated at some point early on, although not necessarily on the first date. For instance, if you really want to get married, don't spend a lot of time with someone who would make a poor match. You will only be misleading yourself and the other person. And if you can tell that your date has intentions that you do not share, speak up. The biggest stumbling block in relationships comes when people fail to communicate what's in their hearts.

- Don't put all your eggs in one basket. At least not until the two of you agree that you are going to be committed to each other. Too many of us have made the mistake of believing that this one is "the one" before even the third date. Give yourselves a chance to get to know one another. Even if you haven't dated in a while, don't hang your hopes on this new flame.

- Leave the expectations at home. Every time you go expecting something from someone, you open yourself up to disappointment. Plus, unless you have clearly established guidelines for your relationship, you can't expect a date to know what you like or want. State the things that bother you, like not showing up on time or not being open to your friends. and get a gauge on what your date thinks about your thinking. Talk openly so that you can come to common ground on what you both expect.

- Be thoughtful. In *The Sistahs' Rules* (1997), Denene Millner cautions sisters about sitting back and soaking it all in without reciprocating. Men and women like to be tended to. Be creative and think of ways that you can surprise your date with a kindness. Millner recommends

A Quilting Story

Down South, during Slavery, our ancestors found creative ways of enjoying their lives. A popular pastime was quilting. Women would get together and produce intricately designed quilts made of scraps of fabric. These quilts were later used for many purposes, including as codes for safe transport along the Underground Railroad. In addition to getting work done, these quilting gatherings often turned into dances to which men came the moment they were invited. In Gladys-Marie Fry's *Stitched from the Soul: Slave Quilts from the Ante-Bellum South* (1990), one aspect of these gatherings was described in this way:

A very important but overlooked aspect of the quilting parties were the courtship games. Two such courtship games (both involving kissing) appeared to be fairly common: In the first, a boy attempted to throw a quilt over one of the girls and catch her, so he could claim his reward of a hug and a kiss; in the second version of this game, the . . . women selected the most handsome male at the party, draped a quilt around him (rendering him immobile), and *all* the women were entitled to a kiss.

This innocent courtship game reminds me of the infamous spin-the-bottle that we used to play as teenagers.

bringing flowers to a first date (or any other) as a wonderful treat for a brother who hardly expects them. African tradition says that reciprocity in relationships is vital to sustaining them.

- Be open. Just because you're not eighteen years old doesn't mean that you have to be set in all of your ways. Be willing to try new things, and allow your date to introduce you to new ideas.
- Practice safe sex. Age doesn't afford immunity from disease.
- Go slow. Especially if you recently ended a marriage or other relationship, give yourself time to heal before being with someone else.

Mature Dating

For many reasons, including death and divorce, older members of our community find themselves dating again. Just like the days of their youth, their initial concerns focus on issues of acceptance and rejection, as well as the potential for loneliness if they don't find suitable companions. In an African situation, companionship would never be the problem. A widower would remarry one of the single women in the village—of any age. A widow would either be supported by her eldest son or taken in by the elder brother of her husband—unless she had financial resources such that she could make it on her own if she so desired. In Western culture, children often take care of their parents as they age or if one passes. But family does not provide for intimate relations. Many elders decide not to remarry after the loss of a spouse or a divorce, but that doesn't mean they don't seek companionship. They can spend time with a suitor, going to the theater or church, visiting with friends or talking on the telephone.

Since older people do not experience sexual readiness as quickly as younger people, their experience of dating is often different. Even with the introduction of such drugs as Viagra, which promises to give a man a youthful erection, the reality is that older people function differently from their juniors—*and* there's nothing wrong with that. One seventy-year-old widow told me that her sexual experiences remind her of her teenage years—and she likes that! Rather than going directly for intercourse, as some younger men who don't understand the subtleties of sexuality do, her mature partner caresses her for hours. The tenderness that she now enjoys interests her far more than the possibility of an instant erection. The dos and don'ts of mature sex really don't differ much from those for anyone else. Just remember to practice safer sex no matter what age you are. Unfortunately, lots of our elders are contracting sexually transmitted diseases from their partners. The last thing you want to do when you reenter the dating scene is to kill yourself in order to have a little fun. Be smart.

It's All About Sex

"What about the women's movement and the Pill? Didn't they make it possible for us to have sex without worrying about the consequences?" These are the sentiments that lots of women and men have these days, even in the face of dangerous sexually transmitted diseases. Trust that this sentiment has nothing to do with a cultural point of strength. Many of the people I have interviewed have "confessed" that they have participated in one-night stands as well as longer-term liaisons that were all about sex. One single woman told me that she had a brother on the side whose job it was to "service" her. "We're friends, of course," she explained, "but our relationship is a once-a-month thing when we get together—you know, to take care of business."

At the risk of sounding like a prude, I have to speak up here, for the ancestors. Having relationships purely for sexual satisfaction points to a crisis in spirit. And yes, it is a symptom of American life—reducing human beings to their sexual function. Just look at the images reflected throughout popular culture; sex is everywhere. That doesn't make it all good. The African worldview actually says that if you are looking for "love" by spending a hot night with somebody, you are bound to be spiritually disappointed. Sobonfu Somé speaks about this beautifully in *The Spirit of Intimacy* (1999):

> Once an intimate relationship is taken out of its spiritual context, it fosters many dangers. A deep disconnection is created, not only at the spiritual level, but also at the personal level between two people. People involved in a solely sexual relationship . . . are completely disconnected from their true self. Their hope is that the person with whom they are involved might give them that connection. More often than not, the person they are reaching out to does not have a connection to the self either.
>
> And so you have two people who are not only disconnected at the spiritual level, they're disconnected at the personal level. The relationship is entirely a disconnected one. It doesn't have any kind of grounding force or any kind of foundation to hold it.

Is this *really* the kind of relationship that you want? Most people said "No." In fact, nine times out of ten when people spoke openly about their intimate relationships, they admitted that what they most want is a loving, committed union. Because that type of relationship has proven to be elusive, they have come to settle for "no strings attached." For the record, such behavior is unacceptable from an African perspective. It is beyond bad manners, entering into the realm of unconscious activity that is completely foreign to the community. Since intimacy is considered as encompassing a relationship that includes Spirit or God, trying to find God within another person without God's support makes no sense at all.

Even as I share this information, I know that many may not heed it, but it is worth considering. If you haven't found peace, happiness or commitment from a partner yet, what makes you think that *getting some* one night is going to make it any better? Your chances are better spending the night in deep contemplation, prayer and meditation. Really. (For the record, I do understand. Sometimes "taking the edge off" is all you really *think* you need sometimes.)

There's another important point to mention. As far as African Americans are concerned, our sexuality has been a volatile issue since our first days on this soil. Sisters have been called Hot Mamas, Sapphires, vixens and more throughout the *Maafa* years. We have been labeled as "loose" or just assumed to be sexually available by white men, so our Mamas worked overtime to make us extra rigid to prove *somebody* wrong. At the same time, brothers have been looked upon as powerful sexual creatures, utter animals in bed, the object of both societal desire and fear. Clearly, we need to let go of these externally inflicted racist fantasies. We need to put down the suppositions, get real with who we are and what we want and then allow ourselves to be satisfied.

Getting to a beautiful place of discovery with each other requires a little vulnerability. There is nothing wrong with expressing that tender quality. In fact, it's a sign of conscious living. Allowing yourself to show what you are feeling rather than masking it in fighting words or silence invites growth, particularly with regard to sexuality. We can choose to be vulnerable and share who we are with our partners without fearing that they will try to take away our power, unless that is their intention.

Same-Sex Relationships

Would it be fair to say that Black folks are often homophobic? I think so. The labels that we often give to the gay community are frightening. Spiritually speaking, there are arguments that go back and forth about the legitimacy of the gay lifestyle. The reality is that many people in the Black community are homosexual. During the course of focus group work, we discovered that African-American homosexuals often feel ostracized from the community and abandoned by their families. Interestingly enough, this is not the way that they were treated in some traditional African societies. Among the Dagara of Burkina Faso, for example, they are given a very special role in the community that is spiritually based. In *The Spirit of Intimacy,* Sobonfu Somé says:

> The words "gay" and "lesbian" do not exist in the village, but there is the word "gatekeeper." Gatekeepers are people who live a life at the edge between two worlds . . . the threshold of the gender line. They are mediators between the two genders. If the two genders are in conflict and the whole village is caught in it, the gatekeepers are the ones to bring peace.
>
> The life of gay people in the West is in many ways a reaction to pressure from a society that rejects them. In the village they are not seen as the other. They are not forced to create a separate community in order to survive. People do not put a negative label on them.
>
> Homosexuality is seen in the village very differently than it is seen in the West, in part because all sexuality is spiritually based.

Although among the Dagara, community ritual is not included as a part of the gatekeepers' evolution, all people are welcomed and encouraged to offer their special gifts to the village. What's more, those gifts are not tied to their sexuality. What has happened in the West, though, is that gay people are defined first and foremost based on the gender of their sexual partners, which is essentially reducing them to sexual beings rather than spiritual entities.

That said, when it comes to dating, a number of gay people shared their heart's issues, which are outlined here:

- The club scene is becoming a drag. Just as for anybody else, finding a partner or a meaningful relationship is unlikely from the dance floor of a smoky, loud nightclub. Because they are still socially ostracized, meeting people in other settings is often difficult.
- Gay stereotypes keep lots of people in the closet. Especially for Black people, one man said, "We spend our formative years in hiding, and there is no one to teach us *how to be* in long-term relationships." A sense of morals is largely absent for gay youth; no one in the family is providing support.
- Honesty is the best policy. As in an other relationship, being up front about your intentions, your level of commitment and your sexual history are key to a healthy life.
- Talk to your family. Find a way to share your lifestyle with your family, so that you do not become alienated from your own village, because this can encourage your spiritual demise.
- Assess whether it's wise to share your sexuality with your place of employment. Just as straight people are discreet about their sex lives,

so should you be. Many lesbians have told me that they rarely let their colleagues know of their personal lives; it's nobody else's business. If you socialize with people from the job, you will need to determine how best to reveal your lifestyle to them.

Sex and Disease

If you look back at different stages in world history, you will see that times of great disease have typically reflected a weakening of the cultural backbone of the community. Does this hold true today? Many would argue an emphatic "Yes." The sexual activity of Western society has seemingly disintegrated to the point that diseases such as HIV/AIDS and other incurable viruses can run rampant. Obviously, the puritanical solution of having sex with only one partner for life is not going to be widely embraced. So what's a couple to do when it comes to protection and intercourse? A lot of people (too many) don't give it too much thought, other than to chalk it up to, "Well, it won't happen to me." These days, people are single longer than their parents were or even the generation between them and their parents. That doesn't mean that they are celibate. The average single Black woman I interviewed said she had had an average of one or two sexual partners each year, starting in her early twenties. If you do the math for a thirty-five-year-old, you can see that her chances of exposure to disease are great. The numbers rise for brothers; those interviewed admitted that their averages were considerably higher than those of their female counterparts—anywhere from four or five to double digits per year. What can you do if you are on the dating scene to protect yourself?

- Ask a potential sex partner about his or her sexual history. Of course, this could immediately cause both of you to clam up. To avoid this, ease into it. Start off by talking about your first sexual experience, if that feels appropriate. Talk about your first and last love. Or get right into it by stating your sexual health (honestly), even if you have a sexually transmitted disease.
- Invite a potential sex partner to go with you for HIV/AIDS testing. You can make the excursion like a date in that you go together and find out your test results together. This may seem like a daunting activity, but it's better to be safe than dead. If your date doesn't want to go through with it, it's a sure way to send a one-hit wonder running.
- Use protection at all times. Especially if you and your partner have not been tested, during all sexual interaction reduce the chances of infection as much as possible, which means the spermicide nonoxyl 9 and condoms.

Guidelines for Safer Sex

- **The safest sex is no sex, or abstinence.** Essentially, this means *don't do it*. Or at least wait until you and your partner get married, and stay monogamous after that. Because people are getting married and/or creating long-term relationships a lot later in life these days, being abstinent is not always a viable option.
- **Use protection.** You can take your pick of many choices, although the nonoxyl 9–lubricated latex (not porous sheep membrane) condom along with nonoxyl 9 foam still ranks as the number one choice for prevention of pregnancy and sexually transmitted diseases, including HIV/AIDS.
- **Avoid the commingling of bodily fluids.** This can be a tough one, as anyone who has ever had sex can attest. Obviously, it means that blood and even nonbleeding open lesions (even as small as a shaving nick) should be avoided by both partners. This includes oral sex. Couples who want to have safe oral sex can use dental dams (worn by women) and unlubricated condoms (worn by men). There are scented and flavored condoms made just for this purpose. Get creative. Sex is supposed to be about fun (on at least one level), right? And there is no need to get embarrassed—that is not *how to be* about sex that *you* want to have. Dying from something that could have been prevented has the potential to make you look far more stupid than shopping for candy-apple flavored rubbers, don't you think?
- **Protect your spirit.** Beyond the physical understanding of safer sex, there is a spiritual aspect that we need to contemplate these days. To have safer sex can also mean to provide a safety net for your feelings toward your sexual partner—what one woman called, "being on the same page." If the two of you share the same level of intimacy and desire, then your sexual experience can be emotionally safe. If either of you goes into your intimate experience with expectations that the other doesn't know or share, one or both of you is bound for hurt feelings. Before you jump into bed with somebody, make sure that you are of one resolve. Then go for it.

When Your Mate Works at Your Job

You've gone and done it—"fallen in love" with someone at work. All the signs are there. You are sweeping each other off your feet. What should you do? *Be careful!*

- Assess early on whether it's worth it to go out with this person. Weigh the odds. In some companies, many couples end up getting married. In other corporate environments, people are looked down on if they get too close. What do your office politics say? And how much does that matter to you? Remember that from an African perspective, your goal is to build community as you make a relationship, not to cause yourself and, in turn, others grief.
- Remember where you are. Work comes first—if you plan to keep your job and your reputation on the job, that is.
- Be discreet. As much as you like each other now, the future is not

guaranteed. If you are discreet, other people won't know what's going on. You can do your work at work, and play after hours.

- Don't lie. If someone asks you about your love interest, it's pointless to deny. The truth always comes out, which would only make it uncomfortable later. At the same time, you don't have to answer the question directly or announce when probed.
- Don't tell your lover all your business. Some couples who work together have found that some business needs to remain confidential or private, for whatever reason. Don't blur the lines just because you're in love. Don't turn confidential business matters into "pillow talk," especially if you and your mate have the potential to be placed into job competition by higher ups. You could be slitting your own throat for a piece . . .
- Be honest about how feel in your relationship. Watch its progress closely. If you ever decide you want out, be up front about it in private so that you avoid complications in front of others.
- If you can, channel your feelings to your work. Many people have turned fast-beating hearts into dynamic projects together that make for powerful and productive interaction but fall short of intimacy.

When Your Date Is White

In the classic film *Guess Who's Coming to Dinner* (1967) we got to see on the big screen what happens behind white folks' doors when the man their daughter brought home was Black. It wasn't a pretty picture, although it was of no surprise to most brothers and sisters, I'm sure. Part of the reason that some white people today say that they move out of neighborhoods when we move in is that they don't want their children getting too close to ours. Witnesses report that it's not so much how close they get when they're toddlers; it's what happens when they come of age and discover their sensuality. Then what?

Well, trust that this cautiousness is not reserved for white folks. Many African Americans are reluctant to let their children date across the color line. Not so long ago, you could get dead by doing this. In many states, for a brother simply to be seen in public with a white woman was enough to get him lynched. Until the 1950s, it remained enough to get him thrown in jail. And then there's what happened (and sometimes continues to happen) to many interracial homes: cross burnings, lurid telephone messages, social ostracization. No wonder our parents, for the most part, have vehemently opposed interracial liaisons. It's not because they have hated white people. Historically, Black folks have welcomed all peoples with open arms and open hearts. But the constant reminders that we have been institutionally *hated* by the very people some of our children are coupling with is cause for alarm. Yes, people find each other and sometimes "fall in love." Yes, many have made loving, healthy families, including some of my relatives. Yes, in this society, you have the "right" to do whatever you want to do. Those choices can backfire, though. I have seen it countless times with the children of interracial couples who often lead tragic and confused lives, trying to figure out who and what they are. Food for thought, eh?

The whole interracial trend began during our enslavement when our beautiful, strong mothers were raped by slave owners both for sport and with the intention of creating color stratification between us—seldom for love. What's saddest of all is that it worked.

A friend in Atlanta told me about a family with three daughters. Their mother was an activist Black woman; their father a white scholar. The three girls were light-skinned, with a serious identity crisis. Their father had split early on, so their mother reared them alone. In the mid-seventies when they were growing up, it seemed that everybody in the country was dealing with the race issue, and that included color. The one trump card the youngest girl frequently used was that she had long, silky hair, light skin and European features. Because she was half-white, she represented a certain elite group at times. On other occasions, she was just odd man out. Muhammad Ali said in his documentary *When We Were Kings* (1996) that Black people in America need to learn to love ourselves—that we need not turn to white folks to make families but instead turn to each other to support our own culture. This perspective is one that is shared by many of our families. But it doesn't take into consideration families like that of the girls in that Atlanta neighborhood and how to support them or the many multiethnic families that are being formed right now. I agree that we should love one another—even when the media say we aren't beautiful or worthy enough. We need to be able to embrace *all* of our brothers and sisters, regardless of parentage. Yet we must be careful as we rebuild our communities that we also keep the focus on each other and find ways to validate ourselves. If we don't see our beauty, who will? We also must respect *any* person who comes to dinner. There have always been white folks who have loved us as brothers and sisters, even to their deaths. When we date and make family with people who truly love and respect us, we can find a way.

Does This Mean He's Serious?

A twenty-something sister recently shared that she had been dating a brother for a few months, a nice guy. Her Jamaican mother had come to town to visit, and the two of them had spent the day shopping.

When they got back to Connie's place, there were three messages on the answering machine from this brother. Without skipping a beat, Connie's Mama gave her daughter a knowing look and said, "I guess he's ready to get married." A few phone calls? Could that really be his message, or was Connie's mother jumping to conclusions? A similar situation happened to a thirty-something sister who had been going out with a brother for one month. One night at dinner he told her that he was ready to spend the rest of his life with her—and that was that. Donna's first reaction was to laugh and ask him if he was kidding. When she noticed his straight face, she started asking more questions.

After several focus groups with brothers about their relationships, I learned that both situations were potentially signs of serious brothers. The group of eighteen- to twenty-four-year-olds said that when a brother starts to call regularly, it means one of two things: either he is really trying hard to "get some" and hasn't scored yet, or he is truly interested in the woman he's calling. Denene Millner, author of *The Sistahs' Rules* cautions that "the only thing better than poontang is new poontang," so beware. Devoted attention does often mean commitment of some sort. The level of commitment marks the big question. Older brothers, thirty and above, said that they tend to be up front about what they want when they are calling. Saying that they're ready to settle down usually means they're serious, some admitted.

Before you go and ask a brother if he wants to get married (something that you certainly are entitled to do if *you* want to get married and are into the idea of proposing), get clear on your own feelings. Ask yourself if you are serious. Do you want to get married? If you do, you can pop the question or create a welcoming environment where he will feel comfortable asking you. If you are not ready or don't want to jump the broom with this man, don't lead him on. What's more, you really should have a sense of the stability of your relationship before you make any move toward marriage. It shouldn't come as a surprise to either of you that you are headed in that direction. Millner recommends that you wait a full year after you have begun to date exclusively before you "strike up the intentions conversation—the one where you feel him out on the marriage thing. If he's clearly not with it, don't push him. He will come around if he's serious about you and your relationship." Neither desperation nor entrapment is appealing.

When Your Spouse Has Died

Recently I got to see the devastating effects of the loss of a spouse up close, when my sister Susan's husband passed away. Even as time ticks by, it's strange not having her George in our lives. He was my brother.

As a thirty-eight-year-old at the time of her husband's death, Susan certainly had plenty of life ahead of her. But what does that mean? That's the same question that another young sister, whom we'll call Linda, asked herself. Married for more than ten years to her childhood sweetheart, Linda discovered one day that her husband was ill. She took him to the hospital, and before she knew it, he was gone. Several years later, Linda still mourns the love of her life and wonders how to go on.

Whether you are young and vital like these two sisters or more mature, learning how to deal with death is one thing; learning how to date again is another.

- **Take time to mourn first.** Author Malidoma Some says that it's important to mourn out loud upon the death of a loved one. Among his people, the Dagara of Burkina Faso, it is imperative to grieve properly, allowing your emotions to run their full course—within the context of the support of the community—so that the spirit of the dead can move on. Otherwise, that spirit lingers and can cause the remaining family tremendous discomfort. By allowing for the full grieving process, you invite the power of the spirit of the one who is gone to support you as time goes on.
- **Don't date right away.** If you're from the old school, you have two choices: either never to date (or marry) again or wait for at least one year for your period of mourning. Traditionally in Western culture, widows wore black for a full year, something that might not even be noticed, now that black is a wardrobe staple. Most people are more relaxed about the black wardrobe now, anyway. (In many African communities, upon the death of a spouse, the husband's brother takes the deceased's wife into his home, providing for her and her children and serving in the intimate capacity of husband on occasion.) Some spiritual advisers suggest that you take time to heal before you go back out into the world again. Your healing time depends upon how you process your loss. Those who have been there recommend a minimum of three months.
- **Turn to loved ones for support.** Your family members, friends and others who love you unconditionally are probably the best ones to help see you through this period. While you are on the mend, experts suggest that you stay busy, even as you take critical time out for contemplation. Your goal is to rediscover balance—*Maat*. At first you may immerse yourself in your work, a favorite hobby, travel, reading or other activities that make you feel good and occupy your time. Be sure to take time out for pampering yourself and introspection. Time and concerted effort will lead you to a place of calm if you work at it. Seek spiritual or professional help for a bridge of

support. Once you have regained a sense of completeness in your own being, you will be ready to go out and possibly discover another life partner—or just have a little fun.

- Practice safer sex. This is an important reminder because so many people who have lost spouses had not needed to use caution during intercourse for years. Remember that as you begin to date again, you *must* protect yourself, regardless of your state of fertility.

When You've Got Children

Whether folks started out as single parents or fate changed their lives, those with children can find dating to be a bit of a challenge. You've got to figure your children into the logistics of dating. There are a lot of funny—if exasperating—stories of single parents trying to carve out private time to be with their dates. Here's where the village comes in. If you intend to date casually you should do so outside the purview of your kids. Enlist the *ndezi,* or baby-sitters of the family, or whomever else you bring in when you have to be away. Take your dates off site, away from your children, until you have a clear sense that you are serious. Know that anyone new who enters your life may be considered suspiciously by your children, because that person may appear to be stealing precious time from them or trying to replace their other parent.

Many dating adults ask if it is okay to invite a date to spend the night when their children are at home. Unless you are in a long-term committed relationship with which your children are comfortable, do not parade sex partners in and out and all around your children's lives. Their peace of mind, respect for sex, other people's feelings and *you* are more important than your libido. Also, don't make them the managers and receptionists of your sex life, insisting they keep people's names straight so you don't get busted either! If you want to have sex, get a baby-sitter, and either go to a hotel or somewhere else or have your sitter take the kids out of the house. When your children are with their other parent is another ideal time for sex at home. Get clear with your date, too, about how he or she feels about being in a meaningful relationship with you and your kids. Mutual respect is key.

Dating in Marriage

This may seem like a misnomer, but it's not. You may have heard wise ones say that once you get married, it becomes routine unless you do something to keep the fire burning. Believe it. As in every other part of your life, your marriage can become humdrum if you don't pay attention to it. Mystery writer Valerie Wilson Wesley shared a brilliant approach with me a few years back. At the time, she and her husband, playwright Richard Wesley, had been married for many years. They both had exciting careers and were rearing two lovely daughters. Yet there was a sameness about their marriage that Valerie wanted to change. Rather than accepting the status quo, she came up with a great idea: to have a weekly date. That's exactly what they did. They made Friday nights their standing night out, thereby creating an opportunity for a weekly breath of fresh air!

I thought this was a great idea and invited my husband to participate in our own version of marital dating one year when I was on the road a lot. We spoke regularly on the phone while I was away and made weekly out-of-the-house dates when I was in town. The discipline of that practice really paid off when I was working on this book too. When I was in final edits, literally working around the clock, I usually took Friday evening off to spend with him. Those end-of-the-week dates enabled us to see each other when we were both awake! I highly recommend it.

There's another idea with great value that we found from E. M. Woods, author of *The Negro in Etiquette* (1899). I caution that you have to look beyond the provincial thinking of a middle-class brother whose ideas were shaped by his times, just post-Slavery:

> Wives, do you not remember how nicely you had everything arranged about the house when John was courting you, and how sweet and clean you looked then, and how everything in the kitchen, dining room and sitting room was in apple-pie order? Ladies, if you keep home clean and sweet, and dress to receive your husbands, I can assure you they will come home earlier.
>
> Husbands, if you would have your wives greet you at the door with a kiss, as she did during the honeymoon, treat her as tenderly, kindly and gentlemanly as you did before marriage, and I assure you that you will not only find the kisses waiting, but you will also find your home happier, the rough edges of life made smooth, and finally arrive at the other shore on the matrimonial sea with no sighs or regrets for the past and ready to dip into eternity.

Before you start screaming, "Don't set me back one hundred years," consider what Brother Woods has put forth and change the word *wife* to spouse. Whoever is taking on the role of homemaker—quite often these days it's a shared responsibility—it is nice to come home to a clean, pretty, welcoming environment. Who wouldn't want to see their spouse looking the way they did when they were dating? It was during the period of dating that you did everything you could to look beautiful for each other. Why stop now? One brother who has been married more than twenty years shared, "You have to work to keep the sensuality going in your marriage. I look for that in my wife. We look for it in each other. It might just be the way she looks at me, or a little gift that she brings home from work—something that makes me feel special. Even after all these years, I need that." The role you take on isn't so much the point. Remembering to nurture the basics is. Homemaking takes two.

Date Rape

From college campuses across the country we hear stories of young women being raped by people they know—men they are dating or men who are otherwise friends. At first glance, this seems like a mistake. "How can it be," some ask, "that he raped you if you were dating him?" The definition of rape is sexual violence, sex against a person's will through the use of threat or force. And, yes, statistics prove that people who know each other do experience rape at shockingly high percentages—often induced by drug and alcohol use.

One of the most widely publicized cases of date rape occurred when Desiree Washington visited boxer Mike Tyson in his hotel room after a fight in the middle of the night. According to Desiree, an eighteen-year-old beauty queen, Tyson forced her to have sex with him. She said she was not in his room for sex, but just to be able to see Mike and talk to him. Tyson ended up spending time in jail.

The Tyson scenario stirred up mixed emotions nationwide. One of the most obvious issues was, and is, *Why was that woman in his room at that time of night?* Although a man can and must be held accountable, so must a woman. The old folks' rules really do work in such situations. Don't put yourself in a compromising situation in the first place. That's not to get a brother off the hook, either. If you're not in a dangerous environment, you can't get hurt there, can you? Being conscious means being aware of the potential result of an action *before* it happens.

Beyond the obvious suggestion that you stay aware of where you are and who is in your company at all times, you still can be the victim of rape. Again, studies point out that many women (and men) who are victims of rape were in environments where they felt safe, and further they were raped by people they personally knew. So, how can you protect yourself?

Women's Responsibilities and Rights

- Be clear about your intentions before you go out with someone. Make a decision as to what you want from the relationship or the date. Then allow your intention to guide your actions.
- Be fully aware of your environment.
- Be clear. Make sure that when you say "No," you mean "No," and when you say "Yes," you're sure you mean "Yes." Men have joked that a woman really means "Yes" when she says "No"—and it might be true in some cases. It's up to you to make your intentions known and to be clear about them yourself. Stay firm and strong. Let your voice and your demeanor emphasize your point. Eye contact can drive your point home.
- Trust your instincts. When a situation doesn't feel right, get out of it immediately, even if that means making a scene to draw attention to a potentially dangerous encounter.
- Know that you always have the right to say "No," regardless of the circumstances in which you find yourself.

Men's Responsibilities and Rights

- It is never okay to force yourself on a woman. Period. This means that you must exercise control over yourself at all times. Regardless of how excited your body may become, your mind has the power over what you will do with it. If restraint is what is called for, then rise to the occasion.
- To force a woman to have sex with you against her will is rape. That includes having sex with a woman who is drunk and unable to provide her consent or say "No." Just because she can't say "No" doesn't mean "Yes" by default. Men have been convicted of rape on this count. Being conscious does not allow for playing dumb. When you are unsure, think about your own feelings. Ask yourself if you really want to have sex with someone who doesn't want to have sex with you. Chances are you don't. And think about how you would feel if it were your girlfriend, wife, sister or mother in the same situation.
- Be clear and honest about your intentions. By saying what you really want in a respectful and tender manner, you can receive a relaxed and honest response. No woman wants to feel that you are just trying to get some—especially if you pretend otherwise.
- Understand that "No" means "No." If at any time a woman tells you she wants to stop, do so. Even if you think she is just teasing and she's being unfair, stop. You can challenge her response later, in a less-charged atmosphere, when you are both dressed and not coming off arousal. Further, you should know that a woman's telling you

she doesn't want to have sex is not necessarily a rejection of you. It simply is a decision not to have sex at that time.

- If you feel a woman is sending you mixed signals, ask explicitly what she wants. Gently but directly address the situation rather than leaving unanswered questions that can lead to hurt feelings or worse. You don't have to spoil the mood in your efforts to find out what she really wants to do.
- Be sensitive. Understand that physical affection, including kissing and touching, does not automatically mean sexual intercourse. Petting does not mean "Yes." Only "Yes" means "Yes." It could, on the other hand, mean that your date would like to engage in some form of intimate activity and enjoys your company. Be in the moment with her. Don't rush and don't push. It's always best to wait until you are both ready.

RAINN (Rape, Abuse, and Incest National Network) is a 24-hour-a-day, 7-day-a-week national hot line for victims of sexual assault. The telephone number is 1-800-656-HOPE.

YOUR QUESTIONS ANSWERED

1. I am involved in a long-term relationship, and I really want my man to be "everything" to me. The problem is that as I am evolving and learning more about myself, my culture and my own gifts, my partner seems aggressively uninterested. What can I do?

Stop looking for complete validation from your man—or from anyone else for that matter. You can't win with that approach. The problem here, according to African scholars, is that we get caught up in a delusion of what "romantic" love is supposed to be, when "romanticizing" really means not being able to see things clearly. A traditional African response would be that we look for connection in "romantic" relationships that we should be looking for in our connection to God. If you find that you are working to establish your connection to God, even as you nurture your relationship, be patient. Do your work with love. And offer your partner support and attention in ways that he can enjoy. Ask the ancestors for guidance. And pray for the ability to find the validation you so desperately seek through the Divine.

2. I am in love with a wonderful man, but my family doesn't like him at all. How can I manage this?

If you comb African literature, you will see that this is a sign to say goodbye. The idea in traditional African societies is that couples come together first and foremost to perpetuate family. Once you become partners, you are married, or about to be so, for all intents and purposes. You represent the joining of two families. Marriage in African tradition represents a union of two families—not of two individuals. And that union must be sanctioned by both families. Everybody has to say "We do!" I know this may seem extreme, but I mention it for a reason. I have interviewed hundreds of African-American couples, in both successful and unsuccessful relationships. A key factor in their success or failure has been support of loved ones. When the family and friends who have been adopted as family have given their blessing, the relationships have had more opportunity to work—what I call the ancestors' insurance policy. Having the support of the people who really know you and love you unconditionally helps tremendously in keeping your bond strong at times when you might be weak. They can serve as sounding boards and give insightful feedback. Since, through ritual, they have acknowledged the sacred nature of your union, they will not start off telling you to leave your partner. In those instances when you have a poor relationship with your family, you will need to assess who your community support system is and rely on those people for this purpose.

3. *My friend's ex-boyfriend recently asked me out on a date. Is it appropriate for me to go?*

The resounding advice from across the country is weigh your options. If you and your friend are very close, consider what it will mean for your friendship if you date her ex-boyfriend. Determine how close they were and what feelings your friend had and has for this person. If their breakup really hurt your friend, seeing you with him may bring up bad memories and make it difficult for the two of you to stay close. If you and your friend are just acquaintances, then it's a different story. You still want to gauge what the relationship was like for the two of them and where they stand now, before you walk into it. But, you need not be as cautious.

4. *I recently started going out with a really nice man who literally showers me with lavish gifts. Every time I turn around, he is presenting me with something else. Is it appropriate for me to accept?*

When I was growing up, nice girls didn't accept expensive gifts from men. It was "unladylike" to do so, because it was considered to be leading him on. The exchange of gifts in African cultures supports this idea. Before intimate relations, a young Gikuyu boy brings gifts to his girl, while a Masai male gives necklaces to his lover after sex. Still, for the Dogon of Mali, the acceptance of a kola nut from a young man indicates that a young woman has agreed to be engaged. What are you agreeing to by accepting lavish gifts? If you don't intend to have sex with the brother, are you leading him on? To what end? You can accept presents, but know when to draw the line.

5. I don't want to come off like a prude, especially since I am still on the dating scene, but I really don't like tongue kissing. How can I handle this?

You're not alone. You'd be surprised how many other people share your aversion. Part of the problem is that people don't clean their mouths well, but that's a whole 'nother chapter. If hygiene is your issue, make it a requirement that you and your partner brush your teeth before you kiss. What you may be surprised to learn is that you are not unlike many other African people. In fact, according to Khamitic scholar Ra Un Nefer Amen, author of *An Afrocentric Guide to a Spiritual Union* (1992):

> In traditional African nations, kissing is called "eating dirt." How would you react if a stranger, or someone with whom you don't have a relationship kissed you on the mouth? How do you react to someone's spit making contact with you?

Just because you don't enjoy tongue kissing doesn't mean that you can't enjoy passionate kissing. The lips come alive when you pay attention to them. And then, of course, there's a whole body to traverse. Be sure to let your partner know how you feel early on, so that this doesn't become an issue. And if you like to kiss, do so. Just use discretion regarding to whom you offer this intimate affection.

6. I have been hanging out with a friend for a few months now, and it's really fun. We laugh and talk about everything. What I like about our time together is that I really feel as if I have a good friend. Now she seems to want more. How can I gently let her know that I want to be "just friends"?

Billy Crystal's sentiment in *When Harry Met Sally* . . . comes to mind now: Can men and women really be friends? According to African wisdom, that's what we're supposed to be—friends as close as brothers and sisters. Sexual interest is considered secondary in the village. The moment you sense that your friend is "romantically" interested in you, set aside some time and discuss both of your feelings. Since attraction is often lopsided, one partner in a friendship can easily be more interested than the other. The kindest thing you can do is to listen respectfully and then make the boundaries clear. Do not vacillate either. For instance, giving in to your friend's desire for sexual intimacy may only hurt her later if you decide to go back to being "just friends."

7. My girlfriend has become superpossessive of me and my time and jealous of all of my friends. Recently she started an argument in public when I spoke to another woman. How should I behave during a public outburst?

I went to a concert at Radio City Music Hall with about 6,000 fine Black folks. As I was entering the hall, headed for my seat, a ruckus broke out. What I saw was disgraceful. Right there before all 12,000 eyes, a brother and two sisters were screaming and shouting at each other. In a matter of moments, the brother had ripped off one of the sister's dresses, knocked her down and proceeded to drag her down the aisle. *What was that all about?* Jealousy. Turns out the brother was two-timing, as the old folks used to say. He had brought one sister with him to the event. His "other woman" showed up as well, and was none too happy to see him already sporting a woman on his arm. Rather than moving away from the situation and dealing with it later (the right action), the "other" woman's rage welled up in her, and she confronted him. He lost his mind and beat her up. Jealousy is one of the most vicious enemies we face in life. It encourages us to distort perception. It utterly forces us to lose our cool because we lose our ability to think clearly. Doubts then drive our actions.

If your partner is exhibiting overly possessive or jealous behavior, ask what's going on. If you know already that your behavior could be making her uncomfortable, don't play dumb. The worst thing you can do to another person is to cause the person pain, spiritual or physical. Instead of allowing your partner to become uneasy because of your actions, be responsible. Make your intentions known from the start. If they change, provide an update—in a neutral setting rather than in a public forum. That's being a friend. Keep your cool in public by keeping your business to yourselves.

8. I am dating somebody I really think is "the one." He's at the end of a serious relationship, and even though I know he can't be spending that much time with her because he's seeing me so often—at least five times a week—the fact is that she's still in the picture. What should I do?

Leave him alone. You will never know for sure if he will be there for you if you don't give him his space. You will be shortchanging yourself if you stick around while he is wrestling with his own issues. He may use you as a crutch. His feelings of why he wasn't able to get love from her may flow over to you. Back off and wait to see if he can come to you as a "free" man.

9. My baby's father and I are not together anymore. He has a relationship and lives with another woman whom my baby knows and likes. When he comes to visit the baby, he wants to get some. How should I handle this?

The most important party in this is the baby. What you want to do is preserve the relationship that the father has with the child, so he will stay in the baby's life. Since the child knows the other woman, you have to stay strong. Be a good example and tell him that his behavior is confusing the child. Invite him to come over during neutral times, such as when others are around. Or go outside. Also, end the visits before dark. Over time, he will catch on.

10. My husband recently passed away. Should I stop wearing my wedding ring when I begin to date?

It depends on you. For some women and men, putting away the wedding ring represents a willingness to move on and allow a new person to be a part of their lives. For others, the wedding ring serves as a security blanket of sorts. Whereas previously it might have been a brother or a father who had to approve of a date for a woman, somehow the deceased husband serves that role. I wouldn't diminish the power of that option either. Many people who have lost their partners have shared that they communicate with their beloved regularly on a spiritual plane—and this from women who weren't previously spiritually attuned with "the other side."

11. I just found out my husband is cheating on me. How do I approach him? Should I approach the other woman?

Before you do any approaching, assess your situation. Based on the information you believe you have, how do you feel? Ask yourself if you find anything lacking in your marriage that you may want to work on. Do you think it's possible to trust your spouse again? Then pick a neutral setting—free of alcohol—and address the topic. Ask your husband what he has been doing of late, and tell him that you suspect he is having an affair. Ask him if it is true. Don't whine or accost him; be direct and even in tone. Listen for the truth. If he admits his behavior, talk about what's going on, and find out whether he wants to make your marriage work. Know that you can't force him to do anything. You can only make up your mind as to *your* next move. If you want to mend your relationship, consider spiritual or family counseling.

By all means, don't approach the woman. Your problem is between you and your husband. The other person really is incidental to the situation in most cases. This doesn't mean that you don't harbor strong feelings about her disrespect for your vows, but it's best to direct your feelings toward your husband as you work out your differences.

12. There's this person I see every day on my way to work. I am wildly attracted to him—everything I like in a person he has. I really wish I had met him before; now I'm married. What do I do?

First off, give yourself a break. Just because you're married doesn't mean you stopped seeing. In focus groups, people admitted that it was sometimes hard *not* to act on their impulses. They also had a few suggestions:

- Acknowledge your own attraction within your own being.
- Keep it to yourself. Telling the person you are attracted to about your hidden feelings really will not dispel them. Instead, it will accelerate them and likely lead to an affair if the other person has been harboring similar feelings or just wants to have a good time.
- Tell a close friend or confidante, someone you absolutely trust, only if you must talk about it.
- Depending on the stability of your relationship and his personality, tell your partner. This will give you the opportunity to work through a real-life challenge so that your marriage becomes stronger.
- Ask God to take the power out of the attraction. Get down on your hands and knees if you need to, and ask for the desire to be removed. It really does work if you believe and if that's what you honestly want.

13. I just found out that the man I'm dating is married. How can I handle this gracefully?

Stop. Do you realize that your man lied to you? We've all heard the statistics about how there are more women than there are men out there. Some men have gotten it in to their heads that they are doing a sister a favor by dating her, even if he does have a wife, because she *needs* somebody. Others just want to have a little fun. One of the promises that two people make to each other when they get married is that they will be faithful to each other. In many traditions, that translates into monogamy. Even in Islam, where men are allowed to marry up to four women, men are supposed to be responsible to each of their wives. That doesn't mean that it's cool to date whomever they want.

Responsibility is the issue here. Put yourself in the wife's shoes. How would you feel if you found out that your husband was going out with another woman? Chances are you would be devastated. This goes for married women who are in extramarital relationships too. So if you are the single person in this liaison, check your motives and your needs. In your heart, you probably don't want to hurt anyone. Though the temptation may be great, resisting is definitely the honorable option in every situation. Leave the relationship now.

14. I recently got involved with a man who wants to keep our relationship a secret. I am not married, and neither is he. What is the proper way to handle a situation like this when we are out in public?

Ask yourself why you would want to be involved with somebody who doesn't want to admit to being in a relationship with you. How can your bond possibly be worth the cost? If you measure your relationship using an African perspective as your guide, you will see that what you should be looking for is a mutually respectful friendship, one that you honor and nurture by including your family and loved ones. This does not mean, however, that it is appropriate to blast the news all over that the two of you are seeing each other. Discretion and honesty are key here. Often when people want to keep relationships secret, it is because they shouldn't be involved in the first place. If that sounds like your situation, let your discomfort give you the strength to walk.

15. I am really at wit's end. I am in love with someone who is questioning our relationship because we don't share spiritual views. What can I do?

That depends on you and how you plan to live your life. One couple faced this dilemma. They had been dating for nearly a year and were feeling at ease with each other. Everything felt like a match until she became a born-again Christian; he was an atheist. Because of her new-found religious practice, Tawanna felt that Robert had to join her church and become part of her spiritual family for their life together to work. Robert agreed to go to church sometimes but was not of the mind to adopt any religious belief. Their relationship reached a standstill.

According to C. Augustus Stallings, archbishop of Imani Temple in Capitol Hill, Maryland, you and your partner do need to share some spiritual point of view. Although ideally that can mean that you practice the same religion, it can also mean that you develop a spiritual practice that you do together at home or in another neutral area that strengthens your relationship. If you are serious about your relationship and intend for it to be long lasting, you need to resolve your issues. One thing that our ancestors knew was that having a protective covenant with the Divine is essential for family life.

16. I am going to a party with my boyfriend, who is white. I am concerned that my friends will be mad at me for bringing him and may be rude to him. What can I do?

Preparation is key. The worst thing you can do is surprise the group with someone who may not be warmly received. Inform your friends that you intend to bring your partner, and talk to them about their feelings in private. If, after your conversation, you still believe they will not welcome your date, you may think twice about bringing him into a hostile environment. If it is important to you that all members of the group become friends; keep that as your goal. Speak to your boyfriend and your friends separately, letting them know how important they all are to you. Appeal to their love—your friends and your boyfriend—so that you may act as a bridge, and they will get to know and respect one another.

Mirror, Mirror

Care of the self begins with our capacity to tenderly and lovingly care for the body. . . . It is important for us to be able to stand naked in front of mirrors and look at our bodies, express our care for them, and our recognition of their beauty.

bell hooks

I N the story of Snow White and the Seven Dwarfs, Snow White gazes into the mirror and asks, "Mirror, Mirror, on the wall, who's the fairest of them all?" This fictional character represents the archetypal European woman—delicate of feature, pale of skin, silky of hair, "fine." Regardless of what she may have looked like, we were supposed to understand that it was just the set of attributes described that made Snow White the most revered, "the fairest of them all"—and fair meant "light." When a darker-skinned, dark-eyed white girl was described by other whites as "fair," this often meant she was being called blond or pretty *in spite of* her dark features—which was to be understood as the ultimate compliment. No wonder Toni Morrison's character Pecola in *The Bluest Eye* was so confused about her identity and so wanted to be different from what she saw in the mirror.

For generations, the supporting notion that "if you're white, you're all right. If you're yellow, you're mellow. If you're brown, stick around. But if you're Black, get back!" has plagued people of color. And we should not believe this is limited to the African-American experience. You can go elsewhere in the world and find the same phenomenon in place as a system of thought and corresponding behavior. If pale skin, light eyes and a tiny build illustrate the quintessential woman, then who is this other woman—the one who is burnished brown, with kinky dark hair and a broad, full body, lips and cheekbones. And further, who is her partner, this man who is a stronger reflection of her, while standing in sharp contrast to Snow White's willowy Prince Charming?

Who are we as people of African descent in the world of appearance, in the land of acceptance and rejection, if we do not look like what others—white people—consider beautiful?

This book, along with countless others that celebrate the human spirit in addition to the external covering, would like to be able to push past the cursory discussion of physical beauty to gain entrée to deeper realms. But reality says, "Hold up a minute." What's real for many people of African descent is that by virtue of the very way(s) that we look, we have been ostracized, maligned, judged and otherwise denied immediate access to many aspects of daily living. The colors of our skin, the shapes and sizes of our features and bodies, the textures of our hair—all of these have served as excuses for discrimination. In the world of visual comparisons, darker skin simply could not be accepted as beauty equal to skin that is "white as the driven snow," even among whites themselves! What that means in real terms for all of us is that we must remember the principle of *Sankofa;* we must take a hard look at the past of ourselves and of others who have the power to make their definitions our reality. In this way, we will be able to affect our present and our plans for the future.

In this chapter, we explore some of the most sensitive nuances of appearance as they relate to identity and navigating in the world. Because the way you look ends up informing the first impression that others have of you, we address this topic and provide suggestions on how you can evaluate your own image as well as the way that you form opinions of others. We also look at the art of grooming—from taking care of the body to skin and hair care, nail maintenance and makeup. Another section is devoted to wardrobe and body adornment.

Keep in mind that the purpose of this investigation is to help you take an honest look at yourself in the mirror to see the person before you. Ask yourself the following questions: *Do I know the person who is looking back at me? Do I feel comfortable with my image? How do I take care of myself, my physical body and my outer adornment? Do I understand what messages I convey with my personal style? Do I understand what is appropriate for different situations?* By engaging in this introspective questioning, you will gain a clear perspective of the messages that you are sending about yourself to others based specifically on how you present yourself. In this way, you will gain the opportunity to refine your presentation so that it can accurately portray and support you in your daily life. Your ability to welcome yourself with love and respect directly affects your relationships with others. It becomes possible to practice conscious living and to embrace the essentials of *how to be* only when you accept yourself, including your vast ancestral heritage, with open arms.

On Being *Black*

My Uncle Wendell, a very, very light-skinned Black man—a civil rights attorney—who has had to prove to everyone that he is of African descent all his life, visited my parents recently. He and my dark-skinned Daddy got into a discussion of what times were like when they were growing up—including what *being* Negro, Afro-American, Black or African American has meant over the years. Their discussion was both lively and unbelievable, as they told story after story of personal head-on collisions that they had experienced with racist opposition on every possible level. Both well educated, both community leaders, these two men have faced racial discrimination at nearly every turn, while also leading inspired lives. Uncle Wendell said, "Well, you know, people will still tell you that the worst thing anybody can call you is Negro." The tragedy is that he is largely right. Being a person of African descent in contemporary culture means that the very society in which you live considers you to be "minority," in nearly every way inferior to white people—less intelligent, less beautiful, less capable, less employable, less lovable. The melanin in one's body, rather than being what it is—a sign of strength and power and a demonstration of evolutionary efficiency of the Creator—has almost been made a scarlet letter. The darker a person is, the less welcome in this society. Even for those who are light-skinned, like my uncle, the weight of being a "minority" isn't lifted. Having to prove your identity to Blacks and whites alike *because* you love and respect your people seems a particularly cruel irony.

I can't help but think of Willie Lynch here. Lynch was the slave owner who in 1713 gave other slave owners a prescription for guaranteeing Black servitude for hundreds, if not thousands, of years. One of his recommendations was to manipulate our complexions through miscegenation in the slave community in order to initiate conflict and jealousies among the enslaved. The clearly outlined plan was that the lighter-skinned Blacks would be given preferential treatment. And we wonder why we have so many problems!

The practice of "passing" is one of many mental illnesses born out of the hatred of Blackness. Passing is what some white-skinned Black people did first as a way of escaping our enslavement—which was cunning—and later to perfect the art of assimilation—a tragedy, an unconscious genocide. Part of the reason that Black people were so carefully scrutinized by whites for identification purposes, leading to such categories as "octaroon" or "quadroon" (one-eighth or one-quarter Black blood, respectively), was to ensure that they remained separate from them and out of the reach of power. Never mind the reason that some ancestors turned out so pale was often the result of rape by the slave owner. The reality was that the slave owner may have made the child but for the most part didn't intend to claim him or her.

When so much information that comes at us says that Black people are ugly, it makes sense that some of us would do everything in our power to change the way that we look. All you need to do is think about a long list of our superstar entertainers. For instance, when I was growing up, I was a huge Jackson Five fan. Michael especially made me swoon. I learned how to dance to "ABC," for heaven's sake. You can imagine my horror as I watched Michael skyrocket to international acclaim as he continued to metamorphose. The degree to which he altered his physical appearance is shocking—including excessive plastic surgery that wiped away all indications of his beautiful African features.

I still love Michael Jackson's music and all that he has contributed to global culture. I also have tremendous compassion for him. In the bigger picture, though, I wonder: Why do our people undergo such tremendous physical transformations? What is it about Western culture that prompts some of us to want to look so different from our natural state? What is influencing our decision making?

In so many ways, we have been taught to think that being Black is a curse. This delusional thinking must stop. With the efforts of so many behind us, including all of the leaders of the Black Power movement, starting with Stokely Carmichael or Kwame Touré, who chanted, "Black is beautiful," and the legendary leaders of Khamit on up through modern history, we have enough examples of great beings of color to be able to shake off our misconceptions. As Tony Browder reminds us in *From the Browder File,* "African Americans have been programmed to think that Black is something to be ashamed of. It's strange that people who gave the world culture, science, religion and civilization, know so little about their ancestral heritage. All we have to do is study our history, and the perceptions that we have of ourselves will change instantaneously." Hence, looking in the mirror really means looking back in time. There is no reason whatsoever to need to erase your cultural identity. You are Black *and* beautiful. Until you accept and embrace this fact, you will not be able to negotiate any aspect of your life effectively regardless of the current color-blind rhetoric. Knowing *how to be* requires knowing all of who you are.

What Are You?

As I was leafing through a catalogue of businesses in Miami/Dade County, Florida, I saw some suspicious statistics. This brochure suggested that more than 80 percent of the population of Miami was white.

The Value of Color

Do you think that traditional African people used to judge each other based on the color of their skin? Historical data suggest not. In *The Miseducation of the Negro,* Carter G. Woodson tells a wonderful story of an African people who cherished "perfectly Black" skin: "We are told that they are so anxious to be Black that if they find one of the group with a tendency to depart the least from this color they go to the heart of nature and extract from it its darkest dye and paint therewith that native's face that he may continue perfectly Black." Contrast that to the contemporary obsession with skin bleaching to whiten it. In 1990 we used $44 million worth of skin-bleaching products, according to Kathy Russell, Midge Wilson and Ronald Hall's *The Color Complex: The Politics of Skin Color Among African Americans* (1992). The use of such products started back at the turn of the century. One advertisement went so far as to say: "Lighten your dark skin. Race men and women, protect your future by using Black & White Ointment. Be attractive. Throw off the chains that have held you back from the prosperity that rightly belongs to you." See anything wrong with this picture? Blackness was defined and accepted as *the problem,* when it actually was and is the *mind* out of which the idea that a physical characteristic can become an excuse for discrimination is the real problem.

Now, I know that white folks make up the majority—in terms of numbers—in most American cities. I didn't think Miami was one of those places. Riding around throughout the city, what I have seen more than white folks are Afro-Caribbeans—largely people from Cuba, the Dominican Republic, Puerto Rico and Haiti. These stats baffled me, so I read on. What I found—in fine print—was that the majority community of Miami is actually Latino, and that the Latino community had checked off the "white" box on the census form—being considered of the *Blanco* (white) class in their countries of origin.

So many issues came up when I saw this. First is one that people have been challenging a lot in recent years: the delineation of race on government forms. Are the choices of Caucasian, African-American, Asian, Native American and Latino enough? Should you choose Latino if you have light skin? How can you really identify yourself on a form if you don't immediately fit the descriptions offered? Are you then simply "Other"? More and more often, people today are seeking to acknowledge that they are of mixed parentage. They say they want to celebrate the "whole" of who they are, without having to choose an ethnicity, a by-product of racism. Lots of people of color are facing this issue now, more than ever before—without support from the polar definitions offered today.

I had a troubling conversation with a woman from the Caribbean island of Montserrat several years ago about this very subject. She is the daughter of an aristocrat. When she was growing up, she had the opportunity to travel around the world with her father and to experience the "finest" things in life. She was also born with very light skin. As a woman who has resided in the West, either Europe or the United States, for more than twenty-five years, she also considers herself to be "white." After all, her skin is pale. One summer day we had the chance to chat about fun in the summer and what we both liked to do. I enjoy being in the sun. I consider the sun to be my greatest healer, actually. When I mentioned this, she cringed, explaining that she never goes in the sun. Since her childhood on Montserrat, she has avoided the sun, to keep her skin as white as possible. In the end, her skin may fare better than mine with regard to the sun's rays, but beyond that physical health concern, I found her underlying philosophy scary. She has spent her entire life becoming a well-to-do white lady, largely devoid of any native cultural expression, including the possibility of acquiring brown skin. What does that say about us, in a larger sense, and our respect for who we are and our ancestral lineage? This woman's story unfortunately is not rare in our community.

It's a Color Thang

Okay, so how many of you think that the color of your skin affects your daily interaction? Raise your hand if you think that your complexion has ever affected your ability to move in different circles, get a date, secure a job, feel safe. Chances are your hand is waving in the air. For the redbones in the house, your ability to navigate may have been physically easier than a blue-black brother or sister. For a sister who doesn't pass the paper-bag test (whose skin is deeper than that midbrown tone), maybe brothers have passed you up for a high-yellow sister no matter how she acted, right? Right and *wrong*. Unfortunately, Black folks are our own worst enemies when it comes to judging one another on the color of our skin. *Light is right, isn't it?* That's actually what many people have thought and still think. Light skin did make it easier to move ahead.

When a group of young brothers and sisters sat down to discuss appearance for this book, I was amazed at how stuck we still are on this issue. People at the turn of the century still hold these to be true—that it is easier to make it if you are closer to white. If that is true, what does that say for the millions of our folks who are obviously Black? And what does that say for the extraordinary accomplishments of those known and unknown of darker hues who have lived exemplary, inspired lives that all can and do admire? We are hypersensitive as it relates to the ways in which we look—and for good reason. Look at yourself in the mirror. Can't you see how beautiful you are?

If you go back and read accounts from the *Maafa,* when our ancestors were placed on auction blocks, you will read about how their bodies were glistening with oil as they stood tall (and frightened) before the huge, raging crowds. Our people were sold *not* because they were considered inferior. Actually, it was their physical beauty and strength that radiated out to everyone and caused a frenzy of activity. The brothers stood strong and fierce before the crowds as the sisters stood firmly planted on their powerful flat feet. Trust that their burnished brown skin was not a turn-off. It was insurance that they would be able to withstand the hot sun. Their muscular bodies promised physical stamina and strength throughout the brutal summer. Our ancestors served as workers in the fields and homes of white folks for so many years *because* they were beautiful and powerful. This we must learn and remember. Out of them we came. Because of their inner and outer beauty and indefatigable energy, we are.

There is no reason to be ashamed of how we look. Instead, we have every possible reason to embrace our many ways of appearing; we even have proof that those who oppressed us for so long saw our beauty too. The problem is that in order to justify the insanity of Slavery, everything had to be twisted around so that it no longer made sense. Our beauty was called ugly. Our powerful bodies were considered raw, wild and unattractive. Our full lips, curly hair and dark, shiny skin were at once envied and rejected by those who enslaved us. In the end, we emerged with a pretty sick sense of self. As Queen Afua affirms, the only choice we have now is to *Heal thyself.* Filmmaker and educator Bridgett M. Davis explored our anguish in her film *Naked Acts* (1995), showing that we must embrace who we are as we are in order to become whole.

You Think You White?!

Black folks have been tearing each other apart for years, based on how we look, how we speak and how we fit into Western class structure. (Although there certainly was infighting between different peoples on African shores, I sincerely doubt that Yoruba and Ibo people stood in the sunshine arguing over who was too dark to live there!)

In this country, conflicts have arisen between us over everything, especially when we seem to have "made it." What has happened to children and adults alike who have "moved on up" is that as they have done so, they often have rejected their roots as others in the community have sometimes rejected them, considering them siddity Black people over there *who think they white.* You know who I mean? (You might even fit into the group. I surely have been given that label on occasion.) They're the ones who live in the fancy neighborhoods, drive expensive cars, send their children to white schools and live the "white life" and probably are light-skinned, right?

Although that stereotype does play out in the Black community where the people who have moved into middle- and upper-class status either became shunned by the folks still in the 'hood or did the shunning, things aren't that simple. The hateful "us" and "them" lines have their roots *not* only in our own desire to tear each other down—that "crabs in a barrel" mentality of which our people are so often accused. Instead, those lines are drawn based on Western class structure—how much money you have, how much education you have and where you live. They also reflect the perception that access to more Western ways of behaving and acquisition of those things that mainstream culture values somehow make you "better." What may be more accurate is that they make you "comfortable." In considering our cultural development in this country, as a people we haven't thought critically enough about what we think of as opportunity. Opportunity shouldn't automatically be viewed as the amount of financial resources or objects that you have. At the same time, being able to live in relative comfort with greater access to resources and the world is a valid goal to have—one that the burgeoning Black middle class is now enjoying.

Clearly it's hard to separate what is really of value when there's so much conflicting information in our faces. Take language, for example. Our ancestors in this country learned that one's ability to flow in America was often directly related to how well the person could speak standard English and be "civilized," which often meant "act white." Today when you hear a brother accuse another brother with, *"You think you white or something?"* it usually has to do with the way the person speaks, the accent, the use of the English language, the intonations or lack thereof, the style of dress—the whole package. When this happens to a brother or sister from the inner city, after going away to an "exclusive" college, that person is not readily welcomed back into the old neighborhood. It's viewed almost like being a traitor. *You left and became one of them!* That's what some people say. Because fear and distrust have often characterized the relationships that Black people have had with the dominant culture, young people who have adopted "their" language "apparently" become one of them—at least to their peers—which isn't wholly true.

Many African scholars suggest that " 'hood folk" know intuitively that Eurocentric or mainstream education is designed to teach the African-American person who's lucky enough to be granted access to it that it is an individual thing and that the curriculum itself is largely anti- or at least non-African. If this is so, it means Black students are often being taught to hate both our image in the mirror and those who look like us who are not participating in this "civilizing" education process. The eighteenth-century Western philosopher David Hume, who is still taught today, actually stated this contention: "I am apt to suspect the Negroes . . . to be naturally inferior to the white. There never was a civilized nation of any other complexion than white; nor even any individual eminent either in action or speculation, no ingenious manufacturers amongst them, no arts, or science." For a more contemporary echo of sentiment, just read *The Bell Curve* (1994).

If you have been taught this kind of nonsense in an institution of higher learning as anything other than an unfortunate and misinformed "opinion" and come away believing it, wouldn't you want to do whatever you could to separate yourself so that you would achieve in that which is defined as "good"? The stuff defined as good, tragically, is commonly considered anything other than Black. No wonder when Black students come home to the 'hood they are greeted with suspicion. They may have just learned institutionalized self-contempt, and they may be unconsciously projecting that out into the very world from which they came. Even with the cropping up of Black Studies programs across the country that celebrate who we are and what we have accomplished, we are still hard-pressed to see consistent positive images of ourselves that reinforce the beauty of who we are in all of our many ways. To become conscious beings who can support our families and our communities now and in the future, we must take the actions that promise that we learn about who we really are. We must read about our cultures, from Africa and all of the Diaspora. We must participate in meaningful dialogue that celebrates our cultural continuum and examines our people with loving scrutiny. Then we will all be able to rejoice in knowing that we are Black—and beautiful! This vital awareness of our inherent value begins with the way that we communicate about ourselves. Language is so very important in this process, as it serves to define culture. We must affirm our greatness in every way that we can. We must look for the good within each one of our brothers and sisters so that we can revitalize ourselves. We also need to accept and learn from the problems that we are experiencing. We must do this now.

Beware of the Idiot Box

When my parents were growing up, they read books, talked to family and elders and sometimes listened to the radio. In their all-Black neighborhoods, they learned about cultivating integrity and character. They got to see the most exquisite spectrum of Black beauty—from the broadest nose and deep chocolate skin to the most "keen" features and lemon-colored skin. Their experience was interactive, allowing for meaningful discussion of issues of concern to the community.

And then came television. At first, what my father calls "the idiot box," was intriguing. You could see all kinds of images that you could only imagine before. What was bad was that the images being projected did not then—and rarely do now—promote positive illustrations of Black people. Writer bell hooks addressed the danger of television in her book, *Sisters of the Yam* (1993): "Learning to identify with the screen images of good and bad, whether looking at Westerns or Tarzan movies, television was bringing into the homes of Black people a message that we were inferior, a race doomed to serve and die so that white people could live well."

Over the years, affirming images of Black folks have been few and far between on television and in film—although many strides have been made. (Think of newscasters Ed Bradley, Bryant Gumbel, Gil Noble and Tony Brown; of actors Bill Cosby, Phylicia Rashad, Cicely Tyson, James Earl Jones, Avery Brooks, Ruby Dee and Ossie Davis, Oprah Winfrey, Della Reese, Danny Glover, Alfre Woodard, Whoopi Goldberg, Angela Bassett, Lynn Whitfield, Sidney Poitier; think of writers Maya Angelou and Toni Morrison.) Still, the devastating effects of constant images of white people succeeding while Black folks act as buffoons, lowlifes and other disempowered "individuals" wreak havoc, particularly on our youth. No wonder many of our children still prefer a white Barbie over a Black superhero.

When it comes to shoring up our self-image, we must monitor what we watch, what we buy, how we spend our time so that we can undo some of the psychological damage of being told we are worthless. Otherwise, it really is impossible to learn *how to be* with others, because we won't have a clue about how to be *with ourselves*. bell hooks intimated that the efforts of the sixties and its talk of universal love did a lot to undo the work of our families to balance the negative images projected in the media. Her challenge to us all is to remain vigilant. I will add that we need to read, study and spend time with other thinking people who see our beauty and celebrate the inherent strength and goodness that we reflect.

Work That Body!

When you look in the mirror, do you like what you see? That may seem like a loaded question. All you have to do is go into the fitting room of any clothing store to see women struggling with the image that stares back at them as they try on clothes. Body image is something we all deal with on an intimate level regularly, even when we don't realize it. For the sister who will never be a size 4 but who wants to be, to the brother who can't understand where those love handles came from, we've all got our issues.

At the top of the list should be how healthy we are, *not* how good or not-so-good we look. We often hear that the body is the temple of the soul. Do you know that God dwells in you? (If you really believed that, would you be able to continue shoveling garbage into a place where God lives?) When we asked brothers and sisters this question, most didn't have a positive response. Some talked about experiencing so much stress due to their tight daily schedules that they don't really pay that much attention to their physical bodies on a consistent basis. Mothers said they defer to their children. Fathers spoke of working two jobs and crashing when they get home. Young adults and teenagers said they don't need to exercise yet. And plenty of others who are already suffering from diseases that are triggered by overeating and lack of exercise had just plain given up. In nearly every Black family there is at least one person who is obese, another who has high blood pressure or diabetes, one who suffers from depression, another who is addicted to alcohol, drugs or cigarettes. As a group, we are not taking care of ourselves to the best of our abilities. We need to start.

To be fair, plenty of our people do get out there and exercise. *Heart & Soul* magazine points the way every month for sisters, and the numbers are picking up. For those of us who aren't as disciplined, we can take a page out of the committed people's book. Byl Thompson, a public relations executive in his mid-thirties, travels more than 50 percent of the year. Even though he is superbusy, Byl says he consistently makes time for exercise when he travels. He usually stays in hotels that have a gym. Just in case, he uses a machine that people used to laugh about when they saw it advertised on television—the Abdominizer. He says it travels well and assists him in doing his workout. Motivation is key. An entrepreneurial sister who used to work out regularly, on the other hand, found herself in a real slump one summer and did absolutely nothing. She sat in front of the pool at her summer house and rarely got in, she says, because she was depressed. Rather than staying in that depression, at twenty pounds heavier after only three months, she decided to do something about it. She got a therapist to help her climb out of the doldrums, and she went back to the gym. Both of these examples prove that there is a way to move beyond seeming obstacles so that you can take care of yourself. Doctors always ask if you exercise as part of your daily regimen. If your answer is "No," change today. You have a powerful will. Turn it on yourself and use that energy to fortify your being.

A Word About Medical Attention

Statistics suggest that African-American people discover medical problems later than other people, largely due to our avoidance of the doctor. We just don't go, at least not until our problems have reached life-or-death proportions. There are legitimate reasons that our people are suspicious of doctors. For several decades, doctors in Tuskegee, Alabama, conducted a vicious experiment on Black men, falsely treating those having syphilis with placebos. They duped hundreds of brothers into believing that they were getting top treatment for their life-threatening illness, when instead they were being fed placebos. It was only in the mid-1970s that the "study" ended, due to a nurse's coming forward to tell the horror story of what had been done to our families. In the light of the many documented incidents where the Black community was supplied with deadly drugs, diseases and other maladies, it's no wonder that we steer clear of "medical" help. The good news is that we are better represented today in the medical profession, and checks and balances are better enforced.

Whether it's fear of the doctor or lack of insurance, we have to take responsibility for ourselves, and that means we have to pay attention to our physical bodies and the needs that our bodies have. So often in this era of modern medicine coupled with holistic methods, safe and effective means of curing disease are saving people's lives. As well, people are preventing disease in their bodies by taking measures in advance of crises so that they can stay strong. We've heard it all before, and it's true. A healthy diet of fresh, live foods (little or no meat), regular exercise, rest and prayer make for a good life. Developing the discipline for any or all of those four in the midst of daily life can seem beyond your reach, but it is possible. We must take a stand for ourselves and become strong human beings who are physically and mentally capable of facing all that comes our way.

How to Be *with Doctors*

For lots of reasons, we get tongue-tied when it comes time to go to the doctor. It is imperative, however, for us to be empowered to manage

Getting the Help You Need

Taking care of yourself is the first step in healthy living. Without a conscious effort on your part to this end, your ability to be polite, thoughtful or otherwise gracious to others is lost. Be respectful of yourself first. If you don't have a doctor and need help, you still can get it. Following are some ideas that can jump-start you to a healthier life:

- **Make a list of your health concerns—all of them.** Add to the list your family history as best you know it, and ask somebody who might know. Next, think about any diseases that may run in your family—sickle-cell anemia, arthritis, high blood pressure, diabetes, glaucoma, Alzheimer's, alcoholism. Write them all down with the names of which family members have the afflictions. Make another list of your health strengths, such as regular cardiovascular exercise and a healthy diet. Be honest. You're not fooling anybody but yourself.
- **Select a doctor who can be your primary health practitioner.** For women, also select a gynecologist. Visit your doctor(s) regularly for the suggested checkups and whenever there is an emergency.
- **Learn about your medical insurance benefits provided by your employer.** If you are a member of a health maintenance organization or other group medical insurance, research doctors in your area who service your particular needs and make an appointment. Be sure you have the proper paperwork before you go. Find out if your insurance pays for homeopathic or preventative care; if not, lead the letter-writing campaign.
- **If you aren't covered by your employer, don't give up.** Identify medical clinics in your area that offer low-cost medical care. In many communities, top doctors with private practices offer their services at clinics each week. Also, research ways to secure medical insurance on your own. Depending on your health, you may be able to purchase basic coverage at an affordable price.
- **When it comes to dental care and your resources are low, contact medical and dental schools to find out about free or reduced-rate programs.** Often students do the dental work under the supervision of seasoned dentists. Although this may seem scary, I know of quite a few people who have been treated through these programs successfully.
- **Get a second opinion when you are in doubt.** Be clear when you communicate with medical professionals. If you feel uncomfortable about their diagnoses, prescriptions or other forms of care, let them know straight away, and seek further help.
- **Seek out holistic health care.** The proliferation of Western drugs that "treat" the symptoms and, further, that approach health care as curative rather than preventative should be reconsidered. The healers in African communities understood that the body, mind and spirit work together in a healthy, balanced body; treating a symptom would be considered ridiculous —like taking cold medicine rather than fasting and purging the germ that's making you sick.
- **As the saying goes,** *Don't put off until tomorrow what you can do today*. When it comes to your health, deal with anything that comes up immediately. With all of the new treatments out there, the chances are great that your illness can be handled successfully if it is diagnosed in time. Here's to your health!

our health. That means that we must go to the doctor prepared to share all pertinent information about our health. Here are some strategies gleaned from medical doctors around the country:

- Pay attention to your health. Keep records of your checkups as well as dates and descriptions of any physical concerns you may have. Bring your records to the doctor, so that you can discuss your health accurately.
- Ask questions until you are satisfied. Don't be intimidated by your doctor or assume that he or she *knows* what's wrong with you. Assume that doctors don't, and be as patient as you need to be to cover every concern. You have to participate in your health care, which means that you must reveal pertinent information and ask every question you think of that will help you to get the help you need.
- Bring a medical notebook. Put all of your medical information into one book that you bring to your appointments. Write your questions down beforehand so that you can run down your list when you visit the doctor. Make a list of symptoms and ailments in the days leading up to your appointment. Most doctors ask you to fill out a sheet. This is not the time to forget a nagging problem because something else is currently bothering you.
- Keep your cool. People often get nervous at the doctor's office. If you can stay focused and calm, you will have a more thorough visit. Remember that your doctor is a person too. Offer your gratitude and support. Your mood will affect your doctor's.

Perfect Posture

The first time I visited the Continent was on a trip to the Ivory Coast with *Essence*. A vanload of us had been in the capital city of Abidjan and were headed to the rural areas just before sundown. It had to be nearly 100 degrees outside, at close to 100 percent humidity. As we headed away from town, I couldn't help but notice lots of local people walking along the side of the dusty road. It was the first time that I had ever seen people walking with baskets balanced perfectly on their heads. What an incredible sight! As I watched the people, dressed in an exquisite mixture of African and Western clothing, I was overcome with awe. Everything that I had been sold about African people from mainstream media since childhood—that they were slovenly, heathenish, lazy people—was clearly untrue. These people were beautiful, regal, proud. And each and every one of them was walking with erect spines and sure footing. They had perfect posture, and it seemed to be effortlessly achieved. That same elongated spine is what "etiquette" teachers strive to develop in their students by having them walk back and forth with telephone books on their heads. Guess where they got the idea!

One of the clearest memories I have of growing up was my mother reminding my sisters and me to *Stand up straight, girls!* At barely five-feet-four, Doris Freeland Cole *knew* she stood six feet. Standing next to our Daddy, who was six-feet-two-and-a-half, she almost looked tall too. It was because she stood head high and proud all the time. And she encouraged us to have good posture at all times. We were to pull our tummies in and stand straight and tall before moving. Her lessons worked. As I have observed other Black folks around the world and throughout the United States, I see that many of us do walk tall and proud, but I also see many of us slouch over, heads hanging low. The submissive posture was all too familiar during our enslavement. It was a requirement that our ancestors walk with heads down, eyes gazing at the ground. Those days are over. Not only is walking tall good for your health, but it is also a great way to inspire positive communication with anyone who crosses your path.

What's on Your Mind?

Take a moment of pause to check in on what you are allowing to happen in your own head. That touchy subject of mental illness is something that most Black folks don't dare talk about. But many of us are living with varying degrees of mental frailty, much of which can be managed simply by paying attention to what's going on between our ears. How many times have you dwelled on a situation that made you angry? How many coworkers, family members, lovers, children, jobs or other situations are bothering you? Do you hold any resentments toward others now? If so, how long have you felt the resentment? Has it been months? Years? What happens inside your body when you experience negative feelings toward others?

You'd be surprised just how damaging to your own mental well-being holding on to negative feelings can be. There was a woman I knew in Philly, Miss Kay, the mother of one of my college friends. Miss Kay's husband got involved with another woman, and the family unit crumbled. Long after the husband moved out, Miss Kay continued to mourn and wait for him to return—not that he ever said he was coming back. Rather than facing reality, Miss Kay took a seat in her misery and stewed in it. Slowly her health began to deteriorate. From headaches to overeating, depression and finally cancer, Miss Kay essentially let herself die because she couldn't deal with the reality of her life. Nobody's saying that it was right for her husband to leave, but sometimes these things happen. And, in life, we have to either accept the things that happen to us or do something about them. Deciding to live in a state of unreality can only lead to personal ruin.

When I think about Miss Kay, I recall times in my own life when I was unwilling to let go of relationships and how I tolerated abuse. Lashing out, harboring ill will—all of that negative stuff—just made me ill, physically ill. And it made me do things that were ultimately self-destructive, such as eating poorly or staying too long in unproductive relationships.

It's true what your Mama told you about holding on to such things: *The only person you're hurting is yourself*. Chances are, when you find yourself in an uncomfortable situation in which you get angry, the person you are mad at isn't even thinking about you at all—at least not for long. The same goes for the person with whom you may be infatuated. I've spoken to quite a few brothers and sisters who have been "in love" with somebody who wasn't quite feeling the same way about them. That feeling for some folks has lasted for years and gotten in the way of the possibility of developing other healthy relationships. Dwelling on what isn't yours, allowing yourself to sit in the "pity pot," as my aunts used to call it, or otherwise letting your mind blow things out of proportion is dangerous. God didn't put us here to drive our own selves crazy. Seek spiritual refuge instead, or professional help.

Our Hair

Entire books have been written about Black folks and hair. As for Medusa, immortalized by Greek mythology (she, by the way, was Ethiopian), our hair has been the source of our strength and our weakness. When you look at a gathering of Black people, male and female, what you see is a range of hair colors, textures and styles that goes unmatched compared to any other people in the world. Our hair is magnificent—and also misunderstood. The first Black millionaire in America was a woman, Madame C. J. Walker, who specialized in Black hair care. This sister invented a chemical means of straightening Black hair that earned her more money than any other Black person before. Why? Because she paved the way for us to have greater options with our hair, including the questionable ability to give our hair what Zora Neale Hurston called "the whitish feel." Then and now, being able to blend in has helped a lot of Black folks get ahead. I'm sure that's why so many of our parents and elders have had such a fit with us about our own hair when it's presented in natural styles.

In a heated focus group session, several young brothers and sisters who were sporting a variety of cultural hairstyles said they had gotten a

A Word from Malcolm X

Malcolm X experimented with processing his hair early in his life. For several years, he wore a "conk," the straight-hair style of the day that required a permanent relaxer. Here is an excerpt of his description of his hair transformation from his book, *The Autobiography of Malcolm X* (1964):

> My first view in the mirror blotted out the hurting [from the chemicals]. I'd seen some pretty conks, but when it's the first time, on your *own* head, the transformation, after a lifetime of kinks, is staggering. . . . On top of my head was this thick, smooth sheen of shining red hair—real red—as straight as any white man's.
>
> How ridiculous I was! Stupid enough to stand there simply lost in admiration of my hair now looking "white." I vowed that I'd never again be without a conk, and I never was for many years.
>
> This was my first really big step toward self-degradation: when I endured all of that pain, literally burning my flesh to have it look like a white man's hair. I had joined that multitude of Negro men and women in America who are brainwashed into believing that the Black people are "inferior"—and white people "superior"—that they will even violate and mutilate their God-created bodies to try to look "pretty" by white standards.

lot of painful flack from their parents over the years. One young woman with twists explained that her father, a career politician, warned her that she would never get ahead "looking like that." A brother with long locks said his father wouldn't let him into the house the first time he saw his son's hair. "Have you gone crazy?" the educator wanted to know. "Nobody will hire you if you keep that style. You're more likely to get arrested."

Our hair issues are serious. No wonder so many artists, writers and scholars have explored its meaning in our lives. For those of us who grew up in households whose parents and grandparents remember the Great Depression plus the endless efforts to keep our people from the opportunity to succeed, we hear echoes of those fathers' words. If we choose to celebrate our natural beauty—that which adorns our heads—will we, by definition of who we are, fail in life? We do have the responsibility to evolve beyond our parents' perspective, don't we?

Bruce M. Tyler, a professor at the University of Louisville, explored this issue in an article entitled "Black Hairstyles: Cultural and Sociopolitical Implications" (1990):

The controversy over Black hairstyles and public conduct is not new. Throughout the nineteenth and twentieth centuries Blacks have conducted a heated internal debate on how they should conduct themselves and what were appropriate public dress and grooming standards. These concerns were vital to many Black leaders who believed that proper conduct and grooming standards would advance Black people's status and citizen rights. Black leaders of various persuasions—assimilationists and Black nationalists—disagreed, often bitterly, over what constituted a respectable "Black" standard. Assimilationists, or integrationists, believed that Blacks should follow the national White middle-class norms.

For the record, the debate rages on. When people consider their appearance and work, tensions especially flare. For instance, I spoke to one human resources executive who said that she hires people who look "palatable" to the potential employers. For her, that means someone with neat, organized hair that does not "distract" from the person's overall presentation—the implication being, not *too* Black.

The first time I really got to see the spectrum of Black hair was when I started working at *Essence* magazine. Before my eyes were all manner of hairstyles that I had not previously seen—not even at Howard University, where I went to college. Back at Howard, sisters were into hair, to be sure. But it was mostly about the D.C. precision cut, the bone-straight relaxer and the sprayed-into-place "do." I was definitely part of that crowd, sporting many different straightened styles during my college years. But when I walked through the doors of the magazine, I entered a whole new world—one that was primarily, if not completely, Black, one that celebrated the way we look in all its forms. As far as hair goes, this meant that back in the early eighties, there was every kind of hairstyle, from relaxed looks to braided extensions to small Afros to weaves. Over the course of the next decade and some, Black women—and men—have continued to explore hair options that have included ways to wear natural styles to work. *Essence* was instrumental in making that transition make sense. Among the many things that I have learned about our hair over the years, the greatest lesson is that however we wear our hair, *we* have to feel good about it. Natural or relaxed, Jheri-curled or braided, our hair needs to reflect how we feel about ourselves. I am generally of the mind that natural is best, but having experimented with all sorts of styles and textures, I think other options can be fun and efficient to explore, just so long as we're clear on the reasons we're doing so.

Historically, brothers and sisters on the Continent have created elaborate and gorgeous hairstyles for men and women. From dying hair with henna and bright red ochre to achieve that ruddy look that so many sisters go for today, to designing long-lasting exquisite braided looks that express a family history, African people have found creative ways to showcase hair that are practical, beautiful and spiritually linked.

Do a little research to see how your hair concerns can be solved using African methods and products like shea nut butter. You're likely to preserve your precious locks in the process. And here are some hair dos and don'ts:

Dos	Don'ts
Take good care of your hair. Keep it clean and moisturized.	Neglect your hair (or any other aspect of your physical self) as you manage the rest of your life.
Select a hairstyle that you can maintain.	Wear a style that is impractical for your lifestyle.
Use natural products that will nurture your hair.	Abuse your hair with harsh, abrasive products.
Consider what hairstyle will be appropriate for your workplace.	Ignore the codes of conduct in your workplace or other environment. Know what is expected, so that you can make an informed decision about how you intend to present yourself.
Work with your stylist to discover ways of caring for natural hair and developing hairstyles for different activities.	Wear black-tie hair to work (unless it's for a special event), or with jeans and sneakers.
Become acquainted with the person who will be doing your hair. Trust your intuition. If you get a funny feeling, find someone else— no matter what kind of success your friend's mother's Aunt Fanny had with him!	Let too many people touch your hair. Our ancestors understood that our hair holds spiritual power and should be considered sacred and therefore off-limits to unloving hands.

Getting Dressed

As far as traditional etiquette goes, what you wear has a lot to do with how far you go in your life. It's amazing to know just how powerful your physical presentation is, especially your clothing. What you wear makes a big difference. That's why the fashion industry is such a booming international business. I often remind people that *nearly every day, everywhere in the world, everybody gets dressed.* There are few other things that everyone does as consistently. In traditional African cultures, the concept of dress was powered by spiritual acuity. Women and men wore specific garments on various occasions because they meant something to the wearer and the community at large.

For Worship

Most Black families reserve special clothing for church—what we call "our Sunday best." Depending on your house of worship, you may have different specifications for dress, but here are some basics from the Christian old school:

For Women

- Wear a skirt or a dress, your Sunday best, with hosiery. (I made the mistake once of going to church without my tights on. My Mama's eyes promised punishment if I forgot again!) Your skirt should be at least knee length. And be sure to wear a slip.
- Find out the policy on pants before you wear them. In more casual churches, women are now allowed to wear dressy pants, especially when worn with jackets.
- Cover your head. Well, this is not a requirement, but in many churches women wear hats. In some congregations, not having one on can make a woman feel naked. Gauge what's right in your spiritual home. Covering the head is common in many spiritual traditions.

For Men

- Wear a jacket and pants with a dress shirt and tie. A suit is ideal, but mixed separates work too. Often men wear black suits to church, especially if they have special roles, such as deacon or lay minister.
- Don't wear jeans. Even when the mood is casual, dress up for worship.
- Wear dress shoes. No sneakers, please!

Dressing for Work

Apart from special events, the other time that your wardrobe really makes a huge difference is when you are going to work. Every job has a dress code, even if it's not written down in any manual. Find out what is expected of you at your job by asking the office manager, the human resources department or your boss—*before* you start your job. When special activities present themselves at work, ask again to see what the dress code will be. For example, if there will be a company party, is it festive, black tie or casual? And what do any of those descriptions actually mean to your colleagues? I always recommend that people come to work looking as if they mean business. Dress as you would for the job that you ultimately want there, so that your presentation affirms your intention. By keeping your goals in mind as you put

Deciphering Dress Codes

The meaning of different styles of dress has begun to blur for a lot of people. Here's a guide to getting dressed that will help to lift the confusion.

Black tie	**Women**—full-length gown or skirt, often ornamented, with evening shoes (peau de soie or other dressy material, often including rhinestones); small matching purse; handkerchief **Men**—black tuxedo with white evening shirt with cuff links, bow tie and cummerbund or vest; black dress shoes
White tie	**Women**—more formal evening gown and accessories **Men**—white dinner jacket with white tie and black tuxedo pants; black patent leather shoes
Semiformal	**Women**—dressy dress or suit in evening fabric, mid-calf in length or shorter, with evening shoes and small bag **Men**—dress suit with shirt and tie; tuxedo not required
Cocktail	**Women**—knee-length or above dress or skirt suit; sometimes dinner pantsuit with evening shoes; small bag; festive accessories **Men**—dress suit or dressy sport coat with slacks and shirt and tie; tuxedo not required
Cultural	**Women**—traditional dress of the themed party, from batik Caribbean print to West African *bubah* **Men**—traditional dress of themed party
Casual	**Women**—sundress or slacks; day bag; shoes and accessories **Men**—shirt and trousers; day shoes (check theme and location of event)

Don't Be a Fashion Victim

Now you know, we love ourselves some clothes! From young people right on up to older folks, we are known for dressing "to the nines," whatever that has meant for each generation. Actually, we're also responsible for setting nearly all of the international fashion trends. Think hip-hip gear (which came partly out of the prison system in California—big, unbelted pants, shoes without laces, etc.), bustle-back jackets and coats (first from the *Khoisian* women of Southern Africa and later Western Africa), textiles such as *kente,* mudcloth and *asooke* cloth on all types of garments (and housewares) and so much more. As you develop your fashion sense, there's no reason to become a fashion victim. You can cultivate your own intuitive sense of style and go from there. Or if you need help defining your style, seek it from an image consultant in your community.

The industry of fashion is designed to change at least every six months just so you can keep going to the store to buy the new "latest." Be mindful of what you spend your money on. Purchase clothing that looks good on you, not just because fashion magazines say it's the "in" look. Also, spend some of your wardrobe dollars on Black designer clothing. In every major city there are Black designers making a wide range of fashion, as well as national and international designers who have risen to prominence with great clothes. You can make your effort at *kujichagulia* (cooperative economics, one of the principles of Kwanzaa) in the Black community by spending some of your money on clothes made by Black hands. One of the greatest challenges is finding out who our designers are. For a partial listing, see Constance C. R. White's book, *StyleNoir* (1998).

---

on your clothes, you will be using an African method to inform your decisions. From the African worldview, nothing is done "just 'cause." There is always a spiritual reason behind an action, especially physical adornment.

If you want to wear culturally inspired clothing to work, follow the same barometer. Gauge how acceptable you think your wardrobe choices will be. Then dress accordingly. If you feel strongly that you want to wear African or African-inspired clothing on a regular basis and your job doesn't appreciate your style, you have a couple of choices. Get creative and add cultural touches to your attire, such as a cowrie shell necklace and earrings or a *kente*-cloth shawl atop a business suit. You can also choose to work in an environment that welcomes your style. What is usually unrealistic is to think that you can change the thinking of your job to adapt to your particular desires. Yet some

African-American professionals have gone to court over such points and won. You can choose to fight for your garb, too. Investigate discrimination laws. Weigh your options before acting.

Casual Fridays

Getting dressed for work got a lot harder when psychologists figured out that people respond favorably to the notion of being able to dress down on Fridays. Some studies prove that job performance has gone up across the nation with the institution of casual Friday wear. The problem is that whereas there are often clear and strict directions regarding work attire for the beginning of the week, the landscape is largely a vast gray area when it comes to what to wear on Friday. For example, on a mid-September Friday morning, I was riding the subway, and two people got on and stood in front of me. One was a forty-something white man. The other was a twenty-something white woman. The man had on jeans and a button-front shirt. The woman had on a short skirt, a T-shirt and sneakers. As the two of them chatted, I figured out that they were both attorneys at large law firms in Manhattan. The young woman was talking about how much more productive she feels on "dress-down Fridays." She explained that having the chance to be casual somehow clears her mind to be creative at work. I have to tell you that she looked as if she were dressed for a Saturday afternoon at the park instead of a day at work at a law firm. Something definitely seemed off, and I couldn't help but wonder what the workday would be like if she were African American—if she would have been able to get away with dressing so casually.

One senior executive at a large insurance company in New York City, Sylvester Green, told me that the crisis of casual Fridays extends beyond the color line, although he agreed that Blacks are likely to have a greater challenge pulling off supercasual clothes at work than their white counterparts. Sylvester explained that many corporations have extremely rigid and crystal-clear guidelines for work wear. But when it comes to casual Fridays, they seem to have thrown in the towel. What you see more now is "anything goes" than any clear direction about what's acceptable. Although executives and human resources departments have yet to define the parameters, here are a few commonsense suggestions:

- Remember where you are going—to work. Dress in a manner that allows you to feel comfortable in any meeting or interaction during the day. That includes an impromptu meeting with your boss, another supervisor or a million-dollar client.
- Don't go to work dressed as if you're going to spend the day working in your garage! Think about it for a minute. A pair of old jeans, a

sweatshirt and sneakers is not appropriate for work under most circumstances. An exception would be if you are planning a move at
your office or some other physical activity that would require such
attire, or you work in the mailroom. And maybe not even then. One
woman explained that a young man started in the mailroom at her
company, but always dressed neatly, with tailored pants, a shirt and
a tie. Soon he was being sent to deliver things to other offices, then
moved to reception, then to administration.

- Use your own filter as you review your wardrobe. Break your
  wardrobe down into business, weekend and evening categories. If
  you need to add categories, do so.
- Do wear clothing that is more relaxed than your normal work attire. In
  this way you will demonstrate to others in your office that you participate in the weekly dress-down activity but that you know the limitations.
- Avoid jeans at work. I know this seems extreme for some, especially
  for people who work in creative fields. Depending on your industry,
  this may not apply to you. But for the most part, jeans characterize
  casual living. If you take your job seriously, wearing jeans may send
  a different message. When jeans are a viable option for you, wear a
  jacket with them to show that you still mean business.
- For men, the first item to go is your tie. Wearing a tie represents formal business dressing. You can also change from wearing a suit—
  matching jacket and pants—to wearing a sports coat and trousers.
  You can wear a long-sleeved shirt with the collar open, a henley or
  polo shirt, a short-sleeved shirt in a very casual office or a sweater or
  pullover under your jacket. Although a jacket is optional, I recommend that you keep a jacket at work in case you need to be more
  dressed up at some point during the day. A vest over your shirt or a
  cardigan sweater may double as a jacket, however, or you may consider an unstructured jacket alternative.
- For women, you can wear soft knits or silk pieces, leaving the con-
  structed business suits for the beginning of the week. In some offices,
  you can go without stockings. Check to be sure. Women should generally stay away from spaghetti straps, ultrasheer clothing or garments
  that are very short, even on casual days. Clearly, this is not *how to
  be* dressed in any office! When wearing a casual dress or slacks,
  keep a jacket around in case you need to look more business-
  like.
- Be aware. Look around to see how others are dressed at your
  office—your peers, your boss, the heads of your company. Depending on your role in your office and your plans for the future, dress

accordingly. If your boss dresses ultracasually on Fridays, stay professional but not too stuffy.

Accessorize

Men and women find accessories one of the most fun parts of getting dressed, because they create an opportunity for your personality to show through. Whether it's the perfect hat, bag or jewelry, you can take the time to cultivate your accessory choices that will give you a signature look. Remember not to let any one item overpower you or clash with your outfit. *Less is more*—although many African people adorn themselves majestically, for spiritual purposes. Let the mirror be your guide.

Be mindful of how your accessories fit your activities. If you are a man, for example, depending upon where you work, you may be better off leaving most jewelry at home. A wedding ring or other simple ring may be fine, along with a watch and perhaps a simple bracelet, but in many businesses earrings are out. Get a sense of what is expected at your job. For women, remember that during the day, jewelry should be minimal. Avoid dangling earrings in most offices; they make noise when you are using the phone.

Accessories add subtle cultural touches to your wardrobe for work—and for elsewhere, too. Men can wear ties with African or Caribbean motifs. Women can wear cowrie-shell earrings, mudcloth printed or batik scarves as accents. There are also many great Yoruba bags for men and women bearing cultural motifs. At some offices, bold cultural outfits and accessories are welcome!

Makeup

Painting one's face is a daily activity throughout the Western world. What's interesting is when people are in the midst of something, they often don't think of it as being what it is. I mean, people often look at images of indigenous people and remark about how exotic they look with their painted markings and other attire. Just imagine what *they* may think when they see us. Are we any less painted?

What you need to remember when you wear makeup is to create a natural look that allows your own beauty to shine through. Supermodel and actor Iman recommends using products such as concealers and foundation to even out your skin tone. Protect your skin with SPF of at least 15 in your moisturizer. Your lip color should enhance your lips without becoming a distraction. Most of all, don't overdo it.

The Eyes Have It

A couple I know had a baby who was born with very light skin, wavy hair and gray-green eyes. Now, both Mommy and Daddy are light-skinned, but neither has light eyes. The joke that Daddy made one evening was, "That better be my baby! I was away right before my wife got pregnant." Another quip he offered was, "Oh, I wear brown contact lenses. I'll be getting him some soon. Just have to wait until he gets a little older." This Daddy was obviously joking. But the subject sparked a volatile train of thought. *Can "real" Black people have eyes that are colored other than brown? Is it okay for Black folks who have brown eyes to wear colored contact lenses in order to change their eye color?* You might be surprised to learn that geneticists teach that any light-colored eye, skin or hair represents a degree of albinism and is genetically recessive. To that end, anyone can produce any of the forms of albinism by a genetic roll of the dice. Dark features are genetically dominant, and most of the people in the world have them. Light eyes also have a higher likelihood of color blindness and light sensitivity.

To the issue of Black people being able to have light eyes, it's obviously possible. Further, Black people don't fit into a lump of any kind. In my own family, my mother has what some call hazel eyes. They actually are a grayish color that changes depending on the season and the clothes she's wearing (Go figure!). Her brother has blue eyes and very light skin. But both of their parents swore that they were "colored" people, which meant they were of African-American parentage. And all of my parents' children have brown eyes, the predominant color for people throughout the world. Although I have to admit that lighter-colored eyes can be interesting to look at, primarily because you can detect all of the details of the eye, I still have to say, "So what?" I, for one, am satisfied with my own eyes as they are—although if I had the chance to make any changes, I would vote for sharper vision versus a different color.

That's not true for some of our people. When that whole colored contact lens phenomenon lit on the fashion scene a few years ago, the lines were divided about whether it was okay for somebody who was *really* Black to be down with changing one's eye color to blue or green or beige. That meant selling out to a lot of folks. And I can understand why. The idea that one's own brown eyes are not adequate presents a problem—that self-hate thing again. Plus, in the early days, the lenses gave a strange quality to dark brown eyes, making them look obviously altered rather than fashionably chic. Even later when we saw such celebrities as Whoopi Goldberg with her long, luxurious locks or supermodel Naomi Campbell strutting down the runway wearing them, many people were still disturbed by the preponderance of this eye color alteration.

To be fair, plenty of sisters said they were just having fashion fun. They argued that they felt confident as individuals who were expressing their artistic license to change themselves aesthetically in the same way that people change their clothes or their hair color, for that matter. Nothing more, nothing less. Still, I sit uncomfortably with the eye-color-swap issue. My main point of contention is that, as wisdom notes, the eyes are the windows to the soul. I wonder what good it does to mask that window so directly. The bigger issue when it comes to altering our appearance has to do with a sense of Self. If the action is being taken to make us somehow different, and therefore "better" than we are naturally, we will likely fail. Why? Because we must embrace who we are now in order to feel good about ourselves. Physical alterations can distract people from deeper self-esteem issues—unless, of course, they are connected to a positive way of exploring those sensitive areas.

The Art of Adornment

One of the most fascinating aspects of our cultural ancestry is how African people have adorned their bodies, always in concert with some spiritual activity. Outer expression of love and grief, triumph and sadness have found their expression in visual and ritualistic forms. This includes the prevalence of body piercing and other demarcations. If you look at art history books or documentaries about African cultures, you will see oval lip plates, rows of earrings including large plugs, nose rings in the nostril and through the center of the nose. In some instances, piercing represents the evolution from childhood to puberty, puberty to adulthood. Some extreme items, such as the lip plates, were sometimes used to make indigenous people seem too odd to be of interest to early slave traders. It was a way of preserving the community. See how creative our ancestors were, all the while turning their experiences into art!

Many Black people are adopting the body piercing traditions of our ancestors—either authentically or in a less permanent fashion. For example, for as many brothers and sisters who pierce their noses, there are those who now use magnetized nose rings that hold the jewel in place. (*A word of caution:* One sister told me she was wearing one of those magnetized rings, and when she sneezed she swallowed the magnet!) Similarly, there are faux ear plugs that adhere via magnets rather than holes that are expanded over years of stretching, as they are done in many African communities. An interesting point to note too is that people of all ethnic backgrounds are embracing the desire to pierce their bodies beyond the traditional single hole in each ear—for females only—that the West has considered acceptable.

How does this translate into everyday life? It depends on where you live and how you spend your time. If you are an artist, it's a lot easier to make what may seem like extreme aesthetic choices to the mainstream of America. But you don't just have to be an artist to adopt such forms of self-expression. Perhaps one of the most important questions you should ask *before* making physical alterations to your body is: *What message will I send if I make this choice?* If you can objectively answer that question and then filter your life's activities through that message to gauge its accuracy, you can make an informed, or conscious, decision about whether you should take the action at hand. Beware of *any* cultural practice that is not indigenous to your own culture and that you do not understand. You could be degrading some ancestral expression or inviting the inappropriate attention of a spiritual force that you are not equipped (initiated) to handle.

Plastic Surgery

There may be no other industry that has grown as quickly in recent years. Being able to manipulate your image surgically is extremely popular in Western society, and its popularity is not lost on Black folks. From breasts to liposuction to noses and lips, we have sat in that chair, waiting for the laser to do its work. Author Laurence Otis Graham wrote all about his nose job, expressing that the reason he decided to get surgery was to "look better," which would make him feel more comfortable around others. He says it worked. I once worked with a beautiful dark-skinned model from London who was just emerging on the fashion scene. She had the smoothest skin and a gorgeous, well-proportioned African body. She also had a broad nose, one that reflected her West Indian—that is, African—heritage. Two years into modeling and a few dollars later, girlfriend went under the knife, believing that having a sharper nose would make her more beautiful and, in turn, appealing to potential clients. For a long time after her surgery, I remember looking at her and thinking that she looked really strange and different somehow. Finally, I figured out that she had changed her appearance permanently.

As far as plastic surgery goes, I think it's dangerous to choose to alter your physical body to make it look "more white." Such an action has got to be damaging to the psyche on some unconscious level. At the same time, in this youth-driven culture, I recognize that other forms of plastic surgery, such as eye and neck tucks, seem to help people continue to work and feel good about themselves. Survivors of breast cancer who require reconstructive surgery certainly should be able to avail themselves of the latest surgical breakthroughs. But to be honest, all of it makes me a little queasy. Sucking out fat that should be reduced through exercise, augmenting healthy breasts so that your lover will like you—all of this seems to detract from the deeper issues that we need to face about taking care of ourselves and accepting ourselves as we are. Modern medicine is not always good, you know. Deep cuts like that of surgery accelerate the body's rate of deterioration, just like a piece of fruit stays fresher longer if you don't break the skin.

YOUR QUESTIONS ANSWERED

1. I am going to a business conference at a tropical resort. What is considered appropriate dress for my one-week stay?

The key word here is *business*. Whenever your primary focus is work related, you need to filter all of your activities and wardrobe around business needs. The type of work you do and the nature of the conference, along with the general attitudes of the group to be assembled, will dictate what is appropriate. I went to a business conference in Florida, for example, and everyone wore business suits to the daytime sessions, even though it was 90 degrees outside and we were in a resort location. In the evening, people tended to dress up—men in jackets and women in more casual evening attire. Contrast that to a brother in the computer industry who went to a technology conference in Palm Springs, where all of the attendees were casually dressed in T-shirts, jeans and khakis throughout their stay. When in doubt, ask someone. Read the itinerary carefully and check to see if there will be any black-tie events. Then ask to see if black tie really means a tuxedo for men and a gown for women or if it just means semiformal. Often at a warm-weather resort, the rules are a bit relaxed. Be sure to bring a cover-up to wear when you leave the pool. It is generally inappropriate to walk around the premises in your swimsuit alone. Also, leave the super-sexy outfits at home. They are more appropriate for an intimate trip with a partner than a business excursion.

2. What should I pack for a weekend trip?

Not your entire closet, that's for sure. Get a sense of the activities for the weekend, and plan accordingly. Generally one casual outfit for each day is great, along with something a little dressier for evening. If you will be staying with other people, be sure to bring a robe and slippers. In this way, you can be with your friends in the morning before you get dressed for the day and still be appropriate. Bring along a sweater, no matter what the season. Evenings get cool, even in the Caribbean, if you intend to go out to eat in an air-conditioned restaurant or other locale.

3. I'm going to meet my girlfriend's [boyfriend's] parents for the first time. We'll be having dinner at their home. What should I wear?

Obviously you want to make a positive first impression *and* be yourself—not always so easy to pull off. First, check to see what the normal family dress code is for dinner. Some families are very casual, others formal. For years my father wouldn't let a male suitor come in for dinner unless he had on a shirt, tie and sports coat. He was strict, and we all knew it. So if a brother wanted to make a good impression, he put on those clothes. Even if that wasn't his normal style, he gave my father his due respect and was able to enter into our family domain easily. On the flip side, to arrive overdressed could make everyone feel uncomfortable. Ask in advance. *A general note:* Be modest—nothing too low cut or otherwise revealing for a woman. This is not a date to turn on your man. Brothers should bring along a jacket, even if you're wearing casual clothes. Such simple details are signs of respect.

4. I am about to go on a job interview, and I don't know what to wear.

Do some research on the company with which you are interviewing. What is the nature of the business, and how do other people there dress? When you are unsure, ask someone you know at the company for pointers, or call the human resources department. You may be able to ask about the dress code without identifying yourself, although your inquiries will point to your seriousness about the position.

Generally you can follow these guidelines:

Men	Women
Wear a dark suit (matching jacket and trousers), with a white shirt and tie, along with polished dress shoes and dark socks.	Wear a dark skirt suit that stops just above the knee or a little longer, with sheer natural-colored hose and dark pumps.
Leave the jewelry at home. A watch and a wedding ring should be the limit in most environments.	Wear minimal jewelry, and avoid anything that makes noise.
Carry a briefcase or other professional bag.	Carry a briefcase, tote or professional shoulder bag.
Avoid casual clothing and bright colors. Better to err on the side of conservative.	Avoid trendy fashion, including anything sheer or for evening.

5. Specifically what type of jewelry is appropriate for a job interview?

Getting dressed for any event extends far beyond the clothes you put on your body. Your accessories, which often represent your signature, make a key statement. For a job interview, stay understated. Don't wear anything that draws the focus away from you and your skills. Women should wear small earrings that are close to the ear and do not dangle, a minimal bracelet or necklace and minimal rings. Avoid nose rings or studs, eyebrow rings or other pierced jewelry other than basic earrings. Unless you know that the environment is open to such jewelry, leave it at home until after you have landed the job and get a sense of what's acceptable there.

6. I enjoy having designs on my nails. Is it okay to wear elaborate nail designs to work?

Once again, it depends on where you work. In some work environments, it's perfectly acceptable to have fun with your nails. In conservative work spaces, you may want to be more subtle. What's more important than the color or designs, though, is the length of your nails. Too often I have seen women with extra-long nails applying for administrative positions who are unable to use a keyboard effectively because their nails get in the way. Be conscious of your environment and the needs of the job. A "French" manicure says professional and pretty in most environments.

7. Is it appropriate for a man to wear an earring to work?

I have seen some fine brothers sporting small hoops or studs in their ears, business suits and all. In some instances, these men have worked in corporate environments, other times in the entertainment or sports industries. Earrings on men actually are rather commonplace, yet that *doesn't* mean that they are acceptable everywhere. Earl Graves, publisher of *Black Enterprise,* draws the line on this point, stating that there is no room in a corporate environment for a brother with an earring. I recommend that you find out what is considered acceptable on your job before you put the earring on.

8. I am thinking about getting a brand from my fraternity, but I'm not sure whether it will work for me later on in life. Any ideas?

The first time I saw a Black person with a fresh brand was at Howard University right after I finished pledging Delta Sigma Theta. Many of the brothers who had pledged Omega Psi Phi and Kappa Alpha Psi had healing brands on their arms that looked terribly painful and delicate. Wincing and all, the brothers were proud of their accomplishment and reaping the reward—a lifetime stamp that proved their membership in the "secret society." Apart from the common keloid, this branding naggingly reminded me of cattle. It wasn't until I was told that branding is also like some of the scarification procedures that are traditional in some African societies where men and women are "branded" at puberty and/or marriage to acknowledge their passage through a significant space in their lives that I began to see the value of this practice. I wouldn't do it, though.

So, should you get one? If you really want to, I see the communal value. Most often these markings are placed on the upper arm so that you would see them only if you were wearing a sleeveless shirt or less. Although new technology does partially remove tattoos, a brand is burned into the skin and ultimately is a permanent mark. So, give it serious thought before you do it.

9. I have trouble shaving because I get razor bumps. Is it appropriate to wear a beard to work?

A well-manicured beard is often acceptable in offices. If you are going to wear a beard, make sure that you keep it neat. Sam Chisholm, president of the Chisholm Mingo Group, an advertising agency in New York City, says that a neat beard can work on a brother who has a polished look. If no one else on your job is wearing one, find out if there are any unwritten guidelines about facial hair.

WhatYouSay?

We should not apologize to anyone for the language of Black folks in America. Our language, our voices, are not only legitimate, but right and necessary. This is not to suggest that as we function in other worlds and words we should not learn other languages; that would be stupid and short-sighted. We have to be able to excel in the languages that oppress us as well as in the languages we work and create in and that will ultimately be liberating to us.

HAKI R. MADHUBUTI

IN October 1996, a rousing rally celebrating African-American children and their future was held in Harlem to raise money for an organization that helps to educate and empower our youth. Speaker after speaker cheered the assembly on, encouraging all to dig deep into their pockets to help the organization reach its financial goal. To express her gratitude for the outpouring of love and support that this capacity assembly had offered, Regent Adelaide Sanford, a legend in the New York City public school system, began, "My beloved ones, I adore you, I trust you, I believe in you," and then she paused. With the broadest smile, she continued, "I wish I could tell you how much I love you in our own language—privately. I have tried to master the language of the oppressor and can say things to you through that vehicle, but I wish . . ."

This sentiment rings true for many. How can we find the words to explain to others what we truly mean? In reality, what Regent Sanford calls the language of the oppressor, American English, is an evolved version of the language that was required of our ancestors during Slavery. It is also true that American English is the international language of commerce. In order for our people to be able to make the strides needed to reach our goals, we must all understand how to use this powerful tool to our advantage. To get to that awareness, in this chapter we look at the roots and paths of language for people of African descent in this country as well as the mechanics of contemporary English as they relate to everyday life.

Our Language

After years of research by leading linguists, sociologists and historians, it is clear that people of African descent living in this country came to develop a way of speaking that dates back to the slave trade, which began in the 1600s. Much like the other ways of *being* that our people have adopted over time, learning the English language was necessary in order to communicate with the slave owner and with each other. You see, traders had discovered early on that they were better off organizing their trade as Captain William Smith described in 1744: "The safest way to trade is to trade with the different nations, on either side of the river, and having some of every sort on board, there will be no more likelihood of their succeeding in a plot, than of finishing the Tower of Babel."

Just as people of foreign tongues who come to America today must learn English in order to function in society, so did they. What our ancestors created was an amalgam of all of their various languages with English, thereby creating what Europeans labeled a *pidgin,* or a language form in which the imposed language vocabulary is placed into the basic idiomatic mold and structure of the native tongue. This pidgin served immediately as the means of communication for commerce. Over time, according to Geneva Smitherman, a linguist from Wayne State University who has studied and documented our linguistic patterns for many years, this new language developed into a more formalized creole—a language that evolves from a pidgin with expanded grammar and vocabulary and functions ultimately as a native tongue. This creole then was passed on from generation to generation. As the majority of our ancestors came from West African countries, this new language became a mix of such languages as Ibo, Yoruba, Ewe, Hausa, Wolof and English. The same phenomenon occurred everywhere Africans were taken and a European language was imposed—Jamaican patois, Haitian and New Orleans creole, Liberian and Sierra Leonian krio. The first documentation of this creole came in 1692 when Justice Hawthorne recorded the language of Tituba, an enslaved African woman in Barbados who used English words in a manner reflective of West African language, such as, "He tell me he God," according to Smitherman. In the later writings of Harriet Beecher Stowe, Paul Laurence Dunbar, Zora Neale Hurston and others, it becomes clear that identifiable language patterns that reflect a lyricism and sentence structure different from standard English did in fact represent the common language of our ancestors. Over time, Africans in this country and their children developed varying abilities of speaking English, using their own dialects and elements of standard English. They created a viable language through which they communicated with each other, as well as with people of various other backgrounds. Those who mastered the enunciation, diction and grammar of standard American English had an easier time managing in the company of people foreign to their native tongue—and still do.

Today we see the same reality. Whether it's considered as a class issue or an educational one, Black people who do not speak standard English are not as readily accepted into mainstream society—or the Black middle class, for that matter. Instead of accounting for Black language differences as common dialect differences, Western academia and science have invented a theory of racial inferiority to explain Black dialect differences, which has become all-pervasive. The question of whether what is now termed *Ebonics* (a term coined in 1973 by Dr. Robert Williams, an African-American psychologist, as a combination of ebony and phonics, which he defines as Black sounds, not Black English) should be acknowledged in the public school curriculum is controversial, to be sure. It is a shame that there was so much said by so many with so little information about what Ebonics really is. I personally heard or read little in the popular media about how the people in Oakland are actually using Ebonics to teach standard English to Ebonics speakers (resulting in higher standardized test scores, among other things), only that it was dangerous and destined to hold our youth back even more. But why would starting from a base of respect for the origins of their language as a means of teaching be bad? Educational psychologist Dr. Asa Hilliard says that "if you can't correct misinformation about your own culture, you are miseducated."

You also can't base self-esteem simply on the way you speak, as some have mistakenly suggested about the pros and cons of using Ebonics. A positive self-image will be achieved only when the truth is being told about our people, *good and bad*. The most important thing we can do for our children, no matter how they speak, is to tell the truth. Chancellor Williams, author of *The Destruction of Black Civilization* (1974), explained:

> We wanted to know the whole truth, good and bad. For it would be a continuing degradation of the African people if we simply destroyed the present system of racial lies embedded in world literature only to replace it with glorified fiction based more on wishful thinking than on the labors of historical research.

To deny that Ebonics (Black sounds) exists is to live with your head in the sand—or at least your ears. How we address it, understand it, respect it, and not become bound by lies about it is our mission. According to African-American linguist Dr. Ernie Smith, Ebonics is a language structure—syntax, morphology, grammar, and phonics—that is West African. Only the vocabulary is English. When we speak Ebonics, we speak our ancestral or silent memory of Africa, using English words. (Regardless of your opinion of it, isn't it noteworthy that people across the country speak the same way? There is a reason for that.) Ebonics should not be confused with slang, and we do ourselves and our legacy a powerful disservice in accepting uninformed opinions about it or anything else that has to do with who we are and what we are doing in the world. This is not to say, however, that we do not need to be fluent in standard American English. As Haki Madhubuti, author, leader of the Black Arts Movement and president of Third World Press, reminded us, that would be "stupid and short-sighted."

How We Speak

As always, the first step is respect. We must understand from where we come in all its depth and complexity and appreciate that. As Madhubuti and Regent Adelaide Sanford, a longtime champion of education for our youth, articulated, we can and must cherish our own language, even as we maneuver through the world using standard English when necessary. Second, we must recognize that English today represents a medley of words and meanings from world culture, *including* those of our ancestors. Words like *fiancé* and *hors d'oeuvres* have been adopted from French, and Americans have embraced them. From our enslaved ancestors and their West African languages, we were given *goober, hoodoo/voodoo, tote, gumbo, banjo, chigger/jigger, okra, bozo* and others that are also part of the American English language.

It is through language that we communicate. Spoken language represents our organized way of expressing what we see, think, feel and experience in a concrete way so that others may be able to understand our thoughts and interact with us accordingly. How do you speak? What do your words mean? How does your manner of verbal communication affect your interactions in life? There's the loving-aunt-from-down-South way of talking that sings you a song when you're down and out. And the lullaby lyrics of your Grandma when all you really want is a hug and some reassurance that everything is going to be okay. And that language comes in phrases, intonations, coos, repeated syllables, intimate love notes. *Don't you worry none, chile. Mama's*

Double-Consciousness

W. E. B. Du Bois wrote about the state of our people in this country at the beginning of the twentieth century, and in some ways, it still applies today. In *The Souls of Black Folk* (1903), he speaks of the inner conflicts facing one he called the "Negro," whom we may now consider as the African American:

> After the Egyptian and Indian, the Greek and Roman, the Teuton and Mongolian, the Negro is a sort of seventh son, born with a veil, and gifted with second-sight in this American world—a world which yields him no true self-consciousness, but only lets him see himself through the revelation of the other world. It is a peculiar sensation, this double-consciousness, this sense of always looking at one's self through the eyes of others, of measuring one's soul by the tape of a world that looks on in amused contempt and pity. One ever feels his twoness,—an American, a Negro; two souls, two thoughts, two unreconciled strivings; two warring ideals in one dark body, whose dogged strength alone keeps it from being torn asunder.

Some African scholars challenge this thinking, reminding us that although we do face significant issues in this country, if we adopt the perspective of our ancestors and look at the world through the holistic window of their cultural grounding, we do not have to feel a "twoness" at all. Knowing your spiritual Self is the ultimate answer.

gonna make everything all right. I been there before, don't need to go back no more. Hush, chile, hush. We cherish that language, the private one that comes to us when we most need it. The songs of our souls, spoken in the ways that we understand.

Rich, sweet sounds are in all of our accents—Southern and Midwestern, Jamaican and Trinidadian, Cruzan and Bajan, Wolof and Shona. Our families sing us familiar songs. Yet as W. E. B. Du Bois explained to us so long ago, we don't live just in the world of our families. We don't exist solely in the shell of our private communities. For most of us, there appear to be two worlds—one private, one public (or at least commercial).

The language of the business world that starts with school and marches on through most of our jobs and daily negotiations has a different pacing, organization of thoughts and positioning of words in sentences. This language is not the same as our ancestral tongue. For some of us, learning the language of the business world began when we were children. Just as for children who move to foreign lands and must learn to embrace that tongue, standard English is easiest to grasp during the formative years, as is any other language, but the process of expanding one's language base can be tough once you've already developed patterns.

Layered Lessons

My mother was a kindergarten teacher before she retired in order to take care of my sisters and me full time. Although her parents had received very little formal education, she went to college, studied education and learned to speak very precisely, using what some call "the Queen's English." What she speaks is basic standard English where subjects and verbs always meet up in the appropriate ways, words are pronounced with a certain inflection and so on. Naturally, my sisters and I speak as she and my father do. We certainly got plenty of practice to get it right, too! Only problem, when we were growing up was that all of our friends didn't have the privilege of living in a home with parents who were as well educated in usage of grammar. So whenever a friend would visit and make a grammatical faux pas, my mother would give this unsuspecting soul a grammar lesson. "Mrs. Cole," my friend Renee once said, "May I *ax* you a question?" Uh oh. I knew it was coming. "What did you say, young lady?" my mother kindly questioned, all the while steering her into the den as she collected a piece of paper and a pencil. This time with a bit of a quiver in her voice, Renee repeated, "May I *ax* you a question?" upon which my mother wrote in big, bold letters A-S-K. She then asked Renee to say the word before her. Slowly Renee stuttered, "*ask.*" Wearing a compassionate yet stern face, my mother then complimented her on her correct pronunciation. She then wrote the letters A-X and told her to repeat that. Finally, she pointed out that this indeed was how Renee had been mispronouncing the verb. By making such a graphic representation of this simple (yet terribly common) mistake, my mother was able to educate my friend (never mind shaming me to no end).

Today, I have to admit that I am no longer ashamed. I am grateful for the education that I received. All of those practice sessions at home on language and speech have served me well. I can speak standard English properly and am not restricted by the language barrier excuse as I work to make my way in the world. Still, it took me some time to relax and learn to respect our speech patterns for all of their inherent beauty and magic. Traveling and listening carefully to people, and then watching others' interactions, especially among the sun-kissed peoples of the world, have enabled me to cultivate greater patience for and appreciate the many patterns of our universal language ways. There was a time, though, when I thought the heavy accents of Black people from the Caribbean and African countries made them low class. I'm sure this came from unfortunate influences from the dominant culture and the media. Black folks have gotten caught up in the sick psyche of judging each other based on "class," a nasty throwback to the days of the "field nigger" and the "house nigger." Instead of pulling each other apart, why not acknowledge that of all the speech patterns that have contributed to American English, Black speech may still have the strongest hold on the collective imagination? Think of popular music—hip-hop and rap, as well as jazz, the blues and soul. We must respect each other for who and where we are. We cannot judge and place labels on each other because of the way that we use language. We can and must acknowledge the value of developing the ability to manipulate the language to our advantage.

The Verb "To Be"

One of the most fascinating aspects of the language patterns of people of African descent as filtered through English is the use of the verb *to be*. From a spiritual perspective, cultivating an awareness of one's state of *be-ing* represents the core purpose of this book. We are all on a search to find the true essence of who we are. As it relates to language, this is very important, because language carries culture. The most commonly used verb (word that conveys action) is that which allows for everything else to happen. William Shakespeare contemplated the complex meaning of this verb in a famous passage from Hamlet, *"To be or not to be; that is the question."* If you take a look at African-American history, you will see that the very act of *being* has been an awesome challenge for many of our people. The obstacles have often seemed insurmountable, yet we have struggled and continued the fight. As far as language goes, some cultural linguists suggest that our historical trauma of surviving has led us intuitively to affirm the state of *being* in its simplest form—using the infinitive of the verb almost entirely in speech. These theoreticians suggest that it's natural for one to say, *"We be going to the store,"* or *"He be tired today."* Declaring our existence as a people with the ability to do the simplest things, they argue, is expressed through articulating thoughts in this manner.

Double Negatives and Other Characteristics of Black Language Structure

Similar arguments abound regarding the use of double and triple negatives. *"He ain't have no business going there no how."* Translation: *Under no circumstances should he have gone there.* The use of triple negatives in this sentence was clearly to illustrate a point. In both sentences, the message gets delivered. By looking at other examples of double and triple negative use, it's obvious that they are employed strategically as points of emphasis. Look at: *"There wasn't no chance he was coming back."* Or *"She knew she couldn't never get away with that."* In both instances, the double negatives make it absolutely clear how definite the actions taken were. Had they been stated otherwise, the import of the thought could have been watered down, thereby changing the meaning. This is the way that African languages often function grammatically and syntactically; only the vocabulary is English. Studying traditional African language structure is a must if we are to gain a clear sense of the origins and scope of Ebonics. Another point to note is that in other languages, double and triple negatives are commonplace and grammatically correct, as in Spanish. For example, if you want to tell someone that you don't want anything, you would correctly say: *"No quiero nada,"* which means, *I want nothing.* When Spanish is translated into English, a Spanish speaker would then naturally use multiple negatives to relay a point.

African-American people are caught in a peculiar situation. We know that the use of Black language structure and slang can be an extremely effective means of communicating a particular message. We also know that in the very same instant as we deliver an effective message, we can be judged by its use. So how can we find a balance? It all has to do with strategy. When you are with family and friends and others who share your familiar language base, you should feel free to speak in the vernacular. Standard English is most appropriate for a professional setting or environment where mixed company is present. *Please note:* Mixed company isn't relegated to white people. Unfamiliar territory represents mixed company as far as I'm concerned. A good guideline is: When in doubt, speak using standard English. At the same time, you may be able to comfortably insert elements of Black English into any conversation if your timing is right. To do so mostly requires that you stay in touch with your own rhythm, along with that of others in your midst. You may also want to consider some additional elements of Black English and its genesis. Here are a few key examples along with their rules, as documented by Joycelyn Landrum-Brown, Ph.D.:

- Indicating habitual action through verb structure, notably using the form "be" as a verb. This use of *be* derives from an aspectual verb system that is also found in many African languages. Its use conveys the speaker's meaning with reference to the qualitative character and distribution of an action over time.

He be hollering at us.
I like the way he be psyching people out.

- Predication with optional copula. The sense of complete predication conveyed by a noun followed by an adjective, adverb, verb, noun or prepositional phrase, common in many West African languages.
He real little.
My sister name Stephanie.
- Pronominal apposition, repeating the subject for emphasis. Common in Yoruba.
My boss, he called me into his office.
- Signaling of possession by context and/or juxtaposition. No use of inflectional (written as apostrophe *s*)
My husband name George.
- Same form of noun for singular and plural.
One child, seven child.
- Singular verb regardless of number of subject.
He go to the store. They go to the store.
She buys the soap. Tim and John buys the soap.

I find it very interesting to learn that there is a language-based reason for this type of sentence structure—other than lack of education. Further, I think that since it is vital for our people to know how to speak standard English, I applaud educators who are starting from an acknowledgment of Ebonics to guide students on a linguistic journey.

The N Word

Looking at our history in this country, I am struck by a baffling issue regarding Black folks and language, namely, the use of the word *nigger* in our music and colloquial speech. *"Yo nigga, whass up?"* is a common greeting among African-American males. Used in this way, it is considered an affectionate greeting. At other times, brothers refer to other brothers using the term *nigger* in disdain. *"That nigger ain't know shit!"* Comedian Chris Rock spent the better part of an HBO special elucidating his philosophy on the subject. He differentiated between Black folks and *niggers* by suggesting that Blacks are hard-working folks who are living life to the best of their ability as individuals, while *niggers* are low-life, shuffling scum not worthy of respect or admiration. As funny as his rendition was, Chris Rock essentially affirmed what certain white folks have been saying about us all along. The only difference was that Rock was able to point out that *niggers* aren't just any old Black person. But doesn't that remind you of "My one Black friend, he's different"—

the inference being "He's not *really* Black?" (followed by the unspoken: *that's why he's good enough to be my friend*).

However we choose now to use this term in relation to ourselves, we have to look at this in context. Historically *nigger* was one of the lowest, most derogatory terms imaginable. Even now, the double standard that Black folks impose seems to suggest that under no circumstances is it acceptable for white people to call us *nigger*, so why do we believe that using the proper inflection of endearment, we can transform it into a loving and familiar term to call one another? For instance, many young brothers say, *"Yo, that's my nigger,"* meaning *"That's my boy"* (another term that white folks aren't allowed to use when speaking about Black men in contemporary times) or *"That's my friend,"* (something that wouldn't be said in that way when speaking colloquially). And it's not just young brothers who use the term. I have heard distinguished African-American business leaders and artists, rappers and educators, musicians and stockbrokers bandy this word about in their vernacular speech. In an essay about the meaning of this word, author Gloria Naylor delineated a number of different ways that the *n* word has been used:

- As applied to a man who had distinguished himself in some situation that brought approval for his strength, intelligence or drive. "Did Johnny *really* do that?" "I'm telling you, that nigger pulled in $6,000 of overtime last year."
- When used with a possessive adjective by a woman—"my nigger"— it became a term of endearment for her husband or boyfriend.
- In the plural, it became a description of some group within the community that had overstepped the bounds of decency. Parents who neglected their children, a drunken couple who fought in public, people who simply refused to look for work, those with excessively dirty mouths or unkempt households—all were all "trifling niggers."

Contextually, it is possible to understand how Black people have learned to embrace the derogatory language and extract loving sentiments as well as adopt similarly antagonistic, venomous approaches. We are a creative people. Yet I can't help but think of recent national reports that cut to the quick using this very term. In 1992, for example, Marge Schott, a white woman who was the principal owner of the Cincinnati Reds, was called to the table (and later cleared) due to incidents when she allegedly spoke of her own players as *"million-dollar niggers."* Former Los Angeles Police Department detective Mark Fuhrman, who testified in the O. J. Simpson murder trial, was found to have consistently referred to Blacks as *niggers* during his years on the police force. And then there's the golf pro Fuzzy Zoeller. Although he stopped shy of using the *n* word, he utterly disrespected Tiger Woods in 1997 after Woods had become the youngest player and first Black to win the highest prize in golf, the Masters Tournament, by warning him not to lower the standards of the golf club by bringing what he considered low-class African-American delicacies to the table. You don't have to look to national news to find racist sentiments. Unfortunately, many of the people interviewed for this book had stories to tell of racist comments and name calling that occur to them regularly on the job, at the shopping center, at the playground with their children.

Rather than restyling stigma and anti-African racial slurs into something that we pathologically embrace, my question to us is, *"Why do we want to be considered in this way?"* and more *"What is an affirming term of endearment that we can use when we speak to one another?"* With all of our creativity that reaches back to the beginning of time, I challenge us to come up with something that will lift us to higher ground. For starters, why not try *brother* instead of the *n* word, as so many African-American people already do? In African languages, I bet we can find something better too. We owe it to ourselves to be free of the language that hurts our people. As Asa G. Hilliard III wrote in *Stolen Legacy* (1976):

> Mental bondage is invisible violence. Formal physical slavery has ended in the United States. Mental slavery continues to this present day. This slavery affects the minds of all people and, in one way, it is worse than physical slavery alone. That is, the person who is in mental bondage will be "self contained." Not only will that person fail to challenge beliefs and patterns of thought which control him, he will defend and protect those beliefs and patterns of thought virtually with his last dying effort.

What We Call Ourselves Matters

My grandmother, who was born in 1889, called herself *colored*. She referred to our people as *colored people*. That term didn't have the same meaning as in South Africa, where *coloured* is the term used for people we would call mulatto, octoroon, quadroon and even (East) Indians, although it included those folks too. (FYI: Most of the people in the world—more than 90 percent—have melanin in their skin! So, who is *colored* anyway?) People of African descent living in this country have experienced generations of inner churning as we have sought to recapture our identity. Why? Largely because our ancestors were stripped of their birth names and given Christian names, whose surnames reflected those of the slave owners. The ability to trace our specific family and clan lineage was obliterated almost entirely in this way. As a result, depending on where we have lived and how we have been received by others, we have been attempting to redefine who we are and what we call ourselves since we arrived on these shores. And we have used many appellations.

In Louisiana, for example, where there is a broad range of peoples, including French, African, West Indian and Native American, delineations are made based on color. At the grand cotillion balls that were so famous, not only for whites but also for us, people of color were called octoroons or quadroons, depending on how much non-Caucasian blood was in them. By law, one was considered to be not white, in the early 1900s, if he or she had one eighth of non-Caucasian blood in his or her lineage. Since our beginnings here, we have been chastised and ridiculed for being "of a darker hue," with non-Caucasian features. At the same time, we have, by force and sometimes by choice, become family with white folks, thereby creating a biracial group of people who are also often struggling to be accepted. The lack of respect for our origins in this country, coupled with the wavering views on who we are based on the color of our skin, shape and size of our features and texture of our hair have in large part led to our self-ridicule and self-deception regarding beauty and identity. (See the chapter "Mirror, Mirror.")

When it comes to what we call ourselves, it's no wonder that the definitions have changed in nearly every generation. What have our names been? *African* (Yes, it's true. Remember the AME Church), *Colored, Negro, Afro-American, Black* and *African American* have been the most widely used. The latest of these, *African American,* received national acknowledgment when Jesse Jackson ran for President in 1984. Currently, there are discrepancies about the differences between the terms *Black* and *African American.* For some linguistic experts, *Black* refers to the people of the Diaspora, or people of African descent in various parts of the world beyond the continent of Africa. In this context, *Black* is a more inclusive term that is supposed to reflect world consciousness. *African American* refers to people of African descent who live in or were born in the United States of America. Scholar John Henrik Clarke maintained that any term that doesn't reorient us to our homeland (land mass) is inaccurate. A further distinction deserves mention here. People living here but hailing from places in the Diaspora are becoming more interested in highlighting their specific land of origin, whether it's Jamaica, Brazil or elsewhere, rather than the Motherland. Thus, many people now refer to themselves as Caribbean American, Jamerican, Latin American, and so on. (For the record, there are hundreds of thousands of our people who speak Spanish as the mother tongue who are also African descended. Let us not fall into the fray of disparaging them for any reason. When we approach everyone, especially people of color, as brothers and sisters, we do a great service to humankind and, more, to ourselves.)

In addition, because many people are not singularly African American, Caucasian, Asian, European or Latino(a), awareness is growing that people of mixed heritage do not want to be defined racially. If your Mama is Jamaican and your Daddy is Chinese, what are you? Still others maintain that their ethnicity points directly to the Motherland; therefore, they are African. Although these people may live in America or elsewhere or were born there, they consider that they are from "the world's first people" and pledge their allegiance to that relationship. As purists, they consider themselves African, subscribing to the view of Malcolm X that "if a cat had kittens in an oven, you wouldn't call the kittens biscuits." Questions about ethnic identity will continue to be contemplated as we all work to honor who we are in relation to our bloodlines, our spiritual base and our contemporary insights.

As you consider the terms that you want to use to describe yourself ethnically, you may also choose to research your family genealogy to discover your true heritage. Some people are able to trace their families beyond North American shores. Others discover strong Native American ties. Still others find living relatives scattered here and throughout the world who have powerful stories to share that enrich all the lives touched. Take the time to find that part of yourself that you can. It has proven to be an amazing and satisfying process for many people. You should know that as meaningful as your connections may be to your other bloodlines, biologically your African connection is really the strongest. African genes are dominant. Science, in fact, has proven that all others recess in their wake. That's why an eighth of Black blood was enough to label you as a Negro down South. If you are looking at your own family and seeing some real light-skinned folk—like I have in my family—know this: Africans come in all ranges of colors on the Continent. As African-descended people, you have the ability to produce children of many different hues. We are a beautiful and diverse people. Let us revel in this knowledge.

Also, be aware of something extremely important. The tendency that many of us have to pursue lineages to the exclusion of our African heritage comes from the fact that we have been made to feel ashamed of Africa and what her civilizations have meant to world culture. A frightening document from the early 1700s shows just how sinister the effort has been to get us to deny our Africanness. Known as the Willie Lynch letter, this speech was presented as a tool to break the will of Africans in the same manner as horses are broken and bred, so that they may be enslaved indefinitely for what he refers to throughout the letter as "good economics." Here is but a tiny sample of this slave owner's hateful words:

> Then take the female, run a series of tests on her to see if she will submit to your desires willingly. Test her in every way because she is the most important factor for good economics. . . . Do not hesitate to use the bullwhip on her to extract that last bit of bitch out of her. Take care not to kill her, for, in doing so, you spoil good economics. When in complete submission, she will train her offspring in the early years to submit to labor. . . . Cross-breeding niggers means taking so many drops of good white blood and putting them into as many nigger women as possible, varying the drops by the various tones that you want, and then letting them breed with each other until the circle of colors appears as you desire. What this means is: put the niggers and the horse in the breeding pot, mix some asses and some good white blood and what do you get? You've got a multiplicity of colors of ass-backward, unusual niggers, tied to backward-ass, long-headed mules, the one productive of itself, the other sterile. . . . Both mule and nigger tied to each other, neither knowing where the other came from.

Every time I read even a sentence out of the document from which this is excerpted, I cringe—and laugh. I laugh as a defense mechanism. It is too painful for me to allow this information to seep into my consciousness. At the same time, it incites me to embrace and learn all that I can about my ancestors right now.

The Issue over Accents

A mystery surrounds certain accents. To hear the melody of a French speaker in the middle of a café in New York City can trigger longing for some people. The authoritative clip of the British accent seems to stir the American heart—as it makes its way back into key positions in this country that control the development of entertainment, publishing, fashion and business. Yet that same provocative mystique does not always translate to longing to speak or hear a Trinidadian lilt or a Nigerian flurry of syllables, a Jamaican or Mississippian turn of a sentence. Double standard? To be sure.

A few years ago I participated in a panel discussion during a powerful Black expo celebration in Chicago. One of the panelists was a successful Black female elder in the music industry. As she shared her personal story, included was the revelation that she had come from a Spanish-speaking Caribbean island and had spent the better part of her formative years learning an American accent. She had adopted standard English that had the no-nonsense accent of "I'm in charge here"—in other words, the accent of American business. While describing her studied transformation, this sister showed a glimmer of remorse. That only slightly nagging feeling stemmed from her misunderstanding as a young person of the beauty of her own identity, even as she felt the need to modify her speaking voice for the working world. As a Black Spanish-speaking woman in the music industry, she knew she had made the only decision she could, because she said she needed to come across as "blemish free." To that end, she even chose to call herself by a representation of her name that made her sexuality ambiguous, thereby not allowing any of the males sitting at the controls to close the door on her before she had her foot in it.

I've listened to a Jamaican brother with a similar story. When he arrived in America at the age of fourteen, my husband, George Chinsee, had a full-out Jamaican accent. His reason for adopting an American accent was for basic survival reasons. George explains, "Every day that I went to school, the kids would ask me to repeat myself again and again, even when I knew they heard me the first time." Rather than having to face this constant badgering, he too learned an American accent (although he readily reclaims his own now when he is in the company of fellow Jamaicans). It's harder to make these transitions if you start as an adult.

During the question-and-answer session of the panel in Chicago, a sister with a heavy Jamaican accent expressed her concern: "How can I, as an adult, get rid of my accent?" Before the audience could attack her question, the woman added, "It's not that I don't appreciate my culture or history. I love being Jamaican. I also want to develop my career." She said that while working at a temporary agency, she got to see first-hand how temps with heavy accents were routinely passed over for many corporate positions, particularly for administrative jobs that require telephone work. First impressions are lasting, and unfortunately our native "accents" are not often welcome for that role.

Although it shouldn't be (and isn't always) necessary, if you think that you need help adopting an American accent for business purposes, many sources are available to assist you. For at-home work, you can purchase tapes that teach English as a second language. Study the accents presented, and repeat the words until you make the intonations your own. Alternatively, you can research classes in your area that feature developing language skills. Contact community colleges, linguistics departments of major universities, secretarial schools and African-centered research centers that should offer the added bonus of sensitivity to your cultural language patterns.

Another option is to build your own businesses that support your cultural identity as it is. In Harlem, for example, there are blocks of African-owned businesses, run by Senegalese and Ivorian brothers and sisters. With their thick African-laced French, Wolof, Ewe, Ashanti, Bambara and Toucouleure accents, they are business owners with thriving companies supported by other Africans who make New York their home. It is possible to be you as you are and make it in America within and outside traditional corporate structure.

Sticks and Stones

Sticks and stones will break your bones, but words can never hurt you. Our Mamas reminded us of the importance of shrugging off negative comments as people hurl them our way. Their warning was valid, although not fully true. You *can* walk away from someone who is bad-mouthing you. I recently heard a beautiful story that illustrates this.

There once was a man many hundreds of years ago who had a great teacher. This teacher was very strict. He would give his students a specific task to complete and then leave them to handle it without further interaction. One of his students was a beloved scholar, appreciated widely in his community. The command given to this scholar was, "Every time you receive an insult, pay the person who insulted you." This was a bit baffling at first to the scholar. He thought he was a good man. He didn't remember straightaway that people insulted him, but as he went about his daily life, he saw that he did encounter insults regularly. And so he began to pay. Three years passed in this way, and the scholar was beginning to go broke. Then one day he came upon his teacher again. His teacher asked him, "Are you still paying for your insults?" "Yes, sir," the scholar replied. "And how long has it been?" the teacher wanted to know. The student knew exactly how long, down to the hour, that he had been paying for each negative comment. To that, the teacher told him to go to the gates of a faraway city, where he would find his real answer. As the student approached the gates, he could hear a man shouting out insults to everyone in his path. When the scholar approached this man, he sat before him. Immediately the enraged man began screaming out terrible words, to which the scholar began to laugh. He laughed and laughed. Finally, the wretched one asked him, "Why are you laughing?" The scholar, who was by that time absolutely broke, said, "I have been seeking out people to pay to insult me, and now I see that even when penniless I can get insulted by someone I don't even know." The lesson the scholar learned was that we needn't look for negative reactions to ourselves, nor should we be affected by them when they come our way. Having evenness of mind regardless of how people treat us is the ultimate way to live. In the purest sense, this is *how to be.*

Until we reach the point of looking beyond people's limited actions to their highest possibilities (as well as our own), it remains true that what people say to and about each other can hurt. A stepping-stone, perhaps, to being free from people's comments, whatever they might be, is to cultivate an awareness of seeing the good in others and choosing to respond to that. *Don't say anything if you don't have something good to say.* And never, ever speak when you are angry; then you don't have to take anything back. Choosing silence is an effective discipline and often the kindest action. To use the practice of silence artfully, consider resisting the temptation to respond to people when they lash out with negative comments—regardless of who they are and what your relationship is to them—and then immediately remove yourself from the situation. Later, after you've been able to process what occurred, you may determine to let it go or to respond in a carefully considered manner.

That's what my sister Stephanie decided to do when she was verbally abused a few years back at a nail salon in Baltimore. While waiting for her nails to dry, Stephanie noticed a white woman of about her same age enter the salon. It was nearing closing time, and the woman very excitedly announced, "I'm so glad that you're still open. I just *have* to get my nails done." She continued in a voice that filled the salon, "You see, I have a date with a dentist tonight, and I couldn't go on that date without getting my nails done." As the woman continued to talk loudly about what a great catch a dentist was, she was seated right next to Stephanie. After some time, Stephanie turned to her and said, "I'm glad you are going to get your nails done, especially since you have a date with a dentist." To which, the woman immediately turned her head and snapped, "What would you know, Buckwheat?!"

Stephanie was shocked. Apart from the fact that the woman had disturbed everyone's peace of mind by including them all in her conversation, Stephanie couldn't believe that such a thing would ever be said to her—certainly not at the end of the twentieth century. Stunned, she looked at the woman incredulously, got up, picked up her bag and walked out. Later, she had mixed feelings about her reaction. She says, "I was so surprised that I became speechless." Rather than dropping it, Stephanie did go back to the establishment, in which she had been a frequent customer, to speak with the manager. Stephanie confronted the manager about the incident, asking why she hadn't addressed the woman's outrageous comment in the moment, since she *had* been present. Naturally, the proprietor said she hadn't heard the woman. Stephanie left the salon saying that she would take her business elsewhere.

Buckwheat. For all intents and purposes we are in a new millennium enduring the same indignities as our ancestors did hundreds of years ago, and as many of our South African brothers and sisters are still facing today on many fronts, including the verbal assaults that label them *kaffir,* a term analogous to *nigger.* The ways that we respond to such outrageous comments depend on the circumstances and our own personal facility with the situation at hand. I polled many people about their reaction to Stephanie's encounter. Most were outraged. Quite a few believed they would have hauled off and slapped the offender (which could have led to a felony charge). In fact, one person said that the woman would've needed an *appointment* with that dentist instead of a date! Dozens thought a good tongue-lashing would have done her right (or would it have been stooping to her low level?). Others opted for creatively putting her in her place with words (a viable alternative). Still others felt it best to walk away. "Why even acknowledge her ignorance with a comment?" one person wanted to know. Clearly, this is a volatile topic. Being slapped in the face with a racist remark should qualify as a crime. Unless we respond to such vicious behavior so that the offender understands that the action was unacceptable, we run the risk of allowing that person to continue maligning our people without reprimand. This we cannot do. Although I do not recommend violence, I do need to point out here that both action and inaction are powerful.

A Meditation Before We Speak

Regardless of how people speak to us, we do not have to respond with verbal retaliation. We can take the high road. To develop the ability to do so, consider this exercise: Sit quietly for a moment and recall a time when someone said something that hurt you. Re-create the situation in your mind. Remember all of the details: what was said to you, by whom, in whose company, how you felt when you heard the stinging words, how you responded, what effect those words had on you in that moment, a day later, years later. Next, remember a time when you said something to hurt someone else. Again re-create the scene. What was going on? Why did you feel the need to lash out? What did you say? With what tone of voice? Who else was there? How did your words affect the person who was your target? How did they affect others within earshot? How did you feel then? How did you feel later? How do you feel now?

Although this exercise can be quite painful—remembering negative situations and feelings is always tough—it is valuable. Whenever I have gone through this process, I have discovered aspects of my personality that I don't particularly like. I find that I lash out at others when I am feeling unworthy, unhappy, less than. My target at those times is often someone who seems to be a safe scapegoat—someone with low self-esteem or some sign of vulnerability. In other words, I unconsciously pick someone who is the easiest to hurt when I am hurting. Even worse, I see that I easily slip into stereotypical thinking about others when I'm in this state. So my heart feeling of *one love for everyone* deteriorates into judgments about others based on unfounded or past impressions of them. The first time I realized that this was my M.O., I was shocked and embarrassed. I thought I was a "good person." How could I do such a thing? From my research, I see time and again that it is during our periods of vulnerability and self-doubt that we are most likely to take action that will hurt others. The easiest way to do that is through our words. As we expand our conscious awareness of our own goodness and that of others, we must cultivate the practice of using our words to reflect positive qualities—those that we know lie within ourselves and within all others, no matter who is in our midst.

Lazy Language

In an effort to be hip or cool, young people of all races don't take language seriously enough to be able to use it to their advantage. Some expressions we hear on television, in songs and on music videos, and in job interviews are: *um, you know, like, you know what I'm sayin',* *yeah.* Frequently, a person will say something like this, "Well, um, you know, I was listening to the radio, and, you know, I heard this dope track. It was, like, the new Erykah Badu joint, and it was the bomb, you know what I'm sayin'?"! Apart from the colloquial use of *dope,* which many worry over hearing so often because of its dangerous, if unconscious, reference to drug use, this sentence is cluttered with unnecessary, meaningless words. Jacob Carruthers of the Khamitic Institute in Chicago would call this *tef tef*—nonsense talk. Actor Will Smith encourages us all to speak efficiently so that we can be understood.

I work regularly with young people, helping them to fine-tune their ability to communicate clearly and effectively. What we have discovered together is that much of the use of such unnecessary fillers is due to a simple lack of thought, along with an improper use of certain aspects of the language. The latter refers most often to the use of the word *like.* It appears with incredible frequency in many young people's vocabularies, often more than once in a single sentence, such as, "I was, like, going to the store and then, like, I saw my friend," and "I was, like, thinking about my exam." As a modifier, this word is effectively used in a simile, a comparison in which one sentiment, idea or object is compared to something else. One might say, "Being in the elevator of that building was like being in a museum." What they really ought to be doing is making analogies: This is *like* that. The comparison is made to paint an immediate picture for someone of your meaning, to create a relationship between two different things that brings an image to life. To use *like* in this way can be a provocative way of getting even the most obscure point across.

Filling your sentences up with knee-jerk utterances, such as *um, you know, whatever, you know what I'm saying* and such is lazy and ultimately mind-numbing to those subjected to it, who do not themselves speak this way. While it is true that you can't judge a book by its cover, and poor use of any language does not necessarily mean a person doesn't have it "going on upstairs," people can be judgmental, and in important situations, one shot may be all you get. When you stop to think about it, you will see that what this language immediately suggests is ignorance (which really means "not knowing")—an unconsciousness on your part more than anything else. To acknowledge that your speech patterns are cluttered with unnecessary verbiage is one thing; to do something about it is quite another. Rest assured, the first step in change is awareness. The second step is action. Use this exercise for support:

- Make a written list of all of the words that you use too frequently. Ask someone you speak with often to help you.
- Post your list at your desk at work and in a key place at home where you're likely to see it regularly.
- Listen to yourself speak. Notice how frequently you say the words on your list.
- Select one word at a time to eliminate from your vocabulary or to use with meaning.
- Consciously choose to fill space with silence rather than useless words or *tef tef*.
- Review your progress weekly.

Profanity

Depending on the situation, profanity can be used artfully, distastefully or sloppily, just like other forms of lazy language. Shy of being a prude here, I must say that people today overuse profanity—in a big way. Our youth may be the biggest perpetrators, although they are hardly alone. No doubt, there is a lyricism to the way that many young people let curse words roll off their tongues. Countless educators attest to the prevalence of profanity in nearly all of their students' vocabularies.

What should our stand be on the use of profanity? Clearly, its use deserves closer examination. Plenty of us have no issues, because we can use it or not, as we choose. Others have cluttered their language to the point that they do not really *think* about what they want to express; instead, they just curse. Let's look, for example, at *"That bitch pisses me off!"* Clearly someone made someone else mad. Why? What happened? Rather than calling somebody a bitch, what do you really mean? It could be, *"That thoughtless neighbor of mine really hurt my feelings when she had a party and didn't invite me."* What about this scenario? *"What she did was f——d up!"* Something foul happened. How could that foul thing be described so that others would understand the import of the indiscretion? What about, *"Spending her money on clothes rather than a gift for her godchild's birthday was inconsiderate."*

Even more than these lazy uses of profanity that really just serve as stronger place fillers similar to *like, um, you know,* the frequent use of profanity to the point that it has become part and parcel of most interactions puts one at a disadvantage. Sometimes it's simply not appropriate. For example, many a musical artist has effectively included profanity in his or her lyrics, and it works (albeit it may be a point of contention). But when being interviewed on television or radio, it's no longer acceptable to fill up their speech with such language. Yet it is true that what we practice is what we preach. So you must realize that however you speak most of the time is how you will likely speak when you are in an unfamiliar environment. You may not find yourself with a microphone in your face waiting to answer a media question, but you may be in a job interview and discover that you slip up and let out a profane word that could wreck your chances. Remember, it's the conscious, artful move that makes a good game, not the sloppy, thoughtless one.

A Word About Slang

With all this talk about speaking standard English, it's important to remember that there is a beauty to our speech patterns that we can and should continue to nurture and use. Language is alive in its myriad forms. Among those forms is slang. Colloquial expressions, in-the-moment ways of saying things—all of this goes into the texture of how we communicate with each other. With each generation, new phrases and expressions arise due to technological innovations, current events, politics and business. By keeping an ear attuned to our communities, we will always be in touch with those intimate and familiar ways that we describe ourselves and our lives. We mustn't allow these nuances to fade away.

Spell It Right

Riding down the streets of nearly every urban center in the United States will reveal a startling fact: many people in this country cannot spell correctly. Billboard advertisements, storefront logos, even street signs regularly feature misspelled words. In Manhattan, where this is so prevalent, it is also true that many immigrants operate small businesses and represent those who speak English as a second language. Nonetheless, the dictionary is a great tool. More of us should use it.

Even if you think you are a great speller, double-check your spelling in the following circumstances:

- When you're creating a résumé. You'd be surprised how many résumés have misspellings. Many employers toss those without further consideration.
- When you are writing a letter to send to a client or potential employer. Be sure to spell the addressee's name and title correctly.
- When you are unsure. When in doubt, look it up or call the person's secretary!
- After you use Spellcheck or any other computer spelling program. Some words are not listed in these computer-based files. Further, you may have mistyped a word that is spelled correctly but does not represent your meaning.

A piece of invaluable advice that I received several years ago may help you: *Check. Double-check. Be clear. Crystal clear.*

Where Is It At? (Behind the Preposition!)

In my proper English-speaking household, we could never get away with certain phraseology, such as allowing a preposition to dangle at the end of a sentence by itself. We took great pains, my sisters and I, to rearrange our sentences rather than say something like, *"Where is it at?"* instead of *"Where is it?"* because such a question would cause my Daddy to give us a lecture about where the *at* belonged—*behind* the preposition. (I still feel like a real renegade whenever I write a sentence ending with a preposition!) One of the trickiest aspects of the English language seems to be the relationship between prepositions and objects. A *preposition* (at, from, on, over, by, to) is a word that is used as a connector between a noun, a pronoun or a word group that functions as a noun to another word in the sentence. The noun, pronoun or word group being connected is called the *object* of the preposition.

Generally prepositions come before their objects. When I was in school, it was unthinkable that an object would ever end a sentence. Although the rules have relaxed a bit, it is best to rephrase sentences so that prepositions can find their comfortable place, which might be nowhere, as in *"Where is it at?"* which should be, simply, *"Where is it?"* *"Where is he from?"* could gently be *"Where was he born?"* if *"From where did he come?"* seems awkward.

The Written Word

Learning to use language effectively is a twofold process, in that you must master use of both the spoken and the written word. Whether for pleasure or for business purposes, everyone has the occasion to compose communication in a written form. Words on paper carry greater weight in many instances than the spoken word, as they last longer than the moment. Because the written word has longevity attached, your written communications deserve extra time and attention. Keep in mind that you want to be clear and direct in all written communication. You should spell all words correctly, especially the name of the person to whom you are writing. When in doubt, check! Although the occasions for writing are endless, here are a few of the key writing necessities, along with suggestions for how to manage through them:

Business Letter

Formality rules with a business letter. Your language should remain upbeat and professional. This letter should be typed on standard business stationery, $8^{1}/_{2}$ by 11 inches. The structure of your letter should be as follows:

Your address
Date
[3 spaces]
[Inside address should give name, address and zip code of the person you are writing; optional when you have an established relationship.]
Name
Address, including zip code
[3 spaces]
Dear————: *[Use a colon rather than a comma, which is reserved for personal correspondence.]*
[2 spaces]

Body of letter
[*2 spaces*]

          Salutation *(Sincerely, or Respectfully yours),*
          [*4 spaces*]
          Your name
          Your title [*Unless it appears on the stationery*]
[*2 spaces*]
cc: [*List anyone whom you intend to receive a copy of this letter so that the recipient is aware.*]
bcc: [*If you intend to send the letter to someone else without the recipient's knowledge, put* bcc, *which means blind carbon copy, on the other party's letter, which informs him or her of the means of delivery of the information.*]

Reference Letter

When someone asks you to write a letter of reference on his or her behalf, it's because that person respects you and your reputation. You must do the same for yourself. Sometimes brothers and sisters decide to "hook a friend up" with a letter that says glowing things—whether the information is really true or not. Be aware that when you write a letter that recommends someone for a particular role, you should be honest in your comments. Consider whether you really think the person is well suited for the task. What qualities does this person exhibit that would be of use in the role? Do you really think the person is up to the challenge? If so, write the letter and include specifics within the letter that illustrate the person's value. If you are unsure about your feelings, let the person know. You may say, "I think it would be better for you to get a letter from someone who knows your skill level better than I do," or "I don't feel comfortable making this recommendation at this time." Although your statement may feel awkward at the time, it's far better than writing a fluff letter to a potential employer that helps no one. (Same goes for a reference call.) If you are going to write a letter of reference, be sure to include these points:

- State your relationship to the person in question as well as your credentials for being able to vouch for the person.
- List the qualities that make the person well suited for the task at hand.
- List any personality traits that make working with this person a positive experience.
- Provide an example of a successful interaction that you and this person may have had.
- Offer to be accessible for additional questions.

Personal Letter

For some people, a personal letter seems obsolete. I recommend a revival of the art. People receive so many bills in the mail that when they come upon a kind letter or note from someone, it really brightens their day. As one who is working at honoring others as you build your life, include the personal letter or note as a constructive and effective tool.

What you need is personal stationery, either with your name printed or blank. Select stationery that distinguishes your personality, by color, texture or other design elements. For women, personal stationery is typically smaller than the standard business letter of 8½ by 11 inches. For men, the paper differs from business stationery, but the size remains the same. When you write a personal letter, remember to be friendly, thoughtful and direct. The form of your letter is as follows:

> Your address [*which may be printed on your stationery, and which is optional*]
> Date
> [*3 spaces*]

Dear _____, [*comma here notes familiarity*]
[*2 spaces*]
Body of letter
[*2 spaces*]

> Salutation [*Sincerely, Love, Yours truly*—select one that is appropriate to your relationship with the person]
> [*4 spaces*]
> Your signature

If your handwriting is neat and clear, by all means write your personal letter yourself. You may also type it for legibility's sake!

The Thank-You Note

Whenever someone offers you a gift, an especially thoughtful gesture or some other kindness, you should send that person a note acknowledging the deed. The correspondence is best written on a piece of personal stationery that bears your name or on a blank note card. *Your note should be handwritten, not typed, no matter how busy you are.* In your note, acknowledge the receipt of the kindness with specificity, although you should not mention specific amounts of money that you receive from others.

Example between friends:

Dear Saundra,

Thank you so much for sending me such a beautiful bouquet of flowers. I received your package at the perfect moment, in the midst of a very full day when I really needed a pick-me-up.

Much love,

Sarah

Example between an employee and a manager:

Dear Mr. Stern,

I really appreciate the beautiful baby shower that you hosted for me and my wife. It means a lot to know how supportive you are during this period.

Thank you for being so thoughtful and generous.

Sincerely,

Robert

Example when you receive money:

Dear Aunt Jane,

I can't even express to you how grateful I am to have opened up your card and received such a generous gift from you and Uncle Wendell. Your gift will help tremendously as I launch my latest project. Thank you so much for your generosity.

Lots of love,

Stephanie

Cards

The greeting card industry is huge. All you have to do is go into a card shop to get a sense of the magnitude of correspondence that passes between people every day. The majority of the cards that are purchased today have prewritten messages on them, which invite you merely to sign your name. On this point, I am from the old school. I believe that when you send a greeting to someone, you should write your own message in your own handwriting. What makes the communication personal is your participation. My recommendation is that you choose a blank card with a beautiful cover. On the inside you can handwrite your message. Because such cards are often precious and expensive, you may want to compose your words on a scrap piece of paper and then record them on the card once your message is clear. If you do send a card with a precreated message, be sure to write a brief message of your own as well.

Example for a farewell card:

I wish you all good things in your new career!

Best, Herb

Example for a Father's Day card:
Dear Daddy,
I love you SOOO much, on Father's Day and every day!
Akilah

Invitations

When it's your turn to send out an invitation to an event, do it with style and clarity. You can create your own invitations or purchase ready-made stationery that will serve your purpose. The formality of the event will determine the type of lettering recommended for your invitation. For example, a formal wedding deserves an engraved or at least professionally printed invitation, while a baby shower can be initiated with the use of a pen on a preprinted card. However you send your invitation, be sure to include the following information:

- Date of the event
- Location, including address and directions when necessary
- Time of event   The more specific you are here, the better. If there will be a cocktail hour followed by a formal dinner, say so on the invitation. Even when the event is casual, such as a summer open house brunch, give beginning and ending times so that your guests have a sense of how to commit their time. Do note, as I was reminded, that in our communities, time is experienced, so events really begin when people get there and end when they leave.
- Dress code   This is very important. Check the requirements of the venue where you are having your event, as well as any specifics that you want to enforce. Then use a creative and clear way of delivering the information. State on your invitation specifically what you want people to wear, for example, "Halloween costumes required for admittance," or "Black tie only," or "Black-and-white, please." Follow up with a call when necessary.
- Who is invited   On the envelope specifically list those who are invited to the event: for example, "The Brown Family," which means you are inviting the whole crew, or "Mr. and Mrs. Brown," which excludes the children, or "Mrs. Swann and company," which means the whole office can come.
- RSVP telephone number and address *with* a deadline.

Politically Correct

Particularly when it comes to language, there is currently a growing concern in Western society about being "politically correct." From members of Congress to researchers at universities across the country, studies are being conducted to determine how best to address people and situations so as to avoid any verbal disrespect, intentional or otherwise. To that end, certain terms and phrases that were once considered appropriate have been altered to more welcoming and encompassing terminology. Following are some examples for getting around sexist language.

For:	Substitute:
Actor, actress	Actor
Anchorman, anchorwoman	Anchor, coanchor
Bellboy, bellman	Bellhop
Businessman, businesswoman	Be specific, such as stockbroker, entrepreneur
Chairman, chairwoman	Chair
Congressman, congresswoman	Representative, member of Congress
Female child (under age twelve)	Girl
Male child (under age twelve)	Boy
Female person (age eighteen and older)	Young woman or woman
Male person (age eighteen and older)	Young man or man
Fireman	Firefighter
Forefather	Ancestor
Mailman	Letter carrier
Policeman, policewoman	Police officer, law enforcement officer
Spokesman, spokeswoman	Spokesperson, representative
Stewardess, steward	Flight attendant, cabin attendant
Weatherman, weatherwoman	Weather forecaster, meteorologist
Workman, workwoman	Worker, wage earner

Here are terms to use that are respectful of people with physical and mental disabilities.

For:	Substitute:
Blind	Visually disabled (unless person is completely blind)
Crippled, handicapped, disabled	Physically disabled
A person with mental problems	Emotionally disabled
A person with severe mental problems	Mentally disabled
Deaf or hard of hearing	Hearing impaired
Mute	A person who cannot speak

YOUR QUESTIONS ANSWERED

1. I have been accused of talking too loud. What is an appropriate tone of voice to use in public settings?

When I have visited African and Caribbean cities, I have noticed that the volume that people use in speaking is much higher than in this country. The same is true for many Spanish speakers. Volume is culturally related. That goes for families too. Many people who come from large families speak louder, because they are accustomed to having to speak up to be heard. That said, the best way for you to control your volume is to listen to others and get a sense of the tone at which they are speaking. Be sure that you speak loud enough so that you will be heard clearly. And use what my sister tells her children is the "inside voice," a soothing tone of voice that carries to the people with whom you are speaking but not farther. Additionally, if you believe that someone is speaking too loud, gently invite the person to speak in a more comforting tone of voice. Describing that voice using anecdote is often an effective way of delivering the information.

2. I was recently out shopping and observed several children yelling and being generally disrespectful to the vendors. Is it appropriate for me to say anything?

It is your responsibility to speak up. A sister elder once said, "This *is* my business. Every Black child is my business. And back in the day when everybody felt this way, fewer of you were laying dead in the street and in jail and on drugs." The village. Don't raise your voice. There is a legitimate concern that the child may be armed, so you may be putting yourself in danger by scolding the child.

3. What can I say if I overhear someone making derogatory comments about Black people?

A young brother said he makes it his practice to remove himself immediately from any situation where people are degrading others. That includes when Blacks folks are doing it to each other. One sister suggested that you immediately ask, "Excuse me. Do you think that nobody can hear you?" Sometimes people need to be introduced to the idea that what they are saying must be considered more carefully. Sometimes you really do need to say something.

4. Someone has an accent too thick for me to understand. What can I do?

Make up your mind that you want to understand what is being said. Attitude is the biggest barrier toward comprehension in any language. Tell the person in the nicest voice that you can that you are having trouble understanding. Don't make it sound as if there's something wrong with the speaker. Ask the person to speak more slowly. As you listen, watch the mouth of the speaker. If you still need assistance, solicit someone's help.

5. Do I have to change my vocabulary when I am speaking with elders?

One woman told me that when she is with her friends, they often use profanity and colloquial language interspersed in their communication. In that environment, such language is natural. When this same sister visits her parents and older relatives, she eliminates the profanity and paints pictures with her language that her elders will understand. Using slang or other language of the moment may not be understood by her elders. Even though they have slang of their own, that does not mean that they either understand or welcome yours.

6. I recently witnessed a neighbor screaming abusively at her young child. How can I intervene?

Unless the child's life is in danger, it's best to address your neighbor when she has calmed down and when she is alone. You may invite her to tea or just for a brief chat. Be compassionate. Let her know that you understand how frustrating it can be at times to manage everything—especially young children. Offer to help out if you can to relieve her burden. Tell a story affirming how other mothers have used calm, even tones to deliver powerful messages. Don't attack her; it won't work.

Beyond Your Doorstep

In Africa . . . buildings are mainly there for sleeping, for ritual space and for storing food. But the actual life of the village is outside.

SOBONFU SOMÉ

I'VE always been told that how you behave when you're at home is your business, but what you do and say when you walk out your front door is another matter entirely. Some of us don't think much at all about this and just go about our business, living our lives. Yet when you consider it for a moment, you will see that life isn't quite that simple—mainly because the world is filled with more people than just you. And each of these people has an agenda, a view of how life is supposed to be and a way of being in that life, whether the person is aware of his or her ways or not. That's why codes of conduct exist, in an effort to create an orderly playing field, so to speak, on which people can carry on with their lives. Without such codes, it can become confusing, frustrating and even dangerous.

At the same time, no one should follow such codes blindly. We mustn't forget that historically these codes have presented many conflicts for our people. So as we explore the appropriate ways of *being* in daily interaction, we must take into account the absolute necessity of paying attention to what is expected. This may require research of many kinds—anything from a telephone call to a confidant, or from an event coordinator to a trip to the library. Next, we must run that information through our own internal filters to identify how appropriate the behavior deemed "proper" actually is for us.

If we take the time to cultivate a space within ourselves to contemplate our lives, we can find honest, kind and empowering answers to all of our questions. In this chapter we explore the many social situations that come up for us in which we want to navigate without compromising our needs or stepping on other people's toes. From the perspective of conscious living, we will consider *how to be* out in the world among others with grace. To do this requires a lot more than avoiding obvious faux pas, although that is important too. It means discovering how to create a balance between your own needs and desires and those of others. Getting to that balance requires that you have a good sense of what is expected of you in any given circumstance early on so that you can judge for yourself how to move forward.

Twelve Commandments for Getting a Good Start

As Brother James Brown so cleverly put it, we *do* need to get on the "good foot," as we navigate in this world. Once you break it down and consider how to make that happen, you'll discover that success lies in being optimistic, focused and informed. And that really isn't so hard! Here are some first-line guidelines:

1. **Center yourself *before* you leave your home.** Sometimes your mind can take you spinning into vivid dreams and fantasies, both opulent and disastrous. Don't get caught up in such distractions. Don't allow your mind to lead you along faster than your feet can carry you. Before you step out into your day, allow your spirit to awaken fully within your body. Welcome vital energy into each part of your physical body, by breathing it in, inviting it into every part of your being, from your toes to the very top of your head.
2. **Be of sober mind and body.** Avoid those substances, people, thoughts and circumstances that throw you off center. Stay away from excessive alcohol, legal and illegal drugs that are abused, too much sugar and anyone or anything that triggers out-of-control behavior on your part. Take a minute to think about what some of those things might be; you may find some secret behaviors that could use cleansing.
3. **Keep good company.** The elders' reminder is so important to healthy living. Ward off negative influences among those people whom you see on a regular basis. Stay away from gossip and intrigue, both of which can lead you away from your goals.
4. **Find out what to expect in a given environment.** What are the codes of conduct that govern where you are going to be today? Who will be there? What are those people's personality traits? What is expected of you? Are you prepared with the

materials, ideas and other essentials for which you will be held accountable? Do you have allies there?

5. **Approach each encounter with confidence.** Always remember that within you are all of the tools to manage your life effectively.

6. **Greet people warmly and sincerely, with direct eye contact.** If it's a business contact, include a handshake, an embrace if it's a family member or friend. Your initial eye contact will put the other party at ease, because you have communicated your goodwill. The only exception is when you are greeting people from countries where direct eye contact is considered rude, such as some Eastern and Middle Eastern cultures. A lowered head and slight bow may be more appropriate then, although businesspeople tend to follow Western traditions more and more often now. When in doubt, observe the way that others extend greetings before it's your turn. One way that African people greet each other is to place their right hand over their heart, sometimes holding the other person's hand while doing so, in a gesture of connectedness.

7. **Dress for comfort.** Find out the dress code for your activity, and then gauge your comfort within those parameters. Do as your Mama did for you when you were young: select your wardrobe the night before. By the way, comfort doesn't mean unfashionable. It means that you can feel free to express your individuality within the boundaries of the situation at hand, so that you can move with ease.

8. **Be honest.** How often do you misrepresent yourself in little ways? How often do you say that you have done something that you have yet to tackle? How often do you tell part of a story while leaving out pertinent details? In the end, the one you hurt when you tell untruths is yourself. That's because over time you come to believe that information is true when it really isn't. When you speak the truth, you can rest easy. You don't have to keep track of what you've said, because the truth is a constant. At the same time, be aware of the information that you share, so that you don't hurt others. Conscious honesty entails thoughtfulness. In some instances, the most thoughtful action is to bite your tongue rather than share hurtful information with others.

9. **When you don't know something, say so, or say nothing.** Be sure also to make note of it so that you can look it up later. To avoid embarrassing situations where you believe you should

know a piece of information and don't, stay on top of current events. Read at least one newspaper per day, including periodicals from and about the Diaspora. Watch the world news for a quick update.

10. **Stay true to yourself.** If you believe that someone is approaching you in a condescending, snide, accusatory or otherwise negative way, work hard not to allow that person's negative energy to affect your state. When a situation becomes hostile, don't stoop to that level. Instead, excuse yourself and move out of that negative space. Even if the person is your boss or parent, you can gracefully exit a situation that is counterproductive. (A great out is an emergency trip to the rest room when nothing else seems to work! You can compose yourself there and return clear-headed.) You want to be able to be alert enough to keep negative energy from interfering with yours.

11. **When interacting with others, consider their motivations and needs.** Often people ask questions or talk about subjects other than their core interests. This happens frequently due to a lack of clear thinking or a hidden fear about revealing one's pure intentions, not to mention a hidden agenda that requires a certain measure of secrecy. Listen carefully. Watch the person's body language. If you can discover the person's question behind the question, you will be better able to serve him or her and yourself.

12. **Recognize that people from other countries and cultures may approach life in different ways.** This includes rural versus urban dwellers, easterners versus westerners, and others. In your initial communication, listen for a common thread of experience that will help you to enjoy clear, open dialogue. Find an interpreter when you get stumped. Avoid slang in these situations. Search for words that explain and define what you really mean.

Now that you've got a good sense of how to prepare yourself to go out into the world and *be* with others, it's time to take a look at some specific environments that have clear parameters for behavior. As you examine these situations, keep in mind that the goal is always to move gracefully and efficiently wherever you are.

Praise the Lord

Lots of unwritten guidelines define how to behave in the house of the Lord. Just as you were taught to put on your Sunday best before you headed toward the sanctuary so that you would honor the holy day properly, you were also informed that you should put on your best behavior. What that behavior is today is a little fuzzier than, say, twenty years ago. A thirty-something sister from Des Moines, Iowa, considers folks' behavior in church today downright shocking. She says she can always tell the young mothers in the congregation, because they are constantly getting up and taking their children in and out during service, even when they are sitting in the front rows. "When I was growing up," says DeLora Jones, "my mother talked to me firmly at the door of the church. She told me that before we took our seats, we were going to make a bathroom stop, and that we weren't going to get up again until service was over. And that's what we did."

Appropriate behavior during religious service ranges, depending on the way in which your house of worship experiences religion (sitting still, call-and-response, "getting the Holy Spirit," shouting). It also has a lot to do with your spiritual orientation. I know in the Methodist Church where I grew up, there was to be no fidgeting, clapping or other outward signs of spirituality. We sat quietly and enjoyed the service. With each faith come a number of customs that you must learn so that you can be comfortable. Whether it's right to make your child sit tight throughout the service or not isn't as much the point as is understanding what's expected and finding a way to honor those rules and take care of your needs at the same time. Here are a few basics that should serve you in almost any house of the Lord:

- Dress conservatively. Usually that means that women have their shoulders and knees covered. One sister said that lap scarves are commonly given out at her church, especially for women sitting in the front row. No distractions, please! Men typically wear suits, or at least sports coats and slacks with a dress shirt and tie at Christian churches. In some modern houses of prayer the rules are relaxed. Err on the conservative side until you learn otherwise. And keep in mind that although going to church can sometimes appear like a fashion show, it is not. The hour of worship is set aside for inner cleansing. Dress so that you can participate comfortably.
- Arrive early. It is respectful to be seated before the service begins. In some instances, you have to arrive early to get a seat anyway. When you have young children, give yourself a twenty-minute window, so that you can all be seated and ready to focus on the lesson of the day when the service begins. Nobody wants you and your family to be crawling over them when it's time to turn the hymnal to the first song. While in the sanctuary, keep your voices down.
- Sit on the side aisle toward the back if you have to get up during the

service. This goes for parents with small children and anyone else who may need to leave the sanctuary early.

- Bring your Bible or other appropriate Scripture. In this way, you can leave the books already there for visitors who may not have one. As well, it will help you to get into the practice of using your own scriptural text on a regular basis. Leading a spiritual life, after all, extends well beyond Saturday or Sunday service.
- Greet others when you arrive, and acknowledge them before you leave. Being part of a spiritual community includes basic courtesies, starting with a welcoming spirit. Allow yourself enough time in your schedule so that you can be with the congregation. And by all means, greet the minister before leaving and reaffirm part of his or her message that struck you.
- As a guest, participate only when you feel comfortable. For instance, if you are visiting a Catholic church and you are not Catholic, you do not have to take communion. If you are at a mosque, synagogue or ashram where certain practices are foreign to you, sit quietly as they are practiced. Before you go to the service, it's wise to read up on the practices of that faith so that you will know what to expect. Make the decision to participate after you have had time to think and consider the meaning of the ritual.

Here are special guidelines for going to a mosque:

- Men and women often enter from different locations and do not sit in the same hall for worship. Removal of shoes may be requested.
- Women must have their heads covered, as well as much of their bodies. Attire is very modest.
- Men often wear robes, such as the *galabeya* that Senegalese brothers wear who parade so majestically in my Harlem neighborhood on the way to prayer. Because Muslims pray five times a day, however they are dressed for work is accepted at most mosques.
- Visitors should call in advance to learn of the guidelines for them. Showing up unannounced is inappropriate.
- Men and women do not touch one another unless they are family. Physical contact is considered far too intimate for relative strangers or acquaintances.

Mind Your Money

When it comes time to do your banking or otherwise handle your money, be discreet. Even now, during the ATM (automatic teller machine) days, people still go to the bank. And whenever it comes to money, tensions can run high, so at the bank people need to be extra mindful of how they manage their attitudes, their wallets and their personal space. News reports prove that when people stroll through banks, drive-throughs and sidewalk ATMs, they are easy targets. Many thefts can be avoided simply by paying attention. Here are some good commonsense reminders:

- Prepare your paperwork in advance. Nine times out of ten, you can organize your deposits and withdrawals before you walk through your bank's doors. By so doing, you will reduce the amount of time you have to spend in the bank and avoid having to wait to use pens or rewrite correspondence. You also will reduce the chance of others knowing your business.
- Stand several feet behind anyone who is using an ATM. Giving a person privacy while transactions are underway is both respectful and safe. Just put yourself in the person's shoes for a moment, and you'll see how much money you really have! Further, you shouldn't take money out of a cash machine or even read your balance if you think that someone is peering over your shoulder. Position your body so that no one can see around you. Look through the machine's mirror to survey the area behind and around you before you push the button asking for money. Once you receive your cash, immediately and discreetly count it and then put it away.
- Be cordial to everyone. Yes, the Golden Rule still applies! Be thoughtful and patient with everyone. In this way, you will be able to conduct your business and leave without experiencing unnecessary stress. As James Brown said when he popularized elder wisdom, *"Don't start none, won't be none."*
- Pay attention to people who are begging for money. Speak to them when you enter and leave the bank. They are people too. Acknowledging others with genuine compassion is both right and safe action. It often disarms people who could mean you harm. Although there is no rule that says you must offer beggars money, consider it. Follow your conscience on this issue. I normally give money to people who are obviously in need. When I can, I give them food or another item of value rather than money.

When You're Driving

Even with all of the literature and laws that provide safe guidelines for driving, lots of people don't pay attention to the rules of the road. Wearing your seat belt is the first and most immediate rule. Even if you're just driving around the corner, wear your belt, and make sure that everyone else in the car with you wears one too. If you are the driver of a car that others drive, be sure to adjust your rearview and side-view mirrors before you begin to drive. Keep the dashboard clear of any items that move. As far as points of etiquette go, here are some that several road trippers had to offer:

- Be mindful of the music that you play in your car when you have passengers. If you have a mixed group, such as teenagers and elders, and especially if you are traveling for long periods of time, vary the music. If the trip is short, play something that will be soothing to your elders or turn the music off.
- Watch the volume. Blasting your radio is rude when you are in earshot of others, not to mention what it does to your own ears. Be aware of others around you, and adjust the volume accordingly.
- Don't eat and drive at the same time. Pay close attention to the road. Apart from avoiding a potential accident, you should give your body your full attention when you eat. Drive to your destination, stop and then eat quietly. Your digestive tract will thank you for it.
- Watch out for other activities that can be distractions. Talking on the phone while driving has caused lots of accidents in the past few years. So has changing clothes. Pay attention to your immediate responsibility. If you must use the phone, invest in a speakerphone that will free up your hands, or pull the car off the road first.
- Keep change handy for tolls when you are traveling. You will avoid holding up a long line of cars while you fumble for money.
- Use your signals. A common courtesy (and a law), this rule will help to maintain traffic flow and ensure your own security as you change lanes. If your electronic signal is on the blink, stick your hand out the window like we did years ago, and let people know your intentions.
- Respect space on the road. Don't tailgate. No destination is so important that you have to mow some other car down to get to it. Calm down. Drive with strategy by looking ahead to see what's happening on the road. Learn alternate routes in case you run into unexpected traffic.
- Reserve your horn for emergencies. Part of being considerate is being quiet. Blasting your horn at a slow-moving car is more likely to start an argument than to get the driver to move faster.
- Drive with a clear head. Another no-brainer, yet thousands of people each year die or are critically injured in automobile accidents due to drunk drivers. Many prescription drugs as well as lack of sleep can distort your perception too. Don't drink and drive.

- Wear your glasses. If you need prescription lenses, get prescription shades or wear contacts with sunglasses when necessary.
- Be mindful of "road rage." Too many people these days are victims or perpetrators of violence on the road, because the roads are over-crowded *and* most people don't leave enough time to get to their destination. Be patient on the road. If a conflict ensues, turn the other cheek!

Public Transportation

Using public transportation systems can be your greatest test of paying attention to your surroundings and acting accordingly. Since I live in New York City, the land of the subway system, I sometimes ride. My husband often reminds me of *how to be* on the train. In fact, I hadn't ridden the train for several years when I had occasion to ride through two boroughs to get to a destination, and I had to take a refresher course on *how to ride*. I thought I was doing fine until my husband pointed out that I looked like a target. I was reading a book with a bag sitting by my side and my feet stretched out in front of me. He pointed out that I should have the strap of my bag wrapped around my wrist to make it less of an invitation to be snatched. Further, my outstretched feet were plopped dead in the way of anyone who wanted to pass. I have to admit I was oblivious to these things. The train wasn't full, so I thought I was okay. The final point was that it was fine for me to read a book but not without looking up at regular intervals to check out my surroundings. You never know who is going to pass through a subway car, and you have to be on guard at all times. In this case, a healthy dose of paranoia works!

I have to tell you, I hadn't been too interested in all of these precautions, but one look at statistics on public transportation made me think again:

- Always be aware of what's going on around you. That includes not wearing too much flashy jewelry or clothing on the subway or on the street. If you want to wear it, conceal it while you are outside.
- Make sure that your money is safely stowed away. Placing your valuables on your body is still the safest way to go. That's what our elders have typically done.
- Cover packages so that their contents will not be seen.
- If you are traveling a long distance, pack carefully so that you carry the minimum amount of luggage. Make sure that you keep track of your parcels throughout your journey.

A Note About the Taxicab

The award-winning play *Bring In 'da Noise, Bring In 'da Funk* illustrated an all-too-common occurrence for Black men in New York City (as well as other big cities around the country): taxicabs often just won't stop to pick up a brother or sister. Being a Black man in America has certain stresses, and this is one of them. Even brown-skinned foreign taxi drivers tend to veer away from brothers, whether they are wearing business suits or hip-hop gear. Some men have resorted to getting their female companions to hail a cab for them. I recommend that they continue to make the effort themselves and attempt to stay calm about it. I have a female friend who will hail cabs for Black men she does not know if they let her. The more Black men who get in cabs and pay their bills without a fuss, the more ridiculous cabbies will find their position to be.

- Do not go to sleep on public transportation. If you are really tired and afraid that you might doze off, stand up during the ride.
- Check your voice level. Your conversation should be your business, not that of the whole bus, train, subway car or plane. Keep your voice down. (See "When You Travel" for more.)

The Shopping Mall

One of the modern world's greatest marketing ideas is the shopping mall. In one huge space, you can find everything (well, almost) that you would want to buy. A bonus is the opportunity for some serious socializing. For teenagers across the country, the mall has turned into fertile dating ground. Whether you're headed to the mall to shop or to check out the cuties in the aisles, you should consider these points:

- Dress comfortably and appropriately for your trip. Consider the nature of your visit. If you are shoe shopping, for example, bring the type of socks or hosiery that you plan to wear with the shoes you want to buy. Avoid being too weighted down with heavy bags that will only get heavier as your day goes on.
- Be mindful of how you present yourself and how it might affect your ease of movement in stores. Being Black in America unfortunately still causes a certain level of fear in others, which ends up causing us lots of problems. In shopping malls, that fear is translated into our looking like suspicious characters. The whole issue over how Black people are looked upon in public places is a source of pain and con-

Pagers, Beepers, Electronic Organizers and Cell Phones

We are living in the age of technology—what African scholar Malidoma Some calls "machine-operated society." Nearly everyone seems to have a pager, a.k.a. beeper, and/or a cellular telephone. In fact, some people are using pager–cell phone combinations now instead of land-line phones. Apart from the alleged health risk of holding so much flowing energy to your ear for long periods, when you use a cell phone, there are some other factors that you should consider when you are traveling about your day with electronics in tow. Be aware of where you are and in whose company. Your electronic gadgets shouldn't be allowed to sound off in every environment. We all know the story.

One example of misuse of new technology that I have witnessed occurred at a Black writers' conference in Atlanta. Six prominent writers were seated on a dais before an audience of approximately three hundred people. As one of the young writers was addressing the audience, his pager began to ring. I thought that upon the interruption, he would have immediately put the pager on vibrate, something that he must have forgotten to do in the first place. Instead, he pulled the pager out of his pocket, raised it above the table and read the information it revealed— while pausing, without apology, in mid-speech. My husband often says to me that people call you when *they* want to talk to you, at *their* convenience. That doesn't mean, however, that *you* have to respond when it is inconvenient for you. This fact is especially important to remember in this age of immediate communication. Stay in the moment.

Here are some guidelines:

Dos	Dont's
Give your pager number to family members, key business associates and others who must reach you.	Put your pager number on your business card unless you use it as a primary source of communication.
Turn your pager on pulse or vibrate when you are in a meeting, in a quiet setting or otherwise indisposed.	Leave your pager on to ring when you are in a job interview, on a date, in a restaurant, at the movies or theater, or other such setting.
Limit your cellular phone calls to the minimum necessary (to keep the bill down and make efficient use of your time).	Allow your phone to ring when you are at a meeting, making a presentation or otherwise preoccupied, unless you inform your party in advance that you are expecting a call.
Use your electronic equipment to remind you of important scheduling concerns.	Program your equipment to alarm in the middle of your day during an awkward moment.

(continued on next page)

Pagers, Beepers, Electronic Organizers and Cell Phones *(cont.)*

Dos

Use 911 only as an emergency code for paging. Devise other numerical codes for other reasons, such as 311 for important but not threatening and 411 for "I have something to tell you."

Be mindful of what you say on your cell phone; the lines are not nearly as secure as land-line phones.

Respect the technology you have, and use it for important purposes.

Dont's

Don't abuse emergency codes or calls to others' electronic equipment when your call isn't urgent.

Don't talk about confidential information, give out credit card numbers or make any other points that should be discreet.

Don't overuse others' pagers or cell phones by calling too frequently. Nobody likes a nag!

---

troversy, but the reality is that we are often highly scrutinized, especially in places of commerce. What are the choices? As ugly as it may seem, if you want to be in an environment where your presence is not particularly welcomed, you may want to "look the part." For some brothers, this means leaving the oversized clothing at home. Others have said they just make sure they are clean and neat, and then they head out with a clear purpose. Even with such accommodation tactics, we continue to face discrimination. There are cases still pending in courts across the country regarding discrimination against Blacks in department stores and specialty shops. In one lawsuit, a Black man wearing a business suit was accosted by store security for shoplifting. The man turned out to be a judge who was merely shopping. He has begun litigation. Clearly, if you are wrongly approached, you should take recourse—but not in the moment. The safe action when you are being approached for any reason is to ask in a clear, calm voice what the charges are. Next, you should comply. It is not worth it to protest and resist arrest, because you may get hurt. Responding to law enforcement officials using phrases, such as, "Yes, sir" and "No ma'am" is not demeaning in these situations, by the way. Speaking so does not mean that you have sold out, either. Instead, it simply means that you understand that these people have the authority to put your life in peril, so you want to give them whatever they need to preserve your life for its real purpose. Stay aware of your environment. If you see anyone, call out to that person so that you can capture his or her attention. An eyewitness can be extremely helpful down the road and in the moment, because the person's very presence may encourage the security or police officer to act civilly.

HOW TO BE

- Park in a well-lit space as close to your entry point as possible. Safety must always come first. Sometimes vandals linger on the periphery of shopping centers waiting to rob or harm unsuspecting individuals.
- Don't go into the parking lot with too many bags on your arms. This could make you a walking target. If you must have lots of packages, travel with a companion. That person can stand inside the building near an entrance and wait for you to pull up with your car to load the packages safely.
- Be mindful of other shoppers. Particularly when the mall is full, be aware of your personal space and that of others. If you are traveling with a baby carriage or another large object, select a clear path on which to travel. Don't stop in the middle of a thoroughfare and clog traffic. Make your selections and wait in line patiently.
- Don't cut in line. One quick way to start an argument is to jump in front of someone who has been waiting in line. Yes, people do it all the time, and it's also true that folks get mad when it happens. If you and a friend are shopping together, one person can hold a space for both. But be mindful. If you have lots of merchandise to purchase and you bring armfuls up to the register at the last minute, you're bound to get sneers from behind. Those waiting are gauging how long they will have to stay in line, and they didn't factor you and your load into the equation.
- Leave any gathering that becomes rowdy. This is a special note to young people who hang out at malls. What can be great fun can also turn on you if you don't pay attention. Traveling in large groups is never a recommendation. But if you find yourself in one, keep your antenna up. If you notice an argument breaking out or another difference of opinion raising voices, step out of the circle.
- Know when it's time to go. That goes in any environment. At a shopping mall, you should leave before the stores have closed and security is decreased. The same goes for when you feel uncomfortable in a store. Don't spend your money where you're not being respected. Leave a store whose employees ignore you or otherwise don't acknowledge your presence. Then follow up with a written complaint to the store's management. It will help ensure that the retailer knows that an infraction has occurred and that you, the consumer, take issue with the action. If the store has something that you really think you want, what should you do? I say you live without it. If any of us accepts bad treatment but still gives the offender money, the cycle of disrespect will continue. Don't pay people to disrespect you. If you do, you essentially will be allowing the Civil Rights Movement to have been in vain—and that's the same as spitting on the ancestors.
- Watch your children. In a blink, children can run off and get lost in a

public space. All you need to do is look at milk cartons to see all of the missing children—many of them Black—to know that you have to pay close attention to your little ones. The news is also filled with horror stories of children who have been kidnapped only moments after they left their guardian's sight. Although you don't want to be overly protective, you do need to know where your kids are at all times in a large public place.

The Library

For those who use the Internet, going to the library may seem like an activity of yesteryear. Think again! Thousands of children and adults frequent public and private libraries across the country for access to all manner of resource information, including computers that hook them up to the Net. As libraries have grown to be technological magnets as well as meeting grounds for young people, the rules that have historically governed these institutions have begun to suffer. For the record, here's what you are supposed to do when you are in a library:

- Be quiet. Yes, that sign should be taken literally. Libraries are designed to be resources for people to conduct research, read and learn. Concentration is a key component of a successful library visit. Laughter, muffled whispers and other audible distractions are noticed. Resist the temptation to speak in areas marked for silence. Identify areas where open but soft or low communication is allowed if you must converse.
- Leave your food outside. To preserve the resources of the library, eating and drinking are typically not allowed. One college student shared how he sometimes sneaks in bottled water or juice and snacks. Because he is careful, he didn't think there was anything wrong with that—until he spilled something on an encyclopedia he was using. Doing the right thing means not sneaking. Check with your library. There often is a snack room or area where you can eat. If not, organize your schedule so that you can eat off premises and avoid damaging precious library materials.
- Follow the library schedule. Be aware of opening and closing times. Especially at the end of the day, prepare to leave a few minutes early. In this way, you will not forget anything, and you will be respectful of others who are leaving, including the staff.
- Don't hog the photocopier. Students and other researchers often need to make a lot of copies to facilitate their work. If you have to make fifty copies and someone arrives who needs to make one or two, be a sport and let the person make the few copies. By showing

courtesy to others in such small ways, you will discover others doing the same for you.

- **Return materials on time.** Why make the library police come after you?! It costs the city (i.e., you) money if your library is public. Further, it's easy to go back to your branch and extend your terms for keeping material rather than incurring fines. Moreover, it is inconsiderate to hold on to books overtime; others may need them.
- **Don't steal.** Obvious maybe, but you'd be surprised how many people have books that they checked out of libraries and never intended to return. If you need something that badly, go to a bookstore and purchase it, or call the publisher with the ISBN and order it. It works to no one's advantage to take something that is not yours. Don't do it.
- **Take advantage of community activities.** Attend as many as you can, from author visits and book signings to reading groups. Check the monthly calendar, and then arrive on time.

At Sporting Events

You might not even think there is etiquette attached to sporting events. Know that there are many unspoken rules, whether you are going to observe tennis, golf, football, soccer, basketball or even hockey. Number one on the list is to be on time, especially if you are seated near the playing field. You don't want to run the risk of disturbing the athletes or the other fans. If you are late, wait until a break in the game to take your seat. Here are a few pointers for specific sports:

Basketball and Baseball

One of Black folks' all-time favorite sports is basketball. When you are going to a basketball or baseball game, do your best to be on time, especially if you have seats that are courtside. Don't stand up and block other people's views during the game. Be discreet as you move about.

The same goes for when you are watching basketball, baseball or any other sporting event on television. Be aware of what's going on in the game, even if you are talking with others in your party. When a big play is happening, put a pause on your conversation. By all means, don't walk in front of the television!

Golf

Gawking at a golfer who is about to tee off can be more than a bit distracting. (Security actually have had to help Tiger Woods out on a few occasions so that he could have enough space to make a play.) The same goes for talking, cheering or otherwise making audible sounds right before a play. In the excitement, it may be hard to contain yourself. Just keep in mind your true reason for cheering: to give the player your moral support. The best way to do that in this sport is to stand in silence during a play and cheer once it is over, and before another player needs quiet to concentrate.

Tennis
This is a sport that requires personal decorum. People have been asked to leave when their behavior and outbursts have proven distracting. A tennis court should resound with utter silence, save the sound of the ball hitting the racket, the net, or the ground or sailing through the air. Of course, people do break out into cheers every once in a while. But stay cool!

Football
Not so strict, primarily because the arena in which a game is held is cavernous, watching a football game mainly requires that you be aware of the people surrounding you. Don't block their view, shout in their ears or otherwise infringe on their space. If you are watching a football game in someone's home, be sure not to block the television screen, talk loudly over the commentators unless those gathered aren't paying attention or strike up an unrelated conversation during a key play.

Hockey
Hockey just might be one of the most violent sports, and hockey fans are known to be unruly at the games. So be careful, and look out for fans who have consumed excessive amounts of alcohol or other substances. It's best to keep your distance from them. If you suspect folks getting out of hand, move to another location or leave the stadium. The dress is casual, and so is the mood.

Boxing
Although clearly a violent sport, the pomp and circumstance surrounding boxing matches, especially those at high stakes, is befitting a black-tie ball. People usually dress up, wearing cocktail attire, if not full-length gowns for women and dress suits or tuxedos for men. When the match begins, everyone should be seated. And you don't get up until a round is over.

Conventions and Other Large Gatherings

Many people travel for work or pleasure to large gatherings, such as national sorority or fraternity meetings and professional, scientific and civic seminars and conventions. Even when you are going just for fun, you will enjoy yourself most if you pay attention to the structure of the event:

- Get a copy of the agenda and study it carefully. You will learn about all scheduled activities, including meals that may be prepaid. When you plan to attend an event, read carefully to learn what is required, including time of the events and dress codes.
- Wear your name tag. At most large functions, name tags are provided to all registrants. This helps people to get to know one another by name more readily. It also serves to inform staff of who has legitimately registered for an event.
- Be professional. Often people go to conventions as representatives of their company—all the more reason for you to be graceful and productive. Make your time count, so that you can go back to work with a glowing report. Don't use this time to party.
- Pay attention during meals. Wait until everyone on the dais is seated and the invocation is made before you eat. You will need to exercise patience, because large luncheons and dinners often take time to get started. At your own table, *you should not begin eating until everyone has been served* unless someone is waiting for a special meal or isn't eating during that course.
- Don't leave the room while the keynote speaker is addressing the audience. Your movement in the room can be distracting. Unless it's an emergency, wait until he or she has completed speaking. The same goes for any other speaker. There's always a short break between speakers when you can discreetly get up and exit the room.
- Dress appropriately. If your convention is work related, you may want to dress more conservatively than when you are on a pleasure trip, especially for evening functions. Find out what the dress code is for daytime and evening activities, and be sure to pack accordingly. Err on the conservative side.
- Follow the order of the room when asking questions. If there is a microphone set up, go to the mike and wait to be called on before speaking. Raise your hand when this is expected, but don't keep your hand raised when others are talking. Pose your question briefly, first stating your name and affiliation. Speak so that everyone can hear you. Listen for the answer. Thank the speaker for addressing your question.
- Follow up. If you meet colleagues, mentors or other interesting people, be sure to write a note of acknowledgment to each of them. Perhaps the speaker at a luncheon inspired you; let that person know in a timely manner. Make your contacts last.

When You Are the Guest

This book talks a lot about what to do when you are in charge. It is also important to focus on how to behave when you are the guest. After all, the list runs long for how many occasions you will have to take on that role—a wedding, a christening, a funeral, a weekend away, a foreign celebration. The way that you conduct yourself when you are not setting the rules and others are hosting you will make a lasting impression. The philosopher Ptahhotep wrote, "Be generous as long as you live. . . . Your kindness to your neighbors will be a memorial to you for years, after you satisfy their needs." By keeping a few pointers in mind, you can ensure that the memory is powerful and pleasant.

The Art of the RSVP

I probably don't have to tell you, but, for the record, Black folks are not known for being prompt when it comes to responding to invitations. Whether it's for a wedding, a party or some other function, we are famous for showing up without letting the host know in advance that we are coming. To be fair, this hands-off attitude with respect to the RSVP is not exclusive to us. If you look at etiquette columns in your local newspaper, you're bound to see mentions of this plaguing problem. As American society has become more relaxed about everything—dress codes, relationships between generations and work ethic—so have we become lax about the basic courtesy of letting people know whether we're going to show.

Thelma Golden, former curator of the Whitney Museum of American Art in New York City, thinks it's high time we woke up to good manners on this subject. "I plan events all the time and take a lot of time making sure that there will be enough food, space and entertainment for the numbers we expect. When people show up without letting us know, then we have to scramble around to find them a seat, especially if it's a sit-down dinner." For Thelma, people who don't RSVP create real roadblocks when it comes to her being able to do her job. For the ones who fail to inform the host of their intentions, it can mean embarrassment upon arrival. For clarification's sake, here are guidelines surrounding the RSVP, which stands for the French words *Répondez s'il vous plaît,* which mean, "Please respond":

- When asked to RSVP by a specific date, it's because your host wants to get an accurate count of how many guests can be expected—a number that he or she shares immediately with a caterer. If thirty people who have failed to RSVP (or even five, for that matter) show up for a formal sit-down meal, there may not be enough food or seating. Out of respect, mail your reply card by the specific date, or call in advance to indicate your plans.

- If you find that you cannot attend an event to which you have RSVP'd, contact your host with that information—even if it is on the same day. I can't tell you how many dinners I have attended where there have been half-tables empty, with wasted food.

- If you receive an invitation that is addressed only to you, do not assume that your spouse, partner, child or other companion is invited too. A conscientious host sends an invitation that specifies who is invited. Should you be unsure, pick up the phone and call to find out if you can bring someone along. Know, however, that you should word your call gracefully. For many events that include food, hosts must be extremely careful in their planning to stay within budget. If they have not already invited you to bring a guest, the omission may have been intentional. Make your call without any emotion attached to it, save compassion for your host.

- Don't play dumb. If you are not invited to an event, don't arrive and pretend that you have RSVP'd when in fact you have not. Instead, if you want to attend an upcoming event, work in advance to secure an invitation. Contact the organization or host directly, and request the opportunity to attend. Express clearly and succinctly who you are and why you believe that you should attend the function. Of course, if you know someone who is part of the planning committee or otherwise has some pull with the organization, you can tactfully ask the person to help you. Be careful, though. You don't want to come off as a nag or a freeloader. *Requesting favors is political.* Assess your desires and determine if your attendance at the event is worth cashing in on a favor.

Place Cards

Casual entertaining has largely replaced formal affairs. For this reason, when you are invited to a formal dinner, you may not know the ins and outs of what to do. Common sense, of course, can be your guide. For some people, the excitement of the moment overtakes them. One obvious faux pas has to do with place cards. Typically, for formal meals the host will have spent a considerable amount of time planning the event. This includes organizing a seating chart that places people near one another in a strategic way. In some instances, the host wants people who don't know one another to be introduced and have an opportunity to talk. Whatever the host's strategy, your role as a guest is to sit where you have been assigned.

You will receive your seating assignment either when you arrive at the event or at some point before the meal begins. Your name will be prominently displayed at a specific table setting. Even if you wish you could sit next to someone across the table, resist the urge to switch place cards. Believe it or not, people switch them all the time, which throws off a host's careful planning and is truly an arrogant act. Stay put, and experience the event fully. You are bound to discover that you are in exactly the right place for you, and you can harvest wonderful experiences if you allow yourself the presence of mind to do so.

At a Wedding

Families put a great deal of money, thought and effort into creating a beautiful wedding that will celebrate the union and make guests comfortable. The success of this big yet intimate event depends on everybody's participation. Here's what you can (and should) do:

- **RSVP on time.** This one simple task cannot be emphasized enough. Let folks know your plans. If they change, even at the last minute, pick up the phone and let the couple know. Your absence could mean hundreds of wasted dollars.
- **Follow the dress code.** For formal weddings, brothers really should wear tuxedos, although many younger men choose not to. Sisters have greater flexibility, but a summer sundress will not replace an evening gown! For cultural weddings, couples often request that guests wear African attire. This can range from a West African ensemble to a batik pocket square. As the wedding becomes less formal, use your discretion, but remember that the occasion is very special and deserves celebratory attire. Women should stay away from white clothes, so that they don't compete in any way with the bride. (See "We Are Family" for more.)
- **Come offering your full support.** A wedding is a sacred event. In African tradition, the guests are equally as important as the couple and the families. The reception itself traditionally represented the offering of the new family to the neighboring community. Through the feast and entertainment, the guests were invited to welcome the couple into their community as extended family. To honor the spirit of the event, you should bring your best wishes and prayers for a happy union. If you are feeling envious or cynical about the nuptials, stay home.
- **Give a gift.** If you are invited to a wedding—even if you don't attend —it is customary to give a gift to the couple. The most thoughtful and practical gift may be something that comes from their bridal registry, which lists the couple's personal choices to start their life together. If you decide to get creative, make sure you keep the couple's taste in

the forefront of your mind. (Our best man, for example, gave my husband and me a wall sculpture with inspirational poems and images about love and marriage that he and his wife designed. It truly is beautiful, and the design elements reflected our personal style.) You can mail the gift to a secure address or bring it to the wedding, if you plan to attend. Many people opt to mail the gift, so that it doesn't have to be transported again from the wedding to another location.

- Don't bring along people who were not invited. When in doubt, ask. The wedding invitation should be clearly addressed to those who are invited. Usually both partners in married couples are invited, as are engaged couples. When you are just dating, your partner is not automatically invited. Children are not always invited either. Not everybody likes kids, and even when they do, they may believe that certain times are reserved for adults, especially the reception. Unless you see their names listed, do not assume that you can bring them. In some instances, couples set up baby-sitting services for young children during the wedding and allow children to attend the reception. Check in with the couple when you are unsure, or make arrangements for your children to be cared for during the festivities.

At a Christening

The best guest at a christening is someone who comes offering love and support for the infant's spiritual well-being. The godparents at a christening, of course, have an integral role in supporting the activities. (See the chapter "We Are Family.") Most of the other people who are invited are close friends and family. Your guidelines:

- Let the family know you will be coming. Usually there is a communal meal afterward that requires planning.
- Come to the sanctuary on time. Christenings often occur midway through a regular church service and are group events, with several children being christened in succession.
- Dress for church, in conservative attire.
- Find out in advance if you can take pictures in the sanctuary.
- Bring a gift. People often give money to the child in the form of cash, checks or stocks and bonds. You may also give personal items.

At a Baby-Naming Ceremony

Guests at this sacred event are expected to come with full offerings of love and support. Family members play a key role in this event, as they are called on to watch over the child throughout his or her life. Guests can participate in the festivities by bringing offerings of food, money and other personal or spiritual items for the child, especially an item of clothing or a wrap for the child. Traditionally, these gifts are left at the doorway of the family home, upon guests' arrival. As this event marks the transition of the child from the spirit world to the world of human beings, it is considered holy and is treated with great respect. At the same time, people have lots of fun. (See the chapter "We Are Family" for more.)

At a Funeral

Death is a fact of life. But in America, it makes most of us uncomfortable. People don't quite know what to do when it happens to someone close to them, a neighbor, a colleague. The appropriate way to respond, *how to be,* as it relates to death is not so easy for us. Part of the reason for the discomfort, some scholars suggest, is that we no longer have a strong base in rituals. Rather than allowing for the grief process to run its course, many of us work hard to stuff our feelings and appear "okay." Even during times of death, real men aren't supposed to cry, right? Well, if you want a healthier approach to death, consider the ways of the Dagara people of Burkina Faso. For them, the ritual of death, essentially the funeral, incorporates all aspects of grieving—from the women shrieking in unison to the elder men preparing sacred space to invite the soul to transcend into the land of the ancestors. People are encouraged to express their grief, with everyone in attendance having a role so that balance ensues.

In this country as everywhere else, the family needs support in so many ways after a loved one dies. Even before the funeral, you can be of help by calling to offer your condolences, inquiring about any needs that the family may have and then following up immediately on fulfilling their requests. Bring prepared foods—your loved ones' favorite dishes—in the first days and over time. Pay attention to the bereaved during the first few days of their loss, as well as in the coming weeks and months. Grief has a long life cycle. For the funeral itself, you can follow these steps:

- Find out the date(s) and duration of the funeral. For a traditional Dogon funeral in Mali, West Africa, the ceremony lasts for six weeks and is a communal activity that occurs only once every twelve years. So although bodies are buried upon people's departure, the actual ritual occurs as a community event. In the Jewish tradition, the body must be buried within twenty-four hours. In this country, Christian families tend to organize funerals as quickly as possible, setting the date for as soon as the farthest-traveling relative can arrive. If that period of waiting lasts for a week, loved ones often visit the family homestead each day and sit with the family to provide support.

- Arrive on time to the wake and/or funeral. Sit quietly upon arrival. Be sure to approach the family, who will be seated on the front pew. Offer to shake hands with each person as you express your condolences. Speak sincerely, from your heart, when you greet the family. Offer your love, support and any brief personal memories that you may have of the deceased.
- Don't feel obliged to approach the body if it is an open casket funeral. You can graciously move directly to the family.
- Sign the guest book. The family will appreciate knowing who has come during their hour of need. Furthermore, they need your address so that they can mail thank-you cards.
- Wear modest clothing. Black used to be required for funerals and memorial services. A dark dress or suit will always work. These days, however, many people choose bright colors in their efforts to celebrate the life of the one who has passed.
- Send a gift. People often order flowers for the sanctuary or the family home. Check with the church or family organizer to see, however, if other requests have been made. Frequently families prefer contributions to be made to a specific charity. (See "We Are Family" for more.)

At a Restaurant

When you are a guest at a restaurant or joining a group of friends, consider these pointers:

- Be on time or even early. If you know that you are running late, call the restaurant to leave a message for the party you are meeting. If you learn of your lateness in time, call the person at home. It can be very awkward for the party who is waiting for you during your delay.
- If you have dietary restrictions, let your host know when you accept the invitation for a private party meal. Otherwise, at a restaurant your needs can usually be accommodated.
- Wash your hands. Germs really do kill. More people than you would like to know have contracted serious diseases due to eating with dirty hands.
- Wait for your host to arrive before you begin eating anything.
- If you are part of a group, it is customary to stand at your seat until all parties have arrived. Only then sit down.
- Be sure to meet everyone in your party before sitting down. If your host doesn't handle the introductions, do so yourself.
- Limit your conversation to pleasant subjects during the meal. Don't underestimate the connection of your thoughts, words and actions.

Speaking about positive topics as you eat will aid in your digestion, as it also helps you to maintain a positive relationship with your host and other guests.

- Bring along enough money to cover your meal, although when you are someone's guest, it is customary for that party to pick up the check. If you are part of a group, decide in advance how you will pay for the meal, then assign someone to be the banker. Collect money or credit cards discreetly, making sure to include the tip for the entire bill, preferably 20 percent.
- If you have to cancel your appearance, don't give the task to an assistant. Make the call to your host yourself.

At a Dance

Years ago, it was all up to the man to initiate dancing at a social event. In early American culture, middle-class women used dance cards that their suitors wrote on to request "the pleasure of this dance." Those days have long gone, as have many of the formalities of dancing in the Black community when the man formally asked the female to dance. At many contemporary dance spots across the country, women dance with women and men with men, while a few couples join up here and there. This actually is a common West African practice. In ritual dancing, people of the same gender often danced together during big celebrations. It was a way that everyone got together without participating in intimate activity in public. Young folks today are returning to that practice. Others are just plain nervous about how to strike up a conversation that will get to square one. What are the new rules?

- Both men and women can invite each other to dance. A woman is generally not considered too forward these days if she goes for it. What she may find, as men have long known, is that the object of her interest may say "No." If that happens to you, move on. No need to pout.
- It's okay to dance by yourself or with others of the same sex. If someone joins you on the dance floor, don't exclude those with whom you have already been dancing.
- Acknowledge your partner when you want to stop, and then leave the dance floor.
- When a slow record comes on, thank your partner and begin to walk off the floor if you don't want to dance.
- Don't lie. If you don't want to dance with someone, don't fake fatigue and then get up two seconds later to dance with someone else. You may hurt the person's feelings. Instead, just say, "Thank you, but not now."

In Another Country

Learn as much as you can about the culture you will be visiting before your arrival. This will allow you to be the most gracious of guests. Read about the country you are planning to visit, specifically the customs that are accepted and those considered rude. Look for literature written by locals, such as the newspaper or magazines from there so that you get a true flavor of the people. If you are not fluent in the language, take a translation dictionary along, and practice a few basic phrases. (See the chapter "When You Travel" for more ideas.)

Overnight Stays

When the opportunity knocks and you are able to take a friend, a coworker, a family member—even a lover—up on an offer to spend the night, the weekend or an extended stay, do it with style. A little bit of forethought can go a long way. Unfortunately, the excitement that people experience when it's time to pick up and go, along with the anticipation of the fun you're going to have, can get in the way of your paying attention to the little, all-important details. That's what happened when a couple came to visit interior designer Sheila Bridges, at her summer home in the Hamptons.

These friends were stranded out on Long Island one summer night. As they were heading back home, they remembered their friend Sheila and "dropped by" without calling ahead (the first indiscretion). Because they had made a long trip in vain, Sheila invited them to stay for a few days, and they did so but then left without showing any consideration for their host. In fact, according to Sheila, "I had to ask them to buy water, because they had used all the water in my house. When it came time for them to leave, they walked out of my house with the water bottle in hand!" Yes, you'd be surprised at how unconscious, and selfish, people can be. This couple simply wasn't thinking about the generosity of their host or her needs.

To keep yourself on track when you go away for the weekend or longer to someone else's home, consider the following pointers that were gleaned from brothers and sisters across the country:

• Be clear on the date(s), time and duration of your visit. For example, if you are planning to visit someone for a long weekend, find out when the weekend starts. In the summers especially, long weekends can begin as early as Wednesday or Thursday afternoon. Rather than showing up on one of those days, clarify the date of the beginning of your stay as well as the end—*before* you arrive. Even if you want to renegotiate your end date, agree on the initial parameters from the start.

- Bring a gift. It is customary to bring token gifts of appreciation for the home when you visit someone's home, whether you stay overnight or not (even when you're staying with family). The practice dates back to ancient African cultures. For nomadic people who often move to follow food and water, a gift to a family that would be providing you with food and shelter represented a peace offering and indicated one's sincere appreciation for the convenience being granted them. Gifts historically ranged from foodstuffs to jewelry and fabric, either for all living in the homestead or at least for the elders. Popular choices today are candles, potpourri and incense, a picture frame, flowers or a good book. If an event will be happening during your visit, you can offer a bottle of wine or a nonalcoholic beverage or dessert for the occasion. The latest CD of your host's favorite artist would be an extra-thoughtful treat. What's important to note here is that the cost of your gift is of the least importance. It's the thought that counts, so make sure to think before you buy. You are offering a gift to your host in gratitude for the invitation and privilege to enter into their private life.

- Be discreet when you have sex. Another obvious point that lots of people forget. You know how it can be. You have finally stolen away from your busy life. Here you are with your sweetie, and you want to be intimate. There's nothing wrong with that. You just have to pick your moments. One couple came out to Martha's Vineyard, Massachusetts, to visit a work associate and her family at their summer home. Knowing that children were on the premises and that other adults were in the house, they still threw caution to the wind. They got busy and *pretty noisy too.* Not only did the host hear their hardly muffled voices, so did other guests. That's downright rude. If you want to have sex, do so quietly and/or when no one else is around. Also be considerate and responsible about cleaning up afterwards.

- Follow the household schedule. Find out if there is an agenda for your visit before you arrive. Families normally have set hours for eating meals, and you should honor these times. If special outings have been planned, determine meeting times, suggested attire and probable cost for each event. Do not assume that your host will be picking up the tab. Be on time. Don't stay in your room all day, either. When you visit someone else's home, you aren't coming to get away, or you should have gone to a hotel. Part of the fun in staying with others is spending quality time with them.

- Pick your conversations carefully. You may want to start out listening to the flow of conversation. As you have topics of interest to discuss, introduce them subtly so that you can engage in meaningful discourse, as opposed to argument. Virtually any topic can become a lively and revealing area of exploration if approached so that every-body feels welcome to participate. Don't judge others' comments as you make your own.

- **Volunteer your assistance.** No matter what your state of mind, you should pitch in and help with the chores of the home, unless there are others clearly assigned to do so. Even so, it is thoughtful, for ex-ample, to offer to help in the kitchen, anything from preparing a dish to making tea or clearing the dishes off the table—and mean it. Being of service is key to a good life.

- **Clean up.** Keep your private space neat and clean as well as what-ever common areas you use, such as the bathroom. There's nothing worse than a slob's staying at your house. Be neat; your hosts will appreciate you for it. Before you leave, make sure that you change the bed and straighten up the room, unless someone else is defi-nitely going to handle those responsibilities.

- **Follow up with a thank-you note.** A brief, handwritten note will suf-fice. Include your gratitude once again for being able to stay with your host. To ensure that you send it in a timely fashion, keep a box of thank-you notes in your bag. You can compose the note on your way home and drop it in the mail right away, before you become preoccupied with the rest of your life.

Long-Term Stays

It used to be that when Black people traveled, we always stayed in somebody's house, whether it was a relative, family friend or solid re-ferral. Hotels and motels weren't traditionally part of our travel experi-ence. When the trips extended for long stretches, it generally turned out fine, because hosts and guests worked out their arrangements for how they would live together. You can take a page out of our elders' book if you are planning an extended stay at someone else's home. First off, get clear on the ground rules right away. Be respectful of how your presence affects your host. Consider these suggestions:

- Make your bed. Basic, right?
- Keep the room the way it was when you got there. Ask for hangers, closet and drawer space, or keep your clothing folded neatly in your suitcase.
- Discuss with your host financial contributions for such things as food, use of the phone or other business machines.
- Be prepared to participate in light housework—clearing the table, doing dishes, and so forth.
- Be clear on the nature of your stay. If you are staying at someone's house because the person is lending you the space, it is very differ-

ent from when you're coming to visit. Discuss with the host what your itinerary is going to be so that you know what days you are committing to spending time with each other. It would be rude to arrive under the guise of coming to visit the person, and then becoming so busy that you don't have any time to spend together.

- You should always check on the times when phone calls are considered acceptable—what time in the morning and what time at night. Be mindful of how long you stay on the phone, particularly if the person does not have call waiting.
- Find out if your host has any "curfews" regarding when you are expected to be at home. If you intend to spend the night out, give the host a call to relieve any unnecessary worry.
- Make sure that you bring your own clock and personal amenities. The only things that you really don't have to bring are towels and toilet paper. Have all other hygienic items with you, including toothpaste.
- Be sure to tidy up the bathroom after you have used it, whether for a shower or bath.
- It's traditional for people to give parting gifts upon their departure. It's not mandatory; it's a nice gesture. And it depends on what else you did while you were there: Did you prepare dinner one night? Go out and buy food? Take your friends to a restaurant? If you're always contributing something, you don't necessarily have to do more. A thank-you note is always appropriate.
- Make sure you are aware of any security or alarm system in the house.
- If you are expecting messages, find out how to retrieve them so your host doesn't become your "secretary."
- If you've rented a car, find out where you can park it, so that you're not constantly causing a problem. Be considerate. If you are staying in an apartment building, make sure you park the car so that you don't get tickets every day.
- Be clear about your arrival and departure times and dates, especially if your host is involved. If your host is providing transportation for you, give your host ample notice of when you have to leave and if you have a delayed flight. Check airline schedules.
- Be clear about inviting other guests to the home. Don't make assumptions about who can come over for meals or to spend the night. Discuss this subject with your host in advance.
- If you want to have sex in someone else's house, get a gauge on how your host will feel about it. A lot of Black folks will take exception to your even thinking about doing it at their house! If you get permission, by all means, be discreet. Make sure your door is locked. Strip the bed of sheets and pillowcases and wash them yourself. (Don't

leave the dirty sheets for your host.) To keep down the noise, one brother suggested, "Bring an apple."

YOUR QUESTIONS ANSWERED

1. If I purchase tickets to an event for two or three people, am I responsible for delivering their tickets to them before the event, or can they pick them up from me?

The most efficient way of delivering the tickets is the solution. Make a decision together as to how your party will receive their tickets. Be clear in your communication and certain that your delivery system is secure.

2. In a movie theater that is crowded, is it wrong to hold a seat for a friend who said she would be coming, even though other people are without seats?

Perhaps the greater lesson here is about timeliness. The fact that you have a question about this means that you may question whether your friend will arrive at all. Use your good judgment. Give yourself a time limit, say ten minutes before show time, to save a seat. Graciously let those who are asking about the empty seat know that your guest will arrive soon. By all means, give up the seat before the film begins.

3. If I accepted someone's invitation to attend an event with him, but I knew I didn't want to go, is it rude to call later and tell him that I've changed my mind?

That's a loaded question. Part of being true to yourself is being honest and up front. It's best to bow out of a commitment *before* you get into it. Although it may feel uncomfortable to tell someone that you cannot attend a function with him or her, go for it next time. If you're already in the thick of it, by all means call as soon as possible and let the person know that you will not be able to attend with him after all. Don't lie, though. If, for instance, you plan to go to the function either alone or with someone else, don't say you aren't feeling well or make up some other excuse. At the same time, you don't have to volunteer the details of your plans.

4. At a dance or large party without assigned seating, is it wrong to put your drink down on someone else's table when you head to the dance floor?

Generally, yes. Imagine if you were sitting at a table and someone rushed over to plunk a half-filled glass in front of you. Take a few extra seconds and place your glass at the bar or at a station set up for collecting used glasses and dishes.

5. When traveling by car out of town with friends, shouldn't you offer to help pay for gas or tolls or to help drive along the way? What if the driver gets a speeding ticket? Do we all help to pay?

Everyone who is getting a ride should contribute to the cost of the trip. Your contribution may come in the form of cash for gasoline or tolls. It can also be a meal that you prepare in advance to bring along. When you're short on dollars, get creative. As you are planning the trip, come to an agreement about the estimated costs of the journey and decide together how to split the expense.

Regarding a moving violation, the kindest action may be to split the cost of the ticket, but it's not a requirement. The conditions surrounding the receipt of the ticket need to be examined. Why was the driver speeding? If other people in the car were encouraging his or her accelerated speed, then you all are morally responsible. If you are driving, though, ultimately you must pay for it.

6. How long are you supposed to wait before leaving and going without a person who is late and hasn't called, when you're going to a concert, theater or other time-sensitive event together?

How important is it to you to attend the event? You will have to answer that question in order to decide what to do. To avoid such a situation, check in beforehand with your companion to confirm your meeting time and location. Then wait to hear from the person until you must leave in order to reach your destination on time. I recommend leaving a message on the person's answering machine stating your whereabouts. If you and/or your companion has a pager, make up a paging code that tells the person if you are at home, just leaving, on your way, or there. If you decide to wait for your companion, try not to get in a huff. You will have made the decision to miss the beginning. Be clear about your disappointment, but don't spoil the time you have together. Instead, state the boundaries you intend to follow next time.

7. If my two friends have already planned to do something fun together and they haven't invited me, is it wrong for me to ask if I can come along?

Yes. Find something else to do. This way you won't set yourself up for rejection, nor will you waste time brooding about being left out. Your worry could be for no reason, too. People have the right to spend time with whomever they choose. Just because you were left out this time doesn't mean that they don't care about you. Alternatively, if this is a pattern, perhaps you should consider cultivating more nurturing relationships.

8. When I'm walking down the street, sometimes men yell out at me with a "Hey baby," or even a whistle. If I don't respond, they often start cursing at me. What should I do?

Sometimes you can keep walking and just offer up a smile, especially if the overture is friendly. When someone is rude, I usually keep on moving, silently sending them some love. One elder told me that on occasion she walks over to the brothers and asks them, "What would your Mama do if she saw you out here acting like that?!" She says it shames them to silence every time.

9. My husband, his brother, his brother's wife and I are going to the same party, but I don't want to be at the same table with them. What should I do?

Don't overthink the evening. Unless you are going to a formal affair that has place cards, which position you next to each other, you have little to worry about. Go with a positive attitude and have fun. If you have issues with your in-laws, address them in the privacy of your home.

10. Sometimes at public functions, I see a former friend. Neither of us can stand the other. How should I react when all of my other friends speak to her?

Why are you holding on to an old grudge? You are hurting yourself—and possibly others—in the process. You may not forget whatever happened to sever your ties with this former friend, but forgive yourself and her for the past. Then, with a clear heart, you can say a genuine "Hello" and keep moving. In this way, you will have dissipated all power from the negativity that had been festering within you. Sometimes, though, when a person has wronged you and still wants to be buddy-buddy in public, as if nothing happened, a cold shoulder may prompt the person to right the wrong, because you are not letting him get away with it.

11. What do I do if I see an old lover when I am out with my new partner?

Be cordial. Don't go out of your way to talk to the person, particularly if you have unresolved feelings. But don't act as if he or she isn't there, either. If you and your partner find yourselves face to face with the old flame, say "Hello," introduce the two and smile. Do not avert your eyes from each other. And it is not necessary to state your previous relationship.

When You Travel

He who does not travel will not know the value
of men.

AFRICAN PROVERB

WHEN I was growing up in Baltimore in the late sixties and early
seventies, traveling was considered a luxury—something we did during
summer vacation in a car. Boy, do I remember those backseat drives!
Nearly every year, my sisters and I would go on an excursion to "the
country" with Aunt Audrey and Uncle Henry, my father's sister and her
husband—road trips that took us to where Uncle Henry was from—a
little-known town called Bumpass, Virginia. Really!

When restlessness would strike me during the drive, I would look
out the window and ask Uncle Henry, "Where is it? How long before
we get there?" He would curl up the side of his mouth with a smile just
big enough not to drop his pipe and answer, "You see those mountains
in the distance? Well, as far as you can see, that's where we're going." It
seemed as if hours and hours passed even after Uncle Henry's assur-
ance, but eventually we reached our destination. My sisters and I got to
"see the world"—well, at least a piece of the rural South. And it was
great.

Being a true city girl, I remember feeling the thrill of anticipation as I
walked along a dusty country road, at the end of which I was able to
watch with fascination as pigs bathed in the wet earth of their pen. It
was on one of those expeditions to Virginia that I gathered up the
courage to climb onto a bike and attempt to pedal it—with no thought
of falling onto hard asphalt. My Daddy wouldn't let me get near a bike
at home for fear of a car's coming along and hurting me, but in the
country I was free!

Farmers lived across the way from Uncle Henry's property. They were white. We used to go over there and milk cows. (I was never very good at that.) But it was worth it, because I got to observe white folks—Southerners no less—up close. They seemed pretty okay to me, different somehow from what I had heard certain people say in school extracted from hushed conversations in the hall. These farmers were good people, and they treated my family right.

That was exactly what my Grandma Carrie had told us to expect. She used to tell us that in their hearts, all people were good, and that they weren't different from each other. Although I surely have had my doubts, I have gotten to see a little more of what she meant with each trip that I have taken. Those journeys of my youth were glorious. And even though I didn't love the bumpy ride that often left my stomach queasy, each time we piled into the packed car and the key turned in the ignition, I felt a tremendous thirst for new sights and sounds, new people, different homes, other lives.

Many a Black child has spent summers down South, or in the Caribbean or with small-town relatives, exploring life from a different point of view. And many of us know from personal experience that those summers and what we learned in our travels often stick with us for a lifetime.

These days, traveling is no longer strictly the luxury of our youth or a once-yearly getaway that we so carefully plan. Many of us regularly cover great distances for work, racking up tens of thousands of frequent flyer miles each year! To be able to see the United States and other parts of the world, as well as visit loved ones on the company dollar, can be quite gratifying if organized well. Many business travelers, however, complain that they are more likely to see the insides of countless convention centers and hotels than historic sites, shopping centers or even the clear blue sky in the cities they visit.

In order to make their trips more interesting, some arrange with their employers to fly to a meeting site during the weekend before their business meeting. This makes sense for the employer too because a Saturday or Sunday arrival usually represents a savings on airfare, which balances out the extra hotel cost. For the traveler, it presents a golden chance to explore the area before getting down to work—a plan that ultimately may help the company too, as the sites can only expand the employee's field of inspiration. A little planning and you can take in the sites and be fresh come Monday morning.

San Francisco furniture designer Cheryl Riley comes to New York City several times a year on business. An entrepreneur, Cheryl plans her trips so that she gets the most mileage out of each visit. Usually her clients cover her flight and accommodations for the duration of her formal meetings, before and after which she stays with friends in the city. She explains, "Not only does this save me money, but actually it gives me a chance to spend time with my friends in their personal space. Since everybody's busy in New York anyway, this makes it easier for us to be together."

Doesn't this sound like what folks used to do? That's partly why there would always be extra food on the stove in many an African-American home—for the visitors who stopped by for a few hours or a few days. Even more, back during the days of Jim Crow (as recent as the early sixties), Black travelers had to seek refuge before dark as they made their way across the country. Those places where our people rested their heads were more often people's homes than motels. The village. Whether it was for work or for pleasure, there was always someone with a helping hand and a safe haven and peace of mind when we hit the road.

There's so much to see and experience that can enrich our lives. It is from this vantage that we grow to recognize the beauty of the world— that which is familiar and different. Much like others I've encountered, the hunger to see the world has never left me. It has led me to points dotting the globe, where I've had the extraordinary opportunity to witness and learn about the ways that other people live. Often the journey has shed new light on the need for flexibility in my own life—for the approach that someone from another city, state or country might bring to a particular task. Patience for the extra time needed to push beyond language barriers. Clarity in my assessment of personal needs so that they may be satisfied without harming another.

As I have grown to see the need to nurture relationships wherever I am, I have also seen that many Americans have failed to honor the ways of other people. This is called *xenophobia*. There is an awful stereotype of "the ugly American"—one who is a bully, who expects others everywhere to cater to his or her needs, who presumes that everyone speaks English, thereby relieving him or her of the need to learn the foreign language, and so on. Unfortunately, this assessment is too frequently true—and it doesn't exclude African Americans. Whether it's due to impatience or, more likely, a simple yet profound lack of knowledge about others, American travelers frequently present themselves in a less-than-gracious or hospitable manner while abroad. What happens as a result is the opposite of most travelers' intentions. Doors close. Opportunities to explore deeper into the lives and history of a particular people or place are diminished. And, on a more practical level, one can end up having a miserable time rather than reaping a harvest of enlightening memories. So, in this chapter, we explore the basics of *how to be* with others when you travel. Know what you must keep first and foremost in your mind. In order to show your hosts the proper respect, you will need to take the time to do your homework and learn about your destination—its customs and people. In this way, you will be able to have a full and pleasant experience, one that is guaranteed to broaden your understanding of the world and yourself (without offending people left and right!).

What You Need to Know

There is an art to traveling right, and not just where you go and how you spend your time—although you should always keep those things in mind. But more, the way that you travel directly reflects the degree of understanding and respect you have for yourself and the trip ahead. What's most important to keep in mind is that you want to be courteous to everyone along your journey's way. To do this, you need to put time into preparation for your trip and patience into the details of the trip itself.

- Do your homework. Find out as much as you can in advance about your destination. Knowing the basics about customs, rules and regulations is a must. Seek out details about what makes a locale unique or special. Find out what you can contribute to the community you will be visiting—perhaps your open attitude or an item that is readily available in your hometown and scarce where you're going.
- Learn proper salutations. Since first impressions can make or break a relationship when you're on the road, take special care in learning how to make people feel comfortable and respected. Even if you haven't mastered the language of a people, you can learn the words to say, "Hello," "Thank you" and "Please."
- Be open. Travel with the gracious attitude that shows that you are open for new ideas, inspirations and experiences. Begin with the attitude that you *want* to understand; that you are going to have a good time and that different doesn't automatically mean *strange*. Especially when someone or something is unfamiliar to you, observe the situation with the willingness to learn. You'll be amazed at how much your attitude will help you to get along with people of all cultural backgrounds. Truly welcoming others is something that you can learn how to do well by traveling, if you take the time.
- Travel light. Resist the temptation to bring your entire wardrobe along—something that's pretty challenging for me, I must admit! Pack what you really need, and leave the rest at home. Don't underpack either. Things you consider necessities may be luxuries or tourist items in your getaway paradise and priced accordingly if they

are available at all. Make a list of the activities you will participate in, followed by a corresponding list of clothing, accessory and business items that are required. As you pack the items on your list, check them off, so that you stay organized.

- **Get your money straight.** There's little that's worse than arriving at an airport, a restaurant or some other port without the proper money. Go to a currency exchange beforehand, and get at least $100 in the foreign currency you will be using. Don't expect change back of a five-dollar bill from someone who makes a living on tourist tips and has been convinced of Americans' unlimited resources. Remember that you will need dollar bills for tips throughout your trip, no matter where you are going. Put small change in a separate container so that you can get to it swiftly. (See below for more information on tipping.)

- **Take care of yourself.** How are you feeling? Tired? Hungry? Lonely? Frustrated? Content? Check in with yourself throughout the trip. Eat when you're hungry. Sleep when you're tired, even if it means taking a nap at midday. This may sound simple, but the rapid pace of travel and the stimulation of new places can make you overlook your simplest needs. Travel can be taxing. Don't run yourself down.

- **Treat others with respect.** This can't be emphasized too much. Just as you must take the time to take care of yourself, so you must also walk with an open heart during your trip. From the bellhop to the toll taker, the concierge to the passerby on the street, be kind and thoughtful. Remember to breathe before you communicate with others. Breathing puts you in touch with your heart.

Being with Others

Whether you will be among people of a foreign town a few hundred miles from home or overseas, you want to adopt a friendly, open attitude toward others. *Xenophilia,* or love of people, is a natural attribute of the African worldview. Draw on your ancestral memory, and show the world the best you have to offer. When it comes to people from other parts of the world, research is key, along with keen observation.

A few years ago, I traveled to Zimbabwe with a crew of about ten people to produce a story for *Essence* magazine. We were there to document the tenth anniversary of the country's independence, and we were on a mission. We had a tremendous amount of ground to cover— a whole magnificent, vast country—in two weeks. During that time, we were to interview many key citizens, from members of Parliament to business and spiritual leaders, to grass-roots folks. With a tight time schedule, we began our work. One of our first destinations was the home of the widow of a leading dignitary. We were visiting her with the intention of photographing and interviewing her at the same time. So in we came—myself, the photographer, his assistant and our guide. We introduced ourselves, shook hands graciously and then asked if we might be able to see her home to find a place to shoot. As she led us into the parlor, she invited us to have tea with her. We thanked her kindly as we explained that we would prefer to pass on tea and instead get right to work. In a blink, the woman's face became stern. She motioned to her maid to bring in the tea service and again invited us to sit for tea. Our guide then whispered to me that in Zimbabwe (which was colonized by the British) it is customary to have tea and share niceties *before* conducting business. To skip over that step was unthinkable. In that moment, I took a deep breath and sat down to show proper respect to this woman in her home. I saw that it didn't matter that *my* agenda involved celebrating her family history in America. If I couldn't shed my Western business get-it-done-now sensibility, the effort would have been fruitless.

I learned an important lesson about flexibility and looking outside of what I had been taught on that trip. To grow in your life, you need both of those qualities, along with a heaping dose of selflessness. These are the real gifts of the road.

Other pointers for being with the local people include these:

- Be patient. If it is your true intent to be with the people, that will shine through and help in melting away any invisible barriers that might make the locals suspect you. Patience is the main ingredient here. You can't expect to come in and be fully accepted immediately. People need time to warm up to you. If you are deep down a snooty person, people will sense it and tighten up.
- Do ask for permission to enter a space or take a picture. If the answer is no, you may need to come back later or graciously ask someone else. Be mindful not to step on anyone's toes when you ask again.
- Don't ignore people when you don't get your way. That's a clear sign of disrespect. Be silent at first and assess the situation. Then select the person most likely to be able to help you with a better approach.
- Don't assume that people from other countries *should* know how to speak English simply because they welcome American tourists.
- Do bring along small items for bartering with vendors and artisans. If you are going to a nonindustrialized country, for example, you might bring fingernail polish, miniature toiletries, notepaper and writing instruments to barter—items that are either not easy to acquire or expensive for locals to purchase. Another great bartering agent is an

instant photo. Many people are hard-pressed to get pictures of them-selves. Bring along an instant camera; you'll be amazed at what you can trade for a picture!

- Don't cheat when bartering. Offer something that may be of value so that you make an equitable exchange.
- Listen carefully and pay attention. When in doubt, be quiet. By ob-serving, you're bound to discover answers to many of your questions.

Visiting the Motherland

The promise of connecting with brothers and sisters across the shores, members of our ancestral family, has drawn thousands of African-American people to the Motherland, the continent of Africa. The expe-riences of Black travelers to various ports of call in the more than fifty African nations range widely. Nearly everyone comes away with a sense that people of color in the world are much more powerful, beau-tiful and interesting than we once had been taught even to imagine. When I first visited Africa, on a trip to the Ivory Coast, my perception about African people changed entirely. I got to see firsthand in the cities and the rural areas that our African brothers and sisters are both beautiful and worthy of our support and respect—not as objects to look at through the window of a tour bus, but as people whose lives and ex-periences I wanted to know and understand.

Everybody doesn't have that experience. Some people leave their so-journs disappointed. That is due, in part, to distorted expectations, some degree of cultural (i.e., American) arrogance and a basic lack of preparation. To pay proper respect to those who live on African shores, African-American people need to do a reality check. Before you go, ask yourself what your purpose is for taking a trip to an African country. What do you hope to accomplish? What do you have to offer? Assess your expectations and filter them through the reality of your length of stay, knowledge about the country and its people and ability to gain ac-cess to the regular folk. So often Americans travel abroad, Africa in-cluded, and never get *to be* with the people. To gain the full measure of travel's benefits, you must devote enough time and space to connect one-on-one with others. You can best achieve a meaningful connection by coming from your heart. Be yourself. Speak slowly if there are lan-guage barriers, which include English dialects. (By the way, a language barrier is just what it sounds like. It doesn't mean that the person you're talking to is either deaf or stupid. It just means you don't speak the same language. So don't yell or huff and puff when you experience dif-ficulty getting your message across.) Be patient and observant. Don't assume that the way that you do things is better. It simply is different.

Watch to see how the local people, officials and hospitality industry interact with you and with each other. Your observations will help you to discover the perfect way to interact for your mutual benefit. Don't take advantage of anyone. This includes buying, selling or bartering something at an unfairly low price. Think about how you would feel if the tables were turned. Be fair with your brothers and sisters. Others attempt to get something for little or nothing all the time. We don't need to do it too!

To make your trip easier, contact the country's American embassy. Many embassies are located in Washington, D.C. Prepare your questions before you call, so that you can use your time—and that of the person on the other line—efficiently. Vital guidelines for any foreign trip include these:

- What are the traditional social amenities? How do people greet one another? Are there specific ways that men and women communicate? Are children included in mixed company?
- Is there a dress code for public spaces? For women? For men? For children? During the day? In the evenings? At the beach? Such rules often differ at resorts and large Western hotels as compared to local hangouts.
- Are there any restrictions regarding hairstyle? Believe it or not, there still are countries that will not welcome visitors who wear their hair in locks. In some Caribbean countries, for example, people with locks have been turned away at the airport rather than allowed entry. Although justifiably infuriating, this policy has hampered many a vacation. To reverse the rules will take more than a confrontation at the airport.
- Are women allowed to travel alone? In some Islamic countries, for example, restrictions apply. In other locations, safety is a factor, particularly at night. Western feminist orientations aside, along with what you think you *ought* to do because you are your own woman, there are some countries that are just not safe for a woman alone. Your independence won't mean much if you are dead. Be smart.
- Are gays and lesbians welcome? Depending on the intention of your trip, seek out a locale that is pleased to serve you or run the risk of getting into a political brawl.
- Get literature. All you can read in advance!
- Ask friends who've visited what they discovered that might be useful for you to incorporate. If you get names of friends or other contacts, follow up with them. Often your loved ones have already placed calls to their contacts. Out of common courtesy, follow up, even if you don't intend to spend time with them.

- Be sure to learn a bit of the local language. You'll be amazed at how pleased people are when you are able to offer salutations and gratitude directly. If you learn how to request basic necessities in the local tongue, you will avoid unnecessary frustration and miscommunication during your stay.
- Be flexible. Once you arrive, you probably will discover that even after preparation you don't know all the rules. That's okay. If you remember to pay attention and be kind, you'll be fine. Observe the ways that people interact with each other to see if you can pick up on social customs. Be mindful that the rules may be different for men and for women. When in doubt, ask. Seek out someone with whom you already had a good relationship, the concierge or someone with a welcoming face and discreetly ask what's expected of you in a particular situation. If you discover that you have done something "wrong," apologize. A sincere apology goes a long, long way. When it's offered immediately, you can then move on to the next order of business without ruffling too many feathers.

Mode of Transportation

Whether you are traveling by car, train or airplane, you are bound to run into the same basic needs. You have to plan your trip carefully—a point that will feel like a broken record by the time you finish this chapter. Preparedness means everything, no matter what vehicle you choose. There are some specifics for different modes of transportation that are worthy of considering too.

By Car

A favorite way for families to travel, car trips can be a joy or a source of constant agitation, depending on your preparedness. To keep the peace and have a wonderful trip, bear these thoughts in mind:

- Plan well. This includes your travel routes, stopping points, tolls—everything else, in fact. If you are one to take spontaneous trips, you are not excluded. Whether your preparation takes fifteen minutes or several weeks, you do need to ensure that you have all the bases covered, including mode of transportation, attire, money and clearly defined route. Otherwise you may waste time, energy and money—precious resources to be sure.
- Clean and service your car. There's nothing worse than traveling in a messy vehicle. And make sure that your car is in optimal condition for your trip.

Getting to Africa

A journey to our ancestral homeland can become one of the most profound and moving experiences that an African-American person can have. Just as Muslims commit to making a *hadj* to Mecca, their spiritual home, so should we all do our best to step onto African soil. For several decades now, tours have been organized to help get people of color to African shores on tours that celebrate our cultural history. To get you started, here is a partial listing of Black-owned tour operators across the country who have you in mind:

Eddie Agboh
Ambassadorway
150 Nassau Street, Suite 1921
New York, NY 10038
(212) 693-0700, fax (212) 233-6583

Idella Blackwood
AARCO Travel
2226 East 71st Street
Chicago, IL 60649
(312) 363-9500, fax (312) 363-7164

Ernie Brown
Brown Travel
2286 Cascade Road
Atlanta, GA 30311
(404) 752-600, fax (404) 752-6101

Shariffa Burnett
Alken Tours
1661 Nostrand Avenue
Brooklyn, NY 11226
(718) 856-9100, fax (718) 856-9507

Eleanor Chatman
African Travel Advisors
9122 South Constance Avenue
Chicago, IL 60617
(312) 374-4199

Helenmary Chiagouris
WTMIC
5307 Hyde Park Boulevard
Chicago, IL 60615
(312) 752-5800, fax (312) 752-5814

Selma Edwards
EZ Tours
1650 Broadway
New York, NY 10019
(212) 246-2116, fax (212) 977-4248

Rosetta Gainey
Gainey & Associates, Inc.
1217 Glenhaven Road
Baltimore, MD 21239
(410) 323-4878, fax (410) 323-2816

David Gartrelle
Sun Tours
109-15 Liverpool Street
Jamaica, NY 11425
(718) 523-1931, fax (718) 283-0630

Betty Graves
Harlem Travel
5002 Fifth Avenue
New York, NY 10027

Jon Haggins
Haggins International
306 West 38th Street
New York, NY 10018
(212) 563-2570, fax (212) 563-2578

Bill Haley
Haley Travel Service
499 North Euclid
St. Louis, MO 35235
(314) 361-2888, fax (314) 361-4913

Gaynelle Henderson
Henderson Travel
900 Second Street, NE, #7
Washington, DC 20002
(202) 789-1211, fax (202) 289-1811

Marquita Hill
Sankofa Tours
15030 Terrace Road
East Cleveland, OH 44112
(216) 761-5229, fax (216) 249-0730

Erna Kassa
African Diaspora Konnection
25925 Harden Circle
Southfield, MI 48025
(810) 557-6159, fax (810) 557-6157

Ed Mascoll
Affordable Elegance
901 15th Street, NW
Washington, DC 20005
(202) 842-3820, fax (202) 842-3837

(continued on next page)

Getting to Africa *(cont.)*

Lauritz Parker
Kamil's Travel Agency
6480 New Hampshire Avenue
Takoma Park, MD 20912
(301) 270-2407, fax (301) 270-2952

Fran Raglin
Elite Travel/Lazarus Travel
1601 Madison Road
Cincinnati, OH 45206
(513) 369-7575, fax (513) 861-8555

Bette Saunders
B. Saunders & Associates
2311 Fifth Avenue, Suite 4DD
New York, NY 10037
(212) 690-2971, fax (212) 283-0630

Rita Tigle
Overseas Express
2705 West Howard Street
Chicago, IL 60645
(312) 262-4971, fax (312) 262-4406

Jo Wilson
Allen Travel Service
1134 11th Street, NW
Washington, DC 20001
(202) 371-8740, fax (202) 371-8747

- Establish rules from the start. Let passengers know if eating is allowed in the car, what you expect them to contribute to tolls and gas and other needs. Don't assume that you and your fellow travelers follow the same rules. Such assumptions have led to unnecessary arguments that feel all the more volatile because they are in such a confined space. Create your own car etiquette, and invite others to follow it. Frequent traveler Jocelyn Cooper says that during group travel, everyone should contribute something. She says, "Someone can be in charge of food, another directions, another tolls." It doesn't always have to be money.
- Designate a copilot when traveling in groups. This person should sit up front and watch the road with the driver. Make an agreement that someone will always be on duty to stay awake with the driver.
- Greet the toll taker with a smile and a "hello." Everyone deserves respect.
- Play music that everyone in the car will enjoy. When traveling with elders, defer to their listening needs, or at least include some of their choices in the repertoire. Pay attention to the composition of your group, and play music that will appeal to everyone. When people are sleeping, don't be selfish. Turn the music down unless you are using it to stay alert!
- Drive safely without tailgating. So many people drive right up on the backs of cars, making it difficult for passengers to relax during the ride. Remember your passengers and the other drivers, and slow down.
- Don't venture too far off your path as you approach evening. For general safety purposes, you want to be near open business establish-

ments after dark. Here's a time when you also need to remember *who you are!* Being African American in certain parts of the country still requires that you proceed with extra caution. Be aware that you may run into people who are not welcoming. Have a plan that includes safe exiting. This goes for brothers, too.

- Pack wisely. Whether it's your car or you are a passenger, consider the number of other travelers, and limit the amount of luggage you bring.
- Travel with emergency provisions, including a spare tire, dry foods, water, garbage bag, tissues. By doing so, you actually are honoring everyone in your vehicle by making the environment comfortable.

By Train

For sentimental and practical reasons, many Black folk choose train travel for long- and short-distance trips. Historically many African-American men worked the railroad in this country. What happened was that many college-educated Black men were denied admission into the professions for which they had been trained. Being a porter became a job of "privilege"—by default—back at the turn of the century. The upside was they got to see the United States develop as it whisked by their eyes. They also successfully organized to secure their rights. One of the first successful Black union efforts was organized by A. Philip Randolph on behalf of the Brotherhood of Sleeping Car Porters. We have a long history with the rails. When it comes to traveling by train today, preparation is everything:

- Enroll the help of the porters or redcaps. If you have special needs, extra baggage, small children or just want to be handled more gently, find a redcap who will take you and your luggage to the train platform before the other passengers board. He will also put you on the train in a convenient seat, near your luggage. You should tip porters a minimum of fifty cents per bag, a dollar if you can.
- Bring essentials on board. Especially when you have children, that includes games and entertainment, snacks and a blanket or throw for warmth.
- Watch your belongings. Keep them near you, and make sure that every package is marked. Keep money, credit cards and any forms of personal identification on your body.
- Create a positive relationship with the conductor. When you are traveling long distances, this is particularly important. Any concerns you may have should go directly to the conductor, along with good wishes. Always be polite, especially when bringing a complaint to the person from whom you expect help.

- Greet your neighbors. Say hello to the people sitting next to you. Gauge the prospect of conversation by their body language. When the moment is suited for quiet, greet them and then give yourselves ample privacy. Don't spread your belongings into others' space. Put away food wrappings as soon as you have finished eating.
- Talk quietly. Whenever you are in a public place, especially one that is confining, lower your voice (use that "inside voice") when you speak to keep your conversation relatively private and to give others peace of mind. This includes when you are using a cellular phone.
- Let the conductor know if your children will be traveling alone. For the safety and comfort of all passengers, the conductor should be aware of all minors' travel and of their seats. You may ask him or her to look out for your precious cargo and make sure that they get off at the appropriate destination—and *not* before!

Air Travel

Whereas flying used to be a rare occurrence in many Black families, nowadays traveling in the air is commonplace in many households. Even many of our children are boarding airplanes from infancy on. You can make flying nearly hassle free by preparing for the journey properly. Many steps need to take place well before you arrive at the airport. Know your needs up front, and work to get them met right away.

- Place special meal orders early, at least twenty-four hours in advance. Airlines serve everything from diabetic to kosher, low-fat and vegetarian meals. Trying to order your favorite at the ticket counter won't work.
- Seat requests need to be early too. Put in your request when you purchase your ticket. You can try to change your seat at the gate, but it depends on how full the plane is. Stay calm no matter what. Being kind to the ticket agent often lands miracles.
- Get to the airport early—an hour before domestic flights and two hours before international. By honoring this rule, you will begin your trip with a sense of ease, as everyone will be able to manage his or her responsibility better. Your check-in will be less of a hassle because you will arrive before the last-minute crowds.
- Secure your bags. Make sure all luggage is closed and locked, if possible. Tag every package you have in case you get separated from your possessions. This sounds obvious, but the many unmarked, lost parcels lying about any airport or bus depot prove that people often don't pay attention.
- Watch what you bring. Your charming smile won't allow you to bring on lots of heavy bags anymore. The airlines have cut back on

weight and number requirements for bags. Follow the rules, and stay out of conflict. When you need to bring along more than is allowed, talk to the ticket agent as soon as you arrive to make arrangements.

How to Work with a Travel Agent

People purchase tickets in many ways these days, from Internet services to the airlines directly and through travel agents. When you are busy, working with a travel agent can still be the most helpful. Travel agencies are set up to help travelers plan trips that will be as cost-efficient, comfortable and effortless as possible. Because they work with many businesses in the travel industry, they are aware of details that can satisfy your particular needs—anything from securing a no-smoking room to a suite with business amenities, travel arrangements for newborns to emergency overseas visits for bereaved family members.

- Find a good agent and establish a healthy relationship. Let the agent know who you are, what you like and dislike and how you like to be treated. Tell the agent the best times to talk to you for travel organization. And find out what he or she needs to help you make your plans. Establishing this respectful rapport early on will help when you have to handle last-minute details in a timely fashion.
- Be clear. Your agent is no mind reader. Talk about what you want for each trip. If you need to make changes, alert your agent right away. It can save you money and aggravation.
- Be gracious. When your trip has been planned, thank the agent for his or her assistance. Whether something great or not-so-inspiring happens on your trip, report it back to the agent. The same goes for an Internet service: let the people know. In this way, you can share the good news that will make the agent know that he or she did a good job as well as the areas needing improvement. Be sure to communicate in a loving manner.

Remembering Your Loved Ones

Have you seen the T-shirts that say, "My Daddy went to Jamaica, and all I got was this lousy T-shirt?" The reality usually is that the family member who receives the T-shirt is thrilled that Daddy remembered her during the exciting trip when he was away. That's the point. When you travel, you get to soak in experiences that those closest to you may never see firsthand. While you are away having a ball, they are at home, usually following their daily routine. There are thoughtful ways to treat your loved ones when you travel:

- Give them your itinerary. J. Walter Fisher, the former chief librarian for Morgan State University in Baltimore, used to travel every summer well into his twilight years. Uncle Walter, as we fondly called him, kept the lines of communication open by creating an itinerary that included the address, telephone number and scheduled date and time of arrival for each stop of his trip. He gave that document to several people, including family members and business associates. He said he felt worry free, because in case of emergency, his support network was in place, so people would know where to start looking in case of emergency. Both for their peace of mind and your own, someone should have a complete listing of your contact information.
- Send a postcard. That's why they were created! They are an affordable and quick way of letting the folks back home share in your experience. A one-liner about the scenery, something fun you just did or what's to happen next is perfect. Do your best to mail your postcards while you're away. A local postmark becomes a treasure for observant recipients.

Traveling with Children

As much fun as family travel can be, any parent will tell you that there is an art to it. As far as etiquette goes, what's important is that you think about the children who are in your care *and* your neighbors. You've seen adults when they are oblivious to the needs of those around them. One child might be crying, while another keeps walking back and forth across the aisle of a very narrow plane. Those sobs and tiny feet can become irritating. That doesn't mean that you should lash out at the children, either. Frustration too often becomes the trigger for bad behavior on the part of adult, parent and innocent bystander. To keep the peace and enjoy your trip, keep these pointers in mind:

- Use a checklist when you travel. Itemize all of the essential things that you should bring along, including several changes of clothes, food and drinks, games, books, blankets, an extra pacifier, toys that don't rattle, beep, bang, honk or squeal and any other necessities. The difference in your child's demeanor when you have a toy or a story to occupy his time versus when you are scrambling for an activity for him directly affects everyone's quality of travel. Plan ahead.
- Plan your trip carefully. Make sure that if you travel by car, you build in ample bathroom breaks and safe stretches. At all times, keep your children off the road. When traveling by plane, reserve special seating early. Request seats on an aisle, so you and your children have easy access to the rest rooms and walking space.

- Let the proper personnel know that you are traveling with children. Upon your arrival at a bus terminal, train station or airport, alert the staff to your special needs. Airlines allow adults with small children to board early so that they can settle down before the crowds begin. Take advantage of this extra time. Everyone on board will thank you for it. On a train, you can ask a redcap to help you board early.
- Speak to your immediate neighbors, and let them know your situation. For instance, if you are traveling with a newly walking toddler, you definitely are going to have to get up during your journey. By letting the people sitting on either side of you know what's going on before it happens, they *should* be more willing to help you. Excuse yourself whenever you have to step over people. There is nothing worse than being stepped over—and on—as if you are not there.
- Discipline your children quietly. When I was a child, a mother's eyes could tell it all to a knowing child. Let your subtle gestures relay disciplinary messages to your children whenever possible. In times of danger, obviously you must speak up immediately. Be kind and clear with your children and with others.
- Exit after others have cleared the way. Unless you run the risk of missing a connection, don't rush to get off a public transportation system. Your delay will make it easier for others, and ultimately yourself, to exit smoothly. You and your charges will also be able to avoid possible injury from others' luggage.
- Find a safe and private place for nursing. In some areas, nursing your baby in public can be quite challenging. Court cases have come up in the past couple of years in the United States for public breast-feeding. If you are nursing a child and you need to do so while you are out, be discreet so that the experience between you and your child will be positive and calm. An Islamic sister recommends keeping an extra shawl around, so that you can create instant privacy. When your trip involves long distances such as on a plane or train, scope out the nearest rest room or changing room before you settle down. If you think you'd be more comfortable nursing without an audience, you can quickly move to that area. When traveling overseas, find out if there are any customs, rules or regulations prohibiting nursing in public. You can check with the American embassy.

Group Travel

Whether your group consists of a number of college buddies who decide to spend a weekend in the Caribbean or a large family gathering

Sharing Our Cultural Experience

For your own benefit as well as your family's, be conscious about the choices that you make for pleasure travel. Without a doubt, seeing the world is of great value. But you can do that only one trip at a time. Your journeys can start right on American soil when you make trips to visit African-American historical sights. Education truly should be at the forefront of each of your actions. Choose to learn more about our cultural history by visiting valuable cultural resources. Here is a sampling:

Afro-American Historical and
    Cultural Museum
701 Arch Street
Philadelphia, PA 19106
(215) 574-0380

Apollo Theater
253 West 125th Street
New York, NY 10027
(212) 749-5838

Baltimore's Black American
    Museum
1769 Carswell Street
Baltimore, MD 21218
(410) 243-9600

Beale Street Historical Tour
Memphis, TN 38126
Call Heritage Tours (901) 527-
    3427

Bethune Museum and Archives
1318 Vermont Avenue, NW
Washington, DC 20005
(202) 332-1233

Charles H. Wright Museum of
    African-American History
315 East Warren Avenue
Detroit, MI 48201
(313) 494-5800

Charles L. Blockson Afro-
    American Collection
Temple University
Philadelphia, PA 19122
(215) 204-6632
Vast collection of rare books, pho-
    tographs and other historical
    documents dating to the begin-
    ning of the United States; par-
    ticular focus on the
    Underground Railroad.

Dusable Museum of African-
    American History
740 East 56th Place
Chicago, IL 60637
(773) 947-0600

John Brown's Cave and Historical
    Village
20th Street & 4th Corso
Nebraska City, NE 68410
(402) 873-3115

King-Tisdell Cottage
514 East Huntingdon Street
Savannah, GA 31401
(912) 234-8000
Has bill of sale for slaves written
    in Arabic by plantation slaves,
    along with African icons and
    carvings.

Levi Coffin House, an Under-
    ground Railroad Station
Fountain City, IN 47341
(317) 847-2432

National Museum of the Tuskegee
    Airmen
6235 West Jefferson Avenue
Detroit, MI 48202
(313) 297-9360

New Orleans Historic Voodoo
    Museum
724 Rue Dumaine
New Orleans, LA 70116
(504) 523-7685

Penn Center
16 Penn Center Drive
St. Helena, SC 29920
(843) 838-2432
By appointment only.

Schomburg Center for Research
  in Black Culture
515 Lenox Avenue
New York, NY 10037
(212) 491-2214

Slave Market, Middleton
  Plantation
Middleton Place, Ashley River
  Road
Charleston, SC 29414
(803) 556-6020

---

away from home, when you are traveling with others you will have to expand your patience and openness. Establishing ground rules will set everybody straight from the beginning.

- Determine policies about paying for meals, meeting times for outings, travel plans and other trip elements.
- When you are unable to pay your way completely, ask family or friends for help.
- When sharing rooms, organize payment plan for meals and incidentals before you travel.
- Even with adults, take a head count before moving from one destination to another.
- Assign someone to be team leader on a rotating schedule, if that will work. This person will have the responsibility of being social events and emergencies coordinator. Put this individual in touch with the hotel concierge or other authority for the best service.

Tipping

I now see the value in hotels that make a flat 10 percent (or higher) rate for all service charges. At such establishments, you never have to give a specific tip to anyone, because it is being organized for you. This is a rarity in travel. What's more likely to happen is that all along your path will be people in service roles who will help to make your trip easier. When I am in doubt about who should receive a tip or how much, I think of members of my own family who were porters, domestic workers and other service employees. Back in those days and now, these people earned a real living based on the additional resources that travelers put into their pockets. Tipping is good manners, for sure. Yet it can get even the most savvy of us confused.

The best overall advice is to be practical and generous. Assess each person who helps you on your visit, from the valet at the hotel to the maid (whom you may never see), to the bell captain. How can these people help to make your visit comfortable? Further, how helpful are they actually being? With that information, you can make decisions

Some Tips on Tipping

Hotel maid	$1 a night or $5 to $10 a week for longer stays
Room service waiter	15 percent of bill (check to see if service is already included though)
Porters, bellhops, airport skycaps	$.50 to $1 per bag
Concierge	$5 to $10 at end of stay if you engage their services
Desk clerk	None (a thank you is great!)
Restaurant waiters	15 to 20 percent of pretax bill (check for a service charge for large parties)
Tour guides	$1 per guide or bus driver per day; $5 to $10 for a longer tour (if not already included)
Valet parking attendant	$1 for a single visit; if you're moving your car throughout the day, $1 minimum at the end of day in an envelope
Cruises	Most gratuities are included, but at the cruise's end, stewards typically get $5 to $6 per day
International	Europe—service is already included, but a small tip is customary United Kingdom—follow American custom of 15 to 20 percent Africa—there is no standard, but a tip is expected Countries that follow French custom have a *service compris,* so you can add a small amount extra; ask your guide about protocol

about rewarding people for their services. Know that most people who receive tips are paid very low basic wages and rely on tips as a significant percentage of their income.

Visiting Family

Whereas once you could visit your relatives just by walking down the hall or perhaps down the street, now our families are spread across the country and throughout the world. What that means in terms of family responsibility and commitment is that we all must make a conscious effort to spend some part of our time and resources to visit family members on a consistent basis. I use a one-to-four ratio. If I take four trips during the course of the year, whether they are daily excursions, a week at a social or political convention or a vacation, I make sure that I build in at least one trip for visiting relatives. When times get busy and exciting, carving out that one trip can prove quite challenging.

Visiting family is unlike any other trip that you will take. Especially if you are visiting your parents after you have established your independence, you can count on some measure of friction over the household's codes of conduct. One woman who lives in Los Angeles used to visit her family back East and stay at her parents' home—that is, until they started to demand knowledge of her whereabouts, which left her unnerved. "I saw that the way that I lived was very different from the lifestyle of my parents," explained Susan. "Rather than getting into a fight with them, since my parents and I don't share the same schedule, I decided to stay at a friend's where my schedule wasn't an issue. I use her house as my base when I go back home and visit my parents."

Whether it's your parents' home, another family member, a close friend or even a hotel, you become the guest when you stay under their roof. That means that their rules have to be honored. You must be aware of what is expected of you wherever you are and act accordingly. As far as family goes, you are treading on tender ground. Your loved ones usually want to make you feel welcome, and they do so by showering you with what they feel is special treatment. To strike a winning balance between your needs and desires and those of your loved ones, consider this:

- Let your family know your expected arrival time. Surprise visits are not thoughtful. (How would you feel if someone rolled up on you, when your space was a wreck? Would you like that? Would they? If you find that you are running late, call so that no one will worry or be inconvenienced. Nobody likes to wait around.
- Ask first before bringing someone along. Especially if your guest is a lover, find out how your family feels about that. My Daddy wouldn't allow overnight male visitors in his house—no matter where they slept—unless they were husbands.
- Be of help. Your family homestead is not a vacation resort. Don't allow your parents or other loved ones to serve you hand and foot. This includes men! (Remember, she's your Mama, not your servant.) Give your family a break, and pitch in.

- Bring modest clothing. A robe is a great start, so that you can dress comfortably no matter what the time of day, and slippers.
- Be patient. As our families grow older, their values often brittle a bit. Look beyond the issues that have made you bristle over the years so that you can see the love underneath it all. By looking for that goodness, you may be able to break down old issues, heal some scars *and* have a wonderful time.

YOUR QUESTIONS ANSWERED

1. Is it rude not to understand the language of the country that you are visiting?

Not exactly. What would be rude is if you didn't take the time to learn any words, particularly the basics of greetings, such as how to say, "Hello," "Goodbye," "Where is the . . ." Make a concerted effort *before* you leave to get a good grasp on these phrases. While on your trip, pay attention. Once you have established a rapport with someone that enables solid communication, you may want to ask how to say a particular word in the local language that you are able to describe in your language. In this way, you can learn from each other.

2. If I don't have time to do extensive research on a country, where can I get quick information on the basics of how to be (the customs, the dress codes, etc.)?

One of the benefits of modern technology is being able to turn on the computer and find a world of information. You can log on to the Internet (at home, at work, or the library) and look up the locale of your choice. You can also go to the U.S. Passport Office if there is one in your home town, or to the local post office for an application. You will find brochures and printouts listing basic protocol, including dress codes and information on currency throughout the world.

3. I have a very traditional, Southern upbringing, which tells me that you shouldn't allow strangers to do your laundry. On extended trips, where I will be staying in hotels, what do you suggest that I do about laundering personal items?

Bring travel-size detergent for hand washing, and don't be afraid to use the shampoo provided by the hotel for that purpose either. Many hotels have retractable clotheslines in the bathtub (they tend to look like little silver discs on the walls on either end of the tub) for this purpose. Don't be afraid to call housekeeping to ask for extra hangers. For larger items or those needing dry cleaning, I recommend that you go ahead and get them cleaned.

4. What happens if I go on vacation, as a single person, and fall "in like" with somebody and want to "get my groove back," as Terry McMillan put it? What is the etiquette on that?

On a health tip, make sure you travel with condoms and foam. These essential items may be expensive, defective or unavailable where you are going. The idea of getting away and having a little fun is exciting; however, you need to keep your wits about you, so that you can protect yourself. This extends far beyond health issues. For example, pay attention to the gender politics of the country. Americans are generally perceived as loose and available, which could put you in a compromising situation. Rather than going off to an unknown destination alone, invite your date to "consort" with you in your hotel. If you decide to go off property, let someone know where you're going—perhaps a concierge or someone with whom you have made friends.

5. How can I worship away from home in a country that is antagonistic toward my religion?

Many destinations around the world have small religious communities that are different from the predominant religion. Ask your concierge for a listing. The concept of worship is the bigger question here. Do you feel that you have to go to church, for example, in order to worship God? The way I've been taught is that you carry your spiritual consciousness in your heart. No matter where you go, you can hold onto your faith and create sacred space. Sacred space is a spiritual and mental condition as well as a physical space that you can designate wherever you are staying where you can commune with the spirit of God. If you prefer, bring religious items—pictures of saints, items of religious jewelry, a candle or incense—to use during prayer.

6. I love the idea of traveling to new places, but I'm afraid that I will not want to eat the food. What can I do?

Start with being a little more flexible, please! Do some research to find out what dishes are commonly served and their ingredients. This should make you feel more comfortable. Be sure to try the local food in reputable restaurants. If you know that your stomach is extremely sensitive, avoid fresh fruits and vegetables while you are away. In major Western hotels, such as the Sheraton, the Marriott, the Hilton and the Holiday Inn, which are in most countries, you can usually get "American-ish" fare. You can also find a fast-food restaurant almost anywhere. Remember to travel with bottled water to most non-European countries. And, *don't use ice, period!* This includes the fanciest restaurants and your hotel room. When you need to brush your teeth, use bottled water. It's better to be safe than contract dysentery. If you get a sick stomach, one or two drops of essential oil of peppermint in a glass of water can calm the queasiest stomach. Queen Afua advises not taking a product that stops diarrhea because your body is trying to get rid of the foreign germ as quickly as possible. She recommends drinking bottled water and fasting until the dysentery stops.

Another stomach calmer is coconut water. I was in Jamaica with my husband when I learned about this natural treatment. One afternoon while we were wandering about, I began to feel ill. George immediately told me that the elders in his family always relied on the fresh water of a green coconut to relieve a sick stomach. He found a street vendor who picked a coconut off a tree, machete'd it open and instructed me to drink the "water." Trust me. I was skeptical back then. But I figured, "Why not." I drank it, and it worked. Ever since then, I have known to look for fresh coconuts as a first resort for stomach trouble in the Caribbean.

BreakingBread

What is in the stomach carries what is on the head.
A F R I C A N   P R O V E R B

W H E N E V E R I told anyone that I was writing a book about etiquette, they immediately asked whether I was going to talk about
where to put the knife and fork. Even as I began to describe all of the
other elements that would make up *How to Be,* they consistently went
back to ". . . but what about 'real' etiquette? You know, how to eat." Depending on the person, the question was fueled either by sincere interest or spirited disdain. There was the brother who believed that
knowing how to navigate in dining waters would help him to get ahead
in the corporate world. And there was the sister who wanted to know
what difference it could possibly make in life if you don't know where
to put the butter knife. Let me answer that question with a question:
Don't you find bad manners distracting? At the very least, people can't
hear what's being said elsewhere if you are smacking and slurping.

Learning good manners alone may not make you a better human
being, but it might prevent others from prejudging you harshly. We all
know that first impressions should *not* be depended on to make important assessments about people. Still, we need to accept the fact that
there are plenty of people who use first impressions to judge a person's
entire worth. You may not like it—what that spoon is for may be really
unimportant compared to what's going on in Rwanda—but lax personal habits can be interpreted as an indication of personal careless-
ness, particularly in a business situation. Help people see the real you
by not making these superficialities an issue (What to do with a finger
bowl? *Come on.*) Learn this stuff, and get it over with so that you can

move on to the more vital aspects of personal human and spiritual development.

That's basically the philosophy that my parents had when I was growing up. Eating at the Cole household in Baltimore was always an experience requiring our full focus and attention. You see, there were all manner of unwritten rules and regulations that my sisters and I had to follow (or else!) when we sat down for a meal with Mommie and Daddy. I suppose it started with the fact that we ate together every day for breakfast and dinner. In the morning, it was the mad dash. Being the late riser, I had to get my act together fast so that I could be seated when it was time for Daddy to say grace. During our meal, Susan, Stephanie and I had to sit up straight in our chairs, fully dressed for school, chew our food (with our mouths closed!) and take turns listening and talking about the news. We reconvened at dinnertime and the routine was exactly the same.

It was during our daily meals that I discovered all sorts of dos and don'ts about dining: *No labels were allowed on bottles when we sat down to eat. No elbows on the table. No chewing and talking at the same time. No picking your teeth or singing at the table.*

And then there were the formal meals. I'll never forget the times that my older sister, Susan, and I would invite a date to a holiday meal. Just bringing a boy to our house meant he better be ready for a sparring match with our Daddy. The dinner table was sacred territory. Both my parents had been taught by mothers who had been domestic workers in service of wealthy, well-traveled white folks for much of their lives, so they had learned the "proper" art of fine dining and intended for us to incorporate these basic behaviors in our lives. That included our dates. So, for starters, Thanksgiving dinner, for example, called for dressing up. For us, that meant a dressy dress or skirt with hosiery and dress shoes. For boys that translated into a shirt, tie and jacket. Anything less? You'd better not think about it! Having to endure Daddy's comments would have been enough to send the young suitor home with an empty stomach. I remember at the time thinking, "Why does my father have to be so strict? Other children don't get such a hard time from their parents."

Today I am grateful. What I learned as a child I now practice effortlessly. I discovered what dressing for dinner meant, for a variety of occasions. I learned that as soon as I sat down at the table, my napkin was to go in my lap. I was taught to ask to be excused before getting up to leave the table. Among the most controversial points, when I was a child, was that I was instructed to eat everything on my plate, as that was a sign of good manners as well as a requirement for good nutrition.

Today in the Cole family home, the rules are a bit more relaxed at times, but the intention is still the same. Whenever my sisters and I come to visit, we all have our same seats. We don't think about eating without blessing the food first. Paper napkins frequently replace linen, but underneath it all, the understanding that mealtime is an opportunity for the family to come together and share a bit of their lives with each other remains the true purpose.

In some communities throughout the Diaspora and right here in the United States, eating as a family unit has not been the norm. Quite often adults eat together while children dine separately, with some female supervision. My Aunt Pearl designed many a holiday meal this way. As kids we even had our own miniature furniture at which we dined, while the grownups ate at the (boring) dining room table. For some Islamic families, men customarily eat with the men and women with the women.

Throughout history, practicality has determined how most people dined. For large families, people have often eaten in shifts in order to have space for everyone to eat at a table that is not large enough to seat the entire family comfortably. These days, what's practical has often been TV dinners or fast food for everyone whenever people can eat. The advent of so many of our families having two working partners or only one parent in the household has resulted in rather erratic eating patterns that too often leave children to their own devices. This often eliminates almost entirely the family bonding that can occur when a family sits down to eat together and the learning that goes along with it. As you reconsider the quality that you want your life to have, particularly when it comes to feeding your families, you will need to question how you can best nourish yourselves on every level. Basically, this means—as the African proverb that begins this chapter echoes—that you need to learn what to eat and how to eat it, so that you can move about with ease.

It all starts with the relationship that you have to your body. For years, folks have been saying that you should treat your body like a temple of God. Reading in the seventies that "you are what you eat" certainly had an impact on the American population. Yet for many African-American people, the way we eat has been a source of disease and pain rather than fortification. For generations in this country, we have eaten in an unhealthful way. Beginning in the days of Slavery, our ancestors were allowed to eat only the parts of animals that the slave owners didn't want. So pigs' feet, ham hocks, chitterlings and tripe— the slave menu—became our delicacies. In their expansive creativity, our ancestors figured out how to prepare these foods so that they tasted delicious. Yet the salty and sugary foods that we have grown to

Guidelines for Eating Well

We must be aware of what we feed our bodies, when we feed our bodies and how we eat. As many chefs and nutrition experts have discovered, it is possible to eat our foods—those with a Southern, Caribbean or African palate—and also be healthy. Many books and articles have been written to guide such food preparation. (See the cookbook list included in this chapter for a few.) Here are suggestions for eating right:

- The U.S. Food and Drug Administration recommends these guidelines for adults:

  Eat at least three servings of vegetables, two of fruit and six of grain products (especially whole grains) per day. Include at least three servings of low- or nonfat dairy products, and at least three servings of lean meat, poultry, fish, eggs, beans, and/or nuts.

  Use fats, oils, and sweets sparingly.

  Salt consumption should not exceed 3 grams (3,000 milligrams) per day.

- Eat fruits and vegetables raw when you can. But if you must cook, don't overcook. Steam vegetables lightly to preserve the nutrients.
- Cut away the extra fat from meat. Remove skin from chicken.
- Don't eat standing up. It doesn't enable your food to digest properly.
- Drink lots of liquids—at least six servings of 8 ounces of water per day, but not with meals or too soon before or after (give yourself thirty minutes) because liquids dilute digestive enzymes, interfering with digestion.
- Chew each mouthful of food at least twenty-five times. Complex carbohydrates are digested by the enzymes in saliva. (Protein is digested by enzymes in the stomach.) You may take a multivitamin/mineral too.
- Avoid excessive alcohol intake. Don't drink alcohol on airplanes. You will experience the effects of alcohol at nearly double the usual rate when you are in the air.
- Don't stuff yourself. Leave space in your stomach for your food to digest.
- Allow at least two hours for your food to digest before going to sleep.

call our own, as Soul Food, have not so much been food for the soul, but often fodder for our discontent and dis-ease. But not every soulful food has a sinful effect. According to Jonell Nash in her book *Essence Brings You Great Cooking,* "Some of the foods we love most are the best medicine against poor health and premature aging. Cabbage, mustard greens, brussel sprouts, broccoli, and cauliflower are proven cancer fighters and belong to the lifesaving cruciferous vegetable family. Sweet potatoes with beta carotene and soluble fibers help lower blood cholesterol and remove toxins."

In this chapter, we explore the fundamentals of eating—everything from guidelines on how to eat to live, to basic table manners and entertaining ideas. Since eating is such an integral part of every person's life, learning how to eat comfortably no matter where you are is key to cultivating a life of ease and grace.

Table Manners

Some things are true about eating no matter where you are. You could be at lunch with your mother on the back porch or at a formal dinner with the president of your company, and your basic good manners can see you through—if you have a good handle on them. Here's a refresher course to help make every dining experience comfortable, especially those that take you outside your home.

Wait to Be Seated

In most situations, you and your dining partner(s) will feel most comfortable if you are seated at the same time. This is especially noteworthy when you are at a formal function and you will be sitting at a table with nine other people. Here are some guidelines:

- When you go to someone's home, a private luncheon in an executive office or a formal affair, custom says that you wait until your host either invites you to sit or sits down himself. If there is a place card with your name on it, you may stand at your seat as you wait for others to arrive.
- If a guest is extremely late, a conscientious host will invite the group to sit, although an order usually will not be placed until the table is full. (That's why it's important to be on time!)
- Generally husbands and wives are not seated side by side at dining functions but usually they are seated at the same table. The same goes for business associates. The idea behind the seat arrangements is to allow guests who are not well acquainted with each other to become so over the meal.

Watch What You Say

Think about where you are before you start to speak. The content of your conversation should be crisp, clear and upbeat during a meal. Leave any controversial or highly detailed subjects for another time, when your listeners can offer their undivided attention. If you are at an event where touchy subjects are considered appropriate, consider saving that discussion until after you eat. Pleasant conversation enables good digestion.

Upon reaching your table, introduce yourself to everyone right away by stating your name and shaking the person's hand. If your host is already at the table, speak to him or her first if possible. Your host may want to do the introductions. If others arrive after you have been seated, introduce yourself to them at your earliest convenience. When food is already on the table, introduce yourself without reaching across the food. Then engage the people on either side of you in conversation.

What to Do with Your Stuff

Why is it so hard to figure out what to do with your napkin, your clothing accessories and lipstick too! I suppose it's because you need to mix a delicate balance of common sense and heightened awareness of your environment to manage. Remember that you are in the company of others before you act.

- As soon as you sit down, put your napkin in your lap. The only exception is if your host has not yet arrived, in which case you wait for your host to take a seat and then place your napkin. Do not put your napkin back on the table until you are ready to leave the table. When you do so, fold it neatly with the soiled areas folded inside.
- As you use your napkin, particularly for women wearing lipstick, use the underside and turn it over so that others don't see any stains and so that you don't soil your clothing.
- Don't put your napkin in your collar unless it is the policy of the restaurant. Normally, at rib joints, crab houses or anywhere that lobster is served, the waiter will bring you a plastic bib to protect your clothing.
- Beware of your lipstick. Don't wear lipstick that is too moist or thickly applied. You should avoid creating a thick lipstick ring on your glass or on your flatware. You don't want to eat your lipstick; you want to eat your meal! Many colorfast lipsticks today can prevent bleeding. Better yet, blot it well before eating.
- At a formal meal, it is not appropriate for a man to flip his tie over his shoulder. He can, however, tuck it into his shirt at a more casual affair.
- At a formal meal where you will be dressed in black tie, it's recommended that women cover their shoulders during the meal. Since only your upper body is in view, you will be more comfortable both eating and talking with dinner guests. A light shawl is a modest and comfortable option.
- Sisters, don't put your pocketbooks on the table. Put your bag in your lap. (Elder wisdom says that when a woman puts her purse on the floor, she will never have any money.) At an evening affair, you may put a tiny bag in front of your place setting. Briefcases belong on the floor.

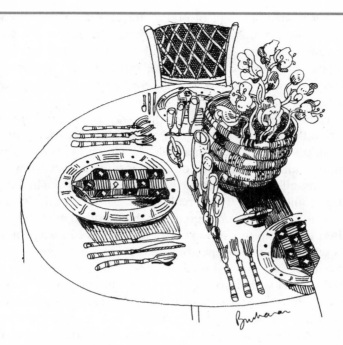

At a formal table as at any other, utensils are used from the outside in. Here the out-side fork is for an appetizer, followed by the salad and main-course forks. Your knives complement the forks. Outside spoon is for coffee or tea, unless soup is served, then a larger spoon is added. The inside glass here is for water, followed by the larger red wine glass, a white wine goblet and a champagne flute.

Using Utensils

Ever feel clumsy when you sit down to eat with others? Even at the most elaborate sit-down dinner, you will be fine if you use your common sense. Pay attention, and enjoy your meal!

- Don't handle flatware or table service items until you are going to use them.
- Follow the rule that you work from the outside in. When in doubt, observe your host.
- It is traditional in the United States to cut food with your knife in your right hand and your fork in your left. Once your food is cut, you gently place your knife across the top edge of your plate, and switch your fork to your right hand to insert food into your mouth. Americans have become less rigid with this rule, but in many Islamic countries it is considered highly offensive to eat with your left hand. At informal meals, lefties should sit at the table ends to avoid bumping elbows.
- Don't use the common butter knife to spread butter on your bread.

Scoop out a small amount of butter, and put it on your bread plate (which should be on your left, just above your fork). Use your own butter knife or regular knife to spread the butter.

- When you are chewing your food or otherwise do not immediately need your utensils, place your knife and fork on the outer edges of the plate.
- When eating soup, spoon the soup away from you, drawing the soup from the middle of the bowl. Never blow on your soup to cool it off—unless you are feeding a child. Don't stir the soup around and around to cool it, either; once or twice is fine, or wait a few minutes. No slurping allowed, no matter how good it tastes. (That applies to all other liquids, too!) If you really want to do it right, follow these directions: Part the lips enough to get the outer edge of the spoon in, and then gently tip the spoon so the soup flows in without sucking. This is why soup spoons are rounded and not pointed.
- When you are not using your soup spoon, do not put it in your bowl unless the bowl is shallow. Put it on the saucer instead. (This applies to tea or coffee as well.) Unfortunately, in many restaurants soup is served without a saucer, in which case you should request one. If you do not receive one, put the spoon in your bowl rather than on the table. Don't hold food in the air, impaled on your fork, as you talk. Eat it.
- Avoid clinking utensils in any way, including when you are stirring in a coffee cup or teacup, cutting on a plate, putting food in your mouth, or replacing a glass on the table.
- Choose utensils over your hands in nearly every situation. When picking fruit from a platter, for example, look for serving utensils that you can use to transfer the fruit onto a small plate or a toothpick that can serve the same purpose. When using a toothpick, do not put the pick in your mouth until after you have retrieved all of the food that you want. If you decide to get more food, get a fresh pick.

Food Service

Pay attention, because you will surely find yourself in the roles of both guest and food server on many occasions in your life. The way you handle the serving and removal of food makes a huge difference in how smoothly a meal flows.

- Food should be served on your left, beverages on your right.
- The server should not reach over others to serve. Instead, he should position himself on the appropriate side for the specific item being served.
- Plates should be removed from your right.

- When you have finished your meal, place your knife and fork together on the side of or horizontally across your plate.
- Your plate should not be removed from the table until everyone has finished the meal, not just when you have finished.
- When removing dishes from the table, do not pile them on top of each other. (Although many people do this, it is not the proper way of doing it.) Instead, take as many dishes as you can (usually two or three) and remove them; then come back for the others.

When Passing Food

Let's start before a single morsel of food is touched. Make sure before you sit down to eat a meal—any meal, anywhere—that you wash your hands with soap. (Just listen: I'm sure you can hear your grandmother reminding you right now.) Think in graceful terms when food is passing your way. Before you take any food from a passed platter, take a quick inventory to see if there is enough food on that platter for the number of guests present. Take your helping with others in mind, but don't be hypersensitive.

- At a buffet or when food is passed, don't pile food on your plate. It's more appropriate to take a second helping later. Piling up your plate suggests that you think your host might run out of food.
- Do not reach over people for items such as salt and pepper or sugar. They should be handed toward you, person to person.
- When you pass something to another person, place the item on the table. Do not put it in the person's hand, as this may easily cause a spill.
- When passing knives, never point the blade at the person. Hold the knife at the top of the handle to avoid touching the blade. (This applies to scissors, too.)
- Don't ever touch the rim of someone else's glass. Pass glasses by holding the stem.

Fundamentals of Dining

Elders and ancestors have been passing along wisdom since the beginning of time. Partly because society has become so casual and partly because people have become more self-absorbed, these fundamentals are often overlooked:

- Always honor the age-old rule of keeping your elbows off the table. Forearms are acceptable, though.
- Don't wipe your mouth with your hands, sleeve or anything other than your napkin.

- Don't lick your fingers or mouth at the table, even when you're eating finger foods, like fried chicken.
- Don't chew with your mouth open, and don't smack your lips while eating.
- Don't blow your nose at the table or in your dinner napkin. If possible, excuse yourself from the table and relieve yourself in the rest room—and wash your hands! You may wipe your nose at the table with a handkerchief or tissue.
- Cover your mouth when you sneeze, cough or belch. Obvious, yes, but many forget to do so, especially at casual functions. Trust that no one wants your germs!
- When someone is addressing a group during a meal, don't get up while the person is speaking (unless you really must). And be very quiet if you're eating while people are speaking.
- Don't touch your hair in the presence of food.
- Something that many people forget: your bread plate is on your left; your glasses are on your right.
- Do not eat off of other people's plates—ever. If you want to share food, separate a portion from your plate and put it on another plate to pass.
- Whenever you are squeezing lemons or limes, cover the fruit with your left hand.
- Eat all of the food on your plate, but don't stuff yourself. Leave room for the food to digest—and for the dessert tray!
- In a formal setting, don't ask for a doggy bag. If you are interested in knowing what will happen to the leftovers, you may inquire with the maître d' and recommend a homeless shelter or other service.
- Don't pick your teeth with toothpicks or fingers at the table. Go to the restroom.
- Generally it is inappropriate for women to apply makeup at the table. However, at a casual meal with a friend, it is okay to apply lipstick—not a full face.
- Use discretion with your affection in public, particularly when dining.
- Don't eat and run. When you arrive, inform your host of any time constraints before the meal; then you won't seem as if you just stopped by to grub. When you have to leave early, arrive on time.
- Be mindful of your alcohol intake at public events. Many people have embarrassed themselves by drinking too much without even realizing it. Especially at events where several courses of alcoholic beverages are served, watch your intake. Drink water before, during and after alcohol. If you are thirsty, drink water before you start drinking alcohol. Sometimes people drink too much and too quickly because they are thirsty.

Let's Toast

When it's time to toast, you really can have fun as you honor the people gathered. Even at a roast for someone that is designed to rank on the person, you still want to be tasteful. You can be funny and even insulting without being crass or profane. Sinbad and Bill Cosby are two of the funniest comedians I've ever heard, and neither curses in a routine. Your words will ring in every person's ears and likely be remembered much later. Make your thoughts count. Planning ahead will help. Logistically, you can get people's attention by clinking a wineglass (Be gentle; glass breaks, you know) with a spoon or other utensil. As they quiet down, raise your glass and begin your toast using a clear, crisp voice. Don't yell, but project your "inside voice." Make your comments brief, specific to the person being toasted, inclusive of everyone gathered—and tasteful. When toasting, it is customary for everyone to touch glasses gently before drinking. If you are part of a large group, you need touch only your neighbors' glasses. You should not toast with an empty glass. A glass of water or any other liquid is fine.

Here are some toasts to get your creative juices flowing:

> I'd like to propose a toast to Jackie, who did a fantastic job bringing us all together and making such a magnificent meal. Jackie, you have created a magical evening for us all. Here's to you!

> To Earl: On behalf of everyone here, I want to congratulate you on a job well done. Your foresight on this project made our company grow twofold in less than a year. We thank you. Cheers.

> Dear Vanessa, it's hard to put in words what we are all feeling today. I've known you since you were a little girl, and now you are about to get married. I trust that your married life will be as full and rewarding as the memories I have of you from so many years ago. On behalf of all of the bridesmaids, I want to wish you all the love, happiness and peace that life has to offer.

> Mr. Johnson, on behalf of all of your students, I want to congratulate you on your most recent honor as teacher of the year. We have loved learning from you. The way that you teach really brings the subject to life. Thank you for everything. Congratulations!

- Don't come to events high. Too frequently people arrive at events reeking of alcohol or marijuana, and it's an automatic turn-off. Arrive at functions clear-headed, so you smell good and everyone can have a great time.

During Your Meal

Allow your body to relax. If you can do that even as you pay attention to your surroundings and the fact that you are eating, you will be fine.

- Excuse yourself whenever you get up from the table.
- Sit up straight when you're eating. Your posture will aid in your digestion and make you appear and be more attentive. Don't lean back or slouch over your plate or bowl.
- Never take yourself to the food; bring the food to you.
- Do not start to eat until your host gives you a cue. Often people say grace before meals. If you choose to pray when others are not doing so, you may offer a silent prayer before eating. If you choose not to pray with the group, you may sit silently as they pray with your head lowered out of respect.
- Don't call your waiter *garçon*. It means "boy" in French and used to be a common practice but is a derogatory term. Never snap your fingers or yell at a waiter to request service. Be gracious. I've heard too many stories of waiters who felt disrespected and got the offenders back by contaminating their food.
- Even if you are really hungry, don't shovel food into your mouth. Eat at a relaxed pace and chew your food thoroughly.

Working Meals

Many business meetings happen around meals. Now, there's a sister-elder school of thought that says you shouldn't talk business while you're eating, which makes such a concept seem incongruous. Yet it does exist. If you find yourself part of a working breakfast, lunch or dinner, you can make the best of it by sizing up the meeting, determining what is expected of you, how well you know the others with whom you are dining, how much talking you will have to do and how much time you will have for your meal. It's always smart to eat food that is not messy when you're on business. You'll be less likely to have a spill or other mishap. Remember your Mama's rule: *Don't talk with food in your mouth*. This holds for any dining experience, but I can't tell you how many people appear oblivious to their own actions. Trust that nobody wants to look at you if what they're seeing is food moving around in your mouth. When dining on business, select food that is easy to chew in one or two bites, that is not too liquidy or stringy (you want to stay neat throughout your meal) and that is not too much for you to manage. You don't want to be wasteful. (I can hear the elders' chorus now: *Your eyes are too big for your stomach, huh?!*)

Occasionally a business associate may invite you to join him for a breakfast meeting. Who pays for the meal? Generally the person who does the inviting (regardless of the time of day) is supposed to pick up the tab, tip included. It's likely that your dining companion selected the restaurant and is therefore aware of the pricing of menu items, so you

Family Dining

Eating at home in America is not always what you might think. For an orthodox Suni Muslim family, the family way of eating included everyone coming together at the same time. A straw mat was placed on the floor. Large communal bowls filled with rice, vegetables and other food were placed in the center of the mat. Each member of the family, beginning with the oldest, took food from the communal bowl and placed food into individual bowls. They then ate carefully using three fingers of the right hand—the middle and index fingers and thumb—as utensils. "We never made a mess or spilled our food when I was growing up," says Aliyyah Abdur-Rahman, a twenty-something young woman who grew up in a strictly disciplined family of fourteen children. It was only when she went to college and was invited to a formal Christian wedding that she began to consider learning Western eating etiquette. "Growing up in a Muslim community, I did not eat with people who used knives and forks, and I didn't know how to handle them correctly. After I was invited to the wedding, one of my best friends taught me. Then later, a friend from Haiti whose family had spent a lot of time in Europe helped me to refine what I had already learned." Today Aliyyah is grateful for her multicultural experiences—and also for her friends' support. Not knowing Western eating habits at a critical moment made her see the importance of learning the etiquette of two worlds. It was also an eye-opener for Aliyyah's mom, who then decided to teach the younger children both ways of dining.

Every environment has its rules of the table, including the family. Even the most typical African-American household has unwritten rules surrounding the family's eating habits. If you have children, you may want to formalize those patterns. Explain them explicitly. No matter how busy you are, find a way to share at least one meal a day with your family. Use that time to tutor your children on good table etiquette and to cultivate a relationship with them in which you discuss the events of the day. By sticking to a disciplined ritual of eating and practicing good manners at home, you will ingrain them in your children so that they will stay with them over the years. You may also want to talk about the ways that other people handle dining situations that are different from your own. By all means, you want to cultivate openness and flexibility in your family, even as you ensure that they have standards you find appropriate to follow.

should feel confident that you can order what you would like—within reason. Don't take this opportunity to order the most expensive item on the menu. Look for what you would like, and then check out the price. If it is within average of the other menu items, feel free to order. For breakfast meetings, don't order alcohol. Drinking at the top of the day doesn't represent good business decorum and can dull your ability to respond effectively during your meeting.

Back to who pays, I always have a backup plan: enough cash or room on my credit card to cover the cost in case I am asked to split the bill or the host doesn't offer to pay. I may offer a tip for both of us to the coatroom attendant. If the meeting includes a number of people, the tip can be one flat sum or each person can tip individually.

Suppose you were invited to a lunch meeting with high-ranking corporate executives at their office. If this is your first invitation from them, you might say: I'm not sure what to wear, how to behave, where to sit—anything—help! First off, relax. If you were invited, that means that the executives want to meet with you. They value you. The key to a successful lunch is for you to remember to value yourself, which begins with being prepared. Consider the executives. What do you know about them? Is the environment strictly blue suits? How do women dress? How do men dress? Dress moderately in a professional style. But don't go too far. You can use the filter of the corporate environment for checks and balances, but remember that you want to represent yourself as yourself. Your personal flair is important.

Knowing how to act in this setting is important. Paying attention is key. From the moment you arrive at the office, observe others to see how they are communicating. Shake everyone's hand firmly but not aggressively. When people get nervous, breathing is the first thing to go. People often hold their breath rather than inviting it to support them through sticky situations. So, breathe! When you enter the room where you will be dining, don't sit down. The host of the meal should indicate where guests will sit as well as when. Typically people sit down after everyone has arrived, which means *do be on time*. There may be place settings that indicate where you will sit, or you may be invited to be seated in a particular place. Don't worry. The time will come, and you will either be told or you can follow your host's lead. Once you are seated, speak to the person on either side of you and in front of you if you haven't already. Wait until everyone has been served before you begin to eat, unless the host indicates that someone is waiting for a special dish and you should begin. Remember to use utensils from the outside in for each course. When in doubt, look at what your host is doing, and follow suit.

Hosting a Dinner Party

So many occasions can prompt a dinner party—anything from a host's wanting to thank a group of people for helping to make a project a success, to a celebration of spring or a chance to get together with friends. Whatever your reasons may be for having a dinner party, make it the best affair it can be by planning carefully. At the top of your mind should be your guests and how you can make them feel comfortable. Of course, that starts with the food. Find out if any of your guests has dietary preferences, allergies or restrictions, so that you can prepare food accordingly.

Jonell Nash elaborates on the challenges facing a host these days in her book *Low Fat Soul* (1996). She says, "Seems almost everyone's on one type of diet or another these days. So what's a hostess to do when planning her menu? It's easier to select foods with a broad appeal than it is to customize to specific individuals. Vegetarians alone fall into three distinct types—varying from those who include eggs and cheese to those who exclude all foods of animal origin, including honey! Simply base a menu around the treasures of the earth—in-season vegetables, fruits, grains and nuts." Create a budget for your meal that includes food, decorations and drinks. Pay special attention to the overall look of your party. It should be festive and immediately reflective of your theme. Then plan your menu.

For the Vegetarian

When the nineties began, my husband and I changed our diets dramatically. For spiritual and health reasons, we decided to give up meat and become vegetarian. I discovered that it actually wasn't that hard to do, because ever since I had lived in New York (since 1984), I hadn't eaten much meat anyway. The downsides of becoming a vegetarian had more to do with eating out and eating a well-balanced meal than anything else. Over the years, I have developed a way of managing both fairly well. In the process, I've also learned that there are all types of vegetarians—from the strictest—vegans who do not eat any dairy, meat or fish—to those who are more relaxed, and eat fish and chicken but no red meat. If you're planning a meal and you expect vegetarians to join you, find out how strict their diets are. Usually the addition of one vegetable side dish and one alternative protein entrée, such as tofu, seiten or a vegetable and cheese casserole will suffice. See the cookbook list in this chapter for menu and recipe ideas.

Note: When hosting vegetarians, be considerate of your guests' dietary needs. Warner Johnson, an entrepreneur in New York City, hosts lots of dinner parties. Warner, who loves to eat meat, has developed a perfect balance for his meat-eating and vegetarian guests. He serves filet mignon along with penne pasta tossed with arugula and tomato. They look great together on his buffet, and everyone leaves happy and full.

Here are some of Jonell Nash's recommendations from *Low Fat Soul* for dinner party fare:

- Vegetarian menu choices. Serve starters, such as spicy black bean dip with crudité, through a main course that includes two hearty vegetables cooked without meat, such as collard greens with sun-dried tomatoes and orange-flavored sweet potatoes and a grain, such as couscous with almonds and raisins. Make mostly vegetable dishes a focal point. Always include a salad that brims with crisp, mixed greens. An array of vegetable dishes adds fresh flavor and vivid color to your party table.
- Meat dishes. Beef is America's favorite red meat—in the form of roasts or ribs (fajitas are a popular choice), though you can easily substitute roasted or smoked turkey breast for beef. Chicken has always been the quintessential party meat in the Black community, and with good reason. It features low-fat appeal and versatility in and with a variety of dishes. All manner of finfish and shellfish make welcome choices too. A whole baked snapper or sea bass stuffed with herbed dressing makes an easy and elegant main dish.
- Dessert. When it comes to dessert—the grand finale—include at least two offerings. If one dessert is rich and gooey, serve it in small quantities. Balance the choice by offering a naturally sweet, fresh fruit cup, strawberry shortcakes or a fruit salad of sliced oranges, pineapple and kiwi topped with toasted coconut. My mother and her friends called this combination ambrosia, and they were right.
- The bar. When setting up your bar, include nonalcoholic beverages such as sparkling cider and seltzer mixed with fruit juices. Add a twist of lemon or lime for zest.

Note: If you do not cook or are not prepared to cook for your party, by all means have the party catered. You can choose from a wide assortment of catering establishments; check with your favorite restaurant too. Whether your party is for five or fifty, most restaurants will be glad to service your needs. Call well in advance to find out how you can best work with the catering establishment. Place your order explicitly, including the time that you want the food either delivered to your home or ready for pick up. Make your food arrival at least two hours before the evening is to begin. You need time to set it up and change your clothes without rushing. Give at least a 15 percent tip to the establishment. If you need serving help, find out if you can hire someone there.

Beyond your menu, here are a few other key details to ensure the success of your dinner party:

- Invite your guests as far in advance as possible—at least two weeks. Give them a specific start time for the meal. You may want to tell them that cocktails will be from 6:00 to 7:00 P.M. and dinner at 8:00 P.M. In this way, your guests will be clear on the deadline for their arrival.
- Prepare your home for your guests, making sure that you have enough hand towels, soap, toilet paper and other essentials for their comfort.
- Create an ambience that will set the mood for the evening. For instance, if your meal features a Caribbean menu, you may want to play soca or reggae in the background and have Caribbean textiles as your table coverings. Your invitations should reflect your theme as well.
- Enroll enough assistance to keep the party flowing smoothly. If your guest list is more than eight people, you will need at least one additional support person to help serve food and clear away dishes. You also may want to have a bartender if you are planning a larger party. Contact your local college to see if there is a bartending service or bartending school. I have found great assistance through colleges at affordable prices.
- Plan an after-dinner activity—anything from watching a video to playing pool, bid whist, dominoes or computer games. Of course, inviting your guests to an area where you can have dessert and schmooze is ideal.

Special Needs for Dietary Concerns

The African-American community has its share of health concerns that relate to diet.

Diabetes

It's no secret that a lot of our family members suffer from diabetes. (It runs in my family as a devastating disease.) At the same time, plenty of diabetics don't take kindly to having to change their diets, particularly on special occasions. As host, we can make it our responsibility to feed our guests in the most healthful manner. For diabetics, that generally means a meal that's low in sugar of any kind, including carbohydrates (which break down into sugar in the body). When you know that you are having guests who have this disorder, include appetizing menu items that will appeal to everyone and feature vegetables and lean meats (if you serve meat). For dessert, natural fruits are winners.

If you find that you need to delay the start of your meal to wait for others, be prepared to feed your diabetic guests on time. Eating on schedule is one of the critical requirements for most diabetics. (Actually, that's why they may have brought along a snack to take care of themselves.) If you're unsure as to how to serve your guests, ask in advance. A call to inquire about what your guests would most like to eat is a gracious and loving gesture—the height of good manners.

Halal

When inviting people of the Muslim faith for dinner at your home, be mindful of some basic guidelines and religious dish restrictions. Most natural foods are *halal* (or sacred), such as vegetables, grains, beans and fruits. Fish and meat, when slaughtered properly and prayed over, are also *halal*. Meat becomes *halal* when it is slaughtered quickly with a sharp knife with the least possible amount of suffering on the part of the animal, as the words *Bismillah* ("in the name of Allah") and *Allahu Akbar* ("God is great") are uttered. Muslims are not allowed to eat the meat of ferocious animals. In addition, cheese and other processed foods are often not *halal* because some are made with animal by-products. Muslims do not eat pork or drink alcohol. Jewish people and Muslims have a few similar religious guidelines with regard to prescribed food rituals of slaughtered animals, which is why kosher meat is also considered *halal*.

Kosher

People who eat kosher do so for religious reasons. Eating kosher foods is part of traditional Jewish life. Substitutions are easy to accomplish, even for international fare. Be mindful of the religious dietary guidelines of your Jewish guests by asking them for their help with the menu so it will be appropriate.

In fact, the word *kosher* means "proper" in Hebrew, and it applies to meat that has been properly slaughtered, as well as foods that have been properly prepared, according to Jewish dietary and religious laws. Some of the laws are found in the books of Exodus, Leviticus and Deuteronomy from the Bible, where verses relate to the issues of *kashrus,* or rituals of holiness. However, the Pentateuch identifies them as *chukkim,* holy statutes, which are faithfully followed for the mere fact that they are grounded in scripture. There are many rules of *kashrus,* which specify the rules for properly slaughtering and preparing foods so they will be kosher. For example, *schechitah* refers to slaughtering meat in the proper manner. Also the mixing of meat and milk products at the same meal is prohibited, so milk and meat must be prepared, served and eaten on two different sets of dishes and utensils. Some Eastern European Jews believe in allowing several hours between eating meat and milk, to let the body properly digest meat.

Kosher foods can be purchased at kosher stores and restaurants. If you are planning to invite Jewish guests—who may be Black, for there's a large Ethiopian Jewish population in the world—you might ask them where to purchase prepared dishes or the proper groceries for the meal. Being respectful of your guests' religious beliefs shows that you care. The gesture will be appreciated.

Lactose Intolerance

A lot of Black folks can't stomach milk or milk products. I'm one of them. People who suffer from lactose intolerance range in the degree that they are affected—from doubling over in pain after drinking a glass of milk or eating a bowl of ice cream to experiencing varying degrees of stomach cramping after eating small portions of cheese or cream sauce included in other dishes. Since your guests may not mention their condition, it's best to provide dishes that take this common ailment into account. Lactose-free milk is a thoughtful option for cream, although a dried nondairy creamer will also work. Check to ensure that your creamer truly is lactose free. Other lactose substitutes are soy—a product used for centuries in the Far East and growing in popularity in the West—margarine, rice and oat-based "milk" and other products.

Hosting a Tea

It used to be that a tea party in the South was a frequent event on hot summer afternoons. Sisters would gather on each other's porches, shaded from the scorching heat, sip iced tea and reminisce for hours at a time. Believe it or not, those days are not over. Tea parties, whether they are outside on ice or inside with steam, are still popular and fun. And they're not just for women, either! What with the decline in alcohol consumption and the rise in entertaining, many folks are looking for alternative ways to spend time with each other. The traditional tea party is a great solution. Any number of Caribbean and African countries were once colonized by the British who brought their love of Indian tea with them. My husband, George, who is Jamaican, drinks tea every day and has introduced me to the practice. If you consider having a tea party, there are a few pointers that can help you pull it off with grace.

- Have an assortment of fine teas—caffeinated, decaffeinated and herbal. The selection is so broad these days that you can have lots of fun selecting them. Earl Grey and darjeeling are favorites in the black tea category. Peppermint, chamomile and lemon are popular herbal teas.
- Make sure that you have a proper tea service, including a porcelain or clay teapot with teacups and saucers and silver for all of your

Great Cookbooks

LOW-FAT COOKING

Wilbert Jones, *The New Soul Food Cookbook* (Birch Lane Press, 1996). Jones, the caterer for Healthy Concepts in Chicago and food scientist for Kraft, wrote this 128-page book, which offers recipes with less salt, cholesterol and sugar, such as unfried hush puppies and collard greens.

Jonell Nash, *Low-Fat Soul* (Ballantine, 1996). Nash is the well-known food editor of *Essence* magazine. In this book, Nash brings a wealth of experience to this subject. The book is filled with delicious recipes and menus for appealing and healthy low-fat meals.

Jonell Nash, *Essence Brings You Great Cooking* (Amistad Press, 1994). Nash organized and wrote this easy-to-follow cookbook with 300 recipes, as well as a listing of the calories, protein, fat, carbohydrates, sodium and cholesterol breakdown for each. This 480-page book outlines all of the major food groups and courses and provides menus and recipes for healthy, good food.

CARIBBEAN COOKING

Yvonne Ortiz, *A Taste of Puerto Rico* (Dutton, 1994). Ortiz is a chef in New Jersey who grew up in Puerto Rico. This colorful 288-page cookbook provides such authentic and tasty recipes as yellow rice with crab and rum cake.

Jay Solomon, *A Taste of the Tropics: Traditional and Innovative Cooking from the Pacific and Caribbean* (Crossing Press, 1992). The owner and chef of Jay's Clinton Café in Ithaca, New York, created this book, which features 139 pages of such basic Caribbean recipes as Jamaican beef patties and kiwi mango flambé. Illustrated.

Robb Walsh and Jay McCarthy, *Traveling Jamaica with a Knife, Food and Spoon: A Righteous Guide to Jamaican Cookery* (Crossing Press, 1995). Walsh, a food writer, and McCarthy, a chef at Cascabel Restaurant in Houston, Texas, wrote this 240-page cookbook after their journey across Jamaica. The recipes were gathered from the kitchens of island cooks and sidewalk cafés and feature homemade dishes such as yam balls and fried plantains with chile.

VEGETARIAN COOKING

Rose Elliott, *The Classic Vegetarian Cookbook: A Classic New Approach to Vegetarian Cooking* (Dorling Kindersley Publishing, 1994). Elliott is a life-long vegetarian and author of more than forty cookbooks. This 176-page recipe guide boasts large color photos and easy-to-follow directions to such foods as falafel and lavender honey ice cream.

Editors of *Vegetarian Times* magazine, *Vegetarian Times Low-Fat and Fast* (Macmillan USA, 1997). The 208-page cookbook features 150 easy, meatless recipes such as tofu chow mein and grilled portobello pita pizza with chili aioli.

SOUTHERN, AFRICAN AND AFRICAN-AMERICAN COOKING

Angela Shelf Medearis, *The African-American Kitchen Cooking from Our Heritage* (Dutton, 1994). Shelf Medearis is an author and historian from Austin, Texas. This 256-page book combines and explains the Caribbean and African influences in recipes from slave quarters to church suppers and family reunions. It provides recipes for such dishes as African fruit punch and Nigerian eggplant.

Barbara Smith, *B. Smith's Entertaining and Cooking for Friends* (Workman Publishing Co., 1995). Smith is the owner of B. Smith's restaurants in New York City, Washington, D.C., and Sag 'Harbor, New York. This book is filled with elegant color photos and entertaining tips with such recipes as jalapeño corn muffins and grilled spiced shrimp with plantains.

Kathryn Tucker Windham, *Southern Cooking to Remember* (Ingram, 1977). Tucker Windham is a famed storyteller and Alabama chef. This 240-page handbook is filled with old favorites such as red velvet cake and fried okra.

Dori Sanders, *Dori Sander's Country Cooking: Recipes and Stories from the Family Farm Stand* (Algonquin Books of Chapel Hill, 1995). Sanders is a renowned Southern cook. Her 240-page guide has basic down-home recipes such as roasted corn on the cob and lemon biscuits.

Norma Jean and Carole Darden, *Spoonbread and Strawberry Wine: Reminiscences of a Family* (Doubleday, 1994). These two North Carolina sisters—Jean, a caterer of Spoonbread, in New York City, and Carole, owner of a family real estate business—drew from their family tree and rich heritage to create this 336-page book filled with photos, stories and recipes for home cooking.

National Council of Negro Women, *The Black Family Dinner Quilt Cookbook* (Fireside, 1994). This book by the nationally respected women's council serves up such old-fashioned favorites as johnny cakes, country chicken and creamy macaroni and cheese.

National Council of Negro Women, *The Black Family Reunion Cookbook* (Fireside, 1991). This 224-page book features such great dishes as shrimp curry and Southern rice cakes.

Carolyn Quick Tillery, *Traditional Recipes and Fond Remembrances from Alabama's Renowned Tuskegee Institute: African-American Heritage Cookbook* (Birch Lane Press, 1996). Quick Tillery is a writer and literary agent in Fairfax, Virginia. This 224-page book features historical photos, facts and recipes such as George Washington Carver salad and buttermilk rolls.

JEWISH COOKING

Faye Levy, *International Jewish Cookbook* (Warner Books, 1991). Levy is a renowned Jewish cook and author. This 368-page guide provides more than 250 traditional Jewish recipes, such as sweet and sour salmon and lentil soup.

Harriet Roth, *Deliciously Healthy Jewish Cooking* (Dutton, 1996). Roth is a well-known cook and cookbook author. The 464-page cookbook provides 350 low-fat recipes and tips for reducing calories when cooking.

guests, as well as a sugar bowl and creamer. If you don't have enough matching cups for everyone, present an assortment of cups and saucers that makes the mood festive. You also need a serving tray or two and cloth napkins. A tea cozy—a fabric cover—is ideal for keeping your teapot warm.

- Sweets are traditionally served with tea, such as scones, other breads and fruit.
- Dress is usually fun and festive.

Coordinating a Picnic

Whether the event calls for just you and your beloved, an intimate family group or a huge gathering of friends, the essentials for a picnic remain the same. You need to have food that can survive a few hours away from the refrigerator, an ample supply of drinks (including water and ice), a grill, matches and lighter fluid, table coverings and/or a surface to serve as a table, lots of napkins, a receptacle for garbage, flatware, disposable dishes and glasses, a cooler and a basket or other container that will protect food from insects. Make a list to check off before you head out on your picnic, so that you don't forget any essentials. If you're headed to a remote place, you may not be able to find that one missing item near your destination. As far as etiquette goes, keep these pointers in mind:

- Pick a location that is not too close to other people, so that you can have privacy.
- If you bring along music or other entertainment, keep the volume at a reasonable level.
- Watch your children. You know how fast they can get away from you. Assign a responsible person, like an older child or young adult, to keep an eye on them if you want to take a break.
- Keep your pets on a leash. Dogs love to search for food. Your neighbor will not appreciate having to deal with your marauding animal.
- Citronella candles can set a beautiful atmosphere and ward off insects. Make sure they are out of the reach of children, though.
- Be sure to pack games and books that will entertain everyone in your party.
- Put all food away as soon as you have finished eating.
- Clean up before you leave.

Holiday Meals

Getting together with family and loved ones during the holidays marks a high point in almost everyone's life. Thanksgiving, Christmas, Kwanzaa, Easter and the evenings of Ramadan are among the most popular gathering times. For these occasions, diners expect cultural delicacies—collard greens and callaloo, corn pudding and curried goat, black cake and rum punch, baked ham and sweet potato pie. People often pitch in to make specific dishes for these large meals. It's best to coordinate with the host of the meal to ensure that you are bringing an item that is needed. If the meal is a traditional family gathering, like in the movie, *Soul Food,* you already know who's cooking what. Sometimes the best contribution you can make to a big meal is to show up early (with permission, of course), pitch in and stay late to clean up.

Frequently these days people who live far away from their families are recreating traditions in their new communities, which means they may be planning a huge meal for the first time. If you are hosting a Thanksgiving meal for a group of friends who won't be headed home, for example, don't panic:

- Talk to your friends to learn of their expectations for the holiday meal.
- Make a list of all that you need to make the meal a success, from the food to the ambience to the entertainment.
- Find out how your friends can contribute, and note that on your list.
- Unless you are a great cook with a lot of time on your hands, don't feel that you have to prepare everything yourself. It's more fun to include others in the process. Besides, if everybody brings something, you know there will be something for everybody to eat.
- Set a realistic time for your meal, and then organize your schedule so that you will be ready when your guests arrive. Get dressed at least an hour before their scheduled arrival.
- Make sure that your home is clean, that you have ample hand towels in your bathroom and that your kitchen is organized so that your friends can help without stumbling over each other.
- Set your dishes and utensils out the night before.
- Unless you have assigned setting the table to someone else, dress the table in the morning well in advance of your guests' arrival.
- Decorate your home with appropriate seasonal items. When in doubt, use candles to set the mood.
- Select soft music that will play during your meal. You may want to make selections from a variety of cultures and genres.

How to Be a Good Guest

- Find out in advance if your children are welcome. Don't assume that they or your date who was not initially invited can come. Some gatherings are casual, and it will be no problem at all to bring your loved ones. At more formal affairs, extra guests could present a problem. The meal could be counted for per person catering; the dining tables may not accommodate additional people; your host may not like children.
- Devote a little extra time to your host by offering to come early to pitch in. Once you arrive, don't get distracted by the television or a juicy conversation. Honor your word and help out.
- Don't come empty-handed. If you have not already committed to preparing a dish or bringing a premade item, come with a bottle of wine or sparkling water, cider or ginger beer, a bouquet of flowers, a fragrant candle, an after-dinner activity or some other thoughtful gift.
- Offer to be part of cleanup duty. Unless a hired helper is assigned to this job, you will be praised forever for helping on the back end of the meal. The host will be exhausted and will appreciate being able to relax with the guests while others take over the kitchen. Be sure to ask permission to help in this way, though; some cooks really don't want anyone else in their kitchens!
- Don't overstay your welcome. As the party winds down, graciously make your exit. Be sure to thank the host for a wonderful meal. Then gather your belongings and leave.

- Survey your home to ensure that all of your cleaning supplies have been put away, all candles are lit and all decorations are in place before your first guest arrives.

Potluck Meals

One of the all-time favorite ways of getting together in the Black community is over a potluck dinner. For this event, everybody brings something—a covered dish, an entrée, bread, a dessert, drinks, appetizers or other items such as table linens, a centerpiece or games for the kids. What's important is that everyone participates. Because so many contribute to this meal, it is wise for the host of the event to do considerable preplanning and coordination. Find out what each participant would like to prepare, and make sure that their suggestions will fill out a well-rounded menu. Write out the list of items being offered, and let people know if you need anything. Follow the other suggestions listed in "Holiday Meals" in this chapter.

Paper Products: Dos and Don'ts

Used to be that you didn't go to a special dinner at someone's home where there wasn't a table set with the finest china the family had. Even for everyday, the table featured "real" dishes and cloth napkins. Disposable was unheard of! Obviously, times have changed. More and more families use disposable items—everything from paper plates and napkins to plastic—to help make cleanup simpler as well as to increase safety for outdoor entertaining or children's parties. Today the choices are vast. You can find all types of party motifs on paper and plastic goods, including cultural icons and designs, which can help make your decorating job easier. At the same time, people are growing more conscientious about waste. To strike a balance, consider using disposable products sparingly—for picnics, late-night meals, big family events or other parties, children's activities (you can protect those little fingers best when there's nothing around that will break) or other times when it might be challenging to wash lots of dishes.

YOUR QUESTIONS ANSWERED

1. If I can't remember all of the functions for a place setting, is it safe to go from the inside out, as conventional wisdom suggests?

Yes. In fact, formal place settings are designed in just that manner. The outermost utensils are the first to be used, for salads and soups generally. Should you skip a course, the waiter in a good restaurant will remove the now-unnecessary utensil. When in doubt, observe your host or neighbor who seems most in the know. One formal dining expert was Patrick Clark, former executive chef at the world-famous Tavern On The Green restaurant located in Central Park in New York City. Chef Clark, a veteran in the culinary industry, managed every aspect of the food, menu preparation, purchasing and staffing for Tavern On The Green. Here is his advice on formal dining. "I think knowing proper dining etiquette is important. Although the air of formality that we had during the 70s and 80s has been pushed aside for a more relaxed dining atmosphere, you will find yourself in situations where that etiquette needs to be known, especially if you get invited to a black-tie affair, where there are multiple courses of food. You sit down to the table and see four forks in front of you and you're wondering, 'Okay, so what do I do with the other three?' " Clark said. "You should work from the outside in, that's basically how a formal table service is set up. Usually, if the people serving the dinner—if their service is correct—each fork and knife or spoon will correspond with the course that's coming. There are also multi-course dinners where they will bring the silver to the table for each course, which is another way of not embarrassing people."

At informal meals, especially those in people's homes, place settings may vary tremendously. Follow your host's lead or what seems practical if you're unsure.

2. In many African cultures, people eat with their hands. I was always taught this was a sign of no home training. How should I respond?

Many of the world's peoples do not do things as they are done here. This is due to cultural differences. When you are dealing with people and their ways of doing things that are different than you are used to because they come from another culture, you should not subject them to standards such as your home training. In this case, the question is not of home training but of culture. I will never forget going to an Ethiopian restaurant with several friends shortly after I moved to New York City. We sat down before a beautifully carved, round wooden table. We each ordered foods that none of us had tasted before. The surprise, though, was less the taste of the food than the way we were expected to eat it. My good friend Jeffrey, a die-hard Baltimorean with Western expectations about everything, nearly fell off his seat when he saw that all of our food was on one plate that was lined with a thin layer of bread, known as *injera*. We were told that it was traditional for us to share our various entrées with one another and tear off small pieces of the *injera* to scoop up the food. The *injera* was fun. The food was delicious. It turned out to be a great experience.

My recommendation, whether you are having a new dining experience that features an unfamiliar cuisine or you are dining abroad, is to find out the proper dining etiquette in advance. If you have reservations about following the customary eating habits, you can request a knife and fork in most situations. Be sure not to judge others. Ask questions and relax a little. The world is large. Good manners are supposed to be about making people more comfortable around you.

3. I've been told that I should arrive at an event exactly on time. What is considered "fashionably late"?

It really depends on the setting. For most dining events, especially those where people will be seated for the meal, you should arrive before the formal meal begins. If you can't prevent arriving a little late, fifteen to thirty minutes is a good barometer for your arrival, although it's best to check with your host to be certain. It's rude to keep people waiting. When it's unavoidable, call to let your hosts know that you will be late and offer your sincere apologies upon your arrival. Your call will allow the host to start the meal without feeling guilty and thus care for her other guests well.

4. What is an appropriate gift to bring to someone's home when I'm invited to a meal?

In the Black community, a covered dish (casserole), delicious dessert, flowers or beverage has been the most favored gift to bring to someone's home, whether it's for a meal, a housewarming or another

Eating Around the World

- Mealtime rules vary depending on where you are in the world. When you are invited to a meal in Zimbabwe, Botswana or South Africa, for example, you should arrive on time to a meal at someone's house, even if you have to wait.
- It is rarely considered appropriate anywhere in the Diaspora for you to eat using your left hand. In some African countries, such as Mali and Uganda, such an act is considered highly offensive, to the point that frequent travelers recommend to lefties that they sit on their left hand rather than commit an offense.
- In many Asian countries, chopsticks are the most commonly used utensils. Since most urban areas in the West have Chinese and Japanese restaurants that offer chopsticks, many of us Westerners enjoy using them. If you're planning to travel East and want to gain dexterity with sticks, practice stateside. It can be great fun. My husband, George, a Jamaican of Chinese descent, decided to learn how to eat with chopsticks as a way of honoring that part of his cultural heritage. Over the years, he has grown to enjoy chopsticks much more than knives and forks. Now I'm pretty good at using them myself. In fact, some foods don't even taste right off a fork!
- Those living in traditional Islamic communities in the United States and abroad often eat from a communal bowl, using bread and fingers as utensils. One Muslim sister shared that when she was growing up, her grandparents, who are not Muslim, came to dinner and were shocked at the way the family was eating. Over time, as they saw the bond that the family was creating at mealtime, they came to appreciate the family practice. The family also made the grandparents comfortable by offering them separate dishes and utensils for their meals. Similarly, many people abroad who eat communally will offer foreigners separate bowls or plates and utensils if they have them.
- Europeans cut food using the knife in their right hand, but don't typically switch the fork from left to right to eat. The fork remains in the left hand when the food is placed in one's mouth. Because so many people travel internationally these days and so many Europeans live in the United States, you may find people using the European style of eating when you are dining. This does not mean that you should change the way you are eating, or that in a formal setting the traditional American rules do not apply (such as switching the fork back to the right hand).

event. My Aunt Audrey's corn pudding was the dish I always waited to see walk in the door. (Now my sister Stephanie makes it!) Even if we had enough food, that family specialty was a guaranteed success. When in doubt, you can ask your host if he or she needs anything. If it sounds as if the meal is fully set and an extra food item would be unnecessary or inappropriate for the planned menu, you might bring a small item for the home, such as beautiful soaps, a scented candle, a lovely picture book or embroidered tea towels.

5. How can I find the time to eat with my family when we are all on different schedules?

It takes a real commitment on everyone's part. Your first step is to recognize the value of having at least one meal together. Then get creative. If you have children, you should certainly start with breakfast.

Get everyone up a little earlier—the same time each day, if possible—and start the day together. Starting off with a family prayer is a powerful way to bless your day.

If your schedule does not permit you to dine together daily, choose a weekend time—for brunch or dinner—when everyone expects to eat together. Each member of your family can have a specific responsibility surrounding the meal—anything from cooking to setting the table to cleaning. Assign each task with great enthusiasm so that everyone recognizes the special nature of all of the preparations for this event. (Giving tasks for each meal helps so that the work gets done more quickly, and your children learn to accept responsibility.)

6. At family gatherings, what is the appropriate way to honor my elders during meals?

Keep foremost in your mind that your elders should be treated with the greatest respect. Make sure that they are seated comfortably. If the meal is a buffet, be sure that you or someone else serves the elders before serving yourselves. Check to see what they can eat, and don't pile too much food on their plates. The host may also choose to invite a family elder to offer the blessing.

7. My family is hosting a large gathering. Usually everyone brings a dish. I don't think I will be able to cook this time. What should I do instead?

Ask the host what is being served and what is needed that can be purchased. Then consider buying a prepared dish from your favorite restaurant, catering service or the deli section of your local grocery store. If you really don't want to bring a dish, let the host know, and suggest that you bring the centerpiece, decorations or other essentials for the meal that don't require cooking (anything from disposable goods to garbage bags). You can also offer to drive family members who need transportation. There's always something that you can do to contribute. Just check in to find out what will be the best use of your time and energy.

8. I am having family over for dinner, but I wasn't planning on inviting everyone. How can I manage this without hurting anyone's feelings?

Our Southern and West Indian sisters will tell you that you should always make enough food for everybody. Even if you have to provide smaller portions to have enough servings, you should welcome everyone. Yet it is also perfectly acceptable today for you to have a dinner gathering to which you invite specific people, even when they are family. Several young couples have told me that they plan small dinner gatherings to which they invite a few people, but they have them often. So over the course of six months or so, they will have welcomed all of their family and other loved ones to break bread with them.

What's most important here is to think clearly about whom you want to invite. If your list includes everybody except for one aunt or cousin, you might consider adding that person to avoid hard feelings. If, on the other hand, these people rarely participate in your life, the omission may be of no consequence to either of you.

9. I was invited to a business lunch and will not be able to attend. How can I bow out gracefully?

That's why people ask you to RSVP. Contact the host via the response card if one was sent or by phone, leaving a clear message that you cannot attend. Ask the secretary or the host directly when you might be able to reschedule. If possible, set a new date right away, and do your best to show up.

If you previously thought you could attend the meal and discover that you have to cancel, call personally as soon as your plans change with a sincere apology. And follow up to reschedule if you are unable to set a date right then. Regardless of the circumstances, you don't want your lunch date to think that you don't respect his or her time.

10. I am often invited to formal dinners, cocktail parties and other events. When is it appropriate to bring my spouse or a date?

It once was a given that a black tie affair meant that you and your spouse or date were invited. For a woman, going out alone to a formal event was considered terribly inappropriate. These days, the rules have changed considerably. Don't assume that your spouse or date is invited to an event. Look at your invitation to see how it is addressed—to you individually or to you and a guest. Sometimes the invitation will say that it is nontransferable for two or for one. If you are unsure, call your host to inquire about whether you can bring someone.

11. How do you eat fried chicken when you're out in public, particularly if it's a formal business environment?

For some people, this question is a nonissue. Depending on who you are and what your sensibilities may be, your response may change. The real question here is whether you can pick up your chicken and eat it with your hands. Folks who were brought up down South know that that's how you eat fried chicken, with one or both hands depending on what's needed. According to the old school, though, at a formal affair, the only food you eat with your hands is that which is passed during the cocktail hour—hors d'oeuvres. Once you're seated, you don't use anything other than your knife and fork to handle food. So when you're staring at that drumstick trying to figure out what to do, just go on and cut it carefully so that you keep the bone from flying off your plate into your neighbor. That may be all well and good, but some folks argue that culturally we learned that you eat fried chicken, especially the drumstick, with your hands. For those who will sit stewing in their chairs feeling insulted by the insensitivity of the host for serving food that should be eaten in hand, you may want to go on and pick it up.

You can also watch your host to see what he or she is doing. You may be pleasantly surprised to see that your host and others have relaxed the formal understanding of eating and begun to use their hands. If you are unsatisfied with the conditions of your meal, discuss your discomfort privately in an even-toned, clear way with your host. Educating others about what's important to us is an essential part of living a comfortable and peaceful life. Even though it may seem tough when you have to approach a potentially embarrassing situation, going for it and finding kind words to get your point across, no matter what it is, allows for clearer communication and mutual respect. Weigh your issue and your timing, though, so that you don't blow a situation out of proportion.

12. I'm no good at small talk, which is why I don't like attending networking events. What can I do to break the ice, especially if I'm at a sit-down dinner?

Before you go to the event, think about your life and what you like to do the most. Consider next the company that you will be keeping and what synergy there is between your interests and those people. Then, when it feels a little rocky to get a conversation going, bring up one of your safety topics. Your sincerity should help to get the conversation going. Avoid politics and religion, at least to start. You don't want to walk into a hornet's nest, as the elders often say.

When you can bring a guest, invite someone who gets along comfortably with others and with whom you have a great rapport. The two of you can ensure that you have a good time and meet all of the guests.

13. I have a friend who sprinkles her food with salt and pepper as soon as the plate is put before her. Isn't that a sign of bad manners?

Not only is it in poor taste, but it's also not good for your friend's health. When you are invited to dine at someone's home, it can be disconcerting to the host if you season food before tasting it. Doing so is an indication to your host that you believe the cooking is not savory enough for your palate. Whether you're in a private home or at a restaurant, resist the knee-jerk tendency to salt your food. Salt has been proven to be a nemesis to our health, even though historically it has been a significant part of Black folks' diets. Start now to limit your salt intake. You'll thank yourself later.

14. Before I eat, I bless my food. In a business setting, is this appropriate?

Of course. You never have to eliminate the spiritual practice of blessing your food. If you think that the others with whom you are dining will be uncomfortable when you pray, you may want to repeat your blessing silently or otherwise do so discreetly. Or you may want to invite the table to participate in the blessing of the food. At an editorial luncheon a few years ago at *Essence,* Susan Taylor asked one of the editors to bless the food. Mikki Taylor, the beauty and cover editor, invited everyone to join hands and bow their heads. Her brief, heartfelt prayer included a blessing of the food and of the staff, in which she asked for guidance and strength for all of the editors to do the work before them with focus and conviction. If you decide to offer a prayer for a group, keep it simple and to the point. Include the purpose of the gathering and ask for grace to support that purpose. Make your prayer general enough to include others' spiritual traditions. If someone chooses not to participate, don't draw attention to the exclusion.

15. I'm having a cocktail party at my home. I'm not sure of the quantities of alcohol I need to be able to serve my guests adequately.

The general rule to follow is that you should have three alcoholic beverage choices per person. A bottle of wine is adequate for three people. A liter of liquor is good for about ten, depending on how strong you make the drinks. Also, have a healthy selection of nonalcoholic beverages, including still and carbonated water, for those who choose not to drink and for minors, if you are expecting any. It's most affordable to purchase alcohol in quantity. Many liquor stores allow you to buy wine and beer by the case and return any unopened bottles the next day, provided you didn't chill them.

16. I'm planning a cocktail party, and several of my guests are Muslim. Should I let them know in advance that we will be serving alcohol?

The definition of a cocktail party is that you will be serving alcoholic beverages. As you make your guest list, you may want to consider how to handle guests who definitely don't drink. That doesn't mean that they should be excluded from receiving an invitation. Know that traditionally Muslims do not drink alcohol. To avoid insulting them or making them feel uncomfortable, definitely let them know that you are planning a cocktail party. Depending on how close you are, you may also want to ask them what they would care to drink as you will be shopping soon to prepare for the party. In some instances, you may find that your friends decline to attend the party. If so, be supportive and let them know that you would like to get together with them another time. Follow up and invite them for tea or another alcohol-free occasion.

Note: When visiting Islamic countries, refrain from drinking alcohol in the presence of practicing Muslims, which would be really anywhere in these countries. It would be highly insensitive to order a drink when you are dining with a Muslim, unless he or she orders one first. Similarly, when in the company of most devout religious practitioners, from

Christians to Rastafarians, select soft drinks unless your host chooses an alcoholic beverage first.

17. I have invited about fifteen people to my home to a cocktail and dinner party. Do you think I need a bartender?

Yes. To ensure that everyone is well served, you should have someone other than yourself serving drinks and cleaning up during the party. The solution may be as simple as asking your spouse, a close friend or a relative to accept the responsibilities. If that's not a viable solution, hire someone. You can ask your friends for references or contact a local university for assistance. Many colleges have a bartending service staffed by students who are supplementing their income. My experience has shown that students can be attentive, focused and trustworthy, in addition to being well trained for the task. Have a talk with anyone you hire in advance of your event, and let them know their responsibilities, the duration of their employment with you, how to handle uncomfortable situations (such as when not to serve a drink), breaks, their fee and the expected attire. Check with them periodically through the evening to see how they're doing. Pay your bartenders before they leave, and definitely include a tip, at least enough to cover transportation to their home.

18. These being the days of the designated driver, what should I do if a friend gets drunk at my party and doesn't have a ride home?

If you are planning an event where alcohol will be served, it's wise to have a general plan in place to protect your loved ones. Is there someone who would be willing to drive an inebriated guest home? Ask that person to be on alert *before* the party begins. Get the number for a local taxi service that will be working when you expect your party to end. Prepare your guest room or even a couch for someone who needs to spend the night.

19. How can I be a good guest at a cocktail party? Sometimes I feel so awkward?

- Go with a winning attitude that says you are going to have a great time.
- Dress comfortably in the style of the event, which may be business or traditional cocktail dress—a fancy dress and heels for a woman and a suit and tie for a man. If your function is a hip-hop event, the dress code will be more informal, though, so check your invitation and call your host if you are unsure.
- Don't pick up more items than you can manage comfortably. So often people get caught with a drink in one hand and a plate of food in another when they are about to be introduced to someone. No hand is free to shake, and the whole situation becomes a bit unman-

Caring for Your Guests

- *Always serve food* with alcohol, especially at cocktail or dinner parties.
- Pay attention to your guests throughout the evening. If you notice that someone is approaching his or her limit, don't offer another drink. Be sure to let your bartender know to do the same. When someone insists on another drink, rather than allowing a disturbance to ensue, offer alternatives such as water, juice or a watered-down version of the original drink.
- Feel free to cut your cocktail hour short if your guests are becoming inebriated before dinner.
- If your assistance goes unheeded and your guest's behavior grows out of control, take action immediately. Remove your guest to a private area, and either ask someone to take him home or call a car service that will escort him to his door.
- Above all, do not get into a discussion about your guest's drinking at this time. You cannot get through to someone who is high. So, focus on taking care of the situation and returning to your other guests as quickly as possible.
- Identify designated drivers at your event and ask for their help. It is definitely not worth it to let someone slide. The drunk driving statistics challenge us to know better.

---

ageable. Eat first (preferably before you arrive). If you prepare a plate at the function, select foods that you can eat in one bite, so that it will be easy for you to talk all evening. Once you have finished eating, you may get your drink. If you can sit down while you eat, it will be ideal. Then both hands can be free as you make your way through the crowd.

- Don't gulp down your drink even if you have to put it down in order to move to the next part of the event.
- Norma Jean Darden, owner of Spoonbread, a catering company in New York City, says, "By all means, don't double dip." When you're eating crudité, chips or anything else that uses a communal dip, you should dip *before* you take a bite. And that's it! If you think you want more dip, you can scoop some out and put it on a small plate or get another carrot stick and start over. Double dipping is unhygienic; actually, it's downright *nasty!*

20. How do I deal with a guest who has overstayed his welcome?

Sometimes your guests are having such a good time that they don't notice that everyone else has gone home. In such an instance, you will need to remind them. One couple in South Carolina had this experience. They walked up to a couple who had been lingering at their cocktail party well after others had left and struck up a conversation as they walked toward the door. When that hint didn't work, they put on their coats and handed their guests' theirs and then told them that they had to run an errand and had to leave. "Do you need a lift anywhere?"

they asked. In that moment, the couple realized that it was time to go home, and they did. Other people use a more direct approach. They start by turning off the music, brightening the lights and standing up. They then thank their guests for coming and let them know that they have an early day tomorrow and must get to bed. Retrieving a guest's coat is usually an effective sign.

21. When is the right time to serve tea and coffee during a regular meal?

Tea and coffee are traditionally served after meals and generally after dessert. They represent the after-dinner refresher that goes along with retiring to another room or area of your home. Nowadays many people couple tea with cigars. Should you not want people to smoke in your home, make that clear. You can do so by not placing any ashtrays. If your gathering is large, post signs that say, "Please don't smoke."

22. I was invited to a black-tie dinner at a fancy hotel. Should I tell my host in advance that I am vegetarian? Do you think there will be a vegetarian entrée on the menu?

It's always good to inform your host of your dietary restrictions. That way, if any arrangements can be made in advance, they will. Most often at four-star hotels (as well as many others), alternative meal selections are available for the asking at affairs with set menus. Alert your waiter as soon as you see him or her, so that your meal can come at the same time as the others at your table. I've experienced several awkward moments when I've asked for a vegetarian plate, only to receive it more than ten minutes after the other guests have been served. To avoid making an uncomfortable situation worse, encourage your host and/or those in your immediate company to begin their meal without you.

23. My family is coming to visit. They still eat a lot of meat, but my husband and I do not. What to do?

When the meal is at your house, you have several choices: prepare a meat entrée that you know they will love or order one in for them. If you keep in mind that you are honoring your guests, it makes sense that you serve them the foods that they love. Your third choice is what my husband and I do every time we have guests, family members and others. We serve vegetarian cuisine that tastes as delicious and familiar as possible. What has happened over time is that our loved ones expect to eat good and healthy food whenever they visit. Since we often have our meals catered by a great vegetarian–West Indian restaurant in our Harlem neighborhood, called Strictly Roots, our family and friends now travel from all over New York City to pick up food from "our spot." You never know, just by staying true to yourself with love, you may be able to encourage others to eat more healthfully.

If you plan to take your family out to eat, ask them what they would prefer. I find it best to go to a restaurant whose menu features both vegetarian and meat or fish dishes. Do your research in advance, so that you have suggestions—with menus, if possible—to offer. You may find that your family wants to have a full experience of the way that you live, especially if they are coming from far away. If so, pick one of your favorite vegetarian spots that has dishes that will taste familiar to them.

24. What do I do when I am at a meal at someone's home, and there's nothing for me to eat?

Instead of deciding not to eat anything, take a closer look. Appetizers commonly include a vegetable crudité, cheese and crackers. Eat up! For the meal, usually salad is served, along with vegetable side dishes and bread. Although this may not appear to be the feast of kings and queens, it can tide you over. With veggie dishes, ask the host discreetly if the item includes any meat or meat stock. For instance, in a traditional Southern home, the greens are prepared with pork, although turkey is fast becoming the substitute of choice. Check out the desserts too. There may be something that you can eat, such as fresh fruit. To ward against finding yourself in such a position, tell your host in advance that you are vegetarian and offer to bring an entrée for the table.

25. I often travel for work. I find it very difficult to maintain my diet when I'm on assignment.

Common sense comes in handy during these times. The first rule of travel for anyone is to go well stocked. Bring along the provisions that you will need, such as dried fruits and nuts, healthy snack bars and bottled water. Whenever possible, do research before your trip to identify restaurants that offer vegetarian menus. Even in Paris, the land of meat and cream, there are wonderful vegetarian restaurants that can satisfy your needs. Most noted restaurants around the world and throughout the United States include a vegetarian plate. Depending on the ingredients, you may need to supplement your diet with additional protein, such as nuts and leafy green vegetables.

GiftingandGivingThanks

Even a little thing brings friendship to remembrance.
GANDA PROVERB

I T was the night before Christmas, and my sister Stephanie and I were tucked under the covers in our bed squeezing our eyes shut with the hope of falling asleep fast so that we could wake up early to see what Santa had sent down the chimney for us the night before. One of the featured attractions was something my Daddy called "the plunder box," a big cardboard box with no outward decoration, save a lot of heavy-duty tape. Funny enough, it didn't actually even come from Santa. The awkward box came from an insurance salesman Daddy knew, but in the tradition of the mythical bearded one, it came every year. As much as we enjoyed the practical and fun gifts that Santa and our family members had wrapped so beautifully for us, we *loved* the plunder box. In it were treasures beyond our imagination—rubber change purses, key chains, tiny little pads of paper, little bags of candy, all manner of writing utensils and more. All of these little things, bearing various company logos, I later learned were promotional items. When I was a child, their origin didn't matter. That we children with our tiny little fingers could dig deep into the heart of the box and pull out lots of goodies was all that counted. Being a writer even way back then, I especially cherished the paper, pens and pencils. Unlike some holiday gifts, these were put to good use, until either they wore out or the next box replaced them with fresh ones.

I've never forgotten the plunder box and the thrill that my sisters and I experienced each year as we unearthed hidden treasures. My parents appreciated the gesture from the small business owner. I'm sure that this kind man and his business were looked on favorably by many families in our city. This simple, unwrapped box points to the core of gifting: a gift given freely reaps many unknown rewards. There truly is no need for pretension. This, by the way, is the central philosophy of Kwanzaa.

A saint once said, "Give whatever you give with love. Then even the tiniest pebble you offer will have great meaning. Its fruit will come back to you a thousand fold, because it is not the pebble that you give, it is love." This philosophy, shared by Grandma Carrie, is what she followed every day of her life. She was always giving a little something to someone that made encounters with her truly memorable. Whenever she would come to visit our home, she had an outstretched hand from the moment she arrived at the door: a yummy treat for our dog; a dollar or two for me, my sisters and my mother; a clipping from the newspaper for my father; a story about her experiences for us all.

It is true that a golden opportunity to give a gift to someone is when your heart is open to do so. The "just 'cause" gift still seems the best to me. (That's why my husband and I keep a closet dedicated to gifts. All through the year, we collect items to share with others at a later point—something I learned from my mother. In that way, we always have something to give, and we don't have to spend a huge amount of money at any particular time to honor our loved ones.) As well, there are many occasions when it is appropriate to give a gift to someone: Christmas and Kwanzaa, birthdays, anniversaries, promotions and retirements, weddings and bridal showers, baby showers, graduations, housewarmings and more.

As we explore these occasions, let us remember why we give gifts to others. What purpose does it serve? How do we feel when we receive gifts from others? How should we respond? These and many other questions gain prominence in our lives as we consider the meaning of a gift. One of the kindest acts that one can make is to offer someone a gift. When shared freely, from one's heart to another, a gift—no matter how small—can brighten a person's day and make the recipient feel honored and special.

African Tradition and Today

Throughout our cultural ancestry, gifting has been an integral part of daily life. Generations ago in many African villages, gifts were offered to the *Orisha* as an invitation for them to protect the community and ensure a resourceful livelihood. Even now, in Congo-Kinshasa, formerly Zaire, people celebrate a farming ritual where they offer ceremonial dishes and raw foods in gratitude for rain and a plentiful harvest.

Similarly, for many farmers in the United States, prayers and offerings are made today to invoke the grace of God to bless the crops and protect the families. Truly, the harvest season represents the time of plenty throughout the world. The tradition of Thanksgiving in this country and the feasts of *Nganja* in Angola, *Newala* in Swaziland and *Homowo* in Ghana honor a community's answered prayers for abundance. Many families today offer the first sampling of a holiday meal in prayer to the Divine, and then share the rest with family and friends gathered. This is a practice of gratitude you can incorporate at every meal while including your children in a devotional moment.

The Genesis of a Gift

People have asked what appropriate circumstances exist for giving gifts. Is it all right to give something so that a person will remember you? Yes and no. Think about this for a moment. Ideally, you give someone a gift because you are remembering that person, not the other way around. As you think of the kindness or generosity that someone has offered to you, you often want to let the person know how grateful you are. Right?

In business people are accustomed to giving their current and potential clients gifts as reminders of them. In these cases, I recommend that you beware. If you can keep the intention that you are thinking fondly of others foremost in your mind when you give, the gift will bear untold fruit. If instead you offer a gift with invisible strings attached—for business or personal reasons—it could actually defeat the purpose on both sides. Why? Because your expectations grow, and if they are not met, it can lead to disappointment. You may wonder, "I thought if I sent her my cake, she would hire me to cater desserts for her next party." If she doesn't hire you, you may discover a resentment building inside. Whenever you find yourself filled with expectations, pause for a moment and consider what you're hoping to gain. Perhaps there's a way to reach your goal other than offering a bribe and hoping to curry favor. When it comes to giving, give freely and live your life. Your reward will come.

To the issue of furthering your business interests, that's what promotion is all about. It's perfectly fine to offer promotional items to your clients. This is different from a straight-out gift. You may want to send along a note that indicates the services that your business provides, along with a discount coupon and an invitation for the recipient to consider you for future projects. The direct and diplomatic approach tends to be the best received! Just be clear that when you plan to give a client a present for a birthday, holiday or other occasion, you do so with that sole intention. Even as I make this point, I remember the plunder box, which was a promotional item. For me as a child, it was the best gift ever.

As we explore the nature of giving and receiving gifts, keep joy at the top of your mind. Run your ideas through the filter of how much pure joy both you and the recipient will experience, and go from there. Because the nature of gifting is so vast, questions abound. This chapter's format is thus somewhat different from the others; questions and answers flow throughout.

The Holiday Season

By the time October rolls in, people are thinking about the holidays and how they will honor their loved ones. So many creative gift ideas are possible—but what's most important is that you give your love.

The holidays are approaching. As I make my gift list, I'm beginning to feel overwhelmed. How can I possibly give a gift to everyone?

Grandma Carrie always told my sisters and me that we don't do anything alone—not really. She said that if we look around, we'll see that other people contribute to our lives in significant ways all the time. For some of us, those people may include a doorman, a baby-sitter, a housekeeper, a bus driver (the one who waits when we're halfway down the block!), the maintenance crew at our apartment building, the janitor at work, the gardener at home, our hairdresser or barber. Once you start to think about the people who help to make your life comfortable, you may discover your list growing long. This doesn't mean that you can't thank everyone kindly, particularly during the holidays, a national time of gift giving in this country. You just need to be practical and alert. A small monetary gift always brightens people's lives, especially during times of high spending. If you decide to give money, cash is best, or a check if you plan to send the gift in the mail. Be sure to enclose it in an envelope with a handwritten note of gratitude. When you can't afford to give cash, consider affordable and thoughtful choices such as making cookies or other sweets. Your hairdresser would probably be pleased with a bottle of the latest fragrance or another great beauty product. If she—or any of the other special helpers in your life—has children, remember them with sweets, a small toy or a book. A thoughtful note or beautiful greeting card is also a wonderful gift for anyone on your list. Be creative. You'll be surprised what comes to mind.

I live in a high-rise apartment building and usually don't give tips to the maintenance staff because it is so large. Do you have a suggestion?

If the maintenance team do a good job, you should remember them with a token of your appreciation. If you think about it, you probably have a relative now as well as in generations past who made a living doing maintenance work. So often we neglect to thank these people who help to make our daily living comfortable. One sister, Donna Rivers, who grew up in New York City, says, "I remember during the holidays or when one of the maintenance crew retired where I used to live, each floor chose a floor captain to collect a $5 to $10 donation from each apartment to be added with thirty other floors to be given to the maintenance staff." In this way, the staff got a handsome monetary gift. Donna says this is key, because "these people maintain the appearance of your buildings by cleaning, even providing plumbing services when your toilet backs up or you have a leaky sink. This type of service should not be taken for granted." In addition to a group gift, you can collectively or individually give a fruit basket or wine as well as a handwritten note stating your gratitude for all that they have done.

Holidays and Work

When the holiday season approaches, people often give gifts to the ones they see the most—folks on the job. If you get a whiff of gingerbread cookies, made by Rhonda, down the hall in Finance, you know the season has begun. Here are ideas on how to give to people at work.

At my job, we often give gifts as a group by participating in what has come to be known as Secret Santa. We set a nominal price ceiling, everybody picks a name and then we are responsible for giving a small gift to that one person each day for a week. I often get the name of someone I don't really know. What's an appropriate gift to give to such a coworker?

Do a little research. Holidays are the perfect occasion to extend extra effort. What holiday does your coworker celebrate? Take a look at his desk. Do you see any indication of hobbies or needs? Like a muffler if he likes to ski or a new pen if his desk is littered with half-empty ballpoints? Remember not to get too personal. Give something that is fun and lighthearted. By all means, do not overspend. Stay within the agreed-upon limits, so that everybody feels comfortable.

Even if you aren't able to attend the formal gathering, be sure to leave the gift for your selected recipient in the hands of someone who will deliver it—or leave it in his or her office or workstation or under the office tree if appropriate. Nothing's worse than participating in a gift-swapping party and not getting a gift!

We're having Secret Santa at work, but I have other friends I want to give gifts. When and how do I do it?

The best thing to do is to participate in your Secret Santa gathering where everyone should receive one gift, then share your other gifts separately. You can organize a time to go out for hot chocolate with your friends or plan another private gathering. You can stop by each person's desk and make hand deliveries. It's better not to swap additional gifts at the formal gathering, where everyone is likely to receive one gift each.

I have several employees and am unsure as to what an appropriate holiday gift might be for them. Right now I'm short on cash and can't afford to give them a bonus. Any ideas?

Think of each of your employees individually. What does each person like? Do you have a sense of his or her personal style or needs? Which holiday(s) the employee celebrates? How he or she intends to spend time off? What contribution each employee has made during the year? Your answers, coupled with a clear sense of your own budget, will help guide your decisions. Further, you should give employees of equal stature gifts of equal value. And no one should be given a personal item or something that hints at a change that you would like to see them make (a bad idea would be a basket of toiletries for someone with body odor). Here are good ideas:

- A gift certificate to a favorite store
- An IOU for a day off (if you can swing it, your employees will be thrilled)
- Tickets to the theater
- The latest bestseller on their favorite topic
- A cultural calendar
- Movie theater coupons for film buffs (AAA offers great rates)

Remember employees who have children. Whenever possible, offer a gift to the little ones as well.

Note: You don't have to give your employees gifts at the holidays. Sending them a note thanking them for their service throughout the year is a perfect idea. Also, you might take them out to lunch or host an end-of-the-year gathering with light refreshments where people get together and enjoy each other's company.

Is it appropriate to give food as a gift to coworkers, friends and others?

In Nairobi, Kenya, employers have been known to give employees a half-kilo of meat as a thank you for service rendered over the year. Similarly, many American businesses have given a canned ham or other substantial food product to honored employees. Today, however, giving meat can be tricky. With the tremendous interest in healthful eating, many people are choosing not to eat meat or are limiting the amount of processed food they and their families eat. So when you think of a food item, be sure you know what the recipient's dietary restrictions are.

Safer than meat, a colorful basket of fruits or vegetables wrapped in plastic and tied with festive ribbon or a box of teas or desserts are great options. Throughout the South and the Caribbean, edible gifts have always been popular. It was one way that our ancestors were able to share their love and appreciation with others even when they were short on cash. Many a covered dish brought from miles away has been served up on holidays and whenever visitors arrive throughout the year to a grateful family. Moreover, the care and attention that we pour into homemade dishes and baked goods cannot be compared to a purchased item.

I want to give my boss a gift for the holiday season, but I don't know whether it's appropriate. Plus I could never afford something as nice as his sense of style.

There is one school of thought that suggests that you don't have to give to your superiors, only to those of equal or lesser status at work. Why? Because it can put your boss on the spot and make it appear unthoughtful of him or her not to reciprocate. Also, it could seem that you are kissing up to the boss rather than making a genuine offering. Rather than chucking the idea entirely, check your motives. If the point of giving a gift to your boss is simply to offer your gratitude and good wishes, go ahead and give an appropriate gift. Think about what your boss likes. Chocolate? A special pen? A new bestseller? A handwritten note? As long as you aren't expecting anything in return, a modest gift is fine. It's the thought that counts, right?

What about office messengers, maintenance workers and other support staff? Should I give them individual gifts?

If you have a personal relationship with any of these key coworkers, you can definitely give them a special gift. Otherwise, you can team up with fellow coworkers and offer a collective gift that they can share in putting together—like home-baked cookies in a decorative box or large tin—or that can be easily managed individually, such as holiday candy for their families.

What is appropriate to give to key clients?

The choices are vast. Today, many people like to give contributions to charities on their clients' behalf. You can also give theater tickets, dinner for two at a local favorite restaurant, a fine bottle of wine or champagne.

Several of my coworkers and I celebrate Kwanzaa. Is it appropriate to have a Kwanzaa celebration at work?

It really depends on the composition and policies of your workplace. More and more companies are hosting multicultural holiday celebrations so that people of different backgrounds and religious traditions feel welcome. If you are having a performance or other presentation during your holiday festivities, you might ask your supervisor if you can make a Kwanzaa addition to the program if there has not been one in the past. Also, you are most welcome to share gifts with your friends in the Kwanzaa spirit.

What kinds of gifts are appropriate to give for Kwanzaa?

For Sonae Fisher of Detroit, Michigan, participating in Kwanzaa has become a community ritual. After she and her husband adopted their son, Sonae began to think about her environment and the state of Black males more critically. She says, "I thought Kwanzaa would fan the flames of unity. I thought this would be a great kick-off for this child, especially to teach him to cultivate pride in himself." Sonae encourages her whole family to participate in the festivities, and she saves gift giving, *zawadi,* to December 31, the day of the *Karamu,* or feast. *Kwanzaa,* an East African Kiswahili word, literally means "the first fruits of the harvest," and is celebrated from December 26 through January 1. Gifts, or *zawadi,* are traditionally given during Kwanzaa, but never out of obligation. *Zawadi* are offered primarily to family members, based on merit. Their intention should be to foster personal and spiritual growth for the recipient; therefore, books written by or about African Americans, ethnic dolls, tickets to cultural events and other educational materials are ideal. Whenever possible, gifts should be handmade. Like Sonae Fisher, many people share gifts at the *Karamu,* or feast, at which a formal ceremony is often presented. (See the chapter "We Are Family" for more details.)

Religious Considerations

A coworker with whom I have a really good relationship is a Jehovah's Witness. I want to give him a gift expressing my fondness for him, but I believe that he doesn't celebrate many holidays. How can I give him a present without offending his religious practice?

Generally people who are Jehovah's Witnesses do not celebrate Christmas or birthdays, or anything else except Memorial, which corresponds to Passover. Yet they live in this world with others who do, which means not to ignore them because you don't know what to do. A woman in Atlanta worked with a man who is a Jehovah's Witness. When the holidays neared, she always experienced discomfort about what to do. She really liked her coworker—more than some of the other people she intended to offer gifts. So she came up with a comfortable solution—a personal note included in a generic greeting card that shared her fond thoughts of him. As it turned out, he was surprised and pleased to receive it, not to mention relieved that he didn't have to return it due to religious conflicts. Greeting cards or handwritten notes are often comfortable and intimate ways of expressing your good intentions to people when gifts seem inappropriate.

When it comes to birthdays, if your friend doesn't celebrate, by all means don't make a fuss about his birthday or waste your energy talking about your own with him. You can, however, invite your friend to a birthday party out of courtesy, even if you don't expect him to come.

Jehovah's Witnesses do celebrate wedding anniversaries, so save the date and do something special at that time of year. And, of course, the "just 'cause" gift that's not attached to a specific occasion is perfect for sharing your affection.

Are there any restrictions regarding gifting in the Islamic faith?

To the contrary, as Aliyyah Abdur-Rahman, a twenty-something Islamic sister, explains, gift giving is an integral part of life. "I don't usually make a big deal of receiving gifts. I make a bigger deal of giving them," she says. "It's because I was raised Muslim." In the Islamic faith, gift giving is an inherent part of daily life. One of the five pillars of Islam, *Zakaat,* or charity, makes giving not merely a gesture of kindness but a requirement of faith. Muslims find a variety of reasons for giving gifts, such as baby naming ceremonies that occur seven days after a baby is born (known as *akikah*) and weddings. On the seventh, the fourteenth or the twenty-first day after a couple is married, the family hosts a *walimah,* which is a gathering and feast. People bring gifts for the newlyweds much as one does for a bridal shower (such showers are not part of their tradition). A beautiful Islamic practice is to give handmade gifts to loved ones rather than those purchased elsewhere.

The time of year that Muslims exchange gifts is during the three-day celebration *Eid,* which follows their holy month of *Ramadan.* There is no set type of gift to offer, so people give freely to their loved ones.

Note: Muslims traditionally do not celebrate Christmas or any other birthdays, including that of Muhammad. It is not the birth of an individual that is considered significant in Islam; instead, it is the life that one leads. Therefore, Muslims would be more inclined to recognize the time of one's death. As with Jehovah's Witnesses, if you would like to offer a gift to a Muslim, a generic card is appropriate. One's work environment can sometimes alter things a bit, though, even for the most devout Muslims. A Muslim woman who works as an obstetric nurse in New York City, for example, gets showered with gifts from proud parents after she has delivered their babies. Often families continue to send gifts of gratitude to her for her assistance in bringing their children into the world safely. She has come to accept these tokens of appreciation as a way to acknowledge the good intentions with which they are given.

My daughter goes to school with a number of Jewish children. How does one celebrate Hanukkah? Are there special gifts offered during this season?

Hanukkah is a Hebrew term that literally means "dedication" or "celebration." Customarily during a Jewish celebration, a menorah, or candelabra, is lit to honor the event. During the era before Christ, there was a war between the Greeks and the Jews that was won by the Jews due to the leadership of Judas Maccabeus. Upon winning the battle, Maccabeus and his troops went to temple to have a *hanukkah,* or dedication ceremony, at which they would light the menorah. The only problem was that there was just enough oil to last for one day, whereas the menorah traditionally was lit each day for eight days (the number of candles it holds). Miraculously, the oil lasted all eight days. Jews worldwide now celebrate this great occasion, remembering it as a sign of faith and freedom.

Traditionally children's Hanukkah gifts are *gelt,* real coins or chocolate wrapped with gold foil. (*Gelt* is the Yiddish word for money, based on the German *geld*.) With the popularization of Christmas and the practice of giving a variety of material possessions, many Jews have expanded the types of gifts offered at Hanukkah. To honor your child's friend, you can give coins or chocolate, as is customary, or offer any other special treat that enables your child to participate in his friend's spiritual tradition.

Mother's Day

> Honor your father and your mother, so that you may live
> long in the land the Lord your God is giving you.
> **Exodus 20:12**

I heard an African sister say once that in Africa every day is Mother's Day. We all have stories about how sweet and strong our mamas are. Every day truly could be Mother's Day in my book. On this national holiday, do remember to honor your mother with a card, flowers or another reminder of your love for her, such as a truly special gift—your time, as one brother in the Midwest did, who gave of himself. Jerry Harris, an accountant in Denver, Colorado, drives ten hours to Des Moines, Iowa, on Mother's Day to help his mother, Jacquelyn Harris, with springtime projects around her house. He helps her transplant flowers, paint the garage and change the oil in her lawnmower and snowblower and makes sure her car is in good running order. "It's just the best Mother's Day present," Jacquelyn Harris said.

Father's Day

Fathers in the African-American community have gotten a bum rap in the media for a long time. Too often we hear stories of how our daddies don't take care of their children and families. Although some may be guilty, we know that more work hard to help their families grow strong. Further, if we recognize the good in *all* of our fathers, we can inspire those who need to show up more consistently that we really care about them and need their input in order to complete the circle in our community development. Remembering all that our fathers have done for us today and through the generations is what Father's Day can be for African-descended people. Make it a moment of celebration in your family—for your father, your stepfather, your grandfather(s), godfathers and elder men who are close to your family. And don't forget young fathers; they need extra support! Taking our fathers out to dinner after church, mosque or your preferred house of worship on Father's Day is a tradition many families enjoy, and a wonderful time to shower your gratitude, fond memories and blessings on your father. If you can't be together physically, send a gift, and call.

Valentine's Day

Here in America, people make a big deal about many holidays, Valentine's Day included. If you have a honey, now is the time to remember him or her—or so American culture says. My recommendation is that you should gauge your decision based on your own views *and* those of your date or partner. I will tell you that some brothers have argued that they shouldn't be forced to celebrate this commercial holiday. They say they honor their partners when they want to, not when they're told to do so. That may be all well and good, but, I ask, Is your view worth it? If you're in a relationship, doing something special on the day that is nationally identified for love can't be all that bad, can it? If you truly don't buy into the practice, make sure you tell your sweetheart early on, so she doesn't get her feelings hurt.

If you want to participate in Valentine's Day, you can determine how personal your gift should be based on how serious and how long the relationship has been going on. For a first or second date, it's probably best to stick to chocolates, although stuffed animals, flowers or a dinner at a special restaurant are great options too. Any number of men as well as women have been known to "pop the question" on V-Day, so some of you may be in for the surprise of a lifetime.

For sisters, you and your man can create your favorite dishes together and dine in a candlelit, incensed room. Or place a handwritten note in his drawer, on a bathroom mirror or in his briefcase, inviting him to a relaxing night alone together.

Birthdays

One busy year I neglected to speak to my sister Susan *on* her birthday, and she admonished me, saying, "It's really important to remember people on their birthdays. That, after all, is the one day in the year that is most important to *them.*" That was a good point. Over the years, I have attempted to remember people's birthdays, although I'm not always good at it. I do recommend that you create a calendar that lists your loved ones' birthdays, so that you can remember them on time.

Celebrating birthdays is a favorite pastime all over the world. Some of the most memorable are your baby's first birthday, your own sweet sixteen, the liberating eighteen and twenty-one, the landmark twenty-five, the eye-opening thirty and so it goes. It's always okay to celebrate your own birthday in the style of your choice as long as you make no requirements of your guests other than to celebrate with you.

When it comes to honoring other people's birthdays, the key thing to remember is *honor.* I've been to surprise birthday parties where the birthday girl was terribly embarrassed to be the center of attention. Similarly, many people do not like to reveal their age. Be aware of this before you sing "the birthday song" and demand that they reveal the new BIG number. With a bit of forethought, you can participate in birthday celebrations with great enthusiasm and help to acknowledge yours and your loved ones' turning points.

Stephanie Stokes Oliver, author and former editor in chief of *Heart and Soul* magazine, and her husband, Reggie, started a beautiful birthday practice when they married. On each of their birthdays, they turn their focus to their parents. They call and send presents to their parents, thanking them for bringing them into the world and sacrificing in innumerable ways so that they could develop into the conscious African-American people they have become.

How personal can a gift be for someone's birthday?

It all depends on your relationship with that person. Often women give each other personal gifts, such as makeup, jewelry or clothing. Men friends often go out together to celebrate over a meal or to attend a sporting event or other favorite activity. Planning and thoughtfulness are the keys here. You want to honor your friend without causing any embarrassment.

Gifts for Family Members

In the tradition of our ancestors, we understand that we must first honor our families. This is true when it comes to gifting as well. For those of us with large families, it can sometimes be a challenge to give every person a gift. Creativity can enter here. Many families put names in a hat and pick. Then, for holidays or other special times when everyone gets a gift, each person will be sure to have a special token, and no one will go broke. For out-of-town family members, send cards or telephone them with your good wishes.

What's the best gift to give to elder members of my family?

Your time. Do something you think they might appreciate, such as taking them shopping or helping them with a project around the house. Vow to spend time with your elders, listening carefully to their wisdom. You might bring along some rosemary or lavender oil and gently massage their hands and shoulders. If you'd like to bring along a tangible gift, be mindful of their dietary restrictions (sugar may not be a good idea) and their eyesight. Large-print books are often best for older people with limited vision. A framed photograph of yourself, of you with the elder or of your whole family would be perfect. Practical gifts can be winners too: warm socks, slippers or gloves; a hat with a broad brim to shield them from the sunlight; a throw blanket for their favorite chair.

I always have a hard time figuring out what to give my father for a gift. Any ideas?

Fathers seem to be either the ones who have everything or the ones we can least figure out. I often wonder, "Could he possibly need another tie?" You can always go for the old standbys—socks, T-shirts, ties, handkerchiefs. Or think about what he might not buy himself—an electric back massager that he can attach to his favorite chair, a book about a historic African leader, a photo album with images of you and your family over the years. Consider your father's social activities and hobbies. A new golf club or camera may be just what he's been wanting. Better yet, a date to spend time together could be the best gift! You can always ask to be sure.

I'm close to only one of my aunts, but I see all of them at the holidays. Do I have to give everyone a gift?

You never "have" to give a gift. But you also don't ever want to hurt someone's feelings. Homemade cookies seem like a good solution. They can be for the whole family to enjoy at the holiday meal or tiny bundles for everyone to take home. For the special aunt to whom you want to give another gift, do so in private so that the two of you share a sweet and unspoiled moment.

Rites of Passage

The purpose of rites of passage is to honor and acknowledge life transitions. Our ancestors often staged elaborate ceremonies that celebrated months and years of preparation, especially for youth transitions.

Is there anything special that should be given to young girls as a coming-of-age present?

In the United States, teenage girls are commonly given a strand of pearls when they turn sixteen (sometimes eighteen). These were traditionally given right before the cotillion—a formal dance that introduces teenage girls to society and that is time honored in the South and the North. Although cotillions are often associated with the dominant culture—and find their roots in European traditions—it turns out that many African-American families have participated in this practice for generations. Social clubs, churches and other organizations plan cotillions where girls wear white tea-length dresses, white gloves and a touch of makeup. The girls work with coaches—their mothers included—to learn social graces, including how to walk elegantly, how to dance (the waltz, two-step and others), how to shake hands, essentially how to be a "lady." At the cotillion, each young woman is introduced to the gathered group and escorted—for the first time—by a young man who is dressed in a tuxedo. Several formal dances follow, and afterward the young woman is allowed to date (with an escort, of course!).

The tradition of giving pearls in the United States translates into gold in the Caribbean. Nilda Cid, a native of St. Thomas, Virgin Islands, who now lives in Maryland, recommends giving jewelry to other West Indians whenever possible. "I remember when my female cousins and I were sixteen, we received a gold-bar necklace from our grandparents."

In African communities, the gifts given to young people who are initiated into adulthood are less tangible. They go through a series of rituals over days and weeks, at the end of which they have received wisdom from the elders as well as status in the community. In many instances, special robes and jewels are given to male and female initiates.

I know that in the Jewish tradition, there is a great celebration when a boy is circumcised. Is there a similar tradition from African culture?

In Judaism, this tradition is called the *bris*. Eight days after a boy is born, he is circumcised. Normally, on that same day or soon after, the family gathers to celebrate the occasion, where they offer gifts to the baby's parents such as those offered at a baby shower. In many African cultures, male circumcision happens much later, at puberty, about age fifteen. Among the Masai of Kenya and Tanzania, right after the circumcision ceremony, families host a big feast and celebration where elders offer the gift of advice to the young man for his next stage in life, the *moran,* or warrior class.

Circumcision and clitoridectomy historically occured in African cultures as a symbol of personal sacrifice and community cohesion. The male sacrificed an aspect of his anatomy that was "female," so that he could join with a woman, whereas the female sacrificed her "male" aspect for the converse reason. Alice Walker and a number of continental sisters have protested against the painful female procedure, calling it abusive in contemporary times, a form of mutilation. Though a current source of controversy, generations ago it was revered. One of the Dogon creation stories, for example, speaks about the fact that the Earth could not become pregnant until her clitoris was removed. Both the male and female operations occur before couples are allowed intimate access to each other. Elaborate celebrations ensue after healing, which include dancing and gifting from the community.

My godchild is getting christened next month. Is there something special that I should give him to mark the occasion?

There is no one set gift for a child's christening. For the godparents—those who will commit during the ceremony to help cultivate the spiritual life of the child and take care of the child in case of the parents' untimely death or other disaster—the gift should be carefully considered. Many godparents offer savings instruments, such as certificates of deposit or stocks and bonds. Others offer spiritual literature, such as the Bible, Torah, Qur'an or other appropriate text. The biggest gift a godparent can offer is love—love and the true commitment to help nurture the child during his or her life.

Christening gifts can be anything practical or spiritual for a child. Remember when buying clothes to purchase clothing one or two sizes larger than the baby, so that the child can get some wear out of it. By all means, if you want to buy christening clothes for the child, check with the parents first to see if they already have the garments or what they want. Many families pass christening clothes down from generation to generation to carry on the family legacy.

I have a friend who is having a naming ceremony for her baby. What kind of gift can I bring for that?

Many Black people have adopted the tradition of celebrating their child's birth and existence in the world through an ancient African ritual, a naming ceremony. Normally such a ceremony occurs seven days after a child is born (See the chapter "We Are Family" for details). You are welcome to bring practical gifts, much like those you would offer at a baby shower, to this celebration—anything from diapers and clothing to bedroom furniture or a stroller. Find out what the family needs, and then stick to your budget.

Weddings

One of the most joyous times to give gifts is when people marry, and gifting begins well before the couple actually gets married.

Contemporary Gifts for Weddings

Countless opportunities are available for gifting at the time of marriage—for the couple, their families and friends. Here's a rundown of them:

- Courtship. Commonly the suitor (the man) gives small gifts of his affection anywhere from over the course of a year to several months or a few weeks before "popping the question." These days, the two are welcome to exchange gifts—none being too precious or expensive.
- Engagement. When the two are certain of their relationship and want to commit to a life together, they ask for the blessings of their families first. This is a vital part of our ancestry that I strongly recommend. If you can take the time to win your family members—parents, siblings, aunts and uncles, even those people who have become your family over the years—you're bound to have a better-fortified union. This may not seem important now, but in the ebb and flow of life, you want some solid support for the dry times.

  Usually the young woman receives a ring from her fiancé upon their engagement. In many African traditions, other jewelry is popular, including beaded necklaces, intricately designed earrings and shawls. So you may consider alternative gifts that you can give to each other.

  Adopt an ancient tradition and make it your own by giving gifts of gratitude to both of your families. Although we don't incorporate a bride-wealth, just imagine how happy your parents would be if they received anything from a heartfelt letter to a beautiful vase or other household treasure.
- Engagement party. Hosted by the bride's family, this party is the formal coming out of the couple to family and friends—the announcement of their intentions. People often bring small gifts for the couple's home, although these gifts should not preclude the later offering of wedding presents.
- Wedding showers. Bridal showers are usually hosted by friends or coworkers. It's not considered in good taste in Western society for

the bride's mother to host such an event. In many African communities, however, it is the bride's family and mother, in particular, who gather loved ones together to give handmade or purchased gifts for the bride herself and the new home. For the hosts, it's best to indicate to your guests what the bride needs, if she is registered and/or has a favorite store.

- Bachelor party. This event is traditionally hosted by the best man and has come to be considered a man's last night "as a free man" in the United States, although countless brothers secretly attest that their bachelor parties were great get-togethers where they got to reminisce with old friends and share good times. As in African tradition, when the men toast the good news, gifts of alcohol are most commonly given at these parties.
- Couple shower. A new tradition that many couples are incorporating is that of the shower where the two of them get a chance to be together and meet each other's loved ones. This event represents a perfect time for guests to give small mementos for the bride and groom that they either need or that conjure up pleasant memories. It can also be a time, like the engagement party, when people give gifts for the home.
- Communion with the elders. We can take a page out of our ancestors' book and organize events for the bride with her female elders and for the groom with male elders. In some African societies, such as among the Bakongo of the Congo, the woman is sequestered for as long as a month, during a "fattening-up" period. While she is away, elder women school her on how to be married—everything from the basics of keeping house to how to satisfy her man. Similarly, among the Samburu of Kenya, young men spend time with male elders learning to be warriors, so that they can protect their new family and their community. In contemporary terms, we can plan a special day with the elders where we listen openly to their wisdom and welcome their blessings for our unions. At such a treasured event, you should offer gifts to your elders—a photo of you and your fiancé, for example, or more personal items, such as a handkerchief. Be sure to videotape such an event. You may want to show an edited version at your wedding reception or at a later family gathering, if it seems appropriate.
- Bridal luncheon. Sometimes the bride hosts a luncheon to which she invites her bridesmaids, the other female members of the wedding party and her mother. This is the time when the bride gives her attendants their gifts (see page 363).
- Rehearsal dinner. Hosted by the groom's family, this dinner usually occurs the evening before the wedding, following the wedding re-

hearsal. Typically gifts are not exchanged at this event, although it's another opportunity in advance of the wedding for the bride and groom to give their attendants their special gifts.

- The wedding. For brides (and grooms), take the time to plan what you need and want in your home. By preshopping with a bridal registry, you can organize your needs and make it convenient for your friends and family to purchase them for you. Be sure to include a range of prices, so that everyone can select comfortably from your choices. Consider registering in a national department store as well as your favorite cultural boutique. Spread the word via your mother or a coordinator. Everyone who participates in and/or attends your wedding should receive a gift of your gratitude. At our wedding, we gave all of the special male attendants hand-dyed silk pocket squares and the females hand-dyed silk scarves in our wedding colors. For our guests, we offered more modest mementos—miniature brooms that were decorated with colorful ribbon by my mother and her friends. In this way, we thanked everyone for their good wishes and also left them with a reminder of our cultural heritage: that our ancestors in this country crafted a way to honor their unions, even when they were legally forbidden, by jumping the broom. Many couples offer sachets with potpourri or sweets. You can offer a cultural kiss with cowrie shells. Found off the coast of West Africa, these tiny shells represent auspiciousness and prosperity (they were once used as currency), and they're quite affordable.

- The wedding party. Each member of the wedding party offers a gift to the couple. Traditionally in the West, the bride's family pays for the wedding, which is often shared in African countries, and more commonly shared by both families and the couple here today. The groom traditionally pays for the honeymoon, often with his family's assistance. The groom's family pays for the wedding rehearsal dinner and the beverages at the wedding reception. Each member of the wedding party gives a gift to either the bride or the groom, depending on their gender—or the women and/or the men team up and offer a collective gift for the home.

- Bride's gift to bridesmaids. A bride should always give her bridesmaids a gift—something personal that they will truly appreciate. Most common are jewelry, spa or beauty treatments in advance of the wedding or toiletries. For a cultural twist, consider a book of African quotations, a bottle of incensed oil or a meditation pillow covered in cultural cloth.

- Groom's gift to groomsmen and ushers. Traditionally in this country, groomsmen receive pens, monogrammed silver money clips or mugs. One brother gave his groomsmen a wall hanging bearing an early twentieth-century African-American illustration. Other cultural ideas are a bow tie and cummerbund set in *kente* or other African or Caribbean cloth, a handcrafted African wallet or money clip or a book about Africa or the Diaspora.

- Wedding performers and other participants. Everyone who participates should receive a little something. For the organist or pianist, drummers and soloists, a monetary payment is appropriate, even when they have offered their services gratis. Be sure to check your agreement in advance of your wedding to ensure no hard feelings. If they truly do not want to be paid or you can better serve them differently, be creative and offer a substantial gift. For your hostesses (those extra helpers who greet guests, handle the guest book and otherwise help out), in addition to a small trinket or other item, offer them each a centerpiece to enjoy at their own homes (if appropriate). Your wedding planner should be compensated and given a special present. By the time your wedding is over, you should have a sense of her taste. Pick out something that lets her know how much you appreciate her support.

- Thank-yous. Everyone should receive a thank-you note soon after your wedding. If you begin sending thank-you notes immediately after you begin receiving gifts—from the engagement party on—it will be easier. These days both husband and wife are encouraged to participate in writing thank-yous for wedding gifts, so by all means, make an event of it and get them written. Send personal notes indicating your gratitude for the specific gift given (unless it's money, in which case you indicate how you intend to spend it). If at all possible, send your thank-yous within two weeks to a month after your wedding. If, for any reason, you don't complete them by that time, keep writing! Whenever your guests receive your note, they will be grateful—for your acknowledgment as well as their possible relief in knowing that you did actually receive the gift.

Getting Married African Style

In some African and all traditional Islamic communities, marriages are arranged by the families. Gifts are traditionally offered to the bride's family from the moment that the arrangement has been made, which could be as early as before the child is born.

The guiding principle of African marriages is that they represent a union of two families, not just two individuals. As such, the families play an integral role in the foundation of the relationship. To honor the bond that unites all of the family members is a universal practice among our African brothers and sisters—the offering of a dowry or bride-wealth, known as *lobola, roracio* and other terms, at the point of engagement. The *lobola* represents in tangible form the groom and his family's acknowledgment of the great blessing they have been given, to be able to welcome the young woman into their family, as well as the understanding that they will be removing an able and vital contributor to the family welfare by taking her away. In Sobonfu E. Some's book, *The Spirit of Intimacy,* in describing marriage ritual for her people, the Dagara of Burkino Faso, the author explains, "In order for the bride to leave her house, her soul has to be transferred from her family to her husband's. This is done by a give-away, a sacrifice of a cow." Among the Burundi of East Africa, bride-wealth traditionally consisted of goods made by the groom's family to give to the bride's family as well as cattle, goats and hoes. The bride-wealth is delivered to the bride's family home early on in the negotiations through which both families agree that the two young people can marry.

Distribution of *lobola* can be spread out over time and vary according to social status and wealth. These gifts also vary depending on which family group is included and what resources are available, but normally the range of items consists of money, fabric for the bride's wardrobe, liquor for the men to share at the meeting of the families when the *lobola* is offered, traditional delicacies and cattle. Among the people of Uganda, for example, young people marry very early, often in their teens. To secure the blessing of their families, the boy must give bride-wealth, which traditionally includes goats, cattle and chickens, although today Western influences have introduced additional items such as electronic equipment, Western clothing and furniture. Should a marriage end or if the wife is unable to bear children, the groom's family in patrilineal societies may request a return of the bride-wealth.

Wedding Traditions Around the World

Throughout the Diaspora, when couples plan to marry, everybody likes to get involved. Depending on a family's resources, the festivities may be simple or extravagant.

In many African countries, the custom is to offer a dowry or what is known as bride-wealth—*lobola, roracio,* and many other terms. You may have read about the concept of bride-wealth or bride-price, as it is sometimes unfortunately called, and gotten the misunderstanding that a young woman is "sold" to her husband's family. This is not true. Gifts are showered on the bride's family in the spirit of community building.

In Grenada and other Caribbean countries, families host a *qwe-qwe* the night before the wedding. At this gathering of family and close friends, the couple is serenaded and showered with presents, particularly cash.

All folks need to know in St. Thomas in the Virgin Islands is that a wedding is about to happen. Immediately a money tree is prepared for the young couple. Some of these trees are quite creatively designed, but the essential materials are crisp dollars (of any denomination), beautiful ribbon and a sturdy plant to which the money is attached. Often the tree is presented at a bridal shower. (This practice is also common for baby showers.)

Housewarmings

I was invited to a housewarming and want to be sure to bring the right gift. Any ideas?

Think of the person and his or her new home. Do you have any idea of your friend's taste in home decorations, housewares, design? You stand the best chance of selecting the "perfect" gift for a housewarming if you focus on the recipient throughout your planning and shopping. Much like wedding presents, gifts for the home are personal. You want the person receiving your present to be able to use it. When in doubt, ask about specific needs he or she might have. Consider your own budget. You should not feel obliged to overspend if your purse strings are tight. Especially down South, it used to be that family members and friends got together and made items for a loved one's new home. If you have the time and inclination, a hand-made quilt could be an extraordinary housewarming gift. Be sure to identify your friend's preferred colors and design scheme, so that you don't make something that really doesn't work in the new home. With any gift, it's best to enclose a gift certificate or keep the receipt in case your friend wants to return it. (And don't get an attitude if your friend doesn't like or need the gift. It's not about you!) Here are some ideas:

- Welcome mat. You can find them in Kuba print, *kente* and mudcloth reproductions.
- Incense to purify the space and welcome the ancestors.
- A spiritual book to invite blessings to the space—the Metu Neter, the Bible, the Qur'an, the Torah, the Bhagavad Gita, a book of spiritual verses.
- A gift certificate for a block of your time when you will help to run errands, put things away or otherwise help to get the new home in order.
- A gift certificate from your friend's favorite home store.

- A subscription to a home design magazine.
- *The Spirit of African Design* (1996), a book by S. Algotsson that explores how to incorporate cultural design elements into your home.
- Wastebaskets.
- Foot stool (or a decorative Ashanti stool).
- Flower vases.
- Floor pillows (a perfect gift to make using fabric your friend already loves).
- Dishes. Check to see if your friend is registered. For married couples, you can add to their wedding pattern.
- Glasses. (We always break them! We can always use more.)
- Plastic containers.
- Pots and pans.
- Knives.
- Linens—matching towels, hand towels, face towels (another opportunity to introduce African-centered treasures).
- Shower curtain.
- Book ends.
- Bathroom accessories—tissue holder, soap dish.
- A gift basket of toiletries—specialty soaps, bath products, loofah.

The Sick and Shut-In

It's customary in the Christian church for the congregation to join the preacher in offering blessings for those in need. When the sick and suffering are people we know, we can also reach out with a token of our love. When I was a little girl, I had an operation and had to be hospitalized for some time. It was pretty frightening to be in a hospital, but everybody was really nice. People sent me cards with sweet inscriptions as well as flowers. The best gift of all, though, was an orange tree—a real, live miniature tree with tiny green oranges growing on it. It came from Judge David Ross (one of Daddy's close colleagues) and Mrs. Ross. He brought it to me and, with his charismatic smile, told me that I could help it to grow and that later it would bear many oranges. Months after I was out of the hospital, that little tree did bear fruit again, and I was so grateful.

Here are other ideas:

- A live plant, particularly for people who will be hospitalized or bedridden for a while. The living plant brings joy and hope.
- An inspirational book of poetry or photographs, or a provocative novel, or a CD player and soothing instrumental music.
- Coloring books and other interactive games for sick children.

- Warm and soft sleepwear—anything from a robe to pajamas and slippers.
- Best of all, your company. If you can visit or call your loved ones regularly while they are ill and for some time after, they will appreciate your presence perhaps the most of all.

Time of Bereavement

Death is considered a high spiritual time in a person's life. It is, in fact, the last action that one takes in this world, when the Spirit—however one chooses to identify it—leaves the physical body. Among Black folks the world over, death is treated with great respect and honor (See the chapter "We Are Family"). Although loved ones commonly grieve over the loss, death has traditionally been considered a time of celebration, when the soul rejoins the Divine in some intangible form. Thus, great death rituals have been born to salute the passing.

Among the Ashanti of West Africa, the final feast always includes the deceased's favorite food. Called *kra aduane,* or food for the soul, this meal is placed before the corpse, which is laid on its left side so that the right hand would be free for eating. Since the Ashanti observe fasting during their period of bereavement, only the children are allowed to eat any of the offered food. Additional gifts include *nsa,* or a donation, that is offered to the family to defray funeral expenses.

Is it appropriate to send a gift to families who have lost a loved one?

Traditionally people send flowers with a note of sympathy and love to the funeral home, where the viewing of the body will be held. You can also send flowers to the site of the funeral or the family home. More and more often, though, families are requesting that contributions be made to specific charities or institutions in lieu of flowers, such as the American Cancer Society or Howard University. You can ask the family when in doubt. Most common in our communities is for family and friends to gather after the funeral at the family home for a huge meal. Everybody is welcome to bring a dish, beverages, desserts or other edibles to share.

Houseguests

Go to most any Southern home, and you'll find that folks will welcome you with open arms. It has been the way of Black families forever, or so it seems. Nearly everybody I know has an Aunt Audrey or Sister Sarah who was known to take care of folks for a while when they needed a place to stay. Whether you're coming to visit for an evening, weekend or longer, heed old folks' wisdom: Don't wear out your welcome. You can start by bringing a small gift upon your arrival. Food is always good; make sure you know the family's taste. Other options are decorative soap for the guest bathroom, hand towels, a beautiful candle, incense, a potted plant or a floral bouquet.

The best advice I ever received about being in someone else's home was to look closely at how that person lives and then honor that way of living. In my sister Susan's home in Los Angeles, for example, my room is not really my room. Susan's rules are that every room always needs to be in perfect order so that anyone visiting can have access to the room, which means that *everything* has to be put away! At first, I wanted to protest, as a middle sister is prone to do. "That's supposed to be *my* room!" But then I realized whose house I was in, after all!

After you've spent an extended stay at someone's home, it's good manners to leave a parting gift. In addition, send along a handwritten thank-you note for your stay. Including a small gift with that letter is a sweet gesture.

Presentation Counts

Black folks are some of the most creative people in the world. When it comes to gift giving, there's no exception. The simplest pair of socks seemed like the best gift ever once my Aunt Esther finished wrapping it in colorful tissue paper, putting it in a hand-stitched bag and attaching a card. One of the magical properties of a gift is that it has a surprise element—even when you already know what it is.

Gifting marks a special occasion, no matter how mundane or unusual that may be. Take the time to wrap your gifts well, so that from the moment the exchange begins, the experience will be exciting and fun. Choose your moments carefully. When you are presenting a gift in person, make the moment special. Avoid super-busy times when the recipient will be distracted. Do your best to give the gift personally. One woman told me that her husband gives her great things, but a lot is lost in the presentation, because he characteristically has someone else do both the shopping and the presenting. Remember that the reason for giving is to remember and celebrate someone. This includes the moment of exchange.

Giving Thanks

Receiving a gift, whether it's expected or a surprise, is a wonderful experience. I have watched many faces light up upon opening a beautifully decorated box. The contents, although important, really don't matter as much as the thought itself. That's why the idiom, *It's the thought that counts.* That sentiment holds true on the other side of the gifting experience. One of the most immediate ways that you can demonstrate your gratitude for the gifts that you receive throughout life is to express your feeling in a concrete and immediate way. Extend your love, especially when it's triggered by a kind act. Offering your sincere gratitude for tangible and intangible gifts is not only appropriate, but also essential for the beautiful cycle of giving and receiving that is part of our cultural legacy. By letting others know how grateful you are for their kindness, both of your hearts open that much wider.

As far as etiquette goes, elaborate systems are in place for such acknowledgment, especially when it comes to weddings and other special occasions. No matter how small or grand a gift you receive may be, your simple act of letting the sender know your sincere appreciation completes the chain of giving, making a circle of goodness. Your action is an integral part of the gifting process and a primary component of good manners. Naturally, the ways in which you let others know your gratitude can vary tremendously, according to many factors, including the nature of the gift received, the personality of the giver as well as your own, your intention behind the thank-you. As you contemplate how to thank the person or institution who has chosen to remember you with a present, don't wait too long. Timeliness is a big factor in completing the gifting process.

A dear friend of mine, Sharon Chatmon, recently participated in an amazing gifting ritual. One moment she was perfectly healthy; the next she was near death. She went from having a bad headache to being hospitalized for emergency brain surgery. Without insurance, she faced enormous medical bills, along with a potentially lengthy recovery time. What was she to do? Thank God, she has good friends. Throughout her hospital stay, friends and family gathered for a prayer vigil that stretched from her hospital room via phone and thought across the country. Upon her release from the hospital, as the bills continued to pile up, two friends organized a party, much like the rent parties that our folks used to have years ago in order to get their bills in order (a viable idea today). Local artisans brought their wares to a restaurant, and special friends were invited to go shopping as well as make a monetary contribution to her medical fund. The event brought together people who had not seen one another for some time. It was a beautiful evening. All of the artisans donated their proceeds to the fund. At the end of the night, Sharon had received several thousand dollars toward her living and medical expenses. Her description of the outpouring of love was that it was nearly overwhelming. To express her gratitude for the many kind gestures, she created a beautiful form letter on her computer, one that seemed personal for everyone. It thanked all who had shared their prayers and gifts with her for their love, and also reminded us of her love and commitment to each of us. Additionally, Sharon gave the two organizers of the special party a gift of massage for their efforts. We all felt honored to be friends with Sharon. Her beautiful note, though not handwritten, had the quality of goodness that represented her personality fully. The paper was special, the font used was delicate and the timing was right. Everyone received her note within two weeks of the event, even though she was still recuperating! With diligence, anything can be done.

When and How to Give Thanks

Whenever you are sincerely grateful for something that someone has done for you, it's appropriate to offer your gratitude. The gift may be a vote of confidence at work when you are having a hard day or a beautiful bouquet of flowers to celebrate the birth of your first child. Whatever the occasion, you can and should offer your thanks. How you do so is of the utmost importance. As you prepare to give thanks, consider your intention. What do you really want to communicate? How can you affirm the giver fully without making him or her uncomfortable? For example, a shy person would not appreciate you announcing over the PA system at work that she sent you a fabulous gift. And someone who gives a generous amount of money to your latest project might prefer a public acknowledgment over a note, although the person should receive the note too. Keep the giver at the top of your mind when preparing your thank-you. His or her personality will guide you to what is appropriate. When in doubt, send a handwritten note immediately, and wait to follow up with something more. Don't confuse your thank-you with another motive, such as a hidden desire to cultivate a more intimate relationship or business arrangement.

The Written Word

The most traditional way to say thank-you for a gift is to write your thoughts in a handwritten note that is affixed with a stamp (not put through a machine) and sent off in the mail within two weeks of receipt of the gift. This is why so many women (and men) have personal note-size stationery. In Western tradition, as soon as a gift is received, the female head of a family must send off a sweet note of thanks. These days both men and women can do the honors.

In reality, it is rare that people send notes that say thanks. If you are one of those many people who drag their feet, it's time to change. My inspiration is Grandma Carrie. She sent hundreds of notes and received just as many. When she was feeling a little low, she would sit quietly and read special notes that she had received over the years. Upon her request, her casket was filled with many of these precious cards and notes. To get started:

- Get stationery. Personalized or not, you need blank paper that you can use to jot off your feelings quickly to loved ones. I love art cards that are blank inside. What's important is your personal message that acknowledges the gift in some specific way.
- Carry stationery with you. One way to get your thank-yous off efficiently is to keep a few pieces of stationery in your possession at all times. One colleague told me that she uses travel time on airplanes to write notes to people who have gifted her recently. When she touches down, she affixes stamps that are also in her bag and drops the notes off in the first mailbox she sees. In this way, she completes the circle before other activities distract her. If you have the time, buy African-American postage stamps or other specialty stamps that reflect the inspiration for your note.
- Keep a record. Your thoughts of thanks can get in the way of the reality of your sending a thank-you note. So make a list of who should receive a note, and check the name off when the note is written and the letter is in the mail.
- Use a form letter as a last resort. If your gift was personally offered, it deserves a personal response. Exceptions occur when the time it will take for you to respond to everyone extends beyond a reasonable limit of one month. Use discipline to complete the task. When you must use a form letter, add a special note at the end of each letter if you can to connect you to each person.
- Don't allow a delay to get in the way. If you are tardy in sending out a thank-you note, still do it. Write the note as soon as you remember. It's never too late to express your gratitude. You can briefly apolo-

gize, but make the core of the note your sentiment of gratitude as it may be a lasting reminder.

The Telephone

Modern technology makes it such that you can say thanks to everyone who has a telephone, and immediately. Although a phone call should not replace a note, it is timely and personal. Plus, if you are one of those people who may not get the note written, communicate your message the best way you can. Since most people receive more telephone calls that are for business, a love call can be a great pick-me-up. Before you place a thank-you call, think about what you want to say. Your sentiments should be expressed succinctly, especially since you run a good chance of connecting to an answering machine rather than a live person. In a clear, upbeat voice, share your good feelings, wish the person the very best and end your call.

A Gift

Another way to complete the chain is with a gift. At weddings, guests come bearing gifts for newlyweds, and the couple, in turn, gives small mementos to everyone as reminders of their union as well as their gratitude for the guests' presence, gifts and love. Similar situations occur all the time. Three friends spent a weekend at a luxurious fitness spa, thanks to the generosity of one friend who treated the group. After a transforming weekend, the two other friends thought long and hard about how they could say thanks. They knew that their friend loved beautiful writing instruments, so they pooled their resources and made a gift of a silver and mother-of-pearl pen to her. The amount of money spent on a gift is not the point here at all. You should not try to match gifts by their monetary value. Instead, think of ways to celebrate the person you are honoring, and then get creative.

Note: Know when to stop. If you receive a thank-you note from someone, you do not have to call to say that you received it, although the gesture would be nice. Once the cycle is complete, you can move on to other concerns. Gifting and giving thanks should be activities that occur with a sense of ease and grace, with no strings attached. Allow the closure to be graceful as well.

Great Gifts

We've heard so often that it's the thought that counts. Below are some gifting stories that prove the point.

Just 'Cause

- According to Nikki, a twenty-something woman from Los Angeles, she and her best friend of eleven years have never formally exchanged gifts. Instead, they always do little things for each other when they feel the time is right.
- A pocket-size quartz crystal was the most meaningful gift for my husband, George Chinsee, because it triggered a ten-year hobby of collecting exotic crystals.

The Opposite Sex

- Sheila Bridges, an interior designer in New York City who loves to travel, says the best gift she has ever received was a surprise birthday trip to the south of France from a man she loved.
- Jill Plair, a college student from New Rochelle, New York, says it took a few tries before she understood that the price of a gift didn't define the quality of her relationship. She says the most treasured gift she has given was a painting made especially for her boyfriend, "because it came straight from the heart."

Hard Luck

- A woman in Washington, D.C., who was having tremendous personal and financial problems cherished the Native American dream catcher that a good friend gave her. The dream catcher promises to make one's dreams sweet.
- A chip of a black stone was enough to make one man smile. When he was out of work, a good friend gave him the stone, which presumably came from a moon rock, and told him it would bring him money. Although the dollars have yet to surface, the warm thoughts keep the man hopeful.

Unacceptable Gifts

When is it *not* right to give a gift to someone? If your gift will make a person feel embarrassed, humiliated, exposed or otherwise uncomfortable, you should refrain from giving it. It bears repeating: Before you select a gift, think about the recipient. What will make him or her smile? How can you make that person happy and comfortable? Keep in mind that if a gift is too expensive, sexually explicit, ostentatious or in poor taste, you're bound to step on toes. At those times, it's best to refrain. Also, if you do intend to give someone with whom you have an intimate relationship an intimate gift, do so in private. In that way, you will keep the intimacy going!

If you're unsure as to what might be unacceptable, consider the following:

- Do not give lingerie to your secretary or other office subordinate— unless the two of you are lovers. Gifts with sexual overtones are offensive and can lead to legal difficulties.
- Refrain from giving alcohol to a recovering alcoholic or to anyone with whom you are not already more than an acquaintance, as many people do not drink at all, while others often have specific alcoholic preferences.
- Do not buy extravagant gifts for people you hardly know. Gifting to impress is a bad practice that usually backfires.

If you receive a gift that is overly offensive, you will need to return it to the sender right away, explaining clearly and firmly why you cannot accept the item. To prepare for what might be an uncomfortable encounter, I recommend taking a few minutes to contemplate exactly what the gift means to you. If anger, frustration or embarrassment comes up, allow it to dissipate. Next, gather your thoughts and formulate your words. Then share your understanding with conviction and calm as you give back the item. Avoid an argument or other explosive discussion, which will only make matters worse. Allow your contemplation to guide you.

OntheJob

In every branch of work, reciprocity is the fundamental principle governing the relationship between a man and his neighbors.

J O M O K E N Y A T T A

O N E of the things that Grandma Carrie and Mommie always used to tell my sisters and me was, "We do nothing by ourselves, girls." They insisted that we understand that whatever work lay before us, it was best handled collectively. If the task was cleaning up the kitchen, it meant one person cleared the table, while another washed the dishes and another swept the floor. That principle of cooperative effort is one that I have maintained in all areas of my life, particularly when it comes to work. Rather than "pretending" to myself or others that I am the one who makes everything happen on whatever project I have undertaken, I make it my business to acknowledge those others who have participated in the process.

The wonderful discovery I made in doing African research is that this fundamental philosophy dates back to our very beginning, with the African worldview. In *The Healing Drum: African Wisdom Teachings* (1989), Yaya Diallo and M. Hall give a beautiful description of the concept of work in African society:

> When the Minianka [of Mali] work, they move rhythmically. When they dance, their movements express the activities of daily life. Most popular, traditional dances in Africa are directly related to work. . . . Work itself can be seen as a dance.
>
> People do not work alone. To do so is considered suicidal . . . partly because of the psychological effects of isolation. A group of friends unite to do a job together. They know at the outset that they

will work at the same speed, eat lunch at the same hour. They must not quarrel during their time of commitment together. No one should be criticized for being slower than the others. The company of each member of the work group is welcome. Even the physically handicapped person has a place. No person's participation should be a source of conflict.

What a beautiful concept. How wonderful that it is our own. It is part of our cultural legacy to consider work as a collective process that follows a natural rhythm and supports everyone who participates. Further, it is inherent in our ancestral ways that women have their own work (not just housework either), as men have theirs. This does not imply that one type of work is more highly valued than another. Traditional African society is structured such that everyone has a role that benefits the entire community.

In the West, the situation is much different, largely because the economy is based upon payment for services rather than people working together to build a community. Knowing this, it is obvious that we must explore the ways of the Western work environment in order to negotiate it to our advantage—which means to the advantage of the entire community, not just ourselves. Being savvy about business, learning to work differently among people of different ideologies, cultivating patience and fortitude: all of these are key ingredients to business success. Although the rudiments are quite simple, mastering them is another task entirely. Again, it goes back to basics, to behavior, to etiquette.

Good Manners at Work

It should come as no surprise that the way you behave at work should be a seamless, if more professional, version of the rest of your life. You've heard it said, *What you practice is what you preach.* Well, this is true, which is why I think my Daddy used to tell us all the time that we had to behave in a consistent manner. We were in training to go out in the world prepared to handle the challenges that came our way. To do so, we were taught, requires listening, studying and skillful use of the information learned along the way. Supporting the African concept of reciprocity and fairness as basic tenets of a work environment, we were taught to follow the Golden Rule on the job, as in every other situation. On the basis of the many interviews and surveys conducted for this book, I assure you that anchoring yourself with a clear grasp of your own morals and ethics is critical at work, even when you have to demonstrate your ability to strategize, outsmart and protect yourself from others. Whatever your job responsibilities, there are ways to remain kind, honest, well meaning and a team player in the process:

- Be nice. This sounds so simple, yet it eludes many people. Kindness is *not* a sign of weakness, folks. It is an aspect of good manners that attracts people to you, makes them feel comfortable and can result in your being better able to meet your objectives.
- Be modest and spare of words. Spending time pumping yourself up in other people's eyes is a waste of time and a huge turnoff. Let your actions demonstrate your abilities. If your credentials are exceptional, people will find out. As the great thinker Ptahhotep said, *Do not be proud and arrogant with your knowledge.*
- Listen. A primary skill of life, listening is an absolute must at work. Don't fall into the pattern of talking just to hear yourself talk or formulating responses in your head while others speak. Instead, seek out people from whom you can learn, ask a question or two and listen for the inevitable wisdom that will follow. Take notes if you can. Further, listen to everything that goes on around you so you can get a sense of the office structure.
- Don't tell on others. Sounds like school, eh? As it should. Unless your coworker has done something that affects your ability to do your job or is illegal, keep your mouth shut. Nobody likes a tattletale, not even the ones you're telling! The offender will get his (or hers) eventually. Work to resolve your own issues rather than focusing on another's shortcomings.
- Be a team player. Look for ways to be of service. The eighties are over and so, I hope, are the times when it was permissible to be totally self-absorbed. Nobody ever really liked the know-it-all or solo runner at work. Nowadays those shooting stars hardly stand a chance.
- Treat everyone with respect. No matter what a person's position, he or she deserves your respect. Speak to everyone.
- Be loyal. You were hired to work at your company because of your ability and interest in doing the job there. If the time comes when you are feeling disgruntled or unhappy, don't bad-mouth your boss or your office in public. You may choose a confidant with whom you can discuss your woes, preferably not a coworker, but blabbering your discontent at work or among a group of coworkers is foolish. Leave if you cannot maintain a healthy level of professional respect for the place that cuts your paycheck.
- Do what you say. This point cannot be emphasized enough. You are defined by your reputation, your word. By living up to your commit-

ments, you will be known as an honorable and reliable person. When you find that you cannot meet an obligation, speak up.

- Remember to say thank you. If someone assists you on a project, holds the door open or takes you to lunch, show your gratitude. A simple "thank you" is often enough. A follow-up handwritten note of gratitude for bigger favors will go a long way.
- Understand protocol. When you are junior to someone, your role is to defer to that person. That does not mean that you kiss butt. It means that you attend to that person's concerns and needs first (an African principle to be applied to everyone regardless of position). If you want something from a more senior person, ask permission to initiate further dialogue. Then *you* follow up. It would be improper for you to ask the person to follow up with you.

Good Conversation

Have you ever felt completely isolated at a business function and the opportunity to strike a conversation seemed impossible? Well, you aren't alone. For Black folks, chances are you have also been the only person of color in the room. What then? This is time when you really need to believe in yourself. Part of good business is cultivating the ability to begin and keep conversation going even when you don't feel like it. When a group gathers before a meeting, during lunch, at an after-work gathering, the company picnic, the holiday party—at any of these functions, you need to be able to participate in light and pleasant conversation. Even the most astute businessperson has a hard time doing this, too (maybe because it is hard to be an active player in what's just short of *tef tef*). That may be why so many people like to have a drink at social events. Some seem to think alcohol can relax them and make them better able to maneuver through what could be awkward conversation. Not so. Actually, alcohol and other drugs have proven to be the death of many business deals, as people sometimes become a little too loose-lipped and say more than what is necessary or appropriate.

To get you going, remember to listen to others as they speak. Unless you are communicating with someone who is completely self-involved, which is possible, your listening first should provide an invitation for that person to listen when it is your turn to speak. Through the art of listening, you can pick up on what others find interesting and discover a natural entrée into conversation.

- Stay abreast of current events. Choose noninflammatory subjects to discuss with others while you are waiting for an event to begin.

When you don't know what's going on, listen and then offer your impression of what others have said. This can be a great way to stimulate deeper conversation. Ask questions, and let people explain what's going on. By all means, don't act as if you know when you don't. That is the thing that backfires like nothing else! Relax, smile and invite the opinions of others. When in doubt, let them talk, and take mental notes. Good listening *is* good speaking.

- Shake hands with each person and look him or her in the eye. Eye contact is important for establishing a bond of trust and respect. Keep in mind that being able to look an employer in the eyes is relatively new for us when it comes to white folks. Well past the dark days of Slavery and beyond Reconstruction into the fifties and in some places even today down South, Black folks were not allowed to look into the eyes of white people, even white children, and certainly not their boss. Don't take this for granted. Being able to stand before someone and greet that person eye to eye shows that you have confidence in your position and an ease about yourself. Lowering your eyes nowadays indicates either timidity or insincerity.

- Be assertive. If you are friends with a colleague, you may touch the person on the shoulder or give what some call a cheek kiss—an exchange usually shared between men and women or women and women when your right cheeks literally touch. Rarely is an embrace appropriate in a professional situation.

- When in doubt, get the person to talk about himself. People are generally eager to do so—it's a great way to zero in on the person's interests and from this formulate conversation. You may find that you have lots of things in common.

- Ask about a colleague's children. Always a safe topic, children, especially small children, light up a discussion and can be the source of delightful exchange. If you are aware of problems with someone's family such as drug abuse or dropouts, however, avoid the topic.

- Talk about seasonal hobbies. Basketball, skiing, golf, tennis and rollerblading are popular choices. Usually more than one person can participate in the discussion. Make sure that if you bring up the topic, you care about it.

- Congratulate a coworker who received a promotion. Celebration is a perfect icebreaker. It also shows that you care about others. Besides, success is nothing unless you have someone to share it with, and you want others to celebrate with you when it's your turn, don't you?

Dealing with Racism

Racism hasn't gone away, even though it may have changed its face a bit since the times of our parents and grandparents. Black folks in America need to be conscious of it as we go about our daily lives, especially at work. Dr. James Jones of the University of Delaware at Newark, in his book *Prejudice and Racism* (1997) defines racism as "belief in racial superiority and inferiority; a doctrine of a . . . national system that conveys privilege or advantage to those in power; systematic attempts to prove the rationality of beliefs about racial differences and . . . policies that are based on [these beliefs]."

We can add to his definition "the power and methods to enforce the system." You can think, believe and say anything you want about people's race. "What I've learned is that until you have the power and the force to make people go along with it," explains African studies scholar, Raven Rowe, "you have rhetoric and maybe propaganda, but essentially, nothing but hot air. This is the key ingredient that precludes any such thing as 'reverse racism.' "

Jones identifies two of the levels of racism as individual racism or racial prejudice, and institutional racism. The best way to handle individual racism (racial prejudice) situations is first of all to learn and know who you *really* are. When you make the decision in your personal life to accept your collective identification as a model for your own, personal, individual success, a pattern will follow. Besides, it can only help your own peace of mind to elevate yourself beyond the same kind of ignorance that most racists suffer about African people—your people. Once again, make the decision to turn off that TV sometimes and start to learn about your *real* history. Five hundred years may sound like a long time, but in terms of *Homo sapiens sapiens* history of at least 200,000 years, 500 years is a drop in the proverbial bucket of time!

You should study our enslavement in this country and the subsequent liberation efforts that got us out of it, on up to the important gains of the Civil Rights and Pan African movements, which can be studied more deeply and understood better and from more perspectives. These can serve as models for the little battles of all kinds that we have to fight each day. There is more to African history than misery and struggle. There are also things like the mathematical principles on which structures like the Herumaket (Sphinx) and the pyramids at Giza in Khamit were built, which no one has been able either to copy or tear down—and not for lack of trying, century after century! There is the Sun ship of Saqqara (a large, 4,500-year-old sailing vessel found at Giza), and the world's first university system, also in Khamit; the Great

Zimbabwe ruins in the southeastern part of the Continent, an enormous complex that has stood for centuries without mortar! In America, there is a harvest of beauty—from the Harlem Renaissance, the birth and development of jazz, rhythm and blues and soul to the art forms burgeoning today. And there is so much more that *your* ancestors did! It was your people—ours—who developed the first systems of writing, philosophy, trade and commerce, maritime travel, the first recorded astronomical observations in the form of stone structures and likely any other subject that could possibly interest you. If learning that it is your people—ours—who are the archetypes of all human civilizations does not give the fortitude to stand toe-to-toe with someone who thinks he is superior to you (and your people) because of the color of his skin, what will? So, if you run into racism in the workplace, remember the following:

- **Argue the specific points.** When you find that you need to school somebody about a particular point, avoid catch-phrases like *prejudice, politically correct* and even *racism*. In the absence of substance, these are just words that convey no meaning, and they can become buzzwords that the "offender" will see as a weapon used in verbal retaliation. Choose the words that best describe what is going on, and be specific. This does not mean you need to defend the race with an entire African civilization lesson. We were not put on this planet to resist racist people. And if a person has decided that he or she wants to believe something, or not, all the information in the world is not going to change that. Pick your battles and conversations wisely.

- **Above all, stay business-like.** Although encounters with people suffering some level or version of individual racism can be uncomfortable, to say the least, these are not really going to matter much unless the person is your boss. Then, depending on your boss's power, his or her individual attitude about anything may conceivably have an effect on what you are "allowed" to do in your employee capacity. Jones says:

When racism goes beyond the level of [the individual, it becomes] the more general, more insidious, and more debilitating institutional racism. . . . Racist institutions are but extensions of individual racist thought in order to achieve racist objective through manipulation of institutions. Thus, for example, "grandfather clauses" and "poll taxes" can be seen as the manipulation of the political process to achieve individual (or collective) racist ends.

Our people have fought long and hard in this country over the issues of race. One result of this protracted struggle is discrimination laws. So while individual racism may be as Earl Graves, publisher of *Black Enterprise,* calls it, a "nuisance factor," which can be overcome by information and your attitude about yourself and your people, for the institutional variety, we have legal recourse in the form of discrimination laws. Never fear, and don't cower. Sue!

How We Speak

Although I address speech issues more thoroughly in the chapter "What You Say?" I find it imperative to restate some basic issues about language and African Americans in this chapter about work. Questions about Black folks and language date back to the days when our ancestors came to this country. They spoke many different languages that had specific accents and language patterns that were not easily translated into English. Many languages have words and concepts for which American cultural language—American English—has no counterparts. There was no Learn English as a Second Language in 10 Weeks course during their time. In fact, they were not allowed formal Western education for many years (so that they could be easily controlled). This meant that they did what many uneducated immigrants do today. Depending on whom they heard speaking the most determined their facility with the English language. Hence, the "house Negro" often spoke something more like standard English, whereas the "field Negro" maintained a more pure form of West African language structure, ergo African cultural retention, than the "house Negro." In all cases, words and expressions from our ancestors' own languages filtered into the English of the slave owner, further evolving English into an amalgam of cultural expressions. Regardless of their contribution to the language, however, the enslaved were immediately differentiated and judged according to their mastery of the language of the people in power.

This basic fact hasn't changed in modern times. Today, the international language of commerce is standard American English. It is the way of communicating used by those who have assumed the position of power. If the French became the most powerful nation in the world, taking on superpower status, we might all begin to speak their language. For many generations, the language of power has been English, most recently American English and immediately before that British English. (Before that, various European languages held that spot as their people fought for land across the globe. What's interesting to note is that we would not use an African example here, because African nations did not share the objective of trying to be the world power. Their context for nation building was and is different.) For this reason, people of all ethnicities who want to grow and build their lives and business opportunities learn to speak the language. As the great philosopher Franz Fanon said, "Mastery of language affords remarkable power." Essentially, it's a survival skill. Yet many African Americans of all classes seem to fall short when it comes to basic survival.

Many of our people cannot speak standard English accurately enough to succeed in the working world. Like an invisible laser beam, the way that people speak often not only separates the haves from the have-nots, but also maintains that separation indefinitely. Fair or not, the reality in the world of business is that anything that can be used against us will be, and that includes our ability to talk the talk. Apart from the lucrative hip-hop industry that celebrates the artistry of individuals who often have limited facility with the English language when speaking, speaking the language of commerce is a basic requirement in the world of working folks. The only way it can change is if we have our own economic base of power, independent of others. And we are far from unified such that this power base is in place.

Unlearning behavior may be the most difficult challenge facing a human being. Stripping away the mechanics of speech and replacing them with new rules is tough. In order to succeed in this effort, you have to understand the value of the goal and develop a disciplined approach to the task. In comes help. Many courses are available to assist people in mastering the English language. If you feel that you need to brush up on your skills, don't be shy. In my business, I often encounter young, intelligent people who have graduated from high school or even college who simply don't speak standard English or write it well. After a frustrating afternoon of working through a grammatical exercise with one of my clients, I listened to the young woman share, "I went to class every day. My teachers never taught me this. I could have learned it if it had been presented to me." Her first inclination was to shut down because she did not know something that was elementary. But her desire to succeed in a job that requires public communication helped her to push on, and she did learn to speak much more precisely—all the while maintaining her own personality in her speech.

A similar situation occurred in my father's office some years back. As a judge, he always needed to have a skilled executive assistant to manage his office. Then one day, in the middle of a busy workweek, his assistant left. A visit to the personnel office gained him a new assistant. As the first point of contact in his office, she needed to be quick and clear. The first sign of concern came when she answered the telephone. Her phone manner was not professional. Her use of language was consistent with African sentence construction rather than standard English, and it simply didn't cut it in that work environment. The reports he received from people who called were that she said things like, "He gone," or "He be back soon," or "He ain't here right now." Trust me, that was painful for my father to hear. The way he handled it, though, proved to be motivating. One day he invited his assistant into his office and showed her a letter he had drafted. He told her, "Now I know if I give you this letter to type, you will do it accurately, because you pay attention. If I ask you to type a letter that I dictate to you, you probably won't get it exactly right, because you don't have a clear command of grammar." At this the young woman's eyes widened. He continued, "You see these degrees I have on my walls? They say that I am highly educated. But I know that that doesn't mean that I know everything. That's why I keep five dictionaries by my side: a medical text, a legal text, a thesaurus, a grammar book and an English dictionary. Whenever I am uncertain as to how to spell a word or use a verb, I look it up, so that I can get it right. I believe that you can get everything right, too, if you do the same thing. All you have to do is put your mind to it, and you'll be fine." With that, the woman went on a mission. She ended up staying in my father's office for eight months. Some eight years later, we're told, she is one of the highest paid, most proficient legal secretaries in Maryland.

Nobody need feel that it is impossible to rise above a lack of skill. No matter where you start, you can succeed if you put your mind to it. That includes developing the language skills needed to succeed in the Western commercial world. To do so does not mean that you become a sellout or that you "become white." Instead, it simply means that you have adopted essential tools to play the game and succeed. By the way, don't think that I'm telling you to develop these skills, because white people have them down. Most people in this country have poor language skills. Just look at spellings on store signs and billboards, and you'll see what I mean.

Giving Good Phone

Now that people communicate on a global level on a moment-by-moment basis, they often never meet in person. Most communication happens either by phone or some other form of electronic interaction. Thus, the importance of making a positive presentation when you use the telephone cannot be underestimated. In a place of business, the person who answers the phone is the lifeline of that enterprise. Depending on how he or she greets people can determine the fate of the entire company. To ensure that you give good phone, consider these suggestions:

- Pay attention to what you are doing. Some people mistakenly think that they can do two or three things at one time, especially when they are using the phone. Not so. It is highly irritating for someone to have to repeat himself or herself because you were distracted in some way. When you pick up the telephone, focus on the communication at hand.

- Don't talk on the phone with food or chewing gum in your mouth. Why be rude? One of the worst sounds that a caller must sometimes bear is gum cracking in his or her ear. Another is speaking through food. The muffled sound of your voice as it is filtered through a sandwich is gross and unprofessional. It has been said that you are not respecting yourself when you eat and speak at the same time, because you aren't giving your body a fair chance of digesting that which allows you to do your work in the first place.

- Be welcoming. The way that you present yourself has everything to do with how the person on the other end of the receiver responds. Your warm and welcoming "Hello" can dissolve the caller's sour disposition. Always remember that people want to connect in positive ways with each other. Your willingness and initiative to embrace the caller with a positive attitude will set the stage for good business.

- Be aware of who is calling. After greeting the caller, listen carefully. If you have spoken to the person before, don't treat the person like a stranger even as you maintain a degree of professionalism. If you answer the phone for someone else, consider making a list of frequent callers so that you will have a system for handling these calls.

- Answer the phone in a timely manner. Telephone answering machines and voice mail ensure that most calls won't get lost, but people do get tired of waiting for someone to pick up or for the machine to engage. Pick up the phone somewhere between the first and the fourth rings. How quickly you respond to potential or actual clients may mean the difference between your success and failure at work.

- Speak clearly and precisely. This point cannot be emphasized too much. Make it easy on the other person by speaking in an inside voice and using standard English with a professional tone. Your bedroom or Little League voice has no place in the office!

- Excuse yourself when you need to speak to someone else while you are on the phone. A common rude action is for a person to start talking to someone else while he or she is already engaged in a discussion on the phone. The interruption is jarring and disrespectful. When you *must* respond to someone else, immediately say, "Please excuse me for one moment. I have to answer a quick question." Then put the person on hold, so that your other conversation is private. If you need more than thirty seconds to complete your communication, go back to the person on hold and ask if he or she can hold a little longer or if you might be able to call right back. Don't forget to return the call.

- Be mindful of using call waiting and the hold button.   Modern technology is good only if you manage it to your advantage. Call waiting and work can spell disaster if your phone rings off the hook all day. Constantly asking callers to hold on while you either take a message or redirect a call can be disconcerting. The same goes for putting people on hold for long periods of time. It's much kinder to limit your telephone conversations to a few focused minutes and let other callers go to voice mail than to juggle back and forth all day long. Use the thirty-second rule of keeping people on hold. That's about how long busy people will wait without getting restless.

- Keep your cool.   No matter what the mood of the caller, remember that the customer (the caller) should always be treated with respect—especially since no one is always right. By maintaining calm, you may be able to assist even the most irate caller and make the person feel better. You don't need to suffer abuse, of course. Instead, you can manage the caller by asking specific questions about how you may be of service, securing a name and telephone number and then letting the person know that you must end the conversation. You can do that by saying, "I'm sorry, but I must take another call. I will be sure to have someone get back to you." Once you hang up, don't forget to pass the message on to someone who can help to handle the situation. Warn the next person of the caller's state.

- Don't be too familiar.   No matter how well you know a caller, maintain a professional perspective when talking on the phone at work. It may be appropriate to share a few niceties, but resist the temptation to say something like, "Hey girl. How you doing?" to the president of a company with whom you do business. The same goes for slipping into colloquial speech just because the person calling is African American. Stay professional. Callers will respect you for it, and so will your boss.

- Keep background sounds at a minimum.   A blaring radio or loud peripheral conversation distracts a caller from the purpose of the call. A professional environment should be relatively quiet, enabling a ripe environment for communication. Soundproof conference rooms are standard in many music industry offices, thereby designating an appropriate space for turning up the volume. If you gravitate toward playing music while you work, don't give it up. Working to the accompaniment of music was a requirement in traditional African life. As Yaya Diallo described in *The Healing Drum,* "If ten villagers are brought together to work without a musician, nothing will be accomplished. A good musician behind the group, who follows the rhythm of each member, will help them all to accelerate." In contemporary work environments, use ear plugs if that's the only way you can get your music on. But be sure to keep the volume low enough so that you can hear what you need to hear—your phone and your coworkers, for example. And, finally, think about what you're playing. Listening to negative rap lyrics, for example, could very well have a negative effect on your ability to get good work done. Think about it.

- When a call is disconnected, the caller should call back. This is basic courtesy. But you should initiate the call when you are *not* the caller if you are on a cellular phone and you must wait until you move into a good receiving area, or if you are otherwise unavailable to talk again at that moment. You should also initiate the return call if you are the one who is in need. Otherwise, you might delay your call further by crossing wires, with both of you calling back at the same time.

- Remember the basics when you are placing a call. Being gracious, to the point and clear will make it easier for you to reach the person you called so that you can engage the business that prompted your call in the first place.

A Word to the Wise

Talking on the phone too much can get you into a jam if you aren't careful. When at work, do your work. Of course, your life includes more than your job, which means that on occasion you will need to accept or make a personal phone call or even a long-distance call. Just be mindful of how often either of those occurs. One relatively new office assistant almost jeopardized his job by abusing his telephone privileges. Throughout the day, friends called him to chat. So whenever his boss walked into his office, he would find this man on the phone, participating in what was obviously not a business call. Over the course of several months, the boss witnessed this chatter and periodically pointed out the excessive amount of personal phone calls to his employee. To fix the situation, the assistant started hanging up as soon as his boss came into the room. That hardly hid the indiscretion. Eventually he told his friends to save their calls for after working hours, a smart keep-the-job move.

Abusing long-distance privileges is equally as negligent, albeit more irritating to an employer because it costs the company more money.

Being called out on your personal long-distance calls is no fun, either. A woman in Cincinnati learned just how uncomfortable that experience could be when her boss showed her a telephone log that tracked more than $300 worth of calls from her line to the Dominican Republic. The woman's boyfriend had recently moved back home to take care of his family, and they had been talking on the phone daily for a month. When presented with the bill, this sister was both embarrassed and nervous. First of all, she didn't have the $300 to reimburse her company. Further, her boss let her know she would be monitoring her performance more closely, since she had been spending a lot of her work time dealing with personal matters.

Trying to "get over"—that is, to con others—is a losing effort, particularly with modern technology. You will get caught in one way or another eventually. When it comes to long distance, think about your own telephone bill. Would you want somebody else to run up your monthly charges? Why do you think your company wants to bear your personal expense? Be smart and honest. If you have an emergency and need to make long-distance personal calls, ask your employer to grant you permission to do so. And then don't abuse the privilege.

Taking Good Messages

One of the most important signs of efficiency at work is the ability to record a clear message. Whether you are the boss or the switchboard operator who answers the phone first, when it's your turn to take a message, be sure to pay attention and think about what you are saying. Be conscious of the activity at hand. These reminders should help:

- Be accurate. Focus in on your responsibility of recording a precise message. Don't allow your mind to become distracted. When you do this, your communication will be briefer and more efficient.
- Remember to be kind. No matter how many balls you are juggling when you have to stop to take a message, speak with a kind and welcoming voice, and give the caller your full attention. Speaking gently to someone else when you feel harried or stressed may be just the moment you needed to calm yourself down and feel better. Some of our greatest gifts arrive when we're doing for someone else.
- When taking a message, jot down the main points; when sharing the message with others, provide a complete thought. This includes the time and date that the message was taken, the correct spelling of the person's first and last name and business affiliation, a correct telephone number (including area code and extension number), a specific, detailed message and your initials. Don't expect the recipient of the message to recognize your handwriting unless you are the

only other person working in the office. Pay attention to your grammar. Every written communication should have correct spelling and subject-verb agreement. When in doubt, look in the grammar book that should be sitting on your desk, or ask a coworker.

- **Don't make assumptions.** If the person gives a first name, be sure to ask for the last so that you can convey who has called. At least three Sheilas call my office on a regular basis. The only way that I will know who has called and how to respond is if my assistant is certain which one it was. When you think you should know who is on the line and don't, graciously ask the person for the last name. You might even say, "I know that my boss knows you, but I want to be certain to give the right message. May I ask your last name, please?" Usually a follow-up question like that meets with little or no resistance.
- **If the caller is a regular, double-check to learn if he or she is at a familiar phone number.** Without being impersonal or pushy, you still need to get clear contact information. You might ask, "Can my boss reach you at your office, or is there another number that you would like to give to me?" In this way, you cover yourself and your boss. If you doubt that your boss has the number required, graciously ask to record it again to ensure a quick call back.
- **Review the message with the caller for accuracy before you hang up.** You'd be surprised how often a telephone number gets transposed or a message is recorded in a garbled manner.

Tip for the boss: Don't assume that your staff knows your expectations regarding telephone etiquette. Outline in writing the way that you want the telephone to be answered, as well as how you want messages to be taken and a list of frequent and priority callers. In this way, you leave no room for misunderstanding.

Voice Mail

Nearly every office today uses some means of recording telephone messages when no one is available to answer the phone. This technological feat helps to free employees from being slaves of their desk and also can make work more efficient. How can you maximize the use of your voice mail system?

- **Don't neglect it.** The first thing that you should do when you come to work is to check your voice mail. Record your messages accurately, and then return as many calls as quickly as possible. Failure to listen to your message is inefficient; you and your business can suffer! Many people have admitted that they have missed important calls and left unnecessary follow-up messages because they weren't up-to-date with their own telephone records.

- **Return calls in a timely manner.** Same-day callbacks are best. Even if you need to ask an assistant to help you, do your best to respond right away. This action accentuates your efficiency and the fact that the call really matters to you. When you are delayed returning calls, apologize for your tardiness when you do call back.

- **Keep your message brief, professional and to the point.** Long-winded messages can be annoying to people who have to wait to leave their message. Included in your message should be a friendly acknowledgment of the call and a promise that someone will return the call if a message is left. If your office will be closed for a period of time, indicate that on your message so that your callers will know when to expect a call. You may also want to leave the fax number on your message.

Restraint of Pen and Tongue

Before blurting out in writing or in speech anything that could insult or offend someone else and, in turn, you, remember to breathe. In this era of instant contact, it is so easy to get yourself in a real jam by not taking a moment and exercising restraint. If somebody upsets you, excites you or otherwise makes your heart beat fast, pause before you initiate any kind of response. A few seconds of pause might save you a professional lifetime of embarrassment or remorse. That goes for quick-mail, e-mail, interoffice memos—anything else that you have to write down. The same advice holds for voice mail. It's actually too easy right now to fire off an incensed message to someone, only to pray later that the person never receives it.

Rather than allowing your emotions to get the best of you, take a few moments to breathe deeply and find your center. Put the impulse in the context of the big picture. Consider what the consequences of your communication might be, and assess whether you are willing to live with them. Pay close attention to wording that you plan to use. Can you replace inflammatory sentiments with more neutral words?

The law makes your recorded communication at work the property of your employer. Keep that in mind when you issue any information whatsoever, including e-mail. Some things truly are better left unsaid. Be smart.

Beepers, Cell Phones and Such

Okay, so we live in a get-it-instantly world. Gotta have everything now, right? If you work in a service industry where you have to be on call twenty-four hours a day, a beeper or pager is an essential part of your job. The other 99 percent of people who carry these devices do so in order to stay in touch with family and friends.

Don't get carried away with any of your electronic gadgets. You can put them to their best use by understanding why you have them and by being mindful of others around you who have to endure them. To keep it together:

- Turn your pager to vibrate mode and conceal it when you are in meetings, the movies or the theater.
- Return pages as soon as possible, especially if the number listed is followed by a 911, the code for an emergency call.
- Turn your cellular phone off or on vibrate when you are at lunch or in a meeting, job interview or other interactive setting. If you must leave it on in any of these situations, let your party know that you are expecting an urgent call, and ask for that person's understanding.

For more, see the chapter "Beyond Your Doorstep."

Respecting Space

In this age of cubicles and open workstations, it is vitally important that people respect each other's space. A journalist at a major newspaper in Boston pretended there was a door at the entrance to her cubicle in order to become free of the distraction of random passersby who stopped to talk to her. At first, it was infuriating, though. "I felt like I had no privacy. People would just come into my cubicle and start talking to me, as if all I had been doing all day was waiting to talk to them." Believe it or not, the same thing happens frequently to people who work behind closed doors. Assistants, bosses and others sometimes barge in when they feel like it. And then there are the people who knock, walk in and start talking before they have been given the go-ahead. Regard for personal space is a huge issue for many people, and the measure of what is acceptable varies significantly based on culture.

Part of the reason that people invade each other's space so frequently is that they are self-absorbed. Their agenda includes only their needs and neglects to consider the needs of others. When the visit backfires, the intruder is often left bewildered and unaware of the mistake that was made. Stepping on other people's toes is not a healthy component of conscious living. Adding a full dose of thoughtfulness to your daily life will help you to fulfill your objectives. When it comes to space:

- Establish your own boundaries. Whether it's your office area or your own physical space, assess your comfort zone. You may want to put a friendly sign on your door that invites visitors to knock before entering. If you are on the telephone when someone approaches, you may need to let the person know through visual cues to wait. Holding your hand up in a halt gesture works, as does handing the person a piece of paper and pen or pencil to record the message. Regarding your body, you may also need to let people know how far they can go. Extending your hand to a coworker or other person on the job will establish a professionally comfortable space and prevent a kiss, for example.
- Let others know in a calm way when you are uncomfortable. Sometimes a simple movement is a telling action. For instance, if a person touches your shoulder or arm, and you don't like it, you can move away. If the action is repeated, you will have to speak up. "It makes me uncomfortable when you touch me that way, Frank," you might say, without any emotion in your voice. You can also use humor, "Now, Frank. What would your wife think if she saw you right now?" When your calm entreaties don't work, reach out to your boss or someone in human resources to help.
- Pay attention. When you are the one approaching another, look for the invitation to enter the person's space. This is a way to develop conscious interactions with others: look first; avoid embarrassment later. Usually you will sense right away if the moment is good for communication. If you are uncertain, you can say, "Excuse me, Mr. Johnson, do you have a moment?" Depending on the response, you will know whether to continue or politely excuse yourself. The same goes on the telephone. You must remember that people place calls when it is convenient for them—not necessarily for the person they are calling. Be courteous and ask the person you're calling if the time is good for talking or if you might set up an appointment in the future.
- Schedule appointments rather than dropping by. One effective way to respect everyone's time is to set up appointments in advance—for telephone conversations, meetings large and small and lunch, for example. Few people appreciate surprise visits. By calling ahead or writing to request some part of another's time, you create the opportunity for open communication.
- Look around. When you are in a public space—whether it's an elevator, an impromptu meeting in the conference room or a gathering

in the hall—look around you and take note of who else is in your space. Make sure that you have allowed room for anyone who should be included in your conversation, as well as for others to escape. Quite often smaller or shorter people get displaced by those who are larger. If you are tall and can see above most other people's heads, invite those whose vision is impaired to stand in front of you. Be kind. It's always worth it.

Dress Codes: How to Honor Them and Be Yourself

What you wear says a whole lot about who you are, or at least who you are presenting yourself to be. That's why what you wear to work is so important. Whether you like it or not, the first impression that you make on someone you meet is visual. Automatically people size each other up based on how they look, and that includes how they are dressed. The suit—two pieces for men and women—was once the universal Western standard. Simple navy or dark gray with an occasional pinstripe was the average wardrobe menu for years.

Now dress codes are more relaxed, and the workforce is facing real challenges when it comes to what employees wear to work. For African Americans who want to add aspects of their ethnicity to their wardrobe, added considerations come into play. Be smart about how you dress. Here are some guidelines to help you make wise decisions:

- Err on the side of conservative in the beginning. At a job interview or the first few days on the job, be conservatively appropriate. Scrutinize the way your peers and your bosses dress so that you will have a sense of the right wardrobe choices.
- Ask for an employee manual. Most companies have written guidelines that include dress codes. Review the manual to get a sense of what is expected for work wear. Often it is outlined in great detail. When in doubt, ask your supervisor or a human resources representative. In general, it is smart to "dress for success"—in the general direction of your boss or the person who has the job you aspire to fill sometime in the future.
- Beware of anything too sheer, too short or too sexy. Gone are the days when the office secretary was "supposed" to wear tight, alluring clothes. At work, as in most other environments, what you want is for your true self to shine through. If a business associate gets distracted by your clothing, or lack thereof, you may have trouble being taken seriously and run into avoidable problems.
- Women should watch their hemlines (and their cleavage). Even as you want to stay in fashion, you don't want to draw all of the attention to

The New Casual Office

When it comes to casual Fridays, office managers, CEOs and everybody else in management, it seems, is in a tizzy about what is appropriate to wear to work. Just as strict as Monday-through-Thursday dress codes often still are, particularly in corporate America, they are vague when it comes to what you wear come Friday morning. The wise want to remind you that you should remember where you are at all times: work. Unless you work in an environment where people stroll in sporting jeans and T-shirts on a regular basis, from the CEO on down, you would do well by yourself to look professional.

As far as the overall trend of casual wear in the office, many American employees of all races are facing the challenge of how casual their dress can be without backfiring. Never lose sight of your purpose from 9 to 5. Dress with your professional future in mind, even if your clothing gets a little more casual. Here are some dos and don'ts that should help everyone stay in check:

Dos	Don'ts
Size up your company to see what your environment considers acceptable for casual Fridays and the rest of the week. You should want to have an impeccable presentation at all times, even if it is somewhat relaxed.	Forget what some people think about what being Black means; being Black is *not* a problem.
When in doubt, wear the most professional attire that your company supports.	Don't let your outfit get in your way. Your body type and overall style define what works for you, not fashion magazines.
Think as a professional and reflect that in your daily appearance.	Don't wear bare arms, spaghetti straps, high-heeled strappy sandals or sneakers all day in a corporate environment.
Use a boss check. Ask yourself: *Would I be comfortable in my outfit if I had a meeting with my boss or another manager?*	Don't throw caution to the wind and wear something that you know your boss will not appreciate.
Wear a jacket. At least leave one at the office in case you need to dress up a casual look.	Don't try to be a carbon copy of anyone at the office, even as you can use someone you admire as a barometer for fashion success.
Save weekend wear for the weekend.	Don't go to work looking as if you're planning to clean your garage.
Incorporate cultural accessories in subtle ways.	Don't wear evening shoes or accessories during the day.

your thighs. Keep your skirt length at a comfortable place on your leg. Sometimes opaque—not sheer or patterned—hose help to mask the shortness of a skirt. Do yourself a favor, and make it easier for your male counterparts to look you in the eye.

- Pants for women still need extra consideration. Basically this comes up in conservative settings. If that's where you work or you have a client who is from the old school, sisters, put on a skirt, suit or dress. Remember that your goal is to make your money so that you can reach your other objectives, such as owning your own business and setting your own dress code, not to fight. If you don't wear dresses, and your superiors don't appreciate pants, consider another line of work.
- Keep jewelry at a minimum. This goes for women *and* men. Lavish jewelry distracts from the person. Unless the day marks a special occasion that allows for dressing up, stay subtle with your jewels. By the way, that doesn't have to mean boring. Instead, it may mean the difference between choosing to wear one very special bracelet versus an armful.
- Men should wear suits. At least in business environments, they should. A dark suit with a dress shirt and tie, dark shoes and dark socks is standard business attire for men. Casual attire means a sports coat, open-collar shirt and slacks. Of course, the influence of hip-hop has brought sweatshirts and oversize jeans into the office. Do note, however, that such clothing is good only in some creative industries. Otherwise, Black men (and women) wearing this style of clothing become immediate targets for the mailroom, regardless of their position in the company.
- Don't dress too far down. Falling into the fashion trap of casual Fridays can mark the beginning of the end for you. Stay professional. Usually that means no jeans, although so many people wear jeans to work these days that you will need to gauge their appropriateness by the nature of your office standards.

The Importance of Education

If etiquette fundamentally is the art of respecting yourself, your environment and others, then education is a key component in fine-tuning that art. One can never place too much emphasis on the value of education. *How to be* in the world is *not* poorly informed. When it comes to increasing one's ability to earn money, education is one of the most important tools we have. Malcolm X once said, "Education is our passport to the future, for tomorrow belongs to the people who prepare for it today." That preparation needs to be ongoing. During my research, I listened to many stories of people who had gotten stuck in their jobs, halfway believing that they would be able to stay put until retirement, only to find out that times had changed. Being out of work over age forty-five, without having cultivated the skills of the new office has meant an old age of destitution for too many people.

Just as you continue to learn how to interact with people, stay abreast of your fields of interest so that you maintain marketable skills. Don't allow fear of change to paralyze you. It's true that you are never too old to learn; keep reading and turn off that television. Your attitude is the number one area that needs constant expansion. As historian Carter G. Woodson put it, "The mere imparting of information is not education. Above all things, the effort must result in making a man think and do for himself." So don't give up. Explore the Internet, find a class, learn the computer, check out the bibliography in the back of this book. The community can't afford any losses.

Understanding C.P. Time

I am because we are; and since we are, therefore I am.

M B I T I

One of the greatest mysteries of the Black community seems to be C.P. time. Well, that may be an exaggeration, but it is a characteristic of Black people of many backgrounds that presents a real challenge in Western culture, particularly at work. C.P. time—Colored People's time, for those who don't know—is chronic lateness. It's the source of many jokes among Black folks. In fact, people tend to laugh it off as just how folks are when somebody rolls into a meeting, party or other event anywhere from fifteen minutes to several hours late. "It's just how it is," I've heard people say, unwittingly chalking it up to our being not as "efficient" as our white coworkers. And I've seen as much as I have traveled around the world. In countries where scorching hot weather demands that people move more slowly, one's sense of time *is* different from that of the industrialized world.

One way that time has been described from the African worldview is as follows, from Vernon Dixon's "World Views and Research Methodology" in *African Philosophy: Assumptions and Paradigms for Research on Black Persons* (1976):

Time has to be experienced in order to make sense or become real. But what is in the future has not yet been experienced, therefore, the future is not real. The future cannot constitute part of time, except as part of the rhythm of natural events. . . . The drive for investment of the future-oriented Euro-American time [by which the African world-view is characterized] also means that time becomes felt and continuous. It is not numerical or linear. Rather there are what Mbiti calls *phenomenal calendars.* Time is a composition of events that are experienced or felt. . . .

The felt time orientation appears in [Diasporic] Africans in America in their operation according to "CP time." Time-scheduled, pre-planned activities simply do not take precedence over a person continuing to respond to other events in which he is immediately experiencing. Felt time rules the day, when the phenomenal world is inseparable from the self.

This explanation may shed light on why we do the things we do, but it doesn't carry any weight when it comes to Western working situations. We go back to the main point of this chapter: in order to play the game successfully—at least as it relates to this commercial and capitalistic world in which we live—we have to know the rules and play by them. This means we have to learn how to function on Western time. Strolling into the office a half-hour late doesn't cut it. Arriving at meetings after the scheduled time with no apology is foolish. If you suspect that you operate on C.P. time, make the decision to consider some strategies to get yourself in sync:

- Use a clock and a watch. Not surprisingly, many people who are chronically late do not use timepieces. Set your alarm so that you will wake up in time to meet your responsibilities. Use your alarm to alert you to other meetings during the day as well. You can set several watches and electronic organizers to sound at an appointed hour that gives you enough time to reach your destination.
- Keep an appointment book. Record the planned activities of your day and week in advance. Then review your schedule every evening before you go to sleep and every morning before you leave for work. In this way, you will be clear about what you must do. Include in your appointments such things as lunch, personal errands and any other activities that require time.
- Call when you know you will be late. People truly appreciate being prepared for potential lateness in advance. They are then free to go about other business that they need to conduct and are not simply waiting around for you. Your call will demonstrate your professionalism and respect for their time.
- Apologize when you are delayed. Acting as if you weren't late doesn't change the facts. When you walk into a situation late, make a brief

apology. Don't lie about what delayed you, although you don't need to announce it to a whole group either.

- **Send a note or small gift.** On occasion, your lateness may mean that you lose your appointment or otherwise cause bad feelings. Follow up with a sincere and brief note of apology. Flowers are another great way to express your interest in maintaining a positive relationship. Be sure that your gesture is heartfelt and not just to smooth things over. That will only leave a bad taste in the person's mouth.
- **Don't do it again.** Your reputation precedes you. Work hard, and discipline yourself to be on time.

Managing the Water Cooler

What you say can and will be used against you at work. Don't forget it. This statement is not meant to make you paranoid, but it is a reminder to remain aware of your behavior at all times, particularly when you are at work in a relaxed environment. Whether it's the water cooler, the lunchroom or the hallway, be mindful of the tone of your voice and the message being delivered. Do yourself a favor, and follow your Mama's advice: *If you don't have anything good to say, don't say anything at all.* Ptahhotep said, "Guard against provocative speech, which makes one great person angry with another. Just keep to the truth . . . Do not malign anyone great or small." This is especially true at work. Chatting about your personal business or that of others—gossip—should find its way out of your experience entirely, but never should be discussed among coworkers when you're on the job. When you want to speak about an upcoming review or any other point of business that should be kept confidential, delay your exchange until you are certain that no one can hear you who isn't intended to listen in on the information being shared.

That goes for the rest room too. You'd be amazed at how many private conversations go on in rest rooms. Never mind that the rest room should be reserved for relieving yourself. Know that sound tends to travel where there is no carpeting. It bounces off the walls, thereby making your private conversation music (or noise) to someone else's ears.

Appropriate Elevator Talk

Have you ever been on a crowded (or relatively empty, for that matter) elevator, only to have to endure details of somebody else's love life during the ride to your floor? It's exasperating, isn't it?! Here is the right way to communicate on an elevator:

- Speak as little as possible. Don't stand there bursting at the seams waiting for the door to open in order to share a point with a colleague. But if you think about the other people who are occupying that tiny space with you for a brief time, you will want to economize your verbal communication. No one wants to know your business that badly. Keep the conversation to a generic minimum.
- Do not discuss confidential matters. Personal life and hygiene details, as well as salary increases, are inappropriate, as are conflicts with your boss or coworkers. You can talk about positive topics, such as your baby's first tooth or the upcoming holiday celebration provided that it's a company-wide event.
- Use your time wisely. Roy Johnson, editor-at-large at *Fortune* magazine, describes advice that he received when he was working to pitch a huge project: "I was told that I should be able to describe my idea fully in the time it would take for an elevator door to close, because that's sometimes all the time you have." If you are making a sales pitch and the elevator is your only chance, you want to make the big sell effectively using the fewest number of words in those precious seconds.
- Don't eat or crack gum during your ride. It's rude. Sharp sounds are piercing in small spaces.
- Keep your Walkman at a volume that only you can hear. No matter how great the latest tune is that you're listening to, other folks shouldn't have to sing along. Some headphones have speakers on them, but be mindful (for your own good as well) of how loud you play the music through them, because others can often hear clearly.
- Be conscious of your personal space in relation to others. Make way for people to get on the elevator, and allow room for them and you to breathe comfortably once inside.
- Be mindful of what you do on an elevator. More often than not there are hidden surveillance cameras transmitting all actions to a guard somewhere in the building. People have been known to adjust their underwear, kiss passionately and other such intimate things, only to walk past the attendant who witnessed it all as they leave the building. Be discreet.

Big Brother Is Watching You!

George Orwell predicted it many years ago, and today it is true. Thanks to surveillance cameras, office computer networks and sophisticated

Netiquette

With modern times has come a whole new form of communicating and therefore the need for a new code of conduct. When it comes to the use of the computer and the Internet, there's a lot that you should know. Here is some sound advice from Eric Easter, chief executive of One Media, a technology company based in Washington, D.C.:

On the Job

- Don't go to any site that you wouldn't look at with your mother, because most workplaces have servers that record which sites employees visit. Further, most businesses have policies prohibiting visiting certain sites that have sexual content or religious cult content or anything else that may be considered offensive. Downloading something from these sites can be tracked back to the corporation as sexual harassment or participation in something immoral, and you ultimately will pay.
- Don't e-mail anything that you don't want anybody other than the recipient to see. When you delete it, it doesn't disappear; it's still out there in cyberspace. This is particularly important at work. Know that your company has the right to review all employee e-mail. (The same goes for faxing.)

In a Chat Room

Etiquette becomes particularly important when you are communicating with others, so the chat room is the main place where you need to pay attention. The reality is you probably shouldn't be in a chat room during work hours. If you legitimately can spend time there, consider the following:

- Anything written in capital letters reads as if you are yelling or placing extra emphasis on something. Use capitals sparingly.
- Don't come into an established chat room without announcing your presence. As soon as you enter, say that you are there. Then wait to participate until after you are clear about the conversation, much as you would at a cocktail party.
- Keep your conversation tight. Because the dialogue is ongoing, you want to speak briefly. Also, don't cut in on a conversation until the one speaking has finished his or her line. Interrupting is rude, even in print.
- If you participate in the Buddy List, a favorite feature on AOL, ask those whom you want to include if it's okay to add them to your list before you do. When you discover that a buddy is on-line, don't just start a conversation with the person. Ask if the time is appropriate to talk before jumping in.

telephone systems, nothing that you do at work is private anymore. A woman walked into her human resources director's office one afternoon and overheard the ambient sounds and conversation of one of her colleague's offices over the speakerphone. This confirmed her belief that her office was listening in on employees' activities. She had often thought that her phone line had been tapped but couldn't prove it.

For the most part, you don't need to prove it unless you are planning a case against your company. And you should know that in most cases you would lose anyway. Your place of business has the right to seize your telephone records, your voice mail, your correspondence. That means you need to be doing your job at work and leaving it at that. Anything that you don't want your office to know about you, your thoughts or your life needs to be kept outside. As tempting as it may be to talk or otherwise communicate about things that may be bothering you, it's not safe to do so. Plus, it's not right action. *At work, you should do your work.* If you have a problem, talk it over with the appropriate people at work at a scheduled time—after reviewing it with your attorney or other confidant off premises. You *can* create a stellar record of upstanding character. In this way, if you do run into a snag, you will have no need to worry about what "evidence" your company has on you. There won't be any!

The Job Interview

Looking for and securing a job has a lot to do with the skills you have—as well as your ability to communicate those skills in a manner that is appealing to your interviewer—who you know and how you conduct yourself. Why all of those factors? For starters, getting to square one, the interview itself, often has a lot to do with contacts. Although many jobs are listed in newspapers and company bulletins, lots of others are made available through what seems like an invisible network of people who know each other and look out for one another. That's why communicating positively with people—wherever you are—is so important. If you are looking for a job, you want to put it out there. Tell people, from your mother's friends at church to the superintendent of your apartment building. Somebody may have a lead that can point you to either the job of your dreams or at least one that will help you to stabilize your life.

Another key ingredient to getting a job is having a good résumé. Your résumé needs to state clearly and concisely who you are from a business point of view, outlining your credentials in easy-to-understand language, with absolutely NO typos. It's amazing how many people labor over their résumés only to have 500 printed with obvious misspellings. Double-check your work, and ask someone you trust to edit it for errors.

When it comes to the interview itself, consider the following as basic rules of etiquette:

- Do your research. Learn in advance all that you can about the job for which you are being interviewed, the company itself and, if possible, your interviewer.

- Be well rounded. Having a good sense of what is going on in the world is important anyway. In a job interview, a tidbit from current events could trip you up if you aren't in the know. That doesn't mean that you should take a crash course on world history. It really means that you should regularly read a newspaper, or, at the least, watch the world news on a daily basis. Buy *Time* or *Newsweek* too.

- Dress for the job. Wear professional attire, even if the job generally allows for casual wear. I'll never forget a callback interview that I had with a very capable young woman. When she walked in wearing an old, linty sweater and jeans to discuss taking on the role of office manager of my company, her chances ended on the spot. What you wear makes a huge immediate impression. Make it count.

- Be confident. Review all of the characteristics that make you a prime candidate for the job in advance of your meeting. Know these points, and walk with the belief that you will be selected for the job.

- Bring an extra copy of your résumé. Even if you have already sent a copy, bring along a copy for the interviewer to review in your presence. You want to make it as easy as possible on the interviewer and show your complete preparedness.

- Be on time. Showing up late for a job interview can and should be the kiss of death. Why would someone choose to hire you if you don't think it's important enough to get to the interview on time? If for any reason you are running late, find a way to contact the interviewer's office to warn of your delay.

- Ask questions. When in doubt, inquire. You are not expected to know everything about a company or a job in an interview. By asking simple, intelligent questions, you will demonstrate your sincere interest in learning all that you can. You can jot down brief bits of information if you like, another sign that you are serious.

- Adopt an air of entitlement. A high-ranking female executive in the music industry once told me that she observed her white coworkers lobbying for positions and raises and securing goals she hadn't even dreamed of, because they entered a room with an air of entitlement. She says that they were certain that whatever it was they were requesting was legitimate and should certainly be theirs. Having that attitude was contagious, she reports. On the flip side, many African Americans (women especially) question our worthiness to get a big raise or be hired for a major job. Rather than questioning your ability, complete belief in your right to enjoy the reward works! Make sure your work and skills are impeccable, and then have the confidence that comes with being your best. And remember humility.

- Thank the interviewer for his or her time. Regardless of how you feel at the end of the interview, be gracious. You do appreciate the time this person took to meet with you. Stand up when the interviewer does, shake hands firmly while making eye contact and offer your thanks.

- Follow up with a thank-you note. A heartfelt, brief note that reminds the interviewer of something significant and positive that you discussed is ideal. Include in it your sincere interest in pursuing the position.

Working with Headhunters

Sometimes a job search can use a jump start. That's what headhunters are for. Executive search firms, personnel agencies, job recruiters—all of these specialize in making good matches between potential employees and businesses. Many people have been successful in their efforts to work with such professionals as they have looked for work. To make the most of a relationship with a recruiter, know this:

- Start off strong. Be assertive when you seek out a headhunter. Use a confident voice when calling, and follow up regularly until you are granted an audience with the recruiter.
- Be prepared to sell yourself as it relates to the available job. Describe your attributes in specific detail, and be enthusiastic. Provide as much information as possible so that the recruiter knows how to describe you to his client, your potential employer.
- Ask intelligent, probing questions that show your interest. Demonstrate to the recruiter that you are thinking about what you are discussing and how your skills can be used effectively.
- Ask for referrals if the immediate job needing to be filled isn't a match for you. Don't be shy!
- Follow up with a note of thanks. Keep in touch as you continue to seek employment.

Pursuing the Temporary Market

One of the fastest-expanding employment agencies in the country is the temporary agency. Because businesses are looking to staff up without paying benefits, temporary employees have become an invaluable part of the workforce. If you are reentering the working world, seeking to make a career change or simply looking for a bit of flexibility in your work schedule, temping may be the answer for you. Becoming a temporary employee does not mean that you get to work on Easy Street. Competition is high. Here are some guidelines for how to make it as a temporary employee, from a veteran in the industry, Ruth Clark, owner of CUP, a temporary agency in New York City:

- **Be prompt.** When you are applying for a temporary position or showing up for a post you have already landed, your timeliness immediately lets your employer and your agency know just how professional you really are.
- **Look professional.** Many temporary positions are in professional offices that require that women and men wear suits. Put your best look forward, so that your image is blemish free. Your hair style and choice of clothing, jewelry and shoes all reflect on your willingness to be part of the team. Let them work for you.
- **Do your work carefully.** Obvious, yes, but some people don't take temping seriously; they consider it an opportunity for quick and easy money. Be smart and recognize that the work that you do is a direct indication of your ability to handle responsibility. The work you do for one or two days in one office will follow you to your other assignments. Plus, the quality of your work is reported back to the agency, which can choose whether to reassign you based on your performance.
- **Be in close communication with your agency.** If you are going to be late, call the agency *and* your employer at once. If your employer offers you a job, let the agency know *before* you make a decision.

Operating a Business from Home

Perhaps the highest growth area for new businesses in America is the home-based business. If you are part of that trend or considering it, keep in mind that discipline must be your best friend. Apart from the details of setting up your business, here are a few pointers on behavior that you should keep in mind:

- Conduct your business during regular office hours, at least when it comes to interacting with others. Avoid making business calls before 9:00 A.M. or after 8:00 P.M. to other home-based businesses especially. Just as you want your privacy to be respected, so do others.
- Establish your own office hours, and use an answering service to enforce them. In this way, others will grow to respect the delineation of time between your work and home life. Consider getting separate telephone and fax lines dedicated to your work.
- Get dressed for work each day, whatever that means for you. Many people have said that they switch into work mode after they shower

and "dress for work." One at-home entrepreneur told me that she made the mistake of working in her pajamas on a day that she had a very important business call. She said that the tone of her voice and degree of familiarity that she used with her client were inappropriate. She believes that had she been dressed for the role, she would have behaved more formally. The bottom line here is to be conscious of your responsibility when you are working.

- Focus on work when you are on business calls. Don't get distracted by personal business or start daydreaming.
- Don't eat or drink and talk on the phone.
- Turn the television off when you are conducting any business.
- Make sure that your home is prepared for in-office meetings.

Keeping Good Company

In every organization you will find a variety of people. You might liken it to the playground. There are kids who want to play fair and others who want to cheat, some who look for creative solutions and others who complain and bully. It's your choice whom you will pick as allies. Selecting people at the office who will be positive influences on you and your work makes smart business sense. As in any other area of your life, the naysayers are all around. That doesn't mean you have to succumb to their influence. Good-hearted folks also exist—of all races and economic backgrounds—who can become part of your support system.

When you start a job, keep your eyes open for people of like minds. If you approach the situation with a positive attitude and intention, you will attract the right people.

Mentors

At the top of your list should be finding a mentor—someone with more experience than you, whose opinion and values you trust. This person or people can be of any ethnic background, although it's great if you can connect with someone of your own heritage. By keeping your eyes open, going to functions and introducing yourself to everyone you meet, you will come upon someone naturally who can be an inspiration to you. As you develop a relationship with this person, you may ask if it would be all right to call on occasion to run ideas by him or her. Often people are flattered that you value their contribution as they are also grateful that you are straightforward about your intentions. Take your time as you cultivate a relationship with a mentor. Share what feels appropriate about your life and work. To make the best of a mentoring relationship, be clear about what you would like to get out of it, and gauge whether the other party shares your vision. Don't be a leech and pretend you made it all up, all by yourself. You will get found out.

You too can be a mentor. Regardless of how full your experience is, there is someone out there with less. Creating a cycle of sharing information and knowledge can be a powerful way of uplifting everyone. You can reach out to a youth organization or to a newcomer at work. By helping another, you will develop more confidence in your own abilities and base of knowledge. Check with your office for information about mentoring programs. If there is none set up to assist the African-American community, take the initiative.

Coworkers

Even if you are the only Black person at your job, you are not alone. There has to be someone there with whom you strike a chord. Keep your eyes open for that person. Rather than being shy and introverted, walk with your own quiet dignity that says that you are in your job because you deserve to be. Self-assurance is attractive and can even break down that invisible color line.

Outside Network of Support

On a regular basis get together by phone or in person with other people whom you respect. Check in with people you have met—at conferences, the grocery store, at church or anywhere else—who share your interests. Ask yourself whose opinion you trust and who seems to keep information confidential.

Joining Professional and Social Organizations

Expanding your horizons beyond your office is a good way to expose yourself to new ideas and opportunities. Many professional and social organizations provide great avenues for real networking—not just passing your business card to the person standing next to you. Whatever your field of interest, there is an organization that brings together others of common interests and professions. Quite often, there is a Black organization in your field as well. For many established professions, from the law to medicine, journalism to engineering, Black people have organized to help each other excel.

Take advantage of these outlets. Do more than pay your dues. Go to the monthly meetings whenever you can. Attend conventions. Participate in the planning of charity events, and demonstrate your skills. Be a team player. You never know what may come of your gift of help. Lots

Our Own Old-School Networks

When it comes to networking, Black folks have long had powerful institutions that support and nurture the development of the community. Sororities and fraternities are thriving across the country and globally, providing opportunities for bright and inspired brothers and sisters to network throughout their lives as they give back something of value to the community. Similarly, national and local social clubs specifically for Black men and women have been in operation for years for this purpose. When I was growing up in Baltimore, both of my parents were involved in a number of social clubs that met on a regular basis. Now, more than thirty years later, my mother and father continue to participate in some of those organizations (from the Boulé for my father to the Smart Set for my mother. The Links and the Guardsmen are longtime memberships for some of their friends). For all of these years, these groups have provided a social and a business outlet for them. Although the late sixties and early seventies saw many a young brother and sister turn up a nose at the prospect of joining these groups, times have changed again. More young adult African Americans are becoming members of our oldest institutions, injecting fresh blood, ideas and enthusiasm into organizations that have fostered intellectual and spiritual growth among the Black middle class for years. As the numbers swell for this burgeoning group of people, the opportunities also grow immensely for members to interact in a meaningful way.

Similarly, our oldest political institutions, such as the NAACP, the National Urban League, grass roots organizations and other groups, are experiencing a renewed interest from young people who are looking for concrete ways to grow and make a difference in their communities. What this says to us all is that we don't have to look outside of what our own people have built to find strength. Instead, we need only point our eyes to that which has fortified us all along to find greater strength to withstand the trials that are yet to come.

of people have gotten real contracts out of serving on boards as well as with other groups of volunteers for a good cause. No matter what the circumstances, put forth your best effort.

The Art of Networking

One of the finer points of doing well in business is learning how to network. This does not mean dropping your business card in a glass jar or slipping it into someone's pocket (something that a number of people said they actually use as a strategy). Your business card means something only when a face, a personality, a track record go along with it. Otherwise, it's one more little piece of paper to be chucked with the evening's trash.

Real networking requires focus and planning. By having a full life that is balanced with work, family and extracurricular activities, you stand a greater chance of establishing healthy networking. Why? As you live your life, you make choices about how you want to spend your time and with whom. It's not so much about trying to be like somebody else as it is working to create a rich life. Your definition of good living likely includes good working. Who are the people who work well? Who does what you would like to do? Who has access to the capital, connection or credibility that you need to leverage your plan? Seek out those people when you are in business and social settings. That's what the closed "good-old-boy" network has always been about: finding casual, personal settings to do deals. We must create our own environments and opportunities for breaking such ground. It can be done first by opening our eyes. Conventions, luncheons, even visits to the grocery store can yield creative solutions to challenges if considered in that vein. One executive pointed out that when he was unable to reach a CEO whom he needed to contact, he made it his business to go to the charity ball that the CEO's wife co-chaired. At that event, he met both husband and wife and established a connection. In some cases, meetings like that are more effective than those at the country club, when whites and Blacks tend to be segregated even though both are present.

Work and Gifts

When it comes time to give a gift to a coworker, supervisor, subordinate or other person on the job, step back for a moment and think about your intention for giving. Usually if you give a gift out of true gratitude or as an acknowledgment of a job well done, you will be fine—at least in the intention department. The nature of the gift is another question. When you offer a gift to someone at work, it can be of a personal nature while not being intimate. Many people bring gifts to coworkers and employees from vacation or a business trip. The opportunities for giving at work are endless. Giving gifts at work, however, is not required. Here are guidelines:

Dos	Don'ts
Send cards and even flowers to coworkers, bosses, secretaries and others for special occasions, including holidays.	Feel obligated to give the boss a gift for the holidays. It's not necessary and can be considered brown-nosing. If you want to offer a small gift to your boss, do so discreetly.
Give a group gift to service workers, such as the maintenance team and messengers. Make sure that everyone can enjoy the gift, such as candy or fruit.	Give intimate gifts to coworkers, especially those of the opposite sex unless you are involved in a sexual relationship. Then do so privately.
Thank anyone at work who gives you a gift with a brief handwritten note that acknowledges the kindness.	Complain about a gift received that you don't like. Unless the gift is offensive, forget about it. You can either give it away (to someone off premises), return it or toss it at another time.

See the chapter "Gifting and Giving Thanks" for more ideas.

Work and Children

Long gone are the days when most families had a Daddy who worked at the office, while Mommy stayed at home with the kids. Truth be told, that was never the real balance for most African-American households anyway. So, what happens when you go to work every day and have children? When health issues pop up, a recital occurs at 11:00 A.M. on Wednesday morning or the day care center is closed, what should you do? Rule number one: Don't panic. Because most Americans with families work, employers are taking a serious look at how to take care of families so that they can maintain healthy relationships and keep profits up. That means many companies are looking for viable solutions to child care issues, rather than ways to fire employees who get pregnant or face family challenges on occasion. Regardless of the kindness of your employer, what you need to do is keep a level head and stay honest.

- Be straightforward when you have a problem. If you wake up and have to take your child to the doctor instead of heading into the office for an 8:00 A.M. appointment, pick up the phone and let your boss know. Don't call in sick if you're not. You will only get stuck in your lie sometime down the line.
- Investigate child care options at work. Is there a facility within your company? Many larger firms offer this as a prime benefit to parents. In smaller organizations, parents are often allowed to bring their

young children to work as needed, so that the work can still get done.

- **Don't abuse the privilege.** Check with your employer. Bringing your child to work on a regular basis can be distracting to fellow coworkers, especially if the child needs to stay all day. Don't allow your needs to affect the productivity of your job. Some people may not like children in general or your child in particular. Be conscious as to how your kid's personality is received by your coworkers.

Time Off

Requesting time off can be a real challenge even when it should be easy. One way to take away some of the tension is to know what is offered. Read your employee manual to brush up on the basics. And keep track of the time you have taken off during the year. Find out how many vacation days you get based on your time on the job. Read the rules about sick days and disability.

If you work for a small or new company that has not already established these guidelines, negotiate your allowed time off before you start your job. Then you will have your agreement in writing. If you're already on the job and are unclear, assess what you really need or want, and ask your boss for the time. Choose wisely, though. If you have had low performance or other aggravating circumstances, requesting what may seem like a favor (whether it is or not) may not be the best strategic move at that time.

When You Are Pregnant

Take it from lots of women who have gotten pregnant while they are working: share the information on a need-to-know basis and only when you need to tell—in other words, when you begin to show. This will make it easier for you to do your work free of the distractions of coworkers' questions, human resources' concerns and your boss's potential worries. Do your job to the best of your ability. Find out what your benefits package contains with regard to pregnancy and childbirth. Keep the details of your pregnancy, such as your physical changes and conditions, to yourself. Remember that you are at work, and your goal should be to do your job. Behave and carry yourself as if you are doing the greatest thing a human can do: creating new life. People will treat you with respect when you behave as if there is no other way to be treated. Don't fall into the trap of accepting pregnancy as a handicap to be defended. Work until you need to take off. Timing will vary from woman to woman. My sister Stephanie worked right up until her ninth month with both of her children, much to everyone's amazement. Because she didn't complain about her job or her physical state, she left no space for cheap jokes or other comments. During her time off, her office was supportive, because they knew she had given her all while she was there—and they knew she intended to come back.

If you are unsure about whether you plan to go back to work after you have your baby, keep your concerns private. Many changes occur in the body and the mind during pregnancy, not to mention the changes in family dynamics, whether you are a couple or a single parent. Do your best to secure your job for your return, and then assess your situation over time. Through maternity or paternity leave, both parents are usually allowed eight to twelve weeks off, with the guarantee of keeping their jobs. During this period, determine your plans. Know that the Family Leave Act provides protection for you as you care for your newborn. Should you decide not to return, go to your office and have a meeting with your supervisor to discuss your decision. An extended leave may be an option. Further, you never know when your paths will cross again. Leave on good terms.

If you plan to return to work, maintain a healthy relationship with your office during your absence. Clearly, your child takes priority, but in the competitive working world, you would do well to secure your position while you are away. Call to see how things are going, and lend your support. Stay abreast of what's going on politically and business-wise. Keep communication flowing between you and your boss. At the same time, don't take on any work projects before you are ready. You will need to be clear about your boundaries, what you will and will not do, even as you plant seeds to secure your future.

Addressing Conflicts

Navigating your way through friction of any kind can be tough. When it comes to conflict resolution on the job, it's important to learn how to manage your emotions and your actions so that you can reach a point of closure on the issue without causing repercussions. What a lot of people do, however, is practice avoidance strategies that serve mainly to frustrate the other party involved and lead to further difficulty. Take Anna, a freelance researcher. Robin, an executive at a small marketing firm, had a really important and sensitive job for which she felt Anna would be perfect. They had worked together extensively in the past and had a great working relationship. After Anna had begun the preliminary research by identifying source materials and their locations, she began to have some time management problems. On the first day Anna was to begin submitting initial search results, she and Robin made an appointment to meet at 10:00 A.M. By midnight, Anna was still a no-show, and Robin had left at least six messages. Robin thought, "Something horrific must have happened!" Well, what happened was that Anna had decided to take on an additional project, which required far more time than she had anticipated and was on a much shorter deadline than Robin's project. Knowing full well how important Robin's work was, as soon as Anna hit a time snag, she panicked and took the least professional way out: the missing-in-action route! For the next two days, Anna returned not one of Robin's phone calls, turned in no work and remained otherwise out of contact. When, on the morning of the third day, Anna left a message for Robin's assistant, Robin's concern quickly turned to anger: the avoidance strategy was in full effect. Giving Anna the benefit, however, Robin continued to leave messages requesting status reports. As you can imagine, with each call, Robin's tone became more and more terse. By the end of the fourth day, Robin decided to find someone else to do the job.

So many things went wrong with this real-life scenario on both sides. Here's a breakdown of dos and don'ts that can keep you out of such a situation when you run into a jam at work:

Dos

Establish a clear understanding of responsibilities on both sides before you begin working on a project. Put your agreement in writing.

Follow up regularly to ensure that things are going as planned.

Speak up if you are falling behind or cannot handle a task. You might be able to get some help, but there's no chance if you don't let somebody know.

Remember to stay focused on the goal and not the personalities when conflicts arise.

Get your mind quiet before you speak, especially when you are feeling anger or fear. Breathe deeply, lower your voice and table it until tomorrow if you can. As soon as you get home, take a bath or meditate.

Don'ts

Start off with a vague understanding of the work you must accomplish. A handshake isn't always enough.

Assume that everything is going well when you are working with someone on a project. Check up on it.

Hide from your boss or coworker when you are late. Own up to your status, and ask for help immediately. The longer you stall, the worse it gets.

Conjure up all the images you can recall of your business associate's flaws. Remain in the present, dealing with the situation at hand. (You should have thought of those other issues before you engaged the person in the work.)

Speak before you think. Lashing out when you are frustrated or otherwise off center will almost always guarantee you negative results. That goes for answering machines and voice mail, too.

(continued on next page)

Dos *(cont.)*	Don'ts
Find a way to laugh. It's one of the best therapies going.	Bad-mouth the person who has let you down. Just move on. Replace your negative emotions with positive action. Have compassion for the person who handled the situation poorly.
Apologize when you are wrong. Whether your mistake had to do with getting the work done or how you communicated with another, immediately accept your part in the matter. In this way, you will clear the air to allow goodness back into your experience.	Hold a grudge. Dwelling on the past will only make *you* unhappy. Forgiveness is a great virtue; even the worst faux pas can be forgiven. Learn from your mistakes and those of others.
Talk to people you respect about the problem, not for the purpose of gossip but for advice.	Feel sorry for yourself. Sitting on the pity pot is a waste of energy that breeds depressing thoughts.
Remember to pray. During times of conflict, especially when you are confused about the right action to take, ask God for guidance.	Feel that you are alone. If you can remember that you are created in the image of God who is perfect, you will never have to feel totally alienated, even when the situation seems dour.

Another word on anger: Of all of the emotions, anger just might be the most dangerous one to experience. It invades the body, mind and spirit and clouds the vision. Instead of seeing what is actually happening, a person who is in the throes of anger sees an exaggerated image of whatever is there. Do your best to let go of anger before you speak or act on a problem. You can do some deep breathing followed by stretching, take a walk, splash your face with water, talk with a mentor about the problem or sleep on it. That angry memo to your boss could cost you your job if you send it today. By waiting overnight and rereading it when your mood has subsided, you may be able to rewrite it using less inflammatory language. Prayer is vital when wrestling anger. Sometimes it is the only way that you can find relief.

Being with Black Folks

An uncanny situation crops up in many corporate offices around the country. You may find that you are the only or one of the only Black people working at your office. All eyes seem to be on you. You feel as if your bosses and coworkers are watching your every move. All of this makes you feel as if you're walking on eggshells half the time. When you do spot another Black person—finally—the sister or brother turns out to be a maintenance worker. What should you do? That there is even a question points to how delusional many of us have become. Yet countless corporate climbers decide to turn their eyes in another direction when the lady with the vacuum walks their way.

Self-hatred is a character defect that runs rampant in the Black community and must be fought with all of the tenacity at our command. Most of our grandparents would be appalled at such foolish behavior. Operating under the mistaken assumption that white people will think less of you if you fraternize with the help is a sick and hopeless belief. *To thine own self be true,* right? For us to grow strong and regain any measure of power requires that we understand that our true self is also reflected in other people of color, regardless of their social or economic position. Remember the Zulu saying, *A person is a person because there are people*. Even more practical, getting to know the maintenance crew can be of tremendous value to you. Who else do you think knows the goings on at your office? You may be able to glean vital information about how you can do your job better if you develop a relationship with them. In turn, you may also be able to help them to reach beyond their current status. I've heard many stories of maintenance workers who secured professional internships for their children after establishing a good rapport with someone at the office. When you find your sense of clarity growing dim on this subject, think about your own family. In nearly all of our families, somebody we love has held a maintenance position. Search within your being for an image of that loved one, and hold that picture close to your heart when you feel the impulse to look away. You may find yourself opening up to a welcoming smile and loving state of being instead. An added bonus is that your white boss will probably respect you even more.

That Delicate Balance

There are lots of names that describe an often-fatal personality trait in the business world: sucking up to a superior, brown nosing or otherwise kissing ass. Whenever you try too hard to please, you are bound for disaster. There is an art, however, to saying the right thing to a person so that you set yourself up for success, and sometimes it requires biting your tongue. You need to discover a way to strike a balance between a sharp tongue and syrupy, false good cheer:

• Think before you speak. Keep this in the forefront of your mind, and your life will run more smoothly. When asked your opinion on something, don't blurt out an answer. Listen carefully first, so that you can repeat the person's words in your head (or back to him or her if need be). Take a few moments, and chew on the topic to see how you can best express your opinion constructively. Ask a clarifying question or two when necessary. This advice stands whether your view is positive or not.

- Consider the other person. How can you best serve that person? Is there a way that you can treat that person with respect and communicate your feelings? Look for that road to travel. There's a big difference between being considerate and kissing up.
- Choose your moments carefully. If you disagree with your boss or a coworker, do so privately whenever possible. When in a public setting, remain silent or say something like, "I have to give that some thought," if you are asked a direct question that would be best supported (in your colleague's eyes) with a resounding "yes" when you strongly disagree. If you can present your view comfortably without dissing the other person, you may share your sentiments in a small group. Don't let the opportunity to hold a microphone tempt you into either singing someone's praises on and on or bad-mouthing the person. In either case, what you really are doing is drawing attention to yourself rather than the situation at hand.
- Decide what is really important. Wise folks often ask, *Is it better to be right or to be happy?* Many executives think that they have to be right all the time. But right is relative. You have to think beyond the moment that you are in to assess the value of your overture in the long run. Speak on what really matters, and let the other things slide. But really let the other issues go. Pulling out old stuff somewhere down the line when you're facing a problem weakens your argument and can make you lose sight of the immediate points.

Dating on the Job

Many business manuals recommend that you keep business and love separate. Reality proves, however, that thousands of couples have found each other through some type of business interaction, quite often on the same job. With a good eight to ten hours devoted to money-making pursuits, most folks simply don't get to do too much other socializing. That doesn't mean that getting involved with someone on your own job is easy. In fact, when Cupid's arrow strikes during your 9 to 5, you had better watch out.

- Do your work. When the magical veil of love falls over your eyes, don't forget your primary purpose where you are: to get your job done. One sister fell in love with a brother on her job and found herself in quite an uncomfortable situation. Every time the two of them saw each other, sparks flew. Their boss quickly observed their romantic interests and commented on it. Although they definitely spent a lot of time behind closed doors in one of their two offices, they made a pact to be superefficient. At the same time, they acknowledged to their boss that they were seeing each other. With all the cards on the table and their work performance up, nobody could complain.

- Avoid married people. This should go without saying. Obviously if you have an affair with a married member of your staff, you are bound for trouble. First off, you have to keep it a secret, which is close to impossible even in a large office. Rapid heart rates are easily detected. Second, one or both of you could lose your job if it gets ugly. What if the wife or husband comes to the workplace, finds out and causes a scene? As hard as it may be to avoid such temptation, do your best to resist it. Immediate gratification rarely pays off in the long run. Chances are not in your favor here.

- Take your relationship off campus. If you really do respect one another, know that there is a time and a place for everything. Work happens at the office. A budding romance enjoys its best chances for growth during your downtime.

- Keep your business to yourself. Avoid sharing blow-by-blow details of your relationship with coworkers. It's none of their business. It infringes on your partner's privacy. And it can prove humiliating for you if the relationship ends.

- Don't lie. It won't work anyway. You can give generic answers to questions about your relationship or simply tell people that you prefer not to talk about it.

- Stabilize your relationship if you can. Once you see that you and your coworker—or boss—want to stay together, calm down. Continue to be professional at the office, leaving your romance for after hours. That's the way that my sister-in-law managed it with her former boss, now husband. My sister-in-law, Gwyneth Whyte, started out as the top salesperson in Jeffrey Shick's Florida-based insurance firm. After a year of just working together, something more seemed to be brewing. Their relationship has blossomed into a family with three children, along with a partnership at work. On the job, it's about performance. Since the lines are clearly drawn, no one seems to have a problem. And Gwyneth and Jeff are proving to be an inspiration for everyone else at their small firm.

- Don't use sex to climb the corporate ladder. A senior executive once told me that having sex with the boss was the way to make it in business. What I didn't know at the time was that I could have sued him. What you should know now is that such behavior rarely works.

Sleeping with the boss in hopes of getting a promotion does more to garner you a reputation as a "ho" than anything else. The way to earn respect is by doing the work, not dropping your drawers!

- If you are asked about someone else's sexual liaisons on the job, keep your mouth shut. Regardless of what you think you know—even if someone has confided in you—you would do best to say nothing. Gossip has gotten many a person in trouble. Discussing your own business should be kept at a minimum. When it comes to somebody else's, adopt the credo that it's none of your business, and you don't know anything. Ptahhotep says, "Don't repeat slander nor should you even listen to it. Slander is like a terrible dream against which one covers the face."

Holiday Celebrations

Many organizations large and small honor their employees by hosting gatherings at the end of the year. Although they are billed as holiday gatherings, by and large these events serve as a good excuse to get together and for the employer to thank the employees for a good year. Regardless of your religious preferences, you should attend the event, at least for a few moments. If the principals of the company plan to speak, be present during that period, and pay attention. Believe it or not, people sometimes are so engrossed in conversation or food that they ignore the speakers. Don't ever forget that you are at work. Listening when you should is a sign of basic common courtesy, as well as smart business sense.

Should your company exchange gifts, as through a Secret Santa grab bag or other arrangement, let people know if you are going to participate. Usually the organizer gives the gift description and includes a price limit, as well as generic recommendations for unisex ideas. Select a gift that can be comfortably revealed in a group setting—nothing too personal or intimate. Wrap the gift that you present creatively. If you intend to give gifts to other members of the staff, do so discreetly if others are not swapping gifts. You don't want to make anyone feel uncomfortable or left out of the festivities. Other pointers for these parties:

- Dress conservatively with style. This doesn't mean you have to look as if you're going to church! It does mean you should remember where you are. Unfortunately, these rules relate more to women than men, but they are real. Common sense can be your guide, but just in case, know that a see-through dress with no bra has no place at an office party. Nor does a dress or skirt that is so short you can't sit down without showing all your stuff! Remember that when the party is over and you're back at work, you want to be taken seriously. And no matter what everyone else is doing, tongues do wag!

- Get there on time. You don't need to open the party, but do arrive within the first hour, especially if the party will run for three hours or less. If you feel awkward when you arrive, make the rounds and greet each person who is there. You can also offer to help. Usually there's something extra to be done.

- Bring a guest if you are allowed. Having someone with you—a spouse, a date, a friend—can help to ease you into the party, because you won't be alone. Think about whom you will invite so that you pick a person who will be comfortable in the setting and makes you feel at ease. Everybody is not right for every event. If you cannot bring a guest, team up with a coworker or group from the office and arrive together. Of course, walking in by yourself is perfectly fine. Just do so with confidence!

- Watch what you drink. Party or not, you are still at work. The office party is famous for bringing latent personality traits out in public. I've heard stories of the president of the company sneaking off with his secretary, people making out on the dance floor, clothes falling off—everything. Excessive drinking triggers loud and ugly brawls on occasion too. Monitor your intake, and keep an eye out for your friends. Alternate alcoholic beverages with sparkling water or soft drinks, and eat before you drink. Start the night with a glass of water so you don't drink the first one too fast because you are thirsty. If you see someone who needs to be rescued, quietly go to that person's aid and escort him or her to a private area.

- Circulate among the crowd. It's easy to stay in a corner and talk to your friends. Instead, be bold and make your way around the room. Approach groups of people who seem to be involved in light conversation (so that you don't interrupt anything private). Be sure to thank the executives of your company for hosting the celebration. Your enthusiasm and confidence will shine through and be remembered long after the party is over.

- Have fun. The celebration was created with good fun in mind. Relax and be yourself, even as you remain professional.

- Leave before it's over. Unless you are part of the cleanup committee, you shouldn't be the last person to leave the party. My Mama taught me years ago that it wasn't ladylike for a female to overstay a party or any other event. Make your rounds, have your clean fun and move on. Your positive performance at the party will make a lasting impression.

Traveling on Business

Whether you're traveling out of town or around town, being Black and traveling make for ruffled feathers.

Do not let obstacles such as taxis that drive by or employees who automatically direct you to the mailroom get the best of you. Racial bias does still exist. It's how you handle yourself and the situation that counts. On the road, it's no different. If you are traveling in the company of white coworkers, chances are you will experience waiters' directing their questions along with the check to one of them regardless of their seniority, as the wait staff ignore you. Attempt to handle the situation with humor. Watch your colleagues to see what they do. Find a way to address the incident lightly; relating it to a constructive way out of a situation is much better than spending an hour giving a soliloquy about how messed up race relations are in this country. Give a minimal tip. You can also let your coworker pay for the meal. What do you really need to prove by spending money anyway?

Beyond dealing with race issues, work and travel present a number of other considerations. Here are a few to keep in mind:

- Men and women should be treated with equality. Chivalry is not part of the work experience these days, which is as it should be. Women should open doors as readily as men, pay for cabs and pay their part of meals just as men should. Junior executives should always take care of tips, cabs and other small expenses in deference to more senior executives. (Just remember to save your receipts so that you can be reimbursed.) It is not necessary to go to extremes to prove a point, though. Call me old fashioned, but I like it when a man extends a hand when I am getting out of a car or holds a door open for me. The acknowledgment of my femininity does not make me automatically think that a man is belittling me; instead, it often feels refreshing and respectful.
- Travel light, travel right. One of the trickiest parts of traveling is carrying only what you need. If you fall into the category of person who packs everything but the kitchen sink, tell yourself that you can adopt a new strategy. Make a list of what you will be doing on your trip, including business meetings, working out and evening activities. Pack one outfit for each activity—nothing more (well, maybe one extra outfit or piece if you are really unsure!). You will look unprofessional if you are lugging lots of bags while your coworkers have one apiece. Be sure to pack a sewing kit; don't depend on the hotel for that, especially when you are packing light.

- Make sure you have your finances in order. If you need an advance, get one. If you will have to charge your expenses, including hotel, to your credit card, make sure that your card will allow you the credit—in advance. Even savvy travelers have on occasion run into embarrassing glitches when they've been on the road a while and haven't checked their credit limits.
- Conduct business meetings in neutral places whenever possible. Particularly if you are meeting with people of the opposite sex, even fellow coworkers who are traveling with you, it's best to have meetings outside your hotel room. Before your trip, find a conference room or private lounge area that may serve your needs. If you must meet in yours or a colleague's room, be fully dressed, no matter what the time of day, handle your business and part ways.

When You Are the Boss

Whether you get promoted into a position of power or you take the plunge and start your own company, becoming the boss means accepting a different kind of responsibility. You are no longer responsible just for your own actions and productivity, but also for that of your staff. To make the most of your position of authority, remember the Golden Rule, *Do unto others as you would have them do unto you.* With that philosophy in mind, you will need to be aware of your way *of being* even as you closely monitor your staff.

- Incorporate the good from your past job experience, and leave the bad behind. You know how your mama used to tell you that you can learn something from any situation? Well, it's true. The workplace is fertile training ground. When you move into the seat of the boss, take time to evaluate how *your* boss worked. Assess the pros and cons of your boss's management style and that of your company. Be especially mindful of the behavior that pushed your buttons. Do your best to determine what exactly about that behavior soured your feelings for your boss. Then make a mental note not to behave in that manner. Spend an equal amount of time outlining what was good about your various work experiences, how your supervisors treated you, how they responded to your needs, how they directed and evaluated you on the job. By making this clear and full review of your experience, you will be better able to bring the best of your experience to your work and your staff. Everyone will appreciate you for it.
- Remember that your employees are people too. Some bosses are so project oriented that they forget the humanity of their staff. Although

you needn't get into long discussions with staff about their personal lives, be sure to ask about their families, their weekends or their holidays on occasion. When someone has been out sick, welcome the person back and inquire about his or her health. If the person is out for a long stretch, call to check on his or her progress, and send a card or gift.

- **Don't get too close.** It is important to be kind and thoughtful to your employees. It is also vital to maintain a healthy distance between you and them. Saundra Parks, owner of the Daily Blossom, a popular florist in New York City, reminds bosses and entrepreneurs with small businesses especially, "Any relationship is subject to change. You have to know the cut-off point with your employees, or else when things turn cold, you won't know how to respond." Balance is key here.

- **Lead by example.** Your employees will follow rules that you follow. You cannot expect anyone to abide by rules that you do not honor yourself, because you have already proven that they are not of value or important.

- **Be available to your staff.** No matter how large or small your staff, have an open door policy in the sense that you take their calls and make appointments to listen to their concerns. Let them know that you want to work as a team to do the best work.

Working with Friends and Family

Take a look at the Korean community and you will see a prime example of how family and friends can work together harmoniously to build an economic base. In many cases, Koreans move to this country, take up residence with each other in small quarters and work tirelessly to reach their clearly outlined goals. Such is no longer the norm among African Americans as it was before segregation ended and integration looked like an answer to a dream, certainly something to fight for. Also, the mentality that "somebody owes me something, so I shouldn't have to work so hard" does a number on a lot of our people. What has happened to cooperative economics and community effort? What can we do to turn the tide?

Choosing to do business with Black people is an essential component of a strong economic base. Yet many Black business owners have complained that they don't reap the same degree of effort that these very brothers and sisters have offered when they worked for white companies. How can this be? When it is so, we must change such misguided behavior by taking an honest look at our thinking and redefining our values. The African work ethic promises that people work together toward a common goal. Many of our family-owned businesses and other smaller companies operate from that premise. At my business, for example, we work as a unit, focused on meeting our goals as we support one another. The sense of cooperative effort creates a level of respect and responsibility that encourages everyone to do the best possible job. Whether the project is large or small, we must put forth 100 percent effort when we work. From the perspective of respect, it's imperative that we look at the opportunity to work with family as a golden chance to give to a common cause that benefits everyone. Being clear about what has to be done is the first step in making the relationship work.

- Clearly outline the objectives. Whether the project is large or small, write down the goals and objectives along with the responsibilities that each person will assume.
- Make a formal agreement regarding the terms of employment. Even when it comes to family and friends, it's best to write it all down and sign off on the agreement. Then there will be no vagueness surrounding the terms at some point in the future. You can always refer back to the document.
- Treat business as business. During office hours, conduct business. Don't take up long periods of time discussing family or personal issues. Formal breaks or time after work can be used for handling these matters.
- Keep the rules the same for all employees. At a family-owned restaurant, the wife's brother tends to be the goof-off, always coming in late, not paying attention to the customers. Everyone knows he's serving up substandard work, and everyone laughs it off—everyone, that is, except for the other staff members who have to take up the slack. What has occurred over time is that resentments build, and staff turnover is high. Because the business owners have not addressed the lackadaisical attitude of their family member, their business is suffering, and they can't keep the good people they need.
- Reward staff on merit, not blood or love. Particularly if you have a mixed staff (family and friends and others), be fair in your pay and bonus structure. In this way, you will provide incentive for good work and avoid possible lawsuits from other employees.

Resignation and Firing

Talk about stress. Whether you are resigning, being fired or doing the firing, your interest in dealing with ending a business relationship is probably no greater than that of severing ties with a lover. For the most part, people avoid it like the plague. Wishing that the situation will change without doing anything about it is foolish. What often happens when people delay the inevitable is that a spirit of discontent and disillusionment sets in, and nobody benefits. In all cases, it's best not to act when you are feeling emotional about the action. Operating from a clear head is the rational and responsible way of handling any situation.

On Resignation

When you know that it's time to leave your job, make a plan. Do you know what you want to do next? Do you have other employment lined up already? Are you interviewing? What do the prospects look like? Do you have any savings? Each of these questions is important, because it will help you to assess when to make your move. Even when the conditions at your job are close to intolerable, devising a strategy for your exit makes good business sense.

Before you can even get to the etiquette of your exit, you need to have a clear head. My sister Susan Cole Hill, who has worked in the recruiting and job placement field for many years, suggests that you will discover your own clarity about your job situation by writing out a list of pros and cons about your job. Somehow looking at it in black and white makes your options seem more real. She also advises people to compose an additional list that describes the work that they would like to do for the short and long term. Once you have these points outlined, you will be amazed at how sure you can become about your next step. That doesn't mean that taking that giant step of leaving your job will be easier, though. So, remember to meditate, contemplate and pray before you act. You may also want to keep these pointers in mind:

- Prepare yourself at work. Get your paperwork in order. Be sure to remove any personal paraphernalia that can easily be taken home in advance. Also, if you have insurance through your job, take care of all of your medical and dental needs that are covered before you give notice. Be ready to walk. Many times when people offer their resignations they are asked to leave right away. You don't want to be caught with boxes and bags of things that need to be transported at the last minute. You must be subtle about your advance packing. Otherwise people will become suspicious, and you could run into an even bigger problem. Keeping your personal possessions at work to a minimum is always best.
- Stay focused and strong without being emotional. Even if you need to practice at home, do what you must to remain professional in all of your interactions surrounding your departure. Tears have no place at work. Do your best to contain them. By having your plan written out

in bullet points, you can refer to your vision when you start feeling ill at ease.

- **Request a meeting with your boss.** Schedule a time for a formal meeting. Bring a typed letter of resignation to that meeting with a date that reflects when you would like for the resignation to be effective, and give a copy to Human Resources. Get straight to the point in the meeting. Even if you have experienced tremendous negativity on the job, it is wise to share what was good about your experience first. Let your boss know how much you appreciate the opportunity to work there. Indicate two or three positive aspects of the job. Keep to a minimum the list of issues that caused you discomfort. Do not allow your meeting to dissolve into a moaning session. Only those negative points that relate to your ability to stay in your job should be mentioned, and then they should be presented from the perspective of business, not personal feelings or emotions. Before the end of the meeting, offer to stay for a specified period of time that might be of help to the company in making the necessary transition. Should your employer request that you leave immediately, stay calm. Agree on a time that will allow you to take care of your personal needs, so that you can go gracefully. If you want a letter of recommendation, ask for it in this meeting. Your chances of securing a positive letter after you go are slim, as your boss will have moved on to other issues. You can follow up with his or her secretary in order to receive it. Before you leave your boss's office, stand up and warmly shake his or her hand. Smile, and say goodbye.
- **Inform your other superiors and your coworkers of your plans.** Since people will find out fast, especially if you work in a small company, let them know that you will be leaving—after you've spoken to the boss. Share only appropriate details with them about your reasons for leaving and your plans. Reinforce the positive with these people. You do not want to be a catalyst for a wave of bad morale there.
- **Follow up with a thank-you note for your experience at the company.** Again, no matter what your experience, chances are you are grateful for something that you learned at that job—even if it is how *not* to do something. A note to your boss and perhaps to the staff wishing them well and letting them know that you are well will spread good cheer. Your reputation is very important. The impression that you leave on people may last forever. Make it count.

On Getting Fired

One energetic employee at a law firm went to her boss to request a raise, only to be told to pack her bags. Apart from being shocked, she was quite taken aback by what she thought was a legitimate request based on her work performance. In her case, further investigation might have disclosed a legal issue that she could fight. For many people who get fired, there's little recourse available. How they respond to their firing, however, is completely in their control. What can you do if it happens to you?

- **Take a deep breath.** One sure way to maintain your physical composure is to monitor your breath. Hearing that your job has been terminated can be hard to swallow, even if you knew it was coming. Before responding, breathe deeply and find your center so that you can speak from that solid space.
- **Ask for an explanation.** You have the right to know the grounds for your firing and can request them in writing. If you consider the reasons unfounded, you can contest them, although doing so in that meeting may not be the most effective time.
- **Keep your cool.** Stay calm and focused throughout the meeting. You may have to use a mind strategy to do so, such as counting your in and out breaths or repeating a silent prayer—whatever will work for you. Do your best to walk with dignity through the meeting and out the door.
- **Find out your termination date.** If your boss says you can decide, set a date at that time. Otherwise, you will have yet another uncomfortable conversation left to endure. Should the date seem unreasonable given what you have to do before leaving, ask for an extension or assistance in packing your belongings.
- **Check your rights with human resources or the Department of Labor.** If you are still on probation, you have no recourse. If your employer didn't follow all of the steps in its codes, you may be able to contest the firing. Find out if you will be offered severance pay. You may be eligible for unemployment insurance, as allowed by law. Don't just walk away.
- **Leave gracefully.** Make the last impression that your coworkers have of you positive. Pack all of your belongings carefully, so that you don't have to come back. Say goodbye to key coworkers, including your boss, before you depart. As you leave your office, keep your head high. Know that you will be all right. As the wisdom goes, when one door closes another one opens. What's next for you will be great. You just need to believe it.

On Doing the Firing

The only thing worse than getting fired sometimes is doing the firing. For most managers, having to tell an employee that the relationship

African Americans and Entrepreneurship

A little-known fact is that since the very start of this country, Black folks have had their own businesses. Some had side enterprises while they were confined to plantation life. Others arrived on these shores as free people who built their dreams in the midst of hatred and few or no rights. Anthony Johnson of Jamestown, Virginia, is considered the first person of African descent to become an entrepreneur in America. He was a landowner. Jean Baptiste DuSable, a wholesaler and merchant who established the first settlement in Chicago in the early 1770s, is a well-known pre–Civil War Black entrepreneur. There is currently an eponymous museum in Chicago built in his honor. Following are some inspiring facts about other African-American entrepreneurial pursuits:

- In 1838, the *Register of Trades of Colored People* listed nearly 100 Black-owned businesses, ranging from bakers and blacksmiths to carpenters, wheelwrights and tailors. (These included businesses owned by Black women.)
- In 1891, Langston, Oklahoma, was formed as the first all-"Negro" town.
- In 1905, Black Wall Street was begun in Tulsa, Oklahoma; the thriving town of more than 600 businesses was destroyed in 1921 in a riot.
- In the early 1900s, catering started in Philadelphia as a viable business for Blacks and quickly spread across the country.
- In 1900 Booker T. Washington founded the National Negro Business League to help promote the development of Black enterprise.
- In the early 1900s, Madame C. J. Walker became the first Black female millionaire, having developed a hair care system.
- Durham, North Carolina, was known as "The Wall Street of Negro America" in the early 1900s. Among the more than 150 businesses that prospered there were traditional service providers, boarding houses, grocery stores, funeral parlors, movie theaters and larger companies such as Banker's Fire Insurance Company, the Mutual Building and Loan Association and North Carolina Mutual Life Insurance Company, to name a few. Some still exist today.
- When the Small Business Administration was formed in 1967, once again African Americans got a chance to develop businesses in broad scope, although major criticism exists surrounding the way that government contracts are allocated and how monies in general are divvied up.
- According to the 1977 Public Works Employment Act, all general contractors bidding for public works projects are required to allocate at least 10 percent of their contracts to "minority" subcontractors.
- A 1989 U.S. Supreme Court ruling in *City of Richmond v. Croson* dealt a huge blow to minority set-aside by not allowing a 30 percent set-aside contract to remain intact. Over the following years, set-asides in general have taken a beating, leaving budding African-American entrepreneurs largely without government support for their efforts.

didn't work out can be devastating. As a result, many managers avoid the inevitable, which prolongs the misery for everyone. Rather than falling into avoidance behavior, take action. There are lots of things you can do to end a relationship that has gone sour—with grace and dignity. Here are a few ideas:

- Find out your company's guidelines on firing. Ask your human resources department about any existing written instructions. Many businesses require that employees be given fair warning of poor job performance before they can be fired. This often starts with a three-month probationary period, a written notice of problem areas, a formal warning and a written strategy for ironing out issues. Only after these or similar steps are taken can an employee be fired in many large companies.
- Be clear but firm. If you are planning to fire someone, be sure to say so in the meeting. Have another manager present as a witness, if possible. Believe it or not, some managers call a meeting with the intention of firing an employee but never get to the point. After having investigated the legal ramifications of your decision, you must tell your employee that you are terminating his or her job—and why. Give a date by which the termination will be effective, along with terms for the duration of his or her time at the office.
- Don't wait too long. I have seen people sit in jobs for years after they and their supervisors knew it was time to go. What happened was ugly. In one instance, the supervisor was too cowardly to ask the person to leave. Instead, she talked about the person behind her back for several years and spoke to the employee with hostility and contempt. The employee's sense of self-worth diminished with each passing month. By the time of the firing, both parties were devastated. It took the employee several years of therapy to grow out of her negative self-image too. It's not worth it to wait. In fact, it's irresponsible.
- Do right by yourself and your business. The rest will follow. If you don't take care of your own needs, which include relieving a staff member of his or her duties, everyone will suffer. It's just like the warning on the airplane. The parent has to take the oxygen first in order to be able to provide for the child. Having the right staff makes all the difference in your productivity and mental well-being.
- Be kind. No matter what the circumstances, you can let a person know that the job is over without attack. Consider in advance what the person's strengths are, and state them in your meeting. Let the employee know that by leaving this job, his or her opportunity for finding the right work fit can happen.

1. I have braids and am worried that I will not be considered for a job because of them. What should I do?

Ask yourself what is more important: your hairstyle or the position for which you are applying. Also evaluate your hairstyle. Many times the style in which you wear braids is the real determining factor in a job situation. Many popular styles are perfectly appropriate for business settings. Keep your braids impeccably clean and oiled. And do them over as soon as they start to get "fuzzy." You always want to look your best—for you! Small braids are a great option, because they can be worn neatly in a bun. In the end, you have to feel comfortable and confident with your appearance in order to win over the job interviewer.

2. I work as an assistant to a powerful man. Sometimes I feel like I don't know anything. How can I develop a good rapport with him?

Remind yourself of your abilities, and make yourself indispensable. Maxine Dally, right arm to Kenneth I. Chenault, president and chief operating officer of American Express, says you should treat your boss like a mentor. Owe him your utmost respect and attention. By putting his needs first you will reap tremendous rewards.

3. My boss gave me a gift that really makes me feel uncomfortable. What should I do?

Weigh your options. How much did it cost? If the gift is too personal, you may feel it is important to give it back with an explanation of why you cannot accept it. Use humor in the exchange. You may say, "Mr. Reynolds, I really appreciate your thinking of me, but my boyfriend would not understand if I brought this home." Even if you are offended by the gift, it's better to avoid confrontation, which usually leads to friction and future conflict. Unless you are prepared to leave your job, a light approach is the best way to go.

4. My Black friends at work have accused me of alienating them, because I have become friendly with a white coworker. How can I handle this?

Check yourself to assess your motives. Are you alienating your Black friends and, in turn, yourself? We always have to educate each other, and that includes folks in the community. Sticking together does not mean that you have to stay away from others. By all means, build your relationships at work with as many coworkers as you can. At the same time, talk to your Black friends about the relationships that you are building, and keep them in your life too. If you think that your Black and white friends will hit it off, plan a lunch date when you can all get together. If not, be kind to everyone, and keep your goals in mind.

Above all, don't use anyone. Generally, be careful about who becomes your friend at work.

5. I overheard someone saying awful things about a friend of mine at work. Should I tell him?

It depends. Assess whether the information being shared is truly hurtful to your friend. Also, consider whether telling him will help him to cope any better in the situation. Put yourself in his position and think about what you would appreciate. If the topic is your friend's personal hygiene or behavior, you may want to make a general statement that indicates that others are aware of his problems, so it's a good time to straighten up. If the information could potentially affect the relationship that your friend has with a manager, by all means let him know so that he can decide how to respond. Be clear, too, that it's best to mind your own business. Don't go off and share what you heard with anyone else. It's easy to start a rumor mill that will only get out of hand.

6. How can I defend myself if I am living in the heat of a rumor?

Stand tall and strong, and be the best person that you can be. It is impossible to disprove a rumor. Once people start to believe something about you, the only way that you can hope to change their opinion is through your behavior. Let your words and actions speak for themselves. Be an example of honesty and integrity. If the rumor is true, you needn't admit anything. Work instead to improve your life and be a strong power of example for others. But don't lie. If the rumor is false and is negatively affecting your ability to earn a living or damaging your family, seek legal action. Be aware, though, that the truth can be hard to prove.

7. I am planning to move to another city and must give notice on my job. What is the appropriate amount of time to give?

Your level of seniority at your job as well as your overall function within the company figure into appropriate notice. Although there are guidelines you can follow, I recommend that you follow your gut instinct the most. For example, you may be a secretary in a small office. Although your position is entry level, the company may have serious difficulty without your presence. In this case, the most thoughtful approach would be to meet with your supervisor at least one month in advance, preferably two, to discuss your intentions. Offer to create a strategy together that will allow you to help identify and train your replacement. For any senior-level employee, a minimum of four weeks is considered acceptable. Check the employee handbook. If you are on uneasy terms with your employer and fear that you will be immediately asked to leave, get all of your work in order before you have your meeting (something that you should do anyway), and still offer to help out in whatever way you can. Be prepared to walk, though.

8. My girlfriend just had a baby. How can I organize for paternity leave at my office?

The law says that you are allowed up to six weeks off from your job when you have a baby—men too. That you aren't married should not figure into your ability to take off. Go to your boss or human resources director early on to announce that you and your partner will be having a child in the coming months. Be proactive and find out what benefits you are offered through your company that will support your family. In most instances, even at small companies, your employer will attempt to help you to take care of your newborn and keep your job.

9. I have worked on my job for three years without a raise. I really believe that I deserve one. Is there a proper way to request a raise?

Check your employee manual to see what the guidelines are for salary increases. If you have friends at work, get a sense of whether others have received raises recently. Next, outline the qualities and skills that you have that make you deserving of a raise. Write these points down, including examples of any projects that you may have helped to succeed. Then call a meeting with your manager. In the meeting, be upbeat and calm. Let your manager know that you believe that you deserve a raise. List the work-related reasons for your request. Stay clear of personal issues that may point to your need for more money. In a professional environment, let the work, not your personal needs, speak for you.

10. I serve as a mentor for a troubled and intelligent young woman. I believe that our relationship is helping both of us to become better people, but I worry that she is becoming too attached to me. How can I establish proper boundaries?

Part of the reason she is getting better may be that she is feeling loved for the first time in her life. Positive reinforcement and a good role model—what could be better than that? Consider your role as a mentor as welcoming another child to the village. You can introduce your mentee to other colleagues, responsible young people who might be good companions and family members. Do you have younger siblings, nieces and nephews, cousins or godchildren who are involved in youth activities or other pursuits appropriate for this person's age? Exposing your mentee to a variety of situations and interesting, supportive people will create a context for the person's self-sufficiency and allow for less pressure for your relationship to be "everything" to her. Conduct your meetings in neutral environments, especially in the beginning of your relationship, so that you can demonstrate how people interact in business settings. Let your mentee know what is expected when the environment changes, such as if you go on a picnic or cultural outing.

Don't be afraid to show warmth. Just keep it simple and familial. Remember, *it takes a whole village to raise a child.*

11. I see my former boss on occasion, but I really don't like or respect him now. How should I behave when I see him?

You need to weigh your options. What will you get out of being nasty? Instead of holding a grudge, forgive him and greet him professionally. As my Mama used to say, "Chances go round." We all must pay for our misdeeds. Don't add to your own. Kindness always pays off.

12. My boss referred to me as "boy" one day. How do I respond to that without getting fired?

Remain calm and clear. If you want to keep your job, you must find a way to set your boss straight without attacking him. Try humor. "Come on, Mr. Charlie," you might jest, "we got off the plantation years ago. Didn't anybody tell you?" (Okay, so this may be a little strong, but the point is to find a lighthearted retort to illustrate your discomfort.) Unless your boss is really dense, he will see how bad his words sounded. You may want to follow up with human resources to file a complaint just in case it happens again.

13. I've been told that men are supposed to walk to the outside of women. Does this hold true in a business setting?

I admit to being an old-school girl here. I do think it is kind and gentlemanly for a man to walk closest to the street when he is walking with a woman, no matter what the setting. Traditionally, men took this position to protect women from traffic and any other potential danger. Obviously, women can fend for themselves. But I happen to appreciate a bit of gentlemanly attention. Of course, if a man doesn't take on this role in a work environment, a woman should not be offended. In your personal life, though, you can feel free to tell your date if you prefer this position.

14. Is it proper for a man to stand up when a woman enters the room?

Again, this is traditional etiquette. In a business setting, it is appropriate for both men and women to stand when someone enters a room. It would be rude to shake hands with someone when you are seated and the other is standing. Meet face-to-face, and offer a warm greeting.

The Almighty Dollar

A people must trust, be dependable, have respect for each other if they are to develop a viable economic system. When they have those kinds of relationships they have a social system, and they can build, and they grow economically.

AMOS WILSON

EVERYBODY seems to want it, but nobody really wants to talk about it. Money. Capital. Or as the hip-hop generation calls it, the Benjamins or Papers. Be it in dollar bills, coins or gold bullion, money is the driving force of the modern concept of economy. It seems to be what separates the haves from the have-nots. In truth, money is not the sole source of power, but it does play a huge part in determining one's ability to flourish in society.

For 400 years, our ancestors here had little or no access to capital. Instead, they themselves were traded as a form of currency. Perhaps that explains why sometimes when we get our hands on it, we do sometimes go "mad," as George Washington Carver put it back in 1931, spending it as if there isn't going to be a tomorrow. One successful businessman, Joshua Greene, CEO of the Maxima Corporation, summed up our situation today by saying, "Black people have lost something from our culture that we used to understand. Our forefathers may have walked miles to make a dollar, but they saved half of it, so that the generation succeeding them would do better than they did." What has happened? The Black middle class has grown to a level never before achieved. We boast a population with more homeowners, car owners, entrepreneurs, corporate executives and millionaires than ever before in our history. Yet if you listen to the reports from our own (Black) media, you will see that our $400 billion or so of wealth isn't doing us enough good. For starters, we don't really know how to hold on to our money. Other communities recycle their dollars, while the "joke" is that Black folks don't even make it past midnight before we've given our hard-earned dollars over to somebody else. There can be no such thing as cooperative economics, the Kwanzaa principle of *ujaama,* if we don't reassess how we acquire, save and spend our hard-earned dollars.

Learning how to honor and respect money should be considered seriously. A unanimous chorus proclaims that Black folks work hard to make it. It's true that we sometimes save it. Even more real is that we spend it. African Americans are among the most active consumers in this country, regardless of the amount of money in our wallets! The bottom line is that there is a tremendous amount of wealth within the Black community, but it is not always put to the best use. Battles over money have broken up many a family—not just husbands and wives, either. Folks who've got a little more than others have, on occasion, taken a high-and-mighty posture when in the company of those without deep pockets.

On the flip side, countless sisters and brothers have donated all of their resources and time to helping others who have less. Finding a balance and establishing a direction are imperatives for our people if we are to make a significant difference in our own lives and of future generations. As the infamous Reverend Ike put it, "The best thing you can do for poor people is never to become one of them." The Reverend's message holds tremendous value. By cultivating wealth (financial and spiritual), we can help each other. By succumbing to poverty, we contribute to greater suffering for all. Being mindful of our postenslavement past and the labor that it took for any of us to reach above poverty status must stay in our awareness, not as a signpost of fear but as a reminder that we must always strive to do better. Controlling our own capital has to stay at the top of the list of ways that we can. It's also important to understand that the history of African people—that includes us—did not start with the slave trade.

We are currently wading through the depths of a 500-year low point along the African cultural continuum. But all you have to do is look a little further back and know that the people of Africa were leaders in every way for more than 100,000 years, nobility, in fact—and that includes the economic arena.

So what does any of this have to do with "etiquette"? Think about it. If you don't have your stuff together regarding your resources, chances are you can't focus clearly on the other aspects of daily living that can lead you to your goals. Discovering *how to be* with money (how to save it, make it, make the most of it and avoid spending it as a way of compensating for inadequacies or filling up character holes with consumer items) is a basic survival skill. We all need to learn *how to be* on a budget. We can even learn *how to be* without money, as many of our families have existed in the past—"poor" but with dignity and with a plan that will ensure that we can move out of poverty into a healthy and sound place. In this chapter, we will take a clear look at how you can assume a responsible relationship with your resources. Only from the perspective of claiming responsibility can we live a conscious life. And the reality is that before you can take care of family, community, elders or anybody else, you have to be able to take care of yourself. On the most basic level, that includes knowing how to manage your money.

Teach Your Children

Learning to manage money can start from as early as when a child is learning how to count. Shortly after a child can count to ten, after all, he or she is on to pennies, nickels, dimes, quarters and dollar bills. It really doesn't take long at all to see that the big numbers are more desirable, and that having the larger bills means that you have power. The savvy four year old who sees this truth may be off to a great start if he or she receives consistent guidance from here on. Yes, this society does say that money is power. And although we can argue back and forth forever about the nature of true power and its relationship to money, the bottom line is that if you learn to respect money, you will have a much greater chance of enjoying financial independence. As far as our children are concerned, we must teach them a tenet of African thought: that balanced interdependence on all levels is the ultimate goal, which means that respect for all of our resources, including each other, must be an essential part of the mix.

The way that most parents teach their children about money is through an allowance. The drill is: *If you do chore x, you will get $x.* Normally, the amount of money that the child receives for the chore is far smaller than any real wage, including minimum wage. And that is as it should be. The understanding of household chores needs to be cultivated as a responsibility of every member of the home, not as work that anyone could be hired to fulfill. At the same time, your child's receiving a reward for a job well done is sure incentive to encourage dedicated effort. So in your child's formative years, he or she can learn to place value on doing work in exchange for cash. Another lesson children should learn is that it takes a lot longer to earn a dollar than it does to spend one. This unsettling fact was true even when my Daddy was doing his home chores back in the 1930s when everything cost a whole lot less, and it's clearly true today. If you can work with your children to teach them how much effort must be expended in order to earn even a single dollar, you will be doing your entire family a great service. It is essential that the Black community learn how to manage its resources more efficiently. This begins at home.

How do you determine a fair allowance? Make a budget for your child, just as you should be doing for yourself. Include in that budget all of the expenses that the child must handle himself or herself: lunch money, snacks, miscellaneous school supplies—whatever you decide on. Arrive at a total of budgetary needs for a week. That amount plus a slight increase to allow for personal items, such as healthy snacks, should be your child's allowance, with an additional 10 percent tagged on for savings. Write the budget down, even for small children. Then review with your child how the money should be allocated each week. Make the establishment of savings a first order of business, followed by tithing or otherwise giving 10 percent to your house of worship as an important spiritual practice. Whether the money first goes into a piggy bank or directly into a commercial bank, it should be put in a safe place that your child knows is his or her nest egg. Any extras that you may add at certain holidays or when your child has done an extra-good job at a particular task should be acknowledged as a bonus with an explanation. This is another opportunity to save 10 percent. You can show your child how saving money does not mean that the child will be deprived of any needs or pleasures. So, when a $10 bonus comes for a specific task accomplished, you can show your child that $1 will be put away for savings, another $1 can be offered to church, and the rest can be used for a special treat for the child. Surely $8 will either be enough for something of value or a substantial addition to current savings.

In order to instill responsibility in your child at an early age, you too must be responsible. This means that you should pay allowances at the same time every week, thereby creating an environment of discipline, order, consistency and trust. Broken promises and deprivation result in distrust, panic and sneaky behavior. You too must save money out of each paycheck and show your child by your own example that by respecting money, one can always have it. A key point here is that this is *not* an African way of viewing or handling resources. Money does not take on as much power as working with others to achieve mutually agreed-on goals. Teaching a child the value of chores would not be attached to money, although small gifts are given to African children for work completed. Instead, it would be shown that the child's effort or lack thereof would directly affect the rest of the family. (For example, if a child has to make sure that millet gets from its storage place to where the women have to pound it, that irresponsibility would show up as a gaping hole in the evening meal—not as an inability for the child to buy a pair of sneakers.) But this is the way that we need to view and handle money in Western situations. Remember that children are learning. Be patient when they don't remember something or fail to complete a task.

Commercial Money Matters

When you think about money today, the image of a bank should come to mind right away. It's where many of our dollars are held. That doesn't mean that everybody knows how to maximize the relationship possibilities with a bank of choice. Actually, many people are not sure of what they can expect of a bank or what a bank expects of them. It is important to know how to interact with a bank in order to set your finances in order without feeling intimidated. Foremost in your communication should be what your goals are, along with questions about how you can reach your goals with the bank's help. When the butterflies come, whether you are opening a new account or trying to secure a mortgage, remember that your money is just as green as anybody else's. Teri Williams, senior vice president of the Black-owned Boston Bank of Commerce, offers these ten tips on how you can move beyond any feelings of intimidation and make your bank work for you:

1. Open a bank account. This sounds very basic, but one-third of African Americans do not have accounts. Check which banks allow minimum deposits.
2. Open your first bank account with a community or Black-owned bank. These banks are more personal, and decisions are made on a branch level. In national banks, decision making is centralized—made at corporate offices, often far away.
3. Introduce yourself to the branch manager and communicate your financial goals. These goals can be as simple as, "I want to learn how to keep a balanced checkbook," to something such as, "I want to purchase real estate." This interaction is important so the manager can get to know you and plan how to make the bank work for your goals and needs.
4. Learn how to balance a checkbook and DO NOT bounce checks. Banks consider bouncing checks a clear sign of financial irresponsibility.
5. After a year of having an account, request a small line of credit for the purpose of establishing credit.
6. Pay all of your bills on time. It is more important to pay the minimum amount on time than to pay a larger amount at a later date. In this way, you establish a relationship of trust with your creditors, showing them that you will honor the agreement that you have made with them consistently. Later,

this consistency may afford you the opportunity to leverage your good credit into a mortgage or other large purchase.

7. Save money—as small as $10 or $15—from each paycheck into a savings account or retirement plan. It is easier to make a small deposit than to come up with a huge amount of cash at one time.

8. As soon as you are financially able, buy a home. The financial and tax benefits of purchasing a home are greater in appreciated value than the stock market. Shop around for a mortgage; many banks offer great plans for first-time home owners.

9. Once your savings account reaches $1,000, ask your bank about mutual funds, an individual retirement account or certificates of deposit. Transfer some or all of your money to one of these accounts. A bank representative can explain these accounts to you and answer any questions that you may have.

10. Maintain a relationship with your community bank as you also open an account with a national bank once you have established financial stability. It is ideal to have two banking relationships concurrently—one with a smaller, personalized bank and another with a national bank at which you can enjoy a host of conveniences, such as nationwide ATM machines.

Credit and You

With as much wealth as the United States seemingly has, it's astounding just how deeply in debt this country is. No wonder most of the country's citizens live their lives as an extension of available credit. We all learn by example. Most often the picture that's painted is, "Charge it today. Pay for it tomorrow—or sometime down the line." This is the nature of the Western worldview: that objects are valued over relationships. Possessing things and resources is of primary importance.

It's rare to hear of people spending their money differently. For many Americans, reckless spending habits start in college. Many students have barely set foot on campus as freshmen when the creditors start knocking at their dorm-room doors, promising them access to the world of consumer products and services—for a mere 19 percent interest. Rather than having any red flags go up, students are generally thrilled by the prospects of being able to live it up a little. Many of them have jobs, after all. Why not enjoy a little "deserved" relief? And so the story begins. By the end of college or at least by the first couple of years out of school, thousands of young people already have a bad credit rating because their eyes were too big for their wallets. The great stuff may have filled up their apartments, fueled fabulous world trips or ended up hanging off their shoulders and hips, but the bills piled up rather than being paid off or down at the end of each month. Those who get a student loan and do what many people don't—that is, pay the loan off on time—automatically get put on another credit card solicitor's list. And so the cycle goes.

What does this mean in the big picture? Depending on how bad your credit profile becomes, you can end up being suspended from having any credit privileges for as long as seven years. A startling statistic says that only 30 percent of the American population is fully eligible for credit, and that the other 70 percent has probably experienced at least one serious blemish on their credit report. No matter what your current financial profile, it's not too late to become financially smart. Being a responsible, conscious adult requires that you get a handle on your money. When it comes to credit, you need to think less, not more. Living below or within your means is vital to building your future; you may need to lower your standard of living, cut your credit cards or otherwise give yourself a reality check, so that you can create a balanced and comfortable life that will last.

Making Good on a Loan

Even the best money managers find times when they could use extra money. Finding an institution or a person to give you money can be challenging. Your credit history will tell a lending institution whether you are a good or a bad risk. Your reputation among family and friends will tell them whether they can trust you with their capital. This is why your word is so important. Doing what you say is essential.

Sharon Johnson of Houston, Texas, says that when she was growing up, she always "borrowed" money from her family but never had the intention of paying it back. They were family, after all. During her high school and college years, she accumulated family debt of thousands of dollars without considering it at all—until it was brought to her attention. Sharon's father approached her about a few specific loans that he had made to her, instances when she had "promised" to pay him back. At first Sharon became defensive and hostile, "Why should I have to pay you back?" she asked her father. "You don't even need the money." What her Dad explained was that the principle of the matter was the issue. If you say you're going to repay a loan, then do so. Otherwise you can't ever come back for more. For Sharon and her father, the issue was resolved when they made a payment schedule that Sharon honored each month until her debt was paid. For other people, a standoff is more likely, because pride gets in the way of talking about the issue at hand. Sharon's way of thinking, by the way, was off the mark primarily because she and her family did not share the same values.

In the African worldview, those who *have* share with those who *need*. Paying somebody back is not of primary concern. Giving when you can is. Sharon's behavior could be considered as African retention (something in her psyche told her that it was okay to take money from her family, no strings attached). Because we have both paradigms to consider—the Western and African worldviews—it's not that simple. Sharon's father and family clearly let her know that she was "borrowing" the money. As you cultivate aspects of African worldview in your life, it is vital to be clear about what you mean by your words and actions. Otherwise, you will run into lots of difficulties. And, for the record, don't try to "get over" or con anybody using the African philosophy, either. It won't work.

Working within the community—which starts with family—to become economically stable and strong is the way that many ethnic groups in this country have grown and prospered. We must learn to respect each other and the value of our contributions. In some instances, the only way that you can possibly move to the next level in your personal or work life is to rely on the help of loved ones. That help won't be available if you don't prove to those you're approaching that your actions are as good as your words. Don't take anyone for granted. You wouldn't want to be treated that way, would you? Another point: If you default on a family or bank loan, own up to your error. Pretending that your failure to pay didn't happen will not make the debt go away. Instead, it will only dig you deeper into a broke, lonely hole. Go forth with confidence and apologize to your creditor. Explain your situation, and pledge to resolve the situation by a specific date.

If you are planning to secure a loan or offer a loan to someone, no matter how close you are, put the agreement in writing. A signed document that sets forth the terms of your agreement will turn what may seem like a personal matter into a business negotiation. In case of default, it becomes a legal document that can be upheld in a court of law.

Cleaning Up Your Credit Report

If you find yourself in the bowels of bad credit, you can't afford to sit there and feel helpless. Even if you have neglected your debts in the past, you can take hold of the reins right now and clean up your record. According to a brother whom many know as the Credit Doctor, Luther Gatling, president of Budget and Credit Counseling Services in New York City, what you need to do is start by taking a good, hard look at your life. He says, "A budget is nothing more than your lifestyle on a piece of paper." When you think of it that way, it makes perfect sense that in order to get your credit in order, you have to start by closely examining how you live. Rest assured, this doesn't mean that you need to feel embarrassed, frustrated or ashamed of your past actions. Instead, you can look at this moment as an opportunity to grow and improve. What can you do?

- Get a copy of your credit report every year. Contact the major credit reporting organizations—Equifax (800-685-1111), Trans Union (718-459-8176) and Experian or TRW (800-682-7654; P. O. Box 2350 Chatsworth, CA 91313-2350)—to determine your status. Listed on your personal credit report will be an itemization of your creditors and your payment status. Late payments, indications of any liens, bankruptcies or other financial difficulties will also be recorded. Be sure to examine your credit reports carefully, as uncomfortable as it may seem, so that you can check to see if all of the information reported is accurate. You can get a copy free within thirty days of being denied credit by any organization.
- Have any incorrect information removed. It may take some effort on your part to correct any mistakes, but be vigilant. You will need to write to the reporting agencies about the item(s) in question, including any substantiating information that supports your request for its removal. Follow up until you are satisfied.
- Don't trust the seven-year statute of limitations. Resolved credit trouble theoretically is removed from your credit report after seven years. Nevertheless, creditors can legally reapply that same information to your report two additional times, thereby giving you credit hell for as long as twenty-one years. That goes for a reported error as well. Paying attention is your only recourse.
- Don't apply for new credit until your report has been cleaned up. Many people discover that they have credit troubles when they apply for a loan or a new credit card. The only problem is that when you apply and are rejected, your declined application goes on your report for two years. Take care of your business first. Then think hard before adding to your debt.
- Get help. Don't be ashamed that you need support. Across the country, agencies such as Budget and Credit Counseling Services exist to help you establish a repayment schedule with your creditors. Counselors will help you learn how to plan a realistic budget for yourself and your family, as they also assist you in finding a way to a more stable financial condition. Help yourself by coming to a credit counseling meeting prepared. Bring all of your current bills, banking

Twenty Steps to Good Credit

1. Pay your bills on time.
2. Limit the amount of bills that you share with others.
3. Resist the temptation to collect credit cards. Keep only what you can afford to manage. Cut up the rest.
4. Live within or below your means. Basically, don't spend as much as *or* more than you make per month.
5. As the old folks say, *Don't rob from Peter to pay Paul.* In other words, don't use resources allocated for one bill to pay another. Don't use credit cards to pay bills, and don't borrow money to pay other debts. It *will* catch up with you.
6. Open your mail. An unopened bill is still a bill, and it will not go away until you handle it.
7. Pay at least the monthly minimum on your credit cards. Know that staying at the minimum payment is not enough to get out of debt, though. You will only be paying the high interest due.
8. Balance your checkbook every month—or more often as needed.
9. Don't carry all of your credit cards with you.
10. Create a realistic budget, and stick to it.
11. Avoid defaulting on loans.
12. Do your taxes on time, even if you can't afford to pay what you owe. It's the law, and many people have been prosecuted who ignore it. Just so you know, prosecution can mean sitting behind bars.
13. Communicate with your creditors. If you know that you will be late paying a bill, let them know in advance, and provide a date by which you will make your payment
14. Return your creditors' calls. Be friendly, courteous and honest. Even when they are nasty and harassing, you *still* should keep your cool. Remember that they are calling you because you have not honored your commitments.
15. If you are taking a vacation, particularly a long trip, be sure to make arrangements to pay your bills during your absence.
16. Review your credit report carefully. Don't hesitate to make every effort to correct any mistakes that may appear on it.
17. Assess your priorities. Shelter, food and clothing (only the essentials!) should come before entertainment, travel and other luxuries. (Remember the image of the brother with the fancy Cadillac back in the seventies who lived in his car because he couldn't afford his rent? No disrespect, but does that brother look like your man today, living at home with his Mama, paying her not one dollar of rent and driving around in a Lexus?)
18. Don't let holiday overspending ruin your life. The spirit of the holidays speaks to giving from your heart, not your wallet.
19. Review your bills and your bank statements each month. Errors do occur. It's better for you to put forth a little effort than to trust them.
20. Seek financial counseling when you first think that you are in trouble. There's no shame in getting help. What's bad is sitting in your mess and doing nothing about it.

and tax records and any other financial information about you. Usually these agencies will manage the payment of your bills for a fee.

- Change your thinking.   The only way that you will be able to maintain good credit once you have cleaned it up is to reassess your values. It really is not intelligent, conscious action to spend all of your resources on things. People these days often use objects and external experiences to fill a spiritual void that plagues them. I've heard it said, "I got mad at my man, so I went shopping." Is that an effective way of dealing with a personal problem? Of course not. What it is is a way of ensuring that you will go deeper into debt. Shore up your spiritual Self. If you make this a priority, you will find that the rest of your life will come into balance.

Black Financial Institutions

One way to secure your financial future and that of your community is to grow your money in a Black financial institution. Following is a partial listing of credible institutions around the country with which you can do business.

Boston Bank of Commerce
133 Federal Street
Boston, MA 02110
(617) 457–4400

Broadway Federal Savings & Loan
4429 South Broadway
Los Angeles, CA 90037
(213) 232–4271

Carver Federal Savings Bank
121 West 125th Street
New York, NY 10027
(212) 876–4747

Citizens Trust Bank
75 Piedmont Avenue
Atlanta, GA 30303
(404) 221–0601

Citizens Federal Savings Bank
300 North 18th Street
Birmingham, AL 35203
(205) 328–2041

City National Bank of New Jersey
900 Broad Street
Newark, NJ 07102
(201) 624–0869

Consolidated Bank and Trust Co.
P.O. Box 26834
Richmond, VA 23261
(804) 771–5200

The Douglass Bank
1314 North 5th Street
Kansas City, KS 66101
(713) 321–7200

Dryades Savings Bank, FSB
231 Carmelita Street, Suite 200
New Orleans, LA 70130
(504) 598–7200

Family Savings Bank, FSB
3683 Crenshaw Boulevard
Los Angeles, CA 90016
(213) 245–3381

First Independence National Bank of
    Detroit
44 Michigan Avenue
Detroit, MI 48226
(213) 256–8200

First Texas Bank
P.O. Box 649
Georgetown, TX 78627
(512) 863–2994

First Tuskegee Bank
301 North Elm Street
Tuskegee, AL 36088
(334) 727–2560

Founders National Bank of Los
    Angeles
3910 West Martin Luther King Jr.,
    Boulevard
Los Angeles, CA 90008
(213) 290–4848

Harbor Bank of Maryland
25 West Fayette Street
Baltimore, MD 21201
(410) 528–1800

Illinois Service Federal Savings and
    Loan Association
4619 South Dr. Martin Luther King
    Drive
Chicago, IL 60653
(312) 624–2000

Independence Bank of Chicago
7936 South Cottage Grove Avenue
Chicago, IL 60619
(312) 722–9456

Independence Federal Savings Bank
1229 Connecticut Avenue, NW
Washington, DC 20036
(202) 628–5500

Industrial Bank of Washington
1317 F Street, NW
Washington, DC 20004
(202) 722–2060

Liberty Bank and Trust Company
3801 Canal Street
New Orleans, LA 60119
(504) 286–8817

Mechanics and Farmers Bank
116 West Parrish Street
Durham, NC 27702
(919) 683–1521

Seaway National Bank of Chicago
643 East 87th Street
Chicago, IL 60619
(312) 487–4800

South Shore Bank
4698 South Drexel Boulevard
Chicago, IL 60653
(312) 451–5900

Tri-State Bank of Memphis
180 South Main Street
Memphis, TN 33103
(901) 525–0384

United Bank of Philadelphia
714 Market Street
Philadelphia, PA 19106
(215) 829–2265

Money and Family

To start, I want to say that I really wish we could readopt the ways of our ancestors here. Although African people didn't live idyllic lives before global enslavement and colonization, they surely seemed to have a better sense of how to get along with each other and how to treat themselves and their families with more respect than folks do today. Points of conflict sparked more often with regard to how people were behaving toward each other than for how much money they were contributing to the pot. Because their philosophical way of looking at the world was completely different from a Western approach, they didn't have the same kinds of problems. In the simplest of terms, their way was to identify how people could support and honor each other such that the individual *and* the community as a whole would benefit. Here in the West, it's all about survival of the fittest. Whoever has the most marbles at the end of the game wins. No wonder we're in such a state about money.

We started off with our hands tied (actually shackled), unable to access any true resources—neither those we valued nor those that the enslaver revered. Over the years, Black people as a whole have been denied access to many of the avenues that allow for "winning" in America. Any number of problems have ensued as a result. Even as more opportunities have become available, the playing field is far from level.

All of the stress inherent in dealing with these issues affects everyone in the community, most prominently the family. What can we do?

Since the rules that we must currently follow about *how to be* as it relates to resources are Western (this is, after all, the economy in which we live), it is important to understand how best to negotiate them to our advantage. Otherwise we end up fighting with our loved ones over something beyond their control. Ask any psychologist, and you will hear that financial issues are at the top of the list of family difficulties, whether the conflict lies between parents and children, adults and in-laws or couples. The biggest issues arise between couples, though. Remember, we live in a capitalistic society that requires that you have money in order to make your way. So when somebody comes up short or otherwise doesn't pull his or her own weight in the financial arena, tensions flare. There is no fail-safe way to eliminate the possibility of financial difficulty. Life happens, and even those who are the best planners can run into a dollar drain. It's how you handle what comes before you that can make the difference between your familial relationship(s) strengthening or dissolving.

- Be honest about your financial condition. You may have to do some homework in order to fulfill this basic task. Assess your financial picture: debt, income, savings and so on. Write everything down. The first step toward a healthy approach to your finances is owning up to their actual state for yourself—independent of anyone else. Although you may not need to reveal all of the details to your children, your spouse deserves to know, and the sooner the better.
- When you see trouble coming, say something. Believing that you have to handle your problems by yourself or, worse, stuff them in a corner because they are too painful to examine will only lead to further misery. A minister once told me that if you can't discuss your financial problems with your spouse, you probably shouldn't be married to that person. Enrolling your spouse in supporting you through the hard times is smart family business. Two heads are better than one, right? Even more, open communication with your spouse and your accountant or money manager should help you to get to the bottom of your difficulty while being supported along the way. Failing to talk about your situation does not mean that your spouse won't notice that something is wrong. Instead, it can cause stresses between the two of you that can lead to the demise of your marriage. The issue here is *not* money, but trust—specifically trust in the ability of the relationship to handle issues outside of romance.
- Accept responsibility for your financial condition. Living consciously requires that you get your finances in order. For some people, bal-

ancing a checkbook is a no-brainer; for others, it's like tackling calculus. Wherever you find yourself, know that you can get organized and clear about your finances, regardless of their condition now. You may need to readdress issues from your childhood about money management or reevaluate the view to which you subscribe regarding men's and women's roles surrounding money. Whatever it takes to become healthy, do the work.

- Don't hide behind being a woman. In traditional African societies, the women's role in the family was just as important as the men's. When it came to financial resources, women in communities that had a market economy, for example, ran the fruit/vegetable/meat/fish stand and handled all of the financial transactions. Men were responsible for hunting, fishing and otherwise gathering the food that the women would sell. The point is that sisters were in charge of the dollars! So what has happened? Even now, in many African-American families women are in the forefront as far as taking care of the finances. For the increasing numbers of African-American women who are staying home to rear their children and manage the household, this doesn't mean you can be unaware of the family finances or how to manage them. Everyone in a household should be able to contribute to the good of the whole. In today's society, not knowing how to deal with your family's resources can be downright dangerous. Too many marriages break up today. Too many inequitable arrangements exist where the homemaker gets the short end of the stick. Ultimately, to live in peace you have to be able to fend for yourself even as you trust your loved ones. As my mother used to say to us girls, "Get an education, so that you will be able to support yourself."

- Make a family budget. Work together with your spouse—and your children when they are old enough to understand—to develop a workable budget that allows for savings, household expenses and investments. Come to an agreement about whether your lifestyle will let you live within the budget you have created, and then check in with each other regularly to ensure that you are following your own guidelines. If you have children, discuss aspects of that budget with them so that they can learn the value and meaning of how resources are used.

Living Together

Managing your money all by your lonesome can be a huge challenge. Doing it with a spouse doesn't guarantee an easy road. Nor does it get any simpler when you are managing a household and dual-income dollars with a live-in partner. Those members of the old school in your family and community have consistently warned against live-in arrangements for many reasons, not the least of which is how you will manage your money. Now, you may not think in old-school fashion, but it is wise to be responsible about your money nonetheless. That means not playing dumb, coy or supertrusting. After all, many studies point to financial issues as being a major trigger for relationship woes. And if you don't have a legal document—a marriage license—to secure your interests, you had better be extra wise about how you handle your affairs. Remember that if you live together and are unmarried, and your name is not on the lease or deed, you have no rights to the property where you live if the two of you break up. And if your partner dies, you do not automatically inherit his or her belongings, including items that you may have purchased together but on his credit card, for example. Instead, those items go to the next of kin or other individuals who are named in the will.

Morality aside, it is clear that you should have a plan when you decide to live with someone. This actually is true whether the person is a romantic partner or just a roommate. Being crystal clear about your plans and intentions from the start will make your living together far easier down the road. Keep these three pointers in mind *before* you move in:

- Write it down. Make a written cohabitation agreement that outlines exactly how you intend to divide all of the household expenses, including rent or mortgage, utilities and other living expenses. Include a clause about how you would settle your finances should you separate and who gets what in the event of untimely death. Know that relatives can be very messy when it comes to things that seem trivial in the light of the situation. Imagine how much more vicious the fight over a dish will be if they resent you and never approved of the relationship. It may seem hard to slow down in the midst of your dreamy-eyed move to secure a few details. Trust those who have come before you: you owe it to yourself to do so. (You'll be glad you did if, God forbid, the dream ends and you wake up to a situation where Prince Charming is really a frog with bad manners!) And be sure to identify how the household duties will be shared, particularly if one partner will be more immediately responsible for such duties in exchange for the financial security provided by the other party.
- Keep your accounts to yourself. Even people who marry are often slow to put their names on shared checking accounts or other financial instruments. For sure, if you are unmarried, financial experts

warn against pooling your resources. Why? Putting your name on a charge card, car or home purchase means that you are fully liable for the entire balance regardless of who created the debt. Further, you can't file your taxes together as an unmarried couple, so you create additional complexity for filing your taxes at the end of the year. At the same time, if you want to buy real estate, the reality may be that you cannot make the purchase without the financial support (and risk) of your partner. If you find yourself in this situation, work with a lawyer to draw up an agreement (much like a prenuptial) that outlines both of your responsibilities. Then get that document notarized and keep it in a safe place.

- **Make a will.** No matter what your age, you should make a will once you begin to live on your own, away from your parents. Accepting full responsibility for yourself includes making a will that will continue to manage your life's assets upon your death. When you are cohabiting, this is a must. Across the country—except in some instances in California—your assets do not go to your live-in partner after your death.

Child Support

When two people come together to make a family, the finances automatically change. Even before there are children, certain expenses get shared by two people who are living together. Once children enter the picture, the expenses grow dramatically. Everyone who has children knows this. It's part of the challenge facing many young families who are juggling to make ends meet, even as they work to provide for the many needs of their growing family. That's why family planning is so important. Although you may not want to wait until every detail is in order, it does make sense to bring children into the world *after* you have your financial house in order.

So what happens if the family breaks up or one of the parents deserts the family? The relationship between adults may no longer exist, but the children are still there, with bellies to feed. This is a cold way of looking at the disintegration of the family structure, but it is real for many of our families. The children too often get treated like costly annoyances. Here again, we can look at an African model for assistance—the Bantu in the Kongo. For these people, according to K. K. Bunseki Fu-Kiau, "The coming of a child in the community is the rising of a new unique 'living sun' into it. It is the responsibility of the community as a whole and of the *ndzi* (babysitter), in particular, to help this 'living sun' to shine and grow in its earliest stage." There is a clear understanding for the Bantu people, as well as throughout the conti-

On Keeping Up with the Joneses

Black folks are famous for working overtime to look the part. The mentality that says that you should have a certain car because your neighbor does, or that you just-have-to-have-that-new-outfit-because-the-upcoming-event-is-going-to-be-so-grand is part of the way of life for many people in the Black community. Never mind that, these same people may not even have a savings account, let alone any real assets. No matter how nice "the good life" seems, you must learn to rethink how you spend precious resources, keeping in mind that providing for the future is imperative. Disciplined spending is a must for long-term good living. A 1997 report in *Money* magazine pointed out that people with real wealth often are the least conspicuous among us. Their clothing and living conditions are generally modest, while their financial portfolios are rich in activity. If there is a choice as to how to spend a dollar, the first thought is either to invest it or otherwise save it, not to spend. Even more, it was noted that the people who become savvy about their finances to the point that they reach well beyond financial security by stepping into millionaire status are often just regular folk. Most millionaires in this country are not trust-fund babies or the children of the privileged class. Instead, they are hard-working, ordinary people who kept their eyes on the prize and focused on making their dreams come true. And a lot of those success stories are African American. In the true sense of keeping up with the Joneses, you can look to those who have really "made it" and emulate their success.

You can take one more step, too, by recognizing that right along with so many other victims of the excesses of this society, Black folks have exchanged our values and are suffering as a result. We must change. Sobonfu Somé explains our state beautifully, if painfully, in her book, *The Spirit of Intimacy:*

> When you don't have community, you are not listened to; you don't have a place you can go to and feel that you really belong. You don't have people to affirm who you are and to support you in bringing forward your gifts. What this does to a person's psyche is that it disempowers it, making the person vulnerable to consumerism and all the things that come with it.

The community Somé is talking about is that of our own people. In truth, instead of trying to keep up with anybody, we must reclaim each other and support our growth so that we don't get caught up in the material race.

nent of Africa, that children are our most precious resource, and that during their childhood, they must be carefully nurtured so that they can grow into responsible members—the foundation—of the community. Because this is so, everyone in the community is to participate in the children's development; that includes both parents, whether they are together or not.

If we can embrace the vision of our children as the foundation of our future, I believe that under all circumstances parents will find a way to support their growth and development. There is no room for dead-beat dads or runaway moms. In the African model, the elders of the community work with couples to counsel them through their difficulties. In a minute, fathers, uncles and cousins, for example, would straighten out a brother who had lost his way. And more, everybody helps with the rearing of the children. If we only went back to what used to work so well for our people, there really would be no reason for child support disputes. Yet they exist. Apart from the spiritual ramifications of not supporting your child through personal contact, the financial repercussions of your not stepping up to your responsibilities can have devastating effects on your own flesh and blood: poor self-esteem, abandonment issues, fear of financial insecurity. Wake up!

To avoid abandoning your children when you leave a relationship, find a way to provide support for them on a consistent basis. For the Bantu people, it was the *kindezi,* which literally means "the art of baby-sitting," which was fulfilled by all of the people who were not in the age of production, young and old. You may need to work with a financial counselor who can help you to structure your income in order to facilitate this basic need. What you will find is that by living up to your duty, you will enjoy peace of mind, and so will your children. By ignoring your responsibility you may damage your children for life, even as you eliminate the possibility of real happiness for yourself. (See the chapter "We Are Family" for more.)

How to Be *Old*

It almost seems like a dream to many people—the prospect of retiring somewhere between ages sixty-two and sixty-five in order to live out the rest of our days savoring each moment of our "golden years." Folks work twenty and thirty years on a job they may not even like just to reap the benefits of a good pension come retirement time. These days, you had better check the terms of your retirement well in advance of retirement day, or you might be in for a nasty surprise. Most people believe that their compensation from social security combined with the pension from their job will be enough for them to live on for the rest of their lives. In many cases, this simply is *not* true. Given that the average financial need is 70 to 80 percent of preretirement income, you will probably need to supplement your government allocation in order to continue to live in relative comfort. In the context of your full life experience, this is something to consider carefully right now. Many older people find themselves in a depressing situation where they must rely on their children, other relatives and other loved ones because they neglected to prepare properly for themselves in later years.

That's what happened to my friend's Aunt May. Having worked in the domestic field for all of her life, Aunt May discovered upon reaching her seventies that she really couldn't work anymore, but that she didn't have enough money to keep on living independently without working. So Aunt May, an independent woman, did what many people today are afraid to talk about. She starved herself to death. Apparently Aunt May lay down on the couch in her cousin's parlor and stopped eating. For three months, she lay there with her lips pursed, not passing more than a morsel of food through her mouth or sharing a word about her actions one way or the other. Her family attempted to feed Aunt May the many soft foods that her cousin would prepare, but nothing worked. Aunt May had made up her mind. She was not going to see a doctor or anything else. For her, that was that.

One of the greatest worries that many old folks have is that they will live longer than their money will carry them. Being a burden on the family—or on anyone else, for that matter—is a role that no one wants to assume. The reality today points to the likelihood that more and more of our own family members will fall into this miserable state, but we don't have to resign ourselves to that. Instead, we can start right this minute to plan for an independent future.

- Plan ahead.   You can secure your future by saving as much of your income as possible and investing it wisely so that it will be available to you in your later years.
- Get creative.   Make an agreement with long-time friends—if you have no family—with whom you can live during your twilight years. You may decide to get a house or an apartment together, like the women did in the popular sit-com *The Golden Girls*. If you put your thinking cap on, you're bound to come up with creative solutions.
- Buy insurance when you are healthy.   Top among challenges for older people is securing health insurance. Rates are often astronomical for what seems like little return. But you need insurance. If you purchase health and life insurance while you are healthy, you will get better rates. Include disability so that you can protect yourself and your family against sudden concerns. (A document known as a liv-

ing will states the circumstances under which you would like doctors not to continue life-sustaining measures. It details at which point you have decided that you would like to die. If you choose to create such a will, do so in the presence of two nonfamilial witnesses, and then give a copy of the document to key family members who may need it should you become gravely ill.)

- Find out what to expect from the Social Security Administration. You can review your contributions to social security over the years and learn about your anticipated benefits just by placing one call. Dial 1-800-772-1213, and follow the recorded instructions. You will soon receive a form on which you will need to provide specific information. Approximately one month after the SSA receives that form, you will receive a benefits estimate. This information will help you to get a sense of what additional resources you will need in order to manage during your retirement years.
- Learn the details about your pension plan. Provided that your employer has created a pension for you, you can learn the details about your anticipated retirement income by asking. Your employer is required by federal law to provide you with a summary plan description—a document that explains the eligibility requirements and means of calculating benefits for your particular retirement plan.
- Work with your company. Invest as much of your salary as you can in employer-sponsored savings plans, such as 401(k)s. These plans allow you to invest pretax dollars that compound tax free until you withdraw them at your retirement. If you start investing $2,000 a year in your twenties, you can have as much as a half million dollars in your sixties.
- Invest in an Individual Retirement Account (IRA). You can set aside up to $2,000 annually in one of these accounts, which will earn you modest income until your retirement.

Wake Up to Investing

Have you ever heard stories about people hiding money in their mattresses? Chances are you have. In fact, there are many people today who have tremendous fear of financial institutions and choose not to entrust their money to anyone other than themselves. But how valuable is that money when it's stashed under the bed or stuffed into a piggybank? The answer is, if you stash $10,000 under your mattress for three years, that same $10,000 will be worth less when you finally decide to spend it. Why? Inflation alone devalues your money by 3 to 5 percent each year. And that's just for starters. This means that hoarding your money is an unconscious act, one that is completely

Africa and the Aging Process

Many of the contemporary ideas about how an American community takes care of the aged would make a traditional African family cringe. How can it be that people would even consider "throwing away" their elders into a nursing home? Even the idea of a nursing home to them is that of a one-way road traveled by those who never come back home. (It's our African retention that makes us so uncomfortable about it when we consider this option.) In traditional Bantu systems, for example, such an institution would be seen as a place for elders to go to die, not to receive any type of care (whether it was offered or not). In this country, as the average age rises higher and higher, people are having to reassess how they treat their elders. And it's not so easy, especially since nearly everything in contemporary Western life revolves around perpetual youth. For the Bantu people, aging is revered as the natural common path of *kala ye zima* or *being* while following the path of extinguishing slowly. From this perspective, elders are considered in the highest way, as a special class of people, *ndezi* (baby-sitters), with a special role based on their lifelong experience. According to African educator K. K. B. Fu-Kiau, rather than being sent away "to retire," they are given two specific responsibilities: (1) to transfer into children's own language the history of the community through songs, stories, legends and games and (2) to explain to these children the path of life, its meaning from *lala* (being, coming to be, to exist in the world) to *zima* (extinguishing the death of the body for change), and the role of the community. In this chapter about how we use our resources, it's worth considering just how valuable our elders are for the development and preservation of our families. Their value can actually be measured in dollars as well as experience, too.

To those who have found it necessary to place their elders in hospices or other facilities that care for people who are ill or otherwise, I am not trying to make you feel bad. I know lots of Black families who have found it necessary to seek help outside their homes for a variety of reasons, including not having anyone at home to care for elders and not having resources to pay for around-the-clock care. Many large Black churches around the country have created retirement and nursing homes that serve our elders for these reasons. The bridge between the ways of our ancestors and the ways of the West is sometimes tricky to build. When it comes to caring for the old folks in our families, what is most important is that we remember and honor them. If our only choice is to put them in a facility, our responsibility becomes ensuring that we attend to their needs while they are there, and that includes personal attention.

uninformed and that will not lead you to financial freedom. In the context of learning *how to be,* you must pursue means of securing your finances in order to be able to support yourself, your family and your community.

What can you do? Consider for a moment: Let's say you have $100 of discretionary income. Ask yourself what you can do with that money. The choices include (1) putting it under the mattress, (2) putting it in a piggybank, (3) spending it, or (4) lending it. When you put your money in a bank account, you essentially are lending your money to that institution. That's why the institution pays you interest for doing it. Basically, you are doing the bank a favor even as you help yourself. How you choose to lend your money is what investing is all about. Your goals and objectives may vary, but the bottom line is that you want to maximize your potential toward the highest earnings.

It's not nearly as hard as you may think. The first step is to adopt the attitude that investing is good and necessary for a full life. Wayne Weddington, president of Penmoyer Capital Management of New York City, says that everyone should invest. "Based upon your current spending patterns," he explains, "unless you have a significant increase in your income, your lack of investing will impinge upon your ability to borrow and spend in the future." His belief is that there is no choice in the matter. Here are Weddington's tips for new investors:

- Be aware of where your money is going. If you work for a major company, chances are the company offers a good pension plan. New laws allow you to have greater discretion as to how your pension benefits are invested. Schedule an appointment to review this information so that you can help direct the growth of your own money.
- Maximize your investments. Learn to live with less so that you can save more. Put as much of your income as you can into any plan from your company, as well as other instruments, such as IRA's, treasury bills, certificates of deposit and traditional savings accounts. If you can save 15 to 20 percent of your income, you will thank yourself when it comes time to retire. If you're just starting out, 10 percent is a good stepping-stone, but you need to save more in order to take care of yourself well.
- Take advantage of the current tax laws. You now can access money that has been set aside in tax-deferred accounts without penalty when the capital is used to purchase a home or pay for tuition for you or your children.
- You are never too old to invest. Depending on your age, you will invest at different levels of risk. When you are young, between ages twenty-five and forty, you can invest the most aggressively because you will not need your money for a long time. From ages forty to fifty-five you want to maximize your tax benefits and invest somewhat more conservatively. In your later years, you want to play it

safer, investing in treasury bills and other instruments that keep pace with inflation.

- **Never panic.** Even after the crash of 1987, the market restabilized within two years. If you have patience and a clear long-term investment strategy, you will be able to weather any storm. The key here is long term, because you lessen your risk when time is on your side.

- **Invest in mutual funds.** Unless you have a sizable amount of money to invest (upwards of $250,000), you're better off putting your money in mutual funds that will expose you to a diversity of stocks or an index fund that invests in the whole stock market. You can invest as little as $500 in a mutual fund or index fund. And there's a world of mutual funds out there from which you can choose. If you want to invest in Black-owned businesses or ecoconscious companies, you can. Hundreds of technology categories are at your disposal. All you need to do is go for it.

- **Get a stockbroker.** Companies such as Charles Schwab, Prudential and Merrill Lynch, as well as many others, work with individuals to help them invest in the stock market. Contact one of them or talk to your bank officer, colleagues or other associates for leads.

- **Get help if you need it.** For first-time investors, the world of finance may seem overwhelming. Some people feel afraid to ask for assistance, particularly if they are not prepared to invest huge amounts of money. Don't allow your budget to paralyze you. Instead, you can look to retail investment companies that will help you to navigate in financial waters. If you pay close attention, over time you may be able to invest on your own. Remember to read, and there are a whole host of investment resources available on-line. Educate yourself, because we're talking about your money and your future. Consider starting your own investment club.

Gambling

Some folks are so hungry for money that they fall into the trap of believing that with a quick roll of the dice, they are sure to acquire more. *Not* a good idea. Contemporary research, in fact, shows that gambling for many people is a dangerous addiction, not unlike drugs or alcohol, that destroys lives when it goes unchecked. That said, why do so many people participate in such a destructive habit? A chance at a better life, of course. It doesn't hurt any that casinos and other gambling institutions have cropped up throughout the world for people's gambling pleasure, either. Or that state governments have created their own ways of luring away taxpayers' hard-earned dollars. The state-run lotteries do fund worthwhile community projects, but they do so at the expense

Adopting a First World Tradition: Bartering

Traveling opens your eyes to a world of other ways of doing things. Chief among them is the way that people in other parts of the world trade a wide variety of goods and services in lieu of currency in order to achieve their goals. It is commonplace in rural communities in Africa, the Diaspora and the United States for people to trade food for clothing or household services for lodging. To make it easy to grasp, consider the American tourist. One thing that many tourists have discovered is that by identifying the items that are least widely available and bringing them on a vacation, they can barter these items for gifts to take back home. Be mindful that you offer gifts of value rather than just junk. This means of transacting business was used by the first slave traders in Africa (and everywhere else), when worthless items were traded for African treasures. Clearly, you don't want to be part of that horrific legacy. The true concept is one of supporting one another rather than getting over!

Bartering can be a saving grace for you at home as well. Plenty of people you know trade their valued possessions for others on a regular basis. One brother in Cleveland, for example, was planning to move from his studio apartment into a larger apartment with his new wife. On the one hand, both he and his wife had great items to decorate their home. Upon closer scrutiny, though, the two of them discovered that they really had more than they needed of some items and not enough of others. Clarence was in luck. He had a friend, Joe, who is a furniture collector and restorer. Joe had long been interested in a quality antique credenza that Clarence had bought a few years before. Clarence needed chairs, and Joe had quite a few beautiful ones in his possession. After several conversations, the two decided to trade these items. In the end, they both were happy because their needs and desires were fulfilled. Best of all, no money changed hands. You too can engineer a similar deal. To get the best or most mutually beneficial barter possible, follow these steps:

1. Assess the value that you place on the goods or services you intend to trade. Check the going market rate as well.
2. Get a clear sense of the value of the goods or services you desire or that are being offered to you.
3. Take the time to check out the "merchandise" carefully to ensure that you will feel comfortable with your decision.
4. If the trade represents significant value, create a written agreement that both parties sign that acknowledges the integrity and legitimacy of the trade.

primarily of the poor—many of our own people who really can't afford to give away dollars on a daily basis even if it is for a dream.

Essentially, the government picked up on a mainstay of the Black community: the practice of playing the numbers. The poorest in our communities kept their hope alive over the years by dropping a dollar or two into the numbers hole. Every week a number would come out, and somebody usually won. Although the earnings often were slim, much like the lotteries that are legally run today, the thrill of adding a few extra dollars to the week's income kitty was incentive enough to keep coming back. Just as with other forms of gambling today, the only problem is that the odds are not in the gambler's favor—ever. If you add up how many dollars the average person puts into the lottery versus how much he or she wins, you'll see that it's rare that even a regular winner breaks even, let alone gets ahead.

Financial analysts prefer to guide people away from gambling pursuits into another high-stakes arena that promises the real possibility of a brighter outcome: the stock market. By working with a competent stockbroker, you may be able to invest those dollars that you largely have been throwing away into companies with long-standing reputations, or into even safer mutual funds or other financial outlets that can earn you money. The risk increases with the opportunity to earn, but at least there's a good chance of making money on the back end. Managing risk is hardly the same as playing roulette, the slot machines or other such gambling pursuits.

If you believe that you or a loved one has a gambling problem, whatever the source of the gambling may be, seek help. In every major city, you can find Debtors Anonymous by calling directory assistance. Other organizations exist as well that will help you get a grip on your finances. Remember, there's no shame in reaching out for assistance. It may be the only way that you can improve your life.

Helping Our Own

One of the most beautiful stories I've heard is of the retired domestic worker down South, Osceola McCarty, who donated her life savings of $150,000 to the University of Mississippi in Hattiesburg so that a young, intelligent Black person would be able to get educated. McCarty received many commendations for her generosity, including the *Essence* Award in 1996. When she was asked about it, she couldn't understand why there was so much fuss about her action. The wisdom of her generation was that it is our responsibility to provide for our youth, so that their lives can be richer than those who passed before them.

That sure was the way that most Black folks lived their lives up until recently. In many of our families, there have been domestic workers, porters, railroad attendants, hard laborers. These people worked tirelessly to save and provide for their children and the children of their communities if they could so that the youth would rise above the status to which they had been relegated. They marched. They got chased by dogs, washed out into the streets with fire hoses and every other sort of activity that placed their lives in utter peril. All of this they did because they had no choice if they were to provide a better life for their families. Our predecessors graduated from being largely relegated to the service industry to becoming educators, nurses, doctors and lawyers. Even then, they faced outrageous injustices. For example, the Black man who discovered the formula for blood plasma—Charles Drew—died on his way to a "colored" hospital because he was not allowed anywhere else. As the fifties turned into the sixties and the Civil Rights Movement accelerated to its full force, the doors of opportunity opened, and many Black folks were able to take advantage of a breadth of opportunity never before considered possible. In the following years, progress has been made. We have seen an African-American woman, Mae Jemison, make it to the moon. We've watched reports of open-heart surgery directed by one of the finest surgeons in the world, Ben Carson, a man who happens to be a brother. We've witnessed a Supreme Court justice, the Honorable Thurgood Marshall, work arduously to turn around our justice system and make it more fair. And the list goes on and on.

What we've experienced has not been all good, though. Replacing Thurgood Marshall with a man with Black skin has not ensured the continuation of a legacy of affirmative action and focused direction toward equal opportunity for Blacks. Instead, he who benefited from it voted against it. Seeing African Americans become doctors hasn't meant that all of our people have access to affordable medical care. Seating a Black man on Wall Street who earned millions of dollars didn't automatically mean more dollars being funneled into the heart of the community. The assumption that many of our predecessors held—that we would provide first and foremost for each other and our children—has not held true for many Black people. More of us than would care to admit it have fallen short on the giving back end of the scale. In order to live in peace, we must create balance in the world. We cannot pull up the ladder once we've made it to a more comfortable place. We must remain conscientious about making a way for those who are still struggling hard to reach a place of stability in their lives and for those who will continue to hold the flame of our legacy once we are gone.

Giving back requires remembering. You don't have to go back that far, either, to start your remembering process. Think about your neighborhood, the people who lived near you, their hopes and aspirations. Consider your school systems—from elementary through your highest level of education. How can you give back to all of the communities that helped to make you the person you are today? It may be by sending a few dollars each month to your local YMCA or youth center, or making a donation to your elementary or middle school. Certainly you can make pledges to your college or university, particularly if it is a historically Black college or university. Earl G. Graves, publisher of *Black Enterprise* magazine, firmly espouses making consistent pledges to your school. "When I first graduated from college, I sent very small amounts of money each month. Over the years, as my earnings have increased, so have my pledges. Being consistent is what has been most important." Graves pledged $1 million to his alma mater, Morgan State University, in 1995, not only because he could, but more so because he had the awareness to give back. This is an important point. Many people feel that if they have only a few dollars to donate to a cause, the contribution will be of little value. This is simply not true. Think of old folks' wisdom here: *How many quarters does it take to make a dollar? How many dollars to make a hundred dollars? And so on.* The smallest contribution, especially when offered consistently and sincerely, will make a real difference.

Beyond your personal context, you may want to reach out more broadly. There is a global community of African and African-descended people who are working to support and strengthen our societies. In nearly every large city, you can find organizations that will direct you to ways that you can contribute your time and other resources to bettering the lives of brothers and sisters around the world. This, too, is helping our own.

Sou Sou *or* Tontine

Knowing how to build an economic base for yourself and your community is critical in learning *how to be*. I can't say it enough: without resources that support not only you but also your community, the effort is not good enough. Many economists, scholars and social leaders have pointed this out. Among them is author and scholar Amos Wilson, who had this to say in *Falsification of Afrikan Consciousness* (1993) about how we view economics and money:

> We're not suffering from any great money problems. We're suffering from the *absence* of an economic system. Money is not a system; money is what it is. A system involves the systematic and organized utilization . . . and distribution of money. Without the pattern, without the system, without the organization, one does not have an economy. An economy exists prior to money. . . . An economic system at its base refers to the nature of the relationship between people. When we lack a systematic way of relating to each other, then we can have

money and still be poor, have money and be robbed—which is what we are.

The good news is that we can learn from some of our brothers and sisters in Africa and other parts of the Diaspora about successful economic systems that rely on the community itself. In the Caribbean and on African shores, there is a system, known as *sou sou* or *tontine,* respectively, that works. Originating in West Africa among the Yoruba people, *sou sou,* which means "cooperative" in Yoruba and "penny by penny" in French, is theoretically a moneymaking venture that relies on the core of the community and its ability to be responsible for others. The way *sou sou* works is that a group of people decide that they want to save money together for a specified duration of time—a period of weeks equal to the number of participants. Everyone contributes the same amount of money each week or month—anywhere from $10 to $1,000 or more. Each week one person becomes the recipient of the entire kitty—the *sou sou.* So if there are twelve members of a group who donate $100 each, each week one member will receive $1,200. Lots are drawn, so that the selection process is "democratic," although participants can agree to throw lots back in or advance a member the kitty early if there is an obvious need. The catch is that each person must supply his or her contribution on time, even after having received the kitty. The *sou sou* is managed by a responsible member of the group who collects and distributes the cash, known as the *main* ("hand" in French).

This practice became very popular throughout the Caribbean, especially among poor people who did not have access to capital from commercial lending institutions. Rather than going without fulfilling their household needs and dreams, they pooled their resources in this safe version of a lottery (not to be confused with a pyramid scheme), which afforded them the chance of leveraging a larger sum of money to access a specific goal. It has worked so well that in recent years in this country participants have been able to start commercial businesses, send their children to school and otherwise make ends meet. Natalee Huey, a Jamaican woman who has lived stateside for many years, explains, "My family and I regularly practice *sou sou,* and it's great, because we agree that we will do our part until the end." If you can find trustworthy individuals, family or otherwise, who would like to participate in this practice, go for it. According to many West Indian people, the concept of cooperative economics, or *ujaama,* that fuels this practice has kept most participants honest and reliable over the years.

Know also that right now in the Cameroons of Central Africa, this same practice, known there as *tontine,* is alive and well, thank-you very much. In fact, in the first half of the 1980s, the economy of the Cameroons had the highest growth rate in Africa, at 7 percent a year. Their success stems from *tontines,* as evidenced by a 47 percent involvement rate versus only a 13 percent participation in commercial savings. The stories are incredible, including one man who wanted to start a business that needed an $850,000 cash flow. He got his money from his *tontine* in just a matter of days, because the kitty in his group is $1 million each month. Imagine, $1 million of accessible cash from people who look like you! We have to believe it in order to make it happen. Next time you get turned down at the bank, think about an African approach to increasing your resources. The responsibility rate is also incredibly high, primarily because social pressure keeps people honest and committed.

Giving to Charities

Deciding how to allocate your financial gifts can be tricky if you don't have a plan. So many individuals and organizations need financial help that you must be clear about your own views, intentions and goals before you write a check. Do a reality check for your life. Ask yourself what organizations and institutions most closely reflect your views and your conscience. You may also consider the following as you are deciding where your resources will go:

- Determine how much money you have to give. If your resources are limited, you should limit the number of entities to which you send money. For example, $100 will go a lot further when it's offered to one organization rather than to four. Knowing that, if you still feel strongly that you want to give to a number of key charities, you may select two or three to which you send portions of that $100.
- Check out the charity's allocation structure. Unfortunately, many organizations spend too much money on promotion, leaving a significantly reduced percentage for the cause at hand. Read the fine print of the charity's literature to assess how much of your contribution will go directly to the cause. When you are unclear, pick up the phone and call, or write for more information.
- Identify charitable organizations that help your community. If we don't take care of ourselves, how can we expect anyone else to help us? That means that you should consider it part of your duty to contribute monetarily or actively through volunteer work to an organization that is benefitting our comunities. Even if you offer other monies to such charities as the local museum, be sure to give something specific that will inspire an African-American child to expand his or

her awareness of the world. Within many civic organizations, such as your local museum, there may be programs specifically targeted to our youth. When that is the case, earmark your check for that specific activity. It is possible for you to direct your dona-tion if you take the time to find out the details on making that happen.

- Remember to report your gifts to the IRS. Your charitable contributions can help you at tax time, yet another sign that giving of yourself reaps more rewards than you might have imagined. You are allowed to deduct up to 50 percent of your adjusted gross income each year, and there are many ways that you can do this. Be sure to give to organizations that have nonprofit status, so that you can receive a legally binding receipt acknowledging your contribution. Among the charitable choices are giving clothing, furniture and other items to the Salvation Army, Goodwill and other resale stores. You may want to give stocks or bonds to your religious organization that will help it to develop community outreach and other programs, and which will save you from having to pay 28 percent capital gains taxes. Of course, you can also give cash. Always get a receipt for your gifts, even if you write a check. The IRS requires that donations of more than $250 be accompanied by a receipt.

Tithing

One of the more surprising suggestions that I have found in my research is that many successful financial planners—real business types—suggest that the proper way to manage money is to skim 10 percent off the top for the Lord. In the Christian church, this practice of giving 10 percent of your income to the church is known as *tithing*. In many other traditions, the same spirit of consistent, planned giving from your financial resources is considered an important spiritual practice. When I was growing up, I remember my mother filling out church envelopes each week and inserting a handwritten check in it. Grandma Carrie tithed up until the day she died, even though we had to mail in her check, because she was unable to get out to go to church. And so it has been for many other families throughout this country. Giving the "first fruits" of your "crops" back to God is common to the Judeo-Christian community. God then promises to "throw open the floodgates of heaven" and pour out tremendous blessings upon you—including a promise to prevent your "crops" from being devoured by pests. (Malachi 3:1)

Many people today continue to tithe or otherwise give financial contributions to their spiritual homes. Yet as more of us have become better educated and moved into the middle class, the practice

unfortunately falls off significantly. Why? For one, the way that education is offered these days, faith comes into question when people receive both education and experience in the world. Work sometimes
replaces the spiritual quest, and people get sidetracked into believing
that they exercise "complete" control of their lives. Obviously, this is
not part of the African tradition of thought nor of Christianity. A healthy
perspective is to recognize that life is a journey best navigated with
God at the wheel. Remembering God by offering part of your earnings
on a regular basis helps to fuel your own trip. It really works that way.
Just ask anyone who has suffered great hardship and made it back to a
place of comfort. The discipline of giving to God first helps you to prioritize and see what is truly important in your life. Taking care of the
inside is essential for managing the outside. (In keeping with the ways
of the West, you also get the bonus that your yearly contributions can
benefit you at tax time, so keep good records.)

Giving to the Brother on the Corner

In every major city, street corners are sprinkled with homeless or otherwise indigent people. The numbers have swelled so high in some cities
that even the kindest and most giving are at a loss for how to respond
to those in need. Shirley Byrd, a sister who lives in Philadelphia, tells
how she got burned a few years back. As she was approaching her office building one morning, Shirley saw a woman who appeared to be
in great need. She had a small child with her and was talking through
real tears, explaining how she had just been kicked out of her apartment because she couldn't pay the rent. Winter was just around the
corner, and this woman seemed desperate. Deeply touched, Shirley
went up to her office and petitioned all of her coworkers to give
money to this woman. By the end of the day, Shirley had raised $300
that she gave to the woman. That night, Shirley felt really grateful for
having been aware and willing enough to help someone else. It all
backfired over the next few months, though. As it turned out, the
woman and her baby were regular fixtures on Shirley's street. Whether
the two were homeless or not, Shirley didn't know. What she witnessed
was the woman sobbing out the same story time and again. Shirley felt
duped.

Naturally, Shirley also became quite skeptical about giving money to
people begging on the street. Her giving heart pretty much closed
down after that, at least for a long while. The same is true across the
country. Whether people are worried about their coins and dollars
going to alcohol and drugs or to the wallets of the slick hustler, many
are turning a blind eye to people who are asking for help. Instead of

completely negating those in the public who are seemingly in need, you have a few options:

- Give food instead of money. People who are really needy may appreciate a good sandwich.
- Give old clothes to individuals or to shelters. Many organizations redistribute goods that are offered to them for needy people.
- Give freely whenever you give. After Shirley cooled down, she had to admit that whether the woman was hustling or not, she definitely had a hard life, and that $300 might have made that day a little easier.
- Participate in programs that reach out to homeless and otherwise indigent people. Getting involved in the fate of others is a great service to humanity.

You and the IRS

Have you heard the saying, "You only have to do three things in this life—die, pay taxes and stay Black"? If the biracial-multicultural option is ever institutionalized on the census, only two will be true. The law says that every person who lives and works in the United States and who earns more than $600 per year must file income taxes on a yearly basis. That's pretty straightforward, yet hundreds of thousands of identified taxpayers don't file, let alone pay what they owe. Once again, you can argue the finer points of where the money goes and question why you should have to pay for such things as the governor's mansion renovation or even that of the White House. Even as you protest, you'd do well to pay. A tax attorney once explained to me, "It is a violation of the law not to file your taxes." That means that you can be hit with a hefty fine or, worse, a jail sentence for ignoring the law.

How can you come to terms with your tax situation? No matter how far behind you are in your taxes, it's never too late to come clean. In fact, there is no statute of limitations on filing, even as there is a three-year statute on receiving any refunds that may be due you from the Internal Revenue Service. (Some things just aren't fair!) Following are some suggestions that should be of help in getting you on your feet:

- Get an accountant. At the top of your list should be securing a capable accountant who is intimately familiar with tax laws. This person can walk you through your financial situation and help you to file your taxes so that you have the maximum protection. If you have limited resources, you can still afford an accountant. Just work out a payment plan that is acceptable to both parties.

- Prepare your papers. Nobody can help you unless you help your-self. Find all of your tax information, including W2 forms from your place of employment, 1099s, interest earned and any other documentation of expenditures and earnings. Ask your accountant for a worksheet on which you can record your financial information. You may also want to purchase a computer program that will guide you through your finances and prepare you to work with your accountant.
- File in a timely manner. That means you should be filing your income taxes no later than April 15 for the preceding year. If for any reason, you cannot file within the time limits, fill in a form requesting an extension. In this case, you must also enclose a check that includes an estimate of what you believe you owe. These simple steps will provide you with the knowledge that you are doing your part, as they also show the IRS your good-faith effort.
- Stay in touch with the IRS if you have a problem. Communication is ideal, because it shows the IRS that you intend to make good on your debts. Adding a human component may also help you to secure a bit of compassion and leniency.
- Let the agent know if you have any unusual circumstances. If you have become disabled, need to be hospitalized or are otherwise temporarily incapacitated, let your agent know. You may be able to extend a time limit for payment, particularly if your income has been suspended. Also, if you are a recovering alcoholic or drug addict, for example, you may be able to enroll help in getting back on your feet if you can bring paperwork substantiating your status. Of course, you must also live up to your new agreement with them. A program called EPHRA is available to help recovering people.
- When you make a deal with the IRS, stick to your agreement. Honoring your commitments is a requirement when dealing with the IRS. Once you have secured a payment plan or some other arrangement, you must consistently pay on or before the payment deadline; otherwise, your deal will automatically end. Then you will owe the full balance at once—which includes accrued interest.

YOUR QUESTIONS ANSWERED

1. I have young children who want to have all of the hip clothes and accessories that their schoolmates have. How can I help them to understand the value of saving their money?

Teach them by example. Look at your own life to see how you spend money on yourself. Do you spend excessively on yourself? Show your children that by budgeting, you can save money *and* enjoy luxury items from time to time. If you work with them so that they see how long it takes to earn enough money to buy designer sneakers, for example, they may begin to think twice before begging you to buy the next greatest novelty item.

2. I've been told that it is rude not *to negotiate with African vendors when traveling abroad. Is that true here in the United States?*

Whenever you make blanket statements without understanding the philosophy behind such differences, you are bound for trouble. Generally, the way that trade is conducted in many West African countries is by negotiation. A price is offered for an item, followed by a counter-offer from the purchaser. Prices are batted back and forth between seller and customer until a mutually agreed-on price can be reached. This does happen in the United States as well, among African vendors and many others. Before stepping into a negotiation posture, it is appropriate to ask a vendor if the price on a particular item is negotiable. Generally, when you don't see a price tag, you can go for it. Otherwise the response you receive will let you know if you can proceed. A word to the wise: Don't waste time negotiating for something that you don't intend to buy. This is insulting. Further, don't try to force a seller into a corner. The art of negotiating a deal is making both parties feel honored when the deal is completed. The way to get the best price is not to look too anxious. Look at other items; be polite *and* prepared to leave your choice behind—for real. Vendors will follow you; the idea is to sell their merchandise. If you say "No, thank you," and mean it, you will likely be offered a better price before you can get away.

3. Is there any code of etiquette that can get me out of credit hell?

Yes. Be assertive. One of the biggest mistakes that people make is to hide from creditors. Trust me, they won't go away no matter how many sheets you pull over your head! The responsible action to take is to contact your creditors individually, by phone and by written correspondence, to let them know the status of your payments. Even if you have no money to send, let them know what's going on with you and what your intentions are for repaying your debt. Then honor the commitment that you make to them. Your responsible communication will go on your record, just as your late payments do.

4. I have significant resources, and I am about to get married. Is it rude of me to want to secure a prenuptial agreement before I jump the broom?

It's not rude, but it can be uncomfortable. Asking someone with whom you say you want to spend the rest of your life for something that seems like a disclaimer can set up a level of mistrust between the two of you. That's not to say that discussing the possibility of a prenuptial agreement is wrong. I recommend that you talk about your financial issues and concerns openly early on in your relationship, so that your feelings don't make your engagement bittersweet. Be open and honest about your intentions—and be clear about your flexibility. The way that the issue of prenuptials has been handled has been a deal breaker for some couples. Even before you begin the discussion with your intended, ask yourself why you feel that you need to protect your resources. You have to come to a place of comfort about this issue in order to communicate effectively with your partner. I recommend that you set aside a time that you agree will be to discuss your plans for the future. During this meeting, have a list of topics that are important to you, including your finances. Start by stating the resources that you have accumulated. Let your partner know where you stand. Then state kindly that you want to protect your property through a prenuptial agreement. To support your cause, you can make reference to some African communities where it is understood that if a couple breaks up, for example, that the *lobola,* or bride-wealth, must be returned to the family of the groom. This is the case because as ties are severed physically, they also end spiritually. For some African people, that means that the spirit of the woman must be given back to her own family so she completes that reconnection.

5. I really think that money is the number one problem in my relationship. I don't know how to be with my boyfriend when we are always fussing about dollars. What can I do?

You can start off by realizing that money is not everything. From an African perspective, you learn that family and community are the most important resources. They come first. This philosophy held fast in Black communities until recent times. Don't fall into the trap of obsessing over money such that it clouds everything else. Instead, work with your partner to cultivate honorable values and practices that will support your life together. If you think that you need help learning how to manage your financial resources, seek it out.

6. I have a very close friend who is terribly irresponsible about money—his own and other people's. One of the worst offenses is that he will "borrow" money—$10 here, $20 there—without ever paying it back or mentioning it again. Since he's my friend, if I have it to give, I don't feel right telling him no when he cries "broke." How can I handle this awkward situation?

Go to the wisdom of the elders. Haven't you heard the saying, *Neither a borrower nor a lender be?* You can sleep better at night if you don't have the weight of owing somebody else money or for waiting for somebody to pay you back at the end of the day. This doesn't mean that you should never give somebody money when the person is in need. That would turn you into a stingy old miser, which would not reflect support of the community. Instead, lend to someone only an amount of money that you can afford to give. In your heart, offer the money as a gift, so that if you don't get it back, you aren't all pushed out of shape.

As this relates to your friend, next time he asks you for a hit, tell him why your answer is "no." Gracefully pull your friend aside and tell him that it makes you uncomfortable in your friendship with him to participate in financial transactions, because he has not honored them in the past. The best way that you see of resolving what has become a plaguing issue is to avoid it altogether. In this way you can preserve your friendship.

7. If my boss and I go to lunch together, should I expect him to pay?

Not unless he specifically invites you to go to lunch with him. Of course, it would be very generous of your boss to offer, but don't make assumptions, and don't get bent out of shape by creating false expectations. Many people at small businesses frequently dine with their bosses, especially when they work through lunch. Your boss doesn't have to pay each of those times. That's not part of his job description. Also, don't assume that if your boss pays for your lunch one day that he will pay every time you get food together.

8. My man asked me to move across the country to live with him. The conditions we agreed on for this move were that he would pay for me to go to school and support me until I finished college. Only problem was, about six months into this arrangement he got tired of it. What is the etiquette for this situation?

Can't you hear your Mama telling you, *Don't move in with no man until you get married!* Aside from that moral viewpoint, there's another one of my mother's reminders that I must offer, too: *Always be able to support yourself.* So what do I say? Get a job. And have a serious sit-down with your man. Find out what is bothering him about the finances. Chances are, things are tight. Instead of coming out and directly telling you that, he's unconsciously blaming you for the problem. By talking openly about your "family" finances, you may be able to solidify your relationship, because you will build a deeper level of communication and trust. By the way, the same thing can happen if you're married.

9. I come from a large family. Over the years, I have built a career for myself and have begun to earn decent money. Everybody in my family thinks that I'm "rich." So one person after another is calling constantly, asking for money. How can I manage what is sometimes an uncomfortable situation from an African perspective?

The African worldview says that family and community come first.

This means that you need to figure out a way to help your family as best you can. One way is to let them know that "you're not made of money," as you also sincerely offer to be of any assistance that you can. You may also want to tell them how you were able to become successful, which may inspire them to pursue ways of their own to develop their own talents such that they are fruitful.

10. I made a purchase recently, and the cashier gave me back incorrect change—$10 too much. Should I have given it back?

If you have to think twice about it, you already have your answer. Living honorably does not include "getting over" on anybody. No matter how small the amount, you should give the money back. Paying attention to financial transactions is an important point to highlight here. Many people don't count their change, especially for small purchases. They often assume that they have been given correct change. What you should do is count your money carefully, so that you conduct transactions accurately.

PoliticalIsCorrect

Leave no one behind.
MARY MCLEOD BETHUNE

HOW TO BE. That's what we are all seeking to discover. How to
live in the world respectful of others, preserving our selves, our families
and our communities. That's what we as people of African heritage
have inherited as both our birthright and our responsibility. When looking with open eyes at the world, we can see that our ancestors literally
were the first beings on the planet. The continent of Africa was inhabited more than 200,000 years ago. This has to mean something to each
of us today, as we attempt to make sense out of a 500-year-old mess
(when the slave trade began) that has left many of our communities
crippled, disillusioned and disempowered. Our legacy is powerful. The
cultural continuum that proves the intelligence, ingenuity and perseverance of our people undeniably points to the promise that if we "wake
up," to use Spike Lee's words from his film *School Daze,* we can reclaim who we are and be the majestic beings that our ancestors were.

Stripping away the veils of illusion that cloud our true Selves can be
excruciatingly painful, especially when the "luxuries" of Western living
dangle so closely before our eyes. But all we need do is look at how
rampant Western values have ravaged not only an entire country, but
much of the rest of the world to know—without question—that there
has to be a better, more balanced way. The way, I believe, is the way of
the ancestors—tapping into the rituals, philosophies and basic decency
of who we were in order to redefine who we are—and then balancing
that within a Western structure.

In terms of politics, on both a societal and a personal level, we have to learn how to negotiate our way in the company of others, so that we can reach our goals. The Honorable Walter E. Fauntroy, former Washington, D.C., delegate to the U.S. House of Representatives, once explained, "Politics is the process of determining who gets how much what, when and where." How can *we* figure out what we even want? Several years ago, I was taught that one of the most useful means of staying focused is to create an *intention*. First, you use the art of contemplation. You sit quietly, pose a question to yourself and search within for an answer; then look deeper by asking the Divine to unlock the true intention that resides in your heart. Know that study is an integral part of discovering the basis of your intention. (So, for example, if you want to know what your purpose is on the planet, you may first think it is to be a good parent. Upon deeper reflection you may discover that your role in life is to help preserve the environment so that it will be healthy for your children and others. That realization should affect the rest of your life—your choice of career, your home site, your political views and actions.) With your intention, you then pray, asking God to show you how it can manifest in your life. Finally, you meditate quietly, listening to your heart as you wait for your answer. Trust that this is not an unattainable process; it does take time, patience and daily practice.

Years ago I used this practice to guide my career. I always wanted to be a writer but hadn't figured out how to make the shift from poetry to something that would sustain me. After graduating Phi Beta Kappa from Howard and landing a secretarial job, I knew I had to reassess my goals in order to make it. Rather than copping an attitude, I prayed for guidance. I saw that all my interests and abilities could be packaged together to support me. My writing could be about fashion—since I had been modeling for years. My goal, then, was to move to New York City to be a fashion writer. As the years passed, my intention sharpened. More than fashion, I wanted to help people. And so through books and images, workshops and seminars, I have designed a career for myself that, I understand, "helps people from the outside in."

Like many others, I am still constantly reassessing my goals so I can grow. Yet many of our people, both middle class and poor, are walking around seemingly in a daze, neither thinking, nor acting. Poet Nikki Giovanni described such a condition as deplorable, saying, "Mediocrity is safe."

So, what are *you* doing? This chapter dips a toe into the question of what political life should be for a Black person in America. Without a power base, the things that we say and the actions that we take can be largely registered as *tef tef,* the Khamitic term for nonsensical talk. In order to establish a way of *being* in the West and on the planet, we must take action. It's the way of the elders. It's the definition of community preservation. The only question is, "What are *you* going to do?"

Your Right to Vote

Even after doing research, I hardly know how complex the issue of voting is for Black people. In a sense it presupposes that we exist in a culture that considers us equal, which obviously isn't true. From another perspective, there are those who firmly believe that the power of the vote is one way of making change, which has been proven over the years. I do know that one of the concerns we face with regard to political and economic power is our ability to make our voices heard. At least in theory, we can make a difference by exercising our hard-earned right to vote. With a hopeful posture, I present this information about voting and how we can participate in our commitment to balance our modern existence with our civil rights legacy.

A young sister from the Bronx, New York, just reached a turning point in her life, a life brimming with great possibility. When she told me that she was turning eighteen, she was so excited. "I'm going to be legal," she beamed. "Legal for what?" I wondered. When I was growing up, becoming "legal" meant you had the right to drink alcohol, something we were all pretty psyched about being able to do. (Now, in retrospect, I realize how warped that thrill was. Having the legal privilege to distort your perception of the world—*what a trick!*) Thank God, that wasn't what my young friend, Whitney Benta, was talking about. (These days, you have to be twenty-one, in most states anyway.) Whitney was talking about the right to vote. A few months before she would reach the legal voting age of eighteen, she had already taken steps to exercise her right; she had already registered to vote at the historic West Indian Day Parade in Brooklyn, New York, over Labor Day weekend. "My mother stressed to me and my brothers when we were growing up that it is essential for us to vote as soon as we are eligible. She used to tell us all the time how she herself remembered knowing Black people who couldn't vote," Whitney revealed, incredulously. "My mom taught us that we need to stay on top of what's going on in our community and make our voice count."

That's exactly what my parents taught me. For them, living in Baltimore, Maryland, they did have the opportunity to vote, thanks to the passage of the Fifteenth Amendment back in 1870. In the East, including those states above the Mason-Dixon line, Black folks did enjoy the privilege of voting early on. But for the thousands and thousands of brothers and sisters down South, only a few years ago being able to vote represented an elusive freedom, something that was guaranteed by the Constitution but that didn't extend to them until 1965, four years after I was born! Hard to believe, but it's true. It took marches on Washington, boycotts, rallies, riots and all other manner of strategic protest before our people's demands were heard, let alone formally acknowledged. Why? This country was founded on the principle that all men (and presumably women) are created equal. Religious and political freedom were the jewels of the great North American plains, attracting thousands from all over the world to start a new life. Most of us came on a different route, one paved in misery and deception rather than hope and possibility. Most of our ancestors were brought to this country forcibly, to work the land (although some came as free people)—as property of greedy landowners who refused even to recognize them as human beings. Property didn't have rights. Property didn't have a voice. Property didn't have a mind. That's why every effort was made during the period of our ancestors' enslavement to keep them from learning to read, write or otherwise become educated. The less they knew, the better off the land, property and business owners would be.

Well, it didn't work. Our people's resilience, ingenuity and thirst for freedom beat down all the efforts to hold them back. And thanks to many great martyrs and freedom fighters, including Sojourner Truth and Frederick Douglass, Dr. Martin Luther King, Jr., and Supreme Court justice Thurgood Marshall, as well as such organizations as the National Association for the Advancement of Colored People (NAACP) and the National Urban League, we have secured many gains through the American judicial and legislative systems, particularly through the Civil Rights Act of 1964 and the Voting Rights Act of 1965. Even with a congressional nod of approval, however, physically taking the steps to vote was much like walking through a field of land mines in the early days. People's lives were threatened and often sacrificed in their efforts to cast their ballot. Myrlie Evers-Williams, widow of slain civil rights crusader Medgar Evers, explained to a group of young people that our people literally walked many miles on foot to get to voting stations, only to find that the locations had been moved in the middle of the night. Further, after the Voting Rights Act of 1965 was passed, Black people still faced outrageous obstacles, including special tests that featured such unanswerable questions as, "How many bubbles are there in a bar of soap?"—designed, of course, to deny our people eligibility.

Some argue that the difficulty that our ancestors experienced in being able to vote led many African-American people to give up. "After all that, why even go to the polls?" some have sighed. As Myrlie Evers-Williams pointed out, "Knowing what we went through, I cannot understand how Black people today cannot understand the importance of voting." We *cannot* give up. Yet as we look across the country at voting patterns, it is apparent that we *are* giving up. Fewer and fewer people on the whole are voting; among Black folks the percentages are critically low.

I know there have been times when I haven't felt much like getting up to vote. My apathy one year made me wonder whether I helped by default to get the "bad guy" in. Just thinking of how vigilant both my parents and Grandma Carrie have been about voting has helped me to commit to get to the polling station on time.

The good news is that even though it sometimes looks dismal, we have made gains. In 1997, there were 40 African-American members of Congress, 417 African-American mayors, hundreds of city council members and more than 641,000 African-American-owned businesses wielding economic clout. And more, it *does* matter to each of us who is elected to a particular office, because those elected officials—their views and their actions—directly affect our families, our livelihood, our well-being, whether we like it or not.

As you consider the effects that politics can have on your life, remember that the road to a fulfilled and honorable life must be paved with a deep and active concern for community. In this context, it should be clear that we must all be willing to engage in some degree of political activity to ensure that the path for our future expands more broadly for those who will follow in our footsteps. In this chapter, we will explore what has happened historically in the political arena for Black folks, and how we can apply the principles of politics in everyday life.

When We Don't Respond

People across the globe fight for the right to make their single vote count. We hear it said that in this country, one vote makes a difference, yet a lot of people don't believe it. In California in 1995, our failure to cast our ballots cost a dear price. Proposition 209 was raised for consideration to the citizens of California. It stated that no longer should preferential treatment be offered to students applying for college based on racial distinctions. This crusade to end affirmative action in the California higher education system was spearheaded by the governor and an African-American public figure. On the one hand, the argument goes that white folks are now losing ground due to reverse discrimination. When a Black person is selected over a white person at a place of employment, at the point of entering college, at any other point, some say this isn't fair. Whites are losing out, some say, apparently disregarding the fact that their rate of employment is better than 80 percent, whereas ours is considerably lower and always has been. Because affirmative action was thrown out in the California higher education system,

African-American student enrollment in California state colleges drop-ped significantly within two years—due to both a dramatic reduction in applications and a higher percentage of rejections.

In the end, in a situation like this and the many others that are crop-ping up around the country that challenge affirmative action initiatives, we are faced with very real issues of *how to be*. The questions that arise are: What is affirmative action? What was its original intention? What were the conditions under which it was originally crafted? Have any substantive changes been made in these conditions? Is it true that dis-crimination in this country has been reduced to the extent that repara-tive opportunities are no longer necessary? Should I feel guilty or less than deserving for receiving an opportunity based on my race?

Kweisi Mfume, executive director of the NAACP and former chairman of the Congressional Black Caucus, has stated that it is ludicrous for the American populace to suggest that discrimination has neutralized to the extent that assistance is no longer necessary. "We must continue to fight," he urges. Earl Graves regularly concurs, "Affirmative action was never meant to guarantee anybody anything. Affirmative action was meant to level the playing field." Graves contends, "If you are coming to the track field wearing track shoes, and I am coming wearing combat boots, the playing field is not even." Affirmative action gave many African Americans who are leaders in this country their start, including controversial Supreme Court justice Clarence Thomas, who later voted in favor of its dismantling. Getting confused about our views based on apathy or newfound financial, social or political comfort is dangerous. So is being misled by misinformation that leads to acceptance of ide-ologies that threaten the very core of the African-American family.

We must remember that it was just in the 1960s that affirmative ac-tion began to make a difference. Before that, many Black people couldn't exercise their right to vote, couldn't shop in the same stores as whites and in some cases couldn't own property or build businesses. Although the Civil Rights Movement of the fifties and sixties reclaimed some basic human rights for us, certainly those few years of "progress" cannot wipe the slate clean. Unless we continue to champion our causes, our gains will slip away. Such inaction would be grossly irre-sponsible.

I recently saw a clip of the Reverend Martin Luther King, Jr., from the television show *Meet the Press,* just days before his historic March on Washington in 1963. King was asked about the struggles of the "Negro" and challenged about the aggressive nature of the efforts that had led up to the march. To the challenge, King asserted that "Negroes" had been waiting at that point "for 346 years" for some semblance of equality, for some flicker of hope that our basic needs would be considered and met—this being the time still of white and colored rest rooms, hospitals, and lunch counters. For King, the time was really overdue but certainly had come for change to occur. The tragedy is that in too many respects we are still waiting.

Become Informed

It's time for a wake-up call. Meaningful participation in the political process begins with *political awareness*. Yes, this *is* part of good etiquette, believe it or not. Being aware of what's going on in your world is a basic requirement of taking care of community. With the proliferation of media in today's society, there really is little excuse for not having at least a working Western knowledge of relevant issues facing your city, state or county. Locally, large and small newspapers carry detailed information on school board, city council and state committee actions. Many cable television systems now use public access channels to carry live coverage of local legislative sessions. The national cable stations C-SPAN and C-SPAN II present live sessions of the U.S. Congress and Senate. Nationally distributed newspapers such as the *New York Times,* the *Wall Street Journal* and *USA Today* provide a broad—if conservative—outlook of issues facing the nation.

But be clear that African-American people cannot stop there. The information disseminated in mainstream media often does not reflect the issues and concerns that speak specifically to people of color in the United States or elsewhere throughout the world. We need to read those publications and view those programs for insight and then turn to other avenues for a reality check. Local, national and global media outlets are essential for discerning a clear perspective. Read African-American periodicals and those from the Diaspora, listen to international radio broadcasts and stay alert.

Take one more step, for those with access to the Internet, and research the topics of greatest interest to you. The Internet has a wealth of detailed information that's available at your fingertips. If you don't have a computer, make purchasing one a priority on your investment list. In the meantime, go to the library to surf the Net. Many African-American resource sites are up and running, so that the lines of communication and access to information can continue to flow.

Historical Highlights

The history of African Americans in this country has been one of constant struggle and triumph. Here are but a few extraordinary moments to remember.

1600–1865	Slavery in the United States
1787	Abolitionist Movement begins
1822	Denmark Vesey Revolt
1831	Nat Turner Rebellion
1857	*Dred Scott* decision (slave is not a citizen, but property)
1861–1865	Civil War
1862	Emancipation Proclamation (the "end" of Slavery)
1865–1877	Reconstruction
1865	Thirteenth Amendment ratified (abolished Slavery)
1868	Fourteenth Amendment ratified (freedom of speech and press)
1896	*Plessy v. Ferguson* ("separate but equal" facilities are legal)
1909	NAACP founded
1910	National Urban League founded
1954	*Brown v. Board of Education of Topeka, Kansas* (segregated schools, etc., illegal)
1955	Emmett Till, a fifteen-year-old boy in Mississippi, was lynched for "wolf-whistling" at a white woman
1956	Rosa Parks sparks bus boycott in Montgomery, Alabama
1963	Martin Luther King, Jr., gives "I Have a Dream" speech
1964	Civil Rights Act passed
1965	Voting Rights Act passed
1966	Watts riots
1967	Thurgood Marshall becomes first Black Supreme Court justice
1968	Martin Luther King, Jr., assassinated
1983	Guion S. Bluford becomes first Black astronaut
1984	Jesse Jackson campaigns for presidency (and again in 1988)
1991	Rodney King beaten by Los Angeles police
1992	Douglas Wilder becomes first Black elected governor (Va.)
1993	Riots erupt in Los Angeles after Rodney King police verdict
1994	Carol Moseley Braun becomes first Black woman elected to U.S. Senate (and is unseated in 1998)
1995	Million Man March in Washington, D.C., sponsored by Louis Farrakhan

Think Globally, Act Locally—Involve the Children

The millennium is here, and it represents great promise. In the twenty-first century, there will be a much greater need to recognize that we are interconnected and interdependent. As the world shrinks through advances in information and travel, increasingly what affects some of us affects all of us. So begin thinking globally by teaching your children the value and richness of other cultures and nations. Become aware of your own prejudices and where you might have acquired them, so that you can break the cycle of ignorance (i.e., not knowing) here and now.

And whenever you can, travel—to other neighborhoods, other states, other countries—to experience how other people live and work. If pursued with a flexible and curious outlook, there is no better education.

Now, it may not be easy tearing kids away from the television set or from their friends. And, yes, children should have the opportunity to play; until they learn to read, that's how they learn. We also need to cultivate in them the discipline of staying abreast of current events—from a very young age. It's never too early to start. You can review articles in the newspaper with youngsters before they learn to read. By discussing pertinent issues over family meals and creating interactive opportunities for the family to stay attuned to current events, you stimulate intellectual conversation and further research. Encourage your children to participate in the electoral process. Follow the debates, and go to rallies and other forums where candidates will be speaking. By researching the fundamental truths of what democracy is supposed to be with your children, you can bring to the light the country's purest goals and encourage your family to strive to make these goals their own. Be sure to teach them about African, African-American and Diasporan studies, first sharing struggles and gains, with the intention of showing them how strong and capable we are as a people. Don't underestimate the need for sharing our cultural truths with them. As Anthony T. Browder explains in his book, *Nile Valley Contributions to Civilization*:

> In light of the extreme difficulties facing African Americans, it is important that new strategies be developed and implemented to ensure our survival. An important part of any plan must include the mental, physical and cultural nourishing of African-American children. They are the ones who will be confronted with racist stereotypes in the media, classrooms and society. A constant diet of hopelessness will ultimately . . . make them believe that their future is bleak and they will . . . develop the self-destructive behavior patterns so many of our youth currently exhibit.
>
> . . . What happens to children who grow up seeing everyone else portrayed as heroes, while they are given a steady diet of images portraying themselves as less desirable? These children grow up falsely believing in the superiority of other groups while doubting themselves. All one has to do is look throughout any neighborhood in the country and you will find groups of unemployed and underachieving African-American males with no real vision of themselves for the future. Images that are formed in early childhood generally stay with us for the rest of our lives. In the final analysis, television and radio are media that are too powerful to be left in the hands of children without proper supervision.

When you introduce a well-rounded base of information to your children, you help to develop a fertile environment in which they can cultivate global ideas and concepts.

Register to Vote

After awareness comes responsibility. The most important political act one can make is to study the history and patterns of thought and behavior in order to get a clear gauge of the actions that you should take to govern your life. One way to effect change is to register and then vote. It's easy to do:

- Legal citizens who are eighteen or older (or who will be eighteen by the date of the next election) may register to vote. *Do it now.* For assistance, contact the board of elections in your home town. Many states may have limited residency requirements, as well as other restrictions, so do your homework regarding your eligibility.
- Many states may have adopted federal "motor voter" laws, which allow residents to register to vote while applying for a driver's license. Check with your local board of elections for the specific rules in your area.
- Once registered, exercise your right to vote at every opportunity. Yes, your vote makes a difference. Elections are won and lost (more often than you might expect) by as little as a percentage point or two, and in some extreme cases, by no more than a handful of votes. One woman in a small town shared this example. Her husband called her from work one morning to report that one of their worst fears had materialized—the local paper headlines announced the defeat of an issue for which a special election had been called. Both she and her husband had strongly supported it, but had forgotten about the election. The issue lost by two votes.
- Read up on the elections, both local and national. Find out who the candidates are and what they represent so that you can cast an informed ballot. Ask questions if you are unsure. No question is a dumb question. The only reason to be embarrassed is if you don't ask when you don't know.
- Stay up to date. When you move, you must update your voting card, just as you do your driver's license and other documents. If you fail to register your new address, you will have to vote at your old voting station or by absentee ballot, until you update your records.
- Cast an absentee ballot if you find that you will be out of the area or otherwise unavailable to vote on Election Day. You can secure an absentee ballot by contacting the board of elections in your city.

- Become a citizen. If you are a permanent resident of the United States and plan to stay in this country, give yourself a voice. By taking this single action, you can become an active participant in directing your future in this country as well as that of many others. Check with your native country. Often you can secure dual citizenship. Contact the Immigration and Naturalization Service for details.
- Keep your voter registration card handy. It can be used as additional identification to help establish residency in an area that is new to you.

Get Political

As you may have experienced, many people shy away from politics, equating the word itself with "the bad guys"—politicians and the legislative process. The images that keep people back are those of cold, marble hallways, smoky backrooms and double-talk. The actual definition of *politics* is not negative. As defined by *The American Heritage College Dictionary,* politics is defined as "the art or science of government." The more telling definition as it applies to our daily lives can be found in its adjective root, *politic,* meaning "shrewd, wise and expedient." If you get right down to it, we all can incorporate the essence of these qualities in our lives, from the workplace to the home.

"Politics is positioning yourself in a certain way to predict or reach a certain outcome," according to Lionel Collins, the chief of staff for Representative William Jefferson (D, Louisiana) and a Capitol Hill veteran known for his savvy. His just might be the best definition of a game for which there are no clear set rules and no set outcomes, for the rules of the game change with every situation—much like life. When you look at it this way, politics can be considered as a way of creating an atmosphere, which makes the odds lean as much in your favor as possible. You need to balance this definition of politics with a clear conscience and an agenda that takes other people's interests and needs into account.

The Reverend Jesse Jackson, president of the PUSH–Rainbow Coalition and a former presidential candidate, is fond of saying, "Politics are personal tics." *Translation:* Understanding politics means understanding people—what drives them, what hurts them, what they fear, what they love, what makes them respond. Similarly, former House Speaker Thomas P. "Tip" O'Neill was famous for his observation that "all politics are local." In other words, what guides the decisions people make are usually issues that are very close to home. In this context, being political is not a dirty concept at all. *Being political* means having a keen, current and, above all, sensitive awareness of the culture, values, desires and motivations of those around you. It further means intelligently and strategically using that awareness to advance the issues that are most important to your people.

Get Involved

Love for politics is an acquired passion and can be viewed as a tool for reaching your goals. The quickest way to develop that passion is to feel the incredible power and satisfaction of having an idea or concern addressed, getting your views heard and seeing your dreams come to fruition. On a deeper level, your drive can come from your commitment to the development and growth of your community—by any means necessary. In the context of the African worldview, this means that those dreams relate directly to empowering and mobilizing the village.

This can best be accomplished at the local level. That means a school's Parent-Teacher Association, the Neighborhood Watch group or one of the hundreds of thousands of advisory commissions, church committees and boards established in communities throughout the nation. Joining these organizations gives amazing insight into important aspects of broader politics, like group dynamics, cooperation, fund raising and leadership, and can provide great credentials and contacts to springboard into a political career.

If you really aren't looking to dive head first into the political world, recognize that nearly everything is political. From that perspective, it is essential to have allies who will support you in whatever your endeavors may be. The best way to gather up your support team is by becoming active in your community, for your community. The only way to make a difference is to understand the absolute necessity to do everything possible to create a firm foundation for your community for the future. As the elders have often said, *Tomorrow is not promised.* In *The Falsification of Afrikan Consciousness,* Amos Wilson says:

> Many of us view history as a continuing progression upward and onward. We have bought the American concept of progress: the idea that things must over time necessarily get better. There is no law in the universe that tells us our future survival is assured; that we will continue to exist now and into the future. There have been races and ethnic groups who have been virtually wiped out on this planet. There is no guarantee that our own group will not be wiped out as well. The idea that we must necessarily arrive at a point greater than that reached by our ancestors could possibly be an illusion. The idea that somehow according to some great universal principle we are going to be in a better condition than our ancestors is an illusion which often results from *not* studying history and recognizing that

Your Neighborhood Association

Used to be that the neighborhood watch consisted of Aunt Etta and Uncle Ted down the block who made sure that nothing out of order happened on their streets. And you better believe, when they were on the lookout, everything was fine. In many towns and neighborhoods, folks do still look out for one another. Whether it's the elders and those working from home who keep an eye peeled for the neighborhood children after school or the brothers who play ball after work with the young men of the community, working to instill solid values in them by being close, we still take good care of our own. But the level of intimacy in many neighborhoods has eroded, due to neighborhoods' changing composition, more people working long hours and greater fear of the potential for crime outside our front doors.

As we know, many citizens across the country are taking a stand against the deterioration that comes to our communities when we lose our neighborhood safety. In many instances, parents have stepped up to the plate inviting other parents and neighbors to create night and day watches during which locals "patrol" their blocks and apartment buildings. Often these grass-roots watches align themselves with the local police department to ensure backup protection when necessary. Posting signs in local stores and other community buildings that alert neighbors and those up to no good about the neighborhood watch heightens awareness on both sides, making crime less welcome.

Communities are fighting back. The Fruit of Islam (FOI), the lay security arm of the Nation of Islam, does an effective job of keeping crime down across the country. Clean-cut brothers dressed in suits with crisp white shirts and bow ties come into neighborhoods when invited and keep a close watch on all comings and goings. In a Black community in Chicago that was riddled with drug abuse and the subsequent deluge of violent crime, the FOI came in and established roadblocks. Only residents were allowed to cross the boundaries unless they had been previously cleared by those they were visiting. Otherwise they had to wait for their hosts to pick them up. Although this measure seemed extreme and inconvenient to some, the results were remarkable. Crime went down more than 50 percent in only a few months, because the environment was no longer ripe for its exploitation.

Unfortunately, these efforts still don't answer the question of how we will protect all of the others of our community from police brutality and racial violence. Think of Emmett Till, Rodney King, Abner Louima, the congregations of our churches all across the South.

> progressions and regressions occur; that integrations and disintegrations occur in history.
>
> History is not a fairy tale wherein certain things are accomplished and people live happily ever after.

Politics in the Office

The 1990s have seen a remarkable growth in the number of African Americans entering the risky world of entrepreneurship. I took the big step in 1995 myself. Many others have done so by interrupting substantial careers in corporate America. While those who make the leap speak often of wanting to "chart my own course" and "be my own boss," the great unspoken benefit of owning your own business is avoiding the trials and pitfalls of office and other people's politics.

To a great number of business owners, all the heartache and false starts associated with entrepreneurship are well worth it if only to get away from the day-to-day infighting, positioning, backbiting and one-upmanship that can permeate the corporate workplace. But not everyone can be the boss. And for the record, when you own your own business, chances are that politics will still crop up. If you're lucky, you just exist above the fray, and it then becomes your responsibility to reduce the levels of friction among your staff.

It *is* possible to work in a harmonious environment. For those who work for others, a little shrewdness and artful maneuvering can make the difference between a rising career and a lifetime of work-related stress and stagnation. That said, I don't mean to diminish the fact that office politics can be taxing and burdensome. Most people would love to go to work, do a great job and have that work recognized for its quality, as opposed to the quality of one's political maneuvering. But particularly in large corporations where employees can seem nameless and faceless, enhancing your visibility and reputation through strategic alliances and positioning is almost mandatory for advancement.

At work, politics is about knowing and understanding how things are done and how to get things done. The rules change from workplace to workplace. But in every situation there is protocol—unwritten rules that one does not break, chains and command of information, laws of hierarchy. Collins gives a classic example of Washington workplace hierarchy in action. "On Capitol Hill, a chief of staff deals with a chief of staff, a legislative assistant deals with a legislative assistant. You would never have a legislative assistant deal with a congressman. A junior staffer would not get a response from a senior official at the White House. A congressman can call anyone." Collins warns, "The biggest penalty for breaking the rules is not getting anything done."

Status and position are important aspects of the corporate culture of the Capitol. But every company, large or small, has its own unique idiosyncrasies, best translated personality. That personality dictates its internal politics—everything from how employees dress to management's attitudes about key business decisions, such as assuming risk or hiring practices.

Winning and advancing in corporate America, then, are about understanding the corporate environment. The key word is *understanding*. In order to comprehend corporate structure, or any other structure, one must grasp the concept of understructure—that which exists beneath or under or behind the scenes, the stuff on which the thing is built. Ask yourself: What is going on beneath the structure of the place where you work? Who is in charge? Who is really in charge? Who does my boss answer to? Is it a private owner or a board of some sort? From where does the money come? Where does it go? No matter how complex something appears, assume that there is always more than what meets the eye. Ask to see the company's original statement of purpose. Find out what philosophy the company is based on. The past holds keys to understanding the present behavior and limitations. It is important to note (especially for those who feel they are selling out if they adhere to policy) that *understanding* office structure and *imbibing* office structure are two different things. In other words, being proficient in office politics does not require changing one's inner structure.

African Americans spend their lives moving back and forth between the Western culture of our workplaces and our own communities and should find this kind of duality familiar. It has been like that for us for centuries. But at the point you feel that your office structure—whether it's government, a corporation, a factory, or the arts—runs strongly in opposition to the values to which you adhere, then that is a sure sign that it may be time to move on. (For more, see the chapter "On the Job.")

The Art of the Favor

In some circles, giving and receiving favors is the absolute bottom line of what politics is all about—whether it's in the workplace, at home or on Capitol Hill. We all have been on one end or the other of a favor and know that it takes thoughtful, strategic moves to negotiate them to our benefit. But remember, as conscious brothers and sisters, we are searching for win-win situations, not opportunities to humiliate, embarrass or cheat. As Ptahhotep said, "Each man teaches as he acts." The lessons of our ancestors, who were duped by broken treaties and disregarded arrangements, teach us to be both honorable and careful. We must cultivate the ability not to cheat and not to allow anyone to cheat us. By defending and protecting yourself honorably, the universe will be on your side.

In politics, favors are not unlike money or capital. Shrewd politicians build war chests of favors—known as *political capital*—as aggressively as they pursue campaign funds. And just like bank capital, the amount and quality of the favors you receive are generally in direct proportion to the amount and quality of favors you can give, or have already given, in return. You should hold onto political capital tightly, spending it wisely and only when necessary. This process is so deeply embedded in political structure that specific laws and enforced rules have been created to keep favor giving within the boundaries of ethical behavior, though the boundaries tend to stretch or shrink depending on who is in charge. Trouble comes, generally, when a person stretches those parameters beyond even their flexible limits.

The following may ring a bell: Favor trading also goes by the name of *patronage*—a system of reward for loyalty and support, and retaliation for opposition. In cities like Chicago and New York, the patronage system is a well-oiled machine where power and influence are gained by lifetimes of building political capital. In such cities, everyone from the mayor to the local cabdriver knows the system well and seems to be at peace with the concept that "to the victor go the spoils." The same is true of our neighborhoods where the local power base is consulted before actions are taken. But in places not so aggressively political, there is a fine line—or no line whatsoever—between what some call patronage and what others call cronyism and, in extreme cases, corruption. So before you set out to practice the art of the political favor, know exactly what kind of place you are in. Listen—a lot. Ask subtle, well-placed questions. Pay attention to everything, and remember what you've seen and heard. Keep your mouth closed. (Think of the Yoruba proverb: *Lip not keeping to lip causes trouble for the jaw*.) Even more, be clear about your intention. You will have a built-in way of measuring your own ethics so that you can avoid crossing boundaries of decency, mutual respect and legal limitations.

The rules do change for each situation, but here are the four basic tenets of the favor-trading process:

1. Know when you are asking a favor. Favors are generally judged by the level of inconvenience it takes to grant them. The greater the inconvenience, the bigger the favor. For example, asking someone for the telephone number of an important contact is generally a minor favor, which comes with little expectation of return. Asking someone to arrange a meeting for you with that same important contact is a much bigger favor.
2. Choose the favors you ask wisely. There are degrees of favors, from inconsequential to major. If you've spent time or energy building up your favor reserves for a major favor from some-

one, don't squander it on something inconsequential. Don't, for example, ask someone who could get you that great job someday for an invitation to some big party next week—unless it seems that it would be no problem to get both.

3. Be certain of your relationship with the person from whom you ask a favor. As a simple matter of course, always take the time to solidify relationships with friends and allies. A phone call here or a note of congratulations there goes far toward keeping the lines of communication open. If you haven't been in touch, it would be unrealistic in most cases to expect any enthusiasm about doing you a favor out of the blue. Take time to reestablish the relationship before you make a request. This truly is commonsense: taking advantage of people doesn't work.

4. If someone cashes in a favor to do you a favor, you owe the person *big time*. Spending your own political capital to do a favor for someone else is the political equivalent of handing over your paycheck to someone who has done no work. Be ready to pay back in a significant way.

Note: With all this talk of favors, it is important to point out that many people do not spend their lives tallying their favors—neither those they have collected, nor those they are owed. To operate in this world out of a place of goodness where you don't keep score is a noble and possible way to live. Even when you practice the art of currying favor, if you do so with a giving heart and with the intention of helping others, you will be able to resist the temptation of becoming bound by a power play.

Getting Your Point Across

Black folks rarely pick up a piece of paper to send a note. We can find an explanation for our methods of communication. One-on-one contact used to be the primary means for delivering information all over the world, certainly in the Motherland. News traveled by personal messenger from home to home, sometimes necessitating long journeys. Even today, to announce weddings in a number of African countries and in the Caribbean, people personally share the news. The legendary *griot, djeli* or *doma* was the conduit for sharing historical information about a people for many generations. This oral tradition extended even further in ancient African cultures by drum. Languages were formed and articulated through the drum, allowing messages to travel across vast distances with a sometimes simple, often complex, always specific beat—understood only by the appropriate listener. Using their cunning and creativity, our ancestors delivered information during the early days of Slavery through the beat of drums (until they were outlawed by English colonists), including escape routes and strategies, until slave owners got wise to them and destroyed this vehicle for getting the word out. We made up spirituals to convey escape routes. "Swing low, sweet chariot" meant Harriet Tubman was "comin' for to carry me home"—to "freedom" up North. The African linguist Theophile Obenga observed in *African World History Project: The Preliminary Challenge:* "From the time of Pharaonic Egypt, the spoken word has been sovereign in Black Africa. From time immemorial, there have been not oral civilizations (as ethnologists and foreign anthropologists call them) but civilizations of the powerful, creative word. . . . It is clear that ancient Egypt was also a high civilization of the mighty and [powerful] Word."

If you need to communicate a message, do it in the most effective way possible. You may have the facility of Al Sharpton, a grass-roots activist in New York City who is constantly leading marches and rallies holding up the flag for African-American's people's rights. Considered by some to be a loudmouth, Sharpton is actually quite effective at getting his point across by being prepared with intelligent arguments to support his premise and inflammatory strategies for engaging the media.

Even so, sometimes you may have to write. In Western situations, it is generally the best choice. Particularly when you are hoping to effect change on a governmental level (but really anywhere), you should make your voice heard through a lasting document that clearly outlines your intentions and recommendations, even if you also employ other means. If you feel at a loss for what to say, think simply. You don't have to write an essay, just a few sentences that state your case.

Keep this in mind: politicians are keenly aware of the power of the voter, whether they admit it or not. As a voter and a constituent, you wield a considerable stick. Yes, you! Although your stick may not be as big as the one carried by powerful lobbies and wealthy corporations, your influence truly is meaningful. And the same goes for your power as a consumer, too. Think about it. Regularly we hear of a housewife from the Midwest whose initial efforts steamrolled into forcing an offensive television show from the prime-time airwaves, based on the strength of a letter. Such is the power of clearly organized protest.

In this world of computers, sound bites and speedy communications, things like writing a simple letter have become rare. In fact, putting pen to paper is so infrequent that doing so has become, ironically, that much more effective. For every letter that a network executive or member of Congress gets, conventional wisdom assumes that thousands of people are represented by that letter. With that in mind, here are a few tips on influencing your mayor, governor, state council member or member of Congress—as well as any other large entity—through the power of the pen:

- Type your letter. Typed letters certainly go a long way toward clarity and image. When presented in a formal, business-like manner, typing is impressive. However, a well-composed, neat and legible handwritten letter can be just as effective—if not more. Use black or blue ink. White or off-white bond paper is preferred, but in a pinch, use what is clean, available and without illustration. Avoid using your personal correspondence stationery, especially if it features designs. Every aspect of your communication needs to be business-like.
- Be brief and to the point. Letters and phone calls should be seen as the starting point to getting results. Action generally follows a process—a letter, a response, a relationship built, a round of phone calls and then the action. It's important to put your best foot forward in a letter, just as you would in a face-to-face meeting. Begin by identifying yourself. Do you represent a neighborhood group, parents' group, union? Are you a resident of the district that the individual represents? Next, succinctly and plainly state your interest, need, concern or grievance. Avoid writing poetry or long, illustrative prose. Think about the recipient of your letter; don't be nasty, and cut out the fluff. Grandma Carrie used to say, "You catch more flies with honey." In this way you will respect that person and his or her time, which will be greatly appreciated and can go a long way toward influencing desired action. If the issue you are addressing makes you angry or upset, write your letter, but then let it sit for a day or two before revisiting it. After you've cooled off a bit, you may find a more neutral and effective way of delivering the same message. Before you put your letter in its envelope, reread it. If you can, get someone to proof it for you for clarity, spelling and delivery. Incorporate appropriate edits and rewrite before signing your final version.
- Package your correspondence professionally. Use a business-size (number 10) envelope for one- to three-page letters. When sending folders of additional material with your letter, you can use a large, clasped envelope appropriate to the size of the documents. Avoid using invitation or greeting-card size envelopes for formal correspondence. Don't write around edges. Include only your return address, the address of your party and a stamp on the outside of the envelope.
- Use the most expedient delivery system possible. An express mail service attaches a greater sense of importance or urgency to your message. This route works well if your letter requires immediate or

swift attention, or contains sensitive information, such as a timely request for resources. Avoid it for normal correspondence.

Actions Speak Louder Than Words

When you see something that goes against what is in the best interest
of the community, complaining among friends or biting your tongue
isn't a responsible way of addressing the situation. Sometimes you have
to stand up and do something. Being a productive member of your
community can mean that you have to take risks—or stand in harm's
way. That may mean giving money—whatever you can afford—to a
local charity, the College Fund, your church's teen summit. We do hear
stories that make people cringe about others' pouring their hard-earned
dollars into political action committees or into presidential hopefuls'
purses. Yet it does cost money to get things done—on Capitol Hill and
everywhere else. When you believe in a cause or support a candidate,
you need to assist in getting the results you desire. And a direct way of
doing this is to make a financial contribution. By reading up on the organization or individual and being clear about that entity's objectives
and capital distribution strategies, you can feel more comfortable and
clear about where your hard-earned dollars will go. You can do more
than make a donation too:

- Volunteer your time and ideas. Politicians, local businesses and community organizations all need enthusiastic supporters. By contributing your personal energy to the cause, you will provide them
  with much-appreciated support, and you will learn a lot at the same
  time.
- Attend rallies and marches. When hundreds of thousands of brothers traveled to Washington, D.C., to show their solidarity in the Million Man March, they also showed the world that Black men can
  stand strong together. By following up in the local Million Man
  March activities, brothers are making their communities stronger.
- Engage in a letter-writing campaign. The campaign to free Mumia
  Abu-Jamal, the United States' only American political prisoner, who
  is facing the death penalty, has resulted in a growing awareness from
  a multicultural base of supporters who have been working toward
  his release.
- Learn what people really need and devote your efforts to helping them.
  For example, as Camille Cosby, wife of entertainer Bill Cosby and
  mother of slain Ennis Cosby, urged people at the 1997 Essence
  Awards, you can stop supporting violent movies as you also monitor
  what your children are watching on television. She said, "There is

One Man's Mission

For some, taking action can mean extreme measures. Only a few years ago South Africa was held in the stranglehold grip of apartheid. Although many people around the world participated in the campaign to unleash this inhumane government, one man lit the flame. Starting in 1982, Randall Robinson, executive director of TransAfrica Forum, a research and lobbying group, and a few others began daily protests at the South African embassy in Washington, D.C., in an effort to bring national attention to the heinous conditions under which our African brothers and sisters were living. The protests called for economic sanctions against the government, and they sparked a national cry for change. Two years later, in 1986, Congress passed the Anti-Apartheid Act over President Reagan's veto. Continued pressure and growing support worldwide ultimately led to the end of the apartheid regime and the beginning of democracy. Dreams came true, including the freeing of Nelson Mandela, president of the African National Congress, who was imprisoned for twenty-seven years for political views and actions. From being relegated as a man with no rights, Mandela became the President of the new country.

Robinson has been a champion of civil rights of the Diaspora for many years. Apart from South Africa, Robinson has been actively involved in the politics of Haiti. In fact, he went on a hunger strike in 1994 that lasted for twenty-seven days in an effort to protest the administration's policy of returning refugees to Haiti without hearings on being granted asylum during the exile of Haitian President Reverend Jean-Bertrand Aristide. Again, his efforts paid off. When questioned about it, Robinson said, "I expressed my own opinion, but obviously if it was a lone opinion, it wouldn't have done so much. I think it dramatized and facilitated the concerns of many across the nation, people who came to learn of this cruel policy through coverage of the hunger strike. If the Administration reacted, I don't think it was so much from me, but Americans who reacted." Robinson added that as a young man growing up in Richmond, Virginia, his parents taught him, "You don't do things because they're successful, but because they're right."

too much violence in the world, and it can have an influence on young minds." Your stand might be much more basic, such as speaking up on behalf of a coworker when he or she is being misrepresented or maligned by another, even if it means that you are putting yourself on the line. In countless small but significant ways, you can make a difference by taking action.

Politically Correct

We hear a lot these days about the importance of being politically correct. Often this refers to watching what you say or do in public so as to avoid offending anyone, whether you mean to or not. In theory, it's a practical tool, though superficial. When you really don't know what to say, it is best to say nothing. Just listen and learn. Being conscientious means looking out for others, truly working to honor yourself and those around you as fully as you can. The hot topics for being politically correct are race, gender, sexual preference, physical disabilities and religion. The going notion is not to broach any of these subjects in polite conversation. For practical purposes, that's good advice. This doesn't mean, however, that you should close your ears and voice to learning. How are we ever going to learn respect for differences if we never learn what they consist of or why they exist? If we approach every situation with love, respect, flexibility and curiosity, we can learn to accept and appreciate differences, not merely ignore them. In the Bible it says, "Let each esteem others better than themselves." (Philippians 213)

On the most profound level, to be truly correct, one must treat everyone with respect and cultivate equality consciousness. It doesn't mean that we have to agree with what other people say or do, or how they choose to live their lives. It doesn't mean that we have to pretend to go along with others when we feel strongly in a different way. It does mean that we need to take the time to look at others to see the best in them. We must ask ourselves how we can honor each person who comes into our path for the value that each brings to the table. We need to develop the facility to look beyond barriers.

Within our own communities, we are not "politically correct." The amount of infighting and dissing, as young folks call it, is outrageous. Whether it's over the color of our skin, the texture of our hair, the level of our income, the size of our bodies, the religion that we practice, the company we keep—we don't have to look outside ourselves to find areas where we can be less critical of each other. We can spend hours dissecting the historical reasons for our self-hatred, much of which is rooted in our introduction to this country. If done with the correct intent, historical inquiries of every sort can be quite liberating. We can then choose to look ahead with a command of the past.

Standing Up for Ourselves

Organizing to save our communities has long been the calling card for our grass-root efforts. Since our first days in this country, the concern has prevailed about how people of African descent are treated—what is fair, what is just. Here is what the Declaration of Independence says:

> We hold these truths to be self-evident, that all men are created equal, that they are endowed by their Creator with certain unalien-

able rights, that among these are life, liberty, and the pursuit of happiness. That to secure these rights, governments are instituted among men, deriving their just powers from the consent of the governed. That, whenever any form of government becomes destructive of these ends, it is the right of the people to alter or to abolish it, and to institute new government, laying its foundation on such principles and organizing its powers in such form, as to them shall seem most likely to effect their safety and happiness. Prudence, indeed, will dictate that governments long established should not be changed for light and transient causes; and accordingly all experiences hath shown, that mankind are more disposed to suffer, while evils are sufferable, than to right themselves by abolishing the forms to which they are accustomed. But when a long train of abuses and usurpations, pursuing invariably the same object, evinces a design to reduce them under absolute despotism, it is their right, it is their duty, to throw off such government, and to provide new guards for their future security.

Black folks have long had to struggle against the very government that has claimed to provide freedom for all, often in dramatic form. What we have not fully comprehended is that this government was not created with us in mind. During Slavery, many of our brave ancestors, including Denmark Vesey and Nat Turner, rose up against the slave owners with violent fights for freedom. An urgent need for building community strength inspired W. E. B. Du Bois to start the NAACP back in 1909. One year later, the National Urban League was founded with the mission of assisting African Americans in the procurement of social and economic equality. During the turbulent 1960s, after Martin Luther King, Jr., President John F. Kennedy and Malcolm X had been assassinated, many Blacks, especially those in the inner city, got fed up and began searching for a new way to change the circumstances under which African Americans lived.

In Oakland, California, community outrage fueled the efforts of Huey P. Newton and Bobby Seale to found the Black Panther party in 1966. Contrary to what many believe, the Black Panther party was not created as a violent response to racism in America. It *was* militant, however, in the tradition of those who revolted during Slavery and at subsequent points in history, believing that their constituency—Black people—deserved their rights to freedom, shelter, education and jobs, as well as the end of police brutality. Fundamentally, this organization sought to foster support and solidarity within the Black community and to educate and feed Black children. Their approach was intense and decidedly controversial. Yet from the perspective of right action, they followed the Constitution of the United States and challenged the way in which African Americans were treated based on the guidelines written in the very document that defines society in this country. Among the good works that the Black Panther party initiated during its brief history were schools for young Black children and nutrition programs in poor neighborhoods. The party also required drug- and crime-free living of its members. History has proven that when the party's following grew, governmental agencies took heed and worked to counter their efforts, and infighting ensued that ultimately led to the dissolution of the party.

The lesson we can take away from all freedom fighters, including the Panthers, is that it is constitutionally acceptable to challenge that which appears to be inhuman, unjust, racist or otherwise detrimental to our well-being. We may not always agree with each other's tactics, just as W. E. B. Du Bois and Booker T. Washington approached education from what appeared to be two different poles. Further, the going will surely be tough and may lead to apparent failure. But every time that we choose to stand in harm's way to defend each other and we keep the good of humanity as a whole in our hearts, we are *being* right, acting consciously. It all takes strategy, willingness and love.

Politics and the Environment

In this new era, it is impossible to look at our lives without examining carefully how we treat the world in which we live. Considering the sum of our circumstances is a prerequisite to responsible living. Unfortunately, in the midst of great technological and industrial growth, too many people have overlooked the environment and the impact that their actions can and will have on it long-term. This is one of those times when it's good to look at our historical legacy. Respect for the earth, for nature, for the seasons, for wildlife, for others' space was an integral part of our ancestors' ritual practice, including Native Americans (many of whom were our ancestors), who with each full moon honored the land for its abundance.

When you take the time, you will discover countless ways that you can be more conscientious about making eco-sense. Here are some ideas to spark your creativity:

- Get excited about recycling. This includes glass and plastic bottles, some boxes, aluminum cans and newspapers. Beyond these, you can direct your purchases to products that are sold in recyclable packaging and then remember to use the packaging for refills when appropriate.
- Don't forget clothing. For generations we've been offering hand-me-

downs to our children. We can do the same with grown-up family members and friends. It can be fun, and the price is always right!

- Eat closer to the earth. Consider moving toward a vegetarian diet. If you eat meat, choose free-range meat (available in health food stores that feature organic food) rather than other selections that might be filled with toxins that can harm the body. (It is argued that many of our children are physically developing too quickly due to the hormones injected in cattle to encourage their growth. That trigger may be passed on to us through a simple burger.) Select organic fruits and vegetables, which are grown without the use of pesticides or chemical fertilizer. They are often more expensive, but they are worth it. If you can, join a food cooperative in your neighborhood where prices will be more affordable, and you and your family will develop discipline by working for your food.
- Don't smoke. Apart from the immediate dangers to your health, you endanger the health of others when you smoke in their company. It's rude and ultimately deadly, so resist. (The list of ailments that you expose yourself and others to by smoking should make you never pick up another cigarette again.)
- Give gifts that support the environment. Dedicate a tree in someone's name. Make a contribution to a holistic health center on a friend's behalf. Send a potted plant instead of a bouquet of flowers. Purchase items whose partial proceeds help promote worthwhile causes.
- Support legislation that preserves wildlife and forest areas.

Our Organizations

Many organizations around the country keep the issues and concerns of African-American people in the light. Following is a partial listing of some national entities that you may want to contact:

Institutions
American Association for Affirmative Action, founded in 1974 to promote affirmative action and equal employment throughout the country.
200 North Michigan Avenue, #200
Chicago, IL 60601
(312) 541-1272

Blacks in Government, founded in 1975 to promote the concerns of Black civil servants working on all levels of government.
1820 11th Street, NW
Washington, DC 20001
(202) 667-3280

Caribbean Action Lobby, founded in 1981 to bring concerns of Caribbean and Caribbean Americans to the Congress.

391 Eastern Parkway
Brooklyn, NY 11216
(718) 773-8351

Congressional Black Caucus, founded in 1970 and comprising the African-American members of Congress, created as the catalyst for economic, educational and social concerns of African Americans, minorities and the poor.

House Annex II
Ford Building, Room 344
Washington, DC 20515
(202) 226-7790

Congress of Racial Equality (CORE), founded in 1942 to challenge overt racism and discrimination in America.

30 Cooper Square
New York, NY 10003
(212) 595-4000

Interracial Council for Business Opportunity, founded in 1963 to cultivate minority economic growth through business development.

51 Madison Avenue, #2212
New York, NY 10010
(212) 779-4360

Joint Center for Political Studies, founded in 1972 at Howard University. This is a think tank and lobbying arm for ideas on African-American culture and life.

1090 Vermont Avenue, NW, Suite 1100
Washington, DC 20005
(202) 789-3500

Leadership Conference on Civil Rights, founded in 1950 by A. Philip Randolph, Roy Wilkins and Arnold Aronson as a coalition of national organizations representing minorities, women, labor, seniors, major religious groups and the disabled.

1200 Massachusetts Avenue, NW
Washington, DC 20005
(202) 842-8686

NAACP, founded in 1909 by W. E. B. Du Bois, the National Association for the Advancement of Colored People has worked over the years through grassroots and legislative means to enable Black people to receive fair treatment in all aspects of their lives, including voter education, housing, equal employment and educational opportunities. Most cities have local chapters.

4805 Mount Hope Drive
Baltimore, MD 21215
(410) 358-8900

National Association of Black Journalists, founded in 1975 to expand and balance media coverage of the Black community and to recruit Black youth into journalism.

> P.O. Box 4222
> Reston, VA 22091
> (703) 648-1270

National Association of Neighborhoods, founded in 1975 to provide information, training and technical assistance to neighborhood groups nationwide and to inform constituent groups about legislation that impacts on neighborhoods.

> 1651 Fuller Street, NW
> Washington, DC 20009
> (202) 332-7766

National Baptist Convention U.S.A., Inc., founded in 1880 as the umbrella for Black Baptist churches in the United States. It currently has 7.5 million members.

> National Baptist World Center
> 1700 Baptist World Center Drive
> Nashville, TN 37207
> (615) 228-6292

National Bar Association, founded in 1925 as an organization of African-American attorneys whose mission is to ensure equal justice.

> 1225 11th Street, NW
> Washington, DC 20001
> (202) 842-3900

National Black Caucus of State Legislators, founded in 1977 as an informational resource and network for Black legislators.

> 444 North Capitol Street, NW #622
> Washington, DC 20001
> (202) 624-5457

National Black United Fund, Inc., founded in 1972 to promote charitable giving within the Black community.

> 50 Park Place, #1538
> Newark, NJ 07102
> (201) 643-5122

National Urban Coalition, founded in 1967 as an urban action advocacy and information organization.

> 1875 Connecticut Avenue, NW, #400
> Washington, DC 20008
> (202) 986-1460

The National Urban League, Inc., founded in 1910 to eradicate racial discrimination and to uphold political and economic equality for African Americans.

500 East 62nd Street
New York, NY 10021
(212) 310-9000

Operation PUSH (People United to Serve Humanity), founded by Jesse Jackson to promote economic and political parity for Blacks and other minorities.

930 East 50th Street
Chicago, IL 60615
(312) 373-3366

Southern Christian Leadership Conference, founded in 1957 to bring moral initiative, spiritual undergirding and mass popular involvement to the struggle against racial oppression.

334 Auburn Avenue, NE
Atlanta, GA 30312
(404) 522-1420

United Negro College Fund, Inc., founded in 1944 to raise money for private, historically Black institutions of higher learning.

8260 Willow Oaks Corp. Drive
P.O. Box 10444
Fairfax, VA 22031

Women's Issues

National Association of Minority Political Women, USA, Inc., founded in 1983 to train minority women and their families in understanding how to make local, regional and national politics work in their individual and group interests.

6120 Oregon Avenue, NW
Washington, DC 20015
(202) 686-1216

National Coalition of 100 Black Women, founded as an advocacy group seeking empowerment for Black women in all aspects of their lives.

38 West 32nd Street, #1610
New York, NY 10001
(212) 947-2196

National Council of Negro Women, Inc., founded to help women improve the quality of life for themselves, their families and communities.

1667 K Street, NW, #700
Washington, DC 20006
(202) 659-0006

Men's Issues

100 Black Men of America, Inc., founded in 1986 to address issues of the Black family, and males in particular. It attracts a broad range of men, from students to scholars, business executives and other professionals who are dedicated to uplifting the Black community.

127 Peachtree Street, NE, Suite 704
Candler Building
Atlanta, GA 30303
(404) 525-7111

Sigma Pi Phi Fraternity (The Boule), the first African-American Greek letter fraternal organization, founded in 1904, with the focus of promoting philanthropic and charitable activity for African Americans.

920 Broadway, Suite 703
New York, NY 10010
(212) 477-5550

Young People

Jack & Jill of America, Inc., founded in 1938 to provide an environment for young people to develop leadership, social skills and camaraderie.

4761 Sylvan Drive
Savannah, GA 31405
(912) 356-2194

Third Wave, a multiracial activist group, devoted to feminist issues, founded by Rebecca Walker (daughter of Alice Walker).

New York, NY
(212) 799-0322

Your Questions Answered

1. I frequently see people addressing their grievances in the media. Is that the best solution to handling difficult situations these days?

Not necessarily. As far as the protocol of the situation, you can create a much more difficult scenario for your issue if you bring it to the public without first attempting to handle it privately. Think about it. If someone is having a problem with you and you learn about it over a news broadcast or even through your network of friends, chances are you will become first embarrassed and then enraged. It is nearly impossible to reason with people when they are angry. A much better strategy is to request a meeting with the party in question and work to hash out your differences face-to-face. To get to that meeting, you may have to place a telephone call, write a letter, enroll a neutral party to help out. Whatever you can do to keep the information as private as possible will help you both in reaching amicable terms. Using the media should be left as a last resort.

2. People in my neighborhood do not respect the environment at all. Any suggestions?

Be a power of example. Select a weekend day when you and your children and a few willing friends clean the streets or tend to the common plants. Have fun together as you are participating in your Respect the Neighborhood campaign. As you see fellow neighbors, invite them to join in. Don't disparage them if they decline. You may go one step further and start a block association. Peggy and Lloyd Toone revitalized their Harlem block association by paying attention to its needs and the development of the neighborhood. In time, other neighbors joined in, and they now have received private funding for restoring some of their historic landmarks—thanks to two people with commitment.

3. I understand how political favors work, but I don't get the impression that others follow suit. How can I get others to play fair?

Jocelyn Cooper, a music industry executive, just shared that she had done at least five significant business favors for someone in the past year, significant to be sure. Yet her one request from this African-American male executive had not yet been fulfilled. Rather than remain frustrated, she simply gave the brother a status report: "I've helped you out with these various things, and you still haven't come through." He responded with what she thought was a lame excuse. She decided not to follow up on his latest request until hers is honored. To answer your question, sometimes people don't make good on the give and take of political favors, but rest assured that nobody forgets where you stand. That's why it's so important to be clear about when you ask and when you give. Also, it is essential that when you give to others, you give generously, from your heart, with no attachments. Do not make the mistake of giving in order to receive later. That action will always backfire on you. At the same time, in business as in the rest of life, reciprocating is essential. It should be a given that someone you help will help you if opportunity knocks. Remember Mama's wisdom: One hand washes the other. You must reach a delicate balance that allows you to remain centered.

4. I recently worked on a project with two white women. At a certain point as we were working, we experienced a serious conflict and they accused me of being "racist" toward them. How should I respond?

Years ago, I was schooled by an elder who explained that it isn't really possible for those without power to be racist. Only those who are in power have the ability to discriminate effectively against others for reasons of race. That said, you can confidently explain that racist you were not. Still, you should examine your actions. What prompted this label? Did you fall into stereotypical thinking about them or behavior toward them? What happened that caused conflict? Can you find the source of the problem? By taking the time to review what actually happened and the possible genesis of the conflict, you may be able to address the irritating concerns and move on peacefully.

5. *Is it "politically correct" to say nothing when I hear people talking badly about others?*

No. To sit in silence when others are bad-mouthing someone unfairly is, in my view, irresponsible. If you do not want to incite an argument, you may invite the people to change the subject or speak directly and say that you consider it inappropriate and rude to talk about people. Your next step can be to leave the situation.

6. *Somebody recently called out to me that I was "H.N.I.C." What does that mean? Is it a compliment?*

H.N.I.C. means "head nigger in charge." It is a derogatory label, to be sure. During Slavery, those brothers who rose to positions of power sometimes did so at the expense of others. In fact, they often were the ones elected to administer public whippings to other African people. Today, when people are called H.N.I.C., it harks back to that sense of achieving at others' expense, something we cannot afford to do.

7. *Is it politically savvy to look at this country in terms of Black and white people and issues?*

No. Although many of the issues that are presented in this book address the sensitivities and concerns that exist between the African-American community and the white community, the content here is not limited to such polar race relations. Nor should your awareness be. In this country alone there are people literally from all over the world. To welcome cultural diversity and cultivate both the patience and the interest to learn about the ways other people think and look at the world requires that you open your eyes. Only with an expanded and growing awareness can you move into the future in a positive and productive manner. Rather than dwelling on the differences among any of us—including people within the Black community—now is the time to learn about the various peoples of this country and the world and treat them all with love and respect.

Postscript

W H E N I think about the global family which our ancestors brought into being, I am inspired. We are so beautiful, so rich, so powerful. And the opportunity lies before us to reclaim our magnificence so that we can be the divine beings whom the Creator put on this planet—to heal it. Regardless of the many efforts that have been made to distract and destroy us, we must keep our eyes on the prize. We must follow the wisdom of the Adinkra symbol *Sankofa* that urges us to stop in our tracks and look back to retrieve the essence of our past so that we may walk with a command of who we are, which provides strength and foundation for our future. The greatest gift that I can share with you is that we must hold each other's hands, firmly and with love. No matter what our spiritual beliefs, our political orientations, our economic classifications, our degrees of education, our facility with language, our disparate views, we must unite.

One of the greatest insights that Nelson Mandela revealed about our people is our fear of being great. Now is the time to shed that crippling veil of fear. To discover *how to be* in the truest sense is to embrace each other and stand united as we reignite the torch of our 200,000-year legacy. With that profound presence of *being,* we can walk tall and proud and in line with the universal mission that our ancestors understood so well: to bring love and peace and honor and dignity and respect to us all.

SelectedBibliography

Afua, Queen. (1992). *Heal thyself: For health and longevity*. Brooklyn, NY: A&B Books.

Akbar, Na'im. (1984). *Chains and images of psychological slavery*. Jersey City, NJ: New Mind Productions

Akbar, Na'im. (1991). *Visions for Black men*. Nashville, TN: Winston-Derek Publishers.

Amen Ra Un Nefer. (1992). An *Afrocentric guide to a spiritual union*. Bronx, NY: Kamit.

Ani, Marimba. (1991). *Let the circle be unbroken*. Trenton, NJ: Red Sea Press.

Blyden, Edward. (1888, 1994). *Christianity, Islam and the Negro race*. Baltimore, MD: Black Classic Press.

Blyden, Edward Wilmont. (1908, 1994). *African life and custom*. Baltimore, MD: Black Classic Press.

Browder, Anthony T. (1994). *Exploding the myths, volume 1: Nile Valley contributions to civilization*. Washington, DC: Institute of Karmic Guidance.

Browder, Anthony T. (1994). *From the Browder file: 22 essays on the African-American experience*. Washington, DC: Institute of Karmic Guidance.

Diallo, Y., and Hall, M. (1989). *The healing drum: African wisdom teachings*. Rochester, VA: Destiny Books.

Fu-Kiau, K. Bunseki, and A. M. Lukondo-Wamaba (1988). Kindezi. Vantage Press.

Ginsberg, Ralph. (1962, 1969). *100 years of lynching*. New York: Lancer Publications.

Hilliard III, Asa G. (1995). *The maroon within us: Essays on African American community socialization*. Baltimore: Black Classic Press.

Among the many authors whom you should read are some who have been so prolific and expansive that it's best to explore their work in detail. These authors include the following:

J. A. Rogers
John G. Jackson
Ngugi Wa Thiong'o
Iyanla Vanzant
Dr. John Henrik Clarke
Dr. Yosef A. A. ben-Jochannan
Dr. Cheikh Anta Diop

Hilliard III, A., Williams, L., and Damali, N. (eds.). (1981). *The teachings of Ptahhotep: The oldest book in the world*. Atlanta: Blackwood Press.

Huang, J. H. (1993). *Sun Tzu. The art of war: The new translation*. New York: Morrow.

Idowu, B. D., and Bolayi, E. (1994). *Olodumare: God in Yoruba belief*. Brooklyn, NY: A&B Books.

Jackson, John G. (1970, 1994). *Introduction to African civilization*. New York: Citadel Press.

Karenga, Maulana. (1984, 1989). *The Husia: Sacred wisdom of ancient Egypt*. Los Angeles: University of Sankore Press.

Karenga, Maulana. (1993). Introduction to Black Studies. University of Sankore Press. Los Angeles.

Kenyatta, Jomo. (1965). *Facing Mount Kenya*. New York: Vintage Books.

La Casas, Bartolomé de. (1992). *A short account of the destruction of the Indies*. London, UK: Penguin Books.

Machiavelli, Niccolò. (1961, 1981). *The prince*. London: Penguin Books.

Michaharic, Draja. (1982). *Spiritual cleansing: A handbook of psychic protection*. York Beach, ME: Samuel Weiser.

Núñez, Luis Manuel. (1992). *Santeria: A practical guide to Afro-Caribbean magic (Opens the Western mind to the Caribbean world)*. Dallas: Spring Publications.

Obenga, Theophile. (1997). *African world history project: The preliminary challenge*. Association for the Study of Classical African Civilizations.

Ousmane, Smbene. (1960). *God's bits of wood*. Berkshire, GB: Cox & Weyman Limited.

Owusu, O. K. (1994). *Origins: Timechart of world civilizations: A wholistic worldview of cultures and civilizations*. Baltimore: Cultural Eye Productions.

Some, Malidoma. (1993). *Ritual: Power, healing and community*. New York: Arkana.

Some, Malidoma. (1994). *Of water and the spirit*. New York: Arkana.

Somé, Sobonfu. (1997). *The spirit of intimacy: Ancient teachings in the ways of relationships*. Berkeley, CA: Berkeley Hills Books.

UNESCO. (1981). *General history of Africa*. (8 vols.). Berkeley: University of California Press.

Van Sertima, Ivan. (1976). *They came before Columbus*. New Brunswick, NJ: Transaction Publishers.

Van Sertima, Ivan (Ed.). (1983). *Blacks in science: Ancient and modern*. New Brunswick, NJ: Transaction Publishers.

Van Sertima, Ivan (Ed.). (1984). *Black women of antiquity*. New Brunswick, NJ: Transaction Publishers.

Van Sertima, Ivan (Ed.). (1995). *Golden age of the Moor*. New Brunswick, NJ: Transaction Publishers.

Van Sertima, Ivan (Ed.). (1996). *African presence in early America*. New Brunswick, NJ: Transaction Publishers.

Van Sertima, Ivan (Ed.). (1996). *African presence in early Europe*. New Brunswick, NJ: Transaction Publishers.

Welsing, M.D., and Frances, C. (1991). *The Isis papers: The keys to the colors*. Chicago: Third World Press.

Williams, Chancellor. (1974, 1987). *The destruction of Black civilization*. Chicago: Third World Press.

Wing, R. L. (1986). *The Tao of power: Lao Tzu's classic guide to leadership, influence and excellence. A new translation of the* Tao Te Ching. New York: Dolphin, Doubleday.

Woodson, Carter G. (1919). *The education of the Negro prior to 1861: A history of the education of the Colored people of the United States from the beginning of Slavery to the Civil War*. Washington, D.C.: Amos Press; reprinted Brooklyn, NY: A&B Books.

Woodson, Carter G. (1933). *The mis-education of the Negro*. Washington, D.C.: Associated Publishers.

Wright, Bruce. (1987, 1993, 1994). *Black robes, white justice: Why our legal system doesn't work for Blacks*. New York: Carol Publishing Group.

Acknowledgments

S O many great hearts helped to shape this book that I must first offer a blanket thank-you to everyone who so generously offered good ideas, warm wishes and blessings. I have needed them all. My family, beginning with Grandma Carrie and continuing from my parents through every family member, have inspired and encouraged me to keep working to make this book a reality. I want to say special thanks to my sister Stephanie, who has been my dearest friend since she was born—a beautiful being who has demonstrated the depths to which unconditional love can grow. I also owe a huge debt of gratitude to my sister Susan, whose firm conviction and no-nonsense manner have awakened me to ever-greater expressions of who I am when I have most needed to believe in me and when I have been most resistant. To Mama Davis, Corey Hills, Gwyneth and Jeff Shick and all the kids for their love and support.

My literary agent, Madeleine Morel, found me years ago and has stuck with me, believing that my ideas are worth publishing. My editor, Bob Mecoy, and his right arm, Pete Fornatale, have been writer/editor dreams. The patience of Bob must come from his Southern upbringing! For his immediate interest, I am appreciative.

I owe so much to my staff—many of whom are acknowledged on the Creative Team page. I began *How to Be* at the same time that I founded *profundities, inc*. Every soul who has stepped through my office has touched this book in some significant way. To all of you I am indebted. Simply being yourselves and giving your best to our work have inspired me in countless ways that find themselves in this book. The same goes for all of my clients, especially those musical artists, from Mary J. Blige to Erykah Badu and Rachid, whose many ways of being have inspired me to dig deeper into my own creative reserves. Earl G. Graves, for being an inspirational mentor. To Andre Harrell, who created the bridge for me between etiquette/presentation training and the entertainment industry, when he was first leading Uptown Records and then Motown. To Delora Jones, for staying by my side through years of research. M. Raven Rowe, for rescuing me right before publication with details of a worldview of African tradition and life whose surface I had only barely scratched.

My friends from childhood and recent years have provided shoulders and wings when I have needed them most. My friend Todd McDaniels stays forever in my heart, proof that even after you have made your transition, your spirit stays close to those you love. I thank you all: my old and new friend, LaJerne Terry Cornish, for many late-night talks. Adriane Birt and Jeffrey Jones, for the roots of friend-faith that have been steadfast over the years. Eric Easter, for being a rock from day one. Susanne Beck, for loving me always, and "Daddy" John Beck, for offering his generous guiding hand. Jonell Nash, whose soft and welcoming presence have provided a sure relief from my imagined boogeyman, for ever reminding me of *The Pledge.* Dwight Carter, Marlowe Goodson and John Pinderhughes, for steadfast support. Sharon Chatmon, a.k.a. *Little Magic,* for shining her sweetness on me. Jocelyn Cooper, for becoming my new sister and demonstrating that you can be friends and business associates at once. Sheila Bridges, for an exquisite respite one summer when I needed to get away and type, and for so much more. My attorney and dear friend, Kervin Simms, who has been there through it all, for helping me navigate my own way of being with unconditional support. Stephanie Stokes Oliver, for hiring and nurturing me into professional adulthood. Sheila Eldridge, for encouraging my entrepreneurial drive from the start. Saundra Parks, for teaching me so much about business. Rashid Silvera, for long ago providing an opportunity for me to cultivate my writing. Ralph Scott, for Sankofa. Cheryl Riley and Charles and Cheryl Ward, for constant encouragement. Jerald Loud and Antonio DaSilva of Andasimo and Patrick Robinson, for so generously outfitting me. Isabel Rivera, for giving me lots of air time and insight. Liz Ross, for her constant and patient direction. Dianne McIntyre, for keeping the flame lit in so many ways. Mrs. Michaela, for just being you. Rhonda Dallas and Delores Stuckey, sorors. To all who have not been mentioned, I love you all. Thank you all.

I offer tremendous gratitude to Essence Communications for being the cradle in which I grew up professionally. Thank you, Susan.

I want to thank my manager and friend, Ramon Hervey, for believing in my vision and helping me to execute my dreams in a productive and effective manner. And my new friend, Rene Scotland, for the constant pep talks. Lauren Summers and Fred Gates, for helping me get the book tour rolling, along with Pam Duevel and Christine Saunders, S&S publicity divas. A huge nod goes to Jackie Seow, the art director who managed to make this world of words inviting to all of you; and to Beverly Miller, my kind and caring copyeditor, and Loretta Denner, the angel in editorial production. A special thank-you to Cindy Riccio and Elise Telloni of L'eggs Products and all of the sponsors who have fortified this book project to help bring a critical message to more people. Forever thanks to Michele Barnwell, Peg Galbraith and Donna Fields for reading these many pages with so much care and love. Even more, I offer my gratitude to all of the people across the country who answered those long surveys and offered their hearts in focus groups and one-on-one meetings.

To my husband, George Chinsee, I offer the most special and sincere thanks for putting up with my endless hours of work and travel in pursuit of my heart's expression—and for working with me to discover *how to be* in marriage—not to mention his exquisite photography that graces the cover of this book.

Finally, I offer my deepest gratitude to my spiritual teacher, Gurumayi Chidvilasananda, whose guidance, inspiration and blessings have fortified and directed me for many years and, who, for this project, has been my most profound inspiration and guide.

Index

at work, 377–79
for youth, 146–50
Cohabitation, 446–48
Collins, Lionel, 480, 483
Colored people, as term, 237–38
Communal worship, 65
Communication. *See also* Language;
  Telephone calls
  acknowledgment of others, 30–31, 34–39,
    147–48, 259, 262
  with elders, 142–44
  on elevators, 399–400
  Four Gateways of Speech, 25
  gossip, 42, 399, 417, 430, 500
  greetings, 30–31, 34–39, 147–48, 259, 262,
    300
  guidelines on, 24–26
  interruption of long conversations at
    work, 46
  introductions, 31–33, 37, 44–45, 279,
    315–16
  listening, 24–26, 378, 379
  with loved ones while traveling, 301–02
  during meals, 280, 315–16
  nonverbal communication, 25, 35, 148,
    259, 380
  and overnight stays, 283
  with politicians, 486–89
  profanity, 42–44, 246–47, 255–56, 321
  in public places, 280, 300
  response to derogatory comments about
    Black people, 255
  small-talk at networking events, 340
  and thinking before speaking, 41–42,
    61
  volume of spoken language, 254–55
  at work, 379–80, 399–400
  yelling by children, 255
Compassion, 29
Conferences, 223, 272–73
Conflicts at work, 412–14
Congress of Racial Equality (CORE), 495
Congressional Black Caucus, 495
Contemplation, 64–65
Conventions, 223, 272–73
Conversations. *See* Communication
Cookbooks, 330–31
Cooper, Jocelyn, 298, 499
CORE, 495
Cosby, Bill, 321, 489
Cosby, Camille, 489–90
Cosby, Ennis, 489–90
Couple showers, 362
Courtship, 160, 173. *See also* Dating
Credit and credit report, 438–43, 466
Cremation, 128
Criticism, 41
Crystal, Billy, 190
Cults, 76–77

Cultural clothing and accessories, 89–90,
  215, 217, 219
Cursing. *See* Profanity
Cutting in line, 46, 269

Dally, Maxine, 428
Dances, 280–81, 285–86
Darden, Norma Jean, 343
Date rape, 186–88
Dating
  adult dating, 172–75, 183–86
  African perspective on, 160–62, 164, 167,
    171, 172, 188–89
  background check on dates, 171
  chaperoned dating, 163–64
  after death of spouse, 183–84, 192
  definition of, 160
  and development of serious relationship,
    182–83
  and different spiritual views, 194
  dos and don'ts for parents when children
    date, 163
  dos and don'ts for persons dating, 169–70
  dressing for, 169
  ending of one relationship before
    beginning another, 191–92
  exit plan for date, 170
  expectations about date, 173
  family's dislike of date, 188–89
  first date, 168, 170
  of friend's ex-boyfriend, 189
  friendship as prelude to, 166
  gift giving and, 190
  by homosexuals, 176–78
  interracial dating, 180–81
  jealousy and, 191
  kissing and, 171, 190
  ladylike or gentlemanly behavior for,
    170–72
  in marriage, 185–86
  married people and infidelity, 192–94, 417
  and meeting date's parents, 172
  men holding doors open for women,
    170–71
  men paying for, 168, 170
  money for, 168, 169, 170
  mutual respect and, 165
  by older people, 174–75
  possessiveness and, 191
  rape by date, 186–88
  romance and, 159–60, 165, 188
  secrecy of, 194
  seeing ex-lover while with new partner,
    287
  self-worthiness and, 165–66
  sexuality and, 164, 170, 175–79
  by single parents, 120, 184–85
  and taking off wedding ring after death of
    spouse, 192

Four Gateways of Speech, 25
Fraternities, 153–54, 226
Freedom, 20–21, 62–64
Freedom Riders, 158
Fried chicken, 339–40
Friendships
    African perspective on, 190–91
    and being left out of fun plans, 286
    borrowing and lending money between
        friends, 467
    before dating, 166
    dating friend's ex-boyfriend, 189
    ending of, 123
    guidelines on, 122–23
    jealousy and, 138, 191
    response to former friends at public
        functions, 287
    seeking dates while out with friends, 138
    versus sexual intimacy, 190
    with whites, 157–58
    working with friends, 421–22
    of youth, 146–47, 149, 157–58
Fruit of Islam (FOI), 489
Fry, Gladys-Marie, 173
Fuhrman, Mark, 236–37
Fu-Kiau, K. Kia Bunseki, 112, 448, 453
Funerals, 126–28, 278–79, 368

Gambling, 455–57
Garnet, Henry Hyland, 26
Garrison, Frank Lloyd, 158
Garvey, Marcus, 26, 47
Gatling, Luther, 440–41
Gays. See Homosexuals
Gender-neutral/gender-fair language, 254
Gifts
    African perspective on, 190, 347–48
    for baby-naming ceremonies, 277–78, 360
    for birthdays, 357
    for christenings, 277, 360
    at Christmas, 117–18, 346–47, 349–55
    dating and, 190
    for elders, 358
    environmentally sound gifts, 494
    examples of great gifts, 373–74
    for families in mourning, 368
    for family members, 358
    for fathers, 358
    for Father's Day, 355–56
    food as, 351–52
    for friends, 123
    for funerals, 279
    genesis of, 348–49
    for Hanukkah, 354–55
    for holidays, 117–18, 346–47, 349–55
    by houseguests, 282, 284, 368–69
    for housewarmings, 366–67
    Islam and, 354
    Jehovah's Witnesses and, 353–54

"just 'cause" gift, 347, 374
    for Kwanzaa, 353
    for lateness, 398
    memorial gifts, 368, 369
    for Mother's Day, 355
    to opposite sex, 374
    presentation of, 369–70
    religious considerations for, 353–55
    for rites of passage, 359–60
    Secret Santa, 350–51, 418
    for sick and shut-ins, 367–68
    thanks for, 370–73
    thank-you gifts, 373
    for troubled times, 374
    unacceptable gifts, 374–75
    for Valentine's Day, 356
    wedding gifts, 93, 276–77, 361–66, 373
    work and, 348–49, 350–53, 375, 409,
        428–29
Gladden, Gwynn, 28–29
Glasses
    for driving, 265
    sunglasses and introductions, 44–45
God. See Spiritual life
Godparents, 105–07, 137–38
Goggins, Lathardus II, 151
Goldberg, Whoopi, 221
Golden, Thelma, 274
Golden Rule, 17, 263, 377, 421
Golf, 271–72
Good judgment, development of, 22–24
Good manners. See Codes of conduct
Gossip, 42, 399, 417, 429, 500
Graham, Laurence Otis, 222
Grandparents. See Elders
Gratitude. See Thanks; Thank-you notes
Graves, Earl, 225, 382, 459, 475
Great Awakening, 50
Green, Sylvester, 217–18
Greene, Joshua, 433
Greeting cards, 252–53
Greetings, 30–31, 34–39, 147–48, 259, 262,
    300
Grocery stores, 45
Group travel, 306
Guess Who's Coming to Dinner, 180
Guests
    in another country, 281
    at baby-naming ceremonies, 277–78, 360
    bringing spouse or date to formal events,
        339
    at christenings, 277, 360
    at cocktail parties, 342–43
    at dance, 280–81
    at funerals, 278–79
    at holiday celebrations at work, 419
    at holiday meals, 334
    houseguests, 282, 284, 368–69
    for long-term stays, 283–85

uninvited guests at, 277
wedding cake for, 90
Weddington, Wayne, 454
Wesley, Richard, 185
Wesley, Valerie Wilson, 185
White tie dress/occasions, 215
Whitening of skin, 198, 199
Whites
  and Abolitionist movement, 158
  appearance of, as beauty standard, 195–96
  Blacks accused of "acting white, 202–04
  conflicts in political work with, 499–500
  as dates, 180–82
  education at majority-white schools, 158
  friendships with, 157–58
  hatred of, 158
  as slaveowners, 158
Williams, Chancellor, 229–30
Williams, Robert, 229
Williams, Terrie, 36, 37
Wills, 130–31, 137–38, 448
Wilson, Amos, 433, 459–60, 481–82
Wilson, Midge, 199
Wilson, Pete, 474
Woods, E. M., 185–86
Woods, Tiger, 236
Woodson, Carter G., 63, 199, 397
Work
  African name versus given name at,
    103
  African perspective on, 67–68, 376–77
  associating with Black people at, 414–15,
    429
  beards at, 226
  beepers, pagers, and cell phones, 391–92
  behavior around former boss, 431
  "casual Fridays" clothing, 217–19, 395,
    396
  children and, 410–11
  clothing for, 214, 216–17, 394–96
  conflicts at, 412–14
  conversations at, 379–80, 399–400, 417
  coworkers at, 407
  cultural clothing for, 217
  dating on the job, 179–80, 416–17
  disagreements with boss at, 416
  discretion about sex life at, 177–78
  earrings for men at, 225–26
  education and, 396–97
  entrepreneurship, 242, 289–90, 405–06,
    427, 483
  with family and friends, 421–22
  firings from, 425–28
  friendship with white coworkers, 429
  getting fired from, 425–26
  gifts and, 348, 350–53, 375, 409, 428–29
  good manners at, 377–79
  gossip at, 399, 417, 429
  guidelines on being the boss, 420–21

hair style at, 428
headhunters and, 404
holiday celebrations at, 418–19
home business, 405–06
interruption of long conversations at
  work, 46
jewelry at, 225–26, 396
job interviews and, 224–25, 394, 402–403
lack of privacy at, 400–402
language for, 231–32, 241–42, 383–85
leaving, 40
loyalty at, 378
maintenance people at, 414–15
meals at business meetings, 322–24,
  339–41, 468
mentors at, 406, 430–31
message taking at, 389–90
nail designs at, 225
netiquette and, 401
networking and, 407–09
and outside support network, 407
paternity leave from, 430
politics at, 483–84
pregnancy and, 411–12
profanity at, 44
and professional and social organizations,
  407
protocol at, 379
racism at, 380–83, 432
rapport with boss at, 428
religious holidays and, 78
requesting raise at, 430
resignation from, 423–25, 429–30
respecting space at, 392–94
restraint of pen and tongue at, 391,
  415–16
and sex for promotion, 417
spiritual life and, 66–69
telephone calls at, 385–91
temporary employees, 404–05
time considerations and, 397–99
time off from, 410–11
traveling for, 289–90, 420
voice mail at, 390–91
Writing
  business letters, 249–50
  cards, 252–53
  to elders, 143–44
  invitations, 253
  note apologizing for lateness, 398
  personal letters, 251
  to politicians, 487–89
  postcards, 302
  reference letters, 250
  thank-you note, 93, 251–52, 283, 364, 369,
    372–73, 378–79, 404, 425

Xenophilia, 292
Xenophobia, 290

THE CREATIVE TEAM
AUTHOR, HARRIETTE COLE

As Grandma Carrie taught, "We do nothing by ourselves." Following are the people who worked so very hard to make this book possible.

AFRICAN RESEARCH EDITOR
M. Raven Rowe

PRINCIPAL RESEARCH COORDINATORS
Ayana Byrd   Delora Jones   Sala Patterson

CHAPTER RESEARCHERS
Aliyyah Abdur-Rahman   Connie Aitcheson   Dawn Baskerville   Paulette Brown
Ayana Byrd   Peggy Dillard Toone   Eric Easter   Yvette Heyliger   Nancy U. Hite
Darin S. Holt   Djassi Johnson   Delora Jones   Paulette Jones   Mana Kasongo
Tina L. Redwood   Linda Tarrant-Reid

FOCUS GROUP COORDINATOR
Eric Easter

JACKET PHOTOGRAPHY
George Chinsee, photographer
Lloyd Toone, photo assistant   Maryse Weeks, Whitney Kyles, stylists   Roxanna Floyd, makeup artist   Julana Chestang, hair stylist   Natalee Huey, prop stylist   Patrick Robinson, fashion designer

ILLUSTRATION
Yvonne Buchanan

ADMINISTRATION
Darin S. Holt